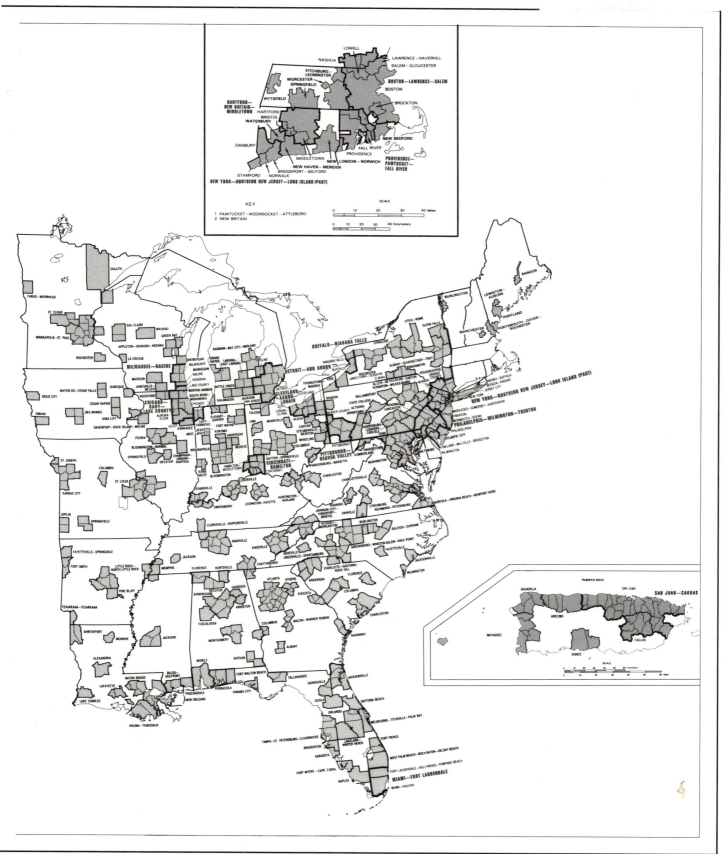

INTERPRETING THE CITY

An Urban Geography

INTERPRETING THE CITY

An Urban Geography

2nd
Edition

TRUMAN ASA HARTSHORN

Georgia State University

Cartographic Design and Production

Borden D. Dent
Georgia State University

Janette Irving Heck
Georgia State University

JOHN WILEY & SONS, INC.

New York • Chichester • Brisbane • Toronto • Singapore

Copyright © 1980, 1992 by John Wiley & Sons, Inc.

All rights reserved. Published simultaneously in Canada.

Reproduction or translation of any part of
this work beyond that permitted by Sections
107 and 108 of the 1976 United States Copyright
Act without the permission of the copyright
owner is unlawful. Requests for permission
or further information should be addressed to
the Permissions Department, John Wiley & Sons.

ACQUISITIONS EDITOR	Barry Harmon
PRODUCTION MANAGER	Linda Muriello
DESIGNER	Lynn Rogan
PRODUCTION SUPERVISOR	Micheline Frederick
COPY EDITOR	Marjorie Shustak
PHOTO RESEARCHER	Elsa Peterson, Hera
PHOTO EDITOR	Jennifer Atkins
PHOTO RESEARCH DIRECTOR	Stella Kupferberg

COVER PHOTOS (top, left) Mexico City; Kal Muller/Woodfin Camp
(top, right) Houston; Mike Yamashita/Woodfin Camp
(bottom) Tokyo; George Holton/Photo Researchers

Recognizing the importance of preserving what has been written, it is a policy of John
Wiley & Sons, Inc. to have books of enduring value published in the United States
printed on acid-free paper, and we exert our best efforts to that end.

Library of Congress Cataloging-in-Publication Data

Hartshorn, Truman A.
    Interpreting the city : an urban geography — 2nd ed. / Truman Asa Hartshorn
 : cartographic design and production: Borden D. Dent and Janette Irving Heck.
        p.   cm.
    Includes index.
    ISBN 0-471-88750-1
    1. Human geography.   2. Urban geography.   I. Dent, Borden D.
 II. Title.
 GF125.H37   1992   91-34874
 307.76—dc20   CIP

 10 9

With appreciation and humility this edition is dedicated to my parents Gailan Oscar and Carolyn Faucett Hartshorn; to sisters Mary Karen DePietro, Lois Marie Hartshorn, and Louise Alice Hartshorn; and to those professional geographers who inspired me to continue my pursuits in a most rewarding field.

PREFACE

What a change a decade can make! Just think about how much the world has changed since 1980, to say nothing about our cities. Poverty and homelessness are more visible today than ever before, even in the midst of affluence and mass consumerism. The information age has created millions of new jobs. Suburban downtowns have come of age. The automobile reigns supreme and the number of vehicle trips has grown dramatically. Lifestyles have changed, the number of persons per household has dropped, and our cities are more ethnically diverse.

The sunbelt concept was unknown in the literature when I wrote the first edition in the late 1970s. And just think about how our attitude about the environment has changed. I recall one reviewer's critical remark concerning the first edition in 1979: "If you have a length problem with the manuscript, the physical environment chapter should be the first to go. . . . It is not necessary." This time around, reviewers offered an entirely different perspective. Repeatedly, the response has been, "Expand the material," "This is important."

During the past few years, as I have become more closely allied with primary, middle, and secondary school teachers through the National Geographic Society-sponsored Alliance movement, I have become aware of how starved our teachers and students are for more geography content. Urban geography occurs in a setting where most students live today, but they are typically taught nothing about it. The city is also the locus of many pressing national problems (poverty, drugs, crime, housing, transportation, growth management), but these issues are rarely dealt with in a systematic way in the curriculum.

College students come to the university unaware of the discipline. They have never experienced a walking field trip to the downtown area in their own or any nearby city. They have not thought about transportation problems other than the goal of buying a car, nor have they attended a zoning hearing. There is just so much to learn about the city, it is no wonder that students taking the urban geography course gain a new excitement and appreciation for the city and urban living.

This second edition mirrors the changing city and the world it reflects. Every page has been revised and updated. Chapters have been moved, deleted, combined, expanded, and reorganized. Chapters dealing with several topics are new: 1) third world urbanization; 2) ethnicity; 3) planning; and 4) economic development. More emphasis has been placed on the historical–evolutionary perspective in discussions of world urbanization, transportation, retailing, and ethnicity. The structural perspective is given more attention, especially in the interpretation of economic development, labor relations, housing, central city–suburban investment tradeoffs, and spatial restructuring. Applied urban geography also receives more attention in the text and in a new feature—boxes—that highlight specific topics related to the chapter.

Many persons provided invaluable assistance in this revision. First, former Wiley editor Katie Vignery signed the second edition several years ago, commissioned market reviews, and provided encouragement to proceed. Successors Stephanie Happer and Barry Harmon kept up the pressure, support, and encouragement. Barry has been very generous with his time and skill at keeping the loose ends together. Without his cajoling and undivided commitment of resources, the book would not be as strong.

Thanks go to Nanda Shrestha for his conscientious and insightful work in producing the third world chapter. Fred Stutz produced the planning chapter and

Instructor's Manual. Several chapter authors from the first edition should also be recognized. First, Tom Bell from the University of Tennessee, author of the central place chapter, can claim the record for promptness and patience. He also assisted with several boxes in this edition. Borden Dent, Georgia State University; Richard Stephenson, East Carolina University; and Wayne Strickland, Fifth District Planning Commission in Roanoke, Virginia: Each authored chapters in the first edition, but played lesser roles in this second edition; they must be thanked for their ongoing interest in this book.

Without the dedication and good humor of my typist June Smith in Atlanta there would be no manuscript; for 12 months she gave up her weekends and evenings to toil over the word processor, printer, and copier, not to mention the countless pickups and deliveries. I benefited immeasurably from the opportunity to spend two weeks in the Library at the Urban Land Institute in Washington, D.C., in autumn 1990. The resources available there are of immense value to the applied urban geographer. Special thanks to Tom Black, Lloyd Bookout, Rachelle Levitt, David Mulvihill, and Diane Suchman for making this time so productive.

Borden Dent once again provided invaluable service in the cartographic design for the book, ably assisted by Jan Heck on the map production side. Jan successfully shifted the majority of "old" art used in this edition to the computer along with all the "new" pieces. All the new maps and diagrams in this edition were produced using Micrografix Designer software and IBM compatible microcomputers. They were printed on 300 dpi laser printers before conventional photographic reduction. This is an example of a technology not available a decade ago that has totally revolutionized map production.

Several geographers have generously provided material, advice, and counsel during the revision process. While I may overlook some, I do want to recognize as many as possible. Included in this group are R. Craig Ham, United States Military Academy; Philip Suckling, University of Northern Iowa; Tom Boswell and Peter Muller of the University of Miami; Harold Rose, and Harold Mayer, University of Wisconsin, Milwaukee; Randy Smith and Edward Taaffe, Ohio State University; Kavita Pandit and James O. Wheeler, University of Georgia; John Adams, University of Minnesota; Roger Zanarini, Fischer Properties; Larry Bourne, University of Toronto; Richard Forstall, Donald Dahmann, and Charles Long, U.S. Bureau of Census; J. Dennis Lord, University of North Carolina, Charlotte; David Longbrake, University of Denver; Thomas Baerwald, National Science Foundation; Robert Lake, Rutgers University; Glenn Miller, Bridgewater State; and Curt Roseman, University of Southern California; Mark Hinshaw.

Many other individuals have assisted with market reviews and manuscript reviews for this edition. I would like to especially thank the following: Frederick Stutz, San Diego State University; David Plane, University of Arizona; Jane Ehemann, Shippensburg University; Richard Greene, Northern Illinois University; Robert Mancell, Eastern Michigan University; Mel Aamodt, California State University–Stanislaus; Howard Adkins, Marshall University; James Hughes, Slippery Rock University; Richard Outwater, California State University–Long Beach; Joseph Leeper, Humboldt State University; Yda Schreuder, University of Delaware; Don C. Bennett, Indiana University; Charles Sargent, Arizona State University; David Hodge, University of Washington.

At Wiley, I am grateful to Micheline Frederick, who supervised production; to Linda Muriello, production manager; to Marjorie Shustak and John C. Thomas for an excellent job in copyediting; to Jennifer Atkins for the seemingly endless task of photo research, and numbering and renumbering to match the manuscript; to Hilary Newman, who also helped with the photo research; to Lynn Rogan for the cover design; to Cathy Faduska in marketing; and to Cynthia Michelsen, who handled endless tasks behind the scenes. Also, thanks to Ishaya Monokoff for his willingness to permit the author such latitude in producing the maps and diagrams close to home.

Finally, I would be remiss if I did not thank my colleagues at Georgia State University for their good humor and support. It does get tiring to answer the queries, "Aren't you done yet?" or "Are you caught up yet?" but anyone who has labored over a book knows it is a never-ending process, and then comes the next edition! Thanks to Richard Pillsbury, Borden Dent, and Sanford Bederman, with whom I have worked for over 20 years. Dean Clyde Faulkner and, more recently, Interim Dean Robert Arrington have been most understanding and supportive. Terry Morris endured endless phone messages with graciousness and aplomb. Catherine McGovern always had a good sense of humor even when exhausted by my last-minute requests. Thanks also go to Deborah Hampton for her boundless energy.

I was ably assisted in the production of the index by Alan DePietro, Louise Hartshorn, and June Smith. In the end, however, the test will be student satisfaction. I can only hope that my classroom experience, research interest, travel experience, and communications style come together to create a meaningful product.

Truman A. Hartshorn

CONTENTS

1

URBAN GEOGRAPHY TODAY

Cities are the centers of power and prestige—economic, political, and social. They are where the action is in terms of innovations and control. Tremendous quantities of capital have been invested in them, and their development and redevelopment represents an ongoing process. At no time in their history, in fact, have larger cities around the world experienced a more rapid rate of growth and change than that which occurs today.

INFORMATION AGE

The postindustrial economy of the 1990s requires rapid access to information (Figure 1-1). We now live in what has been called the *information age*, and the factory for processing information is the office building. Much of this information is fragmented and technical, requiring the clustering of specialists to process it. Therefore, one major function of the city is to process what has been labeled *ambiguous information*.[1] Larger cities possess *agglomeration econo-*

[1]See Edwin S. Mills, "Sectoral Clustering and Metropolitan Sizes and Growth," in Edwin S. Mills and John F. McDonald, eds., *Sources of Metropolitan Growth and Development*, Center for Urban Policy Research, Rutgers University, New Brunswick. See also Edward W. Soja, *Postmodern Geographies: The Reassertion of Space in Critical Social Theory*, Verso, London, 1989.

mies for the handling and exchange of this information, because they have the buildings, telecommunications, transportation, and specialized personnel resources to cope with this flow. In other words, the information age and large urban centers seem to be made for each other and facilitate the generation and exchange of ideas. Perhaps no city better illustrates the information age economy than Washington, D.C., where one finds an incomparable concentration of private sector consultants, sometimes labeled beltway bandits; government agencies; a wide array of business professionals who facilitate the exchange of information, ranging from bankers and legal advisors to engineers; and the full spectrum of business services (Table 1-1). It is no wonder, therefore, that many professional associations also locate their head offices in Washington, D.C., in order to take advantage of this access to people and information.

URBAN PROBLEMS

Notwithstanding the attractive features of cities as places of opportunity, pronounced variations occur within and between cities in terms of prevailing social and economic conditions. Minority laborers and lesser-skilled workers, in particular, have not benefited as strongly as a group from growth and development in recent decades. This problem manifests itself most vividly in the central cities of developed countries and in third world cities. In developed countries, the tran-

Figure 1-1. Satellite Communications Center. The rooftop telecommunications gear on this Hollywood skyscraper showcases the information age economy at the foot of the Los Angeles skyline. This complex incorporates a production studio, network control center, and technical operations center, featuring microwave and fiber optic links. (Courtesy Keystone Communciations)

sition from the manufacturing age industrial-based city, to the information age service-based city, as just discussed, is associated with job displacement and center city decline. In third world cities, opportunities for employment are very limited despite rapid growth. We will deal with these issues in both the developed and developing world in succeeding chapters.

WHY URBAN GEOGRAPHY?

Why do cities grow even when limited opportunities exist for individual advancement? Why have larger cities grown more rapidly in recent years, especially those in the third world with the highest poverty levels? And why has the urban physical environment deteriorated so rapidly in recent years in cities throughout the world?

Training in urban geography helps one to answer these and other questions. It provides the student with a conceptual working knowledge of the location, function, and growth of the city on the one hand and an understanding of its spatial structure or internal organization on the other hand. The urban geographer's approach is that of emphasizing location and space and the study of processes that create the patterns observed. The *spatial* perspective, in fact, provides the central theme of geography. The map adds an extra dimension

to geographic research by demonstrating the importance of place in urban analysis (Figure 1-2).

One of the strongest arguments for the study of urban geography today is the invaluable preparation it provides for careers in planning and consulting related to physical and community development. Many opportunities also exist in the areas of market research, real estate development, historic preservation, and environmental management. We will discuss several traditions of study in urban geography that converge to give this field its current identity among the social and behavioral sciences.

TABLE 1-1
Business Service Functions

Advertising (outdoor, radio, TV)
Credit reporting/collection
Mailing, reproduction, stenographic
Services to buildings
Personnel supply
Computer, data processing services
R & D labs
Management, public relations
Detective, protective services
Equipment rental
Photo finishing

Source: U.S. Bureau of Census.

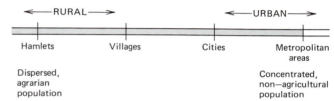

Figure 1-3. Rural-Urban Continuum. Defining the boundary point between rural and urban settlement forms is arbitrary and varies widely throughout the world, making precise comparisons of population statistics difficult.

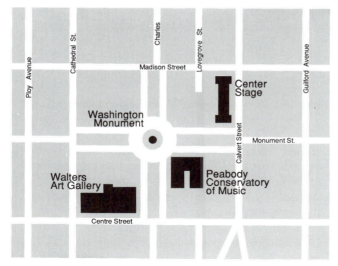

Figure 1-2. Mt. Vernon Circle, Baltimore. This historic site in Baltimore is distinguished by the presence of the Washington Monument in the center of the intersection of two major boulevards, Charles Street and Monument Street. The distinctive architecture of the elegant town homes in the neighborhood and such distinctive cultural institutions as the Walters Art Gallery and the Peabody Conservatory of Music give a distinctive sense of place to this location.

WHAT IS THE CITY?

Defining the city is a difficult task. We usually use vague phrases, such as "a place larger than a village or town," to describe the city. The word *urban* also has a somewhat nebulous connotation. For example, *Webster's New Collegiate Dictionary* defines *urban* as "of, relating to, characteristic of, or constituting a city." Being more specific with either the term *city* or *urban* can lead to arbitrary distinctions, but generally a city can be described as a concentration of people with a distinctive way of life in terms of employment patterns and lifestyle. A high degree of specialized land uses and a wide variety of social, economic, and political institutions that coordinate the use of the facilities and resources in the city make them very complex machines.

Rural–Urban Continuum

Distinguishing the *rural* from the *urban* realm is relatively easy in terms of identifying polar opposites, but determining a critical breaking point between the urban and rural forms is not as simple. A continuum, for

example, can be drawn with rural areas at one end and urban concentrations at the other (Figure 1-3). At the rural end of the urban-settlement spectrum, a dispersed agrarian population, hamlets, and small towns exist. The designation *urban* typically requires a much larger settlement size than the hamlet or town regarding numbers of people. This determination varies widely from country to country. A range in the minimum population size values for urban places in selected nations is shown in Table 1-2. For some nations, the number is less than 500 (Sweden, Denmark); in others it is 1000 (Canada, Australia); 2000 to 5000 (France,

TABLE 1-2
Urban Population Definitions

Country	Minimum Population
Sweden	200
Denmark	200
South Africa	500
Australia	1000
Canada	1000
Czechoslovakia	2000
Israel	2000
France	2000
Cuba	2000
United States	2500
Mexico	2500
Belgium	5000
Iran	5000
Nigeria	5000
Spain	10,000
Turkey	10,000
Japan	30,000

Source: United Nations, Department of Economic and Social Affairs, "Growth of the World's Urban and Rural Population, 1920–2000," *Population Studies,* 44 (1969), 81–84.

METROPOLITAN AREA DESIGNATIONS

The Census Bureau records metropolitan area statistics using several reporting units, including the *metropolitan statistical area* (MSA), *urbanized area, census tract, Zip Code area,* and *census block.* Most of the data are published in printed form, and even more information is available in a computer format.

Metropolitan Statistical Area

The MSA designation, formerly known as the SMSA (standard metropolitan statistical area) until 1983, exists for all cities over 50,000, but smaller cities can be so designated under specified conditions. Metropolitan areas are defined in terms of counties, the number of which is based on their urban population, population density, and share of workers who commute to the central county(ies) of the metro area. Often the outer portion of the metropolitan statistical area is therefore rural in character, but strong urban ties also exist in terms of work, shopping, and socialization.

Consolidated Metropolitan Statistical Area

When strong interconnections, in terms of work trip commuting, exist between two or more metropolitan areas that share a common boundary, the region is defined as a consolidated metropolitan statistical area (CMSA). Each of the metropolitan areas within this designation is then called a Primary Metropolitan Statistical Area (PMSA). Most of the largest metropolitan areas in the country have a CMSA designation. Washington, D.C., and Atlanta are conspicuous exceptions, as they remain designated as MSAs (see Table 4-7 and front endpaper).

Urbanized Area (UA)

The *urbanized area* (UA) definition of the city includes the central city and its immediate suburbs, partially overcoming a weakness of the MSA. This is the built-up area of an urban region, the area in need of urban services provided by municipal police, fire, sewer, water, and solid waste agencies. A weakness of the MSA concept is that it may include low-density, sparsely settled rural areas as well as urban and suburban concentrations because it relies on counties as building blocks. Counties also vary widely in physical extent, and this can greatly distort the areal size and shape of metropolitan areas when county boundaries extend well beyond continuously built-up areas.

UAs were first recognized in 1950. They have expanded considerably over the years because they are defined on the basis of the population distribution at the time of each decennial census. The UA includes: (1) contiguous incorporated place of 2500 or more inhabitants; (2) incorporated places with fewer than 2500 inhabitants, provided each has a closely settled area of 100 dwelling units or more; (3) adjacent unincorporated areas with a population density of 1000 or more inhabitants per square mile; (4) other adjacent areas with a lower population density provided they serve to smooth the boundary or link otherwise separate densely populated areas. It can also include adjacent land devoted to urban uses without any residents, such as industrial parks or railroad yards. Streets, roads, and creeks are used as the boundary units rather than political boundaries as for the MSA.

Typically, there is a UA for each MSA because the central city building blocks are the same. There are more UAs than MSAs because several metropolitan areas include two noncontiguous UAs, and a few UAs do not result in a qualifying MSA, such as Rome, GA.

Census Tract

Census tracts are small areas into which metropolitan areas have been divided for census data reporting purposes. Tract boundaries are established cooperatively by a local committee and the Bureau of the Census. Tracts are designed to be relatively uniform with respect to population characteristics, economic status, and living conditions. The average tract has about 4000 residents. Boundaries are established with the intention of being maintained over a long time so that comparisons may be made from census to census, but tracts are subdivided or combined as population changes warrant. Some other changes are also made over time, such as switching a boundary from an arterial street to a nearby expressway.

Tracts are generally numbered in a consecutive series, with separate numbering formats for each county in the particular metropolitan area. In the past five decades, the number of cities for which tract data are available has multiplied rapidly, from 60 in 1940 to over 350 in 1990. The 1970 census contained nearly 35,000 tracts. There were over 40,000 tracts in 1980, and about 50,000 in 1990. The most comprehensive source of population, housing, and socioeconomic data for the city is available at the tract level. Some nonmetropolitan counties also have census tracts. For 1990, data are being issued for tracts or for similar block numbering areas (BNAs) for all counties. There were 11,270 BNAs in 1990.

Census Block

The Census Bureau reports *block* data for the urbanized portions of all metropolitan areas. Most census blocks correspond to the common usage of the term that refers to a physical area, often square or rectangular in shape, bounded by streets. In rural areas, blocks may be much larger. Block information represents the smallest statistical unit for which census information is published. The data at the block level are primarily housing variables.

The number of blocks reported in census tabulations doubled between 1960 and 1970, increasing to 1.5 million. In 1980, block data were reported by all UAs, as well as for all cities of 10,000 or more outside UAs. In 1990, there were approximately 7 million blocks reported in the United States Census. Block data are being issued in 1990 for the entire country.

United States, Iran); or as much as 30,000 (Japan). These variable definitions make it very difficult to compare urban population statistics among countries.

For smaller towns and cities, the concept of *urban place* defines the extent of the urban population adequately. A settlement of 2500 or more persons constitutes an urban place, according to the U.S. Bureau of Census. But larger cities pose more complex definitional problems. In many cases, cities have grown beyond their *city limits, political city*, or *legal city* boundary. We use each of these terms interchangeably to refer to the incorporated town or city. In such cases, the urban population does not reflect the size of the urban region. We refer to a city as *underbounded* when the city limits area only accounts for a portion of the built-up or developed area. In some cases, cities have merged with counties, creating a situation where the built-up area occupies only a portion of the political city, which is referred to as an *overbounded* community.

Recognizing that many adjacent suburban areas frequently are not part of the city definition, the Census Bureau began a program in the 1950s to identify metropolitan areas, as well as cities, in its reports. The metropolitan area designation used county units as building blocks rather than city limits areas. The city around which the metropolitan area was built became the *central city*, and the *central county* in which it was located the basic building block for the metropolitan definition. Additional counties were then added as appropriate.

Metropolitan area definitions used by the Census Bureau and the criteria used in their determination are discussed in the accompanying box. The student must study and become conversant with this terminology before proceeding to Chapter 2, to avoid later confusion. It is important, for example, to know the difference between the *metropolitan area* and the *urbanized area* of an urban region. The accompanying box provides an explanation of this difference.

The Urban Lifestyle

Sociologists and anthropologists have worked for many generations in an attempt to isolate the fundamental cultural characteristics of the urban lifestyle. The urban pattern generally involves more specialization in the work force, more class distinctions, more formal participation in cultural activities, and, in general, a faster pace of living and tighter organizational structure. Two contemporary symbols of this organization are the traffic signal light that regulates vehicular traffic and the computerized time clock (Figure 1-4). Urban life demands more discipline, firmer scheduling, and precise deadlines—unlike the flexibility and uncertainty more often found in rural areas.

The increasingly dominant urban composition of North America and other highly developed countries, including Canada, Western Europe, Japan, and Australia, had an accelerated impact on rural traditions following World War II. The television, movie theater, and radio media, among others, reinforced the impact of urban values on the countryside. Rural residents

Figure 1-4. **Don't Block the Box.** The traffic light and traffic congestion symbolize the pace and intensity of urban living today. The sign at this Park Avenue intersection in midtown Manhattan warns motorists not to block the intersection when the traffic signal changes. (Yvonne Freund/Photo Researchers)

readily adopted urban cultural elements and attitudes. This cultural transition has been strengthened by a parallel increase in the reverse migration of urban residents to rural nonfarm environments in recent decades.

Growth of industry in rural settings, the expansion of long-distance rural to urban commuting to work, and the greater presence of second homes in remote settings also revolutionized country living standards (Figure 1-5). Transportation and the telecommunications improvements associated with massive road-building programs, greater dependence on the automobile, growing affluence, and other advances in the electronic media also underlie these changes.

EVOLUTION OF URBAN GEOGRAPHY

An early emphasis in American urban geography focused on the *site and situation* of the city (Figure 4-2). This tradition developed out of the man–land philosophical approach practiced in the discipline. Carl Sauer, whose 1925 essay *The Morphology of Landscape* became the benchmark on the subject, is most often identified with this philosophy.[2] Sauer, while not an urban geographer himself, inspired many urban geographers to study the population and economic characteristics of cities in relation to their physical location. Fieldwork was an integral part of this type of research. Many case studies of American cities were produced in the 1930s and 1940s in this tradition.

Hinterland and *trade area* studies represented another early research theme in urban geography, inspired by the rich tradition of regional studies in geography. That approach involved exhaustive research on the physical, economic, cultural, and political underpinnings of an area, showing how it was similar and different from other areas. Studies of newspaper circulation (Figure 5-1) and retail sales tributary areas of cities (Figure 5-3) provide examples

---

[2]Carl Sauer, *The Morphology of Landscape*, University of California Press, University of California Publications in Geography, Berkeley and Los Angeles, 2 (1925), 19–53.

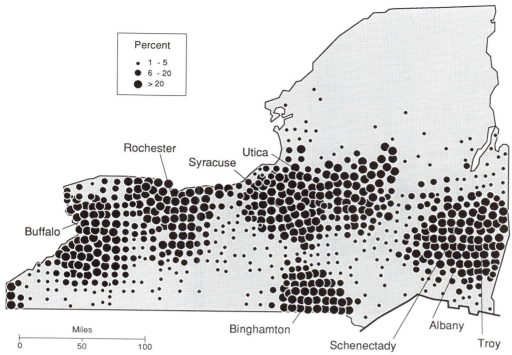

Figure 1-5.   Rural-Urban Commuting in Upstate New York. The extensive commuter laborsheds of Buffalo, Rochester, Syracuse, Utica, Binghamton, Schenectady, Albany, and the Troy area demonstrate the extensive reach of urban influence into the countryside, which has brought virtually all upstate New York into the orbit of urban opportunity. *Source:* Modified after Ronald L. Mitchelson and James S. Fisher. *Long Distance Commuting: Impacts on Population, Employment, and Income Change in Nonmetropolitan areas.* Final Report, U.S. Dept. of Commerce, Economic Development Administration, 1987. p. 68. Washington, D.C.

of such research.[3] In general, the goal of this activity was to explain the function of an area as a market center serving the surrounding region.

Interest at another scale of urban research developed concurrently with the functional studies emphasis. That work focused on the *morphology* or *internal structure* of the city. Land use inventories, involving the classification and mapping of functional areas in the city, such as industrial and residential districts, accounted for much of the early activity (Figure 1-6). This research gradually established an identity for the geographer as an *urban planner*. Extensions of this work into analyses of residential change, suburban growth, and the delivery of urban services, such as the water, sewer, and communication infrastructure, reinforced the association of geography with planning. The con-

temporary interest in *geographic information systems* (GIS) continues the involvement of the geographer/ planner as a data analyzer and synthesizer of diverse information from both the socioeconomic and environmental disciplines.

Locational School

The synergism created by the blending of the internal structure-planning approach and the more regional trade area emphasis created a healthy situation for the field of urban geography. The emergence of the *locational school* of geography in the 1950s, emphasizing systematic quantitative analyses to generate a stronger theoretical foundation for the discipline, also benefited the field. Two research interests, one focused on studying *cities as points* and the other on *cities as areas*, grew in stature from this increasing rigor. Intense scrutiny of census data and insightful comparative studies resulted from large-scale computer-based analyses. Urban studies became the leading research

---

[3]Harold M. Mayer, "Urban Geography," in P. E. James and C. F. Jones, eds., *American Geography: Inventory and Prospect*, Association of American Geographers, Syracuse University Press, Syracuse, 1954, pp. 143–166.

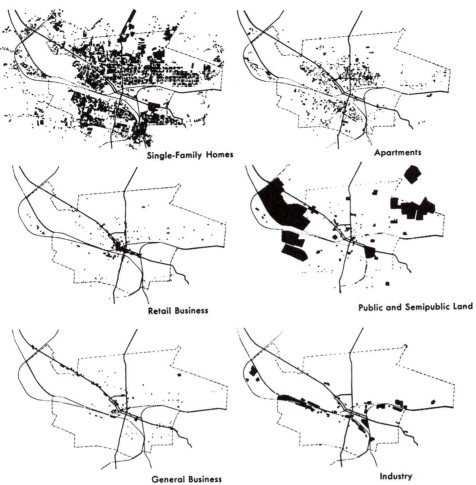

Figure 1-6. **Urban Land Use Maps.** Urban land use follows a regular, predictable pattern. Land uses in a small Tennessee city are shown here on six separate maps, including residential, retail, and, industrial areas. Note the contrasts in pattern among these maps. Why do the uses show such distinctive patterns? *Source:* F. Stuart Chapin, Jr., *Urban Land Use Planning,* University of Illinois Press, Urbana, 1965, after Tennessee State Planning Commission. ©1965 by the Board of Trustees of the University of Illinois.

frontier in geography by the 1970s as a result of this work.[4]

As more powerful inductive statistical and computer applications became available, a wider array of vari-

ables was applied to explain the spatial variation displayed by urban phenomena. Subsequent adoption of mathematical and statistical models had the advantage of making analyses even more realistic, closely approximating the *uncertainty* of individual decision making that underlies most urban activity. The use of simulation models and a systems analysis framework also assisted the development of more realistic solutions and identification of fundamental processes.

Those geographers who first advocated and practiced this *quantitative approach* were mainly associated with the University of Washington (Seattle), the University of Iowa (Iowa City), and Northwestern University (Evanston, Illinois). Among the pioneers in this work were McCarty (Iowa), Garrison (Washing-

[4]The comparative metropolitan analysis project sponsored by the Association of American Geographers and the National Science Foundation epitomizes research produced by urban geographers in this period. Vignettes of 20 metropolitan areas, a comparative atlas of cities, and a policy monograph resulted from this initiative. See John S. Adams, ed., *Contemporary Metropolitan American,* 4 vols., Ballinger, Cambridge, Mass., 1976; Ronald Abler, ed., *A Comparative Atlas of America's Great Cities,* University of Minnesota Press, Minneapolis, 1976; and John Adams, ed., *Urban Policymaking and Metropolitan Dynamics: A Comparative Geographical Analysis,* Ballinger, Cambridge, Mass., 1976. See also Sallie Marston, et al., "The Urban Problematic," in Gary L. Gaile and Cort J. Willmott, eds., *Geography in America,* Merrill, Columbus, 1989, pp. 651–672.

ton, Northwestern), and Ullman (Washington).[5] An excellent discussion of the internal dialogue in geography concerning the merits of several research traditions, including regional geography, the location school, and attempts at model building and quantification, appears in Haggett's *Locational Analysis in Human Geography.*[6]

The first major textbook in urban geography published in North America was the edited volume by Mayer and Kohn in 1959.[7] This collection of previously published journal articles represented the first urban textbook in English published outside Great Britain.[8] The first systematic, original urban geography textbook in the United States, written by Murphy, appeared in 1966.[9] This was followed by the first edition of Yeates and Garner, *The North American City*, in 1971, which became the best-seller in the field in the 1970s.[10]

Emphasis in these early books on land use and economic patterns of the city reflected the training of their authors. Many of the influential pioneer urban geographers prior to the 1960s had been trained as economic geographers or as economists with a strong spatial bias. They naturally brought economic models with them for their urban analyses. Beginning in the 1970s, geographers trained with social and behavioral principles gained prominence. Examinations of housing problems at the neighborhood level, intraurban migration flows, and the perception that individuals have of the city are all examples of this work. Many such studies emphasized individual decision-making processes and helped reestablish the tradition of fieldwork and survey research in the discipline.

Behavioral Studies

The term *behavioral studies* has been given to research focused on decision making. This work represents an

extension of the locational school philosophy.[11] The rationale for this approach is that location and space cannot be fully understood by simply associating similar spatial patterns (as between crime and education). Such explanations are inadequate because they correlate two or more phenomena without incorporating a *process* with which they are associated. They do not answer the question of why such associations exist, nor establish the context within which the decision was made.

Proponents of behavioral studies "believe that the physical elements of existing and past spatial systems represent manifestations of decision making behavior on the landscape, and they search for geography understanding by examining the processes that produce spatial phenomena rather than by examining the phenomena themselves."[12] The appeal of the behavioral theme is that it presents a very realistic framework within which to study the city. It recognizes that activities and land use changes do not just happen but arise from decisions made by individuals and organizations, both public and private.

Attitudes and perceptions are also important in behavioral analyses. Studies of spatial-choice behavior, including those related to consumer shopping habits (Figure 1-7), intraurban migration, variable urban housing market strengths, and environmental perception, all confirm the value of examining the decision-making process when studying change in the city. Notwithstanding important contributions, this approach has been criticized for its emphasis on measurement techniques and a lack of sensitivity to problems of objectivity when the values of the observer interfere with the analysis.

Structural Approach

Dissatisfaction with traditional explanations of urban change, including the limiting features of classic models of urban development, inspired several researchers to posit a new direction in urban geographic research in

[5]James E. Vance, Jr., "Geography and the Study of Cities," *American Behavioral Scientist*, 22 (1978), 131–149.

[6]Peter Haggett, *Locational Analysis in Human Geography*, Vol. 1, *Locational Models*, Wiley, New York, 1977, pp. 2–10.

[7]Harold M. Mayer and Clyde F. Kohn, eds., *Readings in Urban Geography*, University of Chicago Press, Chicago, 1959.

[8]Examples of early British books include R. E. Dickinson, *City, Region, and Regionalism*, Kegan Paul, London, 1947; and Griffith Taylor, *Urban Geography*, 2nd ed., Dutton, New York, 1951.

[9]Raymond E. Murphy, *The American City: An Urban Geography*, McGraw-Hill, New York, 1966.

[10]Maurice H. Yeates and Barry J. Garner, *The North American City*, Harper & Row, New York, 1971; 2nd ed., 1976; 3rd ed., 1989.

[11]For a review of the methodology and accomplishments of this theme, see Chapter 12, "Behavioral Variability and Geographic Reasoning," in Douglas Amedeo and Reginald Golledge, *An Introduction to Scientific Reasoning in Geography*, Wiley, New York, 1975, pp. 347–379; and Stuart Aitken, "Environmental Perception and Behavioral Geography," in Gary L. Gaile and Cort J. Willmont, eds., *Geography in America*, Merrill, Columbus, 1989, pp. 218–238.

[12]Ibid., Amedeo and Golledge "On Laws in Geography," p. 348.

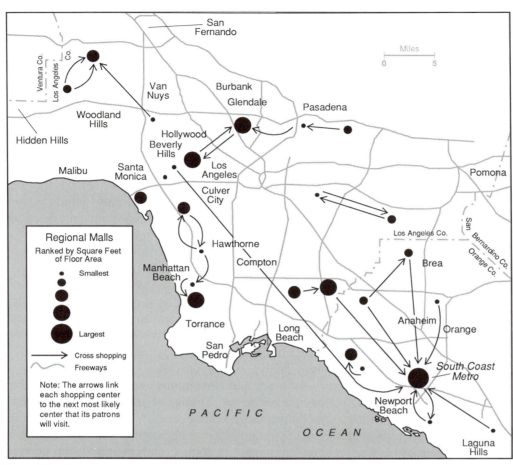

Figure 1-7.   Consumer Travel to Regional Malls. Most urbanites shop primarily at the nearest regional mall. Very large superregional malls such as the Southcoast Metro in Orange County, California (suburban Los Angeles) often draw much more widely, as the map shows. In this instance, the SouthCoast Metro not only draws strongly in Orange County, but also attracts shoppers from as far away as Santa Monica and Beverly Hills. *Source:* Ken Jones and Jim Simmons. *The Retail Environment,* Routledge, New York, 1990. p. 114.

the 1970s and 1980s. Led by the work of Harvey,[13] this revised approach emphasizes the role of uneven development and the political economy of the city as critical factors in understanding urban structure and change. The role of capital investment and disinvestment by the private sector in fostering urban change received special attention in this research. The shift of capital investment from the central city to the suburbs, for example, has been linked to the rapid growth of the suburbs and decline of the central city in recent decades.[14] The growing tendency for capital to be substituted for labor in the high technology age provides a case in point. This phenomenon has been labeled the *deskilling* of the labor force. The structural approach also emphasizes the destabilizing impact of government intervention in the form of subsidies and reallocations of resources that often exacerbate urban problems.

The most significant contributions to urban geogra-

[13]David Harvey, *Social Justice and the City*, Arnold, London, 1973; David Harvey, *The Urbanization of Capital*, Johns Hopkins University Press, Baltimore, 1985; and David Harvey, *The Urban Experience*, Johns Hopkins University Press, Baltimore, 1989.

[14]Robert Beauregard, *Atop the Urban Hierarchy*, Roman and Littlefield, Totowa, N.J., 1989.

phy in the structural approach probably lie in the areas of urban housing research (discussed below), industrial development[15] (Scott, 1982; Markusen et al., 1986), and the transformation of urban economies associated with the emergence of the postindustrial information age (Soja, et al., 1983).[16]

In the area of housing studies, a large and growing geographic literature on gentrification,[17] homelessness,[18] ethnic and cultural issues,[19] and the underclass[20] demonstrates the significant contributions to the structural approach (Figure 1-8). This research appears to be gaining momentum in the 1990s and, together with the growing literature in urban historical geography, comprises some of the most thought-provoking work in the field of urban geography.

Historical Urban Research

Geographers following the historical urban research tradition have examined the origins of modern urban form, the evolution of settlement patterns, the role of ethnic groups, and the significance of transportation as city-shaping forces, among other themes. The works of Vance, Ward, Pred, and Conzen have received partic-

ular attention in this realm.[21] We will introduce this work in succeeding chapters, placing emphasis on the historical evolution of urban form, the impact of transportation modes on urban land uses, and changing ethnicity patterns of the city.

Urban Physical Environment

Unlike other social science disciplines (except psychology), geography bridges both the social and physical sciences and has a rich tradition in physical studies, including the study of the urban physical environment[22] (Figure 1-9). Geographers receive training in both human (social) and physical geography and are uniquely equipped to study the interaction of people and the environment of the city. The physical theme at one time provided the major focus of the entire discipline, especially during the so-called *environmental determinism* era earlier in this century. The environmental determinism philosophy posited that all phenomena could be explained by natural variables. This narrow viewpoint was generally discredited as a viable scientific study in the pre-World War II era. A lesser version of environmentalism, associated with geography as *human ecology*, also flourished at one time.[23] This tradition (geography as human ecology) became prominent at the University of Chicago and led to geography becoming more closely identified with the field of sociology.

In the post-World War II era, human geographers remained very cautious in their treatment of physical

[15]Allen J. Scott, "Locational Patterns and Dynamics of Industrial Activity in the Modern Metropolis." *Urban Studies*, 19(1982), 111–141; and Allen J. Scott, "Industrialization and Urbanization: A Geographical Agenda," *Annals of the Association of American Geographers*, 76 (1986), 25–37; Ann Markusen et al., *High-Tech America: The What, How, Where, and Why of the Sunrise Industries*, Allen & Unwin, Boston, 1986; and William Beyers et al., "Industrial Geography," in Gary Gaile and Cort J. Willmont, eds., *Geography in America*, Merrill, Columbus, 1989, pp. 290–315.

[16]Edward Soja et al., "Urban Restructuring: An Analysis of Social and Spatial Change in Los Angeles," *Economic Geography*, 59 (1983), 195–230; see also Beauregard, footnote 14.

[17]Neil Smith and Peter Williams, *Gentrification of the City*, Allen & Unwin, Winchester, Mass., 1986; Neil Smith, *Uneven Development: Nature, Capital and the Production of Space*, 2nd ed. Blackwell, Cambridge, Mass., 1991; and Demaris Rose, "Rethinking Gentrification," *Environment and Planning D: Society and Space*, 2 (1984), pp. 47–74.

[18]Michael Dear and Jennifer Wolch, *Landscapes of Despair*, Polity Press, Cambridge, Mass., 1987; and Stacy Rowe and Jennifer Wolch, "Social Networks in Time and Space: Homeless Women in Skid Row, Los Angeles," *Annals of the Association of American Geographers*, 80 (1990), 184–204.

[19]John Agnew et al., *The City in Cultural Context*, George Allen and Unwin, London, 1984; Braviel Holcomb, "Women in the City," *Urban Geography*, 5 (1986), 247–254; Mickey Lauria and Lawrence Knopp, "The Role of the Gay Communities in the Urban Renaissance", *Urban Geography*, 6 (1985), 152–169.

[20]W. A. V. Clark, "School Desegregation and White Flight," *Social Science Research*, 16 (1987), 211–228; M. A. Hughes, "Moving Up and Moving Out: Confusing Ends and Means about Ghetto Dispersal," *Urban Studies*, 24 (1987), 503–517.

[21]James E. Vance, Jr., *This Scene of Man: The Role and Structure of the City in the Geography of Western Civilization*, Harper & Row, New York, 1977, revised edition titled *The Continuing City: Urban Morphology in Western Civilization*, The Johns Hopkins University Press, Baltimore, 1990; James E. Vance, Jr., *Capturing the Horizon: The Historical Geography of Transportation*, Harper & Row, New York, 1986, reprinted as *Capturing the Horizon: The Historical Geography of Transportation Since the Sixteenth Century* by The Johns Hopkins University Press, Baltimore, 1990; David Ward, "The Ethnic Ghetto in the United States: Past and Present," *Transactions of the Institute of British Geographers*, 7 (1982), 257–275; David Ward, *Cities and Immigrants*, Oxford University Press, New York, 1971; Allan R. Pred, *City Systems in Advanced Economies: Past Growth, Present Processes, and Future Development Options*, Wiley, New York, 1977; Michael P. Conzen, "The Maturing Urban System in the United States, 1840–1910," *Annals of the Association of American Geographers*, 67 (1977), 88–108.

[22]This interest is illustrated by two books: Thomas R. Detwyler and Melvin G. Marcus, *Urbanization and Environment*, Duxbury Press, Belmont, Calif., 1972; Ian Douglas, *The Urban Environment*, Arnold, Baltimore, 1983.

[23]Harlan Barrows, "Geography as Human Ecology," *Annals of the Association of American Geographers*, 13 (1923), 1–14.

Figure 1-8. Homeless Bag Lady in Manhattan. The rapid growth of the homeless population on the streets of American cities in the past decade reflects weaknesses in the housing market, failures of the mental health delivery system, and structural changes in the economy, posing serious problems for geographical analysis. (Bill Anderson/Monkmeyer Press)

variables, a reaction to the earlier, more extreme position. The recent heightened awareness of the environment, brought about by the greater recognition of the impact of pollution and the degradation of ecosystems, has stimulated urban geographers to restore the study of the environment as a legitimate study topic.

THEMES IN URBAN GEOGRAPHY

Throughout this book, emphasis is placed on the *concepts* that geographers have employed to give meaning to the form and spatial processes present in the city. Classic location models, with their strong economics flair, contemporary decision-making theory, and per-

spectives from the structural interpretation of urban processes all receive appropriate attention.

Every opportunity has been seized to demonstrate how geographers are involved in urban problem solving. Emphasis is placed on current explanations without neglecting the rich heritage of thinking that has developed in this field for the greater part of the twentieth century. Following a thorough study of this book, students will be familiar not only with the content of urban geography, including its literature and leading researchers, but also with the many ways in which geographers solve urban problems at national, regional, and local levels. They will also become keenly aware of the underlying pressures for change in the city.

(A)

(B)

Figure 1-9. Earthquake Damage in San Francisco. Natural hazard research is an important topic for geographic research. The 1906 San Francisco earthquake and associated fire (A) destroyed over 500 city blocks (3000 acres), creating more than $1 billion in losses. This view from Nob Hill faces east toward San Francisco Bay. The 1989 earthquake (B) dealt another blow to San Francisco, especially pronounced in the Marina district due to its location on loose landfill material. (*A*, Courtesy California Historical Society Library, *B*, courtesy American Red Cross/Joseph Matthews)

One general theme that is repeatedly introduced is the tension created by the variable impact of *centripetal* and *centrifugal* forces. These opposing forces are the result of the variable strength of locational and temporal ties of people and activities to specific sites. On the one hand, activities congregate in the core of the city, and on the other hand, they shift to the periphery. This central city–suburban trade-off has become a very important factor in explaining the hardships now faced by central cities in North America, as well as a theme in the expansion of sunbelt cities, which initially developed without high-density core areas but now show signs of their emergence. In Western Europe, the balance has traditionally placed more emphasis on the central city, as has occurred in Japan, in centrally planned economies, and in the third world. Nevertheless, contemporary growth and change patterns evident in North America reappear in Western Europe and Japan. For example, multiple commercial/business centers appear and continually adapt to the growing role of the automobile as a land shaper in all areas of the world.

SUMMARY AND CONCLUSION

The geographer's contribution to an understanding of the city's growing role as a center of power and innovation for the post-industrial information age should be reason enough to become immersed in the field. But the city's role as a veritable hotbed of the production and exchange of information and of growing affluence stands in stark contrast to the simultaneous presence of despair, poverty, and hopelessness prevalent among many urban residents. Here, too, the geographer can offer insights from a spatial and behavioral perspective. The differential impact of capital investment and disinvestment, government intervention, and the growing interdependence of the world system create dynamic forces that continually reshape city form and opportunities or threats to its people. Managing and coping with these opportunities or threats becomes an important agenda for community and economic development planners as well as individuals in the city.

In the following chapters, we will examine the rich tradition of growth and change that weaves the urban fabric as we know it today. We will use a comparative perspective where possible, highlighting the complexity of urban processes around the world. First we will explore the roots of world urbanization, followed by a more detailed look at cities in the developing and more developed world. We will devote the most attention to the internal structure of the city, citing the role of transportation facilities in continually restructuring its form. The importance of ethnicity, mobility, and economic status in residential development and change will be examined. The power and influence of the commercial city, as exemplified by retail, office, and industrial functions, will also receive appropriate attention. And, finally, we will muse about urban growth management and the city of the future.

Suggestions for Further Reading

Abu-Lughod, Janet. *Changing Cities*, HarperCollins, New York, 1991.

Anderson, Margo J. *The American Census: A Social History*, Yale University Press, New Haven, 1988.

Bannon, M., et al. *Urbanization and Urban Development: Recent Trends in a Global Context*, University College, Dublin, 1991.

Beauregard, R. A., ed. *Atop The Urban Hierarchy*, Rowman & Littlefield, Totowa, N.J., 1989.

Bourne, Larry. *Urbanization and Settlement Systems*, Oxford University Press, New York, 1984.

Burtenshaw, David, et al. *European City: A Western Perspective*, Wiley, New York, 1991.

Cadman, D., and G. Payne, eds. *The Living City: Towards a Sustainable Future*, Routledge, London, 1990.

Castells, M. *The Informational City*, Basil Blackwell, Oxford, 1990.

Daniels, Peter, ed. *Services and Metropolitan Development*. Routledge, New York, 1991.

Dogan, M., and J. Kasarda, eds. *The Metropolis Era*, Sage, Beverly Hills, Calif., 1988.

Feagin, J., and R. Parker. *Building American Cities: The Urban Real Estate Game*, Prentice Hall, Englewood Cliffs, N.J., 1990.

Fox, Kenneth. *Metropolitan America: Urban Life and Urban Policy in the United States, 1940–1980*, Rutgers University Press, New Brunswick, N.J., 1985.

Gaile, G., and C. J. Willmont, eds. *Geography in America*, Merrill, Columbus, 1989.

Haggett, Peter. *Locational Analysis in Human Geography*, vol. 1, *Locational Models*, Wiley, New York, 1977.

Haggett, Peter. *The Geographer's Art*, Blackwell, Cambridge, Mass., 1990.

Harris, Chauncy D. "Urban Geography in the United States: My Experience of the Formative Years," *Urban Geography*, 11 (1990), 403–417.

Harvey, David. *The Urban Experience*, The Johns Hopkins University Press, Baltimore, 1989.

Hepworth, M. *The Geography of the Information Economy*, Routledge, London, 1989.

Johnston, Ronald J. *The American Urban System: A Geographical Perspective*. St. Martin's Press, New York, 1982.

Mayer, Harold M., and Clyde F. Kohn, eds. *Readings in Urban Geography*, University of Chicago Press, Chicago, 1959.

Mayer, Harold M. "A Half Century of Urban Geography in the United States." *Urban Geography*, 11 (1990), 418–421.

Murphy, Raymond. *The American City: An Urban Geography*, McGraw-Hill, New York, 1974.

Sassen, S. *The Global City: New York, London, Tokyo*, Princeton University Press, Princeton, N.J., 1991.

Smith, Michael Peter, and Joe R. Feagin. *The Capitalist City: Global Restructuring and Community Politics*, Blackwell, Cambridge, Mass., 1989.

Smith, Neil. *Uneven Development: Nature, Capital, and the Production of Space*, 2nd ed., Blackwell, Cambridge, Mass., 1991.

Soja, Edward W. *Postmodern Geographies: The Reassertion of Space in Critical Social Theory*, Verso, London, 1989.

Taaffe, Edward J. "Some Thoughts on the Development of Urban Geography in the United States During the 1950s and 1960s." *Urban Geography*, 11 (1990), 422–431.

Thrift, Nigel, and Peter Williams. *Class and Space: The Making of Urban Society*. Routledge, New York, 1987.

Vance, James, Jr. *Capturing the Horizon: The Historical Geography of Transportation Since the Sixteenth Century*, The Johns Hopkins University Press, Baltimore, 1990.

Vance, James, Jr. *The Continuing City: Urban Morphology in Western Civilization*, The Johns Hopkins University Press, Baltimore, 1990.

Whitehead, J. W. R. *The Changing Face of Cities: A Study of Development Cycles and Urban Form*, Blackwell, London, 1988.

Yeates, Maurice. *The North American City*, 3rd ed., HarperCollins, New York, 1989.

2

THE ORIGIN AND GROWTH OF CITIES

Urbanization is a phenomenon with both a rich history and a relatively new beginning. Cities first appeared at least 5000 years ago. The following millennia brought many periods of city growth and grandeur as well as failure. From another perspective, that of the predominantly urban nation, city life is of more recent vintage—barely 100 years old. Great Britain became the first urban nation in the late 1800s. Australia also claimed a largely urban population by the turn of the century. Elsewhere, the urbanization rush awaited the twentieth century.

In this chapter, the morphological roots of the city will be traced to their origins in antiquity. World urbanization processes that have led to the present distribution of cities will be examined. A more detailed examination of third world cities will occur in Chapter 3, followed by an analysis of the evolution of the North American pattern in Chapter 4.

EARLIEST CITIES

Cities first emerged between 3000 and 4000 B.C. in present-day Iraq (Figure 2-1), in the fertile crescent formed by the Tigris and the Euphrates river valleys of Mesopotamia near the ancient shore of the Persian Gulf (Figure 2-2).[1] These southwest Asian cities were primarily religious centers, but handicraft functions such as tool making, pottery, and basket weaving often provided an economic base. Eridu is generally acknowledged to be the oldest of these cities. Most of these cities disappeared over the centuries, but one, Damascus, is now generally acknowledged to be the oldest continuously inhabited ancient city in the world today.

A prerequisite for the development of cities in the fertile crescent area was an efficient agricultural system that could produce enough surplus food and fiber to support a nonagricultural class. An elaborate social organization to coordinate the collection, storage, and distribution of the agricultural surplus also became a prerequisite for urban living. An elite priestly or military ruling group usually performed this function. These officials kept the written records and levied the taxes necessary to support the nonagricultural populace, build public buildings and walls, develop elaborate irrigation systems, and supervise artisans and construction workers. Large temples and granaries,

---

[1]Some experts believe that cities in the Indus Valley are older than those in Mesopotamia. They are discussed here in terms of having developed about 1000 years later than those in Mesopotamia.

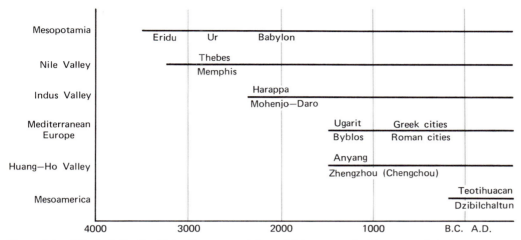

Figure 2-1. Cities in Antiquity. Cities first emerged about 6000 years ago in, Mesopotamia in the Tigris and Euphrates river valleys, (Present-day Iraq), but they also evolved in ancient Egypt (Cairo, Memphis), India, China, Mesoamerica, and in Greece and Rome at an early time. Most of these cities vanished over time. *Source:* Redrawn with permission from Gideon Sjoberg, "The Origin and Evolution of Cities," *Scientific American*, 213, September 1965, 56-57, by W.H. Freeman and Company.

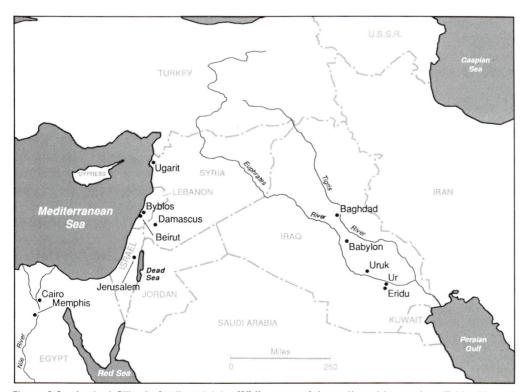

Figure 2-2. Ancient Cities in Southwest Asia. While many of the earliest cities, such as Eridu, Ur, and Babylon in Mesopotamia have disappeared, their ruins typically remain. Damascus is the oldest continuously inhabited city in the world, and in the 9th century, Baghdad had the distinction of being the largest city in the world, with a population of 1 million.

remnants of which still remain, identify the function and level of organization present in these ancient cities.

Eventually, another class of workers emerged—the merchant. This group offered farmers alternative goods, and eventually money, for their surplus product. An expansion in the production of consumer goods also typically accompanied this process, stimulating the growth of an artisan work force. Gradually a trade network evolved out of this activity involving "three urban groups: the merchants, the artisans and the ruling elite."[2]

Most ancient cities were quite small by modern standards, typically no more than 15,000–25,000 in population. The few that did grow to large sizes, by standards of the day, include Uruk, with a population of 50,000, and Babylon, with 80,000 persons.

The development of an adequate transportation network to serve the city's internal and external needs always loomed as a difficult logistical problem and limited urban growth. The provision of fresh drinking water and sanitary services similarly posed serious problems, as did the need for security defenses.

Cities developed in the Nile Valley several hundreds of years after those in Mesopotamia (Figure 2-1). Most likely, a diffusion process was responsible for the spread to Egypt. Two important cities in the Nile Valley were Thebes and Memphis, which flourished around 3000 B.C. Egyptian cities are most remembered for their monumental architecture, popularly symbolized by the pyramid. But Egyptians also excelled in art and urban designs. Unique features of their towns included a series of long, parallel streets, leading from a single corridor, that created a formal city plan.[3]

Around 2500 B.C., cities also flourished in the Indus Valley of present-day Pakistan, again most likely the result of a diffusion process from the Southwest Asian cultural hearth. The Indian cities of Mohenjo-Daro and Harappa were very large administrative-religious centers of approximately 40,000 persons each. Both cities had a similar rectangular grid layout with large citadels positioned on raised platforms about 30 feet high and faced with brick revetment walls. A large public bath has been identified at Mohenjo-Daro. Huge granaries stored small grains for processing in crude flour mills. The desertlike environment associated with this desolate area today masks the potential for wealth and prosperity that once existed in the Indus Valley. Cotton was first cultivated and woven in this area, and the inhabitants also developed a complex system of weights and measures. But the area has been abandoned for centuries. Earlier this century, archaeological work began to uncover these ancient cities. Today, the rising brackish water table of the river in the vicinity of Mohenjo-Daro is eating away the adobe brick construction materials. A restoration effort now underway seeks to minimize the destruction caused by this salt encrustation, including the digging of wells and canals to divert water back to the Indus River.

Cities also existed in antiquity in the Huang Ho (Yellow River) Valley of China, along the Mediterranean Coast, and in Mesoamerica. In the latter instance, they may have developed independently, but those in China and the Mediterranean most certainly evolved from the Mesopotamian heartland. The first cities emerged in China in a region surrounding the middle course of the Huang Ho (Yellow) River in a fertile loess area. Known as the "land within the passes" because of its location between the Lu Liang Mountains and the Chin Ling Highlands, this area supported a growing population in the Shang Dynasty or Bronze Age period (1900–1050 B.C.). Anyang was the major city, located near a bend in the Huang Ho River.

The Maya, Zapotecs, Mextecs, and Aztecs in Mesoamerica developed an elaborate network of cities but apparently did not practice animal husbandry or have the use of the wheel. Neither did the cities enjoy settings in river valleys, but their system did generate considerable crop surpluses from maize cultivation.[4] As the case with all early cities, regardless of location, a powerful religious-political organization strongly influenced their economic-administrative organization.

Greek Tradition

Greek cities emerged in the seventh to eighth centuries B.C., and within 200 years their number had spread widely throughout the Aegean region and westward to Spain and France. Most of these places were small and had little impact, but Greek cities offer tremendous historical significance. Regardless of size, these Greek

[2]R. J. Johnston, "Regarding Urban Origins, Urbanization and Urban Patterns," *Geography*, 62 (January 1977), 3.

[3]Frederick R. Hiorns, *Town-Building in History*, George G. Harrap and Co., London, 1956, p. 13.

[4]Gideon Sjoberg, "The Origin and Evolution of Cities," *Scientific American*, 213 (September 1965), 54–63.

cities are often referred to by the term *polis*.[5] The polis, or *city-state*, was typically a compact region dominated by a walled village or small city. The larger, better-known city-states included Athens and Sparta. Athens, in the fifth century, may have had 100,000 to 150,000 inhabitants. Other important Greek cities included Selinus, Miletus, and Corinth.

Originally, the Greek cities evolved in an unplanned, organic manner around an *acropolis*, a religious and defensive structure. It often contained the entire city area in early stages of development. As the city grew and other activities moved out, the acropolis area often became ceremonial in function. An open, irregular space around the acropolis, the *agora*, served as a circulation and exchange area. As activities dispersed from the acropolis, the agora became more rectilinear and enclosed. It gradually evolved into a multipurpose marketplace and theater complex, as well as a focal point for surrounding residential areas. Residential areas in early times were placed irregularly along curving streets and narrow alleys.

With time, as cities redeveloped, a more formally conceived street network evolved. Hippodamus designed a regular *grid street-block* system for the city of Miletus when it was reconstructed around 450 B.C. Three major sections in Miletus were laid out, one for the artisans, another for the farmers, and a third for the military, each having its own grid.[6] This grid format was also adopted in other cities. Notwithstanding the grid street system, the Greek city was a liberal city in that an elaborate social hierarchy never developed, and residential areas were more ordinary than those that evolved subsequently in the Roman city. House designs were rather plain. Normally, they faced inward away from the street around an open, sometimes colonnaded, courtyard.

Roman Adaptation

The Greek city form became a model for the Romans. Gradually, the Romans went beyond the physical design aspect adopted from the Greeks and made the city function quite strongly as a social machine with a hierarchical order. This was manifest in the placement of administrative and religious facilities in special places to reinforce the notion of an established pecking order.

Ancient Rome itself became an especially ostentatious place, according to Vance, with proper, ordered design receiving a high priority.[7] The health and recreation needs of the population received special attention. At one time, 900 public baths (thermae), 1200 public fountains, and 250 storage reservoirs flourished in and around Rome. But the city grew rapidly, making the implementation of more elaborate plans virtually impossible. As a result, much of Rome came to have a disorganized, organic character.

A typical Roman city displayed a square or rectangular layout. Two perpendicular roads bisected the area at the center, with one axis following a north–south orientation. At the center, an open square, the *forum*, provided space for public assemblies and a market setting for merchants to set up temporary shops (Figure 2-3). As a site for civic and cultural activities, the forum hosted funerals, shows, sporting events, and political functions. Over time, more permanent quarters for stores emerged under porticoes or colonnades on the perimeter of the forum. The nearest thing to a Roman forum today may be the *souk* street market found in North Africa.

Later, *basilicas*, permanent structures housing covered markets, were added adjacent to the forum. The basilica doubled as both a public and private facility, as tribunals or law courts often operated out of them, as did retail shops. Some basilicas became exclusive courthouse facilities. A second type of permanent building in the forum complex, labeled the *curia*, housed the local meeting hall for the governing body, the senate. Other public buildings in the area might include the capitol, or the main temple, other temples, a public bath, and a library. A reconstructed Pompeii, which was buried from an eruption of Mount Vesuvius in 79 A.D., provides an excellent record of the elaborate organizational grouping of public buildings around the forum, including a bath, theater, arena, and gymnasium. Residential blocks surrounded this more specialized core area (Figure 2-4).

The traditional square, single-family Roman house, the *domus*, featured an arrangement of rooms around a central open atrium or court and tile roof. The opening

[5]Norman J. G. Pounds, "The Urbanization of the Classical World," *Annals of the Association of American Geographers*, 59 (1969), 135–157.

[6]James E. Vance, Jr., *The Continuing City: Urban Morphology in Western Civilization*, The Johns Hopkins University Press, Baltimore, 1990, pp. 46–49.

[7]Ibid., pp. 61–77.

Figure 2-3. Ruins of Roman Forum Today. Originally an open market square, the forum became the setting of more formal functions and buildings over time. As a site for civic and cultural activities, the forum hosted funerals, shows, sporting events, and political functions. (Peter Menzel/Stock, Boston)

in the roof of the atrium is shown in Figure 2-5. In larger cities such as Rome, only the wealthy lived in single-family units, whereas the middle- and lower-income families occupied three- to six-story apartments (*insulae*). One impressive type of apartment house recently excavated at the port city of Ostia on the Tiber River, labeled a garden house, contained up to 100 units. Each unit had a central atrium. The Ostia garden house complex included two buildings in the center of a courtyard, surrounded on the perimeter by a solid, irregular rectangle of buildings. Several retail shops faced outward to the street on the ground level in the perimeter buildings. The design of the garden house provides an example of a highly planned complex. An underlying geometric principle, based on dividing a square with a *sacred cut*, strongly influenced the design.

The Roman territorial influence became continental in proportion during the second and third centuries A.D. The Roman empire extended from England (including the early city of London), Belgium, and the Rhine Valley in the north, through France (Gaul), Switzer-land, and Spain, to the whole Mediterranean realm from North Africa through southwest Asia (Figure 2-6). Massive public works programs, including elaborate freshwater aqueducts and sewer canals, serviced this vast network of cities. Remains of these public works can still be found today.

Many modern-day cities on the Rhine and Danube River corridors owe their origin to Roman military camps. Adjacent to these military barracks, market centers called *canabae* emerged. Often when individuals left military service, they chose to remain in the area. The cities of Cologne, Mainz, Strasbourg, Vienna, and Budapest are examples of these military camptowns.

Attention to arts and crafts in Roman cities promoted individual fulfillment and left a great legacy testifying to their prominence. "Statuary, stone-carving, modelled plaster, mosaic work, mural painting, fine metal work, and so on were everywhere."[8] But eventually,

---

[8]Frederick Hiorns, *Town Building*, op. cit., p. 53.

greed and excess among the leaders and citizenry alike led to the downfall of the Roman Empire—and, in turn, to the decay and destruction of European cities as the social order broke down.

Roman institutions began to fail by the fourth century and the army became weaker. Invading German tribes gradually whittled away the territory associated with the Roman Empire. By 410, Rome itself was occupied by invading Goths, and by the fifth century, the Empire all but vanished.

With the decline of the Roman Empire centered on Rome, a shift in political and economic power occurred to the east. The predominantly Christian city of Constantinople, largely free of the pagan influence associated with Rome, became the capital of the Eastern Roman or Byzantine Empire in 395. Gradually the city attained economic and cultural supremacy of the Mediterranean world because of its location astride east–west trade routes.

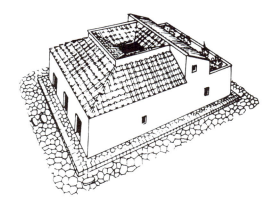

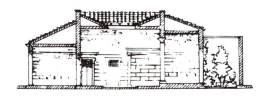

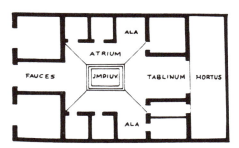

Figure 2-5. The Roman House, or Domus. The traditional square Roman house, the domus, features an arrangement of rooms around a central open atrium or court. *Source:* Frank E. Brown, *Roman Architecture.* Copyright ©1979 by George Braziller. Reprinted by permission of George Braziller, Inc.

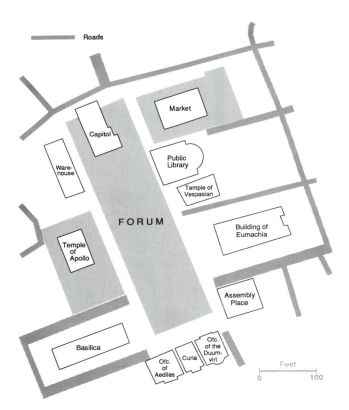

Figure 2-4. Plan of Pompeii. The archaeological reconstruction of ancient Pompeii, which was buried under an eruption of Mt. Vesuvius in 79 A.D., provides an excellent record of the elaborate organizational grouping of public buildings around its forum, including the capitol, market, library, temple, basilica, and political/legal institutions. *Source:* Modified after Pierre Grimal. *Roman Cities.* Translation and edited by G. Michael Woloch. University of Wisconsin Press, Madison, 1983. p. 47.

In 565, Mohammed was born in Mecca. When the prophet died in 632, he left a legacy in his writings, codified as the Koran. Moslems, the followers of Mohammed, eventually established their own empire with its capital in Baghdad. This development led to a division of the East into an Islamic empire, largely based in Persia and focused on Mohammed's teachings, and a Greco-Roman Christian empire centered in Constantinople. In 1453, Constantinople became the capital of the Mohammedan Empire.

Middle Ages

In the Middle Ages, a cultural and economic transition began that eventually transformed Europe from a back-

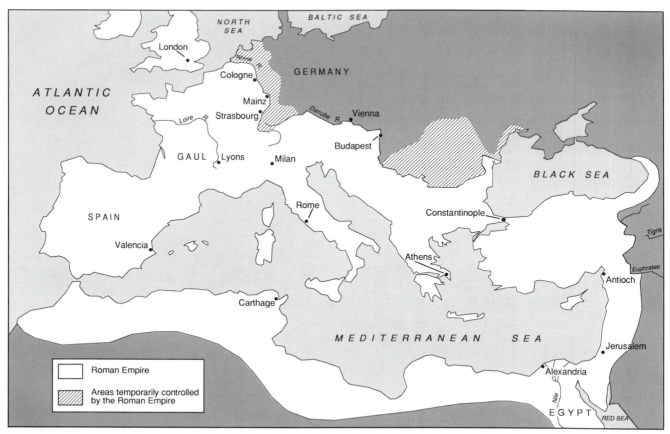

Figure 2-6. Roman Empire, 2nd Century A.D. At its greatest territorial extent, the Roman Empire included much of Europe, North Africa, and Northwest Africa. Many present-day great cities, including London, Cologne, Lyons, Vienna, and Budapest, have origins as Roman cities.

ward, colonial region under the Romans to a leadership role in creating a modern civilization. The focus of innovation and growth gradually shifted from Southwest Asia and the Mediterranean basin to the continental interior. Advances in arts and science, literature, and architecture (Gothic) eventually became an integral part of the change. Christianity played a leadership role in these developments.

This transition in Europe occurred over a period of centuries and awaited the reestablishment of political order following the collapse of the Roman Empire and successive Germanic invasions. Many independent kingdoms rose and fell during the struggle to develop a new order. We still associate the Anglo-Saxons with England, the Franks with France and Germany, and the Lombards with Italy. A Frankish family produced Charles the Great, or Charlemagne, who came to power in 717. He established an extensive Christian empire that represented the beginning of Western European civilization. But the empire disintegrated after Charle-

magne's death and many smaller states or kingdoms reemerged. "To increase the confusion, a new series of invasions struck Europe in the ninth century. Vikings from the North, Magyars from the East, and Saracens from the South plundered the coasts, the plains, and river valleys."[9]

The construction of castles and walled towns became commonplace to defend the countryside. The importance of this development is that central authority vanished and local self-sufficiency increased in this era of civil war. It also produced the institution of *feudalism*. "Essentially it [feudalism] was the rule of bosses (or lords) and their gangs (or vassals). Strong men surrounded by groups of armed retainers took over the government of relatively small districts, and supplied the armed forces and ran the courts [political body]

---

[9]Joseph R. Strayer, *Western Europe in the Middle Ages: A Short History*, Appleton-Century-Crofts, New York, 1955, p. 59.

TABLE 2-1
Leading World Cities, 900 A.D.

City	Population
Baghdad (Iraq)	900,000
Changan (China)	500,000
Constantinople (Turkey)	300,000
Kyoto (Japan)	200,000
Cordova (Spain)	200,000

Source: Tertius Chandler, *Four Thousand Years of Urban Growth,* St. David's University Press, Lewiston, N.Y., 1987. Copyright ©1987 Tertius Chandler. Used by Permission.

which protected their subjects . . . ."[10] While highly variable in areal coverage and control, feudalism became the prevailing governmental structure in Western Europe, especially so in England and France, but also to a lesser degree in Germany and Italy. A typical feudal state was equivalent to a modern-day county unit in size. From 900 to 1100 feudalism experienced its peak. As can be seen in Table 2-1, the leading world cities at the time were located either in present-day Southwest Asia (Baghdad and Constantinople) or in East Asia (Changan, Kyoto, and Hangchow).

By the eleventh century, towns began to grow in Europe, especially in fertile agricultural areas such as the feudal states of Flanders and Normandy in northern France. In Flanders, expanding sheep production led to a wool surplus and the development of a weaving industry, especially at Ghent and Bruges. Coastal port cities also fluorished in Italy, including Venice, Genoa, and Pisa, taking advantage of trade in silk and spices from the Far East. Both the church and feudal lords had difficulties controlling towns, but in some areas towns gained freedoms in exchange for tax and toll payments, which in turn created a stronger centralized economy as was the case in England and France.

The thirteenth century witnessed the flourishing of annual trade fairs in many European cities, which greatly promoted merchant trade. City dwellers became a privileged class. They were called burgers in Germany and the bourgeois in France. The burg was originally a German term meaning "fort," but gradually came to be associated with a walled town. Merchants, bankers, artisans, and small shopkeepers all found expanding opportunities in the burgeoning cities. As *gilds* or associations of similar tradesmen became more

powerful, quality standards developed that further solidified the influence of the city. Crusades launched from Western Europe to Asia also promoted commerce and industry, and European-based sea power expanded correspondingly. Italian seaports benefited the most from growing trade.

Vienna began to flourish in this era as a center of culture and arts. As a crossroads between Italy and northern Europe from the twelfth century onward, Vienna served as a nexus for the transmittal of emerging Renaissance ideas to the rest of Europe. In 1365, a university was founded in Vienna and by 1450, the city had become a veritable hotbed of development, housing not only thousands of nobles and clergy, but equal numbers of merchants, craftsmen, and laborers.

The thirteenth century also brought stagnation to the medieval way of life because of problems in both church leadership and the economy. The setback did not affect Italy as negatively as other areas. Merchant trade and the work of artists and scholars continued to excel in Italy, eventually ushering in the Age of the Renaissance.

EUROPEAN ROOTS OF NORTH AMERICAN CITIES

The design of early American cities was influenced by European traditions brought to the New World by early settlers. Many of these ideas can be traced to Greek and Roman styles, while other philosophies originated in the Middle Ages.

Early American towns were primarily founded as colonial outposts with strong trading ties to the mother country.[11] In the words of Vance, they were primarily merchant towns with very little emphasis placed on ideal rigid plans or a hierarchical social order. The cities were typically founded in a spirit of individualism and equality with the land-subdivision process reflecting this equality. Low priority was given to special treatments for showy public facilities and land lots were rather uniform in size. In contrast, many European cities at the time were ruled by absolutist prices and had an aristocratic flair. Land assignment in them depended on social order, with public buildings placed to empha-

---

[10]Ibid., pp. 60–61.

[11]James E. Vance, Jr., "Was American Urbanization Predictable? Medieval Roots of American Cities," paper delivered at Conference of Urban Geography, Delaware Valley Geographical Association, Philadelphia, April 1976.

size their large scale and to reinforce importance. These structures were often sited at the end of broad vistas or with central court locations and dominated their surroundings.

Vance, the preeminent authority in geography on the morphogenesis of the American city, suggests that five types of American cities exist in terms of origin, function, and layout. These five traditions of urbanization evolved in colonial times nearly simultaneously in various parts of the country. Each will be discussed here separately.

Medieval Organic City

The American medieval organic city form owes its origin to the European bourg and faubourg. The European bourg, originally a castle or walled fortress town, was often built on a hilltop or river bluff location. The faubourg, a merchants' settlement, grew up on the slopes or foothills just outside the bourg, sometimes adjacent to the city gates leading into the bourg. The faubourg settlement did not have any particular established order in terms of housing or underlying street

patterns. Growth occurred in an unplanned, organic manner. The settlement functioned as a trading center located near the bourg because of the security and market potential it offered.

In America, many early coastal merchant towns in New England replicated the medieval organic faubourg. Typically these cities had an elongated street system laid out on the seacoast or along a river. Little evidence of formal organization in terms of design or order existed. In early Boston, for example, houses grew up around many bays and inlets. Other early New England towns exhibiting an organic character are Worcester, Fitchburg, Portsmouth, and Portland, as well as early Salem, Hartford, Providence, and Newport.

Medieval Bastide

The medieval bastide, also a European form, is primarily associated with settlements in southern France dating to the twelfth and thirteenth centuries (Figure 2-7). Today, we would call these cities "new towns," as they were placed in previously unsettled

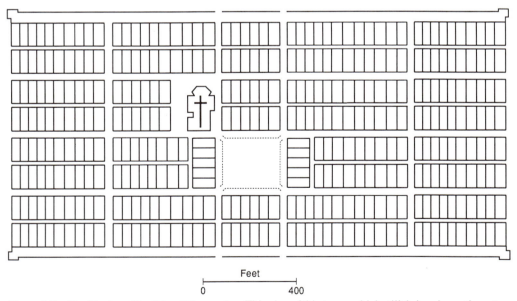

Feet
0   400

Figure 2-7. The Medieval Bastide of Monpazier. This plan of this town, which still thrives in southwestern France, dates to 1284. Inspired by the Roman and Greek city form, bastides possessed a regular street plan with a central square. They were walled and placed as "new towns" in previously unsettled agricultural areas for trade and business reasons. Within this formal plan, land uses followed an irregular arrangement.
Source: Modified after James E. Vance, Jr. *The Continuing City: Urban Morphology in Western Civilization.* Baltimore, The Johns Hopkins University Press, 1990. p. 14. Used by permission.

areas. In Europe, they were established by counts and bishops for economic reasons to increase their wealth from the trade of agricultural products (see box). Merchants promoted trade of locally produced goods such as grain and/or vineyards. Most bastides enjoyed locations in river valleys to assist the export of goods, but some occurred on high ground where military objectives became more important.

Bastides possessed a regular street plan, usually a rectangular grid, but sometimes a radial form characterized the settlement structure. Despite this morphological order, flexibility characterized land use patterns and settlers received equal treatment. Land assignments did not follow a class hierarchy or spatial ordering. The bastide did not experience feudal practices that prevailed in farm towns or the stringent rules of city gilds that evolved in larger, older cities. The bastide served as an economic place, with trade the major function. Vance has said the bastide combined the morphological order of the Roman city with the social flexibility of the Greek city.[12] Streets had equal status in the bastide, which had no central avenues or broad boulevards. Stone walls encircled these towns as a defensive measure, and a market usually occupied a prime location in the central square (Figure 2-8).

No fewer than 315 of these bastide towns still survive in southwestern France between Toulouse and Bordeaux. Bastides occur in Spain, Italy, eastern Europe, and England. The English, in fact, built some of the bastides to the east of Bordeaux. English settlers in the United States in the seventeenth century brought the bastidal form with them, having seen it at places like Salisbury, Hull, Falmouth, Newcastle, and Liverpool. Early examples of this tradition in New England include the cities of Cambridge and New Haven, and French settlements in the St. Lawrence Valley and Great Lakes area extending westward to Detroit, Milwaukee, Green Bay, and Duluth.

In the Ohio–Mississippi River Valley, significant French influence occurred in Pittsburgh (originally Fort Dusquesne), St. Louis, Baton Rouge, and New Orleans. Later, Cambridge, Providence, and Newport also took on a bastidal character. These communities were all designed to be working places, not ideal towns. Like their European counterparts, they often had markets and public squares in the center, but no massive houses or imposing churches. Equality for all residents and activities was emphasized.

Figure 2-8. Villereal Market. The unique covered market in this southwestern France bastide dates to the Middle Ages. "Atop its roof perches an unusual second story, held up by medieval pillars of oak. The addition housed merchants when it was built in 1267 and now serves as offices for a local radio station" (*New York Times*, XX, May 7, 1989, p. 16). (Jean-Marc Charles/Rapho)

Spanish "Laws of the Indies" Towns

The Spanish new town legacy in the New World has been linked to the strong design features of the Roman tradition, as discussed earlier. The Spanish "Laws of the Indies" city building guidelines, issued in the name of King Phillip II of Spain in 1573, codified and extended earlier decrees. The

> 148 ordinances dealt with every aspect of site selection, city planning, and political organization; in fact, they were the most complete such set of instructions ever issued to serve as guidelines for the building of towns in the Americas and, in terms of their widespread application and persistence, probably the most effective planning documents in the history of mankind.[13]

---

[12]James E. Vance, Jr., *The Continuing City*, op. cit., pp. 176–205.

[13]Dora P. Crouch et al., *Spanish City Planning in North America*, M.I.T. Press, Cambridge, Mass., 1982, p. 2.

THE MARKET FUNCTION OF THE MEDIEVAL BASTIDE

The medieval bastide was an orderly place design-wise: grid streets, equal-size lots, walls, and so on, but it was created to be a working town, not an ideal, formal town.

Since trade and artisan manufacture were the two activities for which the towns were established, though walled bastides might stand as strongpoints on the frontier of the realm in times of warfare, the marketplace and the artisan's streets must be given fundamental attention. The bastide plan in its archetypal form was the physical expression of such attention. Always located near the center of the grid layout was a market square [Figure 2-7], one of the modular street blocks left free of buildings and used for the sale of agricultural produce. Typically, this marketplace was apportioned periodically into sites for small barrows and stands on which farmers sold produce. At night and when the market was closed, the square would be swept clean of commercial activity to become a place of social contact among town residents. . . .

Around the square the more fundamental activities of the town—those affairs that kept the citizens busy every day save Sunday—began to show up. Immediately adjacent to the square in the bastides of southern France, and sometimes in Savoy, Switzerland, and other Germanic lands, the houses tended to reflect the selling and buying function carried on there through the construction of a covered arcade in which activities could continue even in wet weather. Sometimes such a shelter stood even in the square itself, now usually termed a market hall, in which certain activities that must transpire whatever the weather could continue. In Villeréal in Périgord, such a structure stands in the center of the square [Figure 2-9], though there are some arcades at the side of the open space. Certainly market halls were not limited to bastides, but they seem to have been common there; unfortunately, most have disappeared in the last couple of centuries, because of their wooden construction.

The real trading life of the towns was located in the arcades at the side. The more important merchants normally resided in the houses fronting the square. In those towns where an arcade, called in the bastides a *cornière*, had been built, those traders seem to have spread their wares brought from distant places under the shelter they afforded. These cornières seem to have been rather consistently possessed of arched openings, both toward the front, giving onto the square, and to each side, leading to the cornières of adjacent houses to create a continuous arcade along the sides of the square. To call these features arcades may be imprecise, as they were probably not actually arched over, save at the openings in the house walls. Under the house itself, the ceiling of the cornière was usually flat, carried by wooden rafters and closed by floorings. In other words, this cornière was essentially a room in the house left open for entrance from the square or movement along its sides. . . .

We may reason that the more successful merchants would tend to take up locations around the squares of bastides employing the cornière both to display the trade goods they used as tender and to collect the staple they might gain in return. Gold and silver were not in common circulation until the Age of Discovery opened the rich mines of the New World. Instead, the exchange of goods facilitated the trade of medieval times. Merchants exercised their function both as distributors and as collectors, and their premises had to be sufficient to comprehend both activities.

If the leading merchants might be expected to take up plots on the frontage of the square, either when the town was being laid out or later, the lesser merchants might be assumed to come to occupy an intermediate economic and morphological position. How many merchants engaged in distant trade would there be in any one bastide? We must fall back on probability to venture that there were never more than could be accommodated in the houses with cornières surrounding the square. Lesser tradespeople, more in the class of artisans than of merchants, came to occupy sites within the town that would best accommodate what was clearly a compromise demand.

On the basis of this logical breakdown of locations within a bastide, we may envisage some characteristic divisions of the land use within the town. Since virtually all these towns had squares, we may designate the first of these land-use divisions as that related to the market square. Within the square itself would be found a periodic market.

More to the point in explaining the origin of the bastide is the second half of the marketplace land-use component—the ring of merchants' shops fronting on the square and often giving on it by means of the cornières. Even in England where the cornière was little used, save in a very specialized form such as the second-story galleries found in medieval Chester, the symbiosis between merchant housing and open marketplace appears to have held. In Bristol's Old Market, the building that served as the piepowder court still stands to attest to this tie, and in many towns the more impressive burghers' houses survive or are recorded as having fronted on the marketplace.

Source: James E. Vance, Jr., *The Continuing City: Urban Morphology in Western Civilization,* Johns Hopkins University Press, Baltimore/London, 1990, pp. 189–193.

Ordinance 114, for example, reads as follows:

> From the plaza shall begin four principal streets: One [shall be] from the middle of each side, and two streets from each corner of the plaza; the four corners of the plaza shall face the four principal winds, because in this manner, the streets running from the plaza will not be exposed to the four principal winds, which would cause much inconvenience.[14]

Other ordinances focused on choosing suitable sites for cities, picking locations for churches, detailed legal, financial, and administrative regulations, and guidelines for dealing with Indians. The impact of these guidelines cannot be overstated.

> Spanish colonization of the New World occupied a vast period of time and extent of territory. The first settlement was made at Hispaniola in the West Indies in 1493, and the last surviving settlement in California in 1781. In North America, Spanish influence is evident from Florida in the east to Louisiana on the Gulf and as far north as St. Louis, and all across the continent to California. The earliest Spanish city of North America, St. Augustine, Florida, was begun in 1565, and was already more than 200 years old when Philip de Neve, governor of Alta California, founded Los Angeles in 1781. During these 200 years, Spanish urban policy had time to grow, develop and be codified.

> Most of the important cities of Latin America were founded between 1506 and 1570 (16 of the 20 largest cities were dedicated by 1580), according to a centralized system of royal planning that encouraged concentration of power, wealth, and resources. Rather than creating a system of cities, each principal city was administratively linked to, and thus dependent on, the government in Spain, and trade among them was not encouraged. We still see the fruits of this dependence in the trade and growth patterns of these cities.[15]

Normally, a grid street plan, focused on a central plaza, prevailed in the Spanish town (Figure 2-9). Land assignment followed the Roman social ordering procedure, with certain sites being reserved for special treatment.

Residential areas developed with a defensive configuration. Narrow streets provided cramped passageways for movement for security reasons and assisted the channeling of air movement for ventilation. Examples of Spanish towns in the United States include St. Augustine (Figure 2-10) and Pensacola, Florida; San Antonio, Texas; and Santa Fe, New Mexico. In California, three types of Spanish settlements occurred: the mission town, the presidio, and the pueblo. The Spanish founded mission towns that combined religious and secular functions throughout California. Converting and educating Indians became a major purpose for establishing these settlements. A church and cloister provided the central focus around which dormitories, a school, and medical facilities clustered. Quarters for Indians and agricultural land rounded out the community. Examples of missions include San Luis Obispo, San Miguel, San Gabriel, San Juan Capistrano, San Fernando, Santa Cruz, Santa Clara, and San Rafael.

The Spaniards also built "four *presidios*, or military communities in California: San Diego in 1769, Monterey in 1770, San Francisco in 1776, and Santa Barbara in 1782. These were stockaded or walled quadrangles containing the barracks, stores, shops, and stables of the military garrison, as well as the houses of a few settlers."[16] Several *pueblos*, or civilian communities, were also established in California following the Laws of the Indies guidelines. The purpose of these settlements was to settle areas with considerable potential for agriculture. Two early examples include San Jose and Los Angeles.

Distinctions among these centers declined over time as did the Spanish tradition in general, as Anglo influences became stronger. Spanish cities in the United States were also located on the margins of Spanish settlement in North America, further weakening their imprint in contrast to their stronger impact in Latin America.

English Renaissance

The European planned city, labeled English Renaissance, is first found in America in the South. Two of these planned cities developed as capitals in the Chesapeake Bay region—Annapolis and Williamsburg. Two others became ports on the southeast coast—Charleston and Savannah. Washington, D.C., may also fit this tradition.

Territorial Governor Colonel Francis Nicholson developed both Annapolis and Williamsburg while serving as the Chief Executive of each of their respective states, first Maryland and then Virginia. Annapolis, granted a charter by Queen Anne in 1708, was laid out

---

[14]Ibid., p. 14.

[15]Ibid., p. 27.

[16]John Reps, *Town Planning in Frontier America*. University of Missouri Press, Columbia, 1980, p. 41.

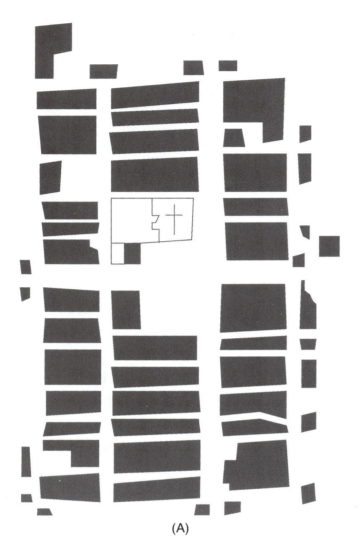

(A)

(B)

Figure 2-9.   Santa Fe de Granada, Spain. The plan of this ancient Spanish city (A) and contemporary photograph (B) show the design concept in the Roman tradition that inspired the Spanish Law of Indies town plan followed in the New World. Built in 1491, the regular plan for Santa Fe de Granada included a grid street pattern and a centrally located plaza with formal placement of the church at one side. Note the traditional look of the architecture of this historic city. *Source:* (A) Crouch, Dora P. et al. *Spanish City Planning in North America.* M.I.T. Press, Cambridge, Mass., 1982, p. 54; Reprinted from *Culture and Conquest: America's Spanish Heritage,* by George M. Foster, Viking Fund Publications in Anthropology, No. 27, 1960, by permission of the Wenner-Gren Foundation for Anthropological Research, Inc., New York.; (B) Office of the Mayor, Santa Fe de Grenada, Spain.

in true elitist style with large lots. A square and two impressive circles with radiating streets became the focal points for administrative functions. In a similar vein, Williamsburg also became a showcase in the early 1700s with a broad avenue, Duke of Gloucester Street, running between the College of William and Mary at one end and the capitol at the other. A palace green open space intersected this corridor midway at a right angle, framing the imposing governor's palace.

Plans for Charleston, the earliest of these towns, date to 1672. Charleston served as an aristocratic center, if not a political capital, for the southern landed gentry. The grand design, developed in honor of King Charles II, never reached completion, but the wealthy Carolina planter class did develop a city in exemplary fashion with their elegant homes. They used the city as a refuge

from the hot, humid interior plantations during the summer months. In this way they transferred the feudal hierarchical order from the plantation to the city. These imposing mansions, with their side porches, still grace the battery section near the waterfront in old Charleston.

The design for Savannah, spearheaded by General James Oglethorpe in 1733, included several formal, but open, public squares. Around the squares, the Savannah Plan called for 40 long, narrow, 60 90-foot house lots on two sides, with larger trust lots for churches and public buildings located on the other two sides (Figure 2-11). Wide, straight streets led to and from the squares, emphasizing their grandeur. Narrow lanes provided access at the rear of all lots. Prior to the Revolutionary War, six wards housed the population,

Figure 2-10. St. Augustine, Florida. Following the classic principles laid out in the "Laws of the Indies," issued by King Philip II of Spain in 1573, the narrow streets of St. Augustine provided cramped passageways for movement for security reasons and assisted the channeling of air movement for ventilation. Picturesque Old Aviles Street shown here is named for Pedro Menendez de Aviles who landed in the area in 1565, claiming the land for Spain and fortifying it against the French. (David W. Corson/A. Davaney, NY.)

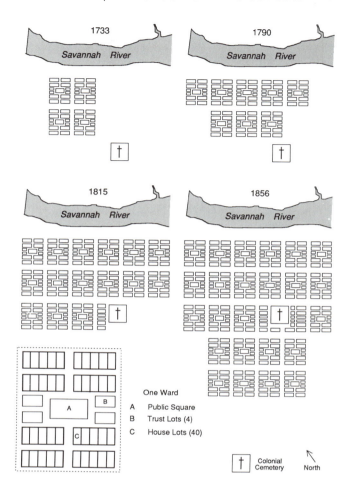

Figure 2-11. The Savannah Plan. Inspired by the rebuilding of London at the time, Oglethorpe laid out the first 4 wards in Savannah in 1733 around squares formed by four large trust lots reserved for large residences, churches, and public buildings, on two sides, and 40 long, narrow house lots in blocks of 5 in two rows on the other two sides. Additional wards were added over time as the map shows, using this same design, creating 24 squares before the plan was abandoned around the time of the Civil War. *Source:* Modified after figure 84 from *Town Planning in Frontier America* by John Reps, by permission of the University of Missouri Press. Copyright ©1980 by the curators of the University of Missouri.

but steady expansion occurred thereafter. In the late 1700s and first half of the 1800s, growth followed the basic plan by adding more wards with squares to the existing space. In the latter half of the 1800s, the plan was abandoned and development reverted to a more informal, speculative format. Today this original residential area comprises the largest officially recognized historic district in the United States, containing over 900 homes. Most of the squares with their gardens, fountains and statues, and surrounding homes and

public buildings, now renovated, still function as they did over a century ago.

As conceived by Pierre L'Enfant in 1791, the expansive new federal city of Washington, D.C., laid out between the east branch and main channel of the Potomac River on land ceded to the government by the states of Virginia and Maryland, provides another example of an aristocratic urban design. Topography was used to good advantage by placing the Congress House (Capitol) on Jenkins Hill, named after the

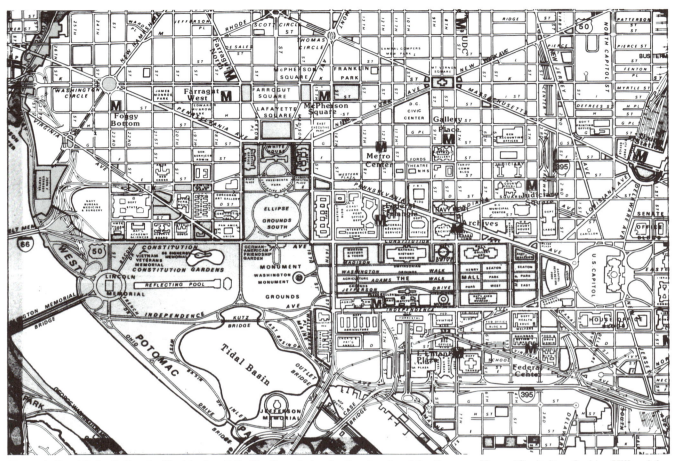

Figure 2-12. L'Enfant's Plan for Washington, D.C. The formal plan for the city placed the Congress House (Capitol) on Jenkins Hill and the President's House (White House) on another ridge overlooking the Potomac. A formal mall joined these focal points. A grid of streets and wide radiating avenues were laid out around the two major landmark buildings. It is still easy to see the imprint of this plan on modern Washington, as this map indicates. Note locations of memorials and museums in mall area which is fronted by government office buildings. *Source:* Courtesy U.S. Park Service.

agriculturalist that owned the land. The President's House (White House) occupied another ridge overlooking the Potomac.[17] A formal mall with large rectangular open spaces joined these focal points. This broad axis of open space was reserved for public use and later became the preferred site for monuments and museums. A tight, rectangular grid of streets was organized around these focal points and a network of avenues was superimposed over them, radiating outward from the two major landmark buildings (Figure 2-12). Squares were laid out at many of the intersections of the radial avenues with the grid streets.

L'Enfant's plan, while never implemented exactly, has had a profound, lasting influence on the city structure. It is still easy to see the evidence of this overall design on modern Washington. The circles, radial streets, and open spaces set aside on the major axes have been only slightly modified with highway tunnels under intersections and one-way street pairs to facilitate traffic movement, and many now accommodate monuments, memorials, museums, federal office buildings, transit stations, and recreational facilities.

Speculators' Town

The one particularly American adaption of the city, according to Vance, was the speculators' town, which

---

[17]Daniel D. Reiff, *Washington Architecture 1791–1861, Problems in Development*, U.S. Commission of Fine Arts, USGPO, Washington, D.C., 1971.

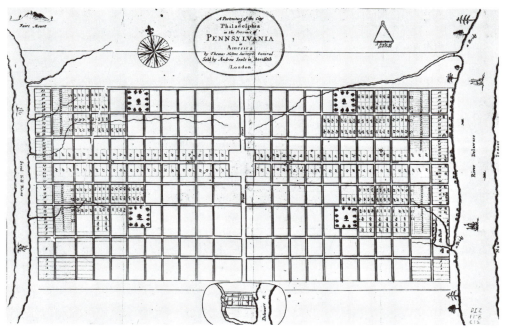

Figure 2-13. Philadelphia, the Speculator's Town. The plan for Philadelphia was developed by William Penn in 1682. Note the expansive grid layout between the Delaware and Scool Kill (sic) rivers with an open square in the center of each quadrangle. *Source:* Map courtesy of Cornell University Libraries. Used by permission.

is typified by Philadelphia (Figure 2-13). William Penn developed the plan for Philadelphia in 1682. He was influenced by the reconstruction plan chosen for rebuilding London following the disastrous 1666 fire. Penn's Philadelphia plan subdivided property into regular and proportional lots. Even though it seems that a formal city grid controlled use, including a 10-acre public square in the center and four 8-acre squares in the center of each quarter, the emphasis in Philadelphia was also on equality. The open spaces were "commons" for the use of citizens.

The plan for Philadelphia encompassed a massive area, two miles by one mile in area, stretching from the Delaware River on the east to the Schuylkill River on the west. This territory encompassed a larger area than the medieval city of London. Because the layout was designed in advance with the future sale of property in mind, land speculation was enhanced. Speculation in land sales itself provided the major force to finance development. Unlike the situation in New England, where land was acquired as needed and subdivided into small parcels, in Philadelphia, land was aggressively marketed for trade and speculation. This arrangement

was quite successful; over 600 houses were built in the three years between 1683 and 1685.

The original Penn plan was modified over time to accommodate topographic irregularities and merchants' needs. For example, an additional street was laid out on the Delaware River floodplain, allowing merchants and traders to live and conduct their business on the waterfront.[18] But the role of speculation and land sales had become entrenched. The speculators' town eventually became the dominant American form with its imprint gradually dominating development patterns in the older organic and bastidal towns of New England, as well as in newer settlements in the interior. Today we still find that urban development is primarily market driven by private sector initiatives; only the breadth and scale of developer operations have changed. Many builders now operate on a national basis and command enormous resources.

---

[18]John W. Reps, *The Making of Urban America: A History of City Planning in the United States*, Princeton University Press, Princeton, N.J., 1965, p. 167.

CONTEMPORARY WORLD URBANIZATION

Large cities were the exception prior to the twentieth century, but a few did exist in antiquity, as discussed earlier (Table 2-1). For example, ancient Rome, Changan (Xian) in China, and Constantinople and Baghdad in the Middle East approached 1 million in size at various times. The list of the largest five cities in the world in 900 A.D., shown in Table 2-1, indicates that three were located in Asia and two in the Middle East, with one (Baghdad) approaching 1 million in population. Big cities subsequently dwindled in the Middle Ages, especially in Western Europe. In the East, Constantinople and Baghdad continued to flourish as leading world cities in the 1600s and 1700s (Table 2-2). Millionaire cities generally did not reemerge until the nineteenth century (Table 2-3).

The world order changed dramatically with the coming of the Industrial Revolution to Western Europe. London and Paris joined the list of leading cities in 1700 as both reached the 500,000 threshold. Only Beijing had topped the 1 million population threshold by 1800, but industrialization and urbanization accelerated in ensuing decades in Western Europe and the United States, allowing many additional cities to achieve millionaire status.

Exceedingly complex support systems are required to employ, feed, and house people in big cities. Only

TABLE 2-2
Leading World Cities, 1600 and 1700

	City	Population
1600		
	Beijing (China)	706,000
	Constantinople (Turkey)	700,000
	Agra (India)	500,000
	Cairo (Egypt)	400,000
	Osaka (Japan)	400,000
1700		
	Constantinople (Turkey)	700,000
	Beijing (China)	—
	Isfahan (Iran)	600,000
	London (England)	550,000
	Paris (France)	530,000

Source: Tertius Chandler and Gerald Fox, *Three Thousand Years of Urban Growth*, Academic Press, New York, 1974.

TABLE 2-3
Leading World Cities, 1800 and 1900

	City	Population (thousands)
1800		
	Beijing	1,100
	London	861
	Canton (China)	800
	Constantinople	570
	Paris	547
	Hangchow	500
	Tokyo (Edo)	492
	Naples	430
	Soochow (China)	392
	Osaka	380
1900		
	London	6,480
	New York	4,242
	Paris	3,330
	Berlin	2,424
	Chicago	1,717
	Vienna	1,662
	Tokyo	1,497
	Leningrad (St. Petersburg)	1,439
	Philadelphia	1,418
	Manchester (England)	1,255

Source: Tertius Chandler and Gerald Fox, *Three Thousand Years of Urban Growth*, Academic Press, New York, 1974.

relatively recently have very large cities (over 1 million population), as a group, been practical and efficient places to live. Technological advancements are a major reason why large cities exist in many areas of the world today. But efficiency and opportunities are not universally associated with cities, as we shall see in Chapter 3. Iron and steel construction technology, which made high-rise buildings possible without huge, thick walls, and the electric elevator represent two important factors in the growth of very large cities in recent times. Improved medicine, transportation (steam engine, railroad), and infrastructure (water supply, wastewater treatment, roads, electricity, etc.) are also frequently cited factors.

The city-building thrust created by the Industrial Revolution must also be placed in proper perspective. The Industrial Revolution, which began in England in the late eighteenth century, generated jobs, increased productivity, and opened up mass markets for goods. Transportation innovations, paced by railroad and steamship advances, made factories more productive, generating additional capital to support urban growth. This circular and cumulative process indelibly linked together industrialization and urbanization processes, thus leading to a significant and lasting city-building era.

London reached 1 million in population around 1810, the first western city in modern times to reach this threshold (Table 2-3). Paris topped 1 million in 1846, and New York in the 1860s; Vienna achieved this status in 1870, and Berlin in 1880. By 1900, there were 20 such large cities in the world (Table 2-4), and these four cities each had populations exceeding 2 million persons. From this small group of millionaire cities in 1900, 57 cities had emerged by 1939, 95 by 1951, 213 by 1979, and 257 by 1985 (Figure 2-14).

Large urban regions today are located in all parts of the world and in areas at all stages of economic development, ranging from the less developed third world to developing and advanced countries (Table 2-5 and front endpaper). Three of the five largest metropolitan areas are found in economically sophisticated countries (Japan and the United States), but examination of the distribution of the 27 remaining urban regions over 5 million in size indicates that they occur in countries at all levels of development, with the majority in the third world. The unique situation associated with cities in the third world, in comparison to developed areas, will be explored in Chapter 3.

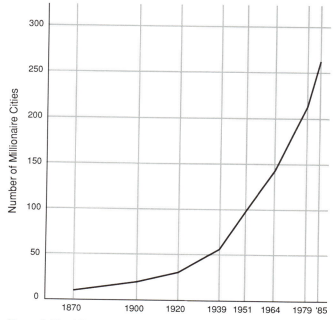

Figure 2-14. **Millionaire Cities of the World.** In modern times, cities over 1 million in population date to the Industrial Revolution in the early 1800s. By far, the most growth in the number of large cities has occurred since World War II. The total number will approach 300 by the turn of the century.

TABLE 2-4
Size Distributions of Millionaire Cities,[a] 1985
(Millions of People)

Size Category	Number of Cities
Over 15	4
10–15	9
5–10	18
3–5	33
2–3	45
1.5–2	46
1–1.5	102
Total	257

Source: 1986 Rand McNally Commercial Atlas and Marketing Guide, Rand McNally, Chicago, 1986, R.L. 92-S-1.
[a]Cities with more than 1 million population.

While about 40 percent of the world's population lives in cities, the city share varies widely between world regions. Nearly 70 percent of the population in highly developed areas lives in cities as a result of the strong and continuous migration to cities that has been under way for about 200 years since the beginning of the Industrial Revolution. In third world areas that are still largely agrarian, slightly less than one-third of the population is urban in the 1990s. Nevertheless, the aggregate size of the urban population in third world areas has exceeded that in developed areas since 1970, because of the large population base in these countries. Currently, Africa experiences the highest urban growth rate, but it is at the same time the most rural continent in the world. East Asia is also largely rural because of the enormous size of the rural population in China. Urbanization rates are expected to increase in the future in China more than in any other area of the world.

Large urban areas in developed countries generally attained the 1 million threshold at, or before, the turn of the century (see Table 2-5). Present-day large urban areas in developing countries generally did not achieve this status until the 1930s or 1940s. Nevertheless, Buenos Aires achieved this status in 1900, as did Rio de

TABLE 2-5
Largest Metropolitan Areas of the World (Millions of People)

Rank	Metropolitan Area	Decade 1 Million Population Reached[a]	1990 Estimated Population
1	Tokyo–Yokohama	1880s	
2	Mexico City	1930s	Over 15
3	New York	1860s	
4	Osaka–Kobe–Kyoto	1900s	
5	São Paulo	1930s	
6	Seoul	1940s	
7	Moscow	1890s	
8	Calcutta	1890s	
9	Buenos Aires	1900s	10–15
10	Bombay	1920s	
11	London	1810s	
12	Los Angeles	1920s	
13	Cairo	1920s	
14	Rio de Janeiro	1910s	
15	Paris	1840s	
16	Shanghai	1910s	
17	Delhi–New Delhi	1940s	
18	Jakarta	1940s	
19	Manila	1940s	
20	Chicago	1880s	
21	Bangkok	1950s	
22	Tehran	1950s	
23	Beijing	1770s	5–10
24	Karachi	1950s	
25	Leningrad	1890s	
26	T'aipei	1960s	
27	Istanbul	1950s	
28	Bogota	1960s	
29	Philadelphia	1880s	
30	Lima	1950s	
31	Madras	1930s	
32	Essen–Dortmund–Duisburg	1900s	

[a]After Chandler and Fox.
Source: 1986 Rand McNally Commercial Atlas and Marketing Guide, Rand McNally, Chicago, 1986, 92-S-1; Tertius Chandler and Gerald Fox, *Three Thousand Years of Urban Growth,* Academic Press, New York, 1974, 365–73.

Janeiro and Shanghai in 1910. Cairo and Bombay were other large third world cities with over 1 million inhabitants by 1920. Beijing, the other major exception, reached the 1 million threshold in 1770, decades before any other present-day metropolitan area.

By the dawn of the twenty-first century, when 50 percent of the world population will be urban (3 billion of the 6 billion world population), the vast majority of the very large metropolitan areas will be located in third world developing areas. A list of the projected leading

TABLE 2-6
Leading World Metropolitan Areas, 1985 and 2000

Projected rank (2000)		1985 Population (millions)	2000 Population (millions)	Projected Growth (Percent Change)
1	Mexico City	17.3	25.8	48
2	São Paulo	15.9	24.0	51
3	Tokyo	18.8	20.2	8
4	Calcutta	11.0	16.5	50
5	Bombay	10.1	16.0	58
6	New York	15.6	15.8	1
7	Shanghai	12.0	14.3	19
8	Seoul	10.3	13.8	34
9	Teheran	7.5	13.6	81
10	Rio de Janeiro	10.4	13.3	28
11	Jakarta	7.9	13.3	68
12	Delhi	7.4	13.2	78

Source: United Nations, *The Prospects of World Urbanization,* Population Studies, No. 101, 1987, p. 25.

metropolitan areas in the world in 2000 appears in Table 2-6. Note that 10 of the top 12 cities in the world will be in third world areas. High rates of rural to urban migration and high levels of natural increase explain this rapid growth.

The projected rapid growth rate of these third world areas in comparison to cities in highly developed areas can also be seen in Table 2-6. On average, the growth rates in the top 10 third world areas will be about 50 percent, ranging from a low of 19 percent in Shanghai to a high of 78 and 81 percent in Delhi and Teheran, respectively. The growth expected in the top two cities represented by highly developed areas, New York (1 percent) and Tokyo (8 percent), pales by comparison.

Megalopolis

The *megalopolis* concept, coined by Jean Gottmann in 1961 for the urban complex in the northeastern United States, where 40 million persons lived in an urban corridor extending from Boston to Washington, D.C.,[19] represents another perspective from which to view the city (Figure 2-15). This megacity definition (*megalopolis* means "great city" in Greek) emphasizes the strong economic ties between and among very large and closely spaced metropolitan areas. High levels of movement of people and goods and telecommunication ties enable a megalopolis to function as a large, if dispersed, galactic city rather than as a series of isolated population centers. In the megalopolis corridor, for example, seven metropolitan areas greater than 1 million in population coexist in a region with over 30 metropolitan areas.

Megalopolis continues to serve as the economic hinge of the United States and exemplifies the viability of the transactional city—created, as it were, by the white collar revolution—and the emergence of the information age. In a paper commemorating the 30th anniversary of Gottmann's seminal treatise on megalopolis, entitled "Geographic Ideas That Have Changed the World" Patricia Gober indicated that "in addition to size and density, a megalopolis implies an expanded scale of urban life, emphasis on information and transactional activities, internal interconnections, and human relationships, and a highly differentiated system of land use including cities, suburbs, small towns, and rural areas."[20] Moreover, Gober suggests that "Gottmann and the concept of megalopolis served as cata-

[19]Jean Gottmann, *Megalopolis,* The Twentieth Century Fund, New York, 1961.

[20]Patricia Gober, "Megalopolis in Geography and Beyond," *Abstracts,* The Association of American Geographers 1991 Annual Meeting, Miami, Florida, Association of American Geographers, Washington, D.C., 1991, p. 68.

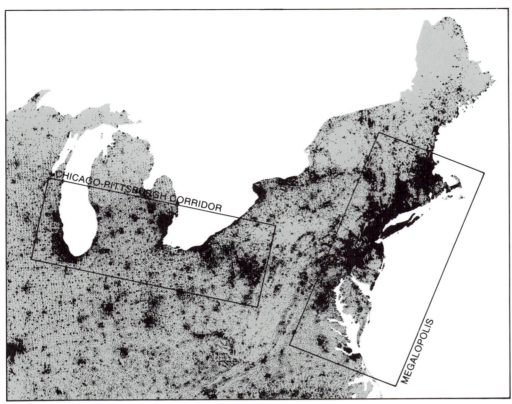

Figure 2-15. Megalopolis and Chicago-Pittsburgh Urban Corridor. The urban corridor extending from Boston to Washington, *megalopolis,* symbolizes the prowess of the modern transational society. High levels of movement of people, goods, and messages enable this large urban region to function as a single, if dispersed, galactic city. The Chicago-Pittsburgh corridor includes the Milwaukee, Chicago, Detroit, Cleveland, and Pittsburgh areas and also functions as an integrated economic unit. *Source:* Adapted from the U.S. Bureau of Census, "Population Distribution, Urban and Rural, in the United States, 1970." GE-70 Series, No. 1, USGPO, Washington, D.C., 1973.

lysts for basic research into the geographic aspects of the post-industrial economic and technological conditions, inspired scholarly and public debate about psychologically viable and physically habitable urban structures, and demonstrated the efficacy of geography and geographic ideas in understanding contemporary urban problems."[21]

Massive urban concentrations in other parts of the world also qualify under the megalopolis umbrella. Examples include urban complexes in the lower Rhine Valley in the Dortmund–Essen–Duesseldorf or *Ruhr* area of Germany and The Hague–Rotterdam–Amsterdam or *Ranstad* area of the Netherlands, the London–Liverpool corridor in Great Britain, and the *Tokaido* megalopolis in Japan, which extends from Tokyo–

Yokohama to Nagoya and Osaka–Kobe (Figure 2-16). Translated literally, "Tokaido" means "east coast road." Separated by several mountain divides, these three metropolitan complexes are linked by expressway, rail, and air connections. The high-speed bullet train dropped travel time between Tokyo and Osaka to just over 3 hours. This latter region now comprises the largest urban complex in the world, containing in excess of 50 million persons.

The large urban population clustered around the lower Great Lakes from Milwaukee and Chicago eastward to Pittsburgh, including Detroit, Flint, Toledo, Cleveland, Akron, and Youngstown is another emerging urban complex in the United States (Figure 2-17). This area is often referred to as the Chicago–Pittsburgh (Chipitts) corridor. The San Diego to San Francisco corridor (Sansan) constitutes yet another megalopolis, as does the emerging suncoast metroplex in Florida that

---

[21]Ibid.

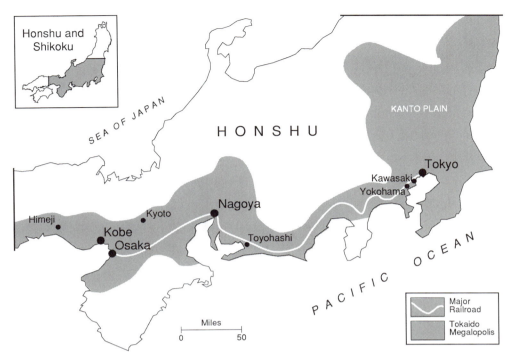

Figure 2-16. *Tokaido Megalopolis.* Literally translated, "Tokaido" means "east coast road." Separated by several mountain divides, the Tokyo, Nagoya, Osaka, and Kobe metropolitan complexes are linked by expressways, rail, and air connections along a narrow coastal strip facing the Pacific Ocean. The high-speed bullet train dropped travel time between Tokyo and Osaka to just over 3 hours when it opened in the 1960s. This megalopolis is the largest urban agglomeration in the world.

encompasses the Miami–Fort Lauderdale–West Palm Beach area.

SUMMARY AND CONCLUSION

Present-day cities can trace their lineage back in antiquity to Mesopotamia, the Nile Valley, the Indus Valley, China, and Meso-America. While continuous urban settlement cannot be associated with most of these sites, the lasting contributions these cities made to urban form and function can be documented. So can their elaborate public works and infrastructure innovations. The urban design concepts introduced in North America in the eighteenth century by early settlers, for example, can be directly linked to settlement types in vogue in Europe at the time, which in turn, can be traced to Greek and Roman traditions in antiquity. The imprint of the *agora, forum, souk, open courtyard,* and *grid* street pattern, among others, can all be accounted for in this way.

Yet another tradition reached North America by way of London in the form of the *speculators' town*. The market-driven development process, as introduced in Philadelphia by William Penn, eventually became the prevailing model for city building in the United States. The city, as conceived in this philosophy, does not exhibit a formal hierarchical order or special building placement. Rather, the needs and demands of the market guide growth and development in true capitalist fashion. In this tradition, the sale of land in the form of building lots provides the capital for financing the infrastructure and land uses are generally allocated on the basis of ability to pay. We will discuss this process in more detail in Chapter 11.

Large cities with over 1 million population represent a relatively recent phenomena in the chronology of urbanization. While ancient Rome may have had 1 million population, and cities of comparable size may have existed in ancient China, it was the Industrial Revolution in the nineteenth century that made large cities more practical. Nineteenth-century advances in transportation (steam engine, railroad), building construction technology (iron and steel, electric elevator), and enhanced worker productivity all converged to make the city a place of opportunity and efficiency. London, Paris, and New York all reached 1 million population by the mid-1800s. But the acceleration in the growth of large cities has been most pronounced in the twentieth century, with over 250 cities achieving this status by the mid-1980s. Today, we find large cities in not only the highly developed world, but also expanding rapidly in a different context in the third world. Third world cities, in fact, are now growing the most rapidly and will comprise the biggest number of very large urban regions (over 5 million in population) by the turn of the century.

This urban growth process has created extensive belts of metropolitan areas in several parts of the world. Each can be labeled a *megalopolis* after its namesake along the northeast corridor of the United States. Each megalopolis also continues to evolve and benefit from the transition to the post-industrial information age, including the *Tokaido* region of Japan, the *Ruhr* of Germany, and the *Randstad* of the Netherlands.

In Chapter 3, we will examine the unique circumstances of the third world city before returning to an analysis of North American urbanization in Chapter 4. As a group, third world cities pose the greatest problems of any urban areas today. Providing adequate shelter, food, and work opportunities for these cities in the face of explosive growth constitutes a never-ending dilemma worthy of closer scrutiny.

Suggestions for Further Reading

Brunn, Stanley, and Jack F. Williams. *Cities of the World: World Regional Urban Development*, Harper & Row, New York, 1983.

Cassanova, Jacques-Donat. *America's French Heritage*, La Documentation Française and the Quebec Official Publisher, Quebec, 1976.

Chandler, Tertius, and Gerald Fox. *Three Thousand Years of Urban Growth*, Academic Press, New York, 1974.

Chandler, Tertius. *Four Thousand Years of Urban Growth: An Historical Census*. St. David's University Press, Lewiston, N.Y., 1987.

Cornelius, Wayne A., and Robert V. Kemper, eds. *Metropolitan Latin America: The Challenge and the Response*, Sage, Beverly Hills, Calif., 1978.

Costello, V. F. *Urbanization in the Middle East*, Cambridge University Press, New York, 1977.

Crouch, Dora P., et al. *Spanish City Planning in North America*, M.I.T. Press, Cambridge, Mass., 1982.

Dogan, M., and J. Kasarda. *The Metropolis Era* (2 vols.), Sage, Beverly Hills, Calif., 1988.

Eldredge, H. W., ed. *The World Capitals*, Anchor Press, Garden City, N.Y., 1975.

Feagin, J., and R. Parker. *Building American Cities: The Urban Real Estate Game*, Prentice Hall, Englewood Cliffs, N.J., 1990.

Finegan, Jack. *Archaeological History of the Ancient Middle East*, Westview Press, Boulder, Colo., 1979.

Gottmann, Jean. *Megalopolis*, The Twentieth Century Fund, New York, 1961.

Gottmann, Jean. *Megalopolis Revisited*, University of Maryland Institute of Urban Studies, College Park, Md., 1987.

Hall, Peter. *The World Cities*, 3rd ed., St. Martin's Press, New York, 1984.

———*Cities of Tomorrow*, Blackwell, Cambridge, Mass., 1990.

Hammond, M. *The City in the Ancient World*, Harvard University Press, Cambridge, Mass., 1972.

Hiorns, Frederick R. *Town-Building in History*, George C. Harrap & Co., London, 1956.

Keatings, Richard W., ed. *Peruvian Prehistory*, Cambridge University Press, New York, 1988.

Kornhauser, David. *Urban Japan: Its Foundations and Growth*, Longman, London, 1976.

Lawton, Richard. *The Rise and Fall of Great Cities: Aspects of Urbanization in the Western World*, Belhaven Press, New York, 1989.

Merrifield, Ralph. *The Roman City of London*. Dover, New York, 1965.

Morrison, Mary, ed. *Historic Savannah*, 2nd ed., Historic Savannah Foundation, Savannah Junior League, Savannah, Ga., 1979.

Mumford, Lewis. *The City in History: Its Origins, Its Transformations, and Its Prospects*, Harcourt Brace & World, New York, 1961.

Nick, Jeffrey, and Malcolm Caldwell, eds. *Planning and Urbanism in China*, Pergamon, New York, 1977.

Pred, Allan. *The Spatial Dynamics of U.S. Urban and Industrial Growth*, M.I.T. Press, Cambridge, Mass., 1967.

Reps, John W. *The Making of Urban America: A History of City Planning in the United States*, Princeton University Press, Princeton, N.J., 1965.

Reps, John W. *Town Planning in Frontier America*, University of Missouri Press, Columbia, 1980.

The National Archives and Records Service. *Washington: Design of the Federal City*, Acropolis Books, Ltd., 1981.

Van Zantwijk, Rudolph. *The Aztec Arrangement*, University of Oklahoma Press, Norman, 1985.

Vance, James E., Jr. *The Continuing City: Urban Morphology in Western Civilization*, Johns Hopkins University Press, Baltimore, 1990.

Yap, Yong. *The Early Civilization of China*, Putnam's Sons, New York, 1975.

3

THE THIRD WORLD CITY*

Urban growth does not automatically bring affluence and prosperity; nor does it necessarily create a large middle class, as third world cities[1] amply demonstrate. Urbanization in the third world, even with the presence of many very large cities, represents a different situation than most Americans associate with the city and merits considerable discussion (see Figure 3-1).

Urban growth in developing areas is proceeding in a different cultural and economic milieu than that experienced by the developed world. Although difficult to conceptualize, the term *false urbanization* captures part of the contrast. It is false urbanization in the sense that less developed regions do not experience a widespread expansion of jobs or opportunities to develop a middle-class market with urban expansion, as has been the case of the more developed nations. Urbanization in most third world countries is primarily driven by demographic forces, particularly rural-to-urban migration, rather than by dynamic economic and industrial forces, as in Europe, North America, and Japan.

One interesting aspect of these contradictions is well portrayed in the movie *The Harder They Come* (1973,

Jamaica), the hero of which is a rural migrant to Kingston, Jamaica. This hero, a reggae singer, is exploited by a musical promoter. In retaliation for this exploitation, the hero confronts the system by killing a policeman and pushing dope ("ganja") in the streets. When pursued by the police, he disappears into the shanty town of Kingston, where he becomes an instant hero cheered by the poor children of the squatter settlement. This story epitomizes the all-too-frequent struggle of the urban poor against urban exploiters, typically consisting of government officials and corrupt businessmen. The most interesting thing the movie reveals is not the contradiction between wealth and poverty, but the tolerance and acceptance of their coexistence side by side, even if occasionally at odds with one another (Figure 3-1). These contradictions are interwoven as two distinctive sides of the same socioeconomic fabric of the third world urban system.

THIRD WORLD URBAN GROWTH

One estimate indicates that there will be over 1 billion urban residents in 300 third world cities larger than 1 million in population by the beginning of the next century.[2] Presently there are only 125 millionaire cities in the third world, which clearly indicates that rapid growth is expected to continue unabated. It has also

---

*Chapter authored by Nanda Shrestha, University of Wisconsin-White-water.

[1]Developed areas constitute the "first" world; the Socialist bloc the "second" world; and developing countries the "third" world, as the term is used here.

[2]Andrew Hamer, "Urbanization Patterns in the Third World," *Finances and Development*, March 1985, p. 39.

Figure 3-1. Poverty and Plenty in Third World City. The contradictions that abound in the third world city are most dramatically illustrated by the coexistence of poverty and wealth. The children shown here in a squatter settlement in the Barrio Sarria section of Caracas live in the shadows of an affluent apartment complex. (The United Nations)

mains the least urbanized third world region, having only 10 large urban areas over 1.5 million in size in 1986. Africa's total population (approximately 625 million) also remains relatively small compared to its land area and in comparison to Asia's total, which approaches 3 billion.

The planning problems caused by the sharp increase in the absolute size of third world cities is demonstrated by the core region of Indonesia—the sprawling metropolis called Jabotabek, which is centered on Jakarta. In 1961, the population of Jabotabek was 6.7 million. During the next 20 years, the growth of Jabotabek was

TABLE 3-1
Third World Cities by Size Category

City Name	Location[a]	Population (In Millions)
Mexico City	LA	Over 15
Bombay	A	10–15
Buenos Aires	LA	
Calcutta	A	
São Paulo	LA	
Alexandria	Af	3–10
Baghdad	A	
Bangalore	A	
Bangkok	A	
Bogotá	LA	
Cairo	Af	
Caracas	LA	
Dacca	A	
Delhi-New Delhi	A	
Jakarta	A	
Johannesburg	Af	
Karachi	A	
Lahore	A	
Lima	LA	
Madras	A	
Manila	A	
Pusan	A	
Rangoon	A	
Rio de Janeiro	LA	
Santiago	LA	
T'aipei	A	
Teheran	A	
Victoria	A	

been suggested that Mexico City will become the world's largest city at that time, with over 30 million inhabitants. In 1990, Mexico City ranked among the four largest metropolitan areas of the world, with over 15 million inhabitants (Table 3-1 and Figure 3-2). Two-thirds of the nine cities in the 10–15 million range in 1986 were also located in the third world, not to mention the majority of the cities in the 5–10 million size range (see Table 2-5 and Figure 3-2).

By region, the largest share of cities over 1.5 million in population in the third world occurs in Asia, where one finds over 30 such cities, with 18 in south and southwest Asia and 15 in east and southeast Asia. The second largest concentration occurs in Latin America, which claims more than 20 such centers. Africa re-

TABLE 3-1 (Continued)
Third World Cities by Size Category

City Name	Location[a]	Population (In Millions)
Abidjan	Af	
Ahmadabad	A	
Algiers	Af	
Ankara	A	
Bandung	A	
Belo Horizonte	LA	
Brasilia	LA	
Cali	LA	
Cape Town	Af	
Casablanca	Af	
Chittagong	A	
Colombo	A	
Curitiba	LA	
Damascus	A	
Durban	Af	
Fortaleza	LA	
Guadalajara	LA	
Hanoi	A	
Harbin	A	1.5–3
Havana	LA	
Hyderabad	A	
Kanpur	A	
Kinshasa	Af	
Lagos	Af	
Medan	A	
Medellin	LA	
Monterrey	LA	
Poona (Pune)	A	
Porto Alegre	LA	
Recife	LA	
Saigon	A	
Salvador	LA	
San Juan	LA	
Santo Domingo	LA	
Singapore	A	
Surabaya	A	

[a]LA = Latin America
Af = Africa
A = Asia

Source: 1986 Rand McNally Commercial Atlas and Marketing Guide, Rand McNally, 1986, 92-S-1.

significantly greater than that of the country as a whole, and by 1981, the metropolitan region had a population of more than 13 million. It has been estimated by the Ministry of Public Works of Indonesia that it will cost the Indonesian government $1.2 billion over the next 10 years to build a public transportation system for Jabotabek. That figure is almost seven times as much as the amount included in the national budget for all forms of public transportation throughout the country from 1984 through 1988. It has also been estimated that to provide an adequate water supply for Jakarta alone will cost an amount equal to 60 percent of the total public investment in water supplies throughout the country under the recent five-year government plan.[3]

In contrast to the situation in the third world, centrally planned economic countries in the Soviet and Chinese realms (second world) are not growing as rapidly, even though they are less developed by Western standards. The monopoly power held by the state has successfully limited the expansion of large cities in this realm by placing more emphasis on rural development and growth of secondary centers which may be viewed as "growth centers," from a conventional regional planning viewpoint. Contrasting situations in North and South Korea vividly demonstrate this point.

> In 1955 the population of South Korea was 21.5 million, 18 percent of whom lived in or near Seoul. During the next 25 years, more than half of the population growth in the country took place in the region of the capital. By 1980, the total had reached 37.4 million and 36 percent of all South Koreans lived in or near Seoul. Furthermore, in 1980, more than half of all the economic production in South Korea took place within 25 kilometers of the center of the capital.[4]

By contrast, in P'yongyang, the capital city of North Korea, growth has been carefully controlled and its population in the 1980s remained under 2 million.

ECONOMIC DEVELOPMENT

The widespread poverty, lack of skills and indigenous technological advancement, and low education levels in developing areas, even in the face of urbanization, are partly due to the rapid rate of population increase resulting from the migration of unskilled rural peasants to the cities, which makes assimilation difficult. In rural areas of developing nations, opportunities for earning a living, other than as a subsistence agricultur-

[3]Daniel R. Vining, Jr., "The Growth of Core Regions in the Third World," *Scientific American,* 252 (April 1985), 45.
[4]Ibid., p. 42.

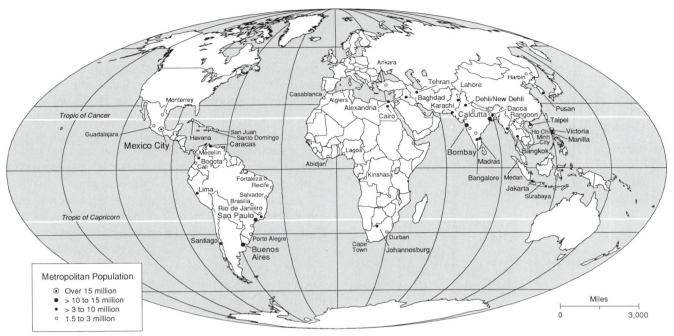

Figure 3-2. **Third World Metropolitan Areas.** Paced by the 15 million residents in Mexico City, and very large cities in India, the 125 millionaire cities in the third world are the fastest-growing metropolitan areas in the world today. The largest concentration of these cities occurs in Asia, and the smallest number in Africa.

alist, often do not exist. In the city, there are other alternatives, even if only to earn a meager income. High dependency burdens, associated with large families and little prospect for advancement, serve to institutionalize poverty. The pressure of continuous immigration of rural families to the city, with little hope of advancement, allows for the maintenance of a low wage structure for the unskilled.

Economic Dualism

Despite expansion of manufacturing activity in major third world cities, unemployment continues to grow because of the rapid influx of rural migrants. Only the *bazaar* economy, often referred to as the informal sector in the conceptual *formal-informal* dichotomy of the third world urban economy, is available to unskilled rural migrants as an employment opportunity. This situation creates an *economic dualism* whereby the formal or capitalist sector coexists with the informal bazaar economy (Table 3-2). The formal sector in-

TABLE 3-2
Income Opportunities in a Third World City

Formal income opportunities
  Public sector wages
  Private sector wages
  Transfer payments: pensions, unemployment benefits
Informal income opportunities: legitimate
  Primary and secondary activities: farming, market gardening, building contractors, artisans, shoemakers, tailors
  Tertiary activities (large capital required): housing, transport, utilities, investments
  Tertiary activities (small-scale distribution): market vendors, petty traders, street hawkers, commission agents
  Other services: musicians, launderers, shoeshiners, barbers, photographers, vehicle maintenance, ritual services, magic, medicine
  Private transfer payments: gifts, borrowing, begging
Informal income opportunities: illegitimate
  Services: hustler, drug pusher, prostitute, pimp, smuggler, racketeer
  Transfers: petty theft, larceny, embezzlement, gambling

Source: Modified after Keith Hart, "Informal Income Opportunities and Urban Employment in Ghana," *The Journal of Modern African Studies,* II (1973), 69. Modified with permission, Cambridge University Press.

cludes relatively large scale retail and service activity operations, in addition to manufacturing activity. The formal sector also includes government workers and other highly paid specialists such as airline pilots.

The informal sector, on the other hand, consists of a plethora of very small scale activities, invariably operated by one person, with little, if any, capital outlay. In fact, its negligible capital investment requirement is what attracts urban residents to this sector as petty entrepreneurs as a means of self-employment and survival. It is predominantly retail in nature with no prescribed work hours. This activity essentially involves the vending and peddling of goods and services in the streets (Figure 3-3). These informal sector activities, such as newspaper sales, shoe shining, and small retail outlets, exhibit some level of locational permanency, generally in public spaces in central locations with heavy pedestrian traffic such as those near movie theaters, downtown parks, bus stops, tourist spots, main street sidewalks, or any open spaces frequented by a large number of people. The use of these spaces requires no rent payments, thus making them more attractive to petty entrepreneurs.

There are a number of reasons why the formal sector, especially manufacturing, has been unable to provide an adequate number of job opportunities. First, industries in the third world have been largely based on advanced, capital-intensive techniques requiring a low labor input. Consequently, an expansion of manufacturing production does not always result in a growth of formal sector employment. Government policies have also inhibited labor absorption in the formal sector. Many developing countries have an artificially high, government-imposed minimum wage in the formal sector (usually in response to demands by trade unions). This high wage prevents industry from em-

Figure 3-3. The Informal Economy in Jadhpur, India. Unregulated informal sector enterprises are operated by one person with little, if any, capital outlay. Much retail work involves the vending and peddling of goods and services in the streets. Much of this activity occurs in public spaces in central locations in city squares. Note the heavy dependence on bicycles and pushcarts. (Peter Menzel/Stock, Boston)

ploying as many workers as it would otherwise. A third reason for the slow labor absorption in the formal economy dates back to the colonial period. Colonial policies discouraged the development of the industrial sectors of the third world. Third world countries attempting to start up manufacturing sectors since their independence have been faced with formidable difficulties, including the lack of capital and the presence of a highly competitive world market. All these factors, combined with rapid population growth and rural-to-urban migration, have meant that the numbers of formal sector jobs have fallen short, forcing the excess labor to join the unregulated informal sector.

Despite the low income, low capital intensity, and unregulated nature of informal sector activities, there is growing evidence that these activities can be important contributors to the urban economy. One reason for this is the dynamic linkages existing between the informal and formal sector enterprises. In the service area, the informal sector provides the formal sector with reliable labor support at a very low cost. The actors in the formal sector can curtail the services provided by the workers in the informal sector any time, without incurring any obligation. Because of the intensive competition that occurs among the people looking for work, wages are severely depressed and remain low, creating a labor cost advantage for the formal sector.

In addition, the informal sector provides small retail outlets for the formal sector. For example, informal sector rickshaw drivers do not own their own rickshaw; they lease them from formal sector participants whose business is to lease out rickshaws to those who want to operate them. In the formal sector, it is difficult to buy goods and commodities in very small quantities, and many people cannot afford to buy them in large quantities. But the informal sector provides very small scale outlets where people can buy things in any amount they can afford, for example, a single cigarette rather than a pack of cigarettes, as mentioned earlier. Small-scale retail operators in the informal sector collectively distribute a significant quantity of goods and buy them in relatively large quantities. It thus generates a large volume of business for the formal sector. This shows how the informal sector is intertwined with the formal sector in a circular loop, thereby sustaining the urban economy by absorbing the excess labor force, as well as generating a large volume of small-scale or petty business.

A number of recent studies have shown that the incomes and productivity of informal sector workers are at least as much as, if not more than, their formal sector counterparts. Further, this sector is much more dynamic than previously thought; for example, the informal sector of Abidjan, Freetown, and Kumasi in Africa have training activities and apprenticeship schemes. Not surprisingly, then, an increasing number of informal sector workers express a preference for this work over the formal sector. This suggests that the informal sector today may no longer be the "refuge" sector as traditionally conceptualized. Rather, many rural migrants to third world cities come with the intention of engaging in informal activities. In terms of government policy, there is a growing notion that assisting the operation of informal sector enterprises is likely to be more effective and less costly than trying to push informal sector workers into the formal sector. Many third world governments, therefore, are now developing schemes to provide training and low-interest credit to informal sector workers.

Import Substitution

As noted above, one important manifestation of the formal sector is industrial growth. In third world cities, skilled labor industrial opportunities and white-collar government positions are expanding and pay competitive salaries, but these opportunities are limited. Developing countries invariably emphasize an *import substitution* policy, focusing on capital-intensive, high-technology industrial expansion that employs relatively few persons (Figure 3-4). Even though export-oriented industrial growth has emerged in some countries of Asia and Latin America import substitution still remains prevalent in the third world. This strategy is part of a prevailing concern to reduce imported goods and make the local economy more self-sufficient. To accomplish this goal, many government controls are invoked, including favorable tax policies for participating firms, trade quotas, and licensing agreements. These measures often lead to an inefficient manufacturing economy and result in more expensive goods as a result of the limited market that exists. The import substitution industrialization process in the third world provides a contrast to the early stages of industrialization experienced by present-day developed countries. In the latter case, industries were largely labor intensive, and geared toward the production of low value added goods such as textiles, clothing, shoes, and food processing. The developing countries, beginning their

Figure 3-4. General Motors Automobile Plant in Brazil. This GM automobile manufacturing plant in *Sao Caetano*, Brazil, symbolizes a weakness of the economic development process in third world cities. Many observers suggest that labor-intensive manufacturing activity would be a more appropriate priority during early stages of industrial development than emphasizing capital-intensive manufacturing. (Courtesy General Motors)

industrialization in the 1970s and 1980s, have had ready access to modern technologies developed over many decades in the West. Their manufacturing sectors, therefore have been based on advanced, capital intensive techniques requiring much less labor than in the past. This *latecomer thesis* suggests that countries that begin their industrialization later in history will have a relatively lower demand for manufacturing workers than did present-day highly developed countries when they were at a similar stage of development. This contrast has already been evidenced in the relative growth of informal and service-oriented activities in developing areas.

To further compound the problem, the import substitution policy encourages premature, rapid urban growth in the cities where the investment occurs, typically in what is known as the *primate city* of the country (Figure 3-5). A primate city is one that accounts for a very large share of a country's population, typically one-third or more of the total (see discussion in Chapter 4). This concentration of growth in one or a few large centers limits the potential for the expansion of secondary growth centers. A favorable *comparative advantage* for development occurs in these larger cities because of poor transportation, communications, and utilities infrastructure in outlying areas. Coupled with financial and banking policies that benefit the primate city, unbridled urban growth typically overwhelms the ability of secondary cities to keep up with expanding infrastructure needs.

Urban growth in third world cities today is also occurring "at much lower per capita income levels than those of developed countries in periods when their growth was comparably fast. Thus, even in the best of circumstances, planners and policymakers in developing nations face more difficult trade-offs than their earlier counterparts in the industrial world in dealing with urban management issues."[5] Per capita incomes must increase significantly, most observers argue, before development will decentralize into secondary centers.

---

[5]Hamer, op. cit., p. 39.

Figure 3-5. Singapore: Quintessential Primate City. The city of Singapore contains 90 percent of the 2.7 million population in the country of Singapore. The city owes its rapid growth to its favorable location at the southern tip of the Malay peninsula astride southeast Asian trade routes. Originally a fishing village, the British discovered the potential of the site for a seaport in the early 1800s. The harbor, the busiest in Southeast Asia, remains the focal point around which the modern skyscrapers have mushroomed. The city has also become an important center of finance and a booming manufacturing center. (Singapore Tourist Promotion Board)

Daniel Vining argues that a country must reach an *economic threshold* of $3000 (1975 dollars) per capita gross domestic product before economic growth will occur in the hinterland of third world cities and the predominant migration flow to the primate city declines.[6] Venezuela's experience during the 1970s appears to support this contention, as Figure 3-6B shows. During the 1970s, the $3000 economic threshold was reached and the flow of population to the Caracas metropolitan area declined. On the other hand, per capita gross domestic product in Thailand barely exceeded $1000 at the same time, and migration to Bangkok continued at an accelerating pace (Figure 3-6A). To better understand the reasons for the contemporary situation in third world cities, it is useful to first examine the unique historical experience these areas have faced in terms of an economic development process.

ROOTS OF URBANIZATION

Curiously, world urbanization began in what became present-day third world cities, and "from these early centers of human civilization, the concept of the city diffused to Europe and then tens of centuries later returned in the form of the colonial city, which was to have such a radical impact and forever alter the urban character of these ancient regions."[7]

Compared to the long traditions and achievements reached by these early urban centers, European and American accomplishments in more recent times seem less striking. Only with the rise of mercantilism in the sixteenth century did European cities begin to emerge as the prominent urban centers of the world. "The major spurt in Western urbanization occurred between the 16th century when colonial conquests began and the end of the nineteenth century when industrialization

[6]Daniel R. Vining, Jr., op. cit., p. 47.

[7]Jack F. Williams, et al., "World Urban Development," in Stanley D. Brunn and Jack F. Williams, eds., *Cities of the World*, Harper & Row, New York, 1983, p. 16.

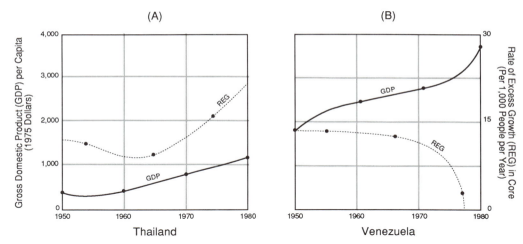

Figure 3-6. Growth Decentralization and the Economic Threshold. Gross domestic product (GDP) per capita must rise above a critical economic threshold ($3000 per capita in 1975 dollars) before growth decentralizes away from the core area in the third world city. In the Thailand example (A), GDP per capita continued to increase in the late 1970s (lower curve). The amount by which the rate of population growth in the core exceeds the rate for the entire country is shown by the upper line. In the Thailand case, it is still rising, but in the Venezuela case (B), once the $3000 per capita threshold was reached in the 1970s (upper curve), the flow of population toward the core declined significantly (lower curve), suggesting Venezuela but not Thailand, had reached a critical economic threshold. *Source:* Daniel Vining, "The Growth of Core Regions in the Third World," Copyright ©1985 by *Scientific American, Inc.* All rights reserved.

and empire-building were the dual motors of development."[8]

In the course of the discussion of the third world cities today, there is a tendency to compare them with the cities of Western Europe and the United States. The comparison generally leads to the categorization and characterization of Western cities as being "industrial" and third world cities as being "preindustrial." These distinctions can be traced to the work of Gideon Sjoberg following the publication of *The Preindustrial City*. This "industrial–preindustrial" dichotomy is often based on the level of technological development, with "industrial" being technologically advanced and "preindustrial" being technologically backward.

Such a comparison dichotomy is useful, but not sufficient, to provide a more complete understanding of third world cities. We also need to examine these cities from a different angle—specifically, in terms of stages in their development. Cities in the third world have served different purposes and provided distinctive roles during various stages in development. With full recognition that third world cities are not a single, homogeneous group and that their internal dynamics as well as external relations vary greatly from region to region, it

is nevertheless possible to distinguish three distinctive stages that characterize their overall historical trajectory of development. Their most important common bond, regardless of location, is their colonial linkage, which yields these stages:

1. The precolonial city
2. The colonial city
3. The postcolonial city

The Precolonial City

The precolonial city existed before the European-based exploration and discovery drive in the fifteenth century. It is safe to assert that many of these cities continued to retain their precolonial characteristics until the expansion of mercantilism in the sixteenth and seventeenth centuries. Some remnants or artifacts of the preindustrial city remain even in modern cities of the third world. In fact, some people might consider cities like Kyoto, Japan; Kathmandu, Nepal; Benaras, India; and Jerusalem, Israel to be precolonial in structure and function in the 1990s.

Simplicity and smallness were the two fundamental characteristics of the precolonial city, and it offered few functions and little spatial variation (Figure 3-7).

---

[8]Janet Abu-Lughod and Richard Hay, Jr., *Third World Urbanization*, Maaroufa Press, Chicago, 1977, p. 38.

Figure 3-7. Kathmandu Valley, Nepal. Simplicity and smallness characterize the pre-colonial city, as it has few functions and little spatial variation. Economic activities are focused on subsistence needs. Kathmandu is generally thought to exhibit these pre-colonial city characteristics today. (Mark Boulton/Photo Researchers)

Population density remained low and the areal extent of development was restricted. No specific land assignment or organization pattern existed and people of all social classes lived and interacted together, conducting different activities informally in a relatively small urban space. Economic activities and functions were only oriented to basic subsistence needs. Trade activities and long-distance interactions occurred on a limited scale, partly because transportation networks were not well developed and partly because there was little need for such contact as a result of local self-sufficiency and the self-contained nature of the city. While the city was not totally devoid of technology, its development indicated only rudimentary applications.

Despite their simple character, precolonial cities were unique and indigenous, features that are conspicuously absent in the later colonial and postcolonial city. Unlike these later cities, the precolonial city developed as a product of the local environment and local initiative, and thus served local needs. These cities were not the product of foreign influences or a replica of foreign cultures and values, although some of them later evolved into colonial and later postcolonial entities; for example, Cairo (Egypt), Calcutta (India), Nairobi (Kenya), Lagos (Nigeria), Bangkok (Thailand), Jakarta (Indonesia), Shanghai (China), Rio de Janeiro (Brazil), and Buenos Aires (Argentina).

The Colonial City

The process of colonial city development began with the rise and expansion of mercantilism in the sixteenth and seventeenth centuries and reached maturity after formal colonization began in the nineteenth century following the Industrial Revolution.[9] Thus, in the evolution of urban development in the third world, the colonial city is a distinctive product of European colonialism, which left a legacy for the succeeding postcolonial period (Figure 3-8).

---

[9]Colonization began in the sixteenth century in the New World.

Figure 3-8. **Shanghai in the 1930s.** The colonial transformation of third world cities unleashed a growth boom. This view of the Shanghai Bund main street along the waterfront shows numerous European style banks and mercantile establishments and western-made automobiles in the bustling city. These buildings still give a European architectural flaire to the city (see Box). (The Bettmann Archive)

The emergence of the colonial city involved a process that transformed many existing precolonial cities, particularly coastal cities. During the transformation process, not only were colonial cultural and economic values implanted, but indigenous technological processes were dismantled. This process occurred most visibly in the field of nonagricultural production technology, thus destroying the potential for further innovations, inventions, and technological advancement of the traditional system. Urban development patterns were altered dramatically and the third world became more dependent on Western technology as a result. The urban development pattern in the third world became associated with "false urbanization" because it failed to generate the positive benefits found with urban development in the Western world, an issue we will return to in a later section.

The colonial city became an economic entity—a European colonial outpost—through which the external colonial ruler exercised economic, political, and sociocultural control over the colony and its citizens. The morphological structure and the sociocultural configuration of the colonial city varied from region to region, according to the philosophical orientation of the

colonial power—Britain, France, the Netherlands, Spain, or Portugal. However, the primary objective behind the establishment of colonial cities became the economic exploitation of their hinterlands. Bombay, India, provides a classic example; it was developed to expedite the cotton fiber production in its hinterlands for export to textile factories in England.

In general, the colonial cities served primarily as commercial entrepôts—points of distribution linking the colony with its colonizing country. These cities were "agents of European imperialism, facilitating trade penetration and acting as gateways for the export of primary products (from the colony) and the import of manufactured goods (into the colony)." To augment the commercial roads of the colonial city, the colonial power developed the necessary railway networks linking the entrepôt cities with the resource bases such as mining centers, and areas producing cash crops such as coffee or sugar in their hinterlands.

In addition to commercial functions, several colonial cities emerged as industrial hubs, such as Calcutta, India; Shanghai, China; and São Paulo, Brazil (see box). Two unique characterizations of industrial development as implemented by the colonial power in these

SHANGHAI: PROFILE OF A COLONIAL CITY

Located near the mouth of the Chang Jiang (Yangtze) River, which nurtures one of the largest and most fertile river plains in the world, Shanghai is the largest city in the People's Republic of China. The core of Shanghai, which can be referred to as the CBD (Central Business District), is situated at the confluence of two rivers: Suzhou Creek (Wusong River) and Huangpu River. The Huangpu River constitutes the city's major water transportation artery, as it connects the city with the Chang Jiang, East China Sea, and ultimately the whole world.

Shanghai is a typical colonial city, that is, a city that gained its prominence during colonial rule as an entrepôt advancing colonial economic interests. Originally a fishing village, the Shanghai county came into being toward the end of the thirteenth century. By the sixteenth century, handicraft, textile, and commerce activity were already quite developed in Shanghai. In 1685, a customs house was established by the Qing (pronounced Ching; also known as Manchu) government—the last Chinese dynasty—to collect taxes on imported as well as exported goods. These historical developments suggest that Shanghai had already emerged as a flourishing seaport attracting the keen attention of European colonial powers. However, it did not attain its prominent position until it came under total colonial domination in the early 1840s.

It is no wonder (or coincidence) that when the British imperial forces attacked and defeated China during the famous "Opium War" (1840–42), the country was compelled to open its major ports, generally known as "Treaty Ports," that is, areas of land under foreign jurisdiction with extra-territorial status and rights, to foreign trade and concessions. The war ended when the Treaty of Nanking (now Nanjing, an important city that once served as the southern capital of China when Beijing was the northern capital) was signed between Great Britain and China. Following the treaty, in November 1843, Shanghai was opened as one of the five treaty ports to foreign trade and concessions, the other four being Guangzhou (Canton), Xiamen, Fuzhou, and Ningbo—all located in southeastern China, south of Shanghai.

Even though the Treaty of Nanjing was unequal and very unfavorable, as a defeated nation China had no choice but to sign it. It was a big blow to Chinese ethnocentrism and their sense of invincibility. In addition to Great Britain, several other foreign powers such as France, the United States, Germany, Russia, and Japan swarmed into Shanghai to capitalize on this great piece of real estate that the Western powers had acquired through the Nanjing Treaty. With the possible exception of Guangzhou and later Hong Kong, Shanghai was perhaps the most important port city, an attribute derived from its central location and enormous economic potential in terms of commercial, agricultural, and industrial opportunities.

Shanghai was partitioned into several foreign concessions or settlements, all maintaining their own rules and regulations and essentially functioning as independent states within a state. Although China was never completely colonized by European powers, Shanghai and other port cities were controlled by foreigners and their economic interests. China had no jurisdiction whatsoever over these settlements. They were extremely segregated, as the Chinese were generally treated as less than second-class citizens in their own land, kept out of the concession areas, and relegated, in stark contrast to fancy European quarters, to the slums made up of thatched sheds and shabby shacks. The Chinese nicknamed their residential areas the "curled up dragon" slums because the dwelling units were so low that people could not even stand upright; they had to curl up to move about.

As a colonial city, Shanghai became not only a commercial market for the foreign powers to dump opium and other imports without any restriction, but also an important operational base for exploiting China's cheap labor and raw materials, including tremendous agricultural resources found in the city's vast Chang Jiang (Yangtze) River valley hinterland.

Nowhere is the colonial economic, social, and cultural imprint more transparent than in Shanghai's architectural styles. Not only do they vividly reflect the diverse Western architectural styles, they also appear to completely dwarf the indigenous Chinese architecture with a rich heritage. Nowhere in the city are these varied architectural styles more prominently displayed in a panoramic fashion than in its most famous section called the *Bund*, a waterfront that stretches about one mile along the Huangpu river (see Figure 3-8).

From the very outset of colonial rule, the Bund was

a part of the concession area. It is noted that ". . . the Bund was not only the foreign powers' bridgehead for political, economic, and cultural aggression against old China, but also the symbol of 'adventurers' paradise.' "[1] The past has left a deep impression on the Bund (and Shanghai), making it an epitaph of Western aggression in the modern history of China. Even today, 40 years after anti-imperial communist rule, the city's urban landscape shows every sign of colonial domination. Somewhat ironically, however in this city, the most graphic symbol of colonialism in China, the First National Congress of the Communist Party of China (CPC) was convened on July 23, 1921, thus solemnly proclaiming the founding of the CPC. It was under the leadership of the CPC that China became liberated in 1949 from the colonial yoke.

With a metropolitan population of over 12 million, Shanghai today is not only the largest city; it also remains one of China's leading commercial and industrial powerhouses, a position it gained during the colonial days. The city boasts a wide range of industries, with over 7000 factories employing more than 4 million workers and staff. Among the important industrial operations are the metallurgical, machinery, electronic, chemical, ship-building, and textile industries. In addition, dozens of institutions have been set up to conduct scientific research in atomic energy, computers, semi-conductors, laser, infrared technology, satellite technology, and many other areas. The value of Shanghai's total industrial output accounts for approximately one-eighth of the national total. Because of their quality and design, products manufactured in Shanghai are more highly preferred by the Chinese then similar items produced anywhere else in the country.

As already indicated, Shanghai was probably the most important and largest commercial center in China in colonial times. During the administrative period of Mao Zedong 1949–76, the great helmsman of China, Shanghai, like other cities and regions, experienced a decline in its commercial vitality, as capitalist commercial operations were shunned. However, since the late 1970s, when the policy of economic liberalization was implemented by Deng Xiaoping under the banner of market socialism, the city appears to have regained its commercial stride. Despite the fact that it still remains centrally controlled under the country's socialist economic command structure, Shanghai is one of the most exuberant commercial cities in today's China. While the signs of growing commercialism can be seen in every nook and corner of the city, the fact is most abundantly visible along Nanjing Lu street, the main shopping strip, and of course along the Bund, where one can even find one of America's favorite fast-food chains: Kentucky Fried Chicken.

---

[1]*China: Shanghai,* China City Guide Series, published by the China Travel and Tourism Press, Beijing, 1983.

---

cities included (1) activity focused on the processing of raw materials for factories in the mother country (this would not only minimize transport costs, but allow the colonizer to take advantage of cheap labor in the colony during initial processing of raw materials which did not require high-skill labor); and (2) factories transplanted in turnkey fashion from Europe rather than developed from within. These industrial development strategies generally did not serve the needs of the local population well and led to continued dependence on the West for both technology and markets in the postcolonial period.

The colonial city also demonstrated a distinctive land use pattern imposed by the colonial ruler. This pattern became evident in a residential use of space "characterized by segregation along both ethnic and socioeconomic lines." Some quarters or neighborhoods were designated exclusively for European colonial settlers and others for the native population and other functions, for example, administrative civil lines or the military cantonment. This segregationist policy led to the creation of a sectoral development pattern in most colonial cities.

The Postcolonial City

The postcolonial city is the most recent phenomenon in the annals of urban development in the third world. It emerged after independence from colonial rule, which generally occurred in the post-World War II period in the cases of Asia and Africa. Although the postcolonial city is one step beyond the colonial city, few structural and functional differences occur between the two cities (Figure 3-9).

While the colonial city was administratively controlled by the colonial power, the postcolonial city is controlled by local elites and power structures. Nevertheless, the colonial influence remains evident in almost every aspect of the postcolonial city; the legacy lives on. The basic difference between the colonial city and the postcolonial city lies not in the type of functions but in their use.

Compared to the colonial city, the postcolonial city is more commercial and industrial, even as the industrial structure continues to depend on Western technology. Many of the cities, for example, Bangkok, São Paulo, Santiago, Lagos, Singapore, Kuala Lumpur (Malaysia), Seoul (South Korea), and Manila (Philippines), have attracted manufacturing facilities owned by multinational companies. In collaboration with the local elites—both within and outside the government—these companies and other state-managed firms control a considerable portion of the production as well as the distribution processes. Many state-controlled compa-

nies emerged following nationalization of former foreign-controlled multinationals.

The postcolonial city also offers a diversified mix of services and performs several economic roles. It is the focal point of administrative control and decision making with regard to national and regional development. Despite all this effort, the city in the postcolonial era has failed to serve as a center of innovation diffusion, which would benefit the hinterland and national economy as a whole—a role performed by urban development in the United States, Europe, and Japan. The postcolonial city, in fact, often has closer ties with cities in highly developed countries than with its own hinterland, further accentuating its dependent relationship with the West.

In spatial extent and population size, the postcolonial city is much larger than the colonial city, mainly because of the rapid influx of rural migrants. Such growth is associated with increased wealth on one hand and expanding poverty and squatter settlements on the other. Despite the existence of considerable residential mixing by social classes, neighborhood separation between the poor and the rich appears to be on the rise. Overall, the postcolonial city, despite its increased

Figure 3-9. New and Old Commercial Sections of Bombay, India. Many post-colonial cities continue to have closer ties to highly developed countries than with their own hinterland. Overall, despite rapid growth and modern downtown skylines, these cities remain colonial in basic structure. (Porterfield/Chickering/Photo Researchers)

number of functions and growing diversity, remains colonial in basic structure. It exhibits a great number of contradictions and dualisms, for example, the coexistence of traditionalism and modernism; and of wealth and poverty. Several of these contradictions have been described earlier. We will now focus more specifically on the housing dilemma.

HOUSING AND SQUATTER SETTLEMENTS

It is a well-known fact that third world cities suffer from severe housing shortages (Figure 3-10). Ths situation condemns the urban poor to poor-quality housing. The problem has been compounded by skyrocketing land prices caused by land speculation and real estate profiteering on the part of those with capital to invest. As has been pointed out, "the operation of the class structure of third world cities is nowhere more geographically explicit than in the composition and working of the housing market."[10]

Urban housing in the third world can be categorized into conventional and nonconventional types. Conven-

[10]J. P. Dickenson et al., *A Geography of the Third World*, Methuen, London, 1983, p. 173.

tional house types include units with a foundation and firm structure, built both privately and by the government. Squatter settlements, on the other hand, are the most familiar type of nonconventional housing constructed by the urban poor—predominantly rural migrants—without government authorization and frequently illegally on land they do not own. These units are typically "lean-tos" constructed out of scrap materials such as cardboard, bamboo sticks, scrap lumber, or galvanized metal roofing material, on sites with no permanent foundation (Figure 3-11). The names of these squatter settlements vary: they are called *barrios, barriadas, favelas*, or *colonias proletarias* in Latin America; *bidonvilles* or *gouibivilles* in North Africa; *bustees* in India; *gecekonou* districts in Turkey; *kampongs* in Malaysia; and *barung-barongs* in the Philippines. Squatter settlements are found in virtually every major city of the third world, from Kingston (Jamaica) to Mexico City to Jakarta and Manila.

Two distinctive social and spatial patterns can be detected in the urban housing market of the third world. Socially, while the upper and middle classes are satisfactorily tucked away in well-constructed, even luxuriously designed and landscaped houses, the poor are spatially trapped in the high-density slums typically on the periphery. One can be seen in the background (or foreground) of another, even coexisting side by side.

Figure 3-10. Squatter Settlements on Steep Slopes in Caracas, Venezuela. Undesirable sites in gullies or steep slopes frequently become homes for squatter settlements in third world cities. This scene shows shacks in the foreground with the modern downtown high-rise skyline of Caracas in the distance. (Owen Franken/Stock, Boston)

Figure 3-11. Santa Fe Dump Squatter Settlement, Mexico City. This garbage dump is home to hundreds of squatters unable to gain access to traditional housing. These units are typically "lean-tos," constructed out of scrap materials, such as cardboard, scrap lumber, or galvanized metal roofing material. (Peter Menzel)

Both slums and squatter settlements represent poor housing, but there are certain distinctions. Slum housing requires rent and is overcrowded—sometimes 10 or 12 people are crammed into one small room. But they usually provide at least some basic, though inadequate, services such as a shared bathroom, water and electricity, and close proximity to work due to their center city locations. Squatter settlements lack all of these basic facilities, although there have been cases in which squatter settlers can gain illegal access to power lines to provide electricity in their settlements. Settlers in Mexico City and other Latin American cities are well known for this type of daring operation.

Squatter settlements are developed in several ways, but each involves some form of invasion of vacant space, public or private. The invasion is sometimes organized by a group of squatters who are predominantly rural migrants and other times it is based on individual initiatives. For example, in many Latin American cities, including Mexico City, squatter settlements are developed literally overnight through illegal land capture and subdivision. Group invasions typically involve large-scale initiatives, whereas those based on individual initiative are small and yield much

less security or permanency because of the lack of group organization and support. Squatter settlements are generally found on abandoned plots, steep slopes, hilltops, swamps, dumps, ravines, or any space that is left unoccupied over a period of time. These settlements are initially illegally developed, some being immediately leveled by government bulldozers. But sometimes the government tacitly legalizes them after a period by providing public services such as water taps, sewage systems, and electricity. Once tacitly approved, they become permanent settlements and are legitimized as the buying and selling of properties creates a permanent land ownership record. Individuals engaged in this type of activity are often admired for their "macho" behavior in solving their housing problems.

As pointed out earlier, the growth of squatter settlements in third world cities has been rapid and spectacular, and undergoes several phases of development over time, from disorganized cardboard shacks to organized and well-established settlements. It is a result of the poor people's inability to pay rent or purchase houses as well as of the government's ineffective and inadequate housing policy. Two governments that have achieved some level of success in housing their poor are Hong Kong and Singapore. Housing shortages and the number of squatter settlements are bound to increase in the future because rural-to-urban migration will not likely decrease in the foreseeable future and the governments will not be able to provide efficient housing.

A vast number of the third world urban population lives in slums and squatter settlements—in some cases up to 90 percent of the total urban population. Table 3-3 shows the percentage of slum and squatter dwellers in the total urban population by geographic region. A map showing the location of some of the major cities with a high percentage of slum and squatter population is presented in Figure 3-12.

One's interpretation of the growth of squatter settlements can be positive or negative, depending on the perspective. While some argue that it represents a negative force in the overall development of third world cities and their economies, others view it as a positive force and a necessary element. No doubt, from a planning point of view, it poses all kinds of problems— uncontrolled development and lack of sanitation, public services, and safety. Overall it is a disgrace, an insult to the elite political structure; a reminder of the government's inability to deal with the problem of massive urban poverty; and a most visible symbol of socioeconomic inequality, especially when it is juxtaposed against a luxury development initiated by and for the upper class.

No matter how one views the growth of urban squatter settlements, they perform certain functional roles.[11] Some of these roles are as follows:

1. They act as a point of entry to the city for migrants, assisting them in their adaptation to the urban way of life.

2. They provide free housing or a minimum rent and an opportunity to establish a foothold in the city.

3. They provide informal or "bazaar" economic opportunities.

4. They provide group, ethnic, or social, and even economic support, which is essential, at least in the initial phase of urban adaptation and assimilation.

Given the poverty status of the affected family, inept bureaucracies and overly high standards for conven-

TABLE 3-3

Slums and Uncontrolled Settlements: Percentage of Total Population in the 1960s

City	Country	Percent[a]
Addis Ababa	Ethiopia	90
Douala	Cameroon	80
Magadishu	Somalia	77
Lomé	Togo	75
Casablanca	Morocco	70
Ouaga dougou	Upper Volta	70
Abidjan	Ivory Coast	60
Bogotá	Colombia	60
Daka	Senegal	60
Kinshasa	Zaire	60
Lusaka	Zambia	58
Blantyre	Malawi	56
Accra	Ghana	53
Dar es Salaam	Tanzania	50
Monrovia	Liberia	50
Guayaquil	Ecuador	49
Mexico City	Mexico	46
Colombo	Sri Lanka	43
Caracas	Venezuela	40
Istanbul	Turkey	40
Lima	Peru	40
Kuala Lumpur	Malaysia	37
Manila	Philippines	35
Calcutta	India	33
Nairobi	Kenya	33
Guatemala City	Guatemala	30
Rio de Janeiro	Brazil	30
Seoul	Korea	30

[a]All estimates are extremely rough.

Source: O. F. Grimes, Jr., *Housing for Low-Income Urban Families,* Johns Hopkins Press for IBRD, London, 1976, Table A2, pp. 118–127.

tional housing serve to maintain the squatter system. Families with restricted incomes often cannot afford what amounts to overdesigned public housing when it is available. For example, in Latin America, only 59 percent of the urban population has piped water, while 17 percent is served by public standpipes. Standards for new housing usually require expensive piped water, which effectively excludes the poor family from the market.[12]

---

[11]Also see Brian J. L. Berry, *Comparative Urbanization,* 2nd ed., St. Martin's Press, New York, 1981.

[12]George J. Beier, "Can Third World Cities Cope?" *Population Bulletin,* 31, No. 4 (1976), 23.

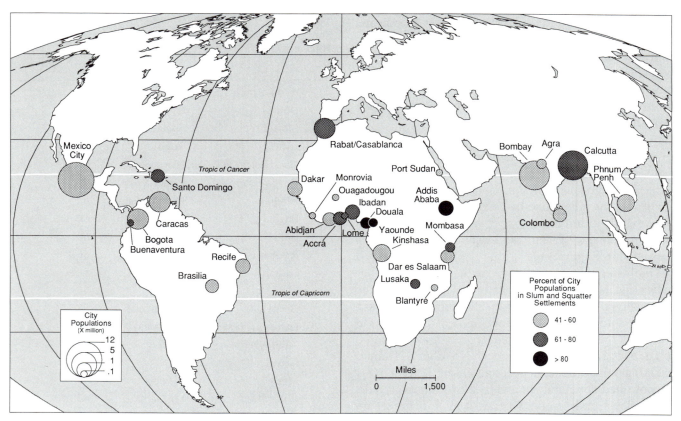

Figure 3-12. **Slum and Squatter Population Shares in Third World Cities.** In many African cities, over one-half the total population lives in slum and squatter settlements. Relatively high shares of squatters also occur in several South American and Asian cities. *Source:* Modified after Dickenson, et al. *A Geography of the Third World.* Methuen, New York, 1983. Used by permission.

Lack of adequate public utility service also discriminates against the poor. Often rationing is required, which gives the wealthy disproportionate access to services and requires the poor to rely on street vendors who provide a lower-quality service at a higher cost. Lack of funds for public service expansion is typical.

The administrative structure responsible for the management of city functions contributes to the urban problems of third world cities. The federal or provincial government is typically responsible for all decision making except for routine services that are supervised locally. The term *fragmented centralization* has been applied to this situation because the necessary resources and infrastructure are typically not available to implement these centrally imposed plans. Moreover, remote bureaucrats in the field make little attempt to become informed about or responsive to local needs. The result is a vacuum in the planning function at the local level and contempt for the process elsewhere.

Rural to Urban Migration

Many *push* and *pull* factors account for the high level of rural to urban migration in third world countries. Often rural migrants perceive that there are more opportunities available in cities, the so-called "lure of bright lights" argument. Coupled with this pull factor is a push associated with rural overpopulation and the poor state of subsistence agriculture and few employment opportunities. In short, economic conditions or motivations explain most of the movement.

In contrast to the situation in Western countries when they experienced the transition from a rural agrarian economy to industrialization, third world countries today have a much poorer agricultural base. Third world countries suffer from the lack of a sound agricultural base that was used at first to boost and later to sustain industrial development in the West. Agriculture is a key element in development because it not only provides raw materials necessary for factories located in cities, but also supplies food and fiber for the labor force. As such, its development is a *sine qua non* for industrial takeoff, but the reality is different.

The agriculture sector has been largely ignored and undercut by various policies in third world areas for a long time. First, in the colonial era it was disrupted by European penetration; and later, in the postcolonial era, it has been similarly overlooked even with the presence of accelerated outmigration flows to the cities. In addition to the lack of necessary investment, the underlying policy of price disincentives for rural farmers stunts agricultural development. Instead of agricultural development, emphasis is placed on capital-intensive manufacturing activity. Multinational corporations and state-owned businesses primarily operate out of large cities, except those involved in mineral recovery or plantation agriculture, and thereby reinforce the attractiveness of the city to migrants.

SUMMARY AND CONCLUSION

Third world city growth and development amply demonstrates that urbanization and affluence and/or urbanization and the growth of the middle class are not inexorably linked. Rather, urbanization often occurs in the absence of job opportunities and access to the good life. The rapid growth of third world cities in the late twentieth century poses many problems in economic development. The weakness of the formal sector of the economy places great stress on the informal to absorb masses of workers in petty business pursuits. Attitudes toward the informal sector, however, are changing. Rather than being treated as "refugee" sectors and ignored, mounting evidence indicates that training and assistance programs could improve productivity and be more effective than encouraging formal sector growth.

Present-day third world countries are experiencing a much different development path than their predecessors as capital intensive rather than labor intensive industries have been emphasized. The latecomer thesis suggests that third world countries will follow their own economic development process which as yet is not well understood. They have bypassed several stages of development that the U.S. and Europe experienced by having ready access to modern technologies. The import substitution industrialization process they have followed creates a lower demand for manufacturing workers at a time when masses need work. A more

productive agricultural sector allowed for capital generation when development unfolded in the U.S. and western Europe but is absent in the third world today. A very depressed and inefficient agricultural sector characterizes many third world countries today. This in turn contributes to the accelerating rural-urban migration flow that fuels rapid urban growth.

The presence of massive quantities of squatter housing on the periphery of third world cities poses yet another contrast with cities in developed areas due to housing shortages, skyrocketing land prices, and a weak infrastructure to support urban development.

A three-stage historical developmental model assists in understanding the distinctive roles third world cities have played over time. The sequence of stages is linked to European colonial involvement with these cities. Essentially, these cities became a product of European-based colonialism in the nineteenth century. They became colonial outposts more closely linked to Europe than their own hinterland at that time, and local indigenous economies were destroyed, a legacy which continues to affect their development. Today, local elites have replaced their colonial predecessors while the city functions much the same, with the juxtaposition of wealth and poverty and related contradictions just as pronounced.

Suggestions for Further Reading

Abu-Lughod, Janet, and Richard Hay, Jr. *Third World Urbanization*, Maaroufa Press, Chicago, 1977.

Abu-Lughod, Janet. "Culture, Modes of Production, and the Changing Nature of Cities in the Arab World," chapter in John A. Agnew, et al., eds., *The City in Cultural Context*, Allen & Unwin, Boston, 1984, pp. 94–119.

Armstrong, Warwick, and T. G. McGee. *Theatres of Accumulation: Studies in Asian and Latin American Accumulation*, Methuen, New York, 1985.

Berry, Brian, J. L. *The Human Consequence of Urbanization*, St. Martin's Press, New York, 1973.

Bradshaw, York W. "Urbanization and Underdevelopment: A Global Study of Modernization, Urban Bias, and Economic Dependency," *American Sociological Review*, 52 (1987), pp. 224–239.

Brown, Larry. *Place, Migration and Development in the Third World*, Routledge, New York, 1991.

Chadwick, George. *Models of Urban and Regional Systems in Developing Countries*, Pergamon, New York, 1987.

Conway, Dennis, "Changing Perspectives on Squatter Settlements, Intraurban Mobility, and Constraints on Housing Choice," *Urban Geography*, 6 (1988), pp. 170–192.

Drakakis-Smith, David. *Economic Growth and Urbanization in Developing Areas*, Routledge, New York, 1990.

——— . *Urbanization, Housing and the Development Process*, St. Martin's Press, New York, 1980.

——— . *Urbanization in the Developing World*, Croom Helm, Dover, N.H., 1986.

Friedmann, John, ed. *New Concepts and Technologies in Third World Urbanization*, University of California, School of Architecture and Urban Planning. Comparative Urbanization Studies, Los Angeles, 1974.

Gilbert, Alan, and Josef Gugler. *Cities, Poverty, and Development: Urbanization in the Third World*. Oxford University Press, New York, 1982.

Gugler, Josef. *The Urbanization of the Third World*, Oxford University Press, New York, 1988.

Lowder, Stella. *The Geography of Third World Cities*, Barnes & Noble Books, Totowa, N.J., 1986.

Safa, H. I., ed. *Towards a Political Economy of Urbanization in Third World Countries*, Oxford University Press, New York, 1982.

Schuurman, Frans J., and Ton Van Naerssen. *Urban Social Movements in the Third World*, Routledge, New York, 1989.

Sharma, Pitamber. *Urbanization in Nepal, Papers of the East-West Population Institute*, No. 110, East-West Center, Honolulu, 1989.

Sjoberg, Gideon. *The Preindustrial City*, Free Press, Glencoe, Ill., 1966.

Turnham, David. *The Informal Sector Revisited*, OECD, Paris, 1990.

4

THE NORTH AMERICAN CITY

By world standards, the urban pattern in North America is of recent vintage. The patterns that evolved in the United States and Canada in the past 200 years initially grew out of the heritage brought from Europe, but they quickly developed their own ethic. Today, the distinctive character of cities in the United States and Canada reflects the imprint of their respective political economies, ethnic traditions, and resource bases, among other factors. We will examine similarities and contrasts in the development patterns in these two countries later in this chapter. We will begin by introducing several concepts and organizing principles that help us explain the regularities observed in the location, size, and spacing of cities.

LOCATION PATTERNS

Three ideal patterns assist in the understanding of the location, size, and spacing of cities.[1] Each pattern results from a distinctive role and support base for the city and has been identified with unique locational settings.

1. *Linear Pattern.* Cities aligned along a transport route (river, rail, or seacoast).
2. *Cluster Pattern.* Relatively close spacing of cities of similar size.
3. *Hierarchial Pattern.* Several sizes of cities arranged relatively evenly throughout a region, with more smaller than larger-sized centers.

Linear Pattern

Cities distributed in linear fashion may occur along a transportation route, such as on a river system, at a base of a mountain barrier, or along a seacoast. They function primarily as *break-of-bulk* centers. This activity refers to the role of providing facilities and services for the transfer of goods from one type of transport to another, as in the shift from water to rail transport that occurs in coastal port cities. Such cities are often called entrepôt centers. Coastal cities, for example, serve as gateways by handling the shipment of goods into and out of the interior. This role of the city has been likened to that of a funnel; the routeways to and from the city are like the tube.[2]

A hypothetical spacing and trade area conceptualization for the linear pattern is shown in Figure 4-1A. Note that linearly aligned cities such as those along a river or coastline are typically closely and evenly spaced and

[1]This threefold classification appears in Chauncy D. Harris and Edward L. Ullman, "The Nature of Cities," *Annals of the American Academy of Political and Social Science*, 242 (1945), 7–17.

[2]R. J. Johnston, "Regarding Urban Origins, Urbanization and Urban Patterns," *Geography*, 62 (1977), 4.

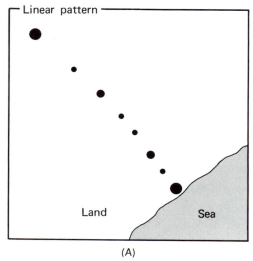

(A)

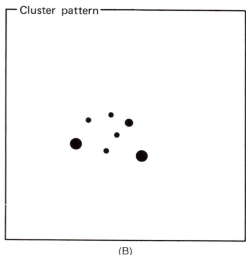

(B)

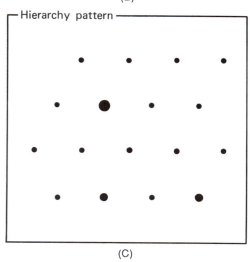

(C)

Figure 4-1. Location Patterns of Cities. The three ideal location patterns for cities assist in the understanding of the location, size, and spacing of cities. Each pattern reflects a distinctive role and support base for the city.

are of similar size, except for those at the extremities of the routeway or at a major interior transportation junction, such as the mouth of a river in the case of the coastal setting. This size and space equity occurs because the cities are not necessarily competing with one another but serve as focal points for the distribution of goods and services in and out of the hinterland. The hinterland refers to the territory linked to the city that is typically elongated at right angles to the route alignment.

An example of the linear pattern of cities occurs along the Hudson–Mohawk River corridor in upstate New York, which served as a gateway for the settlement of the interior in the early 1800s. The relatively even spacing of Yonkers, Poughkeepsie, Albany, Utica, Rome, Syracuse, Rochester, and Buffalo along the waterway corridor formed by the Erie/Barge Canal and Hudson and Mohawk rivers provides a case in point. The gateway cities on the Missouri and Mississippi river system and the early pattern of colonial cities along the Atlantic seaboard in the late 1700s provide other illustrations. In the late 1800s, such linear patterns also evolved along railroad lines in the United States and Canada.

Cluster Pattern

A cluster of cities can occur where specialized resources exist, such as at mineral extraction sites or resort locations (Figure 4-1B). The tightly spaced resort city locations in southeastern Florida (Miami, Fort Lauderdale, and West Palm Beach) provide an example. A close grouping of cities can also develop with the expansion of manufacturing centers at raw material sites. The concentration of relatively large industrial cities near coal-mining sites in Pennsylvania (Scranton, Wilkes-Barre, Hazleton, Bethlehem, Allentown, and Easton) is an example. The grouping of manufacturing centers on the Carolina Piedmont is another illustration. The close spacing and relatively large sizes of Winston-Salem, High Point, Greensboro, Durham, and Raleigh largely occur in response to the manufacturing support base of the cities (textiles, food processing, furniture, chemicals, and tobacco), which create many *localization economies* associated with access to a diversified, skilled labor pool and to a broad array of producer services and equipment fabricators that the manufacturing complex supports.

Hierarchical Pattern

A hierarchical city size and spacing pattern occurs in an agrarian area where the support base relies on the sale of goods and services to a surrounding, largely rural hinterland (Figure 4-1C). Cities providing this function are called central places or service centers. Nonindustrial, relatively homogeneous, agricultural regions provide ideal conditions for the development of the hierarchical pattern. The United States' Middle West provides the best example of this system of cities in the world. The theoretical underpinning of this settlement type and the rich body of central place theory literature that explains the size and spacing of such centers will be covered in Chapter 8.

Site and Situation

The *site and situation* concept emphasizes the importance of both the location of a city and its regional setting. Historically, the choice for the location of a city involved the selection of a favorable site in terms of its physical advantage based on the transportation technology available at the time. For example, a location at the confluence for two or more rivers provided superior access in the era of river corridor transportation. The site of Pittsburgh illustrates such a location at the confluence of the Monongahela and Allegheny rivers. Coastal sites near the mouths of rivers where deepwater ports could be established also illustrate the point. The site then is the physical location of the city. The situation refers to a dynamic that involves the city in its regional context.

The status of the regional economy of which the city is a part, and the nature of technology and transportation factors, all affect the situation of a city at a particular time. Typically a city only prospers if it has an opportunity to provide an expanded array of services to its hinterland. Manhattan Island provided New York with a favorable site as a port city, for example, but it did not prosper until the Erie Canal opened up the interior for trade. Thus the situation of New York changed as the canal era provided a stronger role for it as a trade center. Later, the railroad offered a similar advantage.

The early settlement history of the Minneapolis–St. Paul area of Minnesota also illustrates the importance of both the site and situation concept in accounting for urban growth in the region. Actually, St. Paul was settled first, when the Mississippi River served as the

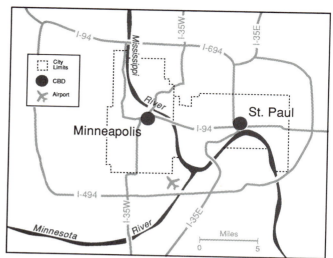

Figure 4-2. Site and Situation of Minneapolis–St. Paul. The historical sequence of settlement of the twin cities area reflects the importance of both site and situation. The St. Paul site offered an advantageous location to ford the Mississippi River, while the St. Anthony Falls location for Minneapolis offered a favorable water power site. The situation facing this area changed dramatically before and after the Louisiana purchase, which opened settlement to the west of the river.

western boundary of the country. Located at an advantageous site to ford the Mississippi River, in an area where the river flows in an east–west direction, the city became a major frontier service center (Figure 4-2). Since the original site of Minneapolis lies to the west of the river, that area was not open for settlement prior to the Louisiana Purchase. As the opportunity to harness the water power potential at a falls location became an important factor in selecting a second site for a city, the St. Anthony Falls site on the Mississippi River presented Minneapolis with an ideal location for urban development.

RANK-SIZE RULE

Groups of cities at the regional, national, or world scale usually exhibit a consistent regularity in size. The *rank-size rule* is an example of an organizing principle that helps account for this tendency. The rank-size concept was first discussed in the literature in the 1920s and 1930s.[3] Since that time, it has been tested in many

[3]Ernest Goodrich, "The Statistical Relationship between Population and the City Plan," in Ernest Burgess, ed., *The Urban Community*, University of Chicago Press, Chicago, 1926, pp. 144–150; H. W. Singer, "The Curbe des Populations: A Parallel to Pareto's Law," *The Economic Journal* (1936), 254–263.

areas of the world for many periods, past and present, and refined to accommodate necessary conditions and limits of applicability. Credit for much of the early testing of the concept in a variety of situations goes to Zipf's 1949 work.[4]

The rank-size rule states that the size of a given city can be predicted by simply knowing its population rank (among all cities in the area studied) and the size of the largest city. One can show this relationship as

$$P_n = P_1 \times R_n^{-1}$$

where

P_n = population of city to be calculated
P_1 = population of largest city
R_n = rank of city to be calculated

For example, one could calculate the size of the third largest city in an area as follows (assuming the largest city had a population of 17 million):

$$P_3 = P_1 \times 3^{-1}$$

$$P_3 = 17,000,000 \times 1/3$$

$$P_3 = 5,666,667$$

This calculation indicates that the third-ranking city would have a population of 5,666,667 persons.

Graphing the rank and size of a group of cities produces a curvilinear relationship as indicated in Figure 4-3A. If the population of the leading center were 17 million, such as that of greater New York in 1970, the population of the second center should approximate 8.6 million. In fact, in the United States two cities approached that size: Los Angeles with nearly 10 million people and Chicago with about 7.6 million. The third-ranking city of 5.7 million population corresponded to the populations of the Philadelphia, Detroit, and San Francisco areas, which all had over 4 million people in 1970. By expressing the numbers on the vertical axis of the rank-size diagram according to log transformations, the extreme variation is collapsed, producing a linear trend as shown in Figure 4-3A, which respresents the classic manner of portraying the relationship as a straight line.

Berry examined the rank-size relationship in several dozen countries around 1960 and determined that the rank-size distribution worked in about one-third of the

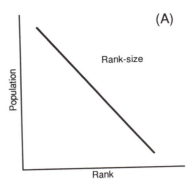

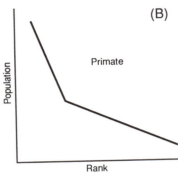

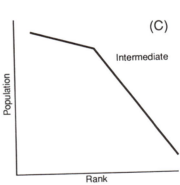

Figure 4-3. **Rank-Size Rule.** Groups of cities at the regional, national, or world scale exhibit a consistent regularity in size. While the rank, size rule works well in areas with a long history of urbanization, exceptions occur. *Source:* Redrawn with permission. From Brian J. L. Berry, "City Size Distributions and Economic Development," *Economic Development and Cultural Change,* 9, 1961, pp. 573–588. Copyright ©1961 by the University of Chicago.

countries studied; in another one-third, a *primate city-size* distribution prevailed.[5] The primate city-size distribution refers to a situation in which one single city houses a large proportion of a country's population, say

[4]G. K. Zipf, *Human Behavior and the Principle of Least Effort,* Addison-Wesley, Cambridge, Mass., 1949.

[5]Peter Haggett, *Location Analysis in Human Geography,* St. Martins Press, New York, 1965, pp. 101–106; B. J. L. Berry, "City Size Distributions and Economic Development," *Economic Development and Cultural Change,* 9 (1961), 573–588; Mark Jefferson, "The Law of the Primate City," *Geographical Review* 29 (1939), 226–232.

30 percent or more. Mexico City, Paris, and Bangkok, for example, all contain a very large share of their countries' inhabitants and exemplify this primate relationship. In some instances, the primate city phenomenon occurs as a result of outside or foreign settlement influences. In many present-day third world countries, for example, primate cities developed as a result of the intervention of a colonial power as mentioned in Chapter 2. Bangkok is an example of this circumstance. In graphic form, the primate distribution appears as a steep gradient because the second- and third-ranking cities are absent (Figure 4-3B).

A third category of countries exhibited an *intermediate-size distribution* in the Berry study (Figure 4-3C). Cities at any one of several levels might be absent in that grouping. For example, Australian cities were included in the intermediate-size category because small cities were missing, while a large proportion of the country's population lives in the large cities. England and Wales were also assigned to the intermediate group because of the absence of middle-size cities. Canada might also be included in this group because of a lack of a dominant center at the top.

A sound and comprehensive explanation of the conditions associated with each of these types of distributions does not exist. However, several generalizations were suggested by Berry as possible explanations. Usually, countries that show a rank-size relationship are large (Soviet Union, United States) and have had a long history of urbanization. Some less developed countries, such as Korea and El Salvador, were also found to follow the rank-size relationship. Primate centers also existed in developed countries, but in general they occurred in smaller nations and in those with a shorter history of urbanization (Portugal, Uruguay).

EVOLUTION OF THE URBAN PATTERN IN THE UNITED STATES, 1790 TO 1990

Even in colonial times, when a rural agrarian lifestyle prevailed, the American city made a significant impact on the landscape. Cities served as important trade centers for both local and overseas commerce.

Coastal City

The first United States census, taken in 1790, identified the leading urban centers of the country as *coastal cities* aligned in a linear pattern along the East Coast. The top 20 cities at that time are shown in Figure 4-4A and Table 4-1. A few inland cities (Taunton, Richmond, Albany, Petersburg) also had large populations in 1790. They provided functions similar to the coastal port cities, and rivers typically linked them to the sea.

River City

In 1830, coastal cities still dominated, but inland *river cities* also gained in stature (Figure 4-4B and Table 4-2) as the settlement frontier moved inland to the West. Note the prominence of New Orleans, Cincinnati, Louisville, Pittsburgh, and Troy in the list of the top 20 cities. Washington, D.C., also first appeared in the list of large cities in 1830.

Manufacturing City

By 1870, the railroad became a major influence in city development associated with the growth of the *manufacturing city* (Figure 4-4C and Table 4-3). Many coastal and river cities experienced this transition to manufacturing cities, but the most dramatic changes occurring at that time were the dramatic growth of Chicago, Milwaukee, Minneapolis, Detroit, Cleveland and St. Louis, which began to frame a *manufacturing belt* in the United States. We will discuss the importance of manufacturing and urban development again in Chapter 7. The emergence of San Francisco on the West coast is also a significant addition to the urban pattern in this period.

National City System

Differential growth rates between prosperous manufacturing centers and declining port cities resulted in a great realignment of leading cities in the early twentieth century. By 1910, dramatic rank increases occurred for several booming manufacturing centers, including Milwaukee, Detroit, and to a lesser extent Buffalo and Pittsburgh (Figure 4-4D and Table 4-4). Several river cities, such as Cincinnati and New Orleans, fell to lower rankings, while others dropped off the list completely (Louisville, Albany). The new cities added to the list at the beginning of the century reflected the continued vitality of cities in the Middle and Far West (Minneapolis, Kansas City, Seattle, and Los Angeles).

Figure 4-4. Leading U.S. City Rankings, 1790–1910. This group of maps documents the historical sequence of urban development at four critical periods in the nation's development. In 1790 (A), a *coastal city* pattern prevailed; in 1830 (B), a *river city* pattern emerged; in 1870 (C), the *manufacturing city* dominated; and in 1910 (D), a *national system* characterized settlement.

During the first decades of the twentieth century, the nation became more urban than rural for the first time, and the present-day national city system emerged. Stretching from coast to coast and filling in the interior, this new alignment of top 20 cities included Los Angeles, Kansas City, and Seattle for the first time. Denver and Salt Lake City would soon join the list.

Central City Dominance Weakens

The surge in city growth in the immediate post-World War II years led to the spilling over of population growth well beyond the city limits in many areas. Annexations of territory to the city slowed, and suburbs began developing independently. Those cities that continued annexing territory, particularly common in the southwest, maintained stronger central cities than other areas.

In the 1950s, central city dominance began to weaken (Figure 4-5A and Table 4-5). The list of top 20 cities in 1950 has been expanded to include not only a listing of central city rankings, but also a metropolitan area listing based on combined city and suburban population totals. The map in Figure 4-5 is based on metropolitan populations. For the most part, the lists are similar with slight rank shifts. Comparing the lists to the 1910 ranking, several dramatic changes can be observed. Los Angeles jumped from 17th to 4th ranking (city) and to 3rd place when comparing metropolitan figures. Washington, D.C. and Detroit also sprang upward due to the growth of the government sector and the expansion of the automobile industry, respectively. A second city from the South (after New Orleans), Houston, also joined the list of leading cities in 1950 for the first time since the colonial days. Foreshadowing harder times ahead, many older industrial cities began declining, including St. Louis, Boston, Pittsburgh, Buffalo, and Cincinnati.

TABLE 4-1
Leading Cities in the United States, 1790

Rank	City
1	New York, N.Y.
2	Philadelphia, Pa.
3	Boston, Mass.
4	Charleston, S.C.
5	Baltimore, Md.
6	Salem, Mass.
7	Newport, R.I.
8	Providence, R.I.
9	Gloucester, Mass.
10	Newburyport, Mass.
11	Portsmouth, N.H.
12	Brooklyn, N.Y.
13	New Haven, Conn.
14	Taunton, Mass.
15	Richmond, Va.
16	Albany, N.Y.
17	New Bedford, Mass.
18	Beverly, Mass.
19	Norfolk, Va.
20	Petersburg, Va.

Source: James E. Vance, Jr., "Cities in the Shaping of the American Nation," *The Journal of Geography,* 75, No. 1 (January 1976), 41–52. Reprinted by permission of *The Journal of Geography,* National Council for Geographic Education.

Suburban Dominance

The intense suburbanization process of the 1950s and 1960s led to a crossing of the population curves in 1970. For the first time, the population of the suburbs exceeded that of the central cities. In 1970, the West became the most highly urbanized region of the country (83 percent), overtaking the previous leader, the Northeast (80 percent urban in 1970), while the country as a whole registered a 74 percent urban population share.

The differential ranking of city and metropolitan listings (Table 4-6 and Figure 4-5B) is accounted for by a combination of the presence or absence of annexation, central city population losses and/or suburban growth. In several instances, the top metropolitan areas in 1970 had relatively small central cities, as in the case of Atlanta. Some metropolitan areas were buoyed in size as neighboring urban areas coalesced, such as the

case of Los Angeles–Long Beach, San Francisco–Oakland, Minneapolis–St. Paul, and Seattle–Everett. Other metropolitan areas seemed to develop rather independently of their central cities, becoming prototype suburban cities, such as Anaheim–Santa Ana–Garden Grove in the Orange County area of greater Los Angeles and Nassau–Suffolk on Long Island in metropolitan New York.

The growth of U.S. metropolitan areas slowed in the 1970s, registering a 7 percent gain overall durng the decade compared with the national growth rate of 11 percent. Ten major metropolitan areas, in fact, experienced significant population losses in the decade, led by an 8 percent decline in Buffalo. Pittsburgh, Cleveland, and New York also sustained considerable losses. Metropolitan areas in the Northeast and Middle West, as a group, experienced very little change. Only Columbus, Ohio, and Minneapolis–St. Paul significantly outperformed the region as a whole.

TABLE 4-2
Leading Cities in the United States, 1830

Rank	City
1	New York, N.Y.
2	Baltimore, Md.
3	Philadelphia, Pa.
4	Boston, Mass.
5	New Orleans, La.
6	Charleston, S.C.
7	Cincinnati, Ohio
8	Albany, N.Y.
9	Brooklyn, N.Y.
10	Washington, D.C.
11	Providence, R.I.
12	Richmond, Va.
13	Pittsburgh, Pa.
14	Salem, Mass.
15	Portland, Maine
16	Troy, N.Y.
17	Newark, N.J.
18	Louisville, Ky.
19	New Haven, Conn.
20	Norfolk, Va.

Source: James E. Vance, Jr., "Cities in the Shaping of the American Nation," *The Journal of Geography,* 75, No. 1 (January 1976), 41–52. Reprinted by permission of *The Journal of Geography,* National Council for Geographic Education.

Nonmetropolitan Growth

A drifting of the urban population away from larger urban areas to smaller cities and nonmetropolitan (rural) areas emerged as a significant counterstream to the more traditional flow toward large cities during the 1970s, as mentioned earlier. The average annual growth rate of metropolitan areas dropped below 1 percent in the early part of the decade, and metropolitan areas over 2 million in population actually experienced a net loss in population from 1970 to 1974. In contrast, areas under 250,000 grew more rapidly in the early 1970s than in the 1960s, except for those in the Northeast and North Central states, which stagnated much as did the larger cities.

The prevailing flow of people from metropolitan to nonmetropolitan areas of the 1970s is remarkable because it represented a complete reversal of a 200-year

TABLE 4-3
Leading Cities in the United States, 1870

Rank	City
1	New York, N.Y.
2	Philadelphia, Pa.
3	Brooklyn, N.Y.
4	St. Louis, Mo.
5	Chicago, Ill.
6	Baltimore, Md.
7	Boston, Mass.
8	Cincinnati, Ohio
9	New Orleans, La.
10	San Francisco, Calif.
11	Pittsburgh, Pa.
12	Buffalo, N.Y.
13	Washington, D.C.
14	Newark, N.J.
15	Louisville, Ky.
16	Cleveland, Ohio
17	Jersey City, N.J.
18	Detroit, Mich.
19	Milwaukee, Wis.
20	Albany, N.Y.

Source: James E. Vance, Jr., "Cities in the Shaping of the American Nation," *The Journal of Geography,* 75, No. 1 (January 1976), 41–52. Reprinted by permission of *The Journal of Geography,* National Council for Geographic Education.

TABLE 4-4
Leading Cities in the United States, 1910

Rank	City
1	New York, N.Y.
2	Chicago, Ill.
3	Philadelphia, Pa.
4	St. Louis, Mo.
5	Boston, Mass.
6	Cleveland, Ohio
7	Baltimore, Md.
8	Pittsburgh, Pa.
9	Detroit, Mich.
10	Buffalo, N.Y.
11	San Francisco, Calif.
12	Milwaukee, Wis.
13	Cincinnati, Ohio
14	Newark, N.Y.
15	New Orleans, La.
16	Washington, D.C.
17	Los Angeles, Calif.
18	Minneapolis, Minn.
19	Kansas City, Mo.
20	Seattle, Wash.

Source: James E. Vance, Jr., "Cities in the Shaping of the American Nation," *The Journal of Geography,* 75, No. 1 (January 1976), 41–52. Reprinted by permission of *The Journal of Geography,* National Council for Geographic Education.

trend in the opposite direction. But as we will see in the next section, this counterflow did not carry over into the 1980s.

The growth rate of nonmetropolitan areas in the 1970s was nearly double that of the metropolitan experience. Spillover of growth from the urban areas into the exurban periphery explained over half of the nonmetropolitan growth. It was an especially prominent factor in the Northeast and Great Lakes region.[6] Elsewhere, growth occurred in locations distinctly separate from metropolitan areas and often did not involve living in the country and commuting to the city to work. This growth represented genuine relocation to rural and small-town environments.

One example of the turnaround from rural decline to

[6]Calvin L. Beale, *The Revival of Population Growth in Nonmetropolitan America,* Economic Development Division, Economic Research Service, ERS-605, U.S. Department of Agriculture, Washington, D.C., 1975.

Figure 4-5.   Leading Metropolitan Area Rankings, 1950–1990. The leading metropolitan areas in the 1950s (A) closely paralleled the top city listing, but as metropolitan growth accelerated in succeeding decades the metropolitan area rankings began to differ significantly, paralleling the growth of the suburbs. The 1970 map (B) and includes two additional cities from the South—Dallas and Atlanta. By 1990 a wider divergence in city and metro listings (maps C and D) became apparent. Note absence of Pittsburgh, Cleveland, St. Louis, Minneapolis, Atlanta, Miami, and Seattle from the top-city group (map D), and the addition of Miami, Phoenix, and San Diego to the leading metro area distribution in 1990 (map C), since 1970 (map B).

growth in the 1970s was provided by the Ozark–Ouachita region, which forms a crescent from southern Missouri to Arkansas and eastern Oklahoma. That growth symbolized the renewed attraction of the rural area for retirement and recreation. The upper Great Lakes area of Michigan, the hill country of Texas, and the Sierra Nevada foothills of California experienced this same phenomenon. In fact, all areas endowed with amenities associated with lakes and reservoirs became favored settlement areas in the 1970s.

Another factor benefiting nommetropolitan growth was manufacturing decentralization, which was especially pronounced in the southern Piedmont. This phenomenon will be discussed in Chapter 7. The growth of colleges and technical schools in small towns also benefited rural areas by promoting cultural activities in them, as well as providing a stronger economic base.

Boom Towns

Perhaps the most remarkable form of nonmetropolitan growth in the 1970s occurred in so-called boom towns that expanded, and even doubled, in population as a result of energy-related projects. This growth was not necessarily rural, because much of it involved expansion of existing communities. Wyoming, a state with no MSAs in 1970, experienced considerable energy-related growth and became a model area for the study of boom towns during the decade. The national distribution of boom towns in the 1970s encompassed an area extending from the Great Plains (particularly the Dakotas), to all Rocky Mountain states (especially Montana, Colorado, Utah, and Wyoming), the Far West, and Gulf Coast states. Coal, oil, gas, oil shale, thermal power plants, and other mineral deposits (uranium, phosphate, trona, etc.) produced the strongest growth

TABLE 4-5
Leading U.S. City and Metropolitan Area Population Comparisons, 1950

Rank	City	Rank	Metropolitan Area[a]
1	New York	1	New York
2	Chicago	2	Chicago
3	Philadelphia	3	Los Angeles
4	Los Angeles	4	Philadelphia
5	Detroit	5	Detroit
6	Baltimore	6	Boston
7	Cleveland	7	San Francisco
8	St. Louis	8	Pittsburgh
9	Washington, D.C.	9	St. Louis
10	Boston	10	Cleveland
11	San Francisco	11	Washington, D.C.
12	Pittsburgh	12	Baltimore
13	Milwaukee	13	Minneapolis
14	Houston	14	Buffalo
15	Buffalo	15	Milwaukee
16	New Orleans	16	Cincinnati
17	Minneapolis	17	Seattle
18	Cincinnati	18	Kansas City
19	Seattle	19	Houston
20	Kansas City	20	Providence

[a]Identified by name of largest city.
Source: U.S. Bureau of the Census.

incentive in these areas. Nuclear power plant investments across the country also created local booms.

The increasing concern with expanding domestic energy supplies and the 1974–1975 energy crisis itself triggered much of this expansion, as did the increasing demand for electrical power and the need for cleaner-burning coal (western coal has a lower sulfur content than the traditional eastern supply) as a result of pollution control guidelines. The boom in many of these areas turned out to be short-lived, as had earlier booms, such as the gold rush a century earlier. By the late 1970s, the price of oil peaked and recessionary times returned to the energy-related (boom) towns, causing many to lose population in the early 1980s.

Sweetwater County, Wyoming

The case of Sweetwater County, Wyoming, typifies the boom–bust cycle. The Union Pacific Railroad was synonymous with the development of towns across southern Wyoming in the late 1800s, when the county was first settled. Cities were initially established as refueling (coal and water) depots; they remained company towns. In the 1950s, automation and a switch from coal fuel to oil spelled catastrophe and hard times for the towns of Green River and Rock Springs, following the closing of mines and the withdrawal of work forces.

In 1970, the population of Sweetwater County was 18,400, just as an energy boom was to break. A power dam opened in the area to the south (Flaming Gorge Dam), oil and gas exploration accelerated, coal mines reopened, trona mines produced, and construction began on a massive coal-fired power plant. These actions converged to create a massive impact on Rock Springs and Green River. Construction employment in the county was 400 in 1970, rising to nearly 5000 in 1974.

TABLE 4-6
Leading U.S. City and Metropolitan Area Population Comparisons, 1970

Rank	City	Rank	Metropolitan Area[a]
1	New York	1	New York
2	Chicago	2	Los Angeles
3	Los Angeles	3	Chicago
4	Philadelphia	4	Philadelphia
5	Detroit	5	Detroit
6	Houston	6	San Francisco
7	Baltimore	7	Washington, D.C.
8	Dallas	8	Boston
9	Washington, D.C.	9	Pittsburgh
10	Cleveland	10	St. Louis
11	Indianapolis	11	Baltimore
12	Milwaukee	12	Cleveland
13	San Francisco	13	Houston
14	San Diego	14	Newark
15	San Antonio	15	Minneapolis
16	Boston	16	Dallas
17	Memphis	17	Seattle
18	St. Louis	18	Anaheim–Santa Ana–Garden Grove
19	New Orleans	19	Milwaukee
20	Phoenix	20	Atlanta

[a]Identified by name of largest city.
Source: U.S. Bureau of the Census.

Similarly, the population zoomed upward to about 36,900 in 1974. An annual growth rate of 19 percent created a severe impact on the resources of the two cities.

Boom conditions continued until the late 1970s, when they collapsed. Services, including retailing and medical facilities, gradually moved into the area to serve local needs, but a development lag of five years endured before this occurred. During that period many problems emerged in coping with growth, for both local government leaders and residents, including gaining access to health-care facilities and personal and professional services. Some companies even paid bonus hardship salaries to families in light of the difficulties they faced before services were available.

Sunbelt Growth

The *sunbelt* received top billing in metropolitan growth in the 1970s, as 10 major metropolitan areas in the South and West grew faster than the United States as a whole. The sunbelt term emerged in the late 1970s as an integrating concept to differentiate and tie together the rapidly growing regions of the South and West. This perspective assisted with the differentiation of that area from the relative stagnation and decline perceived at the time to be overtaking the North. The latter area was variously labeled the *frostbelt* or the *rustbelt*.

Sunbelt definitions vary widely, but the one used here approximates all or part of the 21 states shown in Figure 4-6, where the January mean maximum temperature exceeds 45°F. Some observers have noted that this amalgam of the South and West has benefited the South the most, as its traditional reputation characterized it as an impoverished rural backwater region, whereas the West already enjoyed a positive reputation for growth and prosperity. For whatever reason, the term caught on rapidly and came to symbolize the good life associated with the sun and leisure lifestyle accompanying the booming service economy in the South and West.

Phoenix led the pack in sunbelt metropolitan growth in the 1970s, registering a whopping 55 percent growth

Figure 4-6. Sunbelt Metropolitan Areas. The sunbelt received top billing in metropolitan growth in the 1970s, as 10 major metropolitan areas in the South and West grew faster than the United States as a whole. The boundary line between the frostbelt and sunbelt shown here approximates the January mean maximum temperature of 45°F.

rate, followed by Tampa–St. Petersburg, 44 percent; Houston, 43 percent; Miami–Fort Lauderdale, 40 percent; San Diego, 37 percent; Denver, 31 percent; Atlanta, 27 percent; Sacramento, 26 percent; and Dallas–Fort Worth, 25 percent. Even slow-growing metropolitan areas in the South and West outperformed those in the Northeast and Middle West in the 1970s.

In the South, the largest metropolitan areas grew the fastest, unlike the situation in the rest of the country where the largest centers grew the least. The explanation for this differential is that urban immigration in most of the country did not keep pace with the greater reverse flow from larger to smaller centers and to nonmetropolitan areas. Growth rates for the nonmetropolitan population, in fact, increased nationwide during the 1970s unlike the situation a decade earlier.

Many central cities continued to decline in the 1970s as they had in previous decades. This situation occurred most conspicuously in the Northeast, where an average decline of 10 percent prevailed. In the South the opposite occurred, producing an average increase in central city populations of 9 percent. But there were significant exceptions, as in the case of Atlanta, where a 14 percent decline significantly impacted the central city. The most rapid growth in central city populations occurred in cities with liberal annexation policies such as Phoenix (35 percent growth), Houston (27 percent growth), San Diego (26 percent), and San Antonio (20 percent).

Sluggish overall central city growth rates, in the face of rapid metropolitan expansion growth, has severely eroded the central city share of metropolitan population nationally in the past 30 years. Whereas 49 percent of the metropolitan population collectively resided in central cities in 1960, only 38 percent resided there in 1970. By 1980, only 6 central cities from among the top 34 metropolitan regions in the United States contained over 50 percent of their metropolitan area's population. In some cases, the central city share of the metropolitan population dwindled to about 20 percent of the total in 1980, as in the case of Pittsburgh and St. Louis (19 percent), Washington, D.C., and Atlanta (21 percent), and Miami (23 percent).

A New City-Building Era

Dramatic changes in the ranking of the top 20 central cities again occurred in the 1970–1990 period (Figure 4-5C and Table 4-7). First, rapid upward mobility

occurred with several sunbelt cities, such as Phoenix rising from 20th to 9th position in central city population, San Diego moving from 14th to 6th, and San Antonio from 15th to 10th in rank. Cleveland, 10th in 1970, dropped from the top 20 city list by 1990, as did New Orleans and St. Louis. Significant rank declines occurred with Baltimore, 7th to 13th; Milwaukee, 12th to 17th; and Washington, D.C., 9th to 19th. New cities on the list included San Jose, 11th; Jacksonville, Florida, 15th; and Columbus, Ohio, 16th. Los Angeles also replaced Chicago as the second largest central city in this era, and Houston moved ahead of Philadelphia to occupy 4th position.

But the big story of the 1970–1990 period centers on the precipitous decline of traditional central city greats such as Detroit, which fell from 5th to 7th place, losing about 15 percent of its population in the 1980s alone. Pittsburgh, Cleveland, New Orleans, and St. Louis also lost more than 10 percent of their central city populations in the 1980s. The central city share of the metropolitan population continued to drop in the 1980s. In Detroit, that share fell from 25 to 22 percent of the metropolitan total. The metropolitan areas of Detroit and Cleveland lost about 2 percent of their population at the same time, further emphasizing the ongoing urban restructuring of the country.

The dramatic difference in ranking of several other central cities and their metropolitan area counterparts for 1990 also strikes the reader in Figure 4-5D and Table 4-7. Whereas metropolitan San Francisco ranked 4th nationally in metropolitan size, the city of San Francisco ranked 14th. Boston ranked 20th in size as a city, but 7th in metropolitan area. Cleveland ranked 13th as a metropolitan area, but did not make the list of top 20 cities. On the other hand, there are also examples of cities and their metropolitan areas having similar rankings, as in the case of New York, Los Angeles, Chicago, and Philadelphia. Several cities ranking in the top 20 in the city list but not the metropolitan list include the sunbelt cities with recent histories of liberal annexation (San Antonio, San Jose). In other cases, city–county consolidation has boosted city size, as in the case of Indianapolis (12th ranking) and Jacksonville (15th ranking).

Strong metropolitan growth returned to the United States in the 1980s following the energy-related recession at the beginning of the decade. The foundation of the new city-building era rested on a rapidly expanding entrepreneurial job base, associated with the emergence of the full-blown service economy and the

TABLE 4-7
Top 20 City and Metropolitan Area Population Comparisons, 1990

Rank	City	Rank	Metropolitan Area
1	New York	1	New York-Northern N.J.-Long Island CMSA
2	Los Angeles	2	Los Angeles-Anaheim-Riverside CMSA
3	Chicago	3	Chicago-Gary-Lake Co. CMSA
4	Houston	4	San Francisco-Oakland-San Jose CMSA
5	Philadelphia	5	Philadelphia-Wilmington-Trenton CMSA
6	San Diego	6	Detroit-Ann Arbor CMSA
7	Detroit	7	Boston-Lawrence-Salem CMSA
8	Dallas	8	Washington, D.C. MSA
9	Phoenix	9	Dallas-Fort Worth CMSA
10	San Antonio	10	Houston-Galveston-Brazoria CMSA
11	San Jose	11	Miami-Fort Lauderdale CMSA
12	Indianapolis	12	Atlanta MSA
13	Baltimore	13	Cleveland-Akron-Lorain CMSA
14	San Francisco	14	Seattle-Tacoma CMSA
15	Jacksonville	15	San Diego MSA
16	Columbus	16	Minneapolis-St. Paul MSA
17	Milwaukee	17	St. Louis MSA
18	Memphis	18	Baltimore MSA
19	Washington, D.C.	19	Pittsburgh-Beaver Valley CMSA
20	Boston	20	Phoenix MSA

Source: U.S. Bureau of the Census.

information age. Expansion of high-technology industry and growing affluence fueled this growth, as did an explosion of white-collar office employment and the growth of producer services. Not only did sunbelt cities boom, but many northern cities threw off the shackles of decline associated with their heavy manufacturing past and transformed their economies into innovative and aggressive information/high-technology leaders. Their traditional industrial base also became more competitive by the end of the decade as business leaders took advantage of earlier restructuring, and the decline of the dollar made exports of manufacturing goods more competitive. Boston, Rochester, Chicago, Cincinnati, and Pittsburgh, among others, benefited significantly from this transition, but the national economic slowdown in the early 1990s tempered this expansion.

Sunbelt metropolitan areas, with the exception of those located in the energy states of Texas, Oklahoma, and Louisiana, continued to pace the urban growth race in the United States throughout the 1980s. Florida cities exhibited robust expansion, as did Charlotte, Atlanta, Phoenix, Dallas–Fort Worth, and several California cities. Expansion occurred in Texas and neighboring oil-producing states (Louisiana and Oklahoma) at the beginning of the decade, but within three years an energy recession had severely impacted this "oil patch" region inducing considerable population outmigration. Whereas about one-half of the population growth in the country could be counted in just two states—Texas and Florida—at the beginning of the decade, only Florida remained as a growth leader after the energy setback occurred. In fact, by 1984, 6 of the 10 fastest-growing metropolitan areas in the country claimed a Florida venue, but Phoenix held the lead as the most rapidly growing large metropolitan area in the country.

In the mid-1980s, about one-half of the country's population lived in cities over 1 million in population. These 37 urban centers, while widely spaced throughout the country, also displayed a tendency that harkened back to the 1790s—preference for coastal locations. The largest of these centers still clustered in the North, which claimed three of the five cities over 5 million, while two were in the West. It is significant that no city of 5 million yet existed in the South. One or more such centers will likely emerge in the South early in the twenty-first century. Atlanta, Dallas–Fort Worth, and/or Houston, for example, could reach the 5 million population threshold by 2025, providing similar roles in the national economy to those provided by Los Angeles and San Francisco in the West and Chicago in the Middle West. If and when that occurs, a more balanced urban structure, in terms of city hierarchy, will exist throughout the country.

NATIONAL REDISTRIBUTION CYCLES

The continuous redistribution of metropolitan population that took place on a national scale in the United States in the twentieth century occurred in the context of a rapidly changing economy, which was shifting from an agrarian and heavy industry base to a postindustrial service/high-technology base. A depopulation of the interior and growth in peripheral coastal areas accompanied this transition. Many counties in the

agriculture-dominated interior of the country have experienced continuous decline since the beginning of this century (Figure 4-7).

Large expanses of several states in the center of the nation continued to decline in recent years, as has upper New England, many counties in Rocky Mountain states, and sections of the rural South. This decline resulted in a net population loss for three states in the 1960s—North and South Dakota, and West Virginia—and for two states in the 1970s—New York and Rhode Island. Four states lost more than 1 percent of their population in the 1980s, paced by West Virginia (−9 percent), Iowa (−5 percent), Wyoming (−4 percent), and North Dakota (−3 percent). Other findings from the 1990 Census are reported in the accompanying box.

Coastal population expansion in the last several decades is reflected by the share and density of the population of the country residing within 50 miles of shorelines (Table 4-8). In 1940, about 46 percent of the country lived in this zone at a density of about 129 persons per square mile. In 1976, the share had increased to 53 percent and the density had nearly doubled, rising to 243 persons per square mile. Today, over one-half of the nation still lives in this very small land area in a very fragile and environmentally risky

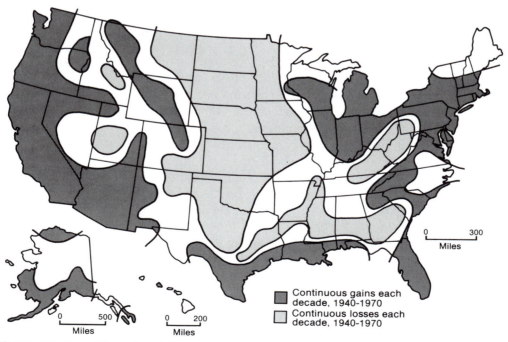

Continuous gains each decade, 1940-1970
Continuous losses each decade, 1940-1970

Figure 4-7. United States Population Trends, 1940–1970. Many counties in the agriculture-dominated interior of the country have experienced continuous decline since the beginning of the century. At the same time, coastal population expansion has increased, especially in the sunbelt.

1990 CENSUS FINDINGS

Metropolitan growth in the 1980s slowed in all parts of the country except for selected areas of a few sunbelt states, most notably southern California and Florida. "Of the 320 officially designated metropolitan areas, 65 actually lost population between 1980 and 1990. Another 116 metros grew more slowly than the 10 percent rate for the national population. Only 73 metros increased by 20 percent or more in 10 years"[1] Overall, metropolitan areas grew at about the same rate as the U.S. population (1.1 percent annually versus 1 percent for the county as a whole). The share of the population in metropolitan areas increased 1 percent during the decade as well (up to 77 percent versus 76 percent in 1980).

"Nine of the 12 fastest-growing metropolitan areas in the 1980s were in Florida; the others were in California, Nevada, and Texas."[2] Naples, Florida, grew by 77 percent during the decade, the fastest-growing metropolitan area in the country. In migration from other parts of the country largely explains this rapid expansion. At the opposite end of the spectrum, Casper, Wyoming, lost 15 percent of its population; Wheeling, West Virginia, lost 14 percent; Steubenville, Ohio, lost 11 percent; and Duluth, Minnesota, lost 10 percent.[3]

Most of the country fell between these extremes, registering little change. "About one metro in four failed to achieve even 2 percent growth for the entire decade. And one metro in nine showed no change whatsoever. This 'flatliner' club gained or lost less than 2 percent of their population during the 1980s."[4] The flatliner group included very large metropolitan areas such as Chicago (0.2 percent population increase for the decade), older suburban refuges such as Nassau–Suffolk, New York (0.1 percent population increase), and many other areas in the Northeast and Middle West.

[1]Joe Schwartz and Thomas Exter, "This World Is Flat," *American Demographics,* April 1991, 34.

[2]Ibid., p. 36.

[3]Ibid., pp. 36–37.

[4]Ibid., p. 37.

TABLE 4-8
Coastal Population Shares in the United States, 1940–1985

Year	United States Population (millions)	Coastal Total (millions)	Percent in Coastal Area	Population Density per Square Mile	Coastal Population Density per Square Mile
1940	131.7	60.5	46	44.4	129.3
1950	150.7	73.5	49	50.8	157.2
1960	178.5	92.7	52	60.2	198.3
1970	202.1	108.5	54	68.2	232.0
1980	225.2	118.4	53	76.0	253.0
1985	238.8	125.0	52	80.6	267.0

Source: U.S. Bureau of the Census, *Statistical Abstract of the United States: 1987,* USGPO, Washington, D.C., 1987, p. 21.

setting at densities four times the national average. This problem will be discussed again in the physical environment discussion in Chapter 6.

Energy-related growth in the Great Plains and Mountain States in the 1970s partially counteracted the coastal migration cycle. But the coastal growth trend accelerated again in the 1980s as Americans moved to more amenity-rich locations for work, recreation, and retirement.

CANADIAN URBANIZATION

Early Canadian settlements, not unlike those in the United States began as trading outposts or entrepôts for the trans-Atlantic trade of furs and fish. Fishing stations existed along the coast of Newfoundland, for example, before 1600, and Quebec emerged as a trade center on the St. Lawrence River around 1600. Soon Montreal, positioned at the junction point of three routes on the St. Lawrence River, also became an important trade center. Both of these French settlements predated any permanent English community in Canada, except for

St. John's in Newfoundland, which also has had a long history (Figure 4-8). Water Street in St. John's, in fact, may be the oldest street in North America.[7] Halifax began as a British garrison in 1749.

By the 1750s, Quebec had become a walled-fortress city of 7500 population. The British captured it in 1759, and France ceded Canada to the British in 1763. At the time, Montreal was much smaller than Quebec City, numbering only 3500 persons. But its strategic location as a trade center served the city well and Montreal grew to 20,000 by 1821, displacing Quebec as the leading city, which only had a population of 15,000.

In 1791, Quebec was divided into Upper Canada (now Ontario) and Lower Canada (present-day Quebec). Loyalists flocked to New Brunswick and Upper Canada following the American Revolution. The Napoleonic Wars in Europe in 1815 brought even larger waves of British immigrants. Toronto also gained population from this migration. Originally known as

---

[7]J. M. S. Careless, *The Rise of Cities in Canada Before 1914*, "The Canadian Historical Association, Ottawa, Booklet No. 32, 1978, p. 5.

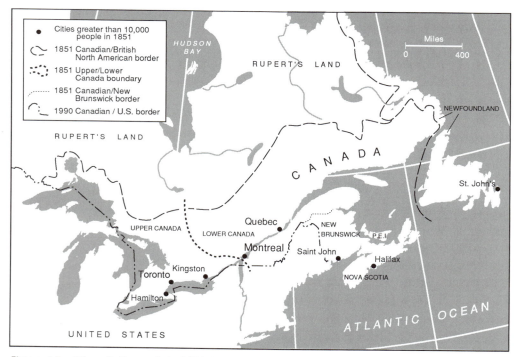

Figure 4-8.   Urban Settlements in British North America, 1851. Early Canadian settlements, as in the United States, began as trading outposts. Both French and English settlements date to the early 1600s in Quebec and Newfoundland. As recently as the 1850s, the St. Lawrence Valley and lower Great Lakes claimed the largest share of population. *Source:* modified after *National Atlas of Canada*, Ottawa, 1974, p. 91.

the city of York, the present city of Toronto served as the capital and military base for Upper Canada. After 1793, the area around Hudson Bay was known as Rupert's Land, having been granted to the Hudson Bay Company in 1670.

Until the 1820s, Kingston, at the mouth of the St. Lawrence River on the east end of Lake Ontario, was larger than York (population 1200). The opening of the Erie Canal in 1825 benefited York by providing an alternative to the St. Lawrence River for the shipment of goods to the East Coast, and the town flourished, reaching a population of 9200 in 1834 when it became incorporated as Toronto.

The 1850s brought the railway age to Canada. The Grand Trunk Railway, completed in 1858, linked Montreal, Toronto, Hamilton, London, and Windsor. Boom times again returned to Toronto and Montreal as the Canadian Pacific Railway spanned the continent in the 1880s.

Settlement in the West predated the railway, but significant growth awaited its arrival. Victoria, for example, located on the Island of Vancouver, was founded by the Hudson Bay Company as its chief western base. A gold rush in 1858 on the mainland made the city a supply depot, but prosperity waned as the railroad from the East never arrived. The railroad

terminated instead at Burrard Inlet on the mainland, the future site of Vancouver.

Settlements in the interior Plains owe their origin to the fur trade. Winnipeg, at the junction of the Red and Assiniboine rivers, for example, began as the Hudson Bay Company's Fort Garry. It was not incorporated until 1873, but rapid expansion came in the 1880s with the opening of the Canadian Pacific Railway (Figure 4-9). Eventually, the city assumed the role of the major wholesale and distribution center on the prairie. Its grain exchange became a major wheat seller. Regina also grew up with the railway and wheat trade became the major growth impetus. The city also served as the capital of the Province of Saskatchewan and the headquarters of the North-West Mounted Police.

Calgary and Edmonton also share early histories as trade outposts (Figure 4-9). The Canadian Pacific Railway gave Calgary a boost in the 1880s, as did the prospering cattle economy. But Edmonton became the capital of the new province of Alberta in 1906 and attracted major rail connections, which reinforced its growth potential. Vancouver gained the most of any western city from the acquisition of rail service, as it was also a port city and became a significant break-of-bulk transshipment point. The opening of the Panama Canal in 1914 boosted foreign trade with Europe,

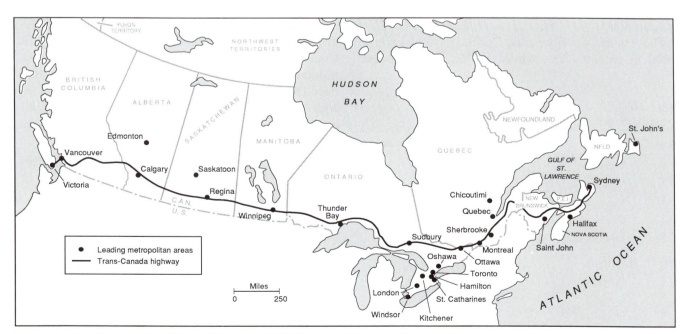

Figure 4-9. Leading Canadian Metropolitan Areas, 1990. Most large Canadian cities occur in a band across the extreme southern section of the country. Many are connected by the Trans-Canada Highway shown here and the transcontinental railway.

and the export of timber, grain, and fish (especially salmon) expanded rapidly.

Over time, industrial development in Canada mainly occurred in the eastern heartland in Ontario and Quebec, as the western and far eastern provinces remained predominantly raw material-based resource centers. This lack of maturity of the Canadian national economy still means that the largest Canadian cities occur in the more diversified provinces of Ontario and Quebec.

Montreal reached a population of one-half million after the turn of the century, Toronto achieved this size threshold in 1941, and Vancouver reached it around 1950. In the 1960s, Toronto surpassed Montreal in population for the first time and has remained larger ever since. Both metropolitan areas are now growing again after experiencing relative declines in the 1970s. In the 1980s, Toronto grew faster than Montreal, widening the size gap. Montreal now has a population just under 3 million and Toronto has 3.4 million. Third-ranking Vancouver, the only other millionaire city in the country, houses 1.4 million persons. These three metropolitan areas now contain 30 percent of the country's population.

In addition to these larger centers, there are 22 other metropolitan areas in Canada over 100,000 in population. The top 10 metropolitan areas in Canada in 1986 are listed in Table 4-9. While the terminology and criteria for metropolitan status differ between the United States and Canada, the regions themselves are quite similar.

The Atlantic provinces and Quebec have lost population in recent years, while the Prairie provinces,

British Columbia, and Ontario have all gained population shares. Saskatoon, Saskatchewan, in fact, grew the fastest of all urban regions in the country in the early 1980s.

U.S./Canadian Comparison

We observe that the early settlement histories of Canada and the United States closely parallel one another. The influence of water transportation on early urban settlement patterns was profound in both countries, as was the influence of the railroad in the settlement of the western frontier in the latter 1800s. Because of a smaller population base (25 million in Canada versus 246 million in the United States) the greater dependence on agriculture and resource production (timber, oil, fishing, etc.) in the interior, the city-size hierarchy is not as well developed in Canada at the regional level as in the United States. Nor does the rank-size rule regularly work as well in Canada at the national level as it does in the United States. Furthermore, Canada does not have a dominant city like New York; Toronto and Montreal each account for approximately 3 million persons, creating two cities at the top of the city-size list.

This relatively unique circumstance of having the two largest cities both about the same size in Canada can be largely explained by the dual ethnic traditions and the settlement history of the country. The Anglo influence associated with Toronto and the province of Ontario, on the one hand, and the French allegiance to Montreal and the Province of Quebec, on the other hand, have placed the two cities in direct competition, with each drawing from its own distinct cultural-economic support base and market area. Ties between each of these cities and their hinterlands are graphically portrayed in Figure 4-10.

SUMMARY AND CONCLUSION

The present pattern of urbanization in North America reflects the imprint of the past, especially the influence of changing transportation technologies—from water, to rail, to automobile. We will return to a discussion of the importance of transportation in urban development in Chapter 9. The changing structure of the national economies of the United States and Canada are also reflected in the growth and development of cities. The

TABLE 4-9
Top 10 Canadian Metropolitan Areas, 1986

Rank		Population (thousands)
1	Toronto	3,427
2	Montreal	2,921
3	Vancouver	1,381
4	Ottawa–Hull	819
5	Edmonton	786
6	Calgary	671
7	Winnipeg	625
8	Quebec	603
9	Hamilton	557
10	St. Catharines–Niagara	343

Source: Statistics Canada.

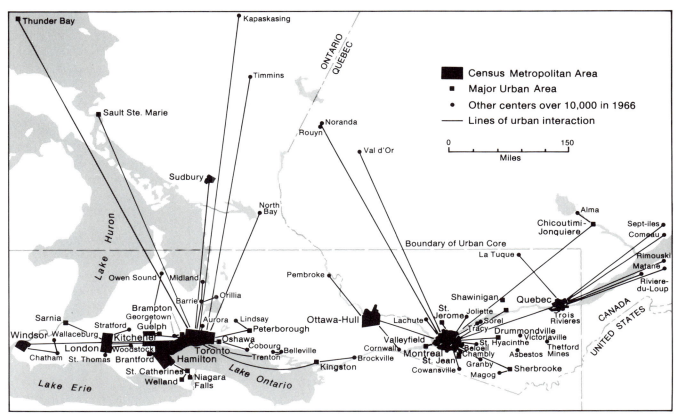

Figure 4-10. Nodal structure of Southern Ontario–Quebec. The anglo influence associated with Toronto and the province of Ontario, and the French allegiance to Montreal and the province of Quebec, place the cities in direct competition, each having strong ties to a distinctive hinterland. *Source:* Redrawn with permission from *Regional Studies,* 8, Larry S. Bourne, "Forecasting Urban Systems: Research Design, Alternative Methodologies, and Urbanization Trends with Canadian Examples." Copyright © 1977, Pergamon Press, Ltd.

industrial age greatly influenced urban growth from 1850 to 1950, while in the past 40 years, the transition to the postindustrial service economy accounts for many shifts in the growth process.

The expansion of large metropolitan areas in the twentieth century and the lure of coastal areas for development have dramatically changed the urban pattern at the national level. The urban hierarchy in the United States more closely follows the rank-size rule conceptualization than does the situation in Canada. The fact that no single city dominates the urban size profile in Canada, due to the relative parity of the two largest centers, largely explains this difference. The prospect for continued urban growth, especially among cities over 1 million population, remains strong in both countries.

Suggestions for Further Reading

Abbott, Carl. *The New Urban America*, University of North Carolina Press, Chapel Hill, 1987.

Beauregard, Robert A., ed. *Atop the Urban Hierarchy*, Rowman & Littlefield Publishers, Inc., Totowa, N.J., 1989.

Bernard, Richard M., and Bradley Rice, eds. *Sunbelt Cities*, University of Texas Press, Austin, 1983.

Bourne, Larry S., and J. W. Simmons, eds. *System of Cities: Readings on Structure, Growth and Policy*, Oxford University Press, New York, 1978.

Careless, J. M. S. *Frontier and Metropolis: Regions, Cities, and Identities in Canada Before 1914*, University of Toronto Press, Toronto, 1989.

Careless, J. M. S. *The Rise of Cities in Canada Before 1914*, The Canadian Historical Association, Booklet No. 32, p. 5, Ottawa, 1978.

Fox, Kenneth. *Metropolitan America: Urban Life and Urban Policy in the United States, 1940–1980*, University of Mississippi Press, Jackson, 1986.

Hooper, Diana, et al. *The Changing Economic Basis of Canadian Urban Growth, 1971–1981*, Centre for Urban and Community Studies, University of Toronto, Toronto, 1983.

Jackson, Kenneth. *Crabgrass Frontier*, Oxford University Press, New York, 1985.

Oliver, John W. *History of American Technology*, Ronald Press, New York, 1956.

Pfouts, Ralph W., ed. *The Techniques of Urban Economic Analysis*, Chandler-Davis, West Trenton, N.J., 1960.

Pred, Allan. *City Systems in Advanced Economies*, Wiley, New York, 1977.

————. *The Spatial Dynamics of U.S. Urban Industrial Growth, 1800–1914: Interpretive and Theoretical Essays*, M.I.T. Press, Cambridge, Mass., 1966.

————. *Urban Growth and City-Systems in the United States, 1840–1860*, Harvard University Press, Cambridge, Mass., 1980.

Reps, John W. *The Making of Urban America: A History of City Planning in the United States*, Princeton University Press, Princeton, N.J., 1965.

Ullman, Edward, et al. *The Economic Base of American Cities*, University of Washington, Center for Urban and Regional Research, Monograph No. 1, Seattle, Wash., 1969.

Vance, James E., Jr. *Capturing the Horizon: The Historical Geography of Transportation Since the Transportation Revolution of the Sixteenth Century*, Harper & Row, New York, 1986.

5

METROPOLITAN DOMINANCE AND MOVEMENT

The impact of large metropolitan areas on daily living over wide outlying territories is essentially a twentieth-century phenomenon in North America. The 1920s signaled a great surge in this involvement as the radio and automobile came into wide use, and since World War II, television and the interstate highway system further reinforced this transfer of influence. Before the modern era of easy mobility and rapid communication, rural areas had little daily contact with urban centers.

Some would argue that cities have always dominated in America, even in colonial times, as indicated in Chapter 4. The point here is not to contradict that generalization but to document the accelerated influence of the large metropolitan area beginning in the late nineteenth century. The "new" influence occurred in at least three ways: (1) accelerated urban growth, (2) decentralization of the city itself, and (3) reorganization of the surrounding countryside following the extension of commuter zones and the emergence of weekend and seasonal recreation activity in rural areas.

METROPOLITAN DOMINANCE

Research on the topic of metropolitan dominance in North America began appearing in print in the 1920s and 1930s, but not until the World War II period did a large literature accumulate. One of the first studies of this impact on the organization of the surrounding territory appeared in 1933.[1] Newspaper circulation patterns for large cities served as surrogate measures of influence. No precise means had been established at that time to select the cities to illustrate metropolitan dominance. Somewhat arbitrarily, the authors chose the 36 Federal Reserve Bank cities, plus 5 others—a total of 41—to illustrate metropolitan influence. The newspaper circulation map in Figure 5-1 reveals interesting findings, many of which still hold. A few large cities, obviously important today, are missing (note the absence of Washington D.C., and Miami). The regions are not accurate in that respect, but the areas over which the cities had direct influence in the 1920s remain essentially the same today.

The largest newspaper tributary areas occurred in

---
[1]R. D. McKenzie, *The Metropolitan Community*, McGraw–Hill, New York, 1933.

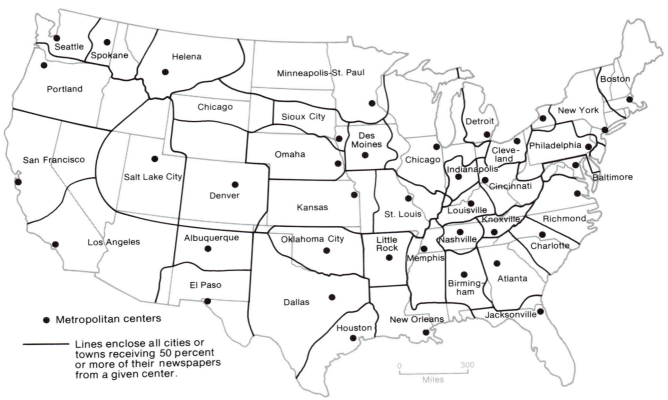

Figure 5-1. Newspaper Circulation as a Measure of Metropolitan Influence, 1929. The largest tributary areas occur in regions with few large cities, due to the lack of competition. Cities are rarely in the center of their market area because circulation is curtailed abruptly in the direction of greater competition. The Dallas and Minneapolis-St. Paul areas provide examples of this directional bias. Note absence of Phoenix and Miami. *Source:* Roderick Duncan McKenzie, *The Metropolitan Community* (1933), Russell and Russell, New York, 1967.

regions with few large cities because of a lack of competition. The expansive zones around Minneapolis, Denver, and Salt Lake City illustrate this point. Cities were rarely positioned in the center of the market region they dominated because circulation was cut off more abruptly in the direction of greater competition. Such a situation occurred to the north and south of Dallas, north of Oklahoma City, and south of Houston (see Figure 5-1). In similar fashion, circulation extended farther in the direction of least competition (to the west in the case of Dallas). One curious point shown on the map is the reemergence of the Chicago paper as dominant in northern Wyoming and southern Montana. This is explained by the relative remoteness of those areas, their low population density, and few ties with nearby cities. Since local news was highly "perishable" and transportation access was relatively poor, the Chicago paper dominated because of its national outlook, offering information on world news and business markets.

These maps delimiting newspaper circulation areas are classic examples of *nodal regions*. Nodal regions or functional regions, as they are sometimes called, are areas focused on a location to or from which movement occurs. In this instance the movement of newspapers from the city outward provides the defining criterion. The boundary of the region occurs at the point where 50 percent of the population receives that particular paper and 50 subscribes to a competing paper.

Further insight into the problem of delimiting urban spheres of influence unfolded with the appearance of studies using several economic indicators simultaneously. One study produced a composite map of urban influence by adding wholesale trade zones and agricultural marketing areas to the newspaper circulation variable.[2]

---

[2]R. E. Dickinson, "The Metropolitan Regions of the United States," *Geographical Review*, 24 (1934), 278–291.

Commuting to central city
- ■ More than 50 percent
- ▨ 5 – 50 percent
- □ Less than 5 percent

0   300
Miles

Figure 5-2. *The Daily Urban System (DUS).* The most populated areas of the United States fall within the daily commuting fields of metropolitan areas. The eastern and southern parts of the country are most completely encompassed in such spheres of influence. *Source:* Reprinted with permission from *Growth Centers in the American Urban System, Volume 1: Community Development and Regional Growth in the Sixties and Seventies.* Copyright © 1973, Ballinger Publishing.

Daily Urban System

Construction of regions around the city on the basis of daily commuting has led to new definitions of the city and its hinterland. The concept of a *daily urban system* (DUS) was originally discussed as a part of a comprehensive study of the Detroit urban area.[3] The idea was later refined and used by Brian Berry.[4] He constructed a DUS map of the entire United States in the late 1960s using commuter information from the population census (Figure 5-2). The concept was defined on the basis of several levels of commuting by workers to core counties of metropolitan areas. Counties sending more than 50 percent of their workers to core counties, those with 5 to 50 percent, and those with less than 5 percent were shown in expanding rings around metropolitan centers. Extensions of this work have led to newer DUS maps based on more recent census data.

Berry determined that the most populated areas of the United States fell within fields of daily commuting to metropolitan areas. Most of the eastern half of the country is encompassed in such spheres of influence. Only parts of the Great Plains and Mountain States, including the Dakotas, Nebraska, Wyoming, Montana, Nevada, and Idaho, do not lie within such zones.

As cities have become more interdependent and commuting flows more complex, the overlapping of commuter fields has also increased, raising questions about the validity of the traditional monocentric daily

[3]Constantinos Doxiadis said the urban Detroit area, consisting of 25 counties in Michigan, 9 in Ohio, and 3 in Canada, with a radius of 85 miles, represented an example of the daily urban system. See Constantinos A. Doxiadis, *Emergence and Growth of an Urban Region: The Developing Detroit Area*, 3 volumes, Detroit Edison Co., Detroit, 1966–1970.

[4]Brian J. L. Berry and Elaine Neils, "Location, Size and Shape of Cities as Influenced by Environmental Factors: The Urban Environment Writ Large," in Harvey S. Perloff, ed., *The Quality of Urban Environment*, Johns Hopkins University Press, Baltimore, 1969, pp. 257–302; Brian J. L. Berry, "Latent Structure of the American Urban System, with International Comparisons," in Brian J. L. Berry, ed., *City Classification Handbook*, Wiley, New York, 1972, pp. 11–60.

urban system commuting region.[5] Many more persons are commuting outward from the suburbs today, for example, and more residents live within the commuting field of more than one urban region. The growth of multiple worker households also further complicates the work trip pattern (see Chapter 9).

Urban Field

The sphere of influence of the city, as constituted by its economic and social zone of control, has also been defined as an *urban field.* When first identified in 1947, this hinterland of the city was described as similar in scope to the German *Umland,* the area around a town which it serves.[6] The writer suggested that surveys of urban fields should be a part of all regional planning reports. Such studies would include examination of the full complement of services the city provides—medical care, higher education, employment, newspapers, goods distribution (wholesaling), and shopping—to illustrate the full impact of each city. More recently the urban field concept has been defined arbitrarily as a zone up to 100 miles around a large city, an area within an afternoon's drive, wherein urbanites recreate, vacation, or build second homes, reflecting a change to larger-scale urban living.[7]

The wider life-space now implied by urban living, the greater choice in living environments, and a wider range of community interests all serve to make the intermetropolitan area a functional part of the city. The list of possible uses for this intermetropolitan area that appears in Table 5-1 suggests that rural land use is really more urban than often acknowledged and basically serves an urban clientele.

Local Tributary Area Studies

The spatial impact of the city has also been examined at the individual metropolitan area scale. Reports of Salt Lake City and Mobile, produced in the 1940s, have become classic case studies of tributary areas.[8] Each of

TABLE 5-1
Uses of Intermetropolitan Periphery

Recreational

Campgrounds	Golf courses
Parks	Ski resorts
Lakes	Hunting preserves
Forests	Theme amusement parks
Wilderness areas	Gardens
Nature preserves	Racetracks (dog, horse, or automobile)
Dude ranches	

Cultural and institutional

Resorts (winter and/or summer)	Conference centers
	Hospitals
Retirement villages	Cemeteries
Vacation retreats	Environmental education centers
Art colonies	
Airports	"Gentlemen" farms
Boarding schools	Communication transmission facilities
Junior colleges	
Universities	High-risk research and testing facilities
Museums	
Historical villages	Sanitary landfills
Second-home areas	Power-generating facilities
Military bases	

those analyses utilized several measures of influence. Various measures of the Mobile hinterland are shown in Figure 5-3. The significance of these works was the revelation that metropolitan influence has a relatively uniform areal extent regardless of the measure used.

A more recent landmark study by Howard Green shed additional light on the problem of defining metropolitan influence.[9] The development of a methodology to establish *boundaries* between hinterlands of the two cities was the main contribution of the study. Several complementary functions were examined to learn how the New York/Boston region was organized: (1) goods flow (by rail, ship, and truck); (2) communication (newspaper circulation, telephone calls); (3) agricultural production; (4) recreation activity (vacation pat-

[5]David A. Plane, "The Geography of Urban Commuting Fields," *Professional Geographer*, 33(2), 1981, 182–188.

[6]Arthur E. Smailes, "The Analysis and Delimitation of Urban Fields," *Geography*, 32 (1947), 151–161.

[7]John Friedmann and John Miller, "The Urban Field," *Journal of the American Institute of Planners*, 31 (1965), 312–319.

[8]Chauncy Harris, "Salt Lake City: A Regional Capital," Ph.D. dissertation, University of Chicago Libraries, Chicago, 1940; Edward Ullman, "Mobile Industrial Seaport and Trade Center," Department of Geography, University of Chicago, Chicago, 1943.

[9]Howard L. Green, "Hinterland Boundaries of New York City and Boston in Southern New England," *Economic Geography*, 31 (1955), 283–300.

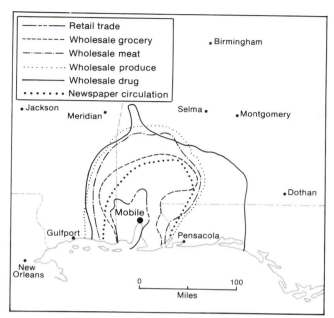

Figure 5-3. **Mobile Tributary Area.** The classic study that produced this comparative study of several measures of Mobile's hinterland in the 1940s helped establish an identity for geography in field work research. Note that the wholesale market areas are more encompassing than the retail trade area for Mobile. *Source:* Copyright by the University of Chicago Department of Geography. Redrawn with permission.

terns); and (5) banking allegiance. The medium composite boundary between the two cities that Green established, based on all the variables just mentioned, equitably split the area into two parts (Figure 5-4). That boundary enclosed an area within which 50 percent of the activity was attracted to one city or the other. At the boundary line itself residents divided their allegiance between the cities equally. In the following sections we will examine more precise ways to measure movement and trade area boundaries around cities.

CONCEPTUALIZING MOVEMENT

One cannot understand the expanding zone of influence of the city without gaining an appreciation of the volume of the movement of goods and services, including telecommunication ties, to and from these centers. Geographers utilize several quantitative and theoretical tools to explain movement, which is typically labeled *interaction*. Interaction is a process referring to many forms of communication and transportation exchanges. The most widespread empirical testing of interaction dynamics has been associated with wholesale and retail

trade area studies. In addition to this marketing application, migration flows, goods movement, and information flows have been explained with interaction models.

As mentioned earlier, Zipf stated that there is a single principle that best accounts for the length and intensity of movement. He called this rule the *principle of least effort*.[10] In fact, he felt that all human behavior could be explained with this principle. In the context of transportation and communication, this rule states that one minimizes distance, selects the shortest path, and chooses the nearest location to obtain a good or service.

Since distance is an inconvenience that must be overcome for interaction to occur, people and their activity are governed by the tendency to engage in the "least average rate of probable work."[11] Human activity in a spatial context exemplified this arrangement at all levels of behavior. The decision to take a shortcut and walk across a lawn rather than follow a "suggested" route along a sidewalk, which may be longer and more circuitous, illustrates the point, as does a highway network that connects large cities directly, bypassing smaller ones rather than zigzagging through them, which would create additional route mileage.

More specifically, the conditions in which movement or interaction occurs between places have been synthesized into three broad categories: (1) *complementarity*, (2) *intervening opportunity*, and (3) *transferability*.[12]

Complementarity refers to the need for both a demand and a supply relationship before flows of a good or service occur. This requirement for interaction shows that having an area that produces a product or service and having another in need of it are both necessary conditions. An example would be the movement of newspapers from a metropolitan center (supply) to the surrounding rural population (demand).

The concept of *intervening opportunity* explains the selection of the source of supply for the item in demand. The intervening opportunity is an alternative source of supply closer to the consumer than the present point of origin. When such an alternative source exists or emerges nearer the final destination, it is normally chosen in place of the original or former source. In

[10]George Kingsley Zipf, *Human Behavior and the Principle of Least Effort*, Addison–Wesley, Cambridge, 1949.

[11]Ibid., p. 6.

[12]Edward Ullman, "The Role of Transportation and the Bases for Interaction," in William Thomas, Jr., ed., *Man's Role in Changing the Face of the Earth*, University of Chicago Press, Chicago, 1956, pp. 862–880.

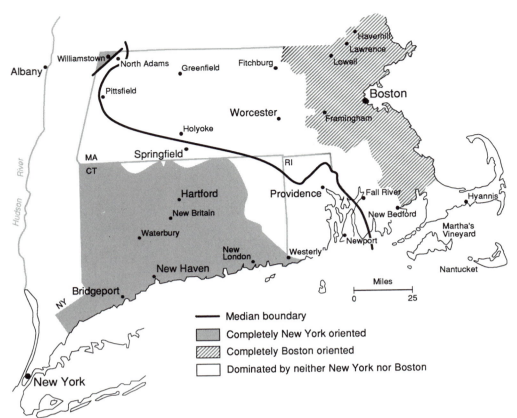

Figure 5-4. Hinterland Boundaries of New York and Boston in the Early 1950s. The boundary line between these major markets approximates the location where residents divided their allegiance between the two cities equally. On either side of the boundary, residents are more oriented to one of the cities, as shown. *Source:* Redrawn with permission. From Howard L. Green, "Hinterland Boundaries of New York City and Boston in New England," *Economic Geography*, 31(1955), 249.

other words, an intervening opportunity normally results in the substitution of a new source area.

The flow of visitors to a theme amusement park complex can serve as an example of the intervening opportunity concept. If only one theme park existed in a region, say in the rural hinterland of a major metropolitan center such as Chicago, all families seeking such a form of recreation would gravitate to it. If another park opened in a more accessible suburban location, many families would switch allegiance in favor of the more local facility because it provides an intervening opportunity.

A third aspect of movement, *transferability*, focuses on the time and cost factor of movement. When distances reach or exceed a critical length, movement ceases because costs and time make interaction economically unjustifiable. When this occurs, another good will be substituted for the one originally in demand. This substitution of one product for another item more locally available results in financial savings. The substitution of a local building material, such as wood, for a more expensive (and prestigious) product, such as marble, is an example of this substitution process.

Some items can withstand more transportation costs than others, depending on their value per unit of weight and the price of transporting each weight unit. Bulky products typically move the shortest distances and product substitution becomes necessary more frequently. High-value-added products such as computers or electronic equipment, on the other hand, can absorb large transportation costs because they are so valuable per unit of weight. Even with long-distance hauls, they do not cost significantly more.

Underlying the conceptualization of the interaction process is the notion of the friction of distance. This concept refers to the resistance to movement over space. An elementary form of this inverse relationship between movement and distance may be expressed as

$$I = \frac{M_a}{d}$$

where

   I = interaction between a location and place a

   M = mass at place a, usually expressed in terms of population

   d = distance in miles between a location and place a

The greater the distance, the lesser the amount of interaction that would occur. Empirical studies have shown that simple distances often do not accurately express real-world situations, because the friction of distance is not large enough. The following modification of the equation is often seen to remedy this situation:

$$I = \frac{M_a}{d^2}$$

Raising the value of the exponent, in this case squaring distance, has the effect of increasing the amount of friction that must be overcome for interaction to occur (Figure 5-5). But regardless of the value of the exponent, friction increases as distances also grow. Raising the distance exponent (2, 3, etc.) refers to a power function. Many empirical studies have focused on determining the value of the exponent for various types of movement, including interregional migration, commodity flows, and travel behavior. The type of product or service, the degree of interconnection, and the capacity and condition of the transport or communication infrastructure (telephone network, highway capacity, etc.) all affect the friction of distance. The distance–decay decline rate in an area with a poorly developed transportation or communication network would be much steeper than in an area with a well-integrated route structure where the friction of distance would be less pronounced. In the former case, the distance exponent would be greater. This friction of distance factor operates at the regional and national scales, as well as at the local level within the city.

Cost and information considerations are both plausible explanations for the success of the distance minimization approach. Critics of the least effort explanation

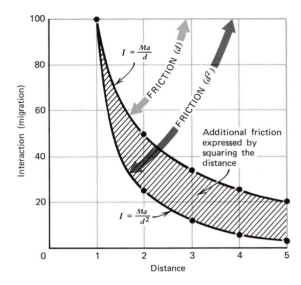

Sample data used to derive the above graph:
$$Ma = 100$$
$$d = 1, 2, 3, 4, 5$$

Computed interactions	Distance (miles)					Distance² (miles)				
	1	2	3	4	5	1	4	9	16	25
$(I) \longrightarrow$	100	50	33.3	25	20	100	25	11.1	6.25	4

Figure 5-5. The Effects of Distance on Interaction. The greater the distance, the lesser the amount of interaction, called the friction of distance. Raising the value of the distance exponent has the effect of increasing the amount of friction that must be overcome, as the diagram shows.

of movement have pointed out that psychological factors, such as emotional involvement, preferences, and habit, may be more important than distance minimization in explaining movement. Consumer shopping behavior, migration distances, and journey to work patterns, for example, do not always conform to the principle of least effort. The behavioral parameters that account for the deviation from the classical interpretation of distance will be elaborated on in succeeding chapters.

SOCIAL PHYSICS

The regularity exhibited by human behavior among large groups of people has attracted a large cadre of social science researchers. *Social physics* is the term generally given to the field of study dealing with the behavior of people in large groups over distance. A pioneer in the development of this philosophy was the astronomer John Stewart, who stated: "We can no longer ignore the fact that human beings, on the average and at least in certain circumstances, obey mathematical rules resembling in a general way some of the primitive 'laws' of physics."[13] This macrogeography approach to behavior over space can be attributed to the work of William Warntz, who extended the study to national and international economics.[14]

Critics of the social physics approach have pointed out that people do not behave according to natural physical laws, and that in their enthusiasm to apply this approach to human behavior, social physicists have overstepped their bounds. Nevertheless, there are valid analogies between the behavior of people in large groups and the laws of physical science.

Gravity Model

The *gravity model* in the social science realm has a likeness to Newton's law of gravitation and evolved from the work of Ernest Ravenstein and others in the field of migration, Zipf in his study of movement minimization, and Stewart studying student migration patterns.[15]

Newton's law of gravitation in physics deals with the attraction of objects to each other. His discovery states that "any two bodies attract each other with a force proportional to the product of their masses and inversely proportional to the square of the distance between them."[16] Newton's law can be expressed as

$$F = K \frac{m_1 \, m_2}{d^2}$$

where

F = force of attraction between two objects
K = constant

m_1 = mass of body 1
m_2 = mass of body 2
d^2 = distance squared (between body 1 and body 2)

In the social science field, mass is typically measured by population, reflecting the fact that the greater the quantity of people, the greater the "force" of interaction.[17] The quantity of interaction becomes

$$I = K \frac{P_1 \, P_2}{d^2}$$

where

I = level of interaction between two centers
K = constant
P_1 = population of center 1
P_2 = population of center 2
d^2 = distance squared (between centers)

The gravitational attraction concept in geographical research has had wide application in the prediction of movement between cities. To predict the volume of vehicular traffic or number of telephone calls, the model suggests that one only need know the population of the centers and their distance apart. Frequently the formula is simply presented as

$$G = \frac{P_1 \, P_2}{d}$$

where

G = gravitational attraction
P_1 = population of city 1
P_2 = population of city 2
d = distance between centers

The concept works remarkably well in empirical application given its simplicity. The population component of the model can be weighted on the basis of income, age, sex, etc., to approximate actual conditions. In a similar vein, the distance factor can also be adjusted. Travel times, rather than physical distances, are often a more realistic indicator. When highway networks are poorly developed or if physical barriers are present, it becomes appropriate to weight distance more heavily, making it more of a negative factor. This

---

[13]John Q. Stewart, "Empirical and Mathematical Rules concerning the Distribution and Equilibrium of Population," *Geographical Review*, 37 (1947), 474.

[14]William Warntz, *Macrogeography and Income Fronts*. Regional Science Research Institute, University of Pennsylvania, Philadelphia, 1965; William Warntz, *Toward A Geography of Price*, University of Pennsylvania Press, Philadelphia, 1959.

[15]Ernest Ravenstein, "The Laws of Migration," *Journal of The Royal Statistical Society*, 48 (1885), 167–235; Zipf, op. cit.; John Q. Stewart, "Demographic Gravitation: Evidence and Application" *Sociometry*, 11 (1948), 31–58.

[16]Harvey White, *College Physics*, Van Nostrand, New York, 1963.

[17]Gerald A. P. Carrothers, "An Historical Review of the Gravity and Potential Concepts of Human Interaction," *Journal of the American Institute of Planners* 22 (1956), 95.

can be accomplished by raising the exponent to a higher power, such as from 2 to 3.

By incorporating the influence of size and distance variables simultaneously, the gravity model recognizes the greater influence of large cities over distance than smaller ones. The model also provides a mechanism for the quantitative assessment of trade areas around cities.

Using this formula to measure the attraction between places, one can observe the simultaneous impact of size and distance as illustrated in Figure 5-6. The figure shows a city of 50,000 population (A), and two cities of 25,000 (B and C).

Substituting the numbers in the formula based on the populations and distances separating the cities, one can determine the intensity of flow expected between different pairs of cities. The greatest level of attraction is between cities A and B rather than A and C due to the closer proximity of A and B (200 miles vs. 300 miles).

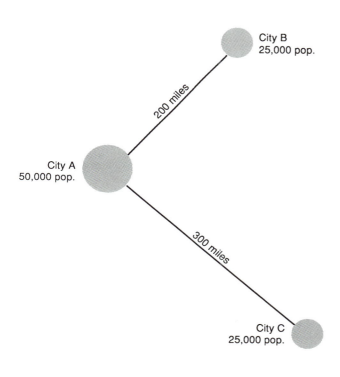

Sample gravitational calculation
between cities A and B:

$$\frac{50,000 \times 25,000}{200^2} = 31,250$$

Figure 5-6. Gravitational Attraction Among Cities of Varying Sizes. The gravity model recognizes the greater influence of large cities over distance than smaller ones. The model offers a mechanism to quantitatively assess trade areas of cities.

One could verify the actual intensity of flows between these centers by checking passenger traffic (by bus, auto, etc.) or the actual number of telephone calls. Discrepancies might occur because of historical ties or highway conditions (capacity of routes, speed limits, etc.) that would foster more or less movement, but given the simplicity of the model, the reliability of the results is generally remarkable. For this reason, utilities (telephone companies, intercity bus lines) use the gravity model to predict future demand as do land developers and highway builders.

Predicting the number of students that might attend a university, based on the size of the home county (in terms of population) and its distance from the college town being studied, represents another application of the gravity model. Stewart successfully predicted enrollment figures for Princeton in the 1940s using this approach. More recently Herbert Kariel successfully predicted freshman enrollment for Western Washington University in Bellingham.[18]

At the national scale, the gravity model can show the expected intensity of migration flows over distance. Movement from Atlanta and Portland is shown in Figure 5-7. The delicate balance between distance and size in attracting migrants is reflected in the similar quantities of migrants leaving Atlanta for nearby Columbus, farther Nashville, and more distant Houston. As the distance between origin and destination cities increases, less movement would be expected. But in the case of Atlanta and Houston, the attraction of the two very large metropolitan areas counteracts the distance factor such that similar movement rates are recorded between them and the much smaller but closer centers of Nashville and Columbus. Movement from Portland is similar. New York and Chicago, because of their size, compete favorably with Denver and Sacramento for Portland's out-migrants even though they are considerably more distant.

More recently, researchers have noted that absolute physical distances are poor measures of actual migration distances. By using more sophisticated calibration procedures relative *functional distances* that influence destination choices can be determined. By using "constrained" gravity models, for example, one can take into account competing opportunity effects. "Doubly constrained models exactly reproduce observed migrant supplies and migrant demands at all origin and

[18]Herbert Kariel, "Student Enrollment and Spatial Interaction," *The Annals of Regional Science*, 2 (1968), 114–127.

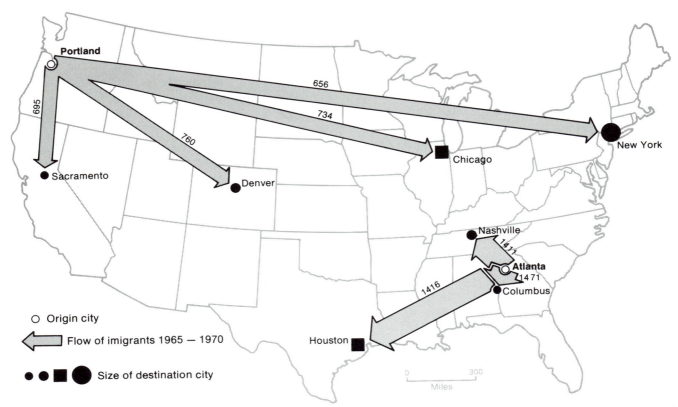

Figure 5-7.   Migration Flows from Atlanta and Portland to Selected Cities. At the national scale, the gravity model can show the expected intensity of migration flows over distance. The flows from Portland to Denver and Chicago, from example, are approximately the same even though Chicago is much farther away, but it is also larger than Denver, creating a greater attraction to prospective migrants. *Source:* From *Human Spatial Behavior: A Social Geography*, by John A. Jakle, Stanley Brunn, and Curtis C. Roseman. Copyright © 1976 by Wadsworth Publishing Company, Inc., Belmont, Calif., 94002. Redrawn by permission of the publisher, Duxbury Press.

destination regions. Thus they are called distribution models because the size of the regional inflows and outflows is not in question, only the pattern of region-to-region interactions."[19]

Reilly's Law of Retail Gravitation

The application of the gravity model to the measurement of retail trade areas has received the most attention, beginning with the work of William Reilly in the 1930s.[20] The law of retail gravitation he developed

allows one to determine trade area boundaries around cities in a precise manner using only population and distance figures. It is obvious that the trade area boundary between two cities of equal size would be midway between them, and that if they were unequal in size, the boundary would be nearer the smaller of the two. But a problem arises in determining the exact location in the latter instance. Using Reilly's law, one can arrive at the location precisely. Actually, the trade area of a city is determined through a series of calculations of the boundaries between successive pairs of cities (see box for modern application).

The trade area boundary between any two places is the breaking point (BP). At the BP, 50 percent of the population trades in one city and 50 percent in the other. The ratio of customer preferences is 1: 1 at that point. By connecting several pairs of BPs, one can

[19]David A. Plane, "Migration Space: Doubly Constrained Gravity Model Mapping of Relative Interstate Separation," *Annals of the Association of American Geographers*, 74(2), 1984, 245.

[20]William J. Reilly, *The Law of Retail Gravitation*, 2nd ed., Pillsbury Publishers, New York, 1953.

APPLIED GEOGRAPHY: TRADEMARK INFRINGEMENT AND REILLY'S LAW

Locational principles can be applied in a variety of situations and, as the following case demonstrates, may even be admissible as evidence in a court of law.[1] A disgruntled owner of a custom picture framing shop located near Oak Ridge, Tennessee, recently sued another frame shop with a very similar (though not exact) name located some 25 miles away in Knoxville, Tennessee, for trademark infringement. The owner of the Oak Ridge business sought compensatory damages for the business he claimed was lost because of supposed confusion about the names in the minds of potential clients.

The name of a business, especially if the name is unique (i.e., not generic like "The Picture Frame Shop"), is protected under Tennessee state law so long as the two businesses are competing in the same trade area. The right to the unique name always goes to the business which has been established longer, and the new business therefore would be guilty of trademark infringement. In this case, the owner of the picture frame shop in Oak Ridge had been in business about six months longer than the business with the similar name in Knoxville. A geographer was called in as an expert witness by the attorney defending the Knoxville merchant who was being sued. The geographer's task was to prove to the judge at the hearing that the two businesses were not really in the same trade area and, therefore, trademark infringement did not pertain in that particular situation. This arena of applied geography is referred to as *forensic geography*. Although it is less common for geographers to be expert witnesses than for doctors and certain other professionals (e.g., physical anthropologists called to identify skeletal remains, traffic safety engineers called to reconstruct the details of an automobile accident), some geographers have served as expert witnesses in cases heard before the Supreme Court.[2]

How close can two competitors be before they are considered to be in the same market? An earlier court case on trademark infringement offered some legal precedent. In 1957, the trade name "Big Apple" was used by separate grocery stores in Chattanooga and Cleveland, Tennessee. Interestingly, the relative size and location of that pair of cities are almost the same as those between Knoxville and Oak Ridge, Tennessee. In the earlier case, the Tennessee Court of Appeals found that there was

> no overlapping of trade areas and little confusion resulting from concurrent use of the name in Chattanooga and Cleveland (*Kirk v. Big Apple Supermarket of Cleveland*, 1957).

As we have learned, however, grocery stores are low order central place activities, and travel accessibility was less in 1957 than it would be today. Are custom picture frame shops a low order activity? Custom framing is low order in the sense that there are lots of them from which a potential customer might choose. But even more revealing is the degree of clustering of these businesses near affluent shopping centers and the pronounced western directional bias displayed on the map.

Knoxville was one of the 148 cities that Homer Hoyt used to develop his ideas for his sector theory of urban residential morphology (see Chapter 11). Even in the late 1930s, the affluent sector of Knoxville was

---

[1]For greater detail on this particular case, see Thomas L. Bell, "Central Place Theory Goes on Trial," a paper presented at the 1989 meeting of the Southeastern Division of the Association of American Geographers, Charleston, W.Va., November 1989.

[2]See, for example, the work of the historical geographer Louis DeVorsey, Jr., who has argued historical boundary dispute cases before the U.S. Supreme Court and other judicial venues. Louis DeVorsey, Jr., "Florida's Seaward Boundary: A Problem in Applied Historical Geography," *Professional Geographer,* Vol. 25 (August 1973), pp. 214–220.

[3]William J. Reilly, *The Law of Retail Gravitation* (New York: Knickerbocker Press, 1931).

[4]William Applebaum and Saul B. Cohen, "The Dynamics of Store Trade Areas and Market Equilibrium," *Annals of the Association of American Geographers,* Vol. 51 (March 1961), pp. 73–101.

the western corridor, and the same is true today. Custom framing is a service that the middle and upper classes seem to use a great deal more than their working class counterparts and, therefore, the shop locations are oriented to this more affluent market segment.

The line of defense on behalf of the Knoxville shop owner was two-pronged—an application of Reilly's breaking point formula[3] and a customer spotting survey.[4] Both analyses were used to support the argument that the two shops were not competing for the same market. The breaking point along an imaginary 25-mile line connecting the two stores in question fell slightly more than 18 miles from the Knoxville loca-tion in the direction of Oak Ridge. Plotting a sample of customer credit card receipts with identifiable ad-dresses revealed that 72 percent of the Knoxville frame shop's customers were located within a 5-mile radius of the shop. Furthermore, the furthest customer (i.e. the outer range of the good) resided 14 miles away, well within the theoretical breaking point delimited by the application of Reilly's law of retail gravitation.

The judge in the case dismissed the claims of the Oak Ridge frame shop owner. In rendering her judg-ment, she remarked on how effective the maps were in supporting the claim of market separability and, there-fore, in influencing her legal opinion.

create a complete trade area around a city (Figure 5-8). The BP is expressed as

$$BP = \frac{d_{ij}}{1 + \sqrt{\dfrac{P_2}{P_1}}}$$

where

BP = distance from city 1 to breaking point
d_{ij} = distance between city 1 and city 2
P_1 = population of city 1
P_2 = population of city 2

Using the example shown in Figure 5-8, where the two cities are 150 miles apart and have populations of 175,000 and 60,000, respectively, the calculation be-comes

$$BP = \frac{150}{1 + \sqrt{\dfrac{60,000}{175,000}}}$$

$$BP = \frac{150}{1 + \sqrt{0.3429}}$$

$$BP = \frac{150}{1 + 0.5856}$$

$$BP = \frac{150}{1 + 1.5856}$$

$$BP = \frac{150}{1.5856}$$

$$BP = 94.6 \text{ miles}$$

The breaking point is 94.6 miles from city 1. Figure 5-8 also shows the BP between cities 1 and 3, and 1 and 4. By connecting all the BPs, a trade area for city 1 is created.

Physical barriers often distort the shape of trade area. In effect, this means that the friction of distance is greater. In Figure 5-9 the effect of an international boundary is shown. The lower level of interaction across the boundary has the effect of lessening the

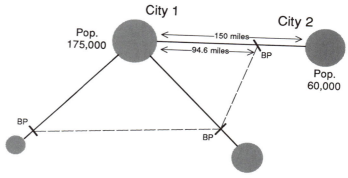

Figure 5-8. Calculating the Breaking Point (BP) Between Two Cit-ies. The law of retail gravitation allows us to determine trade area boundaries around cities in a precise manner, using only population and distance figures.

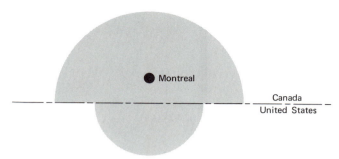

Figure 5-9. The Impact of an International Boundary on Trade Area Shape. The lower level of interaction across the boundary has the effect of lessening the radius of the Montreal trade area on the United States side of the boundary.

radius of the trade area. The trade areas are circular in form on either side of the boundary, with the truncation effect on one side arising because, functionally, the population on that side of the boundary is much less attracted to the city culturally and economically than physical distances alone would suggest.

An exception to the notion of diminution of activity across an international boundary based on an accelerated distance–decay function occurs in the case of daily movement of laborers from Tijuana, Mexico to San Diego for work. (Figure 5-10). These day laborers from Tijuana live close to the border and cross into the U.S. using visitor cards, but once in the United States, fan out in San Diego—working in a myriad of jobs from manufacturing (metal recycling), construction, landscaping, food preparation, hotel service work and associated pursuits. The prospect of obtaining higher paying work in San Diego provides an incentive for travel across the boundary, far outweighing the inconvenience and risk commuters take, as most are working illegally.

The trade area of a city based on Reilly's law is a deterministic endeavor, because a fixed boundary line is derived using distance and population size. In the real world, other factors such as consumer preferences and familiarity with an area might also affect shopping habits. David Huff modified the gravity model to take into account such behavioral characteristics when defining trade areas.[21] He used various probability levels for customers shopping at a particular center, based on the distance they live from the center and its square footage. The calculation of such probabilities will be

covered in Chapter 16, which deals with retailing within the city.

HIERARCHY OF CITIES

A discussion of city hinterlands must also recognize the function of a city in addition to its population and location. For example, a major headquarters city, a political capital, or an important distribution hub will have stronger regional ties than a manufacturing center. The regional hinterland for the largest city in a country, the international metropolis, may be the entire nation or even extranational in scope. Other metropolitan areas play lesser national or regional roles.

The concept of hierarchy shows the relationship among cities to the entire distribution, usually measured in terms of population or employment levels. We introduced this concept briefly in Chapter 2 with the discussion of rank-size rule. Here, we want to be more specific about the roles and impacts of cities in various size groups in a given country. One observer has said that a hierarchical unit (city)

> has two attributes that should be distinguished: its relationships to a higher order unit is one of part to whole, to a lower unit of whole to part. That is, going up the hierarchy, wholes are divided into parts and separated out. Thus, despite the overall characteristics of control, each hierarchical level has autonomy over orders below itself, while being a dependent on those above.[22]

Using this framework, a hierarchy of cities can be discussed with the international metropolis at the top.

International Metropolis

The international metropolis serves as the financial, corporate, cultural, and political headquarters for a nation. Only one city is required for this role, assuming that all relevant activities occur at one place. In the United States, New York City obviously provides this function, but it does not serve as a political capital. The two cities that share the international metropolis limelight in Canada, Toronto and Montreal, do not provide the political capital function either. Notwithstanding this point, New York, Toronto, and Montreal are unique because the whole country of which they are a

[21]David L. Huff, "A Probabilistic Analysis of Shopping Center Trade Areas," *Land Economics* 39 (1963), 81–90.

[22]Fred Lukermann, "Empirical Expressions of Nodality and Hierarchy in a Circulation Manifold," *East Lakes Geographer*, 2 (1966), 21.

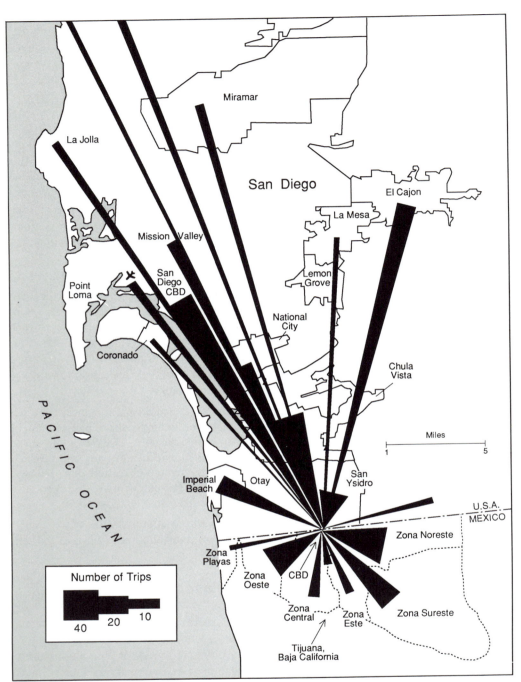

Figure 5-10.   Labor Shed of Tijuana in Relation to the U.S.-Mexican Border. Day laborers using visitor cards living in Tijuana close to the international boundary cross into the United States daily to find work using visitor cards. Once in the United States they fan out throughout metropolitan San Diego. Courtesy Fred Stutz.

part lies in their wake. They are the banking, business, and cultural kingpins of their nations. The intensity of activity in these centers can be measured by the level of nonagricultural employment, the quantity of bank deposits, and the number of libraries, museums, theaters, and music halls. For purposes of this discussion, the leading city of a nation will be labeled a *first-order city* (Table 5-2).

These global cities distinguish themselves as first among equals in the international metropolis category—Tokyo, London, and New York. As the homes of the largest stock markets and financial institutions,

TABLE 5-2
Metropolitan Hierarchy of United States, 1986
(Based on Nonagricultural Employment Levels)

First Order (≤7,500,000)

New York

Second Order (≤1,000,000)

Los Angeles
Chicago
Philadelphia
San Francisco
Boston
Detroit
Washington, D.C.
Dallas/Ft. Worth
Houston
Atlanta
Miami
Minneapolis/St. Paul
St. Louis

Third Order (≤500,000)

Baltimore
Denver
Pittsburgh
Seattle
Phoenix
San Diego
Milwaukee
Tampa/St. Petersburg
Kansas City
Cincinnati
Columbus
New Orleans
Indianapolis
Portland

National Metropolis

A metropolitan area that dominates a smaller territory, but no less completely, constitutes a *national metropolis*, or second-order city. Whereas there were 7 such second-order centers in the United States in 1970, there are now 13 (Figure 5-12 and Table 5-2). A first-order city also serves as a second-order center for a locally defined area. Including New York, there were 14 second-order centers in the United States in 1986.[23]

A relatively uniform spacing of these second-order centers is indicated in Figure 5-12. The figure is a cartogram showing the land area of each state proportional to its 1960 population. The "gaps" in the number and spacing of these cities that would show up on a conventional map, based on land area in the Great Plains and South, largely disappear when states are collapsed or expanded in size proportional to their population. This indicates that each second-order center serves a comparably sized market and that cities are functionally spaced according to this role. The highly populated states "explode" in size in the cartogram so as to approximate the effect of their greater population. This technique provides an excellent visual device to portray the national metropolis role that cities perform as second-order centers.

As a measure of the standing of the national metropolis, one can examine banking linkages, as shown by *correspondent bank* ties. A correspondent bank is a very large metropolitan bank, typically located in the international metropolis (New York) or national metropolis (second-order center), to which banks in other parts of the country maintain ties in order to gain access to a range of banking services. These services include access to mortgage markets, loan sales, and investment advice. The banking ties among the eight first- and second-order metropolitan areas that existed in 1970 are shown in Figure 5-13. Note that Miami, Atlanta, Houston, Dallas, Washington, D.C., and Minneapolis had not yet emerged as second-order centers. At that time, the South had strong ties with New York, given the absence of second-order centers in that region. Chicago dominated the Middle West and Los Angeles and San Francisco dominated the Far West. The pattern of banking linkages today is changing rapidly as the new grouping of second-order cities acquires more specialized banking activity and deregulation of the industry continues.

---

[23] A city of a given order can also serve as a center of the next lower order to its immediate hinterland.

these cities cast a shadow over the rest of the world in terms of asset control and sheer economic clout (Figure 5-11). These activities, in turn, attract a large producer service support system and a large international business community. The enormity of their influence in the areas of international trade, business investments, and international goodwill clearly places them apart from the rest.

(A)

(B)

Figure 5-11. The New York and Tokyo Stock Exchanges. As the homes of two of the world's largest stock markets and many financial institutions, these cities cast a shadow over the rest of the world, along with London, in terms of asset control and sheer economic clout. (*A*, New York Stock Exchange; *B*, Matsumoto/Sygma)

Regional Metropolis

Another layer of urban areas, each labeled a regional metropolis or third-order center, similarly possesses widespread importance. They typically employ over 500,000 persons and provide many roles for their regional economy in banking, retailing, and services. John Borchert said these three levels of cities together are the "cosmopolitanizers" of the country.[24] Culture and technology are delivered to the nation through them and they serve as originators of new innovations, which then filter down to lower-order centers. From an examination of banking linkages among third-order centers, one can observe the regional nature of their impact (Figure 5-14).

[24]John R. Borchert, "America's Changing Metropolitan Regions," *Annals of the Association of American Geographers*, 62 (1972), 355–356.

SUMMARY AND CONCLUSION

There can be no doubt of the depth and strength of metropolitan dominance of activity patterns in highly urbanized nations as exhibited in North America. The present hierarchial structure of the United States has evolved out of the role that cities play in the national and international economy. The concepts of urban field, daily urban system, and hinterland assist in the conceptualization of metropolitan dominance.

An understanding of movement or interaction between and among centers also assists the explanation of expanding urban spheres of influence as one moves up the urban hierarchy. The gravity model, for example, simultaneously brings together the role of size and distance in accounting for movement. Applications of the gravity model assist geographical studies of retail-

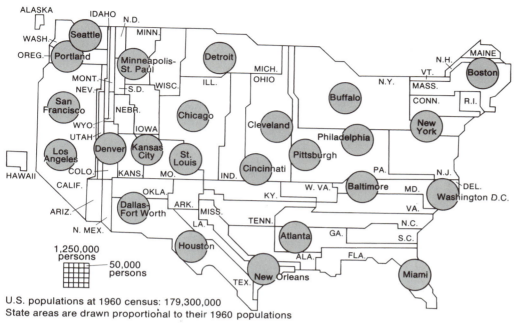

Figure 5-12. Second Order Metropolitan Center Cartogram of the United States. The relatively uniform spacing of second-order centers indicates that they are functionally spaced to serve a comparably sized market. The cartogram provides an excellent visual device to portray this relationship. *Source:* Ronald Abler, John Adams, and Peter Gould, *Spatial Organization: The Geographer's View of the World,* Copyright 1971, p. 337. Adapted by permission of Prentice Hall, Inc., Englewood Cliffs, N.J.

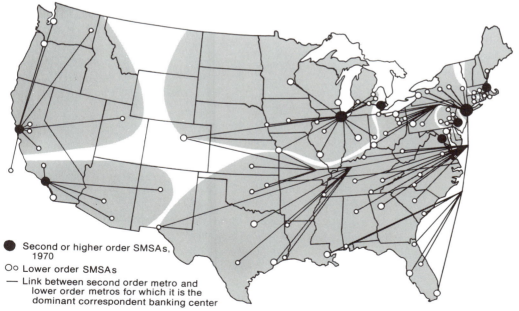

Figure 5-13. Banking Linkages of Second-order Centers, 1970. Banking linkages provide one measure of the standing of a national metropolis, defined here as a second order center. Miami, Atlanta, Houston, Dallas, and Washington, D.C., had not yet emerged as second-order centers in 1970. *Source:* Redrawn with permission from the *Annals of the Association of American Geographers,* 62 (1972), p. 253. J. R. Borchert.

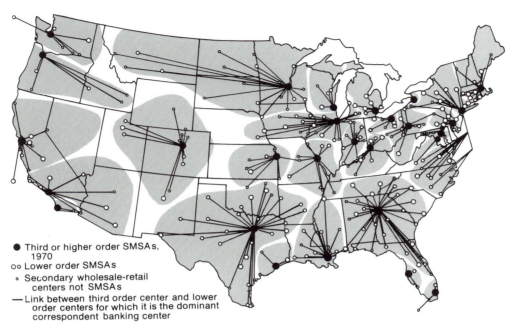

● Third or higher order SMSAs, 1970
oo Lower order SMSAs
○ Secondary wholesale-retail centers not SMSAs
— Link between third order center and lower order centers for which it is the dominant correspondent banking center

Figure 5-14. Banking Linkages of Third-order Centers, 1970. The role of the regional metropolis can be evaluated by mapping the banking linkages of third-order centers. These cities are the "cosmopolitanizers" of the country. *Source:* Redrawn by permission from the *Annals of the Association of American Geographers*, 62 (1972), p. 253. J. R. Borchert.

ing, transportation planning, and migration. The elegance of the model lies in its simplicity and wide applicability. The utility of the gravity model to urban analyses at the intraurban level will be repeatedly mentioned in the last half of the book.

We will return to a discussion of the hierarchy concept in Chapter 8, in the section dealing with Central Place Theory. A greater appreciation of the growth and development of cities will be provided by the discussion of the role of manufacturing in the historical development of the city in Chapter 7. In Chapter 6 we will examine the physical environment as a city-shaping factor.

Suggestions for Further Reading

Abler, Ronald, ed. *A Comparative Atlas of America's Great Cities*, University of Minnesota Press, Minneapolis, 1976.

Berry, Brian J. L., *et al. Metropolitan Area Definition: A Reevaluation of Concept and Statistical Practice* (rev. ed.), Bureau of Census Working Paper No. 28. USGPO, Washington, D.C., 1969.

Bogue, Donald J., and Calvin Beale. *Economic Areas of the United States*, Free Press, Glencoe, N.Y., 1961.

Duncan, Otis Dudley, *et al. Metropolis and Region*, The Johns Hopkins University Press, Baltimore, 1960.

Haggett, Peter, *et al.* "Size Distribution of Settlements," in *Locational Analysis in Human Geography*, 2nd ed., Vol. 1, *Locational Models*, Wiley, New York, 1977.

Huff, David L. "A Probabilistic Analysis of Shopping Center Trade Areas," *Land Economics* 39 (1963), 81–90.

McKenzie, R. D. *The Metropolitan Community*, McGraw-Hill, New York, 1933.

Picard, Jerome. *Dimensions of Metropolitanism*, Urban Land Institute, Washington, D.C., 1967.

Pred, Allan. *City-Systems in Advanced Economies*, Wiley, New York, 1977.

Richardson, H. W. *The Economics of Urban Size*, Lexington Books, Lexington, Mass., 1973.

Zipf, George K. *Human Behavior and the Principle of Least Effort*, Addison–Wesley, Cambridge, Mass., 1949.

6

THE URBAN PHYSICAL ENVIRONMENT*

Why does flooding increase along with urban growth and why has the disposal of garbage become a big urban issue? Answers to these and other questions associated with urban growth and the physical environment lie in a better understanding of the critical links between the physical environment and urban activity. For many decades, this connection between people and the environment has not been properly understood or respected. Fortunately, we now are becoming more sensitive to environmental issues, and actions to correct past neglect look promising. The decade of the 1990s may, in fact, become the decade of the environment.

The present-day neglect of the urban physical environment arose historically from the prevailing philosophy of the superiority of human beings over nature. The notion that nature represented a passive force, which could be easily subdued, gained prominence during the industrial revolution. As bigger earthmovers were built, and more sophisticated technology was applied, the philosophy that nature could be overcome gained even greater prominence throughout most of the present century.

A separation of academic studies into physical versus humanistic areas in American education and research has reinforced the nature–human division. Engineers and architects, for example, have traditionally received very little training in the humanities and social science; philosophers, journalists, and social scientists have received very little physical science exposure. Vocal environmentalists and ecologists, as well as academicians themselves, called increasing attention to the bankruptcy of the traditional educational isolationism of physical and social sciences, which has led to more cross-disciplinary contact in recent years.

In this chapter, the problem and process of the physical impact in the city will be examined. The academic study of the urban physical environment is still in its infancy, and many conflicting and indeterminate research investigations hamper progress. But the parameters of the problem are known; they involve many types of air, water, and environmental pollution, waste, and extravagant misuse. A greater effort in the future must be placed on conservation, recycling, and developing strategies to mitigate negative environmental effects if we are to ensure a livable urban setting.

HISTORICAL EVOLUTION OF ENVIRONMENTAL CONCERNS

European settlers in the New World brought with them a tradition of respect for the natural environment. They

---

*Chapter authored by Richard A. Stephenson, East Carolina University, Greenville, N.C. (in 1st edition; revised for this edition by author).

lived by trial and error, but maintained a balanced existence with nature. Despite this compatibility, their outlook nevertheless promoted a gradual trend leading to greater exploitation of the environment. Wealth to them generally indicated that the work of God was being successfully accomplished. This led to a process of ordering the wilderness to achieve economic gain. Belatedly, the recognition that the wilderness is naturally ordered and not disordered, and that wealth has limited benefits, became the basis of the current environmental concern.

Most of the existing pollution problems are induced by people, such as disposing of industrial and residential waste (Figure 6-1).

> Every five years the average American discards, directly and indirectly, an amount of waste equal in weight to the Statue of Liberty. Municipal solid waste alone accounts for 140 million metric tons per year. The municipal solid waste produced in this country in just one day fills roughly 63,000 garbage trucks, which lined up end to end would stretch 600 kilometers, the distance from San Francisco to Los Angeles.[1]

This and other problems are by-products of an advanced consumer society and are difficult to resolve. Evils such as contaminated air, polluted water, high noise levels, and street debris have long been recognized. But the proposed solutions to the problem have too often been to apply more technology to the target rather than to address the root cause and decrease the need for its existence. Conservation alternatives or simpler lifestyles have not been fully harnessed. Foul air can be overcome by introducing a completely enclosed environment to filter out the contaminants, but this is expensive and artificial. An alternative would be to decrease the supply of pollutants at their source.

LOCATION AND LIMITS TO URBAN GROWTH

Sites for urban settlements were physically as well as economically determined in colonial times. Some urban places began as fortifications on hilltops, at the confluence of major rivers, or at favorable harbor locations. For example, the city of San Francisco was located on a peninsula having excellent ship-docking potential. Manhattan was a good location for a city for similar reasons. In the case of San Francisco, the initial advantage of the harbor access provided by its peninsular locations was lost once rail transportation became a major locational factor. Direct rail access to the eastern part of the country then favored sites in the East Bay area, centering on Oakland, and San Francisco itself became less ideally situated.

Cities that in the past prospered through economic fluctuations, armed conflict, and political strife usually have had optimal physical attributes for development, protection, and expansion. Because of their socioeconomic dynamism, many urban places, such as San Francisco, were able to adapt to change by shifting their major function and modifying the physical environment to promote growth. The filling-in of the waterfront and the use of the land for office and finance activities illustrate this adaption.

Figure 6-1. Trash and Debris on the Beach. Managing vast quantities of debris and trash has become a national priority, but finding a solution is difficult, as the number of landfills has declined significantly and new sites are difficult to open. This beach on Staten Island graphically portrays the dilemma. (Barbara Alper/Stock, Boston)

[1]Philip O'Leary, et al., *Managing Solid Waste, Scientific American*, 259 (December 1988), p. 36.

Limitations to urban growth are much less pronounced today than at the dawn of the Industrial Revolution. Several hundred years ago a swamp or salt marsh would have remained unsettled. Only limited use would be made of a river floodplain. Steep slopes would remain wooded. Dunes and beaches would remain in their natural state, with settlements located in more protected environments. With modern engineering skills and the advent of large earthmoving equipment, development was no longer restricted by nature. Developers could easily flatten the terrain, fill the wetlands, and construct dikes and bulkheads (retaining walls) to transform the coastline. Lands capable of being developed were created in Boston, for example, by filling in wetlands and shallow waters. The construction of retaining walls and backfilling them to reclaim land from the sea drastically changed the size and shape of the city (Figure 6-2).

The altering of the landscape to fit urban needs has multiple effects on environmental processes. Stream regimes have been changed by modifying watersheds. Currents and longshore drifts adjust to new artificial shoreline configurations. Groundwater flow becomes more variable as more land is covered with concrete and asphalt. Natural habitats for aquatic life are virtually eliminated when marshes and swamps are de-

stroyed. In many situations, the magnitude of alteration is so great and the natural processes so blatantly ignored that environmental hazards have increased.

THE URBAN ECOSYSTEM

An ecosystem consists of sun energy, earth materials, air, and water, interacting with plant and animal organisms. Complex interactions occur among these elements, which in turn create a dynamic stability in the system. The urbanization process tends to simplify these interactions and removing or altering natural processes increases instability.

A conceptual framework identifying linkages among the various components of the urban ecosystem appears in Figure 6-3. Feedback loops that operate among these factors are identified. A feedback loop shows the influence of an element on itself as a result of interactions with other elements. Some feedback loops are positive and others are negative. Positive loops induce

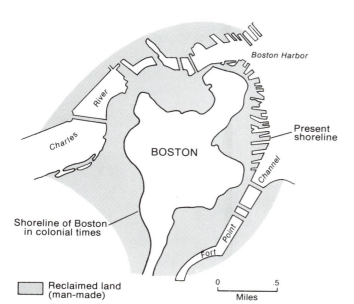

Figure 6-2. Land Reclamation in Boston. In the past, vast quantities of developable land were created in Boston and other coastal cities by filling in wetlands and shallow coastal waters, drastically changing the size and shape of the city, as shown here. *Source:* Reprinted with permission from *Boston: A Geographical Portrait.* Copyright © 1976, Ballinger Publishing Company.

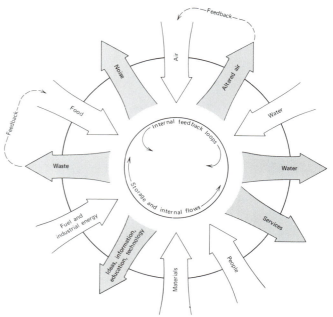

Figure 6-3. A Model of the Urban Ecosystem. The connectivity of the urban physical environment, including ties between people, water, air, food, fuel and materials, and their by-products, such as noise, solid waste, and sewage, as shown here, suggests that we live in an environment with many complex interactions. *Source:* From *Urbanization and the City: the Physical Geography of the City.* By Thomas R. Detwyler and Melvin G. Marcus, and Contributors. Copyright © 1972 by Wadsworth Publishing Co., Belmont, Calif. 94002. Redrawn by permission of the publisher, Duxbury Press.

changes in a circular cumulative manner and upset the balance of nature, while negative loops decrease variations and encourage an equilibrium or steady state.

THE URBAN LAND SURFACE

The natural landscape is often completely transformed by urbanization in densely developed portions of metropolitan areas. This transformation represents the epitome of human impact on the environment. As distance increases from the city center, a transition from an artificial cityscape to a more natural landscape occurs. Many areas in cities have been transformed by developers during one or more periods of construction. During this process the terrain can be modified, native vegetation obliterated, soils removed or covered, and open streams enclosed by conduits. Although there are many factors we could consider here, the discussion will be limited to the impact of urbanization on water features, waste generation, and atmospheric change.

Runoff

A reduction of vegetation in urban places induces quicker water runoff, accelerated erosion, greater flood potential, and increased sedimentation. As land cover is stripped away at construction sites, it is common to notice increased erosion, including muddy sediment-laden creeks and rivers (Figure 6-4).

Natural drainage typically becomes more difficult to find as streams are encased following urbanization. An example of the decreasing incidence of streams has been observed in Washington, D.C. In 1913, the Rock Creek drainage basin contained approximately 102 km of open streams compared to less than 43 km of open streams today. Converting open streams to enclosed conduits allows for landfilling and creates greater quantities of developable land. This process hastens runoff, and in turn induces flooding. As more impervious surfaces are created as buildings and pavement cover a greater proportion of land and more storm water sewers are constructed, the greater is the speed of discharge, and the lower the rate of percolation of water into the ground.

Flooding

Flood magnitudes typically increase in a regular manner as the transition from rural to urban land uses occurs. The degree to which cities are at risk to flooding varies considerably depending on location and topog-

Figure 6-4. The Silt Fence and Runoff Protection at Construction Sites. Federal and local environmental controls now require that steps be taken to ensure that erosion is minimized at construction sites. At this new highway and transit corridor being cleared in suburban Atlanta, the plastic silt fence confines runoff to the project site. Note noise-containment wall under construction near office building and house in distance.

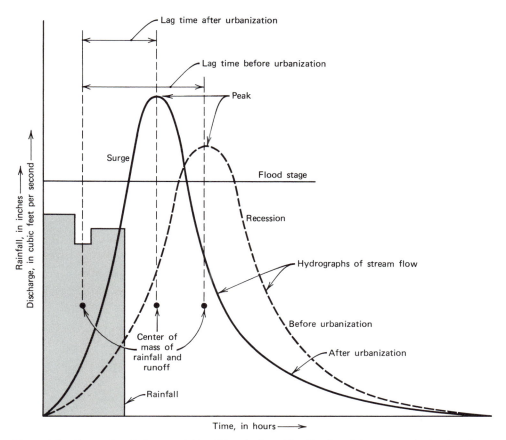

Figure 6-5. Streamflow Before and After Urbanization. The flood peak is greater, the lagtime less, and the flood surge is more rapid following urbanization. *Source:* Redrawn from Luna B. Leopold, *Hydrology for Urban Land Planning—A Guidebook on the Hydrologic Effects of Urban Land Use.* Geological Survey Circular No. 554, USGPO, Washington, D.C.

raphy. A study of 26 urban areas in the United States has indicated that the amount of territory in floodplains varies dramatically, from 2 percent for Spokane, Washington, to 81 percent for Monroe, Louisiana.[2] The amount of development on the floodplain ranges from 11 percent for Lorain–Elyria, Ohio, to 96 percent for Great Falls, Montana. Floodplain areas have been and continue to be prime land for urbanization because of ease of development and accessibility, even though floods are an inevitable occurrence because they serve as a natural storage area for floodwater.

A graph can be used to show the relationship between stream discharge, measured in cubic feet per second (cfs), and time, expressed in hours (Figure 6-5). As land use changes, the curve also adjusts. One can

observe on the hydrograph that the flood peak is greater, the lag time is less, and the flood surge is more rapid following urbanization. An increase in impervious surfaces will quicken the surge, increase the peak, and decrease the lag time. Consequently, potential flood damage is more likely in urban areas. For example, in the winter of 1969, a part of southern California between the Santa Ana and Santa Ynez rivers received intense storms and subsequent flooding. The aftereffects attributed to this occurrence, in January alone, amounted to 92 deaths and $62 million in damage.

Federal law now requires local governments to regulate land uses in flood plain areas. The National Flood Insurance Program (NFIP), passed in 1968, sets standards to limit property exposure to flood damage. In 1979, the Federal Emergency Management Administration (FEMA) was formed to oversee NFIP. "The NFIP established the 100-year flood as a regulatory standard and distinguished two hazard areas: the *flood-*

[2]W. J. Schneider and J. E. Goddard, *Extent and Development of Urban Floodplains*, Circular 601-J, U.S. Geological Survey, USGPO, Washington, D.C., 1974.

Figure 6-6. Hurricane Hugo Hits the South Carolina Coast. Residential communities on the waterfront bore the brunt of the tidal surge, wind, and rain associated with landfall of the hurricane on September 12, 1989. This beach house, built on piers to withstand a potential flood, was devastated by high winds during the storm. (City of Charleston, Department of Planning)

way and the *floodway fringe*. The 100-year floodplain is an area with a 1 percent probability of being flooded in any year. . . . The NFIP established minimum federal standards requiring that any new residential construction be elevated to the level of the 100-year flood and that new construction not obstruct floodwaters in such a way as to raise the level of the floodway by more than one foot. Houses built in non-coastal floodplains typically are elevated by using fill dirt to raise building sites to the required elevations; in coastal areas, buildings are placed on pilings."[3]

Local governments have been slow to implement federal standards in limiting floodplain development, but development is becoming more sensitive to the potential risk. Floodplain areas make good locations for parks, playgrounds, and natural open space. Removing existing buildings from floodplains poses another set of problems. Often local and federal standards are not enough incentive. In Kansas City, for example, major flooding in 1977 and 1984 along the Blue River

floodplain led to the permanent removal of structures from the floodplain.[4]

Coastal flooding is usually related to storms at sea. But coastal flooding has commonly occurred in the Pacific Ocean basin from sudden movements of the ocean bottom causing *tsunamis*. These huge tidal waves crash against the seashore and inundate low-lying areas. It is not uncommon to have a storm surge of 10 to 15 feet above normal sea level, and occasionally waves more than 100 feet high. The rise of the storm tides, coupled with winds in excess of 100 miles per hour, can cause millions of dollars in property damage, not to mention lives lost, in a matter of minutes. The damage caused by Hurricane Hugo on the South Carolina coast on September 21, 1989, provides a case in point (Figure 6-6).

But aside from storms, we know that sea levels are rising worldwide over time and that some coasts are being slowly submerged. While hurricanes and typhoons create occasional crises, the long-term effect of a rising sea level, due to possible global warming

---

[3]James M. Holway and Raymond J. Burby, "The Effects of Floodplain Development Controls on Residential Land Values," *Land Economics*, 66 (1990), p. 260.

[4]Stephen Driever and Danny Vaughan, "Flood Hazard in Kansas City Since 1980," *Geographical Review*, 78 (1988), pp. 1–19.

caused by enhancement of the greenhouse effect, may create more severe problems for urban areas (see later section). With 21 of the world's 25 largest urban areas on or near the coast, rising sea levels would be an important widespread problem.

Debris and Solid Waste

The magnitude of urban debris and solid wastes, including that produced by industries, is increasing at a rapid rate. The cost alone of solid waste disposal is enormous, and simply finding satisfactory depository sites presents an increasing problem. A study of urban street debris indicated that 5 to 8 pounds are generated per 100 feet of curb per day. The average varied from about 5 pounds per day per 100 feet of curb in commercial areas to just over 2 pounds per day per 100 feet of curb in single-family residential areas. Dust and dirt are the most significant components of street debris in terms of water pollution potential. An additional problem in many cities is the accumulation of dog feces. Urban ponds and lakes become highly polluted from animal waste. Other sources of street debris include spillage from trucks, yard refuse, debris from construction or demolition sites, roadside dumping, poor use of trash receptacles, and pedestrian littering.

Urban street debris is commonly washed down storm sewers by runoff or street washers, eventually finding its way to streams, lakes, and the ocean. Its effect on the environment has been largely ignored, even though sediments, salts, and toxic chemicals are present. The combined storm and wastewater sewers present in most older sections of cities are also a problem, as will be discussed later.

Solid waste materials generated by Americans amounts to 4 to 4.5 pounds a day, or over a half a ton annually (Figure 6-7). This does not include the additional problem of disposing of over 9 million automobiles a year in the United States.

> From 35 percent of volume in 1970 refuse, paper has burgeoned to 50 percent. The most common variety is newspapers; despite our recycling efforts they occupy 12 to 15 percent or more of landfill volume in the East and Midwest and 10 to 12 percent on the West Coast, where export to Asia promotes recycling.[5]
>
> New York City generates the nation's largest waste stream—27,750 tons of garbage a day—and disposes of

most of it in the world's largest landfill, the 3000 acre, 30-year-old dump on Staten Island with the ironic name of Fresh Kills. An environmental monstrosity, Fresh Kills has problems with seagulls and leachate, and it operates at all only because the state's Department of Environmental Conservation has given it a special dispensation.

> Within a dozen or so years, Fresh Kills will be the highest point on the eastern seaboard south of Maine, rising 500 feet above New York Harbor, half as high as the Chrysler Building, half again as high as the Statue of Liberty, and likely to become one of the wonders of the world—an ugly, stinking symbol of urban civilization.
>
> If Fresh Kills were exhausted tomorrow and New York had to ship its 8 million tons of waste to Ohio at $120 a ton, as many of its neighboring communities do, it would cost the city a staggering $1 billion a year, equal to twice the city's current Sanitation Department budget. And Fresh Kills is not really atypical. Forty percent of the U.S.'s solid waste goes into 157 large landfills, most of them also becoming saturated.[6]

Integrated Solid Waste Management

Disposal of municipal solid waste continues to be a major concern in urban areas where generation rates are high in a relatively small area and disposal sites occur at some distance. Disposal concerns affect everyone including all levels of government, business, and industry, as well as individuals.

To deal with integrated solid waste management, municipalities should develop solid waste management plans. These plans outline methods for dealing with the waste stream. The integrated system can be designed to address specific disposal methods in various settings. More and more communities are encouraging recycling as a means of reducing the amount of waste for disposal in either a landfill or burned in a combustion facility. Landfills are designed and constructed as secure land burial facilities and include pollution control and monitoring equipment (see Box).

Disposal costs have increased dramatically in the past few years due to an increased number of landfill closings as a result of existing permits expiring, groundwater contamination concerns, and decreasing capacity. Tighter regulations governing the siting of new waste facilities has also become a contributing factor and existing facilities must be upgraded to obtain permit renewals.

[5]William L. Rathje, ''Once and Future Landfills,'' *National Geographic*, 179 (May 1991), 122.

[6]James Cook, ''Not in Anybody's Backyard,'' *Forbes*, Nov. 28, 1988, pp. 172–173.

SITING PROCESS FOR MUNICIPAL SOLID WASTE LANDFILLS

As regulations governing the siting of landfills become stricter, the ability to find sites for new landfills becomes more difficult. Historically, landfills or open dumps have gained a bad reputation in that dumps or "uncontrolled landfills" pollute groundwater, cause unsightly mountains of garbage while being filled, and cause explosions as a result of the buildup of methane gas below the land surface.

Today, landfilling refers to placing compacted layers of waste in cells or contained areas in the ground, and covering the waste daily with soil. Protective layers of natural and synthetic material are placed around the perimeter of a landfill to try to minimize the escape of contaminated material.

Costs involved in siting a landfill are ever increasing because of expenses related to acquisition of land, engineering and design, preparation of the site for disposal of waste, hauling and disposal, daily and final cover material, and costs related public participation of siting a landfill and offering benefits to the host community where the landfill is located.

Federal regulations initiated in 1979 attempted to set forth criteria for new and existing landfills. However, the criteria were neither strict nor effective, and in 1988 regulations were changed to govern the design and operation of new and existing municipal solid waste landfills. The revised regulations included location restrictions, facility design restrictions based on performance goals, operating criteria, groundwater monitoring requirements, and corrective action requirements for groundwater contamination. Financial assurance requirements for closure, post-closure and known releases of contaminants, closure standards, and post-closure standards were also included in the revised regulations.

Location restrictions include prohibitions on sites at or near airports, floodplains, wetlands, fault areas, seismic impact zones, and unstable areas. Some states have regulations that are stricter than the federal regulations. Furthermore, some states have decided to restrict landfills as a last option after waste reduction, recycling, and waste combustion (incineration). There are still portions of a waste stream in which no other alternative is available except to use landfills for disposal. However, by having the reduction and recycling alternatives available, the amount of material that must be landfilled is drastically reduced.

In order to select the most acceptable site for a landfill, a site selection study is usually prescribed. This includes selecting a study area and omitting the areas that are restricted (airports, wetlands, and so on). Then other factors such as large population centers, highways, bodies of water, agricultural areas, and areas of endangered species are taken into consideration, and these areas generally are omitted as a potential landfill area. Once an area is selected, other criteria such as subsurface conditions must be acceptable. Testing for an acceptable site includes installation of test wells to determine the type of soil and depth of various subsurface formations. Monitoring wells sample the ground water and determine background conditions. If all the criteria are acceptable, the site is selected and an environmental impact study completed to set forth the issues. This involves public participation so objections and controversies can be resolved. Once the environmental impact statement is accepted, a permit is usually granted by the permitting agency and site preparation can begin.

Site preparation begins with the installation of liners along the bottom and sometimes the sides of a landfill. Protective layers of natural material including clay and/or synthetic material such as rubber, polyvinyl chloride, or various polyethylenes are utilized. These are used to contain and/or minimize releases of waste and contaminated liquids called *leachate* into the environment. The protective layers are placed below the area to be filled, around the perimeter of the waste area, and in a few instances on the top of the waste. The amount and thickness of the natural and synthetic layers depend on the regulations governing the site and the type of subsurface conditions. On top of the natural and synthetic material, contractors install a drainage area comprised of crushed stone. On top of the crushed stone another layer of synthetic and natural material and another drainage layer for the leachate collection system occur. These layers intercept the leachate, or contaminated liquid. The leachate is collected from drains intersecting the site and treated for disposal. This can be either treated on site and then discharged back to the environment via a stream or nearby water body, or sent to a sewage treatment facility. On top of the leachate collection system is a protective fiber material layer and then the municipal solid waste deposited above. The various layers below the waste can be up to eight feet thick lying over the virgin soil. The waste is deposited at the site in layers and covered daily with soil. Daily soil cover usually controls disease vectors and vermin, and minimizes odor and fires. Upon completion of the compartments or cells, another layer of soil is placed on the material. This continues until the site has reached the permitted height and slope and is then closed according to regulations. Proper cover material is important to expedite the growth of vegetation, to minimize leachate outbreaks, and create a visually acceptable environment once landfilling has ceased.

During the disposal of material, the monitoring wells, which were installed prior to placing waste disposal at the site, are sampled at predetermined intervals for parameters outlined in the permit. If contamination is found in the wells, procedures are initiated to determine the source of contamination and to stop the flow of contamination.

Another concern is the buildup of methane gas. In large quantities, methane gas can cause explosions. Gas venting and/or recovery systems are generally installed in landfills. Gas venting systems are designed to allow the methane gas to escape from the site. These pipes are usually placed vertically through the waste with an opening at the top to disperse the gas into the atmosphere. Gas recovery systems recover the methane gas generated within the landfill for processing.

Most permits issued for municipal solid waste landfills require post-closure care that includes site inspections, restoration to the cover material if needed, leachate treatment, methane control, and sampling of the monitoring wells for contamination. Some permits for municipal solid waste landfills require up to 30 years of monitoring following closure to ensure that contamination does not adversely affect human health or the environment.

Louise A. Hartshorn, Environmental Management Council, Monroe County, Rochester, N.Y.

The number of municipal landfills will decline steadily in the future (Table 6-1); from a total of 5,499 in 1988, the total is projected to fall to 2,720 by 1998. Opposition to the siting of these facilities has increased dramatically due in part to the NIMBY (Not In My Backyard) syndrome. Fears of lower property values, contamination, and exposure contribute to the increasing opposition to these facilities. To entice communities to accept these functions, attractive compensation packages or host benefit plans are being presented. These host benefit plans allow the community accepting the facility to dispose of waste at dramatically reduced fees or free of charge and compensation to the community per the amount of waste disposed. Disposal fees, called *tip fees*, vary from region to region and state to state depending on the availability of waste disposal facilities, but they rose dramatically on average in the late 1980s (see Table 6-2).

Municipal solid waste—waste that is generated at residences, commercial establishments, and institutions—consists of paper and paperboard, glass, metals, plastics, rubber, food wastes, yard wastes, and miscellaneous inorganic wastes (see Figure 6-8). Approxi-

mately 80 percent of the municipal solid waste generated goes to landfills.[7] However, with landfill space decreasing, new techniques for disposal are appearing. The technique of *integrated solid waste management* involves the management and disposal of the separate components of waste. The components include: *source reduction, recycling, combustion*, and *landfilling*.

Source reduction involves reducing the amount of waste produced or generated at the source. This includes the packaging of products using less material and manufacturing a product with a longer lifetime and/or reuse capabilities. Decreased consumption of products with excess packaging can also be an integral part of source reduction. Education programs, financial incentives and disincentives, and technology advances can assist in source reduction.

Recycling techniques include the separation of waste materials for reuse in manufacturing processes to make other material or products. Material being recycled

---

[7]U.S. Environmental Protection Agency, *Decision-Maker's Guide to Solid Waste Management*, Office of Solid Waste and Emergency Response (OS-305), EPA1530-SW-072, U.S. G.P.O., Washington, D.C., 1989.

Figure 6-7. **Sanitary Landfill, St. John's, Oregon.** The 5000 landfill sites remaining in the U.S. receive 80 percent of our trash. It is difficult to build new landfills, as no one wants to live near them and environmental controls restrict their siting. (John Maher/Stock, Boston)

today includes paper, aluminum, glass, ferrous metal, plastics, and batteries. Improved collection programs, an informed citizenry, and markets for the products are all necessary to have a successful recycling program. Recycling also includes the composting of yard debris (grass, leaves, branches) and food wastes. Recycling

TABLE 6-1
Projected Municipal Landfill Operations, 1988–2008

Year	Number of Landfills
1988	5499[a]
1993	3332
1998	2720
2003	1594
2008	1234

[a] 1988 figures reflect projected closings of 535 landfills during 1987.

Source: U.S. Environmental Protection Agency, *Report to Congress: Solid Waste Disposal in the United States, Vol. II,* EPA/530-SW-88-011B (Washington, DC: October 1988).

TABLE 6-2
Landfill Tip Fees (Average for national sample)

Year	Tip Fee (per ton)
1982	$10.80
1983	$10.80
1984	$10.59
1985	$11.93
1986	$13.43
1987	$20.36
1988	$28.93

Source: C. L. Petit, "Tip Fees Up More Than 30% in Annual NSWMA Survey," *Waste Age* (March 1989), p. 101. Copyright © 1989 by National Solid Wastes Management Association. Reprinted with permission.

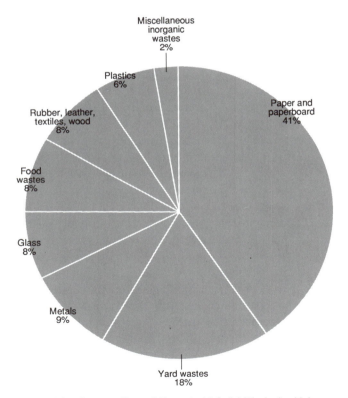

Figure 6-8. **Composition of Household Solid Waste by Volume.** The largest sources of household waste (paper, paperbound, and yard waste) can be recycled or composted, drastically reducing the quantity of landfill material. Recycling and composting other materials (metals, glass, food wastes, and plastics) also reduces the pressure on landfills. *Source:* U.S. Environmental Protection Agency.

these products keeps them from taking up valuable landfill space. Recycling yard debris can take place in the homeowner's backyard in a compost pile or at a central location.

Combustion of municipal waste includes the reduction through the burning of waste and the production of energy (i.e., steam or electricity). Combustion of municipal solid waste must take into account the type of waste, its quantity, and the disposal of the ash residue. Several types of combustion facilities include *mass burn* and *refuse derived fuel*. Mass burn facilities are designed so that little or no preprocessing of waste is necessary. The waste is burned to reduce volume, resulting in ash which is then landfilled. Most new facilities are designed so that the heat generated in the process can be converted to usable energy, labeled an energy recovery system. Refuse derived fuel (RDF) facilities typically handle pre-processed municipal solid waste. The waste is processed into a "fuel" that is then burned. The fuel that is produced (powder, fluff, coarse, dense) varies by design of the facility and the design of the burn facility accepting the "fuel." Air emissions and ash management at these facilities are concerns that must be addressed with regard to their environmental impact. Such concerns are raised by residents when opposing the siting of such facilities in their communities.

Landfilling occurs in more and more areas only after source reduction, recycling, and/or combustion strategies have been accomplished. Landfilling is also required for items when no other disposal method is available. Because of dwindling capacity, in the future very few landfills will exist for disposal of wastes where no preprocessing of the waste occurs.

ATMOSPHERIC CHANGE

As urban land use intensifies and land cover is removed, atmospheric elements such as temperature, moisture, and heat transfer or radiation are affected. The impact of rural development on the generation and dispersal of pollutants is equally strong. A rural–urban comparison of many air quality indicators is shown in Table 6-3.

Urban Heat Island

Higher temperatures are common in central city areas as compared to the suburbs and rural habitats. The presence of taller, darker buildings and the abundance

TABLE 6-3
Air Quality Indicators

Atmospheric Factor	Comparison of Urban with Rural Area
Temperature	
Annual mean	1 to 1.5°F more
Winter minimum	2 to 3°F more
Cloudiness	
Clouds	5 to 10 percent more
Fog, winter	100 percent more
Fog, summer	30 percent more
Precipitation	
Amounts	5 to 10 percent more
Days with 0.2 inches	10 percent more
Wind speed	
Annual mean	20 to 30 percent less
Extreme gusts	10 to 20 percent less
Calms	5 to 20 percent more
Radiation	
Total on horizontal surface	15 to 20 percent less
Ultraviolet, winter	30 percent less
Ultraviolet, summer	5 percent less

Source: After Helmut E. Landsberg, "City Air—Better or Worse," in *Symposium: Air Over Cities,* Tech. Report A 62-5, Taft Sanitary Engineering Center, Cincinnati, no date, cited in Irving Hoch, "Urban Scale and Environmental Quality," in Vol. 3, *Population Resources and the Environment,* Research Report of the Commission on Population Growth and the American Future, USGPO, Washington, D.C., 1972.

of vertical walls, paved streets, and parking areas in urban areas trap radiant energy in the urban environment. This situation creates a *heat island* where temperatures up to 15° Fahrenheit or higher may occur in the center of large cities on calm, clear nights when compared with nearby suburban and rural areas. Even small cities will experience temperatures a few degrees warmer than their rural surroundings on calm, clear nights.

The urban *heat island* refers to the relative temperatures in the city in comparison to either preurban conditions or local rural–urban temperature differences. The greatest contrast in rural–urban temperatures occurs at night, contradicting the perception based on conventional wisdom. "Surface heat islands achieve maximum values near midnight and remain fairly constant through the remainder of the night [in mid-latitude areas]. Heat islands then decrease after sunrise and become weak urban 'cold islands' during midday."[8] Thus, rural–urban surface temperatures

---

[8]Robert D. Bernstein and Tim Oke, "Influence of Pollution and Urbanization on Urban Climates," *Advances in Environmental Sciences and Engineering*, 3 (1980), 186.

show small differences during the day. Because of the thermal properties of urban buildings, the absorption of heat by large exposed surfaces, and the retention of this heat, little nocturnal cooling of urban surfaces occurs between sunset and midnight in cities, as compared to rural areas. Both rural and urban areas then cool at a similar rate from midnight until sunrise.

In the morning, solar heating causes more rapid warming of rural surfaces as compared to urban surfaces as a result of the thermal properties of building materials. Other factors that retard early morning warming of urban surfaces include shading by the tall buildings and increased solar attenuation, or weakening of the sun's rays associated with elevated pollutant layers. During calm wind conditions, this heat island assumes a domelike form hovering over the city. During windy conditions, the form becomes plumelike, with the warmer air extending downwind from the city.

More erratic precipitation patterns are also normally present in and near urban areas, as are wind bursts. The cooling of the warm air as it rises, associated with the heat island phenomenon, in combination with greater amounts of particulate matter, may induce more cloudiness and convectional precipitation in and downwind of the city. "Precipitation is generally increased due to the physical, thermal, and mechanical uplift of air flowing over the city and to increased numbers of condensation nuclei."[9] Downdrafts and updrafts around buildings can be particularly troublesome to pedestrians. The presence of buildings actually intensifies air movement patterns as natural flow processes are interrupted and/or magnified.

Temperature Inversion

Atmospheric temperature normally decreases as altitude increases. This is known as the *normal lapse rate*, which is a decrease of 3.5° Fahrenheit for every 1000 feet of elevation. In some areas, because of the terrain, air pollution, and other atmospheric conditions, this upward cooling is thwarted, resulting in temperature inversions. In effect, a lid of warmer air is placed over cooler air, preventing the latter from rising. This promotes air stagnation and an intensification of pollutants in the atmosphere. If temperature inversions are prolonged, illnesses and deaths can result. Numerous

episodes such as the Donora, Pennsylvania, disaster of 1948 and the New York City disasters of 1953, 1962, and 1963 show how inversions can trap an unbreathable mixture of gases and particulates over a city and intensify human respiratory ailments, such as asthma and emphysema.

Air Pollution

In the United States, over 200 millions of tons of waste are released into the atmosphere annually. About half of this amount originates from fuel burned for transportation purposes. Some improvement occurred in air pollution levels in the United States in the 1980s, due to the impact of air quality standards established in the previous decade. The six pollutants that currently comprise the National Ambient Air Quality Standards (NAAQS) established by the federal Environmental Protection Agency are listed in Table 6-4. These standards occur at two levels: 1) Primary—designed to protect public health, and 2) Secondary—to protect the public welfare, including the impact of air pollution on vegetation, materials, and visibility.

Less sulfur oxide, carbon monoxide, and volatile organic compounds were found in the air in United States metropolitan areas at the end of the 1980s than at the beginning of the decade. Nitrogen oxide from fuel emissions (motor vehicle and smokestack) did increase. Lead in the atmosphere has also decreased significantly in the past 20 years, as it has been removed from gasoline and paint. Nevertheless "about 84 million people in the United States reside in counties which did not meet at least one air quality standard during 1989."[10]

In the period 1987–1989, over 90 metropolitan areas in the United States failed to meet ozone standards. The most serious problem exists in the Los Angeles basin of southern California, but other large metropolitan areas also experience problems in meeting standards, including the megalopolis area of the northeast, Chicago, Houston, San Francisco, and Atlanta. In many cases, the highest levels of ozone concentrations occur downwind from the major metropolitan area. In the case of Chicago, for example, the peak values occur in the vicinity of Racine, Wisconsin.[11] This occurs because

---

[9]Ibid., p. 186.

[10]Environmental Protection Agency, *National Air Quality and Emission Trends Report, 1989*, EPA-450/4-91-003, Office of Air Quality, Research Triangle Park, N.S., February 1991, pp. 7–15.

[11]Ibid., pp. 4–15.

TABLE 6-4
National Ambient Air Quality Standard (NAAQS)

Pollutant Categories	Primary Source(s)	Human Impact
1. Particulate matter (PM_{10})	Industrial processes; transportation (motor vehicles); fuel combustion	Breathing and respiratory problems; aggravation of cardiovascular disease; damage to lung tissue
2. Sulfur dioxide (SO_2)	Coal and oil combustion; refineries; paper mills	Breathing and respiratory problems; aggravation of cardiovascular disease; asthmatics affected
3. Carbon monoxide (CO)	Transportation (motor vehicles)	Enters bloodstream, disrupting delivery of oxygen to organs and tissues
4. Nitrogen dioxide (NO_2)	Transportation (motor vehicles); electric utility plants, industrial boilers	Lung irritant; lowers resistance to respiratory infections such as influenza; precursor to acid rain
5. Ozone (O_3)—ground level	Chemical reaction between organic compounds and nitrogen oxide in sunlight; organic compounds produced by motor vehicles, chemical manufacture, dry cleaners and paint shops	Breaks down biological tissues and cells; reduces lung function
6. Lead (Pb)	Motor vehicles	Accumulates in body, causing neurological impairment; associated with high blood pressure and heart disease

Source: Environmental Protection Agency, *National Air Quality and Emissions Trends Report, 1989,* EPA-450/4-91-003, Office of Air Quality, Research Triangle Park, N.C., February 1991.

ozone levels increase during the day as organic compounds produced by motor vehicles and industry, and nitrogen oxides interact with the sunlight and are carried downwind in the atmosphere. Ozone also shows seasonal variation with the highest levels during the warmer summer months.

Southern California also does not meet particulate matter standards or established carbon monoxide guidelines. As a result of these air quality problems, a region-wide Southern California Air Quality Management district was created in the late 1980s to address this issue and has established a program to improve the air quality in the region by imposing restrictions on automobile emissions, limiting the use of gasoline engines on lawn mowers, etc., and the burning of charcoal in barbecue grills, among others, to address the problem.

The growing awareness of the negative impact of air pollution on the public health demonstrates the need for its careful monitoring and the continuous revision of standards. As shown in Table 6-4, the primary impact of these pollutants on humans is breathing and respiratory problems, as well as cardiovascular disease. Asthmatics and individuals with lung and heart disease are very susceptible to increased pollution levels. The

young and elderly are also more often affected, as well. These pollutants, especially nitrogen oxide, can also be cited for their indirect effect on human health as a result of increased levels of acid rain and associated crop and tree damage.

The spatial variation of air pollution in Philadelphia (Figure 6-9) illustrates the association to land use. The highest pollution counts occur in the central business district (CBD) and over low-lying industrial corridors along the Schuylkill and Delaware rivers. Suburban residential areas to the northeast and northwest have the least polluted air. Carbon monoxide levels are generally highest where the greatest concentration of automobiles occurs and the downtown area readings are the highest for this pollutant. The highest ozone levels in Philadelphia occur across the Delaware River to the East in New Jersey.

Acid Rain

Scientists in the past 30 years have detected an increase in the acid level of rain, a problem most acutely felt in the northeastern United States, eastern Canada, and Central Europe, particularly in Germany and Scandina-

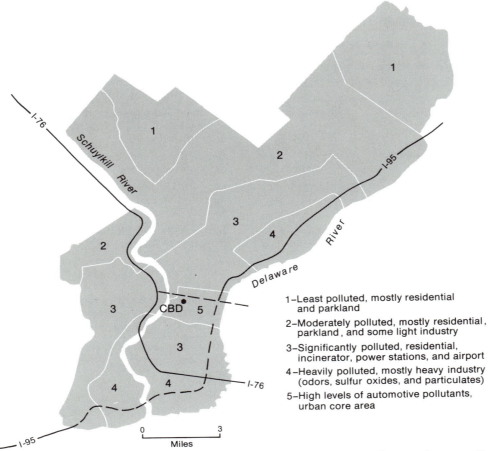

Figure 6-9. Air Pollution in Philadelphia. Significant spatial variations in air quality occur in metropolitan areas. Higher levels occur in the central business district and in industrial areas due to motor vehicle and industrial emission concentrations of carbon monoxide, particulate matter, and nitrogen oxide in these areas. Ozone counts are generally higher downwind, as in the case of the area east of the Delaware River in New Jersey in the Philadelphia region. *Source:* Redrawn and modified from Council on Environmental Quality, *The Delaware River Basin*, USGPO, Washington, D.C., 1975. p. 29.

via. Sulfur and nitrogen oxides emitted into the atmosphere from the burning of fossil fuels, especially coal, create the problem. In the United States, electric utility companies produce up to 65 percent of the sulfur dioxide and nitrogen oxide introduced into the atmosphere from the tall stacks of their coal-fired power generating plants. This material collects in the upper atmosphere and returns to the earth's surface during rainfall many miles downwind. Because of prevailing westerly wind flows, the problem is the worst in the Northeast, which is downwind from the Middle West industrial region. This acid rainfall eventually kills trees and plant life and reduces crop yields. Lakes in severely impacted areas no longer support fish, and the toxicity problem induces accelerated corrosion and deterioration of exposed building surfaces in cities.

Greenhouse Effect

Concern heightened during the 1980s that the slow rise in the earth's temperature observed over the past century may be due to the enhancement of the so-called *greenhouse effect*, which is intensified by human activity. One estimate is that the temperature rose as much in the 30 years from 1950 to 1980 as it did in the 70 previous years, 1880–1950.[12] The greenhouse effect refers to the trapping of heat by the Earth's atmosphere. Any enhancement of the effect may cause global warming with changing weather patterns and also cause the sea level to rise. Theoretical models of this phenomenon show that the increases in temperature should be

[12]Craig Mellow, "Who's Afraid of the Greenhouse Effect?" *Across the Board*, May 15, 1988, p. 30.

greater in higher latitudes. Melting of sea ice and glaciers, along with thermal expansion of water in the oceans, accounts for the suggested rise in sea levels. Agriculture patterns may also change as rainfall patterns change.

The primary contributing factor to the enhancement of the greenhouse effect is the increasing carbon dioxide level in the atmosphere. It traps radiation emitted by the earth within the atmosphere, acting as a thermal heat blanket. The greater the level of carbon dioxide, the more heat that is trapped and the warmer the planet becomes. "Roughly 75 percent of the increase is generally attribute to fuel emissions and 25 percent to the ongoing destruction of the world's forests."[13] Trees and other plants, of course, remove carbon dioxide from the air and emit oxygen. Emissions from coal-fired electrical generating plants are a major contributor to the carbon dioxide problem. The National Academy of Sciences estimated in 1983 that within 50–100 years the level of carbon dioxide in the atmosphere would be twice its preindustrial level.

Unless corrective steps are taken to lessen the global warming effect, sea levels may rise by two to three feet in the next century and beach erosion will accelerate even more. Already the coastline in some areas on the East Coast of the United States has eroded significantly such that beach nourishment programs involving the pumping of sand from coastal waters back onto eroded beach areas have been required, as in the case of Miami Beach. "The shoreline at Cape Hatteras, North Carolina, for instance, is eroding at a pace of 15 feet per year."[14]

In addition to the problem of increasing carbon dioxide levels, chlorofluorocarbons (CFCs), including synthetic chemicals such as Freon, which is used as a refrigerant, are destroying the ozone in the upper atmosphere. Levels of other trace gases, such as methane, and nitrous oxide levels are also increasing as by-products from the agriculture industry. These gases also contribute to enhancing the greenhouse effect, and this combination may be of greater importance than increasing carbon dioxide over the next century.

Noise

Recognition of noise as a pollutant occurred relatively recently by environmental scientists. Not until the 1960s were precise noise standards formulated in the United States. Traditionally, Americans have associated noise with progress, expansion, and growth. We have especially expected noise in the city. In contrast with other sources of pollution, it is not as permanent, and it has been easier to overlook. Noise also dissipates with distance from the source, and this too has prolonged, until recently, a permissive attitude.

In 1968, the first federal noise guidelines were issued by the Federal Aviation Administration (FAA) for airports. In 1970, congressionally mandated clean air guidelines instructed the Environmental Protection Agency (EPA) to establish standards for noise as well. In the few years that followed, many other federal agencies became involved in setting standards. For example, the Department of Housing and Urban Development (HUD) developed noise-related guidelines for residential, commercial, and industrial properties in 1972. These guidelines were more restrictive for residential land use than for commercial and industrial activity. They included ratings of acceptable levels of noise for both interior and exterior environments.

The measure of noise is a very technical undertaking and requires sophisticated monitoring devices. Readings are normally taken on a decibel (dB) scale, which is expressed in cycles per second. There are several scales used, but the A scale—dB(A)—is used most often because it most closely approximates the impact of noise on the human ear.[15] The dB(A) scale ranges from 0 to 150 (Table 6-5). The lowest value is the threshold for hearing a noise by the human ear. Light auto traffic produces a 50 reading, while freeway traffic at 50 feet creates a rating of 70, and a pneumatic drill has an annoying reading of 80. Above this level, sound becomes very disturbing. The threshold of noise-inducing pain for humans has been estimated to range from 120 to 140 dB(A). Prolonged exposure to noise at 90 dB(A) induces permanent loss of hearing, and it is possible that lower levels may induce a hearing loss. Note that many of the upper ranges of dB(A) levels are commonplace within urban areas, although varying spatially from one area to another.

The impact of noise on human health is not fully understood, but it is known to affect hearing. It may also lead to long-term health problems. It is believed that continued exposure to loud noises could cause hypertension or ulcers. Some persons may not be

[13]Ibid., p. 30.
[14]Ibid., p. 32.

[15]Clifford R. Bragdon, *Noise Pollution, The Unquiet Crisis*, University of Pennsylvania Press, Philadelphia, 1970.

TABLE 6-5
Weighted Sound Levels and Human Response

Decibel Level (dB(A) Scale)	Representative Sources of Sound	Human Response to Sound Level
150		
140	Jet flights from aircraft carrier deck	Painfully loud
130	Limit of amplified speech	
120	Jet takeoff at 200 feet Discotheque Auto horn at 3 feet	
110	Riveting machine Jet takeoff at 2000 feet	
100	Shout at 1.5 feet	Very annoying
90	New York subway station	
90	Heavy truck at 50 feet Pneumatic drill at 50 feet	Hearing damage (8 hours)
80	Freight train at 50 feet	Annoying
70	Freeway traffic at 50 feet	Telephone use difficult
60	Air-conditioning unit at 20 feet Light auto traffic at 50 feet	Intrusive
50	Living room	Quiet
40	Bedroom Library	
30	Soft whisper	Very quiet
20	Broadcasting studio	
10		Just audible
0		Threshold of hearing

Source: Council on Environmental Quality, Department of Transportation, 1970.

affected by noise at all, while others are very sensitive to certain types of sound or loud and unusual noise.

WATER DEMAND AND SUPPLY

The importance of the circulation of water in the hydrologic system has already been discussed, as well as the impact of urbanization on this process. The biggest problem associated with water and urbanization is the provision of an adequate quality supply in the face of greatly accelerated demand. Urban areas obtain their water needs primarily from streams, lakes, and wells (Table 6-6). As cities grow and water demands increase, reservoirs, aqueducts, and more and deeper wells must be constructed. An example of these problems is found in the various water projects in California that are designed to serve the large demand.

Figure 6-10 shows the complexity of supplying water to urban and agricultural areas from remote source areas. Three major aqueducts transport water to southern California alone to satisfy the need.

A direct, positive relationship exists between urban growth and water demand. Water use by urban inhabitants, including commercial and industrial demands, continues to increase, but interest in conservation has also gained momentum. The total per capita water withdrawal from ground and surface sources in the United States totaled 1400 gallons per day in 1985. About 20 percent of this total goes to municipal and business use. Irrigation and thermoelectric uses account for most of the rest of the withdrawal. In the past, residential water use was primarily limited to drinking and cooking in the home, but today vast quantities of water are also used for automatic dishwashers and clothes washers, baths and showers, sewage disposal,

TABLE 6-6
Common River-Quality Problems

Primary Causative Agent(s)	Usual Streamflow Condition	Likely Occurrence	
		Time	Place
Dissolved-Oxygen Depletion			
Municipal and industrial wastewater discharges	Low flow	Summer, high temperature	Slow-moving pools and tidal reaches
Excessive Algal Growth			
Aquatic plant nutrients from municipal, industrial, and agricultural wastewater effluents	Low flow	Summer, high temperature	Shallows or in euphotic zone of slow-moving pools and tidal reaches
Toxicity			
Toxicants from industrial, municipal, and agricultural wastewater discharges; swamp drainage	Low flow	Summer, high temperature	Slow-moving pools and tidal reaches
Salinity			
Salt-laden agricultural, industrial, and municipal wastewater discharges	Low flow	Summer, high temperature	Lower reaches, especially those with very long detention time
Thermal Pollution			
Waste-heat discharges (industry, power plants)	Low flow	Any time, but usually summer, high temperature	Any reach below waste-heat discharges
Microbial Pollution			
Microbes from poorly disinfected municipal or industrial waste-waters; seepage from animal feedlots; combined sewer overflows; urban runoff	Any flow condition	Any time	Any reach below sources
Sedimentation and Turbidity			
Accelerated erosion resulting from land-use activities	High flow	Rainy season, commonly winter or spring for most rivers	All reaches, but especially those proximate to heavy erosional activity

Source: W. G. Hines, et al., *Hydrologic Analysis and River-Quality Data Programs,* Circular 715-D, U.S. Geological Survey, USGPO, Washington, D.C., 1976.

lawn sprinkling, and car washing. Industrial and commercial uses have changed as well. The use of water for industrial cooling processes, air-conditioning, and waste removal has grown rapidly. North Americans are not running out of water, but ready access to a quality supply has become a severe problem. Water quality is continually decreasing and the problem is rapidly becoming national in proportion.

Urbanization decreases the rate of infiltration of water into the ground and accelerates runoff, and stream sedimentation (Table 6-7) at the same time as demand for water is increasing. Cities using deep wells for supplies often find that recharge has decreased as pumping lowers the water table. In the case of coastal cities, seawater encroachment increases and subsidence occurs as pumping lowers the water table. Many cities along the East and Gulf coasts have experienced

severe problems of this type, especially in Florida. Several areas must now look farther inland for water to replenish the groundwater supply.

In 1900, the Miami water system served 1680 people. By 1925, with a population of about 300,000, the city needed new and larger well fields. Preventive measures to control saltwater intrusion were also necessary. Concrete-lined drainage-ways and bulkheads reduced saline water encroachment. However, increases in impervious surfaces covering the land gradually decreased the recharge rate of the well fields. To compensate for this loss, canals were built westward into the interior of the state to bring more surface water to the well fields.

In 1960, over 1 million people lived in metropolitan Miami and used 145 MGD of water. The consumption rate in the late 1970s rose to 250 million gallons per

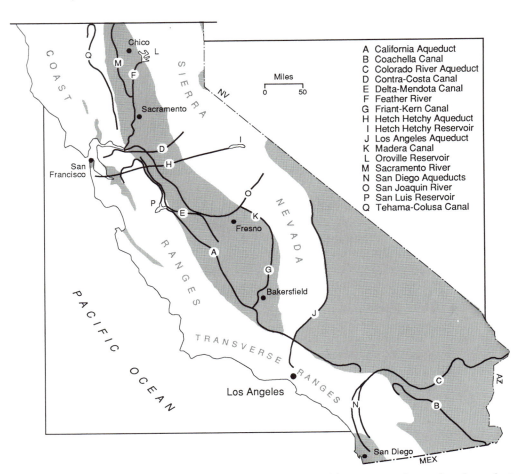

A California Aqueduct
B Coachella Canal
C Colorado River Aqueduct
D Contra-Costa Canal
E Delta-Mendota Canal
F Feather River
G Friant-Kern Canal
H Hetch Hetchy Aqueduct
I Hetch Hetchy Reservoir
J Los Angeles Aqueduct
K Madera Canal
L Oroville Reservoir
M Sacramento River
N San Diego Aqueducts
O San Joaquin River
P San Luis Reservoir
Q Tehama-Colusa Canal

Figure 6-10. Water Supply Sources for Southern California. An elaborate reservoir, canal, and aqueduct system blanketing the state supplies water to urban centers and agricultural land in southern California. Following years of drought, a stricter water rationing program began in the region in the early 1990s.

TABLE 6-7
Hydrologic Changes Associated with Urbanization

Change in Land or Water Use	Possible Hydrologic Effect
Preurban to Early Urban Transition Stage Removal of trees or vegetation; scattered house construction; well drilling and septic tank installation.	Decrease in transpiration; increased sedimentation of streams; lowered water table.
Transition from Early to Middle Urban Stage Massive earth removal; filling large-scale subdivision housing; street paving; abandoned culvert construction wells; sewage discharged into streams.	Accelerated land erosion and stream sedimentation; decreased infiltration of water into soil; increased flooding; increased water pollution; decreased water supply and quality; death of fish and aquatic life.
Transition from Middle Urban to Late Urban Stage Population increases demand for public utilities, including water supply and sewage treatment; distant reservoirs used as water source.	Further increases in stream pollution and additional degradation of water to downstream users; increased flood damage; overloading of sewers and other drainage facilities.

Source: John Savini and J. C. Kammerer, *Urban Growth and the Water Regimen,* Water Supply Paper 1591-A, U.S. Geological Survey, USGPO, Washington, D.C., 1961.

day. By the year 2000, the expected population will be over 4 million, requiring an estimated 1.4 billion gallons per day (BGD). As a result of this growing demand, Miami has had to impose "water hours" and consider time-of-day pricing, as well as expand the network of recharge canals that stretch westward into the Everglades and Lake Okeechobee. While water management practices have averted hardships to date, controls on growth in the area may be necessary in the future.

As of 1975, water use in the United States was 420 billion gallons a day (BGD). This amount represented a doubling in use since 1950. Notwithstanding the Miami situation just discussed, water supply problems for most communities do not exist except in drought conditions. Most urban areas have been very successful in projecting for their future needs and taking measures to provide for those needs. But in the area of maintaining high quality levels, success has been more elusive.

Water Quality

While water quality is generally good in the United States, many municipal water supply systems are operating with potentially harmful contaminant and pollutant levels. Between 1961 and 1973, over 200 outbreaks of disease or poisoning caused by contaminated drinking water occurred. It is estimated that 8 million people are using potentially dangerous water from about 5000 community water supply systems.[16]

Present municipal water treatment systems were not designed to cope with the current quality of their raw water. Most treatment systems in use today were primarily designed to remove the bacteria produced by animal and human wastes from relatively clean water. The harsh chemicals and other dissolved toxic substances frequently found in water today are frequently not treated. In a 1975 survey, the EPA found that 80 cities had small quantities of organic chemicals in their water supplies.[17] Although the survey found very low concentrations, their mere presence was cause for concern.

One example of the presence of pollutants in streams used for a local water supply is provided by the Detroit region.[18] The Detroit River and its outflow into Lake Erie, where southern sections of Detroit and the cities of Wyandotte and Monroe obtain their water supply, have high bacterial counts and ammonia levels. Algae growth has also caused serious problems. The pollution that degrades the water for these communities comes from the mouths of the Detroit and Raisin rivers. These streams yield many different industrial wastes, such as chlorides, oil, and phosphates. The various toxic chemicals, suspended and settling solids, coliform bacteria, and other wastes contribute to *eutrophication* or the depletion of dissolved oxygen in the water. Growth of slime bacteria or "sewage fungus" occurs in such environments.

Storm Water Drainage

Another source of stream pollution in urban areas is storm water discharge. Debris on impervious surfaces and the erosion of storm drainage channels contribute a high proportion of the total water pollutants. Of particular concern are bacteria, solid wastes, and chlorides, which adversely affect the biological life of streams and lakes. In urban areas located in the snowbelt, the impact of highway deicing compounds used to keep streets and roads free of snow and ice is becoming a major problem, as the runoff pollutes streams and rivers. Healthy trees that once lined city streets in northern cities have also been damaged by the salt, as have soils and other vegetation.

Most storm drainage systems are designed to carry away excess water runoff. Some cities have separate storm and sanitary sewers, but often they constitute a single combined system. Such combination sewers are not recommended because of the high cost of treating all street runoff in traditional sewage treatment plants. During rainstorms these treatment plants are easily overloaded. As a short-run solution, during heavy rains, floodgates are typically opened and massive amounts of sewage are released untreated. It is also a common occurrence for combined sewers to back up into homes, businesses, industries, and streets during flood peaks. Garbage, human and animal feces, sediment, and other pollutants are then left behind as the flood recedes.

Wastewater Treatment

Water tumbling over rocks or flowing through porous media tends to purify itself naturally, and for centuries wastes have been cleaned in this manner. But the

---

[16]U.S. Environmental Protection Agency, *A Drop to Drink: A Report on the Quality of Our Drinking Water*, Office of Public Affairs, USGPO, Washington, D.C., 1976.

[17]Ibid.

[18]Ibid.

threshold for natural purification is easily exceeded in urban areas, resulting in considerable damage to the environment. Artificial wastewater treatment speeds up the natural process of purification. Up to three levels of treatment can be involved in this process: primary, secondary, and tertiary. Primary treatment removes solid wastes from the water after they have settled out. Thirty percent of the municipalities in the United States give only primary treatment. This is considered inadequate by many public health officials and researchers, who recommend treatment at least through the secondary level. Secondary treatment removes about 90 percent of the organic matter in sewage by using a natural bacteria process and then adding chlorine. After the effluent leaves a sedimentation tank in the primary stage of treatment, it flows into a trickling filter or an activated sludge aeration tank where bacteria break down the organic matter. This effluent then flows into another sedimentation tank for chlorination.

The advanced tertiary methods of waste treatment are considered necessary in many areas as new processes in manufacturing, and the increased use of industrial chemicals, create more complex pollutants. Such wastes almost defy cleansing by traditional methods. Tertiary methods involve processes such as coagulation, flocculation, absorption, and electrodialysis.

While many cities do not need to treat all of their wastes with all three levels, it is nearly impossible to preclassify the target effluent to ensure adequate treatment.

A recent recommendation regarding waste treatment has been to encourage the return to more natural processes, thus decreasing the dependence on technology. The European sewage farm used in medieval times provides the model for this solution. In modern terminology this approach is called land application or spray irrigation (Figure 6-11). Essentially, it involves spraying wastewater on the ground and letting natural percolation processes remove the wastes. The nutrients found in such wastes also boost soil productivity, increasing farm and forest production. Such a system can be a viable solution for both large and small municipalities. In the former instance, vast acreage may be necessary, but this arrangement is compatible with strategies to preserve open spaces and return to more natural recycling processes.

A SOLUTION TO POLLUTION?

Given the scale and diversity of the urban environmental ills, one might wonder if a solution to the problem is close at hand. The answer is that considerable headway

Figure 6-11. Land Application Waste Water Disposal. This process involves spraying previously treated wastewater on the ground and letting natural percolation processes remove the wastes. Note wastewater storage lagoon in foreground, where water can be stored prior to land application. (Courtesy of the USDA, Soil Conservation Service)

has been gained. Enforcement of stricter regulations and greater public support for a cleaner environment now exist. But further reduction in pollution will be difficult because the easiest, most cost-effective steps have been taken. More advanced treatments and stringent controls will be very expensive and less effective because "the very process of pollution control produces pollution. The chemicals that are added in advanced water treatment are often troublesome, even toxic, pollutants (ordinary chlorine, for example, is now known to combine with certain organic material to form chloroform, a known carcinogen)."[19]

Eventually more emphasis will have to be placed on conservation and recycling, as well as on the use of more natural processes to treat waste. The interrelatedness of various physical and human phenomena must receive more recognition before the problem will be solved. Treating one aspect of pollution alone often has many unintentional deleterious side effects. Land use changes and growth itself are among the root causes of environmental problems. The traditional association of new technology and rapid population and employment growth as progress may need reevaluation, as does the quick-fix approach.

Environmental legislation, for example, has had a negative effect on energy resources, directly and indirectly. The direct effects include: "increased consumption of fuel; changes in patterns of fuel consumption; investment in pollution-control equipment; delays in construction of energy facilities; increased prices and rates; and land-use conflicts."[20] Gasoline mileage from automobiles, for example, decreased as a result of emission regulations in the early 1970s, but it later increased dramatically in response to price hikes in the mid and late-1970s. While automobile mileage improved again in the 1980s, it appears to be plateauing again in the 1990s.

Considerable switching from coal to cleaner burning oil has occurred as a result of the introduction of sulfur oxide emission standards. Unfortunately, oil is not as plentiful as coal, and this has accelerated the rate of depletion of petroleum and increased the dependence on imports. Land use conflicts have occurred when environmental regulations prohibited the development of ports, pipelines, and power plants. It is now clear that we must return to more dependence on coal for

fuel, but the price of this shift may result in greater *acid rain* problems. We will discuss environmental issues and urban development again in Chapter 9, which deals with transportation.

SUMMARY AND CONCLUSION

The natural physical environment has always operated much the same as it does today, but we are still learning to appreciate its complexity. Following a period of total neglect (most of this century), we as a nation began to give environmental issues increased attention in the mid-1970s and 1980s and now give them critical national priority in the 1990s. We also understand that preserving an adequate environment is part of a greater scenario relating to quality of life issues, mobility, and urban design itself.

Recognition that the city is a biological as well as a physical system has led people to be more sensitive to the requirements for its continued viability. This has also led to better use of relatively inexpensive natural processes to maintain and preserve a sound ecosystem. Despite this progress, much remains to be done to right the ills of the past. But the city lives on because, like people, it has an enormous capacity to cope and adapt, even in the face of adversity.

Suggestions for Further Reading

Baumann, Duane D., and Daniel M. Dworkin. *Planning for Water Reuse*, Maaroufa Press, Chicago, 1978.

Bennett, R. J., and R. J. Chorley. *Environmental Systems: Philosophy, Analysis, and Control*, Princeton University Press, Princeton, N.J., 1978.

Bernstein, R. D., and T. R. Oke. "Influence of Pollution and Urbanization on Urban Climate," in *Advances in Environmental Science and Engineering*, Vol. 3, Gordon & Breach, New York, 1980, pp. 181–202.

Berry, Brian J. L., and Frank T. Horton. *Urban Environmental Management: Planning for Pollution Control*, Prentice Hall, Englewood Cliffs, N.J., 1974.

Burby, Raymond J., and Stephen P. French, et al. *Floodplain Land Use Management: A National Assessment*, Westview Press, Boulder, Colo., 1985.

Burton, Ian, et al. *The Environment as Hazard*, Oxford University Press, New York, 1978.

Caris, Susan L. *Community Attitudes toward Pollution*, University of Chicago, Department of Geography Research Paper 188, Chicago, 1978.

Cook, Earl. *Man, Energy, Society*, Freeman, San Francisco, 1976.

---

[19]Tom Alexander, "It's Time for New Approaches to Pollution Control," *Fortune*, November 1976, p. 230.

[20]Daniel P. Beard, "United States Environmental Legislation and Energy Resources: A Review," *Geographical Review*, 65 (1975), 229–244.

Coppock, J. T., and C. B. Wilson. *Environmental Quality with Emphasis on Urban Problems*, Wiley, New York, 1974.

Corson, Walter H., ed. *The Global Ecology Handbook*, The Global Tomorrow Coalition, Beacon Press, Boston 1990.

Detwyler, Thomas R., and Melvin G. Marcus. *Urbanization and the Environment*, Duxbury Press, Belmont, Calif., 1972.

Douglas, Ian. *The Urban Environment*, Edward Arnold, London, 1983.

Driever, Steven, and Danny Vaughn. "Flood Hazard in Kansas City since 1880," *Geographical Review*, 78, 1988, 1–19.

Ferguson, B. K., and T. N. Debo. *On-Site Stormwater Management: Applications for Landscape and Engineering*, 2nd ed., Van Nostrand Reinhold, New York, 1990.

Greenberg, Michael R., and Robert M. Hordon. *Water Supply Environmental Impact*, Center for Urban Policy Research, Rutgers University, New Brunswick, N.J., 1979.

Greenberg, Michael R., *et al. A Primer on Industrial Planning: A Case Study and Systems Analysis*, Center for Urban Policy Research, Rutgers University, New Brunswick, N.J., 1976.

Hammond, Kenneth A., George Macinko, and Wilma B. Fairchild, eds. *A Sourcebook on the Environment: A Guide to the Literature*, University of Chicago Press, Chicago, 1978.

Landsberg, H. E. *The Urban Climate*, Academic Press, New York, 1981.

Lave, Lester, and Gilbert Omenn. *Clearing the Air: Reforming the Clean Air Act*, The Brookings Institution, Washington, D.C., 1981.

Liroff, Richard A. *Reforming Air Pollution Regulation: The Toil and Trouble of EPA's Bubble*, The Conservation Foundation, Washington, D.C., 1986.

Leopold, Luna. *Hydrology for Urban Land Planning: A Guidebook on the Hydrologic Effects of Urban Land Use*, Circular 554, U.S. Geological Survey, Washington, D.C., 1968.

Marsh, William. *Environmental Analysis for Land Use and Site Planning*, McGraw–Hill, New York, 1978.

Mather, John R. *The Climatic Water Budget in Environmental Analysis*, Lexington Books, Lexington, Mass., 1978.

May, Daryl N., ed. *Handbook of Noise Assessment*, Van Nostrand Reinhold, New York, 1978.

McPherson, M. B. *Hydrological Effects of Urbanization*, UNESCO Press, Paris, 1974.

Mellon, Margaret, *et al. The Regulation of Toxic and Oxidant Air Pollution in North America*, C C H Canadian Limited, Toronto, 1986.

Oke, T. R. *Boundary Layer Climates*, 2nd ed., Methuen, London/New York, 1987.

Oke, T. R. "The Urban Energy Balance," *Progress in Physical Geography*, 12 (1988), 471–508.

Organization for Economic Cooperation and Development. *Environment and Energy Use in Urban Areas*, OECD, Washington, D.C., 1978.

Organization for Economic Cooperation and Development. *Urban Environment Indicators*, OECD, Washington, D.C., 1978.

William L. Rathje, "Once and Future Landfills," *National Geographic*, 179, (May, 1991), 116–134.

Spirn, Anne. *The Granite Garden: Urban Nature and Human Design*, Basic Books, New York, 1984.

U.S. Congress, Office of Technology Assessment. *Facing America's Trash: What Next for Municipal Solid Waste?* OTA-0-424. U.S. Government Printing Office, Washington, D.C., October 1989.

U.S. Environmental Protection Agency, Office of Solid Waste and Emergency Response (OS-305). *Decision-Maker's Guide to Solid Waste Management*, EPA/530-SW-072, U.S. Government Printing Office, Washington, D.C., November 1989.

U.S. Environmental Protection Agency, Office of Solid Waste and Emergency Response, Franklin Associates, Ltd. *Characterization of Municipal Solid Waste in the United States, 1960–2000* (Update 1988), Final Report, U.S. Government Printing Office, Washington, D.C., March 30, 1988.

Wyman, Richard. *Global Climate Change and Life on Earth*, Chapman and Hall, New York, 1991.

7

CITY DEVELOPMENT: THEORY AND PRACTICE

No dominant theory of urban economic development exists, but the link between development and urbanization occurs very frequently in all conceptualizations. *Economic base* studies associate growth with the sale of goods outside the community, typically manufactured products. A second approach, *growth pole theory*, ties socioeconomic expansion to the prowess of large urban areas in providing self-generating expansion. *Industrial development* and urban growth is a third perspective that overlaps the first two approaches. Finally, current thinking also places more emphasis on seeking access to information as a reason for urban growth.

Urban economic development patterns in much of the highly developed world, over time, provide evidence in support of each of these approaches as a means to modernize traditional economies. A similar process, operating today in several *newly industrializing countries* (NICS),[1] appears to follow a similar sequence, but for much of the third world, urban economic development has not had the same impact on national economies, as discussed earlier in Chapter 3.

ECONOMIC BASE THEORY

As urbanization accelerated and the planning profession emerged in the post-World War I era, interest grew in predicting urban growth and in explaining the mechanism that propelled this expansion. This growth was typically measured in relation to the strength of (1) the industrial sector of the urban economy and (2) the level of services. In 1927, a report of the New York Regional Plan Association distinguished between "primary" and "ancillary" employment.[2] The former referred to industry and the latter to service activity. By the 1930s, a more formal statement of economic base theory appeared. An article in *Fortune* magazine in 1938 and a 1939 study by Homer Hoyt promulgated the new terminology and analytical framework.[3]

According to the economic base approach, the foundation of support for a city came from the sales of goods or services outside the community (Figure 7-1). These sales were called *exports*. Revenues that such sales produced, according to the scenario, assisted local expansion by providing dollars to support service activities. Goods or services produced for sale outside the

---

[1]No consensus exists as to which countries should be included in this group, but most lists include Mexico, Brazil, Spain, Portugal, Greece, Yugoslavia, Taiwan, South Korea, Hong Kong, and Singapore.

[2]Robert M. Haig, *Major Economic Factors in Metropolitan Growth and Arrangement, Regional Survey of New York, and Environs*, Vol. 1. New York Regional Plan Association, New York, 1928: reprinted by Arno Press, 1975.

[3]"Oskaloosa vs. the United States," *Fortune*, April 1938; Arthur M. Weimer and Homer Hoyt, *Principles of Urban Real Estate*, Ronald Press, New York, 1939.

Figure 7-1. Flour Mills in Minneapolis. Economic base theory links growth with the sale of goods outside the community. Flour milling was a mainstay of the Minneapolis economy in the late ninetenth and early twentieth century. Remnants of that export industry lined the Mississippi River in this 1950s photo. The area is now redeveloped as a mixed-use commercial and residential area. Downtown Minneapolis at top left. (Minnesota Historical Society)

local urban area were called *basic*, and employment related to local sales in the home community was labeled *nonbasic*. Economists at the time typically attributed urban growth to the basic portion of total employment, relegating services to a backup role and arguing that they developed after basic activity expansion.

Stages of Development

Wilbur Thompson's scenario of growth, using the basic–nonbasic dichotomy, describes a series of stages in the development of a city.[4] The first stage of *export*

---

[4]Wilbur Thompson, *A Preface to Urban Economics*, Johns Hopkins University Press, Baltimore, 1965, pp. 15–16.

specialization appears when a local economy emerges under the aegis of a single manufacturing firm, and begins selling goods for export outside the community. A second stage, *export complex*, unfolds as additional companies begin production to supply inputs or purchase outputs from the original enterprise. Again, the focus is on the sale of goods to the outside world. The growth of a local service sector (retailing, wholesaling, transportation) signifies the presence of the third stage, *economic maturation*. As growth continues, the city may become a wholesaler and financial center for other, once rival, cities that now become its satellites. Cities that reach the fourth stage, *regional metropolis*, provide many services to the regional hinterland. A fifth, elite stage, *technical-professional virtuosity*, signals national or international preeminence for a city (Figure 7-2).

The role that gives major metropolitan areas great stature is often quite obvious. For example, Detroit is associated with the automobile, Boston with education and research, and Miami with retirement and the financial hub for the Caribbean market. Thompson, while stating that these stages are arbitrary and impressionistic, argues that they show the sequential, and expanding, roles that cities play as they grow. Not all cities experience the full sequence of developmental stages; some lose momentum because of competition from other centers, poor location, or the lack of leadership. Others prosper, whether from chance, local boosterism, location, or favored resource availability.

Economies of Scale

Economies of scale refers to the efficiencies a firm can experience from a larger operation, which allows for more specialization in the production process, better prices for materials associated with larger purchases,

and more competitive pricing of products for the market. As firms grow, classical location theory suggests that economies of scale would provide them with greater returns on their investment. Large cities offer advantages to firms that reinforce economies of scale. These opportunities have been labeled *urbanization economies* and *localization economies*.

Larger cities can offer advantages to the firm through larger labor markets, greater access to financial resources, a broader range of infrastructure support, and other advantages that, collectively, we call *urbanization economies*. Often, start-up firms obtain advantages by locating in such larger areas, but it is also true that costs are higher in larger cities. Often, firms decentralize away from such centers, as they grow, to minimize costs.

The role of urbanization economies in attracting growth, however, may be overexaggerated, as there is also evidence that *localization economies*, not urbanization economies, attract industries. This means that like concentrations of industries frequently occur in cities and that they are there not because of the large size of the city, but to take advantage of skilled labor

Figure 7-2. Georges Pompidou National Center of Art and Culture, Paris. Major metropolitan areas are known for their technical-professional virtuosity in one or more areas. Paris, for example, is known for its cultural heritage as expressed in its architecture, museums, and art galleries. This innovative building, opened in the 1970s, houses the largest museum of modern art in the world. Note the exterior placement of elevators, escalators, and utilities. (Charles Kennard/Stock, Boston).

markets, to foster intrafirm cooperation/communication, as in keeping abreast of innovations, and to take advantage of opportunities for greater levels of specialization.[5] Indeed, most industries do exhibit a clustering of firms, supporting the notion that localization economies do operate. Witness, for example, the clustering that occurs in the aerospace, steel, automobile, carpet, and machinery industries, wherein a few cities capture most of the employment in these sectors.

Basic/Nonbasic Ratios

In the 1940s and 1950s, geographers and economists widely heralded the economic base approach as a key to unlock the mystery of urban growth.[6] The terms *primary, external, basic*, and *town-building* came to be used interchangeably to describe *basic* sector jobs. At the same time, *secondary, ancillary, service*, and *town-serving* tags were applied to *nonbasic* jobs. Determining a specific *basic/nonbasic ratio* linking industrial and service jobs shares became a topic of great concern. Proponents of this approach thought future growth could be promoted by increasing the number of basic (industrial) jobs, which in turn would spin off more nonbasic employment.

Basic/nonbasic ratio analyses revealed a systematic variation with city size (Table 7-1). In smaller cities a greater share of employment was typically basic in nature. For example, the ratio revealed for Oshkosh, Wisconsin, was 100 : 60. This means that 100 basic jobs created 60 nonbasic worker jobs. In larger cities the ratio adjusted downward to a level where each component contributed equally. For example, 100 basic jobs created about 100 nonbasic opportunities in cities of 100,000 population, such as Albuquerque. In the largest cities the basic sector was overshadowed by the nonbasic component, as occurred in New York, Cincinnati, and Detroit, which had ratios of 100 : 215, 100 : 170, and 100 : 117, respectively. This suggests that larger cities depend more heavily on their service role than on manufacturing.

In the real world, growth does not occur as uniformly as the economic base interpretation might imply. The

TABLE 7-1
Basic/Nonbasic Ratios for Selected Cities

City	Population (thousands)	B/N Ratio
New York	12,500	100 : 215
Detroit	2900	100 : 117
Cincinnati	907	100 : 170
Brocton	119	100 : 82
Albuquerque	116	100 : 103
Madison	110	100 : 82
Oshkosh	42	100 : 60

Source: From John Alexander, "The Basic-Nonbasic Concept of Economic Functions," *Land Economics*, 32 (1967), 69–84. Copyright © 1967 by the Regents of the University of Wisconsin.) Reprinted with permission.

expansion process is highly selective and only works in areas experiencing special circumstances. Few options exist for most areas to induce growth. With all communities in the country actively recruiting new export activity, most cannot be successful. Those areas that do acquire new firms often learn that new industry just provides jobs for local residents who formerly commuted elsewhere to work, rather than inducing growth by attracting new residents from outside the region.

Another interpretation of the basic/nonbasic approach is also available. Basic activity need not refer solely to industrial employment; it can also be interpreted to be *any* activity that sells its goods or services to people or businesses outside the city, bringing revenue into the local area. Whereas manufacturing could be a basic activity for some cities, tourism may provide the same role in others. Basic employment can also refer to activities that receive their funding and or clientele support from outside the community such as a military base, medical complex, or university. Retirement income or transfer payment (social security, welfare, or alimony) monies can also operate in the same fashion. This interpretation has gradually led researchers to the conclusion that for every activity in the city, some of the employment is basic (for export) and the rest nonbasic (for local support), and manufacturing need not be the primary export activity.

Problems with Economic Base

Criticisms leveled at the economic base approach involve both pragmatic measurement problems and philosophical issues. The problem of how to determine

[5]J. Vernon Henderson, *Urban Development: Theory, Fact, and Illusion*, Oxford University Press, 1988.

[6]Richard B. Andrews, "Mechanics of the Urban Economic Base," *Land Economics*, 29 (1953), 161–167; Homer Hoyt, "Homer Hoyt on Development of Economic Concept," *Land Economics*, 30 (1954), 182–191; John W. Alexander, "Basic Concept of Urban Economic Functions," *Economic Geography*, 30 (1954), 246–261.

the boundaries of the local as opposed to the export area has always plagued the researcher. The larger the size of the local area, the smaller the export component, and vice versa. It makes a great difference if the local area is defined as the city limits, the urbanized area, the MSA, or the daily urban system. The decision to assign an activity to either the basic or nonbasic category is also arbitrary. Many so-called local services such as doctors, lawyers, and government workers also serve clients outside the local community, and this problem becomes more prevalent when studying larger cities.

In technologically advanced industries, confusion also exists from the presence of intermediate goods brought into and out of the area to be fabricated into more sophisticated products. Subdividing each and every activity to parcel out those jobs that are basic or nonbasic is a very subjective and arduous undertaking. In many smaller communities, it is foolish even to attempt to separate employment between basic and nonbasic categories because there may not be such a structure.

An Alternate Economic Base

Criticisms of economic base have inevitably led to substitute interpretations of the growth process. One opponent of the traditional approach of the technique, Hans Blumenfeld, presented a very forceful and appealing alternative. He stated that the traditional economic base approach possessed a mercantilistic trade (import–export of goods) bias in favor of money earning that did not look at total monetary flows in the community. He indicated that it overlooked inputs from tourist dollars, retirement transfer payments, and unemployment or welfare payments by emphasizing more traditional work types.[7] Blumenfeld said that the traditional interpretation could be meaningful only in small communities. He correctly indicated that as cities become larger and more diverse, the nonbasic sector increases in importance. Moreover, he stated that the service component of the city is always in place, as we will see in Chapter 8, whereas industry (export activity) comes and goes (Figure 7-3).

The fact that an array of services (schools, utilities, retailing, and others) becomes a permanent fixture of the economy of a city is important. Services are typically less susceptible to business cycle fluctuations and may pay lower salaries, but opportunities have grown tremendously in this area in the past 25 years. These observations are the basis of a compelling argument against viewing such functions as nonbasic. Another important point worth repeating is that *any* export activity, whether it be specialized services (major league sports, television commercials, tourism, or higher education) or manufactured goods, creates money flows and influences the growth rate of the city.

GROWTH POLE THEORY

An alternative economic development philosophy that highlights the importance of the city is *growth pole theory*. Growth pole theory is an umbrella term referring to a series of concepts related to development rather than a comprehensive theory.[8] But compared with the economic base approach to economic development, growth pole theory is far more elegant, both theoretically and empirically. Planning implications of the theory have proved worthwhile in many environments and led to significant changes in governmental development policies. The theory is dynamic and applicable to many stages of the development process.

Francois Perroux first discussed the growth pole philosophy in a paper pointing out the role of cities in fostering economic development in the mid-1950s.[9] French planners and regional economists at that time were generally dissatisifed with traditional growth theory because it did not fit the development experience of their country. The growth pole (pôle de croissance) approach was more realistic and had several behavioral applications in terms of priorities for resource allocation. Perroux recognized that growth was not balanced but disproportionately concentrated at certain points, forming the basis of his conceptualization.

At the scale of an individual firm, one can observe the impact of the effects of a development pole in its most elemental form. This form, called a *propulsive industry*, generates growth from its own purchases and sales. The larger and faster growing it is, the greater the effect. A high level of intense interaction with other

[7]Hans Blumenfeld, "The Economic Base of the Metropolis," *Journal of the American Institute of Planners*, 21 (1955), 114–132.

[8]T. Hermansen, "Development Poles and Development Centers in National and Regional Development, Elements of a Theoretical Framework," in A. R. Kuklinski, ed., *Growth Poles and Growth Centers in Regional Planning*, Mouton, Paris, 1972.

[9]Francois Perroux, "Note sur la Notion de Pôle de Croissance," *Economie Appliquée*, Nos. 1–2 (January–June 1955), 307–320.

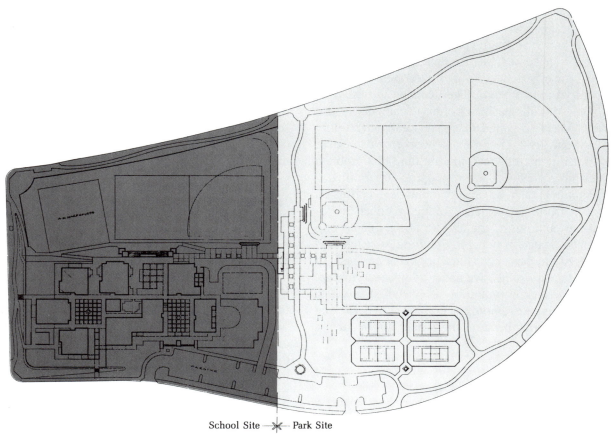

School Site —✳— Park Site

Figure 7-3.   Schools and Parks as Basic Activities.   Unlike industry, which can come and go, services are a permanent fixture in the city. In this example, the developer of Rancho Santa Margarita, California, designed a park and an elementary school adjacent to one another so they could share playground equipment and ballfields.   (Courtesy of Urban Land Institute)

firms (purchases and sales) also enhances growth. This process has been labeled *circular and cumulative causation* (Figure 7-4).[10] The expansion of a business or industry, for example, will create a *multiplier effect*, as increased purchases of materials and greater employment levels create additional jobs as money flows through the economy. These job increases may occur in several areas, such as manufacturing, transportation, retail sales, and other services. This expansion may, in turn, lead to population growth and will increase the likelihood of a new invention or innovation that, in turn, can induce yet another round of growth in jobs and population; hence, the reference to a circular and cumulative process.

At another scale, the pole could be a metropolitan economy, such as greater Paris. At that scale the availability of services and the infrastructure (transportation network, electrical and telephone utilities, etc.) become important factors in encouraging the concentration of activity.

Polarization and the Trickling-Down Process

Concentrating investment in one area usually leads to *polarization* of development (Figure 7-5).[11] As growth accelerates in the urban area, the hinterland experiences a parallel decline. This latter circumstance was labeled by Gunnar Myrdal as a *backwash* involving the

---

[10]Gunnar Myrdal, *Rich Lands and Poor*, Harper & Brothers, New York, 1957.

[11]Albert O. Hirschman, "Investment Policies and Dualism in Underdeveloped Countries," *American Economic Review*, 47 (1957), 550–570.

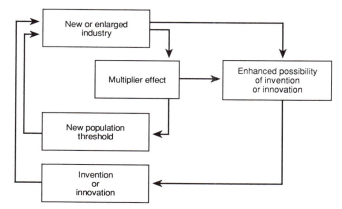

Figure 7-4. Circular and Cumulative Growth: Industrialization and Urban Development. The expansion of a business or industry creates a multiplier effect, leading to more jobs and business, as money flows through the economy. This growth increases the likelihood of a new invention or innovation, creating another round of expansion. *Source:* Reprinted from *The Spatial Dynamics of U.S. Urban-Industrial Growth, 1800–1914*, by Allan R. Pred. By permission of the M.I.T. Press, Cambridge, Mass. Copyright © 1966 by the Massachusetts Institute of Technology.

outmigration of rural residents from the hinterlands to take advantage of urban job opportunities.[12] Financial resources (bank deposits, investments) often vacate rural areas in favor of the development pole in early stages of development. The net result of this process is that the hinterland can become more impacted and less able to meet local needs, such as the provision of health and educational services. The migration process itself is also highly selective, with a disproportionate share of the younger population moving away, leaving an older, more dependent clientele in peripheral areas.

As time passes, a *trickling-down process* (in Albert Hirschman's terminology), or *spread effect* (in Myrdal's terminology), counteracts the initial depletion of human and financial resources in the hinterland. "Growing markets, new technology and friction of distance, combined with congestion, pollution, and diseconomies of scale in the heartland and the amenities of the hinterland, make outlying areas more attractive to the development (over time)."[13] Just as *centripetal* forces encourage concentration of growth in the center as first, *centrifugal* effects gradually begin to provide increased opportunities in outlying areas as

centralization pressures increase. The impacts of the latter process are much weaker than the *centripetal* forces and can take a half century or more to appear.

Application of the Growth Pole Theory

Growth processes in several underdeveloped countries have been shown to fit the growth pole conceptualization particularly well. Less developed parts of industrial countries may also conform to this developmental sequence. In some instances the growth pole approach has been used to describe the development process within the context of the existing hierarchy of cities, while in other instances it has been used as a guide for developing new, planned cities as focal points for development in depressed areas. Such a planned pole, for example, was implemented in Brazil with the creation of Brasilia in the late 1950s.

The Guyana Plan, drawn up in 1958 in Venezuela, also adopted this heartland–hinterland model, sometimes referred to as a *core–periphery* model. Than plan aimed to revitalize the eastern one-third of Venezuela. Development of a major industrial complex, Cuidad Guyana, based on iron ore, hydroelectric, and natural gas resources, was envisioned. Between this new core region and existing urban centers, development corridors were proposed in the periphery.

MANUFACTURING AND URBAN GROWTH

Manufacturing played a prominent role in the growth and development of North American cities in the nineteenth century, continuing through the early post-World War II era in this century (see Box for definitions).

The bulk of the manufacturing expansion in the late nineteenth and early twentieth centuries developed in an area now generally referred to as the *manufacturing belt* (Figure 7-6). The growth of this belt in the Northeast and Middle West fits the Pred circular and cumulative growth scenario very well. That area, first identified in 1919, remains the core area of manufacturing activity in the country, but its share of activity has declined to less than one-half the total from a peak of over two-thirds of manufacturing activity in the country. Larger MSAs in the region contribute significantly to manufacturing belt dominance, even though many have declined as industrial centers in recent

---

[12]Gunnar Myrdal, *Economic Theory and Underdeveloped Regions*, Duckworth, London, 1957.

[13]Truman A. Hartshorn, "The Spatial Structure of Socioeconomic Development in the Southeast, 1950–1960," *Geographical Review*, 61 (1971), 269.

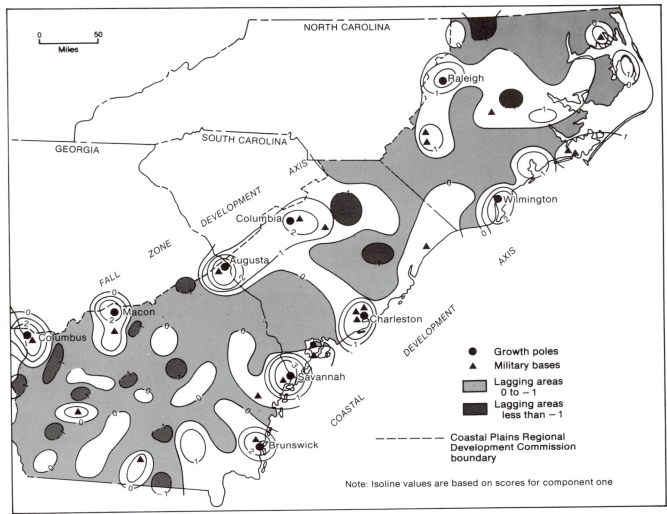

Figure 7-5.   Growth Poles and Lagging Areas in the Atlantic Coastal Plain, 1960. The importance of larger cities as growth poles is shown here in a band along the coast and along the Fall Line Zone in the interior. Lagging areas dominated the area between these two corridors except the emerging development axis connecting Augusta, Columbia, and Charleston.

years. New York, Chicago, and Philadelphia placed in the top 5 MSAs in the United States in terms of value-added by manufacture in 1982 (Table 7-2). Moreover, 6 of the top 10 manufacturing centers in the country today are identified with the manufacturing belt.

The relative stability of the manufacturing prowess of the Northeast and Middle West in the past 100 years is demonstrated by the fact that only three changes occurred in the list of leading centers. One city—St. Louis—missed out in 1982 by merely dropping to 11th place. The other two cities failing to return to the leader list in 1982 are Baltimore and Pittsburgh. Newcomers are the sunbelt cities of Los Angeles, Houston, and

Dallas. Los Angeles currently ranks number two nationally, and Houston and Dallas are 8th and 9th, respectively.

All recent additions to the top-10 list lie outside the traditional manufacturing belt, demonstrating that significant manufacturing activity decentralization away from the traditional core area has occurred. Newer high-technology activities (see Box), which we will discuss later in the chapter, are not as closely tied to the traditional resource base, and expanding markets in the South and West have broadened the locational field for manufacturing activity in recent decades. High-technology activity has gravitated to many large urban centers, but the most pronounced associations today

MANUFACTURING ACTIVITY DEFINITIONS

Value-added/Employment

Value-added by manufacture is an excellent measure of the importance of manufacturing activity in an area. It is defined as the difference in the dollar cost of producing a product (raw materials, power, labor, etc.) and the value of the finished product. The value-added measure is preferred over figures for employment or capital investment because some industries are very labor-intensive, while others are more automated, and each of these measures can be misleading. For example, the apparel industry employs many persons per unit of production, while the oil-refining industry is more heavily capitalized and automated. Comparing only employment figures for the two industries, therefore, might understate the importance of oil refining vis-à-vis apparel manufacture. Value-added figures, on the other hand, give a more balanced perspective on the importance of the product in the economy.

High Technology

Although a precise definition of high technology activity is not possible, it is possible to distinguish activities on the basis of their employment profile. The U.S. Department of Labor has developed three categories:

1. Research and development (R&D) spending in relation to sales is twice the industry average. This definition identifies theory-driven firms with a heavy emphasis on R&D, such as biotech and computer development.

2. Firms employing a greater-than-average proportion of engineers and scientists and a ratio of R&D spending equal to or above average. This definition is not as restrictive as above and identifies firms that manufacture products as opposed to R&D.

3. Firms with a science and engineer work force proportion 1.5 times the industry average. This definition is the broadest of the three and is general enough to include firms producing high technology items for the mass market.

---

occur in the silicon valley of the San Jose metropolitan area south of San Francisco (Figure 7-7) and in the greater Boston area (see later section).

In recent years the transition to a postindustrial society brought declines to traditional heavy industry strongholds such as Cleveland and Milwaukee. Manufacturing job losses, in fact, led to economic stagnation in the Middle West and Northeast in the 1970s, but restructuring involving the transformation of economies to a service base, adding a high-technology manufacturing sector, heavy capital reinvestment, and downsizing traditional activity restored competitiveness in most areas by the dawn of the 1990s.

Pred's Model of Urban–Industrial Growth

The growth incentive created by manufacturing expansion in the United States in the late 1800s prompted Allan Pred to describe it in the context of *circular and cumulative causation.* This conceptualization, originally developed by Myrdal to explain the economic development process in an underdeveloped nation, captured the essence of the urban growth syndrome. The Pred model posits a dual set of reinforcing chain reactions, as shown in Figure 7-4. Central to this process of growth is the *multiplier effect.*

The multiplier effect shown in Figure 7-4 illustrates the priming effect created by increases in local demand for goods and services that initiate the growth process. This demand emanates from both the manufacturing facility itself and the purchases of its employees. These purchases create additional jobs in the service sector as well as additional demand for the manufactured good as money flows through the economy. In turn, a new population-size threshold occurs as the city grows. As industry expands, greater opportunities for new innovations unfold, adding to the potential for growth as the outer loop of Figure 7-4 shows. The possibility also exists for a new spin-off industry related to the first firm

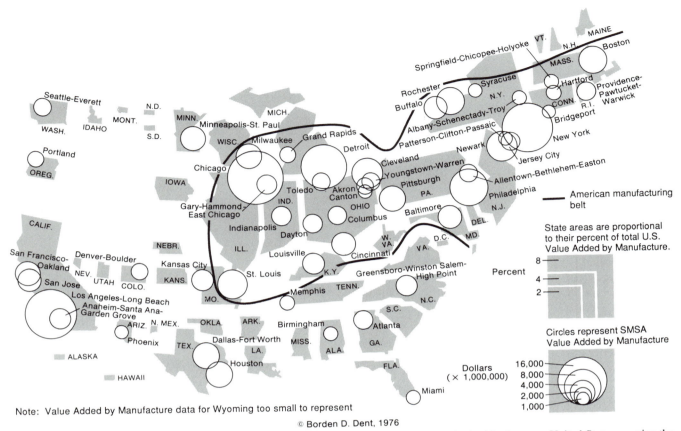

Note: Value Added by Manufacture data for Wyoming too small to represent

© Borden D. Dent, 1976

Figure 7-6. American Manufacturing Belt. First identified in 1919, the manufacturing belt in the Northeastern United States remains the core area of manufacturing activity in the country, but has declined in dominance since World War II. The top 6 of 10 manufacturing centers in the country today are identified with the manufacturing belt. *Source:* Redrawn with permission of Borden D. Dent.

The Emergence of the U.S. Urban–Industrial Economy

Whereas only two cities in the country, New York and Philadelphia, had more than 25,000 manufacturing employees in 1860, the size and scope of the urban–industrial machine changed dramatically in the United States immediately thereafter. First, the needs of the Civil War drove the demand for war material, and thereafter, growing markets, technological advancements, and greater capital resources interacted to generate expansion. Manufacturing began to grow in the interior faster than in the older coastal centers. Interior river hubs and emerging rail centers benefited the most from this expansion. In fact, railroad transportation

crossroads cities became the important industrial centers in the late nineteenth century.

The rail-hub function served Chicago most dramatically. In terms of value added, industrial output in Chicago zoomed from $5 million in 1869 to $283 million in 1890, giving it third place in the United States, behind only New York and Philadelphia. Chicago's 300,000 industrial workers displaced second-place Philadelphia in manufacturing employment in 1900 (Table 7-3). The number of industrial workers in Chicago actually doubled in a short six-year span, 1884–1890, rising from 105,000 to 210,000.

The dramatic increase in value-added by manufacture (see Box) figures for Chicago in the period 1860–1890 tell an even more dramatic story (Table 7-2). By 1890, five cities exceeded $100 million in value-added, each having grown rapidly in the previous 30 years, but none experienced the whopping 50-fold expansion that Chicago registered. Several cities with a smaller initial

TABLE 7-2
Value-Added by Manufacture in Major Cities, 1860, 1890, and 1982 ($ in millions)

	1860		1890		1982	
	$	Rank	$	Rank	$	Rank
New York	92	1	612	1	61,548	1
Philadelphia	70	2	298	2	21,161	5
Chicago	5	7	283	3	36,363	3
St. Louis	9	4	120	4	—	—
Boston	18	3	118	5	17,529	7
Baltimore	9	5	76	6	—	—
Pittsburgh	6	6	64	7	—	—
San Francisco	2	8	64	8	26,315	4
Cleveland	2	9	53	9	12,804	10
Detroit	2	10	40	10	18,381	6
Los Angeles	—	—	—	—	54,168	2
Houston	—	—	—	—	16,946	8
Dallas	—	—	—	—	14,691	9

Source: Allan R. Pred, *The Spatial Dynamics of U.S. Urban Industrial Growth: 1800–1914*, MIT Press, Cambridge, Mass., 1966, p. 47. Copyright © 1966 by the Massachusetts Institute of Technology. Used by permission. *Census of Manufacturers, 1982.*

base also rose dramatically, including Pittsburgh, San Francisco, Cleveland, and Detroit. Shifts in population ranks from 1860 to 1910 provide further evidence of the strong association between population growth and manufacturing expansion (Table 7-4). Emerging manufacturing centers such as Chicago, Cleveland, Pittsburgh, Detroit, and Milwaukee all moved up in rank, while the former leaders, the coastal port and river cities such as New Orleans, Cincinnati, Louisville, and Charleston, lost significant ground.

Metropolitan Industrial Mix

The mix of manufacturing in most metropolitan areas is remarkably diverse, substantiating the circular and cumulative growth conceptualization. In Chicago, for example, the top five industries in 1972 each contributed about 12–14 percent of total metropolitan value-added totals, indicating that no one activity predominated.

Manufacturing activity in New York City, while also demonstrating considerable diversity, is skewed in favor of the printing and publishing and apparel industries. Second-ranking Los Angeles, primarily a trans-

Figure 7-7. Silicon Valley High Technology Complex. The roots of this high technology complex, which specializes in electronics activity, lie with spin-offs from military contracts held by Stanford University in Palo Alto for weaponry research in World War II. Note the quality of design and landscaping in this low density setting of 1- and 2-story buildings. (Steve Proehl)

TABLE 7-3
Manufacturing Employment in Major Cities, 1860–1900 (thousands)[a]

1860	Employees	1880	Employees	1900	Employees
New York	106	New York	282	New York	511
Chicago	—	Chicago	79	Chicago	298
Philadelphia	99	Philadelphia	186	Philadelphia	266
		St. Louis	42	St. Louis	93
		Boston	59	Boston	81
		Baltimore	56	Baltimore	85
		Pittsburgh	43	Pittsburgh	98
		Cleveland	—	Cleveland	64
		San Francisco	28	San Francisco	46
				Detroit	51
				Louisville	33

[a]Cities with more than 25,000 manufacturing employees are listed; cities are ranked according to 1900 population size.

Source: Allan R. Pred, *The Spatial Dynamics of U.S. Urban Industrial Growth: 1800–1914,* MIT Press, Cambridge, Mass., 1966, p. 114. Copyright © 1966 by the Massachusetts Institute of Technology. Used by permission.

portation equipment manufacturer, also has two activities dominating its mix: aircraft and automobile assembly. To a lesser extent, Dallas–Fort Worth is also a transportation equipment center, supplemented by a strong electric and electronic machinery component. Houston stands out as an important chemical-energy center. The Greensboro/Winston-Salem/High Point area, lying in the core of the Carolina Piedmont manufacturing complex, is identified relatively equally with textiles, furniture and fixtures, electrical machinery, food products, and chemicals. These diversified areas also have an advantage in withstanding economic downturns compared to those that rely on a single sector—e.g., Detroit or Flint, Michigan, with their automobile emphases.

Industrial Restructuring

A massive restructuring of the U.S. economy has been under way over the past 30 years—a transition as fundamental as the Industrial Revolution itself some 200 years ago. On the one hand, the knowledge-intensive service economy is certainly creating a new city-building era as discussed in Chapter 2, and on the other hand, a restructuring process is reordering the traditional manufacturing economy. In many ways, labeling the current restructuring process a transition to a postindustrial economy is misleading and only partially accurate. To be sure, over two-thirds of Americans now work in the service economy, but just as importantly, high-technology activity represents a major industrial undertaking and a major portion of the high-order management/administrative function occurring in cities today involves firms engaged in manufacturing activities (Figure 7-8).

TABLE 7-4
Cities with a Significant Change in Population Rank, 1860–1910

	1860 Rank	1910 Rank	Net Change in Rank
Increase in Rank			
Chicago	8	2	+6
Cleveland	19	6	+13
Pittsburgh	15	8	+7
Detroit	17	9	+8
Milwaukee	18	12	+6
Decrease in Rank			
New Orleans	5	14	−9
Cincinnati	6	13	−7
Louisville	10	22	−11
Albany	11	44	−33
Charleston	20	77	−57
Mobile	25	90	−65

Source: Allan R. Pred, *The Spatial Dynamics of U.S. Urban Industrial Growth: 1800–1914,* MIT Press, Cambridge, Mass., 1966, p. 47. Copyright © 1966 by the Massachusetts Institute of Technology. Used by permission.

Figure 7-8. Changes in the Manufacturing/Service Employment Mix in the United States. As the post-industrial service economy gained momentum in the 1970s, a fundamental change occurred in the manufacturing/service employment mix. While the biggest shifts occurred in the northeast, where there was a decline in manufacturing employment, the modest gains in manufacturing employment in the rest of the country were far overshadowed by service economy growth. *Source:* Modified after Allen J. Scott, *Metropolis: From the Division of Labor to Urban Form,* University of California Press, Berkeley, 1988, p. 21. Used by permission.

Semantics aside, a major shift in the urban economy did occur in the 1960s and 1970s as traditional manufacturing activity entered a crisis stage and a new economic order emerged. Plant closures and layoffs occurred in the textile, steel, and automobile industries, among others, resulting in net employment and population losses in several metropolitan areas. Why did this occur? A Marxist interpretation of this economic restructuring suggests that excesses associated with industrial capitalism sowed the seeds of instability. Insight into this process can be gained by examining the role of labor in industrial output and by examining the traditional structure of the *fordist* industrial system itself.[14]

Fordism refers to the system of production developed by Henry Ford in the automobile industry, which later came to dominate manufacturing processes in all sectors of the economy—indeed, in all lines of business, including service activities. This system breaks down and routinizes various operations in the fabrication process and uses assembly-line and mass production processes to facilitate efficient production.

Economies of scale in the production process occur by standardizing output and specializing work tasks. By automating the production process, the role of labor becomes a less intensive part of the manufacturing process and more routine in nature. Labor unions have responded to this tendency by bargaining for protective work rules and higher wage levels.

The fordist industrial era spanned the 1920–1970 era during the heyday of traditional industrial dominance of the manufacturing belt in the U.S. economy. Coupled with fordism, scientific management principles, often referred to as "Taylorism," after its namesake Frederick Taylor, led to unprecedented industrial growth in the Western world in the post-World War II era.[15] Scientific management strategies led to the cre-

---

[14]Allen J. Scott, *Metropolis: From the Division of Labor to Urban Form,* University of California Press, Berkeley, 1988.

[15]Frederick W. Taylor, *The Principle of Scientific Management,* Harper, New York, 1947; rev. ed. Norton, New York, 1967.

ation of middle-management staff positions in industry to coordinate more efficient production strategies.

> Underlying this wave of growth were new sources of energy and new methods of production. These methods, which included the introduction of "scientific management" or "Taylorism" and the flow-line principles of Henry Ford, were particularly important in the newly developing consumer goods industries, and they raised labor productivity so that real wages and profits could rise simultaneously. . . . Consequently, workers found their incomes and jobs were more secure and they were able to purchase the new commodities either directly or through the growing number of lending institutions.[16]

Over time, this growth cycle slowed as opportunities for greater productivity declined.

> The reasons for the ending of the wave of growth in Western Europe and America lie mainly in the exhaustion of the possibilities for raising labor productivity and profitability within the fordist labor processes in the production of mass private consumption goods.[17]

More intense international competition exacerbated the situation by squeezing profits and creating an excess supply of goods. In response, some businesses collapsed financially, some scaled back operations, and other operations were relocated to cheaper, peripheral production sites within the United States in the South, or to Mexico or other overseas locations. Pressure for more automation in existing plants accompanied this process, further displacing labor.

Given these circumstances, conditions existed for the establishment of a new economic order, the coming of the so-called *post-fordist* era. Both new and traditional industry experienced this transition. The restructuring that occurred in the manufacturing belt and the expansion of high-technology centers, such as the silicon valley in California, illustrate the process. The vertical integration of firms, wherein all stages of production, from raw material sourcing to assembly and marketing of the finished product, traditionally occurred as an integrated process, gave way to the *vertical disintegration* of business. This term refers to the breakup of the traditional firms by either buying components from other specialized independent producers or by subcontracting specialized operations to save labor costs and take advantage of specialized skills. This process, in part, reflected what has been

labeled an *economy of scope*, wherein particular businesses specialize in a particular know-how and serve as suppliers of a specialized product to several firms. In this way, the end user firm can save costs and time by buying products from a more specialized firm, a process often labeled *outsourcing*. Flexible manufacturing production techniques and just-in-time manufacturing systems, which demand more flexible manufacturing schedules, reinforce the advantage of *outsourcing* parts.[18] Flexible manufacturing techniques involve moving computer-driven machine tools and automated fabricating machines to the factory floor so that changes in product output can be changed rapidly. Just-in-time manufacturing systems refer to computer driven production processes that screen and order parts as needed eliminating the need for large warehouse inventories. Frequently, independent producers supplying specialized parts are nonunion businesses and much smaller operations than the buyers to whom they sell goods.

Manufacturing activity is still clustered in this system, but more independent units and subcontractors exist in such an environment. Often, this activity occurs in the suburbs or urban fringe rather than in the central city. Newer high-technology areas also demonstrate this dispersion of facilities, and it is also an emerging trend with more traditional industries, such as the automobile industry, which rely today on more subcontractors.

HIGH TECHNOLOGY

Having discussed recent changes in the national economy in conceptual terms, it is now appropriate to discuss high-technology activity in more detail and to examine more specifically the challenges and uncertainties associated with restructuring a traditional economy, as has happened in the past 20 years in New England.

High-technology firms place far more emphasis on research and development (R&D) than traditional manufacturers (see Box for high technology definition).

The silicon valley (Santa Clara valley) south of San Francisco in the San Jose area is the best example in the world of a high technology region as mentioned earlier. As elsewhere, that high technology area benefits from the presence of a nearby research university

[16]Allen J. Scott and Michael Storper, *Production, Work, Territory*, Allen & Unwin, Boston, 1986, pp. 249–250.
[17]Ibid., p. 250.
[18]Ibid., p. 252.

TABLE 7-5
Selected High-Technology Centers in the United States

Name	Location	Nearby Research University
Silicon Valley	San Jose, Mountain View, Sunnyvale, Palo Alto, Cupertino, Milipitas, Santa Clara	Stanford
Route 128, I-495 "A.I. Alley" (artificial intelligence)	Boston	MIT
Research Triangle	Raleigh, Durham, Chapel Hill	N.C. State, Duke, University of North Carolina, Chapel Hill
"Silicon Prairie"	Dallas–Austin corridor	University of Texas at Austin
"Bionic Valley"	Salt Lake City	University of Utah
Route 1 "Silicon Valley East"	Princeton, N.J.	Princeton University
Space Coast	Orlando	Florida Tech University
Peachtree Corners "Technology Alley"	Atlanta	Georgia Institute of Technology
"Silicon Desert"	Phoenix	Arizona State University

Source: Table adopted from *Silicon Valley Fever* by Everett M. Rogers and Judith K. Larsen. Copyright ©1984 by Basic Books, Inc. Reprinted by Permission of Basic Books, a division of HarperCollins Publishers Inc.

(Table 7-5). The roots of the silicon valley high-technology complex, which specializes in electronics activity, lie with the spin-offs from military contracts, held by Stanford University in Palo Alto, for weaponry research in World War II.

In addition to electronics goods and miliary weaponry, a host of other high-technology fields also exist, including pharmaceuticals, chemicals, biotechnology, medicine, genetic engineering, telecommunications, robotics, and space technology, among others. In fact, these high-technology aspects are involved in nearly every industrial grouping today.

As we have noted, firms in the post-fordist economy operate much differently than they did in the past. Automated machine tools and robots have replaced the line worker on the factory floor in the traditional factory. Pittsburgh, Buffalo, and Cincinnati, among others, have shifted their economies to a new high-technology base to offset earlier losses. Growth industries in those areas today include robotics, electronics, and flexible manufacturing systems.

Boston and the New England economy illustrate the transitions that occurred in the past 20 years in the rustbelt to create a new high-technology base. After decades of declines and losses in the textile, shoe, and related manufacturing industries, New England yearned for a new economic base. For years, the region suffered from a lack of cheap energy sources, such as oil or coal. The high cost of labor also deterred manufacturing investment. But in the high-technology era, former handicaps became assets.

New England suddenly became a lower-cost environment in which to recruit a highly skilled labor force for the high-technology industry. An excellent education system, from preschool through the university level, the favorable regulatory atmosphere on the part of government, and good labor–management relations gave the area a comparative advantage for high-technology growth in the 1980s.[19] When coupled with the presence of venture capital and entrepreneurs eager to apply new technology to the work place, all the critical ingredients came together to generate jobs in an array of fields such as computers, software, artificial intelligence, biotechnology, electronics, medical equipment, plastics, and defense apparatus.

The catalytic impact of the traditional applied focus of the Massachusetts Institute of Technology (MIT) in the process cannot be overlooked. The university had earlier spun off many companies dating to the turn of

[19]David R. Lampe, ed., *The Massachusetts Miracle*. MIT Press, Cambridge, Mass., 1988.

the century, including Arthur D. Little, Raytheon, and Polaroid. World War II stimulated the research and development industry in the region with the influx of federal dollars to assist with the war effort. Among the firms dating to this era, one finds the Lincoln Laboratory, Draper Labs, and the MITRE Corporation. Later, Data General, Digital Equipment, Prime, and Wang computers came to represent the most robust minicomputer production concentration in the country. Defense and space-related work connected to NASA also evolved in the area, along with biotechnology firms.

In the period 1975–1983, high-technology jobs increased by 47 percent in Massachusetts. Between 1950 and 1986, no fewer than 400 new high-technology firms emerged in Massachusetts, employing over 175,000 persons. The Route 128 and I-495 technology corridors in suburban Boston benefited tremendously from this expansion. *Producer services* tied to high-technology firms, including data services, management consulting, software, advertising, and public relations activities, grew even faster, especially in the Boston suburbs.

This growth process received widespread scrutiny during the 1988 presidential campaign. Governor Michael Dukakis of Massachusetts, the Democratic presidential candidate, became associated with the "Massachusetts Miracle" and it became a model for other areas to emulate. As elsewhere, small business created the most new jobs in this era. In 1983, 88 percent of the business establishments in Massachusetts had fewer than 20 employees. Such statistics have been used to illustrate the strength and importance of the entrepreneurial spirit to the U.S. economy.

The restructuring of the economy of Lowell, Massachusetts, from a textile-dominated manufacturing past to an electronics-driven economy for the 1990s provides another perspective on economic change.[20] This reindustrialization program received a boost from an extensive training program for labor funded by several governmental agencies. The existing buildings and infrastructure available in Lowell, as in many other New England towns, provided an excellent resource base for the new industry. Renovated textile mills, for example, provide excellent facilities for computer and electronics manufacturers (Figure 7-9).

Notwithstanding the textbook example quality of the redevelopment of the Massachusetts economy, and the tremendous impact of high-technology activity on local economies in New England and elsewhere, the shallow staying power of this segment of the economy became painfully evident by the end of the 1980s. Saturation of product in the computer industry led to declining sales, global competition grew in the computer field, layoffs related to defense industry research increased as the Cold War came to a close, and the high cost of doing business in New England, including high taxes, came back to haunt the area.

A severe recession gripped the region by the dawn of the 1990s and the Dukakis administration came to a close, leaving behind a massive state budget deficit. Analysts suggested, however, that this downturn would be temporary, as "the north-east's underlying strengths remain. It has a well-educated work force, underpinned by the country's best higher-education institutions. It is well-placed to benefit from the export boom that America must go through to correct its trade deficit, especially if it is directed to a newly-resurgent Europe."[21]

SUMMARY AND CONCLUSION

Urban growth remains an enigma in many ways, because it is difficult to explain even though we can observe and monitor its presence. In earlier times, we accounted for it simply on the basis of the sale of goods outside the community, which would in turn bring money into the market to support the expansion of that activity, and/or create conditions favorable to creating other employment opportunities. These economic base interpretations did not explain why some cities grew much larger than others, or why development occurred unevenly. Growth pole theory partially overcame the latter problems by emphasizing the role of larger urban markets as growth leaders and conceptualized an uneven development process as well as the conditions for decentralization of activity.

The most pervasive and historically sound notion of why development occurs relates to the connection between manufacturing activity and urban growth. The expansion of industrial output in the late nineteenth and early twentieth centuries, for example, has been associated with the strongest and most widespread city-building era in the history of civilization. Pred's model of urban–industrial growth captures this connection

[20]Patricia M. Flynn, "Technological Change, the 'Training Cycle' and Economic Development," in John Rees, ed., *Technology, Regions, and Policy*, Roman & Littlefield, Totowa, N.J., 1986, pp. 282–308.

[21]"The Boom That Went Away," *The Economist*, May 5, 1990, p. 30.

Figure 7-9. **New Life for the Old Mill.** This renovated textile mill in Lowell, Massachusetts, now houses the offices of the Wannalancet Office and Technology Center. This shift in uses reflects the restructuring of the New England economy from a low technology to a high technology base. (Courtesy of Wannalancit Office and Technology Center and James Higgins).

very convincingly. Even the transition from the industrial to postindustrial age, or the shift from the fordist to the post-fordist economic system, has slowed neither the pace of urban growth nor the massive internal restructuring of growth within the metropolitan area.

The reason for the continuing strong association between urban growth and economic development lies in the ongoing need for the clustering of activity to take advantage of skilled labor pools, markets, and information. The administrative control function in modern society, in fact, assumes a much more important role in coordinating and directing business activity, and it remains highly concentrated in larger metropolitan markets. The strong tie between this activity and the banking/finance industry and other producer services accounts for this urban connection. In conclusion, the future for the growth of larger, if more decentralized, metropolitan areas remains strong. Even in an era of improved, instantaneous electronic communication, clustering of activity promotes and stimulates economic development.

In the next chapter, we will examine the role of cities as service centers that provide goods and services to the market areas they serve. Central place theory provides the guiding principle to unraveling the complex pattern of city size and spacing. The implications of this theory for understanding the location of retail and service activity in the city, among others, run deep, not to mention regional planning implications.

Suggestions for Further Reading

Brecher, Charles, and Raymond Horton. *Setting Municipal Priorities, 1990*, New York University Press, New York, 1989.

Brotchie, J., et al. *The Spatial Impact of Technological Change*, Croom Helm, London, 1987.

Cronon, William. *Nature's Metropolis: Chicago and the Great West*. W. W. Norton and Co., New York, 1991.

Friedmann, John. *Urbanization, Planning and Regional Development*, Sage Publications, Los Angeles, 1972.

Goodall, Brian. *The Economics of Urban Areas*, Pergamon, New York, 1972.

Hamilton, F. E., and G. J. R. Linge, eds. *Spatial Analysis, Industry and the Industrial Environment*, Vol. 1, *Industrial Systems*, Wiley, New York, 1979.

Hansen, Niles O. *Growth Centers and Regional Development*. Free Press, New York, 1972.

Hartshorn, Truman A., and John Alexander. *Economic Geography*, 3rd ed., Prentice Hall, Englewood Cliffs, N.J., 1988.

Henderson, J. Vernon. *Urban Development: Theory, Fact, and Illusion*, Oxford University Press, New York, 1988.

Hepworth, Mark. *Geography of the Information Economy*, Guilford Press, New York, 1990.

Hoover, Edgar. *The Location of Economic Activity*, McGraw-Hill, New York, 1948.

Isard, Walter. *Location and Space-Economy*, Wiley, New York, 1956.

Isard, Walter. *Methods of Regional Analysis*, MIT Press, Cambridge, Mass., 1960.

Jacobs, Jane. *The Economy of Cities*, Random House, New York, 1969.

Jacobs, Jane. *Cities and the Wealth of Nations*, Random House, New York, 1984.

Kuklinski, A. R., ed. *Growth Poles and Growth Centers in Regional Planning*, Mouton, Paris, 1972.

Lampe, David R., ed. *The Massachusetts Miracle*, MIT Press, Cambridge, Mass., 1988.

Markusen, Ann. *Profit Cycles, Oligipoly, and Regional Development*, MIT Press, Cambridge, Mass., 1985.

Markusen, Ann, et al. *High Tech America*, Allen & Unwin, Boston, 1986.

Noyelle, Thierry J. *Beyond Industrial Dualism: Market and Job Segmentation in the New Economy*, Westview Press, Boulder, Colo., 1986.

Noyelle, Thierry, and Thomas Stanback. *The Economic Transformation of American Cities*, Allanheld Osmun, Totowa, N.J., 1983.

Pred, Allan R. *The Spatial Dynamics of U.S. Urban Industrial Growth: 1800–1914*, MIT Press, Cambridge, Mass. 1966.

Pred, Allan R. *City Systems in Advanced Economies*, Wiley, New York, 1977.

Sawers, Larry, and William Taff, eds. *Sunbelt/Snowbelt: Urban Development and Regional Restructuring*, Oxford University Press, New York, 1984.

Scott, Allen J. *Metropolis: From the Division of Labor to Urban Form*, University of California Press, Berkeley, 1988.

Scott, Allen J., and Michael Storper. *Production, Work, Territory*, Allen & Unwin, Boston, 1986, pp. 249–250.

Smith, Michael Peter, and Joe R. Feagin. *The Capitalist City: Global Restructuring and Community Politics*. Basil Blackwell, New York, 1987.

Taff, William, and Larry Sawers. *Marxism and the Metropolis*, Oxford University Press, New York, 1984.

Thompson, Wilbur. *A Preface to Urban Economics*, Johns Hopkins University Press, Baltimore, 1956.

Tiebout, Charles M. *The Community Economic Base Study*, Committee for Economic Development, New York, 1962.

8

CENTRAL PLACE THEORY*

Central place theory provides a conceptual mechanism for understanding the role of the city as a *service center*. When viewed as the focus of a complementary region or hinterland, the city becomes a supplier of goods and services to the surrounding countryside (tributary area). It depends on the inbound cash flow produced by the spending of the hinterland population to support the complement of goods and services offered. The city and its surrounding complementary region therefore constitute a mutually interdependent system.

CITIES AS SERVICE CENTERS

A German geographer, Walter Christaller, recognized the economic relationship between cities and their hinterlands. He developed an economic theory to provide an explanation for the size, spacing, location, and functional content of cities. Christaller tested his theoretical notions empirically in southern Germany as a part of his doctoral dissertation.[1] Christaller, not satisfied with the previous explanations for the location of cities that traced the history of a unique city from its inception and treated location as a consequence of physical characteristics, looked for more satisfying answers. While not denying the importance of physical features in the siting of cities, Christaller thought such explanations of city locations missed a vital point.

People congregate together in cities to exchange commodities and ideas. Cities exist for economic reasons; many are the articulation points that facilitate the exchange of goods and services. As such, Christaller viewed his theory as a complement to the earliest location theories of Johann von Thünen on agricultural land use around market centers (discussed in Chapter 11).[2] Christaller's theory addresses tertiary activities or the service sector of cities that, as we learned in Chapter 1, now represents the largest urban employment grouping. To understand Christaller's theory, it will first be necessary to introduce some important concepts related to the theory.

The Central Place

Christaller made it clear that not all settlements could be considered central places. A central place exists to provide goods and services to a surrounding hinterland population. There are some settlements for which a distribution center function is of little consequence.

*Chapter authored by Thomas L. Bell, University of Tennessee, Knoxville.

[1] Walter Christaller, *Die Zentralen Orte in Süddeutschland*, Gustav Fisher, Verlag, Jena, 1933; translated as *Central Places in Southern Germany*, by Carlisle W. Baskin, Prentice Hall, Englewood Cliffs, N.J., 1966.

[2] Peter Hall, ed., *Von Thünen's Isolated State*, Pergamon, London, 1966.

Christaller placed mining settlements and resort places in this category. Such resource or amenity-bound settlements did not depend primarily on a hinterland population for their support, and so these specialized function places were not addressed by his theory. Similarly, manufacturing centers do not qualify as central places.

Assumptions

In order to control for any factor of central place location other than economic forces, Christaller assumed the countryside was a flat, homogeneous plain in which there were no barriers to movement, thus permitting uninhibited travel in all directions. Christaller also assumed a dispersed rural farm population regularly spaced over this uniform territory and an ideal spacing of settlements. It can be shown mathematically that the greatest dispersion between points (individuals, farmsteads, central places) is achieved when each point is located at the vertex of an equilateral triangle.[3] Mathematicians refer to this optimal spacing as *close-packing*.

In central place theory, there are also two assumptions made about human behavior. The first states that consumers will always purchase from the closest central place that offers a particular good. The second states that whenever threshold purchasing power for a good is obtained at a central place, an entrepreneur will offer the good; whenever demand for a good drops below threshold, the good will be no longer offered.[4] These assumptions imply that actors are economically rational in their behavior and have perfect knowledge of all shopping alternatives. Consumers always minimize distance by patronizing the closest central place opportunity, and entrepreneurs have such knowledge of the business environment that they will make rapid adjustments to changes in purchasing power.

Centrality

Christaller recognized that two settlements of exactly the same population did not necessarily function as equally important central places. Population size is positively correlated with the importance of a settlement as a distribution center (central place), but the correlation is far from perfect. The term *centrality* was introduced to distinguish between the size of a place and its central place importance. In Christaller's empirical test of the theory in southern Germany, the number of telephone connections in a place became a surrogate of centrality. When Christaller developed his theoretical notions, very few private telephones existed in southern Germany. Telephones were used almost exclusively by businesses. Christaller therefore argued that this surrogate would be a better measure of central place importance (centrality) than the population of the settlement. Measures such as sales tax receipts, the number of retail and wholesale stores, or retail employment would be more appropriate modern surrogates of centrality.

An important economic concept, *threshold*, refers to the amount of purchasing power required in the region to support a person engaged in a tertiary business activity. Threshold has been defined as the minimum amount of monetary support (in the form of sales) necessary for such an entrepreneur to break even on business investments.[5] Merchants, wholesalers, and professionals have a certain amount of overhead cost, including rent on space and inventories, that must be paid in order to remain in business. The money spent by consumers on the purchase of the business's merchandise or services must be at least sufficient to recoup the entrepreneur's investment or the business will fail.

Some goods (e.g., groceries) are purchased with such regularity by consumers that small stores carrying a limited selection of these items can survive if they are conveniently located (accessible) to a consumer market. Goods that are frequently replenished are called *low-order* goods. The emergence of the franchised convenience grocery store is a recent retailing response to such demand (Figure 8-1). In the same manner, the small, locally owned, corner grocery store ("mom and pop" store), in older urban neighborhoods and small

---

[3]The dispersion of points may also be illustrated by a physical analogue model. If small magnets are placed on corks and the corks in turn are placed in a tub of water, the repulsion of opposite poles of the magnets will force the corks to disperse as far as possible from each other. Equilibrium is achieved when all the corks form a pattern such that they are at the vertices of equilateral triangles. See Peter Gould, "The New Geography," *Harper's*, 238 (March 1969), 91–100.

[4]For a more detailed analysis of the deductive logic of central place theory, see Gerard Rushton, "Postulates of Central Place Theory and Properties of Central Place Systems," *Geographical Analysis*, 3 (1971), 140–156.

[5]For a discussion of threshold and its relationship to Christaller's concept of the range of a good, see Brian J. L. Berry and W. L. Garrison, "A Note on Central Place Theory and the Range of a Good," *Economic Geography*, 34 (1958), 304–311.

Figure 8-1. Convenience Store. The franchised convenience store offers low order retail goods in a neighborhood setting. Convenience stores have a low threshold support level. These stores are the modern-day counterparts of the mom and pop corner grocery store. (The Southland Corporation)

towns, represents a similar lower order in the distribution channel. Retailers who distribute such low-order convenience goods have low threshold levels of economic support. More specialized items, such as appliances, automobiles, or furniture, would not be available in these local centers because they are high-order goods and require a large *threshold* support level.

High-order goods and services, such as jewelry, gifts, or tax consultants, are purchased less often and involve larger expenditures per trip in both time and money. For these reasons, such activities are usually offered only in larger cities. A large trade area is required to keep business volume at an acceptable level for these activities along with a high threshold support level.

Threshold, like centrality, is an easy concept to understand but difficult to measure. Monetary flows are replaced in most empirical tests of the theory by the number of customers because of the difficulty in obtaining billing data. In such cases, threshold is operationally defined as the minimum number of people needed for a central place activity to remain viable. An example of the number of persons required to support various activities is reported in Table 8-1. Berry and Garrison identified the number of persons required to support a variety of *central functions* ranging from filling stations (196) to health practitioners (1424) in Snohomish County, Washington, several decades ago.

A central function is a retail or service activity found in a service center. Central functions reflect current technology and behavioral situations. For example, the frozen-food locker mentioned in the table formerly provided an important role in smaller towns before the advent of the home freezer. Similarly, a fast-food franchise restaurant is not reported in the table because it is of more recent vintage.

Range of a Good

The threshold concept introduced by Berry and Garrison has a spatial corollary in Christaller's notion of the *range of a good* (Figure 8-2). The range refers to the market area for the good or, alternatively, the distance people travel to purchase a good. Travel distances to purchase low-order goods are generally much shorter than those for high-order goods.

Size and Spacing

Typically, five sizes or levels of communities exist in a central place system. The smallest of these, the *hamlet*, occurs most frequently. Moving up the hierarchy, one encounters a *village*, *town*, *city*, and *regional capital*. Most areas that we will study, such as the Middle West

TABLE 8-1
Central Functions and Threshold Sizes

Group	Central Function	Threshold Sizes	Group	Central Functions	Threshold Size
1	Filling stations	196	2 Cont'd.	Freight lines and storage	567
	Food stores	254		Veterinarians	579
	Churches	265		Apparel stores	590
	Restaurants and snack bars	276		Lumberyards	598
	Taverns	282		Banks	610
	Elementary schools	322		Farm implements	650
2	Physicians	380		Electric repair shops	693
	Real estate agencies	384		Florists	729
	Appliance stores	385		High schools	732
	Barbershops	386		Dry cleaners	754
	Auto dealers	398		Local taxi services	762
	Insurance agencies	409		Billiard halls and bowling	789
	Fuel oil dealers	419		Jewelry stores	827
	Dentists	426		Hotels	846
	Motels	430		Shoe repair shops	896
	Hardware stores	431		Sporting goods stores	928
	Auto repair shops	435		Frozen food lockers	938
	Fuel dealers (coal, etc.)	453	3	Sheet metal works	1076
	Drugstores	458		Department stores	1083
	Beauticians	480		Optometrists	1140
	Auto parts dealers	488		Hospitals and clinics	1159
	Meeting halls	525		Undertakers	1214
	Feed stores	526		Photographers	1243
	Lawyers	528		Public accountants	1300
	Furniture stores	546		Laundries and laundromats	1307
	Variety stores (5 & 10)	549		Health practitioners	1424

Source: Brian J.L. Berry and W.L. Garrison, "Functional Basis of the Central Place Hierarchy." *Economic Geography*, 34 (1958), 150.

of the United States, which has become a classic laboratory in which to study central place principles, were settled before the advent of the modern automobile. Settlements were therefore more closely spaced than we would expect if settled today. Hamlets were typically evenly spaced at a distance of 5–7 miles. Rural residents could comfortably make the round-trip to and from such a center by horse on a regular basis. Market areas for hamlets are shown in Figure 8-2. They would offer only low-order convenience goods such as groceries. The market, or trade area, for the hamlet is shown as both a circle and a hexagon in Figure 8-2. Note that the circle indicates either an overlap of trade

areas or an area not assigned, which would violate the principle that the consumer would travel to only a single center, which would be the closest, whereas the hexagon assigns the space completely without overlap or underlap. This situation is also illustrated in Figure 8-3.

CENTRAL PLACE MARKET AREA GEOMETRY

If central places are located at the vertices of equilateral triangles (i.e., maximum spatial dispersion), and the evenly distributed consumers always patronize the

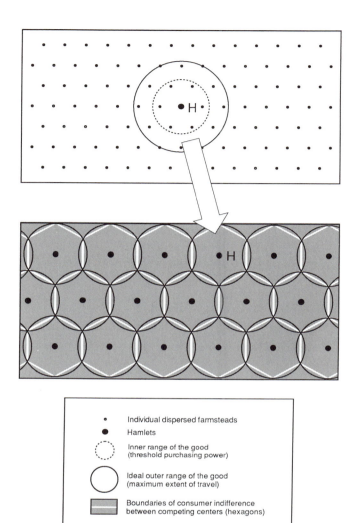

Figure 8-2. **Hamlet Market Areas.** Either hexagonal or circular market areas can be drawn to approximate the extent of the market area for the hamlet. The even spacing of the hamlet is evident.

closest central place, then we can deduce that the real market area will be a *hexagon*. The hexagon offers the best balance of geometric packing properties and most closely approximates the area of the ideal circular market area, as mentioned in the previous section.

If consumers each patronize the closest central place, the market-area boundary between any two central places can be determined by drawing a perpendicular bisector on an imaginary straight line connecting two central places. By successively drawing bisectors among pairs of central places, the whole region can be assigned to a given central place. Three of these perpendicular bisectors always meet together, forming a trade area boundary. The hexagonal shape of the market areas arises because of the interaction of (1) the initial conditions of the landscape (i.e., the triangular latticework of central places) and (2) the consumer behavior assumption (i.e., patronizing the closest place offering the good).

The Marketing Principle of Central Place Theory

To understand the hierarchy and spacing of settlements in Christaller's landscape, let us develop a system of three levels of central places offering goods with different thresholds (Figure 8-4). In this example, we will include hamlets, villages, and town-level central places. A farmers' cooperative commands the highest threshold value in our example and will locate in the town. A dry cleaner might be an example of an activity located in the village, and a general store plays a function that would be sited in the hamlet. Note that

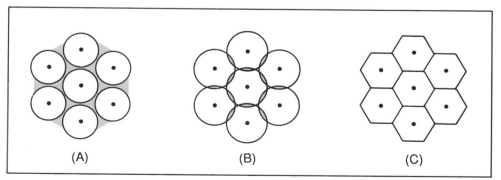

Figure 8-3. **Comparison of Circular and Hexagonal Trade Areas.** The hexagon offers the best balance of geometric packing properties (C), while the circle poses problems of either overlap (B) or underlap (A).

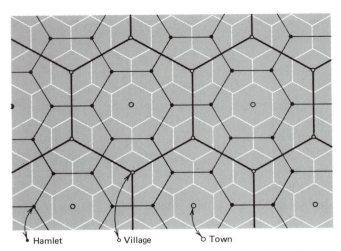

Figure 8-4. Central Place Hierarchy with Three Levels: The Hamlet, Village, and Town. Each place of a specific order is surrounded by six centers of the next lower size. The size and spacing of centers follows a regular pattern.

hamlet- and village-level funtions can also operate in the town, as each successively larger place also functions as a lower-order center. Notice also that places of lower order (e.g., hamlets and villages) in Figure 8-4 are more numerous over the landscape than higher-order places (towns) and that the distance between lower-order settlements is less than the distance between settlements of higher order. Each place of specific order is surrounded by six centers of the next lower size. The spacing arrangement makes intuitive sense. Parts of the United States have been shown to approximate the theoretical model, especially the agricultural Middle West. It is in such an area that the conditions of the theoretical model of central places are most closely approximated. John Brush, for example, found that the average distance between hamlets in an agricultural portion of southwestern Wisconsin was approximately 5.5 miles, the average distance between villages was 9.9 miles, and for towns it was 21.2 miles of separation.[6]

A five-level hierarchy of central places in southwestern Iowa appears in Figure 8-5. The Council Bluffs–Omaha area is indicated as a *regional capital* (the highest order). The second order of places, *cities*, is represented by Atlantic, Red Oak, and Glenwood. Consumer travel patterns to these and lower-order centers are shown in Figure 8-6. In this study area, rural

[6]John E. Brush, "The Hierarchy of Central Places in Southwestern Wisconsin," *Geographical Review*, 43 (1953), 308–402.

residents patronized all central place levels for lower-order goods such as groceries. The lines radiating from each community in Figure 8-6 are called *desire lines* because they show actual travel preferences of residents. The lines link up the patron's origin (home) with a destination (market center). By comparing shopping preferences for a variety of goods or services (groceries, lawyers, hospitals), it is possible to see how large centers gradually emerge as the dominant places for the more specialized goods and services. The overwhelming importance of Council Bluffs–Omaha as a destination for hospital services is shown by the desire lines focusing on the regional capital. Only Atlantic, Red Oak, and Harlan seem to be viable competitors for this type of service in the area.

Ordering Principles of Central Place Theory

Christaller stated that the hierarchical arrangement depicted in Figure 8-4 followed a *marketing principle* because each trade area at every level was as small as possible. The aggregate distance traveled by consumers to purchase central goods and services was at a minimum because of the existence of the maximum number of centers at each level. The marketing principle was also called the $K = 3$ system, where K refers to a constant. Market areas at a given level of the central place hierarchy are three times larger than the market areas of the next lower order in the $K = 3$ system. The distance between centers at a given level is equal to the square root of 3 times the distance between the centers immediately below them in the hierarchy in this system. Finally, the number of central places at each level of the hierarchy also follows the progression of "threes." If, for example, there were 2 cities within a particular study area, there would be 6 towns, 18 villages, and 54 hamlets.

The relationship between level in the hierarchy and market-area size can be illustrated by examining the difference in the market areas of two centers such as those in Figure 8-7A. Contained within a single town-level (higher-order) hexagon is one complete village-level (lower-order) hexagon plus one-third of the area of six other surrounding village-level hexagons. The higher-order trade area contains one complete lower-order trade area plus one-third of six surrounding lower-order trade areas. By adding up the equivalent

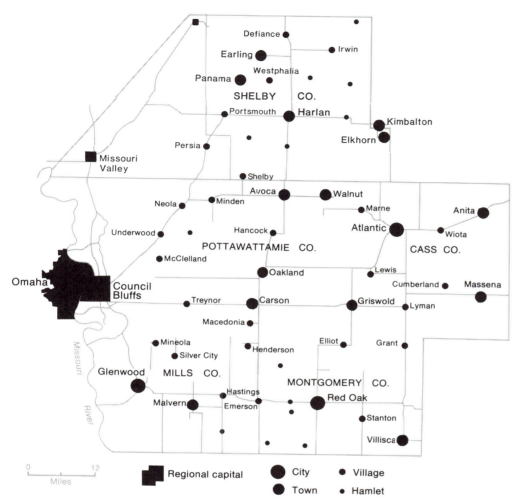

Figure 8-5.   Central Places in Southwest Iowa. A five-level central place hierarchy occurs in this market area. Note travel patterns to these centers, shown in Figure 8–6. *Source:* Brian J. L. Berry/John B. Parr, *Market Centers and Retail Location: Theory and Applications* ©1988, p. 4. Adapted by permission of Prentice Hall, Englewood Cliffs, New Jersey.

Figure 8-6.   Consumer Shopping Preferences in Southwest Iowa. The desire lines shown here for three different functions show increasing trip lengths for successively more specialized goods or services. *Source:* Brian J. L. Berry/John B. Parr, *Market Centers and Retail Location: Theory and Applications,* ©1988, p. 12. Adapted by permission of Prentice Hall, Englewood Cliffs, New Jersey.

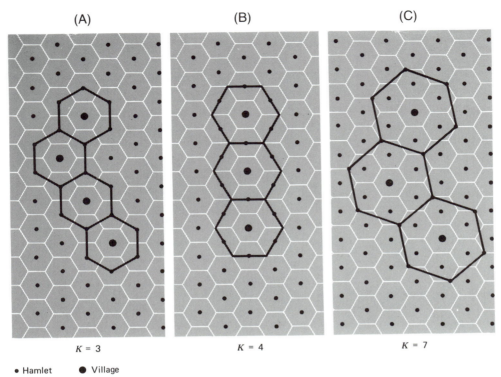

(A)   (B)   (C)

$K = 3$ $K = 4$ $K = 7$

● Hamlet   ● Village

Figure 8-7. **Building the Central Place Hierarchy According to Various Ordering Principles.** The K-3 system (A) corresponds to a marketing principle, the K-4 system (B) to a transportation principle, and K-7 arrangement (C) to an administrative principle.

lower-order trade areas incorporated within the higher-order center, one finds a sum of three.

$$1 + (1/3 \times 6) =$$
$$1 + \quad (2) \quad = 3$$

There are circumstances when the marketing principle ($K = 3$ system) is not the most advantageous spacing of settlements. Christaller described two other ordering principles, which he called the *transportation principle* ($K = 4$) shown in Figure 8-7B and the *administrative principle* ($K = 7$), depicted in Figure 8-7C. In the $K = 4$ system, market areas of a given level in the central place hierarchy are four times larger than the market areas of central places of the next lower order. In Figure 8-7B, the market area of each town-level center contains the equivalent of four village-level market areas. One complete village-level hexagon is contained within each town-level market area plus one-half of six other surrounding hexagons, or the equivalent of four village-level centers. This is calculated as before:

$$1 + (1/2 \times 6) =$$
$$1 + \quad (3) \quad = 4$$

Likewise, the $K = 7$ system depicted in Figure 8-7C contains seven complete village-level hexagons within the market area of each town-level center and the trade area of the higher-order center increases by a factor of seven:

$$1 + (5/6 \times 6) + (1/6 \times 6) =$$
$$1 + \quad (5) \quad + \quad (1) \quad = 7$$

In the administrative principle, the higher-order trade areas closely approximates the boundaries of the six surrounding lower-order trade areas so that the territory included in the higher-order trade area completely dominates that of the lower-order system. Lower-order centers are not assigned to several higher-order centers. This system is best for administrative or political purposes because it minimizes the jurisdictional problems of boundaries and maximizes the number of lower-order centers within the territorial control of a higher-order place as can be noted in Figure 8-7C.

Evidence supporting each of the central place order principles was found in Christaller's study area in southern Germany. In the $K = 4$ system, the village-level central places are located midway between the vertices of the town-level hexagon rather than at the vertices, as was the case in the *marketing principle* ($K = 3$). The hexagons themselves are rotated 45 degrees from the $K = 3$ arrangement to create this situation. Christaller said that the geometric spacing of the $K = 4$ system made it possible to interconnect a greater number of high-order places with straight-line transportation routes than was possible in the $K = 3$ system (where the lower-order centers are staggered). In regions where the minimization of transportation lines is important (e.g., the mountainous areas of southern Germany), the $K = 4$ system will be predominant, wherein higher-order places are arranged in linear fashion (see Figure 8-7B). Christaller found evidence of the $K = 7$ settlement pattern in areas of southern Germany where the patchwork quilt of the tiny principalities that made up the former Holy Roman Empire was especially influential.

ANOTHER CENTRAL PLACE THEORY: LÖSCH

Christaller's system was rigid. A town in his formulation *always* had all the goods present in a village. Some central place researchers contend that this ordering of the central place within the hierarchy is not as important as the tributary market area for the particular central place. One might, for example, find a dentist in a tiny hamlet if the exclusive trade area of that hamlet encompassed sufficient population to meet the threshold requirements for a dentist. For this reason it is more accurate to talk about the central place *theories* than to limit the discussion to Christaller's formulation of central place theory. The breadth of current central place applications demonstrates this point.

The German regional economist August Lösch developed a theory for the size and spacing of settlements that differed in many significant respects from the one derived earlier by Christaller.[7] Lösch also began his

theory with very simple initial conditions. Self-sufficient farmers were evenly dispersed in farmsteads (or agricultural villages) over a homogeneous plain. Lösch was also attempting to derive a theory in which economic forces explained the basic settlement pattern. But he differed from Christaller in his basic philosophy and this led to differences in the settlement pattern ultimately derived. Lösch was a socialist, and his main concern was to develop a pattern that maximized consumer welfare.

Christaller's rigid hierarchical arrangement of central places led to a condition in which entrepreneurs engaged in the distribution of particular goods or services could accrue excess profits solely because of their location within the settlement fabric. Lösch assumed that excess profits for entrepreneurs were inconsistent with the goal of consumer welfare maximization. He did not attempt to describe the *actual* pattern of central places in an economic landscape, but formulated a theory that would describe an *ideal* landscape. In this ideal environment, consumer travel required to obtain needed central goods and services would be minimized, while business profits would simultaneously be held to a level that returned only a normal profit from investment.

The Geometry of the Löschian Landscape

The three K-systems of Christaller's theory previously discussed were the three smallest market-area size arrangements posited in the Löschian version of the theory. Lösch developed a mathematical sequence that included several high-order K-systems (e.g., $K = 9$, $K = 12$, $K = 13$).

To eliminate the "tyranny of space" inherent in the Christaller hierarchy, Lösch allowed one central place to possess all the central goods and services present in the economic system. He called this privileged central place, with the highest degree of centrality, the "metropolis" of the economic landscape. All the hexagonally shaped market-area networks for each of the K-systems coincided at the metropolis; other centers offered fewer goods. The good with the lowest threshold value had a $K = 3$ distribution network, the next higher-order good had a $K = 4$ distribution network, and so on up through the K-system progression.

Rather than assuming that only one type of K-network operated in an area, Lösch considered that many operated simultaneously, each for a particular

---

[7]August Lösch, *The Economics of Location*, translated by W. H. Woglom and W. F. Stolper (originally published in 1939), Yale University Press, New Haven, Conn., 1954; reprinted by Wiley, New York, 1967.

good. Hence, he superimposed the networks. To locate central place service centers in his theoretical economic landscape, Lösch rotated these nets of hexagonally shaped *K*-systems about the metropolis of the economic landscape in such a way as to produce the least number of centers. This rotation created more higher-order centers in some sectors than others. The rotation of hexagonal nets produced twelve alternating 30-degree sectors radiating away from the metropolis of the economic landscape (Figure 8-8). One of the 30-degree sectors distributed mainly low-threshold goods. The transportation network (infrastructure) connecting central places in this sector was very poorly developed. Lösch called this the *city-poor* sector. Alternating with the six 30-degree city-poor sectors were six 30-degree *city-rich* sectors. Within the city-rich sectors, central places distributing higher-order goods were located. The transportation network was densely developed in these latter areas.

Functional Content of Löschian Central Places

Allowing each activity to be offered in central places of any order breaks the rigidity of the Christaller hierar-

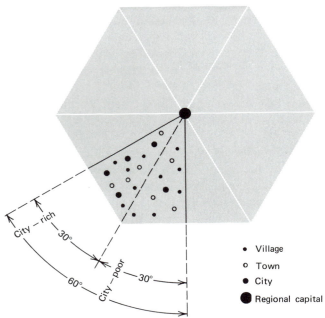

● Village
○ Town
● City
⬤ Regional capital

Figure 8-8. Löschian City-rich, City-poor Sectors. Lösch superimposed several networks and rotated the hexagonal nets about the landscape to produce the least number of centers. *Source:* Adapted with permission from August Lösch, *The Economics of Location,* © Gustav-Fischer (original *Die räumliche Ordnung der Wirtschaft*), Stuttgart, 3rd ed., 1962.

chy. The predictability of central place offerings also disappears.

The area-serving principle of Lösch may minimize excess profits, but it also discourages consumers from making multiple-purpose shopping trips. The typical bundle of goods that was present in the Christaller functional content hierarchy is not part of Lösch's theory.

CHRISTALLER AND LÖSCH COMPARED

The findings of the two theorists are vastly different, considering that they began with the same initial environment. It is quite likely that real-world central place systems contain elements of both theoretical principles. Recent evidence from a comparative study of central Iowa and southern Minnesota indicates that some activities, especially agricultural services, conform closely to the area-serving principle of Lösch, while others, most notably lower-order consumer goods that are purchased with regularity, conform closely to the hierarchical ordering principle of Christaller.[8] Table 8-2 summarizes the major differences between the central place theories of Christaller and Lösch.

MODIFICATIONS OF THE THEORY

The two versions of central place theory just discussed have stimulated considerable interest among scholars seeking a theoretical framework with which to interpret settlement patterns. Hundreds of articles purported to be "tests" of central place theory have been published.[9] Many studies have been conducted on settlement patterns in Europe and Asia as well as in North America.

Adding Realism to the Consumer Behavioral Postulate

Christaller assumed that consumers travel to the closest central place opportunity. If that were a realistic de-

[8]Thomas L. Bell, Stanley R. Lieber, and Gerard Rushton, "Clustering of Services in Central Places," *Annals of the Association of American Geographers,* 64 (1974), 214–225.

[9]See Brian J. L. Berry and Allan R. Pred, *Central Place Studies: A Bibliography of Theory and Applications,* Regional Science Research Institute, Philadelphia, 1964. Reprinted 1965 (with supplement through 1964 by H. G. Barnum, R. Kasperson, and S. Krucki).

TABLE 8-2
Christaller and Lösch Compared

Structure of Central Place Theory
A. Environment—Assumptions of uniformity
B. Behavior—1. Propositions regarding consumer spatial behavior
2. Propositions regarding entrepreneurial behavior
3. Assumptions regarding the linkages between goods

Christaller
A. Assumed initially uniform environment
B1. Demand invariant over space
B2. Order of goods defined by threshold levels
B3. Linkage between goods was cumulative and hierarchical

Lösch
A. Assumed initially uniform environment
B1. Allowed demand to vary through space
B2. Entrepreneurs to make only "normal" profits
B3. Linkages between goods ignored

Deduced Theorems
1. Uniform spacing of central places
2. Content hierarchy
3. Spatial hierarchy
4. Goods have distinctive levels of entry in centers

Deduced Theorems
1. City-rich and city-poor sectors (nonuniform spacing of centers)
2. No content hierarchy
3. No typical order of entry of goods in centers

Source: Thomas L. Bell.

scription of actual shopping behavior in North America today, then hamlets in many rural regions would still be the viable trade centers they were a half century ago, but they are not. The emergence of the automobile as a means of personal transportation and a vast interurban highway network have decreased travel times to more distant centers. Rural residents today can easily bypass a nearby hamlet or village in favor of shopping at more distant towns and cities using the same travel time formerly required to reach the local site. Rural consumers often perceive that larger central places offer better selection, quality, and lower prices than smaller centers. It is not surprising, therefore, that hamlets and villages have lost much of their retail function even though they may be stable in population or even growing.

The institution of rural free delivery (RFD) mail service during the 1930s, coupled with the wide application of mail-order catalog retailing, hastened the functional decline of hamlets.[10] As mail began to be delivered door to door, rural households no longer journeyed to town to pick up mail from the local post office. Before the advent of RFD, rural residents often

minimized their travel by purchasing needed supplies in the hamlet at the same time they picked up the mail. The supplies were normally low-order convenience goods and services that needed frequent replenishment (e.g., groceries, gasoline, agricultural products, and services). This type of shopping behavior is called a *multiple-purpose trip*. Because the multiple-purpose trip was the norm, the demise of the hamlet post office had significant repercussions on the hamlet's retail structure.

A Preference Structure Description of Consumer Behavior

If central place theory is to be useful for understanding modern settlement patterns, it must reflect actual behavior. It is realistic to assume that shopping behavior represents a trade-off between the size of a place and the distance that the consumer must travel to shop at the place. Specifying the exact nature of this trade-off is a problem.

Gerard Rushton developed a methodology that determines the *consumer preference* trade-off between central place size and the journey to shop for different central goods and services.[11] His technique treated

---

[10]See, for example, P. H. Landis, *The Growth and Decline of South Dakota Trade Centers 1901–1933*, Bulletin No. 279, South Dakota Agricultural Experiment Station, Huron, 1933; C. E. Lively, *Growth and Decline of Farm Trade Centers in Minnesota 1905–1930*, Bulletin No. 287, University of Minnesota Agricultural Experiment Station, St. Paul, 1932.

[11]Gerard Rushton, "The Scaling of Locational Preferences," in Kevin Cox and Reginald Golledge, eds., *Behavioral Problems in Geography: A Symposium*, Studies in Geography, No. 17, Department of Geography, Northwestern University, Evanston, Ill., 1969, pp. 197–227.

town size and distance as psychological stimuli scaled in the mind of the consumer. Using a sample of rural farm and nonfarm residents distributed throughout the state of Iowa, Rushton determined which central place was patronized for each of 86 different goods and services. He then generalized town-specific shopping information into a set of choice situations in which the sample population chose between different combinations of the two relevant stimuli (size and distance). When a town of a certain size range within the shopping radius of a household was present but not patronized, it was assumed that the consumer consciously made the choice to ignore that shopping opportunity.

The nature of the trade-off between the two stimuli varied among central goods and services in the Rushton study, but several generalizations regarding preference structures can be made. First, both distance and town size are relevant stimuli for consumer shopping behavior. This finding differs from the classic theory in which only distance is considered. Second, as consumers shop for progressively higher-order activities, they are more willing to bypass nearby small places for more distant larger centers. Third, consumer preference structures are fairly stable over both time and space.[12] Finally, the preference for larger, more distant shopping opportunities over their smaller, more proximate counterparts holds true only up to a certain critical size level. That is, given a choice between shopping at a town of 30,000 and an equidistant city of 200,000, the rural Iowa resident actually expresses a psychological preference for the former. Perhaps the potential of congestion, lack of available parking, and the perceived stress of the trip to a large city lead to the lower ratings of metropolitan centers by rural residents.

Spatial Implications of Consumer Preference Structures

Preference structures may be graphically represented as a family of consumer *indifference curves*.[13] The indifference curves (isosatisfaction lines) in Figure 8-9, based on Rushton's work, show combinations of the two stimuli for which a consumer is indifferent (equally

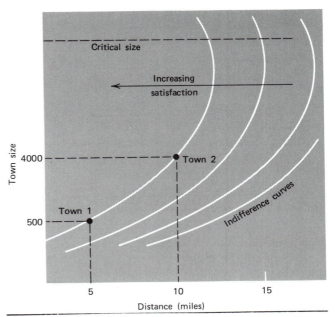

Figure 8-9. Consumer Preference Structure, after Rushton. A consumer would be equally satisfied to shop at Town 1, located 5 miles away, or at Town 2, 10 miles away. An isosatisfaction line to the left of another would be preferable because it would result in higher total satisfaction for the consumer. *Source:* Adapted by permission from the *Annals of the Association of American Geographers,* 59, 1959, pp. 391–400, Gerard Rushton.

satisfied). For example, a consumer would be equally satisfied to shop at Town 1 (population 500) located 5 miles away or at Town 2 (population 4000) located 10 miles away. Any isosatisfaction line to the left of another would be preferable because it would result in higher total satisfaction for the consumer.

What would market areas look like if a person shopped at the central place opportunity *highest* on his or her preference structure?[14] To answer this question, a model is needed that is capable of allocating any consumer to the central place opportunity with the highest preference structure value. When such an allocation model was devised and applied to a study area in central Iowa and compared with a Thiessen polygon allocation (which assigns all areas to the nearest place),[15] dramatic differences were found between the Thiessen polygon delimitation and the preference

[12]Gerard Rushton, "Temporal Changes in Space-Preference Structures," *Proceedings of the Association of American Geographers,* 1 (1969), 304–311; Gerard Rushton, "Preference and Choice in Different Environments," *Proceedings of the Association of American Geographers,* 3 (1971), 146–149.

[13]An indifference curve is a line on a two-dimensional graph, along which equally satisfying combinations of variables occur. These curves can also be called isosatisfaction lines.

[14]For a probabilistic reformulation of preference structures, see John L. Girt, "Some Extensions to Rushton's Spatial Preference Scaling Model," *Geographical Analysis,* 8 (1976), 137–156.

[15]In a Thiessen polygon, all areas within the boundary lie closer to the center than to any other center. See Peter Taylor, *Quantitative Methods in Geography,* Houghton Mifflin, Boston, 1977.

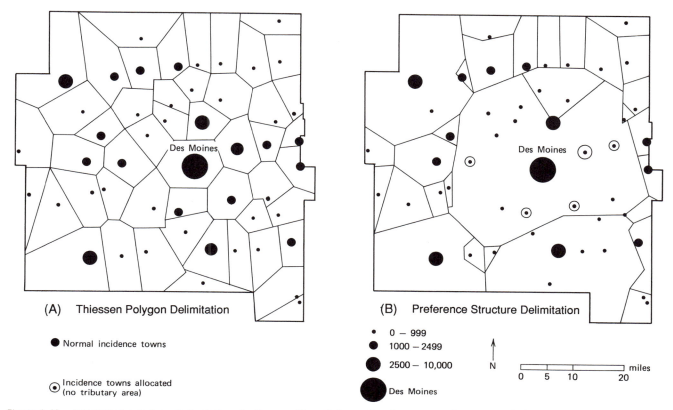

(A)   Thiessen Polygon Delimitation

● Normal incidence towns

⊙ Incidence towns allocated
(no tributary area)

(B)   Preference Structure Delimitation

· 0 — 999
● 1000 — 2499
● 2500 — 10,000
● Des Moines

N
0   5   10   20   miles

Figure 8-10.   Alternate Trade Area Delimitations for Grocery Stores in Iowa. Small towns near larger central places (A) lose customers of the higher order places (B) if residents shop at the central for which they expressed the highest preference. *Source:* Redrawn from Thomas L. Bell, "Central Place Theory as a Mixture of the Function Pattern Principles of Christaller and Lösch: Some Empirical Tests and Applications," unpublished doctoral dissertation, University of Iowa, Department of Geography, 1973, p. 293.

structure delimitation as shown in Figure 8-10.[16] Even for a lower-order central good such as groceries, consumers often preferred to bypass the closest central place opportunity.

The solid graduated circles in Figure 8-10 represent the 47 central places among the 68 total places that had at least one grocery store in the seven-county study region centered on Des Moines. Comparison of the two allocation methods illustrates that some of the central places would lose all of their tributary area if residents always shopped at the central place for which they expressed the highest preference. Small towns that are close to larger central places (i.e., within the zone of functional attrition of the larger central place) are the most disadvantaged. Isolated central places located at

some distance from their nearest competitor seem to fare rather well.

The tributary areas shown in Figure 8-10 illustrate what Lösch abhorred in real-world distribution systems. Two places of the same size vary in centrality because of the effect of relative location and spatial competition. Lösch called this disadvantage the "tyranny of space" and sought to eliminate such competitive forces in his model.

Cultural Differences in Consumer Behavior

Rushton's preference structure method of modeling consumer behavior assumes, as did the theory of Christaller, that consumers have similar tastes and preferences for the consumption of central goods and services. That is, the behavior of all individuals can be aggregated to develop a preference function descriptive of average behavior. Rushton's method does not preclude the development of different preferences for

---

[16]Thomas L. Bell, "A New Operational Definition of Threshold Population Based upon Preference Structures," *Proceedings of the Association of American Geographers*, 5 (1973), 14–17.

different subgroups of the population.[17] For example, the individual differences in shopping patterns between two cultural groups in Ontario, strikingly revealed in Robert Murdie's study of consumer behavior, can be accommodated with Rushton's preference structure method.[18]

Murdie hypothesized that differences between a group of "modern" Canadians and a group of old-order Mennonites who, for religious reasons, shun the material wealth of modern society, would be reflected in their *journey to shop*. While only minute differences between these groups occurred in the journey to shop for low-order convenience goods such as banking services, higher-order shopping distances did differ. For lower-order goods, both groups minimized distance by shopping at the closest central place. When the good was a high-order shopping activity, such as a clothing purchase, "modern" Canadians traveled longer distances to regional centers, bypassing closer shopping opportunities. Presumably the selection of clothing in the larger center was greater and an increased opportunity existed for obtaining the desired merchandise at a cost lower than in a closer small-town alternative. Old-order Mennonites shopped for clothing and yard goods in several smaller towns and cities and ignored the larger center almost completely. Not being as fashion- and style-conscious, and being more self-sufficient (in making their own clothes), the Mennonites found everything they needed in the smaller, closer center. The negative value placed on modern automobiles and commuting long distances among the Mennonite group reinforced the local shopping preference.

Observations concerning Mennonite and modern Canadian shopping behavior support the theoretical work of both Rushton and Christaller. The old-order Mennonites had travel characteristics akin to rural residents in southern Germany in the 1930s. The travel behavior of this cultural group, for clothing and yard goods (cloth) purchases, closely resembled the Christaller distance-minimization assumption. Because accessibility to many central places is available to the modern Canadian, the range of travel for clothing purchases more closely resembled Rushton's preference structure trade-off between town size and distance. Christaller's postulate may have been a fairly realistic reflection of consumer behavior in the 1930s and for more traditional self-sufficient groups, but Rushton's postulate is apparently more closely identified with shopping behavior of most Americans today.

Cultural differences between two so-called modern groups have also been analyzed in the bicultural area of eastern Ontario (between Ottawa and Cornwall), where a comparison of travel patterns between English and French Canadians was conducted.[19] The study indicated that when convenience shopping gives way to comparison shopping, proximity becomes less important and the cultural differences begin to play an obvious role in travel behavior. For higher-order shopping goods, English Canadians shopped in English settlements geographically separate from French ethnic communities even though longer trips were made.

THE ENTREPRENEURIAL BEHAVIOR POSTULATE: A NEGLECTED ASPECT OF CENTRAL PLACE THEORY

Christaller assumed that wherever and whenever threshold purchasing power was present, a good would be offered. In a dynamic sense, this postulate would mean that an entrepreneur adjusts instantaneously to changes in the business environment. There are too many imperfections in the market distribution system for this postulate to be reflective of actual behavior. In reality, entrepreneurs have less than perfect knowledge of their market, and there may be a significant lag time between environmental changes and entrepreneurial reaction to those changes.

Turnover Rates

A high mortality rate of new business operations and an increasingly mobile population have a strong impact on central places. Within the first year of operation many new businesses are eliminated from the retailing system. The average life span in most retail categories has traditionally been less than a decade.[20] This high *turnover rate* severely reduces the economic efficiency

[17]Gordon O. Ewing, "An Analysis of Consumer Space Preferences Using the Method of Paired Comparison," unpublished Ph.D. dissertation, Department of Geography, McMaster University, Hamilton, Ontario, Canada, 1970.

[18]Robert Murdie, "Cultural Differences in Consumer Travel," *Economic Geography*, 41 (1965), 211–233.

[19]D. Michael Ray, "Cultural Differences in Consumer Travel Behavior in Eastern Ontario," *Canadian Geographer*, XI, No. 3 (September 1967), 143–156.

[20]Temporary National Economic Committee, *Problems of Small Business*, Monograph No. 17, USGPO, Washington, D.C., 1941.

of the distribution system and has a disruptive effect on the social welfare of consumers.

Many of the firms that drop out of the retail milieu are marginal businesses. Their elimination may increase retailing efficiency in some instances, but an abnormally high turnover rate is not desirable in the long run. One of the reasons for high turnover is the lack of information feedback concerning the causes of failure. Pred notes that retail trade is characteristically *imitative* in its behavior rather than *innovative*.[21] Without adequate information flow, a selective learning process—in which entrepreneurial decisions become better as business people learn from the mistakes of their predecessors—is thwarted.

The Periodic Market in the Third World

Some of the best theoretical work on entrepreneurial behavior has been undertaken in the non-Western, developing world. In many developing countries, the purchasing power of the consumer is so low that the entrepreneur must make dynamic adjustments in order to stay in business. James Stine, for example, studied the *periodic market*, a common feature of the distributional structure of developing nations, in the context of central place theory.[22] Small towns and villages in many developing countries normally do not have commercial establishments open on a daily basis. Certain market days are set aside for shopping purposes, hence the term periodic market. Entrepreneurs come from other villages and towns to sell their wares on the market day(s). Stine's study of Korea and William Skinner's study of rural market networks in China demonstrate the periodic nature of these markets.[23]

Stine explains the periodic market as an example of rational entrepreneurial adjustment. Since the buying power of rural peasants is low, their ability to travel is restricted due to a lack of access to modern mechanized transportation. Therefore, not enough potential activity exists in the market area to sustain retail stores on a daily basis. Primitive transportation facilities reinforce

the periodic nature of marketing. In such situations, the retailer moves from village to village on a regular schedule. The mobile entrepreneur can capture sufficient purchasing power among several villages to meet threshold requirements. Stine also feels the periodic market benefits the consumer. If consumers can wait until market day, they can minimize the length of their shopping trip.

PLANNING APPLICATIONS

Central place concepts have considerable utility as planning guides (see Box). Berry suggested, for example, that the basic principles of a *nested hierarchy* of shopping opportunities is also appropriate to an understanding of the hierarchy of retail centers within the city.[24] The intraurban hierarchy of nucleated shopping centers would range from the isolated "mom and pop" street-corner grocery store (the counterpart of the hamlet), to the neighborhood center (counterpart of the village), to the community and regional shopping center (the counterpart of the town and city, respectively). Most feasibility studies for shopping centers show great sensitivity to both the location of customers and other competition when estimating potential sales. Generalizations based on central place theory form the framework for assessments of both primary and secondary markets for these centers (see Chapter 16 for further elaboration).

Central place theory can also assist in planning new settlements for developing areas. A *nested hierarchical arrangement* of communities has been developed in this context in both the reclaimed polderland of the Netherlands and the Lachish region of Israel.[25] In both of these cases the settlements were planned from "scratch"—there was no veneer of settlement on which to build. Rather, settlements and the transportation system were deliberately created. Polder reclamation in

[21] Allan R. Pred, *Behavior and Location: Foundation for a Geographic and Dynamic Location Theory, Part II*, Lund Series in Geography, Ser. B., No. 28, Lund, Sweden (1969), pp. 17–19.

[22] James H. Stine, "Temporal Aspects of Tertiary Production Elements in Korea," in F. R. Pitts, ed., *Urban Systems and Economic Behavior*, University of Oregon Press, Eugene, 1962, pp. 68–78.

[23] G. William Skinner, "Marketing and Social Structure in Rural China, Part I," *Journal of Asian Studies*, 24 (1964), 3–43.

[24] Brian J. L. Berry, *Commercial Structure and Commercial Blight*, Research Paper No. 85, Department of Geography, University of Chicago, Chicago, 1963.

[25] Ch. A. P. Takes and A. J. Venstra, "Zuyder Zee Reclamation Scheme," *Tijdschrift Voor Economische en Sociale Geografie*, 51 (1960), 162–167. The Operation Lachish report in the Israeli case states:

> Each group of farm villages will be served by a sub-district center which provides their source of supplies, service and maintenance for their machinery and equipment, and their cultural and educational facilities. All of these groupings are to be linked to the main center of the region which will be the market town where their produce is sold, processed and packed for shipment. (United Jewish Appeal Report, 1959, p. 2).

HOW EFFICIENTLY LOCATED WERE THE REGIONAL CAPITALS OF PHARAOH RAMESES THE GREAT?

Central place principles of efficient service provision need not be confined to modern market economies. Using settlement data from Egypt during the reign of Rameses the Great, it can be shown that this pharaoh, who ruled during the time of Moses, was a clever administrator of his kingdom, as well as the superlative monument builder we know him to be.[1]

Based on archaeological evidence and on trade interactions among settlements written on papyrus reed paper, the geographer/archaeologist Karl Butzer was able to reconstruct the settlement system present in Egypt during the time of Rameses from the first cataract of the Nile at Philae to a point just south of present-day Cairo, a distance of 873 kilometers.[2] The Nile has shifted its course in the millennia since the reign of Rameses the Great (about 1200 B.C.), destroying many east bank settlements. Despite this shift, Butzer was able to identify 128 settlements of the period. These settlements ranged in size from the national capitals of Memphis and Luxor to small agricultural villages. Egypt was organized into political units called *nomes*. The settlement pattern included 23 nomes (22 in upper Egypt and 1 in lower Egypt located just below the Nile delta region). Each of these nomes had a capital. Textual evidence about trade interaction indicated that Rameses organized the country very efficiently and that the organization might be characterized as a centralized bureaucracy. The historical evidence for this assertion is somewhat meager. We might ask, "Can archaeological settlement data be used to either confirm or deny the textual evidence for a centralized bureaucracy during the time of Rameses?" The answer, based on efficient central place

spatial organizational principles, is "yes." A mathematical model based on central place principles was developed to determine the 23 best centers to serve all of the settlements along the Nile and its tributaries in Egypt.[3] Such an optimal pattern of efficient centers could best dispense the Pharaoh's favors or, alternatively, extract the maximum amount of tribute from the populace.

At best, the 23 nome capitals can "cover" (i.e., serve) 123 of the 128 settlements along the Nile and its tributaries within a distance deemed reasonable for a peasant farmer to walk or ply by barge along the Nile in a day's journey. It might seem that since there was such a high proportion of capitals relative to non-capital settlements (about one in five), any 23 settlements chosen at random might do just as well as a set of efficient service centers, but this is not the case. In his research, Butzer chose 23 settlements randomly from among the 128 possibilities and determined how efficient they would be as a set of service centers (i.e., central places). These choices were made 5000 times. The average solution covered or served only about 82 total settlements. The solution chosen by Rameses, on the other hand, was very efficient. His 23 nome capitals covered or served 91 settlements. A coverage value of this magnitude could occur by chance fewer than 2 times in 1000. The mathematical model, which is based on central place principles, confirmed what archaeologists studying the textual records had concluded. Pharaoh Rameses could indeed have ruled Egypt in a very controlled and bureaucratic manner. Furthermore, his locational choices of nome capitals were very shrewd.

---

[1]See Rick Gore, "Rameses the Great," *National Geographic Magazine,* Vol. 179, No. 4 (April 1991), pp. 2–31, for a discussion of Rameses' monumental construction program; and Richard L. Church and Thomas L. Bell, "An Analysis of Ancient Egyptian Settlement Patterns Using Location–Allocation Covering Models," *Annals of the Association of American Geographers*, Vol. 78, No. 4 (1988), pp. 701–714, for an analysis of Rameses' bureaucratic efficiency.

[2]Karl W. Butzer, *Early Hydraulic Civilization in Egypt* (University of Chicago Press, Chicago, 1976).

[3]This model, called a location set-covering model, was applied to three separate sets of settlement data: 1) settlements treated as unweighted points to be served; 2) settlements ranked by their position in a four-level central place hierarchy; and 3) settlements weighted by their "population" (i.e., presence of certain types of ceremonial architecture, important local dignitaries such as mayors, extent of the built-up "urban" area). The discussion here is limited to unweighted settlements. For elaboration of the application to settlements weighted by rank and/or "population," see R.L. Church and T.L. Bell, ibid.

the Zuyder Zee has a longer urban history and can be used to illustrate mistakes that can be made if the theory is interpreted too literally.[26]

Planning for the first of five planned polder developments on reclaimed land in the former Zuyder Zee began in the early twentieth century (Table 8-3). By the late 1920s, the land was drained for the first Wieringermeer polder (Figure 8-11). Using their best instincts and a conceptual framework provided by central place theory, planners sought to use the land primarily for agriculture and create four villages to provide services for the rural farm market. Actual settlement began just before World War II. As mechanization changed agricultural practices and transportation accessibility improved with the increased use of the automobile, it became obvious that farm parcels were too small and that too many small service centers had been created. Building on this experience, changes occurred in the settlement structure in the Northeast polder in the 1950s. Larger farm units, and a bigger town in the center of the polder, Emmeloord, reflected these considerations. The 10 smaller villages encircling Emmeloord (Figure 8-11) completed the settlement system.

Projections indicated that Emmeloord would reach a population of 10,000 and the entire polder 50,000 persons. But mechanization continued to lessen the need for the large number of agricultural laborers originally envisioned, and transportation advances limited the potential for villages to grow. Moreover, residents commuted to centers off the polder in larger numbers than anticipated for more specialized goods and services. These factors combined to produce slower population growth for the area, especially Emmeloord, than expected.

Again, building on the mistakes of the past, significantly fewer settlements reached the drawing board stage when plans for the Eastern Flevoland polder unfolded in the 1960s. A city-level center in this polder, Lelystad, occupied the top of a three-level hierarchy of communities. The second-level town of Dronten, surrounded by three smaller villages, completed the settlement system. By the time settlement began, land use priorities for this polder had changed in the direction of assigning more land to urban, conser-

TABLE 8-3

Polder Settlements in the Ijsselmeer Region of Holland

Polder Name	Dates Drained
1. Wieringermeer	1927–1930
2. Northeast	1937–1942
3. Eastern Flevoland	1950–1957
4. Southern Flevoland	1959–1968
5. Markerwaard	Under discussion

Source: Henk Meijer, *Zyder Zee, Lake Ijssel* Information and Documentation Centre for the Geography of the Netherlands, Utrecht/The Hague, 1981.

vation, industrial, and recreational uses and less to agriculture.

In recognition of the potential of Lelystad as a growth center in the greater "Randstad Holland" urban complex, especially as a destination for residents moving from Amsterdam, a population of 100,000 was projected for the city. By 1988, Lelystad had grown to a population of about 60,000. Over half the workers in Lelystad commute from the city to work, primarily to Amsterdam. Greater congestion levels on roads leading to Amsterdam and the slowing of employment expansion in Lelystad have, nevertheless, dampened future growth prospects for the city in recent years.

The fourth and most recently settled polder, Southern Flevoland, continued the trend toward fewer, larger settlements and less land devoted to agriculture. The city of Almere, planned for 125,000–250,000 population, will house most of the population. Only one other settlement, Zeewolde, an agricultural service center and recreation community, was planned for the polder. In a short 10-year span, 1978–1988, the population of Almere reached 50,000, whereas Zeewolde grew to 4,000.

Located closer to Amsterdam than Lelystad, the Almere growth center has an even larger commuter population. About 70 percent of its inhabitants relocated from Amsterdam, and an even larger share of population continues to work there. If and when the Markerwaard Polder is drained and settled, it will be much smaller than originally envisioned. Environmental concerns and debates over open space, recreation uses, and finance issues, have all slowed the project. The original plan for a 60,000 hectare polder were later scaled back to 41,000 and most recently to 23,000 (57,000 acres).

In summary, central place theory principles have important applications to present-day settlement plan-

---

[26]A. K. Constandse, "Reclamation and Colonization of New Areas," *Tijdschrift voor Economische en Sociale Geografie*, 54 (1963), 41–45; Henk meijer, Zyder Zee, Lake Ijssel, Information and Documentation Centre for the Geography of the Netherlands, Utrecht/The Hague, 1981.

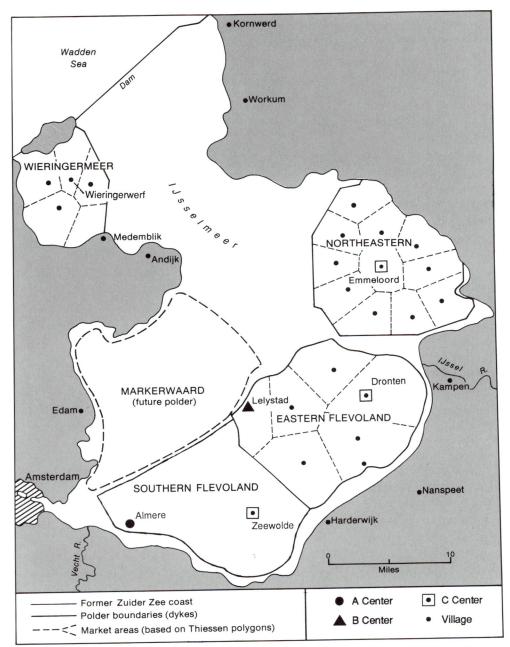

Figure 8-11. Planned Settlements in the Netherlands. Central place concepts have guided the settlement planning process in the polders. More recently, settled polders have fewer, larger centers, owing to improved transportation and longer distance commuting to existing urban cities such as Amsterdam. Less land has been devoted to agriculture in more recently settled polders. *Source:* Modified after A. P. Takes and A. J. Venstra, "Zuyder Zee Reclamation Scheme," *Tijdschrift voor Econ. en Soc. Geografie,* 51, 1961, p. 163; and Henk Meijer, *Randstad Holland,* Information and Documentation Centre for the Geography of the Netherlands, Utrecht/The Hague, 1986.

ning. Due to agricultural mechanization advances and transportation improvements associated with the automobile and improved highway access, the size and spacing of settlements appropriate today is much different than it was as recently as the end of World War II.

The influence of mature metropolitan areas on the settlement system, such as that which occurs in the vicinity of Amsterdam, also influences the urban hierarchy more significantly than in the past. To their credit, the Dutch have been quite successful, over time, in adjusting their polder settlement policy to reflect these changes.

ARCHAEOLOGICAL APPLICATIONS OF CENTRAL PLACE THEORY

Archaeologists consider central place theory a useful research tool to unlock the puzzle of the settlement pattern of bygone civilizations. Applications in such disparate areas as the Diyala Plans of Iraq and the lower Yucatan Peninsula of Mexico have confirmed central place theory's validity in understanding such historical settlement patterns.[27]

One researcher, in describing an application of central place theory to an explanation of the settlement pattern of the Maya Indians during their late Classic period (A.D. 600–900), states:

> Around these capitals [the four regional Maya capitals of Copan, Tikal, Calakmul, and Palenque] developed the familiar hexagonal lattices of secondary centers predicted by the Central Place Theory; tertiary hexagons developed around these secondary centers and around these were villages and hamlets whose overall patterns probably shifted with the fallow cycle in slash-burn farming.[28]

SUMMARY AND CONCLUSION

Despite the elegance of central place theory and its wide applicability to a variety of consumer-behavior situations, it has shortcomings. One critic of central place theory, James Vance, notes that even though it may work in explaining retail activity, it does not satisfactorily account for wholesaling.[29] Therefore, he describes it as a special case, not a general model. The reasons for this breakdown in the wholesale arena are that agents of trade are involved and outward trade away from existing places is necessary. An open *exogenic* system, rather than Christaller's closed *en-*

dogenic model, is required, for this to occur. Vance says that the central place model does not relate to change induced externally and is not dynamic. For the case of wholesaling, Vance suggests a more general *mercantile model* to explain settlement systems. A fuller treatment of wholesaling activity will be presented in Chapter 18.

Rushton's preference-structure description of modern consumer behavior has extended the applicability of the theory. Murdie and Ray both demonstrate that cultural differences can add complexity to real-world shopping behavior. The operation of central place systems has also been examined in developing nations where dynamic adjustments to low-threshold purchasing power have been made.

Central place theory still needs some improvement and refinement. In the end, the utility of a theory is demonstrated not in its mathematical elegance or esoteric theorems, but in its relevance in resolving real-world problems. Central place concepts such as *threshold, range of a good, centrality, size and spacing*, and *functional hierarchy* are important elements in the structure of urban marketing systems used by geographers and other urban researchers. Planners incorporate these concepts when they develop retail nucleations within cities and when they lay out entire city systems. Archaeologists have also found utility in central place theory: it provides hypotheses about the settlement patterns of ancient civilizations. We will look at the pervasive impact of transportation on urban structure in Chapter 9.

Suggestions for Further Reading

Baskin, C. W. *Central Places in Southern Germany*, Prentice Hall, Englewood Cliffs, N.J., 1966; translation of Walter Christaller, *Die Zentralen Orte in Suddeutschland*, Gustav Fischer Verlag, Jena, 1933.

Beavon, Keith S. *Central Place Theory: A Reinterpretation.* Longman, London, 1977.

Berry, Brian J. L. *Geography of Market Centers and Retail Distribution*, Prentice Hall, Englewood Cliffs, N.J., 1967; Berry, Brian J.L., et al., *Market Centers and Retail Location*, second ed., Prentice Hall, Englewood Cliffs, N.J., 1988.

Berry, Brian, J. L. *Growth Centers in the American Urban System*, Ballinger, Cambridge, Mass., 1973.

Berry, Brian J. L., and Allan R. Pred. *Central Place Studies: A Bibliography of Theory and Applications.* Regional Science Research Institute, Philadelphia, 1964; reprinted 1965 (with supplement through 1964 by H. G. Barnum, R. Kasperson, and S. Krucki).

---

[27]Gregory A. Johnson, "A Test of the Utility of Central Place Theory in Archaeology," in *Man, Settlement and Urbanism*, Peter J. Ucko, et al., eds., Schenkman, Cambridge, 1972, pp. 1–17; Norman Hammond, "The Distribution of Late Classic Maya Major Ceremonial Centers in the Central Area," in *Mesoamerican Archaeology*, Norman Hammond, ed., University of Texas Press, Austin, 1974, pp. 313–334; Kent V. Flannery, "The Cultural Evolution of Civilizations," *Annual Review of Ecology and Systematics*, 3 (1972), pp. 399–426.

[28]Joyce Marcus, "Territorial Organization of the Lowland Classic Maya," *Science*, 180, 4089 (June 1, 1973), pp. 199–916.

[29]James Vance, Jr., *The Merchant's World: The Geography of Wholesaling*, Prentice Hall, Englewood Cliffs, 1970.

King, Leslie. *Central Place Theory*, Sage, Beverly Hills, Calif., 1984.

Lösch, August. *The Economics of Location*, translated by W. H. Woglom and W. F. Stolper, (originally published in 1939), Yale University Press, New Haven, 1954, reprinted by Wiley, New York, 1967.

Marshall, John U. *The Structure of Urban Systems*, University of Toronto Press, Toronto, 1989.

Meijer, Henk. *Randstad Holland*, Information and Documentation Centre for the Geography of the Netherlands, Utrecht/The Hague, 1986.

Vance, James, Jr. *The Merchant's World: The Geography of Wholesaling,* Prentice Hall, Englewood Cliffs, 1970.

9

TRANSPORTATION PROCESSES

U rban transportation geography is concerned with the many factors that shape and temper city form, including the interaction of transportation accessibility and land use and various policy issues related to mobility. Such issues include the appropriate balance of various transportation modes in the city, their environmental impact, cost, and equity considerations. An emphasis will be placed on the historical evolution of various technologies and changing urban structure in this chapter. The force exerted by the automobile in shaping land use in the present-day city will receive extensive coverage, especially the planning process associated with highway building.

TRANSPORTATION AS A SERVICE

An understanding of the role of transportation in our cities is necessary at the outset so that its effectiveness can be evaluated. In the simplest terms, transportation is a service. It involves the movement of individuals and/or goods from one place to another to satisfy human needs. In fact, a spectrum of transportation services exists, the number and intensity of which vary

considerably with the levels of economic development of a region.

At one end of the continuum, shown in Figure 9-1, are traditional economies, and at the other end are the highly developed nations. The right portion of Figure 9-1 indicates a highly interconnected transportation network such as occurs in highly developed areas. In such an environment people and goods can be moved directly to and from many dispersed origins and destinations. Activities such as housing, employment centers, or commercial services can be concentrated in a few locations or widely dispersed, depending on the particular economies of scale and socioeconomic or technical objectives involved.

A partially interconnected network is portrayed in the left portion of Figure 9-1. Less direct connections occur in areas where, when facilities are not available or when movement costs are high and/or activity linkages less complex, less need for interaction exists. Many third world countries fall into this category, as do sparsely populated areas of highly developed countries, including isolated parts of the United States and Canada.

Because of their potential for greater efficiency and reduced travel times and costs, improved technologies that lead to more rapid mobility have great appeal. Such advances create in turn a *time-space convergence*. This concept refers to the increased distance that one can move in a given time period following a transportation

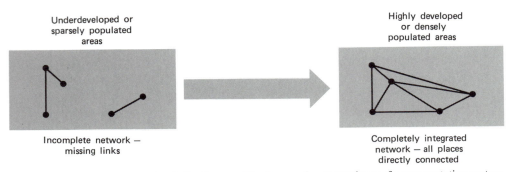

Figure 9-1.   Transportation Network Continuum. The degree of connectedness of a transportation system reflects the level of economic development of an area. The two networks shown here illustrate such a contrast between underdeveloped and developed areas.

improvement, which in effect decreases the friction of distance. We have already discussed this situation in Chapter 8 in conjunction with the discussion of central place theory and the impact of travel times on retailing in centers of various sizes.

Each stage in the development of transportation in the United States has led to a time-space convergence, at both the national and intraurban scale. The relative shrinkage of the United States since 1912, for example, is shown in Figure 9-2. The sequential impact of rail service, the piston airplane, and jet travel is readily apparent from the diagram. Within the city, the electric streetcar lines in nineteenth-century Boston, Chicago, and Milwaukee created a similar impact as they enhanced much slower travel times associated with horse-cars and the omnibus.

For the greatest part of the twentieth century, the emphasis in highly developed areas on more advanced vehicular technology and massive investments in expanded transportation networks has made urban transportation cheaper, faster, and more ubiquitous, greatly enhancing the intensity of movement. Good service has also been a factor. The automobile became the most successful form of travel because it was personal and flexible in that it could take one anywhere there was a roadway. In short, the automobile provided superior service and created a further time-space convergence at the metropolitan scale.

TRANSPORTATION AS LAND SHAPER

Within an urban area, a maze of countervailing forces related to transportation continuously reshapes land uses. Each mode of transportation creates an impact based on its service characteristics. This situation substantiates the old adage that transportation does more to shape the city than any other force. This was true previously in the waterway, railroad, and streetcar eras, as it is today in the automobile and air travel period. The present automobile era has in fact totally recast urban structure. Before turning to the present, let us look more carefully at earlier stages in the historical evolution of transportation technology and its impact on the city.

A four-stage structural-evolution model presented by John Adams emphasizes this change and significant technology innovations on city structure.[1] The walking city forms the first stage of the Adams model.

Stage I: Walking/Horsecar Era

For centuries the city depended on rudimentary water transportation, horse-drawn vehicles, and walking to move its residents and the various goods produced and consumed. As a result, the city retained a relatively compact and high-density form (Figure 9-3A). Even today European, southwest Asian, and other third world cities still retain an imprint of their compact walking-city scale from the past. It is still possible to walk between major historic public places in Rome, for example, and to stroll across a traditional city from one gate to another in those formerly enclosed by a wall, such as Munich, Vienna, and Rouen. In Vienna, the

[1]John S. Adams, "Residential Structure of Midwestern Cities," *Annals of the Association of American Geographers*, 60 (1970), 37–62.

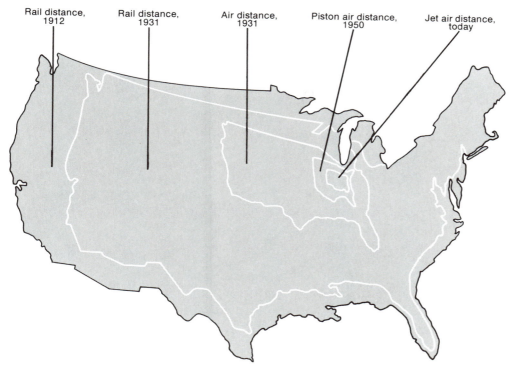

Rail distance, 1912   Rail distance, 1931   Air distance, 1931   Piston air distance, 1950   Jet air distance, today

Figure 9-2.   The "Shrinking" United States, 1912–1970. Each stage in the development of new transportation technologies in the United States has led to a time–space convergence. The sequential impact of rail service, piston airplane travel, and jet travel is shown here. *Source:* Redrawn with permission. From Marion Clawson, *America's Land and Its Uses,* The John Hopkins University Press, Baltimore, 1972, 13. Copyright ©1972 Resources for the Future. the Johns Hopkins Press, Baltimore, Maryland, 21218.

ringstrasse circular roadway network, along with many public buildings, now forms a circumferential belt previously occupied by the city wall, which was dismantled in 1887 (Figure 9-4). Not until the advent of the trolley and rail technologies of the late nineteenth century did the city change significantly in size.

In its earliest format, public transportation occurred as an *omnibus*, perhaps best characterized as an urban stagecoach (Table 9-1). Popular in London, Paris, and New York in the 1830s, the omnibus did permit urban residents the option of living beyond walking distance to work, but lines were short and few passengers were served. Moreover, the unpaved roads of the day inhibited travel and even at its best, omnibus service was slow.

The omnibus initiated a trend, amplified by successive technology advances, that led to more specialized land uses in the central business district and more separation between residential and commercial land uses. The downtown area benefited from its "crossroads" location for various omnibus routes. This accessibility advantage became more obvious in the horsecar

era that followed. Owing its origin to a prohibition against operations of steam trains in central Manhattan, the horsecar began simply enough as a horse-drawn passenger railcar connecting segments of the New York and Harlem railroad. But its use spread rapidly as the rail allowed the horse to draw a larger vehicle at higher speed, and line lengths expanded accordingly.

To accommodate the *horsecar* on city streets necessitated that agreements, often institutionalized as exclusive franchises, be drawn to permit the private use of a public street. In turn the rail company paid a fee, laid the rails, and became responsible for maintaining, even paving, the streets that its vehicles traversed. Improved service alternatives to the relatively expensive and slow horse-drawn vehicles became a priority by the 1850s. However, the horsecar continued to flourish as demonstrated by the fact that 39 streetcar companies operated in Philadelphia at one time.

By the 1870s a viable mechanical substitute for the horsecar came in the form of the *cable car*. First introduced in San Francisco in 1873, the cable car opened the Nob Hill and Russian Hill areas for settle-

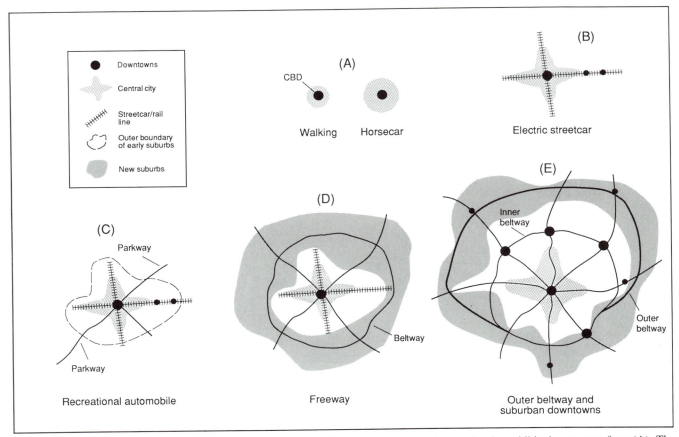

Figure 9-3. Transportation and Urban Form. Before the advent of mechanized transportation, the city exhibited a compact form (A). The streetcar technology of the late nineteenth century created a star-shaped form with development following route alignments (B). The automobile opened up interstitial areas between rail corridors for development in the 1920s and 1930s (C). Freeways and beltways in the post-World War II city led to new waves of development (D), which led to the development of suburban downtowns and outer beltways (E).

ment (Figure 9-5). The technology involved a continuous cable running below street level, driven by machines located in a central power station. The cable car itself, similar in design to the horse-drawn trolley, either "grabbed" or "dropped" the cable when it needed to either move or stop. Only the system that developed in San Francisco still survives in the United States, but many cities used such a system at one time. Chicago, for example, operated the largest system in the world in the 1880s. That cable car system in fact led to the early concentration of commercial activity in downtown Chicago, later defined as the "loop" when the elevated rail system became integrated into the transportation network. A disadvantage of the cable car centered on the enormous initial construction costs. By comparison, operating costs were lower than those for the horsecar, so once built it offered relatively inexpensive service.

Stage II: Electric Streetcar Era

The *electric streetcar* became a third, and most influential, public transportation innovation in the nineteenth century. The significance of the electric streetcar is that it represented a technology breakthrough in the form of the electric traction motor. This innovation truly revolutionized transportation because for the first time mass transportation became available to everyone at an affordable price.

Population densities increased considerably in cities in the last quarter of the nineteenth century as industrialization, rural to urban migration, and immigration combined to generate considerable growth in all rapidly developing countries in Western Europe and North America. The trolley in effect became a safety valve permitting residential population decentralization and escape from the increased congestion and greater pol-

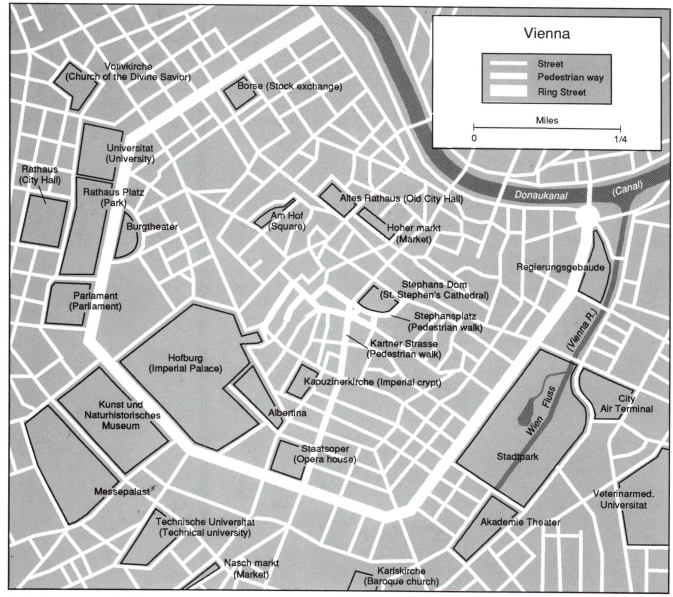

Figure 9-4. Ring Road in Vienna. A ringstrasse circular road now forms an inner-city beltway around the city on an alignment previously occupied by a wall, which was dismantled in 1887. That corridor now showcases many public buildings, such as the Opera House, museums, and government offices.

lution levels in the core city.[2]

Mass-scale suburbs also emerged along the trolley lines catering to the rapidly expanding working and middle class markets. As Figure 9-3B indicates, a star-shaped urban region replaced the circular one in

this era, owing to the accessibility advantage along the streetcar corridor that encouraged the stretching of development along the line. Cheap 5¢ fares meant that the masses could now afford transportation.

The earlier initiatives in public transportation that preceded the electric streetcar could not match the winning combination of favorable service characteristics provided by the streetcar, including, speed, mass mobility potential, line lengths, and low fares. As a result, these earlier forms declined rapidly once the

[2]Truman A. Hartshorn and Peter O. Muller, *Suburban Business Centers: Employment Implications*, Final Report, Project No. RED-808-G-84-5(99-7-13616), 1986. Department Administration, U.S. Department of Economic Commerce, Washington, D.C.

TABLE 9-1
Pioneering Public Transportation Modes

Type	Beginning Dates	Average Speed
Omnibus	1830	3 mph
Horsecar	1832	4 mph
Cable car	1873	5 mph
Electric streetcar	1883	10 mph

streetcar gained a foothold. The cost advantage of this system over the cable car, combined with an operating cost advantage over the horsecar, spelled impending doom for both of those approaches in most cities.

The first electric trolleys were simply horsecars retrofitted with electric motors, but after Frank Sprague developed a new approach in his system in Richmond, Virginia, in 1888 the new era began with a vengeance. Sprague's streetcars used an overhead wire as a power source, a spring-loaded pole mounted on the roof of the trolley to contact the wire, and an improved control system in the trolley. Within two years of its introduction in Richmond, this same system had been installed on over 1200 miles of electric street railways in the United States.[3]

The added service benefits of the electric streetcar also provided many advantages to the rider. Not only did it travel faster than earlier models (10 mph average), but line lengths increased to five miles or more and routes criss-crossed, thus improving cross-town flows. Many transit companies also engaged in the land development process by extending a line to undeveloped tracts that they owned and then used streetcar access as a marketing tool to sell building lots and houses. The electric streetcar therefore became an instrument to direct urban growth.

The heyday for the electric streetcar, in retrospect, came and went quite rapidly. In the period 1880–1910 the streetcar seemed invincible, but by the beginning of World War I the seeds of decline had been sown. In 1907, 94 percent of all urban passenger trips occurred by streetcar.[4] Steadily increasing competition from

---

[3]Ruth Cavin, *Trolleys*, Hawthorn Books, New York, 1976, 6ff.

[4]Arthur Saltzman, "The Decline of Transit," in George Gray and Lester Hoel, eds., *Public Transportation*, Prentice–Hall, Englewood Cliffs, N.J., 1979, p. 29.

Figure 9-5. San Francisco's Powell and Market Street Cable Car. The cable car, first introduced in San Francisco in 1873, opened up the Nob Hill and Russian Hill areas for settlement. That system still runs today, serving as a major tourist attraction. (Peter Menzel/Stock, Boston)

motorbuses occurred in the 1920s and the streetcar industry began to suffer from its aging equipment and a lack of new capital investment.

In this era the exclusive franchises owned by private investors that controlled the streetcar industry became known as "transit trusts" and the public began to question their integrity. Public ownership of transit in the United States did not become a factor until many decades later. As competition increased and profits declined in the streetcar business, consolidations increased. Gradually utility holding companies emerged as the controlling interest in the transit industry. These same companies controlled electric power, gas, water and transit utility systems in many cities. The connection with the electric utilities may not be obvious to us today, but at the time the streetcar business typically consumed the largest quantity of electricity in the city. Often transit operations were subsidized by profits from other utility operations controlled by the transit trust, and this policy became controversial.

The 1935 Public Utility Holding Act, which became effective in 1938, changed the ground rules for interlocking utility operations by requiring separate operating companies for each utility. The impact of this legislation created a death blow to streetcar transit. It also came at a time when competition with motorbuses had intensified. We will return to this topic in a later section.

Two other rail-based mass transit systems providing passenger service in the late nineteenth century also influenced the growth pattern of the city: (1) commuter rail and (2) interurban service. Both forms had ties to the national intercity rail passenger system. Commuter rail service began when long-distance passenger trains seized an opportunity to bolster ridership by offering service to suburban residents along the rail lines. They opened new stations on the urban periphery and offered riders discount or "commuted" fares, hence the term *commuter* that we now associate with all long-distance work trip travel. The early residential growth of Long Island in suburban New York, for example, can be largely explained by the commuter service provided by Long Island Railroad. Similar operations occurred in other large cities serving as rail hubs, such as Chicago, Philadelphia, Boston, and Atlanta.

The second type of operation, the *interurban*, represents a hybrid form, a cross between the electric streetcar and the commuter rail (Figure 9-6). Whereas commuter rail service typically involved steam trains, interurban lines were electrified. Power to run these

trains came from overhead wires or a "third rail." They typically provided service between smaller cities and towns and larger metropolitan areas. The passenger cars, lighter than traditional rail passenger cars, resembled upgraded streetcar vehicles, but they traveled faster and provided more comfortable seating than streetcars. Close station spacing increased their attractiveness to the rider. Elaborate interurban networks evolved in the Middle West and Northeast before the turn of the century. The Los Angeles and San Francisco urban regions also boasted large networks.

The spatial impact of both of these systems on the city occurred in similar fashion, complementing that of other rail technologies. Simply stated, rail commuter lines created *beads of settlement* along the lines (Figure 9-3B). In other words, suburban settlement intensified around the stations, while rural land continued to exist between the stations. Typically, station spacing decreased near the city and increased at greater distances. The extent of suburban development was determined by the availability and frequency of commuter service.

A stimulus to introduce new rail technologies in the city came from the increasing congestion on city streets as the number of vehicles multiplied and conflicts between pedestrians, streetcars, and horse-drawn vehicles increased. After the turn of the century, private automobiles and motorbuses added to the confusion. In 1898 a streetcar subway opened in Boston, and it evolved into the first underground rail system in the United States. Subways opened in New York and Philadelphia in 1904 and 1907, respectively. But the world's first system opened in London much earlier in 1863, in the form of an underground steam train.

Electrification of urban rails began in the 1890s and became the origin of what we now call heavy rail rapid transit systems. Owing to high construction costs and the need for mass patronage, these systems became viable only for very large metropolitan areas. Few lines were built in the United States after 1920 as a result of increased competition from buses and automobiles. But they reemerged as urban transportation alternatives in the 1970s as federal funding became available in response to growing public pressure to offer an alternative to the automobile.

Stage III: Recreational Automobile Era

While the earliest automobiles evolved in the 1890s and before in Europe, they soon became identified as an

Figure 9-6. **Electric Interurban Rail Line.** The electric interurban is a cross between the electric streetcar and commuter rail. Power came from an overhead wire, as in this case, or a "third rail." They provided service between cities, or from small towns to larger urban centers. Elaborate networks existed in the Northeast, Middle West, and California in the early twentieth century. (Courtesy Southern Pacific Electric)

"American" product. Sales escalated faster in the United States than overseas at the turn of the century, following price reductions and the introduction of mass production manufacturing processes. In Europe, artisans continued to make automobiles by hand through the World War II era, keeping their prices relatively high and the market more restricted.

A vast array of independent and widely dispersed carriage makers made the first cars and they were a novelty on both sides of the Atlantic. Every conceivable mode of power drove these vehicles—steam, electricity, diesel oil, and gasoline. The internal combustion gasoline engine eventually became the standard as vehicle reliability and design and propulsion innovations occurred.

Wealthy families became the early patrons of the automobile, primarily using them for weekend outings, hence the early label "touring car" for many models (Figure 9-7). These early vehicles were wood-framed horseless carriages and poor roads and bad weather created handicaps for their wider use.

Nevertheless, many buyers sought these vehicles for racing purposes. In 1895, for example, an automobile race of over 700 miles took place from Paris to Bordeaux. Another race, won by the pioneer car manufacturer Charles Duryea, occurred in Chicago on Thanksgiving Day that same year. For the first 20 or 30 years following its introduction the automobile did not become a factor in commuting. Rather, it became a conveyance for weekend and summer recreational use and for occasional use for shopping or social trips. Often caravans of vehicles were organized for long-distance recreation travel.

In 1920 nearly 90 percent of urban commuting still occurred by streetcar and the remainder by rail transit. Not until after World War II did a massive shift from transit to automobile commuting begin. In the interim, motorbuses gradually replaced the streetcar as a commuter vehicle. In some cities, conversions to the trolleybus also occurred. The bus simply used the same overhead power source as had the trolley.

Emergence of Bus Transit

As early as 1905, motorbuses provided service on regular routes in New York and London. This type of service gained in popularity in major European cities

Figure 9-7. The Touring Car on Weekend Outing. Wealthy families were the earliest patrons of the automobile, using them for weekend trips into the country. This photograph shows F. Major and family in an auto in Dorrance, Kansas, September 21, 1910. (Kansas State Historical Society, Topeka, Kansas)

even faster than in the United States, in part because of the unwillingness of "transit trust" operators in America to make the switch. Improved bus designs came in the 1920s and predecessors of the modern-day rear engine diesel bus arrived in the 1930s. Some electric streetcar operators first used buses to feed their transit lines, while others converted entire routes to bus service.

Generous incentives encouraging conversions to bus service in the United States came from manufacturers such as General Motors, who not only acquired stock in operating companies as compensation for financial and management services, but also bought outright entire streetcar and interurban operating companies.

General Motors established itself as the leading bus manufacturer in the country after purchasing the Yellow Bus and Coach Company in the 1920s. Another General Motors subsidiary, the Hertz Omnibus Company, converted transit systems it purchased in several cities from streetcar to bus operations. Ties between the National City Lines firm and General Motors also existed. By 1946 National City Lines had acquired nearly 50 transit systems, which served as the largest market for General Motors' buses. After a slowdown in

conversions to buses during World War II, the transition from streetcar to bus became nearly complete in the 1950s.

In some cities, transit companies opted to convert streetcars to trolleybus operations to save money and continue using as much of their existing capital investment as possible. Trolleybuses used overhead wires as a source of power to run their electric motors. The advantage they had over the trolley came from greater mobility on the street, since the rubber tires were freed from the fixed rail technology. In the long run, however, high maintenance costs for vehicles and the electrical distribution system led to the abandonment of this hybrid technology, but remnants of this system still exist in some cities such as San Francisco.

As the rivalry between buses and automobiles intensified in the post-World War II era, bus service faced severe curtailment. Greater levels of suburbanization accompanied by improved road networks encouraged lower population densities, creating a less competitive environment for bus operations. Ridership on buses declined and operating company deficits increased. Therefore, the primary service area for buses was limited to higher-density central city areas and express routes linking city and suburb along major arterial highways.

Rail transit systems also lost favor in the post-World War II period as the shift to the automobile became stronger:

By the 1960s only a few cities could boast any survivals of the previously extensive system of a rail-guided rapid transit. Suburban commuter railroads were restricted to Boston, New York, Philadelphia, Chicago, and less significantly, Baltimore, Washington, Cleveland, Detroit, and San Francisco. Trolley lines disappeared from most cities, surviving only where trolley cars were used extensively in subways, as in Boston, Pittsburgh, Philadelphia, and San Francisco, and in New Orleans, where the St. Charles line took on the quality of a tourist attraction. New York and Chicago continued their subway and elevated routes but did away with their surface lines. Thus, significant fixed-plant transit was to be found in only four cities in the United States—Boston, New York, Philadelphia, and Chicago—with bits in a few other places such as Newark, Pittsburgh, Cleveland, New Orleans, and San Francisco."[5]

The Automobile City

The automobile opened up interstitial areas between rail corridors for development in the 1920s and 1930s as more middle- and upper-class buyers acquired vehicles (Figure 9-3C). Some of these areas were initially settled as "country home" areas, primarily for seasonal use. In other cases the automobile became a feeder vehicle connecting the home with the rail or streetcar line, the primary means for work travel. The so-called "station wagon," which we now associate with suburban family living, got its start as a vehicle designed to carry workers to the station for a trip to work on the train.[6] In still other situations entire subdivisions catering to the automobile emerged and long-distance automobile commuting began.

The housing boom that occurred during the 1920s brought many new innovations in both building and subdivision design in response to the automobile. Lots became larger and wider, because of the need for a driveway and garage, but also to maintain a country landscaped look in the suburbs that were often designed with curvilinear streets. The need for closely spaced

housing units on small lots vanished with the enhanced access provided by the automobile. Cape Cod, bungalow, and smaller boxy homes could now be purchased in greater numbers by a wider clientele as transportation access problems declined and building lots became more affordable.

The first automobile-oriented shopping center, Country Club Plaza in Kansas City, also appeared in the 1920s (Figure 9-8). More a hybrid center than the regional mall we now find in the suburbs, this center set a precedent for the decentralization of commercial activity (see Chapter 16 for a more thorough discussion of retail activity). Demands for offstreet parking also increased, especially in newer shopping districts. The setbacks of storefronts on commercial streets also set a new design standard by allowing for parking in front of the stores. Even to this day we can identify residential and shopping areas as dating either to the automobile or streetcar era on the basis of the presence or absence of driveways (residential areas) or store setbacks for parking adjacent to the street (shopping). The first structured parking decks catering to the automobile also appeared in the 1920s.

The *good roads* movement dating to the 1890s promoted the greater use of the automobile. With roots in two areas of need—that of improved pathways for bicycles and paved farm-to-market roads to assist farmers—this promotion gained a strong constituency among urbanites in the early twentieth century. Gradually the responsibility for improving roads shifted from the local government to higher levels, including state and national authorities. Road designs and traffic controls advanced rapidly in the 1920s and 1930s. Limited-access, divided, four-lane highways in fact date to the 1930s, but few were built before World War II.

Engineering advances that vastly improved the vehicle in the 1920s also greatly assisted the growing popularity of the automobile. By mid-decade enclosed vehicles replaced the traditional open "touring" car. Electric starters, pneumatic tires, safety glass, and more powerful engines dating to that period also added additional convenience, reliability, and safety features to the car. Moreover, increased sales kept prices low, broadening their market appeal.

During the 1920s the number of registered automobiles practically tripled in the United States, rising from 8 to 23 million. Per capita automobile ownership levels did not rise as fast in cities as in the country as a result of the continued competitiveness of street railway systems in urban settings. Per capita automobile sales also

---

[5]James E. Vance, Jr., *This Scene of Man*, Harper's College Press, New York, 1977, p. 367.
[6]Ibid., p.408.

Figure 9-8. Country Club Plaza Shopping Center, Kansas City. This automobile-oriented shopping center set a precedent for the design of the retail center and the decentralization of higher order retailing away from the downtown area. Note the curb parking on one side of the street and diagonal parking in front of the stores in this historic photograph. The plaza still flourishes as a retail center; see Figure 16–10. (Plaza Merchants Association)

varied by city size, with the largest cities such as New York having lower rates than cities like Chicago and Boston. One of the highest per capita registration levels occurred in Los Angeles, where one in three households possessed a car by 1930. That metropolitan area experienced the most rapid growth among large urban areas in the country in the 1920s, and also crossed the 1 million population threshold during that decade.

Liberal extensions of the streetcar and interurban rail systems at the turn of the century in Los Angeles provided the initial impetus for rapid suburban growth. In Los Angeles,

> a syndicate formed by Henry E. Huntington purchased 50,000 acres in the San Fernando Valley alone, and he developed thirteen brand new towns in the metropolitan region between 1902 and 1917. Largely as a result of such real estate promotions, by World War I Huntington's Pacific Electric Railway Company was the most extensive interurban system in the world."[7]

As a result of such intense growth, rail corridors soon became saturated with traffic, necessitating other solutions.

Dissatisfaction with the operations of rail franchises, including safety problems, poor service, and high fares, created an increasingly bad reputation for rail transit in the early 1900s in Los Angeles. Moreover, the automobile gained the reputation of a "democratic piece of urban technology" and a symbol of progress.[8] Rail transit ridership began dropping rapidly in Los Angeles after 1914 as a result of this dissatisfaction. Interestingly, the *jitney* contributed to this decline.

Jitney service began when an automobile driver offered to pick up riders and carry them to work for a cheap (often 5) fare. Since these jitneys traveled the same routes as streetcars, they directly competed with them. This automobile-based service typically outclassed transit because of the greater flexibility it offered to navigate congested streets. Personalized service could be offered in terms of pick-up and drop-off locations. Drivers also benefited as the service provided enough income to pay for their own travel. Transit operators objected to this unfair competition because they had much higher overhead costs to bear (taxes to pay, franchise fees, street maintenance, etc.)

[7]Mark S. Foster, *From Streetcar to Superhighway: American City Planners and Urban Transportation*, Temple University Press, Philadelphia, 1981, p. 17.

[8]Scott R. Bottles, *Los Angeles and the Automobile: The Making of the Modern City*, University of California Press, Berkeley, 1987, p. 15.

In short, the "automobile jitney offered flexibility, convenience, and speed to those disappointed with streetcars."[9] By 1915 jitneys carried 150,000 daily riders in Los Angeles. Even though jitneys provided superior service for many short trips, they were forced out of business by the city government following successful lobbying efforts by transit interests. Jitneys were banned altogether from the downtown area of Los Angeles and were forced to post schedules and follow specific routes.

The most intense competition to transit in Los Angeles eventually came from the private automobile, not the jitney, but the favorable service experience of the jitney served to make automobile usage even more popular.

In 1915, Los Angeles had one car for every eight residents, far more than the national mean of one per forty-three citizens. By 1925, every other Angeleno owned an automobile as opposed to the rest of the country where there was only one car for every six people. By 1924, nearly half of all those entering the Los Angeles central business district arrived by automobile. To illustrate the point that Los Angeles was unique at its time, consider that only 20 percent of workers in Pittsburgh drove their cars to work as late as the 1930s. Automobile registration in Los Angeles county increased nearly fourfold between 1918 and 1923 from 110,000 to 430,000.[10]

The decentralized form of development created by the interurban and streetcar systems in Los Angeles created a perfect environment for the automobile. Several independent suburban communities, including the San Fernando Valley area, Westwood, Hollywood, and Pasadena, developed under the influence of rail service. Once the long downtown commute by rail became congested, the switch to the more flexible and personal service offered by the automobile occurred rapidly. It then even became possible to create other newer suburbs based on the automobile both farther from the downtown area and in vast areas between the rail-served corridors. Beverly Hills, between downtown Los Angeles and Santa Monica on an interurban line, also became a prototype automobile suburb in the 1920s.

A California-inspired adaptation to the automobile—the freeway—grew out of the then unique decentralized nature of metropolitan development in Los Angeles. As automobile traffic increased, concern with vehicular congestion, safety, and the ugly specter of commercial development along arterial corridors intensified. To combat these problems, proposals for limited-access landscaped parkways (freeways) gained acceptance.

Construction on the Arroyo Seco Freeway (later renamed the Pasadena Freeway) began in 1938. This pioneering 6-mile route connecting downtown Los Angeles with Pasadena was dedicated in December 1940. A second early freeway, the Cahuenga Pass, linked the downtown with the San Fernando Valley. Part of the inspiration for these roads came from the parkway concepts developed for New York City as a part of the recreation automobile era.

The first of these was the Bronx River Parkway, conceived as early as 1906 and opened in 1921. By the end of the decade, largely through the political efforts of regional planner Robert Moses, nearly 100 miles of four-lane limited-access parkways stretched deep into Westchester County on the north and Nassau County on Long Island to the east [Figure 9-9]. Many of the weekend motorists must have been pleased with what they saw because significant numbers of them began to move into the many new tract housing subdivisions which soon sprang up alongside of these suburban parkways.[11]

Stage IV: Freeway Era

The concept of the freeway as a solution to urban traffic problems gained favor in the 1930s throughout the country. The newly built autoban in Germany became a model to emulate in this country. In addition to the initiatives taken in New York and Los Angeles mentioned earlier, discussions and plans unfolded for superhighways in all metropolitan areas. Because of the lack of funding alternatives, tollroads became the only viable solution in many states. Construction of such a network began in Pennsylvania just before World War II and picked up momentum in several states after the war. Chicago was the only city to lay a rail line in the 1930s, so pervasive had the dependence on the automobile become in American cities.

As the freeway era dawned in 1945, no comprehensive national system of roads existed. Owing to their origin as recreational highways, most early improved roads led from the city into surrounding rural areas and

---

[9]Ibid., p. 49.
[10]Ibid. p. 93.

[11]Peter O. Muller, *Contemporary Suburban America*, Prentice–Hall, Englewood Cliffs, N.J., 1981, pp. 41–42.

Figure 9-9. The Long Island Motor Parkway, circa 1910. The landscaped parkway concept inspired the early design of motorways during the Recreational Automobile era. Designed for weekend pleasure driving by the affluent, these parkways soon attracted residential development along the corridors they traversed. (Nassau County Museum Reference Library)

no comprehensive financing mechanism to build them existed.

A commitment on the part of the federal government to cost sharing in financing highway construction dates to the 1916 Federal-Aid Road Act. That bill also established the principle still followed today in which federal money flows to state highway departments to handle construction. A federal-aid Primary Highway system became a reality with the 1921 Federal-Aid Highway Act. Over 260,000 miles of roads received this designation. Later, in 1936 and 1944 a much larger 600,000-mile network of federal-aid Secondary Highway road system received support. Many of these roads are the so-called farm-to-market roads and the rural mail route corridors built during the New Deal years. It is also significant to note that the U.S. Bureau of Public Roads was housed in the Department of Agriculture in its early years, reflecting the federal commitment to rural highways.

Several developments in the 1920s also increased the need for a national road network. First, hard-surface paving became more common with the half-million miles of paved roads that existed by 1926. Prior to that time, muddy and heavily rutted roads severely limited long-distance travel. Second, several named highways of continental proportions emerged. The Lincoln Highway, for example, espoused by the Lincoln Memorial Association as early as 1913, grew from its eastern

terminus in New York City westward to Philadelphia, Pittsburgh, Fort Wayne, Omaha, Salt Lake City, Reno, Sacramento, and San Francisco. Red, white, and blue stripes on utility poles identified this route. As a standardized road numbering system became a reality in the late 1920s, this corridor became U.S. Route 30, the major east–west road across the country. Interstate highway 80 now generally traverses this same corridor from Ohio westward across Indiana, Illinois, Iowa, and Nebraska to Wyoming, Utah, Nevada, and California via the same major cities. The Dixie Highway, another of the 250 named routes that grew up by the 1920s, extended from Sault Sainte Marie, Michigan, to south Florida.

By the 1930s it became obvious that a more comprehensive, national approach was necessary to fund road construction and improve safety. Such support in the form of planning and survey studies came as early as the 1934 Federal-Aid Highway Act. But most initiatives before World War II primarily occurred at the state and local levels. A precedence for construction subsidies existed from the earlier experience in building the railroad network, but never before had the public sector been so extensively involved as it would soon become in engineering and construction of a federal road system.

As an outgrowth of studies during World War II, the concept of a "National System of Interstate and Defense Highways" emerged. The 1944 Federal-Aid Highway Act called for such an initiative but no action was immediately taken. Following another comprehensive study during the Eisenhower administration and the authorization of a Highway Trust Fund to pay 90 percent of the cost at the federal level, the Interstate Highway Act of 1956 implemented what was to become the biggest public works program in U.S. history—building a 41,000-mile interstate highway system in a 16-year period, from 1956 to 1972.

In this time period, transportation improvements in North American cities consisted solely of highway projects, with one or two exceptions. Only 16 miles of urban rail transit were built in American cities from 1945 to 1970. The pent-up demand for automobiles, housing, and the better life converged after the war to induce a tremendous wave of urban development that led to suburbanization at a scale never seen before. America was well on its way to becoming a suburban nation. An era of apparent never-ending investments in highway construction to accommodate growth unfolded as congestion levels continued to mount.

Changing Urban Form

Decreased travel times became the primary justification for massive highway investments. The twin goals of adding enormous capacity to previously existing highway corridors and creating many new routes guided this program. The freeway era in fact gave us metropolitan complexes with highway networks permitting virtual random access among any two points, via the automobile or truck. The highway building program was extremely successful in allowing cities to grow rapidly, and at the same time to decrease travel times between places, thus vastly improving urban mobility. For example, travel times from the city center to any given outlying point in a metropolitan area declined considerably in the post-World War II era, especially during off-peak hours.

In addition to improving access to the downtown, this latest innovation created major accessibility advances in suburban locations, where radial and circumferential or beltway highways intersected (Figure 9-3D). Overall, a total restructuring of the metropolitan area was accomplished in the 30 years following the passage of the Interstate Highway System legislation in 1956 (Figure 9-3E).

The three diagrams in Figure 9-10 illustrate hypothetical high-rise building profiles in cities developing under varying combinations of rail and automobile access. The low density of the automobile city (Figure 9-10C) contrasts sharply with the profile of a city that developed under the influence of a rail transit system (Figure 9-10A). The former profile describes a sunbelt city built under the influence of the automobile such as Phoenix or San Diego. In the latter case, high densities in central locations and along the major routes are shown by the greater vertical development profile and lesser development intensity between the radial lines. Chicago and Boston, in prefreeway days, are examples of such densely populated cities. Figure 9-10B represents a hybrid city that has developed under the influence of both transit and the automobile. Downtown densities, and those along high-accessibility corridors, are somewhat higher than in Figure 9-10C, but strong suburbanization is also evident. Perhaps Detroit and San Francisco in the 1950s and 1960s provide examples of this scenario.

FREEWAYS AND SUBURBAN DEVELOPMENT

The goal of new freeway routes in the 1950s and 1960s within metropolitan areas emphasized improved downtown access as an antidote for declining central cities. These new radial highways in fact helped suburbia more. Freeways turned out to be two-way streets, creating new access for suburban locations for housing and jobs. Over time this decentralization process intensified, encompassing all forms of economic activity. Eventually this process completely turned the metropolitan region inside out, refocusing the majority of the residential and employment activity in the suburbs. In its most elaborate manifestation to date, this transformation has generated suburban downtowns in our larger urban regions that now serve as virtual coequals to the formerly dominant central business district. A five-stage model of land use change captures the essence of the impact of the automobile on suburban landscapes in post-World War II America. We will use that framework in the following sections to assess metropolitan change.

Stage I: Bedroom Community

As the suburbanization process gained momentum in the 1950s, residential areas mushroomed outside the

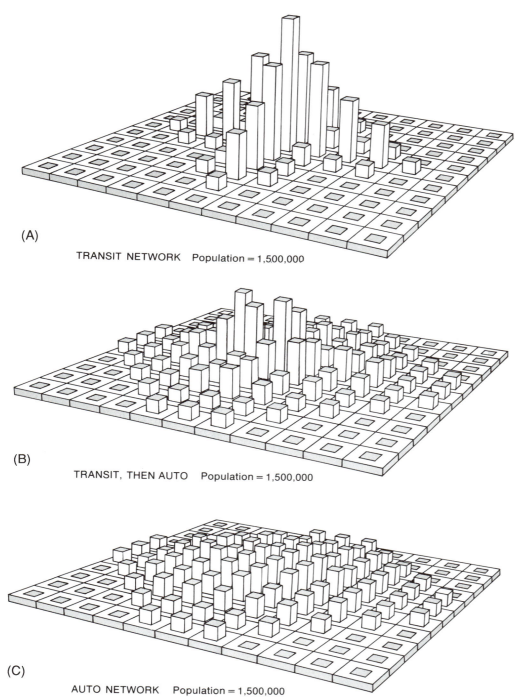

(A)

TRANSIT NETWORK   Population = 1,500,000

(B)

TRANSIT, THEN AUTO   Population = 1,500,000

(C)

AUTO NETWORK   Population = 1,500,000

Figure 9-10. Transportation Modes and City Skyline Profiles. These diagrams illustrate hypothetical high-rise building profiles in cities developing under the influence of varying combinations of rail and automobile access. The low density automobile city (C) contrasts sharply with the profile of the city developed under the influence of a rail transit system (A). A hybrid city developed under the influence of both transit and the automobile is shown in (B). *Source:* Redrawn and adapted with permission. From John R. Hamburg, et al., "Impact of Transportation Facilities on Land Development," *Highway Research Record*, 305, Highway Research Board, Washington, D.C., 1970, p. 177.

central city. Suburbs that evolved in this period were mercantilistic settlements in that residents "imported" their incomes by commuting to and from the central city while living in lower-cost spacious suburban settings. Tract housing, identified with bungalows, split-level, and ranch homes, expanded throughout the country at a voracious pace. In southern California this decentralization process was well underway before the beginning of World War II. In most other parts of the country this phenomenon did not accelerate until after the war. Levittown on Long Island well illustrates the rapidity at which this transformation of hitherto rural land occurred. On 12,000 acres of former potato fields, William Levitt built 17,000 modest-priced homes from 1947 to 1951 (Figure 9-11). This community depended

Figure 9-11. Tract Housing in Levittown. William Levitt developed this innovative automobile-oriented mass-produced subdivision of 12,000 acres on Long Island, 1947–1951. The 17,000 modestly priced houses, developed on former potato fields, sold well. The complex included schools, playgrounds, shopping centers, and good highway access. Hempstead Turnpike at left in this view looking East. (Nassau County Museum Reference Library)

completely on automobiles for access. Schools, playgrounds, and shopping centers provided all necessary services for its residents, who moved into the area from New York City. In some cases cities annexed these rapidly growing areas, but the more typical scenario involved separate incorporated places or *urban counties* providing urban services to these unincorporated areas. Urban counties refer to the situation present when the county not the municipality provides water, sewage, school, and other public service functions. In such cases suburban areas remain largely unincorporated units: the urban county concept has been very popular in suburban Atlanta, among other locations.

Stage II: Independence

Fast on the heels of residential growth came jobs and higher-order retail activity to suburban areas. In the 1960s, industrial and office parks sprung up in suburban settings in response to the increased accessibility offered by the expanding freeway system. Industrial parks increasingly catered to light industry and the distribution/warehouse function, both of which actively sought imageable sites in landscaped parks with ready freeway access (Figure 9-12).

Expansion of industrial parks came at the same time as manufacturers began seeking alternative locations for businesses formerly located in deteriorating multistory, congested, railroad corridor locations in the central city. Associated tenement housing, vandalism, crime, and poor automobile and truck accessibility commonly plagued these older industrial sites. A simultaneous change in preference from vertical to horizontal manufacturing processes occurred as manufacturers introduced new production techniques.

The shift away from railway dependence to trucking as a mode of freight transportation also required more docking and parking space than was typically available in older central city locations. The so-called *truck–auto–freeway* trilogy concept captures the importance of the interstate highway network in promoting suburban industrial expansion, the attraction of improved employee access, and the addition of highly visible and imageable settings for firms striving to enhance public awareness. These changes occurred at a time when a vast expansion occurred in light industry itself, together with a cessation of growth of the belching smokestack industries often associated with traditional manufacturing. Again, trucks served growing light-

Figure 9-12. Industrial Parks Bring Independence to the Suburb. Originally associated with the railroad, the industrial park came of age as it expanded at locations with freeway frontages in the 1960s. These parks catered to light industry and the distribution/warehouse function, both of which actively sought imageable sites in landscaped parks with easy freeway access. (Steve Proehl)

industry firms better, due to the greater flexibility provided and lesser dependence on bulky raw materials. Associated warehouse and distribution facilities geared to trucking services also gravitated to these industrial park settings. In chapter 18 the industrial and distribution function will be discussed thoroughly.

Suburban office park facilities initially catered to firms having an emphasis on intensive clerical operations, involving routine paper-processing tasks such as the back offices of banks and insurance companies, as well as regional sales offices, which preferred the intercity highway accessibility provided by outlying locations. These types of operations experienced savings from lower rental rates in suburban offices and a high level of worker satisfaction with the lower-density work environment.

Back-office operations mainly depend on internalized transactions, but telephone, postal, and electronic data transmission techniques readily provided needed external contact. Sites in the suburbs therefore provided attractive work locations for employees without sacrificing efficiency for the employer (Figure 17-5). Often, suburban expansion involved splitting up office operations, with the clerical functions breaking away

from middle- and upper-level management and research and development functions, which clung to downtown locations. We will discuss this process in more detail in Chapter 17.

To complement the office and industrial function, often in adjacent physical settings, developers built *regional shopping centers*, with department stores and other specialized shopping goods outlets offering an alternative to downtown shopping for the suburbanite. The role and impact of the regional shopping center are discussed in chapter 16.

Stage III: Catalytic Growth

The development of suburban landscapes continued to evolve in the 1970s and 1980s with the expansion of high-income housing and the growing tendency for more specialized office functions to migrate to emerging suburban business centers with expressway exposure. In some cases these centers took the form of corridors with linear belts of high-rise offices and hotels lining expressways. In other cases clusters emerged as rings of offices encircled regional malls

Figure 9-13. **Lenox Square/Buckhead Suburban Downtown in Atlanta.** As the catalytic growth stage unfolded, rings of office/hotel buildings began encircling the regional mall, creating a diversified economic base for the emerging suburban downtown. In this case, offices and hotels frame Lenox Square (center). Peachtree Road cuts across top, Lenox Road to right and MARTA rail station at bottom center. J.W. Marriott luxury hotel at lower center, and Nikko hotel at top left. (Copyright © 1991 by Dillon-Reynolds Aerial Photography, Inc.)

(Figure 9-13). A third type of complex, the large-scale mixed-use center, provides retail, office, and hotel facilities in a single master-planned complex often built by a single developer.

Whatever form these centers assumed, the occupant/tenant profile typically included middle- and upper-management personnel overseeing regional and national headquarters firms. As the business center skyline began to offer more recognition and prestige for these centers, they also began competing more directly with the downtown for the most specialized office functions, such as mortgage banking, corporate legal offices, and accounting services, once thought to be immovable bastions of downtown enterprise. Luxury hotels also joined the list of businesses seeking a growing share of the suburban market, together with additional specialized retail outlets that further complemented the office function.

Stage IV: High Rise

As the process of business center differentiation continued in the 1980s, suburban areas became functional equals to the central business district. Their high-rise buildings designed by nationally renowned architects offered luxury accommodations for their corporate tenants in a prestigious setting. In addition to the increasing use of postmodern architecture, more color, and decked parking, leasers demanded larger blocks of space. Luxury hotels, specialty retailers, and upscale restaurants joined other professional office personnel attracted to these areas, including legal, accounting, and management firms. Suburban Orange County is perhaps the quintessential example of this type of development. We will discuss this area in more detail in Chapters 16 and 17. Chicago, Dallas, Houston, Atlanta, and Washington, D.C., also boast significant suburban downtown developments. In suburban City Post Oak in Houston, for example, one finds the tallest suburban office building in America, the 65-story Transco Tower (Figure 9-14).

Stage V: Town Center

As we enter the 1990s, it is clear that suburban downtowns will continue to evolve and mature. They are increasingly acquiring greater roles as cultural, civic, and entertainment centers as the *town center* role evolves. Considerable retrofitting is also occurring as "found" space formerly used less intensely is developed. The introduction of parking structures, for example, frees land formerly used for surface parking to

Figure 9-14. Transco Tower in City Post Oak Suburban Downtown in Houston. This 65-story structure is the tallest office building in suburban America. Located on the I-610 west loop expressway, this mixed-use center came of age with the opening of the Galleria Regional shopping center in 1970. High-rise hotels, residential towers, and other office buildings and retail activities now distinguish this area. (© Richard Payne AIA 1989)

allow for more intensive development. This "rounding out" of development creates a true town center atmosphere in these suburban downtowns. Increasingly, private business associations have taken initiatives to solve community problems, thus giving these downtowns a greater sense of self-governance. Often these areas have histories of living in political limbo as they lie astride local governmental jurisdictional boundaries and lack the "official" status that a postal address or incorporation would bring. Among the problems addressed by these business-based organizations are transportation and amenity issues. Other infrastructure weaknesses can also be addressed, such as water and sewer services.

Traffic management associations (TMAs) and community improvement districts (CIDs) are two mechanisms often set up by these associations to resolve local problems. We will discuss these initiatives in a later section on suburban mobility. The addition of a town center core commercial district in Reston, Virginia, in the early 1990s is an example of a suburban downtown taking on a new identity, which illustrates the kind of change that occurs in this stage of evolution of the suburban downtown.

HIGHWAY PLANNING

By today's standards the early (pre-1950) planning process for new highway projects appears quite primitive. An entirely new methodology had to be developed and standardized to predict automobile-based urban travel needs and these procedures evolved over time on a piecemeal basis, primarily guided by federal legislation. Federal funding expanded significantly in support of planning and construction in the pre-war era and a shift in emphasis from rural to urban road needs occurred.

Not until the late 1950s did a comprehensive metropolitan transportation study for a single region reach completion. That study, the *Chicago Area Transportation Study* or CATS, became a model for metropolitan analyses in the 1960s.[12]

Other notable planning advances occurred much earlier. In 1944, an origin and destination (O&D) traffic survey procedure was adopted by the Bureau of

---

[12]*Chicago Area Transportation Study, Final Report*: Vol I, *Survey Findings*, 1959; Vol. II, *Data Projections*, 1960; Vol. III, *Transportation Plan*, 1962.

Public Roads. This process called for interviewing a sample of households concerning their travel patterns and using their demographic characteristics to make travel projections. The Housing Act of 1951 included Section 701 that funded an urban planning process, an important step forward in federal policy planning. This program required that urban transportation planning be conducted on a regional basis.

In the 1960s, procedures became more precise and the process broadened to include mass transit initiatives. The 1962 Federal Aid Highway Act, for example, required that planning in urban areas be conducted on a *continuing, comprehensive*, and *cooperative* basis (called the 3C process) in order for local areas to qualify for federal construction funds. The Department of Transportation became a cabinet-level program in 1966. By the end of the decade, the National Environmental Policy Act NEPA (1969) required that environmental impact statements be prepared prior to initiating major federal transportation projects.

Mass transit funding gained in importance in the early 1970s as dissatisfaction with automobile-based solutions diminished and gasoline shortages and price increases necessitated a broader perspective. We will discuss the more technical aspects of the highway planning process in succeeding sections as well as consider mass transit initiatives. First, it is important to review several conceptual aspects of highway travel.

Highway improvements typically generate more traffic. This factor refers to the *latent demand* for transportation. Decreased travel times encourage longer trips and more trips, and create access to places that were not as close, relatively, before travel times decreased. This situation has a *cascading effect* because more centrally located places receive more intensive development, generating even more trips to such locations, while at the same time diverting trips away from other places previously less accessible.

The realignment of retail functions following transportation improvements is an example of the cascading effect. Major regional shopping centers often benefit disproportionately in comparison to the traditional shopping streets or more local neighborhood convenience centers, which decline as trip attractors, as route capacities are enhanced. Shoppers routinely bypass neighborhood retail centers in favor of more distant regional shopping centers that can be reached just as easily as the former locations following transportation improvements. This situation not only increases dependence on the automobile but also compounds traffic problems and usually results in another round of pleas for expanding the capacity of routes to counteract "new" congestion.

In a way, the process of expanding capacity for the automobile trip has become self-defeating. Added capacity just creates more demand. It is partly for this reason that traditional highway engineering has been labeled a *tautology*. That is, when engineers indicate that great increases in flows will occur between two points and say that this warrants new or expanded capacity, this in fact does occur once the improvement is completed. The forecast is thus proved true, hence the tautology. The increased flow occurs because new capacity created it.

Journey to Work

The traditional focus of transportation planning has been the *journey to work*. In the past, this trip typically involved daily movement to the downtown area by the head of household and, in the aggregate, produced a *conflux pattern*. Planners concentrated on this trip because it was the most regular of all trips and because it caused the biggest problems. The high number of work trips generated during the morning and evening, at the start and close of the workday, became identified with the *peak load problem* (Figure 9-15). During this peak period the greatest street congestion occurred and the clamor for more highway capacity typically revolved around this issue.

An obvious response to the peak load problem was to expand highway capacity through capital construction and to implement engineering solutions such as one-way street pairing to handle more traffic. On the negative side, liberal capacity additions are expensive and generate excess capacity at times other than the peak hour. Many severe social costs also occurred as a result of this building strategy and these impacts have not been evenly spread.

Lower-income central city residents have been most negatively affected by highway building programs. Attempts to add to the *gateway capacity* of downtown areas, in order to eliminate congestion and lower the peak load, often displace disadvantaged inner-city residents. Social benefits are generally more widespread and mainly accrue to persons living away from downtown areas. The disparity between the incidence of *social costs* and *social benefits* is shown in Figure 9-16. Adverse environmental and pollution effects associated

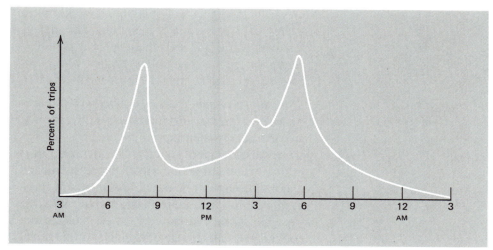

Figure 9-15. The Peak Load Problem and the Journey to Work. Most urban traffic congestion is created by the peaking of traffic during the morning and evening work trip rush hour(s). The clamor for more highway capacity typically focuses on this issue. Note the secondary peak during the late afternoon, which corresponds to school trips.

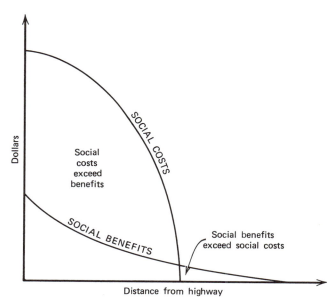

Figure 9-16. Social Costs and Social Benefits from Highway Construction. Residents located closest to a highway bear the heaviest social costs due to the localized impact of adverse environmental costs (noise, light, air pollution, and runoff problems, and so on). These residents would also benefit from the new road, but costs would exceed benefits. Only those living at some distance from the highway would experience benefits exceeding costs. From *The Urban Circulation Noose*, James O. Wheeler, copyright © 1974, Wadsworth Publishing Co., Inc., Belmont, California 94002. Redrawn by permission of the publisher, Duxbury Press.

with capacity expansions added to the evidence condemning this solution. Advocates of alternative solutions often suggested the use of higher-capacity transportation modes (buses, rail, etc.) and better management of existing capacity, especially during the peak hours.

Another problem confronting the planner today is that the journey to work is more dispersed in terms of origins and destinations and not as uniquely determined or predictable as in times past. The increased participation in the labor force by women has created more than one worker per household, which means the journey to work is less likely to be a single trip from a given household. Second, job permanence has decreased, with both skilled and unskilled employees changing work more often, making the home–work trip less stable and reliable as a planning tool. The traditional assumption that workers attempt to minimize the length of this trip may be valid but it is no longer mainly based on the distance to the CBD, but rather to any number of alternative workplace nodes in the city and suburbs.

Multiple Work Flows

The complexity of journey-to-work flows in modern cities is indicated by four types of major journey-to-work commuting patterns (Figure 9-17).

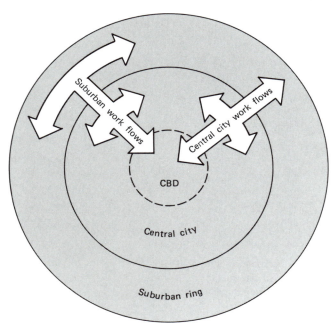

Figure 9-17. Primary Urban Work Trip Flows. Four flows characterize commuting patterns today: 1) city to city; 2) city to suburb; 3) suburb to suburb; and 4) reverse commuting (city to suburb). Over one-half of the work trips in metropolitan areas today are suburb to suburb flows.

1. *City to City.* The city to city work trip form embraces flows within the central city to major work centers, the most important of which is the CBD. Many of these trips involve public transit and less skilled workers, but the automobile is the most important mode of travel, and all income levels depend on it. The trip accounts for about 20–30 percent of all urban work trips in an urban area with 1.5 million population and has stabilized in importance. In cities in the Southwest with a tradition of liberal annexation policies, such as Houston or Phoenix, higher shares of central city employment constitute the norm.

2. *Suburb to City.* Trips originating in the suburbs and ending in the central city, mainly the CBD and surrounding work areas, comprise *suburb to city* work trip form. The trip typically involves travel via automobile on expressways or arterials. In medium to large cities, express bus service or commuter rail transit supplements the automobile. The trip is well served by the radial freeway system that normally focuses on the CBD. It is popularly believed to be the largest work trip flow in the metropolitan area, but it is not. It accounts

for about 25–30 percent of all urban work trips in a city of 1.5 million population. The trip is relatively long and the clientele is a predominantly affluent white-collar group having incomes much higher than the citywide median.

3. *Suburb to Suburb.* *Suburb to suburb* travel is typically a journey from an outlying residential area to a nearby suburban employment center, but some crosstown movement is also involved. It is primarily an automobile trip on expressways and major arterials as few public transit routes serve such outlying locations. It is a rapidly growing trip type, with a broadly based clientele. Blue-collar, clerical, managerial, and professional workers all contribute to this journey as a result of the growing variety of suburban jobs.

   In many metropolitan areas this trip involves multiple conflux patterns produced by relatively compact *labor sheds* surrounding major work nodes. A labor shed is the area from which a workplace draws its employees. A clustering of suburban residences relatively close to employment centers is evident in Atlanta, for example, as shown in Figure 9-18. The maps show desire lines linking residents with workplaces for a manufacturing center, an industrial park, and an office park complex. Typically, 75 percent of the work trips to each of these centers originate from the same quadrant of the region as the workplace, with very little cross-CBD travel.

   The share of metropolitan work trips in this suburb-to-suburb group has grown rapidly since 1960. Over 50 percent of all work trips now follow this pattern in a city of 1.5 million population. A contributing factor to this growth has also been an increase in sales work, which is unique in that no specific workplace location is involved. For many salespeople, the journey to work is a continuous daylong process involving multiple client destinations.

4. *Reverse Commuting.* Reverse commuting originates in or near the city center and ends at suburban downtown locations or dispersed arterial highway employment centers. Neither freeways nor transit serve this movement well and the trip might better be described as involving inside-out movement rather than a commute because it is inadequately served by existing route systems that typically end in residential areas in the sub-

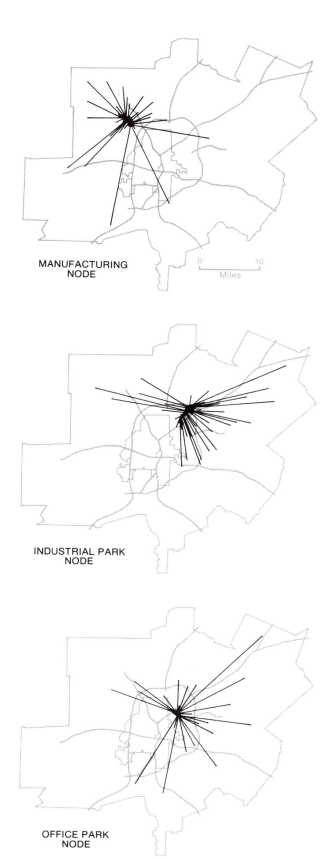

MANUFACTURING
NODE

0   10
Miles

INDUSTRIAL PARK
NODE

OFFICE PARK
NODE

Figure 9-18. Suburb to Suburb Work Trips in Atlanta. Typically, 75 percent of the work trips to a suburban work place originate in the same quadrant of the urban area as the workplace, with very little cross-CBD travel. These trips create a relatively compact labor shed around each major work center. Atlanta city limits are shown in center, with major employment centers located on or near I-285 beltway, which encircles the region.

urbs rather than at employment centers.[13] The trip is typically slow and circuitous, involving arterials and collector streets. Those not traveling by automobile but by public transit often have to ride downtown first and then transfer to an outbound vehicle, which adds to the inconvenience. This trip is patronized primarily by blue-collar employees, many of whom are minority workers. It is also a rapidly growing trip type, but remains the smallest of the four discussed here, accounting for 15–20 percent of movement to work in a city of 1.5 million population. The dominance of the automobile as a work trip mode remained strong during the 1980s. Fully 84 percent of metropolitan workers commuted by car, truck, or van in 1980, 65 percent of whom drove alone (Table 9-2).

Recent growth in urban travel has occurred as a result of a dramatic rise in the number of vehicle miles traveled. Vehicle miles traveled has increased up to five times faster than population growth or the expansion of motor vehicle registrations in some areas. Greater affluence, job decentralization, and the larger number of multiple-worker households partly explain this growth. The expanding share of nonwork trips and the decline of transit ridership in both relative and absolute terms also help account for such growth. In metropolitan areas with strong transit systems up to one-third of all work trips to the central business district occur by transit, but that area only accounts for 10–15 percent of metropolitan employment in U.S. metropolitan areas today. Overall, only 8 percent of work trips occurred by transit in 1980 (Table 9-2).

Most of the growth in vehicle travel is occurring in the suburbs, as discussed in earlier sections, and these areas are more dependent on the automobile. Rarely do

[13]John Meyer, "Myths and Realities in Urban Transportation Planning," in A. Hamer, ed., *Out of Cars/Into Transit: The Urban Transportation Planning Crisis*, Research Monograph No. 65, School of Business Administration, Georgia State University, Atlanta, 1976, pp. 75–82.

TABLE 9-2
Journey-to-Work Modes for Metropolitan Area Residents in the United States, 1980[a]

Mode		Percentage of Total
Private car, truck, or van		84
Drive alone	65	
Carpool	19	
Public transportation		8
Bus or streetcar	5	
Subway or railroad	3	
Walk		5
Other		2
Work at home		2
	Total	≈100

[a]For workers living in MSAs.

Source: U.S. Bureau of the Census, *1980 Census of Population,* USGPO, Washington, D.C., 1980.

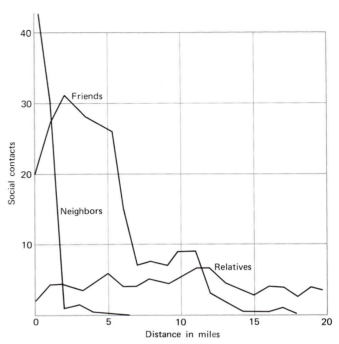

Figure 9-19. Spatial Structure of Social Trips. Three major groups of social trips have been identified based on intensities of contact: 1) friends; 2) neighbors; 3) relatives. The structure of these trips in San Diego suggests that the greatest volume of trips involves friends. These trips vary in distance, with most less than 10 miles in distance. Trips to visit neighbors are the shortest, and visiting relatives typically involves the longest travel. *Source:* Redrawn with permission. From Fred P. Stutz, "Distance and Network Effects on Urban Social Travel Fields," *Economic Geography,* 49 (1973), 134–144.

suburb-to-suburb work trips by transit exceed 1–2 percent of total travel. Moreover, building densities in these areas exist at lower levels than in the traditional downtown, which also limits transit solutions. Nevertheless, many relatively untapped transportation options could be implemented in these areas and will be discussed in a succeeding section on suburban mobility.

Nonwork Trips

Over two-thirds of a household's vehicular trips were work related 40 years ago. The great increase in personal, social, shopping, recreation, and education trips associated with the growth of multiple-car households and growing affluence limits journey to work trips today to half their previous level in terms of their relative contribution to movement. More leisure time, and the role of driving itself as a form of recreation, has also fueled the growth of these *discretionary trips.* The term discretionary travel refers to the full range of nonwork trips.

The Saturday shopping trip in suburbia, for example, often contributes as much to traffic congestion as the peak-hour weekday work trip. Despite its importance, the nonjourney to work trip is largely neglected in the transportation planning process.

Social Trips

At least three major groups of social trips have been identified based on intensities of contact: (1) visits to friends, (2) contact with neighbors, and (3) travel to visit relatives.[14] Perhaps the "friend" category is the most important of the three because of the number of contacts and range of activities involved. Friends and acquaintances made in connection with one's employment constitute the bulk of this network, but social clubs, community service, church, and other cultural contacts provide additional affiliations. The spatial structure of social trips in San Diego shown in Figure 9-19 indicates that the bulk of interaction with friends involves relatively short trips (less than 5 miles), but that many of the trips are also 10 miles or more in length. Even formerly local trips to church

---

[14]Frederick P. Stutz, *Social Aspects of Interaction,* Resource Paper 76-2, Association of American Geographers, Washington, D.C., 1976, pp. 3–6.

have been replaced by long-distance travel in many metropolitan areas so that parishioners can maintain their ties with preferred congregations.

The most localized social trips are those involving neighbors, as one would expect. In the San Diego case few of these trips were more than 2 miles in length. The third type of trip, that to relatives' homes, typically has the longest average distance, but the distance–decline relationship is relatively flat, suggesting that nearly as many long-distance as local ties are maintained.

Unlike work trips, social trips are more of a weekend and evening phenomenon. A study of Lansing, Michigan, for example, found that about two-thirds of such trips occur on Saturday and Sunday.[15] These trips also decrease as a percentage of all travel with higher-income households. Part of the explanation for this situation, which runs counter to the prevailing trend for all travel, is that "low income individuals substitute interresidential social interaction for other leisure activities requiring greater cost. Lower income individuals have greater kinship interaction than higher income individuals and this interaction is usually home-based."[16]

Shopping Trips

Shopping trips are exceedingly complex to study because they are highly variable in length, depending on the distribution of opportunities, the type of good being purchased, and whether a single- or multiple-purpose and/or multiple-place trip is involved. Distance is a good initial predictor of trips because most are responsive to the friction of distance. Explanations of shopping trip behavior have benefited from the use of behavioral choice parameters. Selecting a shopping location, for example, involves a certain degree of individual preference, which in turn depends on the individual's perception of the choices, information availability, and experience. The attractiveness of a particular *shopping opportunity* to an individual depends on expectations and actual attributes of the shopping opportunity. For example, the following measurements of shopping destination attractiveness have been utilized: (1) variety (range of merchandise and stores); (2) quality (prestige of store); (3) satisfaction (store atmosphere, compact area, helpful salesper-

TABLE 9-3
Steps in the Urban Travel Forecasting Process

1. Population and economic forecasts.
2. Land use forecast (activity allocated to zones).
3. Trip generation (number of trips each area contributes).
4. Trip distribution (connects trips generated to a destination).
5. Modal split (separation of trips by mode of travel).
6. Traffic assignment (allocates trips to specific routes).

Source: U.S. Department of Transportation, "Urban Transportation Planning Short Course, Forecasting Land Use and Travel," USGPO, Washington, D.C., 1974.

son); (4) value (good prices, availability of credit, "specials"); and (5) parking.[17] We will discuss consumer shopping behavior in more detail in Chapters 15 and 16.

FORECASTING LAND USE AND TRAVEL

Transportation planning requires a good working knowledge of anticipated future land use patterns, and land use modeling is widely used to assist in this process. Six steps employed in the forecasting process are given in Table 9-3. In order to forecast future land uses, estimates of national and regional shares of population and employment are required, and then used to estimate local metropolitan growth. Once these global forecasts are made, projections are disaggregated (broken down) and growth is assigned to small areal units (zones) within the city to show how much activity (population and employment) will take place in each at various future time periods.

Trip Generation

Population and employment growth projections assist the determination of the number of trips that will be made to various land use areas. This procedure is called *trip generation* (Table 9-4). It is very difficult to estimate precisely where trips will begin and end but generalizations can be made. Trips vary significantly by land use type, location, and the intensity of activity. Residential trip generation depends on factors such as

---

[15]J.O. Wheeler and F.P. Stutz, "Spatial Dimensions of Urban Social Travel," *Annals of the Association of American Geographers*, 61 (1970), 371–386.

[16]Stutz, op. cit., p.8.

[17]Frank S. Koppleman and John R. Hauser, " Destination Choice Behavior for Non-grocery Shopping Trips," paper presented at the Transportation Research Board Meetings, Washington, D.C. January 1978.

TABLE 9-4
Nonresidential Trip Generation

Land Use	Number of Trips	Percentage
Commercial	2,449,468	53
Public buildings	781,960	17
Manufacturing	779,340	17
Public open space	314,833	7
Transportation	280,270	6
Total	4,605,871	100

Source: Chicago Area Transportation Study, 1959. Adapted from Alan Black, *Comparison of Three Parameters of Nonresidential Trip Generation,* No. 114, p. 2, Highway Research Board, Washington, D.C., 1966.

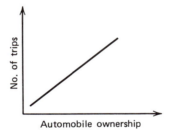

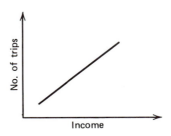

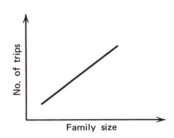

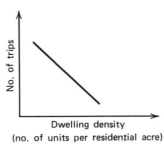

Figure 9-20. Residential Trip Generation and Socioeconomic Variables. Residential trip generation rates increase as the following characteristics increase: 1) automobile ownership (top diagram); 2) income (second diagram); and family size (third diagram). Trips decline as dwelling unit densities decline (bottom diagram).

automobile ownership, family income, and household size. Decreases in trip generation rates generally occur as population densities increase, according to the relationships shown in Figure 9-20. Auto ownership rates, income, and family size have the opposite effect on trip generation in that they are positively associated.

Nonresidential trip generation is usually estimated using one of three measures—*land area* (acreage), *floor area* (square feet), or *employment.* Each of these indicators is best suited to predict trips to a particular land use. Floor area works well for estimating trips generated by commercial activity, employment best predicts flows from manufacturing uses, and land area is most suited for estimating trips to public buildings and facilities. Commercial activity is the most important generator of nonresidential trips, frequently accounting for over half of the total number (Table 9-3 and Figure 9-21). Trip generation rates for the various land uses are highly variable throughout the day (Figure 9-22). Office and industrial trips peak in the morning, shopping trips peak at midday, and residential trips are relatively uniform throughout the day.

Trip Distribution

Once trip generation procedures are complete, analysts turn to *trip distribution* decisions (Table 9-2). The trip distribution calculation involves a geographical process whereby trips originating in one zone are allocated to other zones within the study area. In general, most trips are relatively short (Figure 9-23) and assume a J-shaped distribution. The allocation procedure often follows a *gravity model* format. Since the likelihood of a given zone receiving trips depends on the amount of activity in that zone and how far it is from the other zone, the gravity concept is well suited to this prediction problem.

The attractiveness of a zone for trips can be based on any number of measures (population, employment,

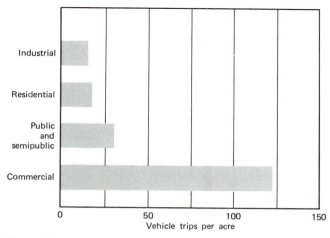

Figure 9-21. Land Use and Trip Generation Rates. Trip generation rates vary significantly by land use type, with commercial uses by far the largest generator. Industrial, residential, and public land use are much smaller generators. *Source:* Redrawn with permission. From Paul W. Shuldiner, *Nonresidential Trip Generation Analysis,* The Transportation Center, Northwestern University, Evanston, Ill., 1965.

Modal Split

Another step (Table 9-2) in the travel forecasting procedure is a *modal split* determination. The modal split calculation separates automobile trips from public transit trips and estimates the proportion of travel by each. The share of transit trips usually varies with city size and service levels available. Larger cities usually have more transit trips and a greater share of total trips by transit. The number of trips on transit typically decreases as car ownership and income increase. In most United States cities today, no more than 10 to 15 percent of total trips are by transit and the percentage is relatively stable or declining slightly following many years of significant decline following World War II (Figure 9-24).

Traffic Assignment

The final procedure in a travel study is the *traffic assignment* process (Table 9-2). This mechanistic procedure assigns trips to specific route segments that link origins and destinations in a route network. Calculations can be completed by hand, using maps and tables, but since many alternatives must be considered that require complex interrelated decisions given the maze of possible routings, automated evaluations are usually preferred. Sophisticated computer programs are now

acreage). Inhibitors to movement also can be measured in several ways (distance, travel time, cost, etc.). The ability of the gravity model to include both attractive (population, income) and negative (distance, travel time) factors simultaneously is the key to its predictive power in this case. Allocation procedures can also be refined by treating various trip purposes separately (social trips, recreation trips, work trips, etc.).

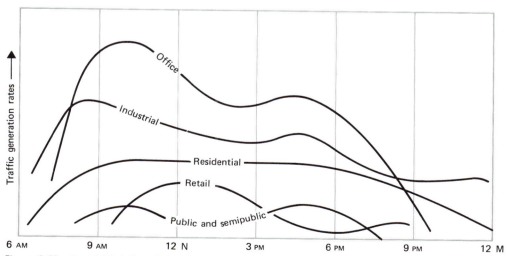

Figure 9-22. Hourly Variations in Traffic Flows by Major Land Use. Trip generation rates for various land uses are highly variable throughout the day. Office and industrial trips peak in the morning, shopping trips peak at midday, and residential trips are relatively uniform throughout the day.

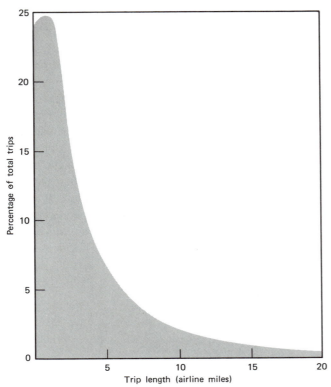

Figure 9-23. Trip Length and Percent of Total Trips. Most trips are relatively short, creating a J-shaped curve due to the rapid drop-off of trips at greater lengths. As shown here, most trips are less than 5 miles in length, with very few in the 15–20-mile range. *Source:* Redrawn with permission. From Roger Creighton, *Urban Transportation Planning,* University of Illinois Press, Urbana, 1970, 31, copyright © by the Board of Trustees of the University of Illinois.

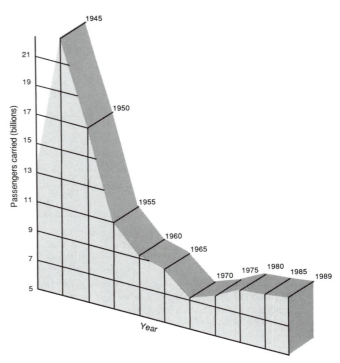

Figure 9-24. Transit Ridership in the United States, 1940–1989. Ridership on transit declined precipitously after World War II. The greater dependence on the automobile explains most of this decline. The greater interest in and support for transit in the past 20 years has reversed the decline, but growth in ridership has been modest. *Source:* After American Public Transit Association, *Transit Fact Book, 1990,* USGPO, Washington, D.C., 1990.

available to execute the route assignment process in an optimal fashion. This involves finding the *shortest path*. The shortest path itself can be defined in several ways (travel time, distance, cost, etc.). The end result of this step is the production of several *trip tables* showing simulated traffic volumes with various routings and capacity restraint relationships for different future time periods. These tables and the traffic assignment process in general can then be used to determine critical problem areas or bottlenecks in the traffic network.

Environmental Impact Statement

Largely in response to negative public reaction to highway building programs, federal (and in many instances state) laws now require that environmental impact statements be prepared outlining possible effects of highway projects and nearly all other public works construction programs, including mass transit projects. A general checklist of items often included in such statements is shown in Table 9-5. The federal legislation mandating environmental statements dates to the 1969 National Environmental Policy Act. The regulation emphasized the need for a more responsible decision-making process, one that involved comprehensive study of present conditions in the area to be affected and a consideration of all possible impacts, positive and negative. It required evidence that mitigative measures had received attention to lessen adverse impacts, if any, as well as thought given to alternative actions to the proposed program. The "lead agency" or primary sponsor of the project must initiate the impact study. Most programs involving federal funding for local projects must also be reviewed by local areawide planning agencies (see Chapter 19).

Environmental impact statement guidelines were vague at first, but they have gradually been refined through additional recommendations by agencies such as the Council on Environmental Quality, the Environ-

TABLE 9-5
Outline of a Typical Environmental Impact Statement

1. Description of project

   Location, purpose, status

2. Description of existing environments

   Physical conditions (soils; climate; vegetation; wildlife; air, water, noise pollution; infrastructure—water supply, sewerage, energy resources)

   Social environment (population, housing, education, community facilities, racial composition)

   Economic conditions (employment, income, transportation)

   Historical (archeological sites)

   Aesthetic environment (visual conditions)

3. Impact on environment (of proposed project)

   Impact on above conditions evaluated

4. Adverse environmental effects

   Unavoidable physical, social, economic, historic, archeological, and aesthetic impacts

   Mitigative actions taken or recommended

5. Alternatives to proposed action taken

   Alternate sites, alternate designs, modifications

6. Long-range impacts

7. Irreversible and irretrievable communities of resources likely to result from implementation of proposed project

Source: Compiled by Truman A. Hartshorn, based on National Environmental Policy Guidelines and selected model environmental impact statements as reported in Robert W. Burchell and David Listokin, *The Environmental Impact Handbook,* Center for Urban Policy Research, Rutgers University, New Brunswick, N.J., 1975.

mental Protection Agency, and court opinions. The result has been favorable overall. Greater consciousness of environmental effects of development now exists.

In summary, the transportation forecasting process, like the prevailing engineering strategy, has been primarily concerned with adding capacity to city streets and highways to accommodate the automobile. Traffic management strategies and transit options are considered as alternatives but are frequently dismissed too readily, typically because they offer too little capacity building potential (as in the case of management) or because of lack of funding. A variety of alternative priorities will be discussed in a later section.

Adverse Transportation Effects

Transportation is more than simply a movement and land-shaping process because it also creates costs as mentioned earlier. In addition to social and economic costs, environmental costs are also significant. In *The Accessible City*, Wilfred Owen noted that transportation keeps things moving, but in the process creates depressing environmental conditions, natural resource pollution, and the erosion of many of the amenities of urban living.[18] These include such problems as noise pollution, loss of property values, and neighborhood isolation, when communities are cut in half with new routes. Freeway construction is often placed in the category of a *noxious facility* by residents who are directly affected. They suffer the major negative impacts from the facility, even though the whole urban region benefits.

Freeway programs have been halted in nearly all major cities because of their negative impacts. The nonuser effects of such construction must now play a greater role in the decision-making process, not just the benefits to be derived by the user.

Two decades ago planners and engineers emphasized user benefits as a justification for projects, but this narrow interpretation of the freeway impact usually ignored citizen opinion and neighborhood effects. The more vocal middle class that became increasingly affected by proposed construction in the 1960s was much more effective in getting itself heard than inner-city residents who have previously felt the major impact. In many states and cities, transportation departments lost the confidence of local citizens in the 1960s because these citizens were typically consulted only after projects reached advanced stages of design.

TRANSPORTATION INVESTMENT PRIORITIES

Efficient service is assumed to be the overriding concern in providing effective transportation for urban residents. The advantage of various technologies of travel can be debated but the service they provide is the crucial factor in attracting ridership (see Box). For example, people will leave their cars only when the alternative provides equivalent service, but the problem is that the car provides the best service for most Americans.

The choice of transportation investment priorities depends partly on the size of the metropolitan area, but many alternatives are appropriate for all sizes of places.

[18]Wilfred Owen, *The Accessible City*, The Brookings Institution, Washington, D.C., 1972.

MYTHS AND FACTS ABOUT TRANSPORTATION AND GROWTH

Myth 1

Stopping development will stop traffic growth.

Fact 1

Even with no new development, traffic would increase due to the population's growing mobility (see Figure 19-5).

Myth 2

Growth is unpredictable, and therefore adequate planning is impossible.

Fact 2

Growth is generally predictable; plans made in advance are essential to cope with it.

Myth 3

Growth in a community primarily serves newcomers.

Fact 3

Much of the development in growing areas is needed to serve existing residents, not people moving in.

Myth 4

Reducing densities will reduce traffic.

Fact 4

Limiting density of development does not reduce traffic, except in the immediate area. Lower-density residential, retail, or office projects generate more, not less, overall traffic.

Myth 5

Urban transportation's major challenge is improving commuting to downtown jobs.

Fact 5

In most growing areas, a diversity of transportation needs—dispersed suburban employment, reverse commuting, and nonwork travel—are as important as, if not more important than, the problem of downtown commuting.

Myth 6

Suburbanites do not ride buses.

Fact 6

Suburbanites do ride buses when the service is reasonably fast and convenient.

Myth 7

Overall, new rail transit systems are needed to reduce traffic congestion.

Fact 7

Rail transit works best in high-density cities that already have it. It is an expensive and ineffectual way to reduce congestion in a city that does not develop around rail transit.

Myth 8

New roads should not be built, because they will only fill up with traffic.

Fact 8

Highway improvements are essential to a balanced regional transportation system. Their use is an indication of the need for them, not a sign of their failure.

Myth 9

Highways can no longer be built in urban areas.

Fact 9

New roads can, and are, being built in urban areas all over the United States.

Myth 10	Fact 10
People must change their attitudes so that they depend less on the automobile.	Commuters' choices are based on comparisons of cost and convenience, not on abstract values. It is not attitudes that must be changed, but the relative service and cost of options offered to commuters.
Myth 11	Fact 11
We should not make capital investments because they will be outmoded by new technology.	Transportation options for the near future will be much like those available today. We should continue to work with these options while seeking better technologies for the more distant future.

Source: adapted from Urban Land Institute, "Myths and Facts about Transportation and Growth," ULI, Washington, D.C., 1989.

In nearly all cities, for example, improved traffic management is appropriate. Bus operations also have a wide range of applications in various parts of the urban area and in all metropolitan areas above a certain threshold size, say 50,000 in population. High-cost, high-technology solutions, such as heavy rail or light rail rapid transit, are appropriate in larger areas.

In the future a more "balanced" transportation system is envisioned, one in which more modes are represented than at present, but high-technology rail solutions will not be as important as projected as recently as the 1970s. Each mode will provide service in the particular realm in which it operates best. In this way those people and areas who are not well served by the automobile will have a greater access to other parts of the city and those with automobiles will have suitable alternatives.

The real total costs of automobile transportation, including services, parking, road construction, police, purchase price, interest, insurance, etc., as opposed to operating costs only, show that it is far more expensive than popularly believed. Most drivers assess their cost in terms of operating costs and not total costs. They typically only consider weekly gasoline costs and parking fees when evaluating the cost of automobile transportation. Real total costs are hard to estimate, but the American Automobile Association estimated that the cost of owning and operating a car was 33¢ per mile in 1990 based on an average of cars of all sizes driven 15,000 miles a year and in service four years.

Traffic Management

Federal transportation policy is gradually shifting away from the highway "build" strategy, particularly in urban areas. Relatively low-cost, short-run *traffic management* solutions are receiving more attention. *Transportation system management* (TSM) plans are now required as a condition for continued federal funding. They include projects to conserve energy, promote transit usage, and provide a greater priority for *high-occupancy vehicles* (HOVs) (Figure 9-26). Some management strategies simply involve more effective traffic control and engineering, including:

Parking restrictions

Reversible lanes

Turn controls at intersections

One-way streets

Signing, signaling, and computerization

Stricter traffic enforcement

Banning deliveries and/or trucks during rush hours

Contraflow lanes (traffic flowing in reverse direction of normal flow during peak hours)

Turn lane flyovers into major employment centers

Goods deliveries restrictions in curb lanes

One solution to the morning/evening peak problem, for example, is to use more one-way streets to improve the flow, introduce reversible lanes (increase the number of inbound lanes in the morning and switch to more outbound lanes in the evening), ban street parking where applicable, or restrict truck deliveries during rush hours. Other possibilities include priorities for higher-capacity vehicles (carpools, vanpools, buses) or increased parking fees. The federal TOPICS (Traffic Operation Program to Increase Capacity and Safety) program is one example of an incentive package offered to local areas for management solutions. Such undertakings have a low cost, can be completed with minimal disruption, and are more consistent with the goal of revitalizing central cities than most "build" strategies.

The consensus of many observers is that the costs of automobile usage and supporting facilities (parking, route networks, etc.) need to be controlled in order to make other systems more competitive and to ensure that the automobile pays for more of the costs it creates. This would provide a more equitable framework within which other transportation strategies could operate.

The area where cars could most effectively be controlled is downtown. The availability of alternative modes of transportation to the automobile, such as bus service or rail transit, occurs most frequently to and from the downtown area. By limiting street and lane usage, charging higher parking fees, eliminating parking, or any combination of these policies, the car would have less of a competitive advantage over other forms of transportation. Many commercial business interests fear that restricting the downtown use of the automobile would be detrimental to their operations. The negative impact of such changes may be more perceived than real, as the European experience has shown.

> "There is firm evidence that limiting the use of automobiles is politically, commercially and technically feasible in urban areas."[19] Public transportation improvements must accompany such policies in congested areas. Over 100 cities, mostly in Europe, have now banned traffic from portions of their downtown areas and turned them over to pedestrians (Figure 9-25).

Carfree streets in American cities are becoming more common as well. Most involve downtown shopping malls, but others exist on university campuses and some in historic areas. The response of American downtown areas to restricting cars may not be the same as in Europe, because retailing is not as strong downtown to begin with in the United States.

Perhaps the most widely known example of success-

---

[19]Organization for Economic Cooperation and Development, "The Impact of the Automobile on the Environment," *OECD Observer*, 66 (1973), 37.

Figure 9-25. Car-free Pedestrian Street in Munich. Neuhauser Strasse is a major pedestrian corridor, lined with retail shops and restaurants. Note street furniture, including planters, lights, and seating. The Karlstor Gate dating to the 14th century is shown in distance. (German Information Center, New York)

ful car use restriction is the traffic-restraint system in operation in Gothenburg, Sweden, a medium-sized city of 500,000 population. Gothenburg has 70 route-miles of light rail transit (see later section) and 250 route-miles of buses. The radial routes of the light rail tramway system carry most of the city's transit passengers. In the early 1960s, several alternative strategies for upgrading downtown Gothenburg were contemplated. Large capital expenditure programs (parking structures, rapid transit, major expressways) were dismissed as too costly and time-consuming. Proposals to ban cars downtown altogether failed, but a compromise solution to restrict traffic but not access succeeded. A subdivided core area with five zones or compartments bounded by major streets resulted.

Beginning in 1970, cars could enter or exit downtown Gothenburg only in the zone in which they were situated and no between-zone movement was possible. Car traffic circulated freely within a particular zone. Through-town auto traffic disappeared with this innovation and auto, pedestrian, and transit conflicts declined. Ring roads serviced through traffic. Bus and tram routes were upgraded.

Implementing the restraint system proved inexpensive and produced successful results in Gothenburg. Street traffic decreased, transit ridership increased, and most citizens and businesses were pleased. Only one group, the taxi industry, suffered at all. The lesson is clear. Traffic management can produce results that were formerly dismissed as fantasy.

Paratransit

Paratransit is a hybrid form of transportation intermediate between personal and mass transit. Actually it is a host of services that provide *door-to-door, demand-responsive service* (following no predetermined routes or schedules), including *taxis, jitneys, carpools, vanpools, dial-a-bus*, and *subscription buses*.

Taxis carry far more people daily in urban areas than is realized. In fact, they may be the largest form of public transit in America, but hard data are difficult to gather because one-third of taxis are individually operated and no comprehensive statistics on them are available.[20] Taxis offer effective door-to-door service similar to that of the private automobile and this

explains their popularity. But taxis are relatively expensive, typically three to five times as costly as other transit trips. Taxis are frequently heavily utilized by the poor and the transportation dependent who do not have access to a private auto. In Pittsburgh, for example, 60 percent of taxi riders are homemakers, students, the unemployed, the retired, or the handicapped.[21] City threshold sizes to support taxis are low; hence, they can be accommodated in very small as well as large cities. In small towns they are frequently the only form of public transit.

As discussed earlier, *jitneys* were more common in America prior to World War II than at present, but they remain popular in many underdeveloped areas. Vestiges of jitney service remain in San Francisco, Atlantic City, and Pittsburgh. Airport or hotel limousine services and dial-a-ride programs for the handicapped and elderly are other forms of jitneys.

Interest in jitneys is now returning because they are particularly well suited to the needs of suburban areas with low population densities in the 2,000–6,000 persons per square mile range. In 1976, dial-a-bus systems operated in over 50 cities in the United States. Such systems are also well adapted to serving as feeders to other transit forms, but most systems now operate in small and medium cities with little or no fixed-route transit service.

Many types of *demand-responsive* systems were introduced in the 1970s to assist the delivery of many human services with the aid of federal funds. Transportation-support services were introduced, agency by agency, to assist Head Start programs, mental illness projects, the handicapped, the elderly, and day-care centers, among others. Much duplication and fragmentation occurred with these programs because each agency had separate fleets of buses or vans and catered to only one type of client, rather than to the whole spectrum of needs in a neighborhood. The agencies themselves knew little about transportation operations, and the high incidence of idle vehicles and poor maintenance produced considerable wasting of funds. Attention then turned to consolidating these fleets to provide more comprehensive and cost-effective services. Often the primary transit provider in the metropolitan area became the provider of these services.

Vanpools and carpools increased in the United States following the Arab oil boycott in 1973–1974. Several initiatives were taken by federal and state departments

---

[20]Martin Wohl, "The Taxi's Role in Urban America: Today and Tomorrow," *Transportation*, 4 (1975), 143–158.

[21]Ibid.

of transportation at that time to encourge carpools for the work trip to concentrated employment centers such as the CBD or major manufacturing facilities. These projects were gradually expanded in the 1980s but have not yet reached their potential. Only in cities with immense traffic congestion problems, such as Washington, D.C., or in areas with strict growth control measures as in California, have such programs received strong commitments to date.

State and local transportation departments or major employers frequently offer their services as a *broker*, matching potential users by obtaining addresses and schedules of potential ride-sharing customers by questionnaire so that optimal pairings can be made. This brokerage service overcomes some information and communications barriers, but since participation is voluntary, the success of the program depends on individual motivation. Considerable turnover in pool ridership occurs in most cities, but in general ridership is growing. Some employers have encouraged carpools by offering free or reduced-cost parking to cars with two or more riders. In some instances, carpools have diverted work trip riders from buses rather than from automobiles, but transit authorities are often also experiencing peak ridership during the peak load rush hour and welcome this diversion.

Vanpools offer a similar service to the carpool, but normally the vehicle is owned by the employer or transit agency rather than the rider, as in the carpool case. Vans have a higher capacity than the private automobile and are very well suited to work commutation. They offer an excellent ride with plenty of room for passenger access and can be elaborately outfitted with bucket seats, stereos, etc. Often the driver of the van is a company employee and receives free transportation and use of the van on weekend as compensation. One problem associated with vanpools is the question of the liability of the driver in the case of an accident and the prohibitive cost of insurance for such operations, but such institutional handicaps are gradually being overcome.

Another incentive that promotes pooling is the "guaranteed ride home." This concept refers to a program offered by employers that provides a carpool rider a ride home in case of an emergency (child sickness, etc.). This program reduces anxiety or uncertainty among potential participants in a carpool network.

Both vanpools and carpools offer an excellent substitute for bus transit service for the work trip in low-density suburban areas. Many projects were initially justified on the basis of reduced energy consumption and less air pollution but they also provide direct employer and employee savings and social amenities. Use of one van, for example, takes five to eight cars off the city streets during rush hours. Participants generally like vanpools because they provide social contacts, financial savings (no need for second car), and a more relaxing jorney to and from work. Employers in turn do not need to provide as much parking space and they benefit from not generating as much traffic, making it easier to meet trip reduction goals.

Vanpools also offer possibilities for nonwork trips such as recreational uses and as substitutes for evening or off-peak-hour bus transit service in smaller towns as a means of saving money. Shared-ride taxis can also be used for such service. A demonstration project funded by the U.S. Department of Transportation in Westport, Connecticut, demonstrated that children constituted one of the largest markets served by a shared-ride taxi program. Formerly, their mothers provided the chauffeur service.

Another variation of the demand-responsive concept, the *subscription bus*, provides effective long-distance (10–50 miles) journey to work service (e.g., suburb to the center city). When travel times by subscription bus are comparable to auto commuting times, this service can be competitive. This form of work trip travel requires about 50 people in an area with common schedules.[22] Guaranteed seating, avoidance of parking costs, and fewer driving hassles all serve this mode well. Usually private operators or employers offer this service by utilizing full-size buses with many amenities. A community group in Reston, Virginia, for example, has offered this type of service from suburban Fairfax County to downtown Washington, D.C., since the late 1960s.

Notwithstanding the subscription bus service example, most demand-responsive transit is provided in van-type vehicles or small buses (15–20 passengers). Fares are typically intermediate between those of taxis and fixed-route buses and operating costs on a vehicle-hour basis are similar to that experienced by fixed-route buses. These vehicles can be used very effectively because of flexible routings. Most of the vehicle fleets are small (less than 10 vehicles) and service areas are relatively compact. It is now generally agreed in the

---

[22]Ronald F. Kirby and Kiran U. Bhatt, "An Analysis of Subscription Bus Service," *Traffic Quarterly*, 19 (1975), 403–425.

industry that the key to a successful vanpool program in a particular urban region depends on the enthusiastic involvement of major employers. When they endorse and implement vanpool strategies, considerable mode-shifting from the private automobile occurs. It is also true that less than 10 percent of total trips are typically diverted to carpools and vanpools. But when coordinated with other programs such as raising parking fees, subsidizing transit fares, etc., they become an important part of a package to reduce the number of vehicles on the road. The number of persons per vehicle also increases as parking fees increase, making traditional automobile commuting more effective as well.

Bus Transit

Bus Transit systems carry 70 percent of transit riders (excluding taxis) in the United States and they dominate ridership even in cities with rail transit. Buses also carry very high portions of the peak-hour travelers on city streets, but primary service areas for buses are typically confined to the central city. Radial routes that focus on the CBD predominate. Limited peak-hour radial service may also extend into surrounding inner suburban areas.

Even though most central city workers still live in the city, ridership on bus transit has declined tremendously since World War II. The popular conceptualization is that decentralization of workers and jobs has contributed most to this decline. It has also been suggested that the massive decline in transit ridership is not primarily due to decentralization, but rather to the greater convenience offered by the automobile. The point is that a market for bus transit in the central city still exists. Central city residents are generally the poorest metropolitan residents and could benefit most from transit.

Aging of the rolling stock, the lower socioeconomic groups that rely on such systems, and larger operating deficits have similarly combined to give the bus a bad image.

Buses can be supported in a wide range of city sizes, down to communities with only 25,000 population. A much larger city with 250,000 inhabitants could also use the bus effectively, with express routings and an elaborate network of central city routes. Buses are very flexible and adaptable to many different needs, corridor densities, and service levels. Some would even argue that buses can carry passengers effectively on very high-demand routes nearly as well as a rail system, and

certainly more cheaply in terms of capital cost and operating budgets.[23] Over 185 public transit systems operate buses in the United States. The cities represented by these systems provide over 90 percent of total bus ridership in the country.

The fact that buses can carry more people per vehicle than automobiles and yet maintain the flexibility of the car has made them attractive for priority treatment on existing streets and freeways. Many cities now have *bus priority/freeway transit* in the form of reserved bus lanes on city streets (the so-called diamond lanes) and/or lanes restricted to high-occupancy vehicles on freeways.

In some cases, innovations in bus transit involve overdesign because great attention has been given to constructing exclusive bus lanes, whereas more efficiency could be gained from simple operational treatment priorities on existing routes. For example, some cities offer exclusive *busways*, typically freeway lanes in the median of expressways devoted exclusively to bus traffic (Figure 9-26). Such facilities are cheaper to build than rail transit systems and can be constructed incrementally, with existing freeways or arterial medians serving as the right-of-way. The problem is that busways do not necessarily serve passengers well, especially pedestrian access, and the opportunities for intermediate stations are severely restricted, not to mention the excess capacity they have most of the day during off-peak hours.

One area where bus priorities could have great payoff is downtown. Buses can have time advantages over automobiles in high-activity zones. Many cities have express bus operations that work well until they enter the CBD, where time is then lost because of competing traffic. The case of the Shirley Highway in Washington, D.C., the median of which is a rapid busway operation, is a good example. The routeway itself is excellent, but a major problem exists in getting to it from the downtown area. Special bus distribution systems in inner-city areas such as tunnels, intersection flyovers, and turn priorities would make buses more competitive.

One strategy involving more effective bus usage of existing freeway facilities involves *metering freeway ramps* and giving buses priority. The metering process prohibits additional automobile access once the capacity of the routeway is reached, and so cars are held back

---

[23]Andrew M. Hamer, *The Selling of Rail Rapid Transit*, Heath, Lexington, Mass., 1976.

Figure 9-26.   Express Bus Lanes on I-395 in Arlington, Virginia. Bus transit systems carry the bulk of transit riders in the U.S. and can be adapted to very high load capacities when given priority treatment. Busways running in the center lanes of expressways are cheaper to build than rail transit and can carry similar loads. They can be built incrementally and offer the flexibility of the automobile in terms of the collection and distribution of passengers. (Virginia Department of Transportation)

until space allows. This prevents congestion from lowering the performance ability of the route to carry traffic. As a further incentive to leave the car and ride the higher-capacity bus, parking lots offered near freeway ramps encourage commuters to board a bus rather than wait for access to the routeway by automobile. By limiting additional automobile access, congestion is relieved, speeds stay higher, and load capacities are enhanced. Priorities given to higher-capacity vehicles permit the freeway to carry more people. Los Angeles, Minneapolis, and other cities have used ramp metering on a few freeways as a means of improving service access.

Two final points concern who is served by improvements in bus routings and how bus lane priorities affect congestion. The CBD-bound suburban resident usually benefits more than those living closer to the CBD (5 to 6 miles from downtown) from freeway transit programs (such as busways). Upgraded bus service on arterial lanes, the creation of bus streets, etc., would serve central city residents better. Finally, if a street is already congested, changing lanes from cars to buses will not help but rather adds to congestion levels because more cars will be using fewer lanes, and the bus lane will not be at capacity most of the day. A more acceptable approach to the public is to reserve lanes for

high occupancy vehicle (HOV) operations at the time of new construction rather than removing existing lanes. Carpools and vanpools also share the use of bus lanes, busways and HOV lanes in many situations.

Light Rail Transit

Perhaps the least understood transit form, and the one that dominated at the turn of the century, is *light rail transit* (LRT). This mode of transit began with the 1890s streetcar and perhaps the horse-drawn rail cars and trolleys that preceded it (recall the earlier discussion). In 1939 only 2,700 miles of trolley lines remained in the United States (compared with 20,000 miles at the turn of the century) as buses and cars gradually took over this service. Remnants of such lines remain in Philadelphia, Boston, San Francisco, and New Orleans, but buy far the best examples of interurbans and trolleys are now in Europe. Of the 300 cities with these systems in the 1970s, virtually all were in Europe, including a large number in West Germany. In the late 1970s and 1980s, several new systems of this type opened in the United States and Canada, including: Calgary, Edmonton, Vancouver, Baltimore, Portland, San Jose, and San Diego (Figure 9-27). In the

Figure 9-27. Light rail transit in San Diego. One advantage of a light rail system over heavy rail is that it does not need a totally separate right-of-way; it can operate on existing streets, as the case here. Light rail transit provides better service than the bus for line-haul trips on medium-to-high density corridors. (Courtesy of Sandra Small)

early 1990s, several others opened, including in Los Angeles, and a system was under construction in Houston.

One advantage of a light rail system over rapid rail is that it does not need a totally separate right-of-way as it can operate on existing streets. Construction costs are far less, design standards are lower (it can navigate steeper grades and sharper turns than rapid rail), and it can be built incrementally while rapid rail cannot. Light rail does not have the capacity of rapid rail nor can it travel as fast. Because of closer station spacing and the sharing of rights-of-way, speed and hauling capacities are lower for light rail than for heavy rail transit.

LRT systems have lower space requirements than a comparable bus network, are more environmentally compatible and durable, and offer better performance. By linking vehicles together, trains with much higher capacity can be formed. LRT is better than bus service for line-haul trips on medium- to high-density corridors and is particularly well suited to the needs of medium-sized cities. In many ways LRT is similar to the busway but a different technology is involved. Construction costs are similar ($4–5 million per mile), but LRT provides better line-haul service and downtown distribution when the tunneling option is used.

In Europe, LRT systems are used in both medium and large cities. In the latter they serve as feeders to rapid rail lines and provide secondary distribution in the central city. This means that line lengths are relatively short (4.5–8 km), and in order to provide good center city service, stations are relatively closely spaced (350–800 m). Interest in LRT increased in North America in the 1980s to the point that several cities built new systems and those that had systems of this type upgraded service and equipment (e.g., San Francisco, Philadelphia, and Pittsburgh). Several of these systems have not lived up to their expectations in terms of ridership levels, suggesting that competing with the automobile is an uphill battle. Even though light rail systems cost much less to build, total costs per passenger carried are not significantly less than those for rail systems, as Table 9-6 indicates. Costs per passenger range from $5.40 in Portland to $10.73 for the Buffalo system. The reason for such high costs is primarily due to disappointing passenger loads, which typically fall far below the design capacity of the system. The Sacramento network, for example, carries only 13,000 passengers a week. Because of these weak performance statistics, federal and local enthusiasm for these systems has waned.

TABLE 9-6
Comparisons of Transit Ridership, Capital Costs, and Operating Costs for Selected Transit Systems

	Light Rail			Heavy Rail		
	Buffalo	*Portland*	*Sacramento*	*Washington*	*Atlanta*	*Miami*
Weekly passengers (thousands)	28	20	13	386	179	37
Capital cost (millions of 1988 dollars)	$722	$241	$188	$7968	$2720	$1341
Annual rail operating expense (millions of 1988 dollars)	$11.8	$5.5	$6.9	$198.9	$40.0	$37.9
Total cost per rail passenger (1988 dollars)	$10.73	$5.40	$6.94	$8.74	$5.92	$16.73

Source: Don H. Pickrell, *A Comparative Analysis of Forecast and Actual Ridership and Costs for Ten Federally-Supported Urban Rail Transit Projects,* U.S. Department of Transportation, Washington, D.C., 1988.

Rapid Rail Transit

The greatest advantage of *rapid rail transit* (RRT) is its very large line-haul capacity. Such capacity is only appropriate in very densely populated corridors of large metropolitan areas. Several rules of thumb related to size and density have been suggested as criteria on which to base a decision for implementing rail rapid transit:[24]

1. Metropolitan population of 1 million, preferably 2 million.
2. Central city population of 500,000–700,000; central city density of 10,000–14,000 persons per square mile.
3. 300,000 daily destinations downtown per square mile of CBD.
4. 25–50 million square feet of floor space in CBD.
5. CBD employment of at least 100,000.

The performance and reliability of heavy rail systems are very good when properly maintained, and rides are smooth. Most United States systems are radial, except in New York City, where an extensive grid system exists. Most systems are very old, dating to the early twentieth or late nineteenth century, but several new systems have been built in the past 25 years, including those in San Francisco, Washington, D.C., Atlanta, Miami, and Baltimore. Line lengths are

usually very long (10 to 20 miles) and stations are widely spaced. The wide spacing is especially pronounced in the San Francisco system constructed in the early 1970s (Figure 9-28) and the Washington system, which opened in the mid-1970s. Large excess capacities exist on many systems except at peak hours. Wide station spacing increases speed (station to station) but hinders collection and distribution of passengers and makes service levels (door-to-door travel times) relatively poor.

The harshest criticism of rail systems is that they are expensive to build (50 million dollars or more per mile), are fixed in place, and do not go, or may not go in the future, where people want to go. They are usually focused on the central city and typically do not link major suburban job centers, nor do they provide good service to the user in terms of access at either or both ends of the trip, which invariably requires a second trip by another means (car, bus, long walk, etc.).

As with light rail systems, ridership levels rarely meet projections and operating costs typically exceed estimates. Ridership levels on the Miami system vividly demonstrate over-optimistic projections as they only register 18 percent of the forecasted level. Even more revealing, the total cost per rail passenger carried exceeds $16.00 per trip, necessitating very large operating subsidies (Table 9-6). By comparison, the Washington, D.C., and Atlanta systems cost $6.00–9.00 per passenger trip. Since fares cover only a fraction of total costs, questions about who pays the subsidy and how much have become more difficult to answer. Federal funding for transit construction declined significantly during the decade of the 1980s as disillusionment with rail solutions grew.

[24]W.S. Smith, *Manual on Urban Planning*, Chapter VII, "Transportation Planning," *Journal of the Urban Planning and Development Division,* ASCE, 93, No. UP2 (June 1967).

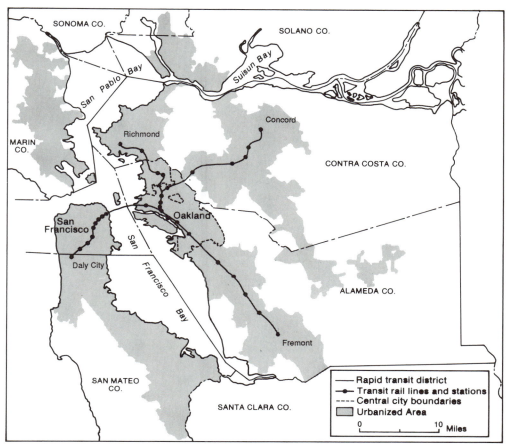

Figure 9-28.   San Francisco Bay Area Rapid Transit (BART) System. The greatest advantage of the heavy rail transit system is its large line-haul capacity. Only the most densely populated corridors of the largest metropolitan areas meet the minimum criteria for such a system. The long line lengths and wide station spacing of the BART system, whose lines cross in Oakland, give it a suburban emphasis. The highest density area in the region (the city of San Francisco) is served by only one line.

People Mover

The *people mover* concept is not a grandiose public transit network but a more refined pedestrian aid appropriate to a high-density localized area. People movers use guideways and stations (stops) are usually on the line, thus simplifying routing. Speeds are moderate (10–20 miles/hour) and lines are usually short. These systems are particularly well suited to downtown areas, airports, shopping centers, and amusement parks, where concentrations of activity exist and only short hauls are needed. Many examples of this form of transport are already in place, ranging from monorails (Disneyland and Seattle) to horizontal elevator-type shuttle operations (Tampa Airport) or rubber-tired ve-

hicles navigating a circuitous path (AIR-TRANS at Dallas–Fort Worth Airport).

The U.S. Department of Transportation funded several downtown people mover demonstration programs in the late 1970s. Only the systems in Miami and Detroit materialized, both completed in the mid-1980s. These people mover systems form downtown distributor loops that connect major activity centers (transit stations, hotels, office buildings) and supplement existing pedestrian, auto, and transit service. It was hoped that they would stimulate downtown redevelopment but since they have opened, results have been disappointing. The outlook for the people mover is not totally bleak, however, as it may also have an application in suburban downtowns as a secondary distribution system.

Urban Design

A most promising long-range goal for urban transportation would be to reverse or stabilize the trend toward more and more dependence on movement that has characterized the twentieth-century American city through better *urban design*. It has been said that we use transportation to cure design mistakes. The process of gradualism (adding more and more transportation capacity, especially roads and freeways) that we have subscribed to in the past was based on the philosophy that urban mobility is best served by road builders following the developers and entrepreneurs into suburbia and integrating their projects into existing networks. This often meant that little planning or coordination of the location decision process occurred and that improved access to poorly located facilities had to be overcome through new route construction.

Bad facility planning has required massive and unending transportation investments. Decentralization of activity and incremental transport improvement programs require continuous capacity expansion of the highway system. Journey to work trips have increased in length, and growing affluence has placed more demand per household on existing facilities in the form of more cars, more trips, and higher design standards.

We suggest here that better urban design, not more transportation, is needed. Rather than increased separations between workplace and home, residential areas need to be interspersed among employment nodes, thus decreasing the journey-to-work trip length. The emphasis should shift to higher-density activity nodes in suburban areas, including housing such as occurs in suburban downtowns, which uses land more intensively. Less segregative zoning that would permit mixing compatible land uses in the suburbs, such as building neighborhood retail centers in subdivisions, would also help. Combining various housing styles and densities in such an area, such as intermingling single-family detached units with mid-rise and high-rise accommodations, would also benefit traffic congestion.

Some planners envision a future city that is totally free of the auto and other vehicular conveyances. High-density living in Soleri's three-dimensional *arcology* is an example (see Chapter 19). Realistically, future living will probably not be at such high densities in most cities (except perhaps in Tokyo or New York), but certainly a more energy-conscious design will be needed to accommodate higher densities than in the past.

In the past decade, people have come full circle regarding urban transportation priorities. Whereas the clamor used to be for more roads and more parking, it is now for more coordination in the development of transportation improvements. The aggressive construction programs of the past were fine as long as they could be afforded and roads were easy to build, but we now have a much more complex environment and funding priorities necessitate more caution.

The automobile will likely remain the most important transportation vehicle in North America and it will continue to be the primary mode for most trip types (recreation, shopping, social, etc.), but alternatives for the journey to work seem to be evolving and are most promising. Since the work trip is the most structured (time of day, volume, and direction of flow), it seems to be the easiest and most logical trip for which transportation alternatives can be found.

Suburban Mobility

Paralleling the great boom in the size and scale of suburban work trip growth in the 1980s was the gradual reduction in federal funding of road construction. Local and state governments absorbed some of the slack but were not prepared financially or logistically to fill the void. The predominant response has been a slowdown in new construction and accelerated dependence on private sector financing even as massive capacity improvements were needed.

Local governments today typically ask developers to bear a greater share of the costs of transportation improvements as a condition for project approval. These exactions, typically called *impact fees*, provide funds for additional lanes, overpasses, signal improvements, and/or freeway interchanges. Another technique, referred to as a *community improvement district* or CID, involves property owners in an area taxing themselves to pay back bonds sold to finance transportation improvements, ranging from additional lanes and interchanges to people movers and local automated light rail transit systems. The advantage of this approach is that existing as well as new property investors help pay for improvements. Of course the CID technique can also be used to finance a variety of other initiatives, not just transportation. Traffic management associations, discussed in the next section, represent a third partnership approach in handling transportation facility coordination.

In California and elsewhere, increasing traffic congestion levels and the lack of new freeway programs have led to growth moratoriums in several cities. Frequently developers are asked to maintain present or improved traffic conditions after their project is completed. This situation requires close attention to adding additional capacity to corridors and instituting better traffic management, including carpool and vanpool programs, parking management plans, and the inclusion of housing initiatives in development plans. Linkage programs increasingly call for the construction of a certain number of housing units tied to a specific level of commercial investment. Mandatory trip reduction ordinances in some California communities in fact require that no new construction occur until traffic problems are resolved.

Toll roads also appear to be gaining favor as a financing mechanism. Tolls not only help pay for the investment but also serve as a management technique and will likely gain favor in the future as privatization occurs in the transportation field. Increased gas taxes and sales taxes represent other mechanisms to finance transportation improvements. The South Coast Air Quality Management District Plan in California now requires that all companies with over 500 employees show how they are going to reduce commuting in order to curtail automobile-induced air pollution. Electric or fuel-cell-powered cars will also be required in California after the turn of the century as restrictions on fossil fuel burning become more stringent.

In time, a fully autonomous motor vehicle will also evolve:

> Such a vehicle would be capable of operating in any traffic environment and traveling portal to portal without driver intervention. Lateral guidance would probably utilize machine vision and pattern recognition. A number of other highly sophisticated sensors and communication devices would provide navigation, collision avoidance, and route optimization capability.[25]

In the future, motor vehicle drivers will probably be required to bear a larger share of the costs of supporting the transportation system, including both highway usage and parking facilities. More automation will greatly increase the cost of developing and maintaining roadbeds. The smart roads that are coming will be able to handle traffic better, detect and manage accidents more smoothly, and relieve pressure on the driver. New metropolitan highways, funded at the local level, will likely be designed as *super street arterials*, "wide multilaned arterials with limited access provided from intersecting streets."[26] They will also be less intrusive and disruptive than their freeway predecessors.

A more participatory planning process is also envisioned involving community leaders, local elected officials, professional planners and engineers, major employers, developers, and transportation management association professionals. Coordinating work schedules of employees at major employment centers to decrease the congestion at traditional peak hours will also become a more common strategy to coordinate traffic.

Traffic Management Associations

Transportation Management Associations (TMAs) rose from obscurity to become a major player in the metropolitan traffic picture in the 1980s. Over 50 such organizations existed nationwide at the end of the decade, with about half concentrated in California, where the concept first took root.

> Transportation Management Associations are partnerships between business and local government, created to help solve transportation problems associated with rapid suburban growth. TMAs give the business community a voice in local transportation decision making, build a local constituency for better transportation, and serve as a forum for public/private consultations on a variety of issues such as highway funding priorities, traffic flow improvements, changes in transit service, and traffic mitigation. TMAs enable developers, employers and property managers to pool resources and address transportation problems on a joint basis, thus benefiting from economies of scale. In unincorporated suburbs, TMAs act as a combination of a shadow transportation district and a civic establishment advocating the interests of the otherwise unrepresented area. . . .
>
> Some TMAs focus on policy leadership and advocacy, and aim primarily to influence public decisions about transportation. Others assume a more operational role: They facilitate ridesharing, coordinate alternative work hours programs, administer parking work hours programs, administer parking management programs, operate shuttle buses and help their members comply with local traffic mitigation requirements through demand management programs. Some "second generation"

---

[25]Institute of Traffic Engineers, *A Toolbox for Alleviating Traffic Congestion*, ITE, Washington, D.C., 1989, p. 34.

[26]Ibid., p. 35.

TMAs have evolved into broad purpose organizations which, in addition to their transportation responsibilities, manage a variety of shared-tenant services such as day-care, security, and telecommunications.[27]

SUBSTITUTING COMMUNICATION FOR TRANSPORTATION

A question arises regarding the possibility of *substituting communication* investments for transportation inputs in designing the future city. Advances in accessing information remotely through data networks, high-speed fax copiers, and other telecommunications devices have assisted many businesses in cutting back vehicular travel. The widely dispersed metropolitan service economy may also be an ideal environment for telecommuting to prosper. Telecommuting refers to working at home or at a decentralized work center, either of which is linked by a communication network to a central office complex. Such an arrangement offers considerable promise in highly congested environments such as southern California. A side benefit from promoting telecommuting would be to cut back on air pollution emissions. In fact telecommuting is an option being studied carefully by the Southern California Air Quality Management District mentioned above.

Social trips and recreational travel may even increase rather than decrease with improved communications. Increased leisure time, affluence, and automobile ownership, coupled with more knowledge about places, frequently induce more travel. Over time there is also a tendency for decision making and the bureaucratic machinery to become more complex, which has increased the demand for travel. Telecommunication improvements can perhaps offset this trend for more travel for many information-based transactions. Innovations have already loosened the ties these activities formerly had with downtown areas, showing that face-to-face contact is not as crucial today.

There are limits to the ability of communcations to become a substitute for transportation. The two may only complement one another and not be substitutes for many firms. For example, "telephone calls precede a meeting and the meeting itself (for which travel is still necessary) provides topics for further communi-

cation."[28] Also, many companies rely comparatively little on communication and information linkages. Resource extraction, manufacturing, and the wholesaling functions depend far more on transportation. For these industries, telecommunication is not as crucial as transportation.

If telecommunication does become more sophisticated in the future, it may even increase dependence on transportation by encouraging functions to disperse. On the other hand, it could provide a land-shaping tool if planners could designate only certain areas for improved communication access. The most likely prospect is that demands on transportation will continue to increase, as will the need for improved communication. Even though the latter may be easier and cheaper to install (communication improvements are less controversial), it is unlikely they will ever become interchangeable, and even more remote that transportation systems will be superseded by communication networks.

SUMMARY AND CONCLUSION

The role of the transportation system in the city continues to evolve but remains as central as ever as a land-shaping force and public policy instrument. More emphasis is placed on managing the system today and in finding alternatives to the single-occupancy automobile trip. The renewed interest in mass transportation and paratransit forms will serve the older core city well into the future and create higher densities in emerging suburban areas. The emphasis in the past, on gradualism, associated with liberal expansion of route capacities, will be replaced by more deliberate policies to get the most efficiency out of the network in the future.

The construction and maintenance costs of more facilities will be supported to a greater degree in the future by the private sector. User fees (e.g., tolls) will not only provide a greater part of the financial support for these facilities, but also discipline the demand for access during peak demand hours. More operations of existing publicly supported transit systems also will be privatized in the future as a cost-saving measure.

The polycentric city created by the automobile is here to stay. Existing suburban downtowns increas-

---

[27]Association for Commuter Transportation, *Transportation Management Association Directory*, ACT, Washington, D.C., 1989, p. iii.

[28]Richard C. Harkness, "Communication Innovations, Urban Form and Travel Demand: Some Hypotheses and a Bibliography," *Transportation*, 2 (1973), 155.

ingly will be retrofitted with the addition of transit facilities, which in turn will lead to a greater concentration of activity at the crossroads locations that characterize these areas. A better balance of jobs and housing must also evolve in these areas in order to minimize additional stress on the transportation network. Improved telecommunications facilities will temper somewhat the demand for added transportation capacity, but rapid mobility will remain a cornerstone for the continued economic development of metropolitan areas.

Suggestions for Further Reading

Bastan, Fred. *Beverly Hills: Portrait of a Fabled City*, Douglas–West Publishers, Los Angeles, 1975.

Bottles, Scott L. *Los Angeles and the Automobile*, University of California Press, Berkeley, 1987.

Broth, Christy. *Mankind on the Move: The Story of Highways*, Automotive Safety Foundation, Washington, D.C., 1969.

Cavin, Ruth. *Trolleys: Riding and Remembering the Electric Interurban Railways*, Hawthorn Books, New York, 1976.

Cervero, Robert. *America's Suburban Centers: The Land Use–Transportation Link*, Unwin–Hyman, London, 1989.

Creighton, Roger. *Urban Transportation Planning*, University of Illinois Press, Urbana, 1970.

Cross, Thomas B., and Marjorie Raizman. *Telecommuting: The Future Technology of Work*, Dow Jones–Irwin, Homewood, Ill., 1986.

Crump, Spencer A. *Ride the Big Red Cars: the Pacific Electric Story,* 17th ed. Trano-Anglo Books, Glendale, Calif., 1988.

Dearing, Charles L. *American Highway Policy*, The Brookings Institution, Washington, D.C., 1941.

Fielding, Gordon J. *Managing Public Transit Strategically*, Jossey–Bass, San Francisco, 1987.

Flink, James J. *America Adopts the Automobile, 1895–1910*, MIT Press, Cambridge, Mass., 1970.

———. *The Automobile Age*, MIT Press, Cambridge, Mass., 1988.

Foster, Mark, S. *From Streetcar to Superhighway: American City Planners and Urban Transportation,* Temple University Press, Philadelphia, 1981.

Garreau, Joel. *Edge City: Life on the New Frontier.* Doubleday: New York, 1991.

Gray, George E., and Lester A. Hoel, eds. *Public Transportation: Planning, Operations, and Management*, Prentice-Hall, Englewood Cliffs, N.J., 1979.

Hamer, Andrew M. *The Selling of Rapid Rail Transit*, Heath, Lexington, Mass., 1976.

Hansen, Susan, and I. Johnston. "Gender Differences in Work-Trip Length: Explanations and Implications," *Urban Geography*, 6 (1985), 193–219.

Hansen, Susan. *The Geography of Urban Transportation*, Guilford Press, New York, 1986.

Hebert, Richard. *Highways to Nowhere: The Politics of City Transportation*, Bobbs–Merrill, New York, 1972.

Hilton, George W. *The Cable Car in America*, Howell–North Books, Berkeley, Calif., 1971.

Hodge, David. "Geography and the Political Economy of Urban Transportation," *Urban Geography*, 11 (1990), 87–100.

Jones, David W., Jr. *Urban Transit Policy: An Economic and Political History*, Prentice–Hall, Englewood Cliffs, N.J., 1985.

Kirby, Ronald, *et al. Para Transit: Neglected Options for Urban Mobility*, The Urban Institute, Washington, D.C., 1974.

Middleton, William D. *The Interurban Era*, Kalmbach, Milwaukee, 1961.

Muller, Peter O. *Contemporary Suburban America*, Prentice Hall, Englewood Cliffs, N.J., 1981.

Pisarski, A. *Commuting in America: A National Report on Commuting Patterns and Trends*, Eno Foundation, Westport, Conn., 1987.

Puscher, J. "Urban Public Transport Subsidies in Western Europe and North America," *Transportation Quarterly*, 42 (1988), 377–402.

Stutz, Frederick P. *Social Aspects of Interaction*, Resource Paper 76-2, Association of American Geographers, Washington, D.C., 1976.

Warner, Sam Bass, Jr. *Streetcar Suburbs: The Process of Growth in Boston, 1870–1900*, Harvard University Press/MIT Press, Cambridge, Mass., 1962.

Weiner, E. *Urban Transportation Planning in the United States: An Historical Overview*, U.S. Department of Transportation, Washington, D.C., 1983.

Wheeler, James O. *The Urban Circulation Noose*, Duxbury Press, North Scituate, Mass., 1974.

Wohl, Martin, and C. Hendrickson, *Transportation Investment Pricing Principles: An Introduction for Engineers, Planners, and Economists*, Wiley, New York, 1984.

10

PERCEPTION AND QUALITY
OF LIFE ISSUES*

The city as a "human artifact" contains many structures and activities for the conduct of business and leisure. But urban places are more than concrete, glass, and steel configurations; they are forums for complex interactions among people—for purposes of work, relaxation, and cultural stimulation.

Geographers in recent years have become interested in exploring the perceived images of cities. Human spatial behavior within the city is largely attributable to the way individuals mentally view the city's internal parts. The way these areas are perceived is fully as important as the physical-structural components themselves. Strong positive images evoked at a place produce satisfaction with and attraction to it (Figure 10-1).

Physical forms (i.e., structures and other physical objects) characteristic of a place present environmental cues that aid in the determination of the relative location of urban activities. Familiarity with an area can facilitate movement, including avoidance decisions (Figure 10-2). The level of satisfaction or psychological uncertainty varies with knowledge of an area.

Negative perceptions of parts of the city, based on reports of high crime rates and deviant behavior, for example, often lower the level of social interaction. Positive connotations associated with other images, such as the downtown skyline, can enhance interaction.

In this chapter, we will review several concepts that help us understand the ways we evaluate the city and how important these perceptions are in guiding human behavior. We will also review several elements that collectively comprise the quality of life of an area. While such a determination represents a very subjective process, it is indeed an important undertaking because decisions and evaluations of cities are made on the basis of such factors. Moreover, strong variations in these characteristics exist from place to place and have become the focus of popular publications that "rate" cities as places to live.

ELEMENTS OF AMERICANS' PERCEPTIONS

Americans possess many idealized images and visual stereotypes that help explain the structure and design of the city.[1] Perhaps most important is the great credibility that has been given to *size*. Big projects (urban renewal, parks, garages, etc.), big buildings, and big cars have

---

*Chapter for first edition authored by Wayne G. Strickland, Fifth District Planning Commission, Roanoke, Va., revision by author.

[1]David Lowenthal, "The American Scene," *The Geographical Review*, 58 (1968), 61–88.

Figure 10-1. Historic Elfreth's Alley in Philadelphia. Images one possesses of an area of the city shape the way that area is evaluated. Strong positive images, such as those produced by this historic street, produce satisfaction and attraction to the area. (Courtesy Teri Leigh)

past is idealized and some places are set aside for special treatment to preserve history. Examples are Greenfield Village, Michigan; Old Sturbridge Village, Massachusetts; and Williamsburg, Virginia. Often replicas are treated with more reverence than the real thing. Walt Disney World's idealized New Orleans in Orlando, Florida, for example, may be preferred to the real Bourbon Street in the Vieux Carré (French Quarter) section of New Orleans because it has been "cleaned up."

The belated sense of historic preservation in the United States, which became a front page issue only in the past two decades, reflects this lack of commitment to the past. This traditional lack of commitment to preservation contrasts strongly with the situation in Europe, where the opposite philosophy prevails. A stronger planning and permitting process in European cities places a much higher priority on maintaining the integrity of the older buildings (Figure 10-5). Nevertheless, most cities in the United States now enforce historic preservation ordinances and offer special protection for historic districts. Such actions received a boost at the federal level with special tax concessions for preservation initiatives in the late 1970s. Many state and local areas also provide such incentives, as well as low interest loans for renovation programs.

A variable sense of *beauty* is another characteristic of American life. Certain select landscapes, particularly monuments and public buildings, are often set aside for priority treatment in terms of landscaping, gardens, lighting, or special manicuring, while other nearby places are allowed to deteriorate and become eyesores. This double standard is partly explained by the emphasis placed on certain individual parts rather than on the whole. It is also due to a preoccupation with the functional utility of an activity or place rather than community aesthetics.

all received disproportionate attention. The dinosaur is frequently used as a symbol because it exemplifies this preoccupation. The grid street pattern found in many cities emphasizes distance and size by channeling visual sightlines along a street to the horizon (Figure 10-3). Size and space can also be dramatized by architectural style. Of course, the skyscraper is one such example, but a strong statement can also be made by the building style itself, as in the case of the *flatiron building*, popular in the late-nineteenth-century city. The term "flatiron" comes from the triangular shape of the building, which can be "shoehorned" into a narrow triangular block. Often such buildings exhibit massive front footages built out to the sidewalk but hollow interiors or rear quarters (Figure 10-4).

Another characteristic of the American psyche, according to David Lowenthal, is a love for the *new*. Americans live in the future, so to speak. They tear down the old and live in throwaway "stage sets." The

TWO APPROACHES TO PERCEPTION RESEARCH

Historically, research concerning the perception of the city has been organized around two distinct philosophies: (1) the structural approach and (2) the evaluative approach.[2] The major works in the field of perception

[2]Roger M. Downs, "Geographic Space Perception: Past Approaches and Future Prospects," *Progress in Geography*, 2 (1970), 65–103.

Figure 10-2. Graffiti in the Inner City of Philadelphia. Graffiti suggesting hostility can lead to decisions by outsiders to avoid an area. Negative perceptions of parts of the city, based on reports of crime rates and deviant behavior, often lower the level of social interaction. (Courtesy Roman Cybriwsky)

have focused on these themes as a means to formulate hypotheses concerning the way persons organize thoughts about space within the city and how these thoughts are utilized in decision-making processes.

Structural Approach

The *structural approach* focuses on the identity and form of geographical space perception and how information about the environment is obtained. The manner in which thoughts about space are organized, including the orientation process in learning about locations in the city, provides a major focus for this research. The impact of learning processes on behavioral decision making is also central to this theme.

In the early part of the century, research was conducted to learn about confusion or "disorientation" in people's experience in unfamiliar regions.[3] An imaginary map was utilized in this research, which involved respondents locating major cities in relation to distance and cardinal direction from New York City. From this survey the author developed a typology of imaginary maps. Each of these groups was composed of those individuals that made similar distance and direction assessments.

Little effort was made to examine imaginary maps in detail until Kevin Lynch published his research in *The Image of the City* in 1960.[4] Lynch's work focused almost entirely on the physical structure of the city and its relationship to an individual's orientation. The

[3]C. C. Trowbridge, "On Fundamental Methods of Orientation and Imaginary Maps," *Science*, 38 (1913), 888–897.

[4]Kevin Lynch, *The Image of the City*, MIT Press, Cambridge, Mass., 1960.

Figure 10-3.   The Grid Street Pattern of Salt Lake City, circa 1971.   The grid street pattern emphasizes size and distance by channeling visual sightlines along the street to the horizon. Note Mormon Tabernacle Church spires at lower center. (Courtesy Edward Lile)

legibility of the cityscape was used by Lynch as a term to show how one could fit various parts of the city together, creating a coherent and recognizable pattern. He emphasized the importance of environmental cues to aid movement. These cues provided an individual with a sequence of directional instructions. For example, the initial direction is normally followed on a trip until reaching such a cue, which might be a building or landmark. This cue mentally indicates to the observer whether or not a turn is needed to arrive at a prescribed destination. One continues to follow this series of mental signals until arriving at the destination.

While the study of orientation has been a major topic in the structural approach to perception, other emphases have also been stressed. The role of highway design on the perception of the environment provides one example. Roadscapes are very important in making an urban area more comprehensible to the traveler. By manipulating the design of roads, the engineer affects the way one identifies with the city, how it "is orga-

nized, what it symbolizes, how people use it, [and] how it relates to [the traveler]."[5] The construction of roads near historic sites may give the traveler a sense of historical continuity between the existing cityscape and the architecture that predominated in the past.

The placement of buildings, their living spaces, and architecture can also affect human behavior. It has been contended that physical and social space within any neighborhood are inextricably linked together in the minds of residents.[6] The type of building configuration can modify social interaction in a housing project. For example, the location of an apartment within a multiunit structure can dictate the level of social interaction or social isolation. Increased social interaction can occur in apartments situated in central locations, while

---

[5]Donald Appleyard, Kevin Lynch, and John Meyer, *The View from the Road*, MIT Press, Cambridge, Mass., 1964, p. 2.
[6]Terrence R. Lee, "Psychology and Living Space," *Transactions of the Bartlett Society*, 2 (1964), 9–36.

Figure 10-4. Flatiron Building in New York City. Architectural styles often dramatize size by emphasizing massive front footages built out to the sidewalk. Note the triangular shape of this building, which is "shoehorned" into a narrow triangular block. (Ray Ellis/Rapho/Photo Researchers)

apartments located at the end of the structure are more isolated. Even the placement of stairwells can affect interaction. Individuals on upper stories are typically more familiar with one another than ground-floor residents who often have private access to their units and are not required to share corridors or stairwells.

Evaluative Approach

Compared with the structural approach to perception research, the *evaluative* approach goes one step further in the organization of space by placing emphasis on the manner in which individuals respond to information

from their perceived environment. More specifically, the evaluative approach is concerned with the behavioral-spatial impact of the environment on individual activity.

The fundamental idea underlying the evaluative approach is that people have the capability of perceiving the most important elements in their environment, and the recognition of these elements (in order of importance) affects their decision-making process. "An implicit assumption is that the perceived world is one of the fundamental criteria or bases used in making a decision which is then expressed as behavior."[7]

Evaluative studies have dealt with the perception of *natural hazards*. From interviews with private individuals and proprietors of commercial establishments (as well as from data obtained from newspaper and public records), one such study compared the disruption of a snowfall in western and midwestern cities.[8] In the Midwest, public officials reacted rather quickly to dispatch snow-removal equipment following a storm, while the response in the West was found to be much slower. Apparently, public officials in the West did not perceive snow to be a hazardous problem. The prevailing philosophy in the West was that coping with snow was an individual problem, while in the Middle West it was viewed as a community or group problem that must be eradicated as soon as possible.

Another example of the evaluative approach is illustrated by a coastal environment study.[9] Local citizens' views toward storm hazards and the effect of their perceptions in adjusting to this natural hazard were studied along the outer shore of Megalopolis. The author found that only minimal hazard-reduction measures were taken, even though most residents elected to live in places exposed to considerable risk from storms. The desire for coastal amenities overshadowed the need for conservation measures (i.e., the construction of seawalls to enhance safety).

Studies utilizing the structural and evaluative approaches have resulted in a better understanding of human spatial behavior. Continuing research has been initiated using both approaches (or a combination of the

---

[7]Downs, op. cit., p. 80.

[8]John F. Rooney, Jr., "The Urban Snow Hazard in the United States," *Geographical Review*, 57 (1967), 538–559.

[9]Robert W. Kates, "Perception of Storm Hazard on the Shore of Megalopolis," in David Lowenthal, ed., *Environmental Perception and Behavior*. Research Paper No. 109, Department of Geography, University of Chicago Press, Chicago, 1967, pp. 60–74.

Figure 10-5. Piazza Navonna, Rome. European cities impart a stronger sense of the historic and a greater sensitivity to the pedestrian than their American counterparts. A stronger planning and permitting process in European cities places a much higher priority on maintaining the integrity of older buildings. Note the fountain in the center of the square around which artists and musicians gather to sell their wares and entertain. High-income residential quarters surround the square. (Tom Bross/Stock, Boston)

two). As studies have increased in sophistication, geographers and planners have realized the potential for such research to contribute to practical applications. Planners, in particular, have recognized the significance of investigating human reaction to various environmental stimuli and have incorporated these approaches in their fieldwork.

IMAGEABILITY OF THE CITY

The growing literature focused on the analysis of perception and cognition by geographers has benefited from joint research efforts with architects, psychologists, and planners. The term *imageability*, sometimes referred to as *legibility*, refers to the mental reading one gets from exposure to the city. The phrase *environmental cognition* has been given to this field. "Environmental cognition is the study of the subjective informa-

tion, images, impressions, and beliefs that people have of the environment, the ways in which these conceptions arise from experience, and the ways in which they affect subsequent behavior with respect to the environment."[10] A pioneer book in this field, *Image and Environment* by Roger Downs and David Stea, appeared in the 1970s, emphasizing *cognitive mapping* and human spatial behavior (see later section in this chapter).

Current perception studies of the city often focus on the interpretation of human spatial behavior as related to the use of structures and open space within the city. For example, geographers and planners have attempted to discover why various urban sites are utilized more

---

[10]Gary T. Moore and Reginald G. Golledge, "Environmental Knowing: Concepts and Theories," in G. T. Moore and R. Golledge, eds., *Environmental Knowing: Theories, Research and Methods*, Dowden, Hutchinson and Ross, Stroudsburg, Pa., 1976, pp. 3–24.

extensively than others. By analyzing human use patterns of specific sites, a better understanding of factors that encourage activity can be obtained. This type of research is useful in describing ways in which the image of undesirable locations in the city may be enhanced.

Earlier perception studies, which emphasized organizing and identifying information critical to the study of city landscapes, found that *orientation* was a critical problem. Lynch built on this work by concentrating on the image of the city, which was evaluated in two ways: (1) the physical form of the city and (2) the cultural image (i.e., the social meaning, function, or history) of the city. Both images were found to play a part in the overall development of a total city image.

Physical Form

Humans, as mobile animals, obtain cues from the city environment similar to the way other animals receive cues from the natural environment. In the natural environment, these cues help bring animals out of hibernation or signal impending danger. The external cues in city environments, such as visual sensation of color, shape, or motion, provide some indication of relative location within the city. By recognizing these cues, orientation is made easier (Figure 10-6). Lynch classified the contents of a city's image into five types of elements:

1. *Paths.* Channels of movement for the observer. A path may be a highway, sidewalk, or transit line. The paths that remain most predominant in the mind of the observer have concentrations of activities or special uses that draw the user to the path. Paths tend to be the predominant city element because they promote observations.

2. *Edges.* Linear elements associated with the boundaries between two differing areas. The most pronounced edges are usually prominent, continuous in form, and impenetrable. An edge may take the form of a river, a rail line, a large wall, or even forested green space.

3. *Districts.* Relatively large city areas that the observer mentally enters. At times these areas are

Figure 10-6. Hyde Street Pier, San Francisco. External cues in city environment provide an indication of relative location in the city. By recognizing cues, orientation is made easier. Note the cannery at right (renovated warehouse, now serving as restaurant and shopping arcade), and Alcatraz across the bay. (Courtesy Bruce Kleiwe/Jeroboam)

easily identifiable as a result of their similar internal characteristics (e.g., the central business district or an industrial park). Districts may be difficult to delineate as a result of a lack of continuity in internal character (i.e., commercial strip developments).

4. *Nodes.* Strategic focal points that an observer can enter. The focal points may be junctions of paths or areas where particular activities are concentrated (and as a result are similar to districts). Normally, nodes are smaller in scale or more concentrated than districts. The junction of paths usually creates a very strong image and therefore makes nodes distinctive in the observer's mind. Highly visible structures surrounding the node enhance its positive image. A shopping area or an office building is an illustration of a node.

5. *Landmarks.* Physical elements that can vary widely in scale and represent point references that tend to be external to the observer. Landmarks, similar to nodes, become stronger images if they are located at the junction of paths. This element is often used by the observer as a trigger cue that can help guide travelers through the city.[11]

The various elements outlined here, if developed in an interrelated fashion, can reinforce a positive image of a city. City planners are becoming more aware of the need for a strong image of the cityscape and often incorporate the principle in their land use and transportation plans.

Emotional Security

An individual's knowledge of a specific location in relation to other areas in the city provides for a sense of *emotional security.* The lack of understanding of a city's physical organization could be devastating: "The very word 'lost' in our language means much more than simple geographic uncertainty; it carries overtones of utter disaster."[12]

City legibility has an immediate impact on the behavioral attributes of its residents and visitors. If individuals cannot orient themselves to various parts of the city, their spatial range of movement is impaired.

That part of the city in which daily movement occurs comprises the *action space* of the individual. In the case of a small town or city, the action space might comprise the entire area, but as a general rule, citizens only interact in a portion of their city, typically an area anchored by their homes and workplaces. The action space of an individual also changes over time to correspond with life cycle changes, socioeconomic status, and mobility characteristics (see Chapter 14). The elastic nature of action spaces of urban residents, according to age, income, and physical condition, are represented in Figure 10-7. Note that adults have the most comprehensive action space, which grows over time from that of a youth, only to contract again for the elderly. The more constrained action spaces portrayed for the poor and handicapped reflect decreased mobility for these groups.

An individual's action space will normally dictate where that person lives, shops, or even works (see Chapter 14). Without adequate knowledge of a particular area, a person may be hesitant to travel there. It is partly for this reason that outer city dwellers prefer to satisfy their shopping and cultural needs in the suburbs

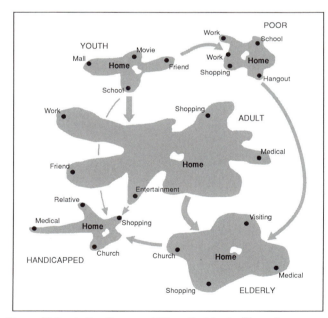

Figure 10-7. Action Spaces of Urban Residents. The action spaces of individuals expand and contract as a function of age, socioeconomic status, and physical condition. Home, work, school, entertainment, and medical facilities frame this space. Note the variable size of the action space for various groups. *Source:* Modified after Frederick P. Stutz. *Social Aspects of Interaction and Transportation,* Resource Paper No. 76-2, Association of American Geographers, 76-2, 1976, p. 30. Used with permission.

---

[11]Lynch, op. cit., p. 47.

[12]Ibid., p. 4.

Figure 10-8. Independence Mall, Philadelphia. The juxtaposition of the open and intense creates an appealing atmosphere in the city. Note the open, parklike atmosphere around Independence Hall (bottom center) and the single-story building that displays the Liberty Bell (center). Intense commercial activity surrounds the area. A trolley line follows 5th Street at right. (Courtesy John Pultz)

rather than in the center city. The central city may represent nothing more than a maze of streets and anonymous large buildings to the suburban dweller—a place to be feared because of its enormous size and complexity.

Inviting Human Activity

In addition to the emotional security gained from a distinctive and legible city environment, a positive mental image can heighten the intensity of the human experience. An environment that emphasizes or evokes images through an individual's sense of sight, sound, and smell will invite more human activity. With their interesting mixtures of open and intense spaces, for example, city landscapes create an appealing atmosphere (Figure 10-8).

> The appeal of cities lies in large part on the juxtaposition of the cozy and the grand, of [sic] darkness and light, the intimate and the public. . . . [M]uch of the attraction of old European cities resides in the juxtaposition of

crowded residential quarters (the dark warrens of life) and spacious public squares.[13]

Lynch's work, conducted in Boston, Los Angeles, and Jersey City, has been replicated in other parts of the world, including the Netherlands.[14] The latter study found that problems in orientation resulted when street patterns displayed an irregular, poorly integrated form. The lack of a connected street network thwarted the development of a mental map of the city. Other research in Tripoli, Lebanon, provided yet another dimension to the Lynch framework. That study demonstrated the importance of sociocultural associations, rather than visual cues, in the construction of individual images of a city.[15]

---

[13]Yi-Fu Tuan, *Topophilia*, Prentice Hall, Englewood Cliffs, N.J., 1974, p. 28.

[14]Derk DeJonge, "Images of Urban Areas: Their Structure and Psychological Foundations," *Journal of the American Institute of Planners*, 28 (November 1962), 266–276.

[15]John Gulick, "Images of an Arab City," *Journal of the American Institute of Planners*, 29 (August 1963), 179–198.

Cultural Screening

One possible flaw in the work of Lynch is that the images of a city vary among different age and cultural groups. The same environment may be perceived and experienced differently by different groups. The teenager who spends time within the confines of physically segregated (and age-graded) institutions can be expected to have a radically different outlook from that of an adult. Blacks, Chinese, and American Indians similarly possess contrasting perceptions of the city as a result of past traditions and cultural nuances. Socioeconomic variations also play a major part in city image development. In Rome and Milan, group differences in city images have been demonstrated between middle- and lower-class residents.[16] The middle class tend to place less emphasis on streets and more emphasis on districts, while the reverse is true of lower-class groups.

The Los Angeles Department of City Planning investigated this differing perception of socioeconomic groups while developing the report *The Visual Environment of Los Angeles*.[17] Planners found distinctive contrasts in city images among three different socioeconomic groups: (1) low-income Spanish-speaking; (2) black inner city; and (3) white upper middle class. The images of these groups are shown in Figures 10-9, 10-10, and 10-11. Both the black and Spanish-speaking groups tended to be oriented to their immediate residential area, with knowledge of the entire city very limited and cramped. The upper-middle-class group, on the other hand, had a more comprehensive image of Los Angeles, which included a wealth of information about neighborhoods other than their own. Ethnic status may not have been the overriding factor for the distinctive perceptions, but mobility was significant. The more traveled, affluent, white group apparently benefited from its broader territorial base.

The problem of mobility for inner-city dwellers as related to image formation is critical. Very often inadequate access to services (medical, dental, legal) poses problems. A limited *action space* typically hinders familiarity with the location of service facilities (see Chapter 14), and limited knowledge of (and access to)

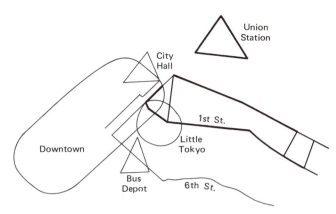

Figure 10-9. Los Angeles as Viewed by Low-Income Hispanic Residents (Boyle Heights Community). Thicker lines delimit areas of more familiarity. Note limited areas of familiarity. *Source:* Redrawn with permission from Los Angeles Department of City Planning, *The Visual Environment of Los Angeles*, Los Angeles, 1971.

citywide services promotes dependency on the immediate neighborhood. Even if service facilities are available at a relatively short distance, they may be irrelevant to the family that is unaware of their existence. As a result, city governments have to expend large amounts of money informing citizens of the location and availability of services.

The Urban Mental Map

Lynch's methodology for obtaining information about images of cities is based on the relatively simple idea that an individual carries around in his or her head a cognitive (or mental) map that helps navigation through the city. These maps are not comparable to road maps, which provide precise street locations. The cognitive map is characterized by a series of mental images combining streets with other physical features into a relatively detailed action space (see Figures 10-9 to 10-11).

Mental maps are the links that tie the physical form of the city together with an individual's action space so that daily activities can be conducted (Figure 10-12). The city images discussed previously are expressions of an individual's mental maps. The maps define a person's behavior space and provide an indication of the importance of one area (or physical feature) in relation to another.

Cognitive mapping is "a process composed of a series of psychological transformations by which an

[16]Donata Francescato and William Mebane, "How Citizens View Two Great Cities: Milan and Rome," in Roger M. Downs and David Stea, eds., *Image and Environment*, Aldine, Chicago, 1973, pp. 131–147.

[17]Department of City Planning, *The Visual Environment of Los Angeles*, Los Angeles, 1971.

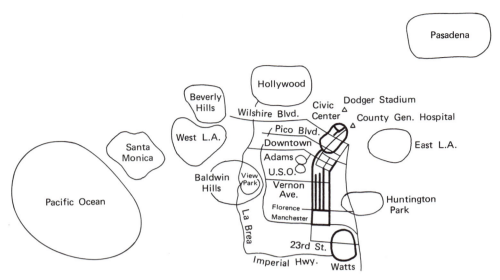

Figure 10-10. Los Angeles as Viewed by Black Inner-City Residents (Avalon Community). Thicker lines delimit areas of more familiarity. Note emphasis on corridor between downtown and the Watts area. *Source:* Redrawn with permission from Los Angeles Department of City Planning, *The Visual Environment of Los Angeles*, Los Angeles, 1971.

individual acquires, codes, stores, recalls, and decodes information about the relative locations and attributes of phenomena in his everyday spatial environment."[18] Cognitive maps are reinforced by daily travel throughout the city. If the urban traveler decides (or is forced) to digress from familiar streets, a sense of direction may be lost because visual cues (i.e., streets and structures) are foreign.

In mental mapping problems, respondents are often requested to draw, from memory, maps of their city on a blank sheet of paper. The participants are given only minimal instructions as to the kinds of features to be included. This technique allows the researcher to determine how well an individual knows the city (i.e., the general legibility of the cityscape) as well as to extract those elements within the city that provide strong images to the observer.

The comprehensiveness of a mental map is based on the mobility of the observer. The presence or absence of fine details may also be a reflection of the cultural background of the observer. For example, North Americans tend to be less "space" conscious and more "time" conscious than the Japanese and therefore more concerned with distance between spatial units rather than

with what occupies the space between the units.[19] This may explain why Americans, in developing their mental maps, often leave vast spaces within cities unidentified, whereas the Japanese would no doubt label these blank spaces. A study conducted with university students found that there were major gaps in mental maps of Atlanta.[20] Residential areas and social institutions rarely represented a significant portion of the students' mental maps; instead, they tended to defer to the larger-scale "hardware" components of the city (monuments, airports, and stadiums).

Psychological dimensions of perception, such as interest/excitement and uncertainty/fear, have real existence on mental maps. In research on an inner-city neighborhood in Philadelphia, for example, residents were surveyed to determine which parts of their community they considered dangerous.[21] The author postulated that areas considered stressful by the residents governed their spatial behavior (i.e., residents would

---

[18]Roger M. Downs and David Stea, "Cognitive Map and Spatial Behavior: Process and Products," in *Image and Environment*, op. cit., p. 9.

[19]Forrest R. Pitts, *Japanese and American World Views and Their Landscapes*, Proceedings of the IGU Regional Conference in Japan, Science Council of Japan, Tokyo, 1957, pp. 447–452.

[20]Truman A. Hartshorn, "Images of Atlanta," unpublished manuscript, Department of Geography, Georgia State University, Atlanta.

[21]David Ley, *The Black Inner City as Frontier Outpost: Images and Behavior of a Philadelphia Neighborhood*, Association of American Geographers, Washington, D.C., 1974, pp. 220–221.

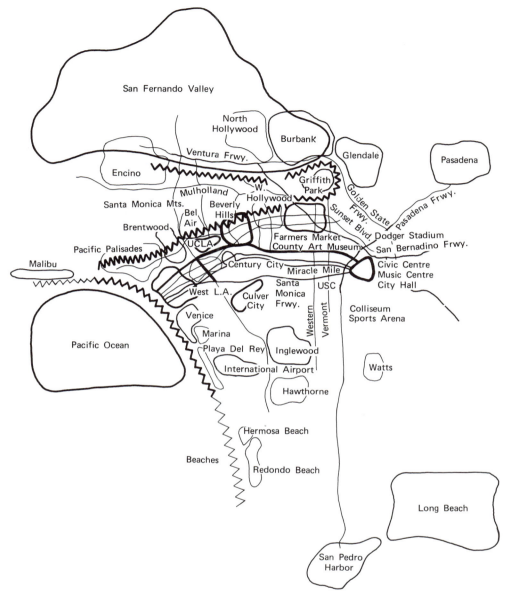

Figure 10-11. Los Angeles as Viewed by White Upper-Middle-Class Residents (Westwood Community). Line thickness varies with intenseness of familiarity. Note extensive area of awareness extending from Long Beach in the south to the San Fernando Valley in the north. *Source:* Redrawn with permission from Los Angeles Department of City Planning, *The Visual Environment of Los Angeles*, Los Angeles, 1971.

avoid traveling through such areas). Locations considered dangerous by the residents were mapped, showing that high-stress areas occurred largely on the perimeter of a neighborhood near the turf of another community (Figure 10-13).

Urban geography students at Georgia State University in Atlanta, when asked to develop their mental maps, were requested to indicate areas in which they felt uncomfortable or fearful. The central city was found to have a mixture of inviting and undesirable areas. The downtown multiuse office skyscraper complexes produced strong positive images. Other parts of the city center near mixed-use centers (megastructures) were often designated as "hazardous" areas. Students

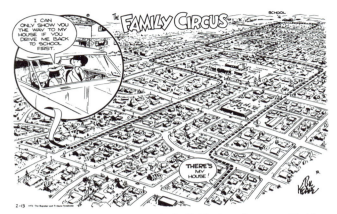

Figure 10-12. Family Circus. An individual carries around in his or her head a cognitive (or mental) map that helps navigation through the city. The map of the suburban elementary school student shown here is an example. *Source: The Family Circus* by Bill Keane, reprinted courtesy of the Register & Tribune Syndicate, Inc.

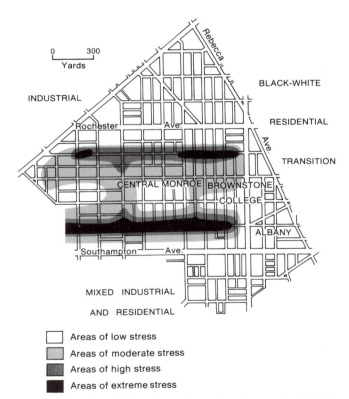

Areas of low stress
Areas of moderate stress
Areas of high stress
Areas of extreme stress

Figure 10-13. *Spatial Variation of Fear–Stress Surface in an Inner-city Neighborhood.* Locations considered dangerous by the residents of this inner-city neighborhood community of Philadelphia occur predominantly on the perimeter of a neighborhood near the turf of another community. *Source:* Redrawn by permission from the Association of American Geographers Monograph #7. *The Black Inner City as Frontier Outpost,* 1974, p. 221, David Ley.

probably feared these areas either because they were unfamiliar with them or because they felt that the streets were unsafe due to the presence of homeless persons.

Urban mental mapping was used too late in a project of the City Planning Commission in Philadelphia. The agency contemplated the construction of a park in a low-income area. A central location was selected so that the largest number of children could utilize the recreational site. After completion of the park, the planners found that children were not using the facilities, and so they called in consultants to study the situation. This research revealed that the park had been constructed on an imaginary boundary line separating two rival street gangs and, as a result, children feared for their safety in that area. Subsequent research revealed that "the youngsters knew that the region was no-man's-land, but unfortunately, the park planners did not."[22]

Mental mapping techniques are potentially useful to practitioners of architecture and city planning, for the mental map indicates those areas or features that have weak images. Weak images may result from the lack of architectural clarity and strength. Planners, as illustrated in the Philadelphia park example, can also benefit from utilizing citizens as a source of information for planning community facilities. Very often planners devise boundaries for neighborhoods by following census tracts or blocks that are, unfortunately, rarely comparable to the boundaries perceived by local residents.

Cognitive Distance

The relationship of perceived distance regarding the location of elements within an individual mental map is critical. The importance of research in *cognitive distance* lies in its power to explain many types of spatial behavior more effectively than real distances.[23] Researchers have shown that there are often major distortions in mental maps with respect to distance.

Research in Dundee, Scotland, indicated that students consistently estimated distances toward the downtown area as shorter than those away from the city

[22]Charles Panati, "Mental Maps," *Newsweek*, 87 (March 15, 1976), p. 71, as quoted by Peter Gould.

[23]R. G. Golledge, R. Briggs, and D. Demko, "Cognitive Approaches to the Analysis of Human Spatial Behavior," in William H. Ittelson, ed., *Environment and Cognition*, Seminar Press, New York, 1973, pp. 59–94.

center.[24] The author felt that the students' perceptions were based on heightened interest generated by the downtown area and that this interest provided a focal orientation leading to a foreshortening of perceived distances in the inward direction. Other researchers found the opposite to be true. In a Columbus, Ohio, study it was found that distances toward the central business district (CBD) were commonly overestimated, while distances away from the downtown area were understated.[25] The authors attributed this perception to the denser packing of land uses toward the CBD in conjunction with increased congestion and travel time. The discrepancy between the two studies may be the result of travel mode utilized by respondents.[26] The Scottish students apparently estimated walking distances, while Americans referred to driving distances. Other work has suggested that familiar locations tend to be perceived as closer than less familiar points that are an equal distance away.[27]

Reading the City

A more colloquial interpretation of the city has been developed to describe several distinctive features that we *read* when moving about the metropolitan area.[28] *Fixes* refer to perspectives we develop of a city landscape. In years past, the village represented a fix with which to identify urban living, but now the fix is more appropriately based on the metropolis. The skyline is an example of a fix we have of a particular city (see Chapter 15).

Epitome districts are "special places" in the city. Such areas carry significant symbolization and pull together emotions, energy, or history into confined space. They trigger in the observer an awareness of the larger surrounding scene and tend to open up views of the city that may be hidden. They "stand for things; they generate metaphors; they are the sort of places, that, ideally, help us get it all together."[29]

The concept of *strips* normally refers to linear commercial developments along highways. Strips project strong images and emotional memories as identity districts. "American Graffiti," the popular mid-1970s movie of the American scene as it was in the 1950s, provides a good example. In that movie, teenagers are shown cruising city streets by automobile as a form of evening recreation and socializing. This represents an expression of emotional attachment to the strip. Teenagers also develop a pecking order of strips. They know where the police are located, where to find their friends, and where to find the best fast food.

Turfs represent both civic and private territories in the city. "Turf is landscape spelled out; it says who goes where, who belongs, and who does not; it is admonitory and administered."[30] Turfs are defined by property lines, hedges, fences, walls, or curbs. They also are expressed by signs, symbols, or markers. The implication of a turf is not only that it is occupied by a particular group, but also that it is inaccessible to others.

THE SOCIAL PERCEPTION OF THE CITY

Within any city many different ethnic and income neighborhoods exist. Each of these residential groups has varying, but distinct, perceptions about other communities. Socioeconomic status often dictates where a group lives, as well as the type of cultural and leisure activities in which it becomes involved. Misconceptions concerning the value and lifestyles of other groups often arise from the association of a particular behavior pattern with a stereotyped image. For example, whites may view the racial change in a neighborhood as detrimental to property values, even though research has proved this myth not to be true (see discussion in Chapter 13).

Social Distance

The level of interaction among groups depends on the *social distance* between them. Social distance is a concept that refers to the degree of separation between individuals, families, and groups, in terms of contact and communication. When applied to communities, it refers to the way that one group perceives another. If

[24]Terrence Lee, "Perceived Distance as a Function of Direction in the City," *Environment and Behavior*, 2, No. 1 (June 1970), 13–39.

[25]R. G. Golledge, R. Briggs, and D. Demko, "The Configuration of Distances in Intra-urban Space," *Proceedings of the Association of American Geographers*, 1 (1969), 60–65.

[26]Thomas G. Saarinen, *Environmental Planning*, Houghton Mifflin, Boston, 1976, p. 126.

[27]Ibid.

[28]Grady Clay, *Close-Up: How to Read the American City*, Praeger, New York, 1973.

[29]Ibid., p. 38.

[30]Ibid., p. 153.

the social distance is great (as is frequently the case among racial groups), it becomes more difficult for groups to be assimilated.

Social distance is important in neighborhood evaluations. If high-income residents perceive a particular community as inhabited by a lower-income population, it is very likely that this latter community will be regarded negatively by the high-income group. Once the image of a neighborhood is established by a particular group, it is very difficult to change. Old in-town neighborhoods are often perceived as being crowded, congested, and highly undesirable by middle-class suburbanites. These attitudes then pass from generation to generation. For example, the younger-generation suburbanite may become accustomed to believing that revitalization efforts in older neighborhoods should be given low priorities based on negative perceptions. Banking institutions and realtors can reinforce this perception through their actions. The impact of those institutions will be discussed in later chapters.

Studies of prejudice and social distance at the high school level indicate that the perceived separation of groups is not perfectly reciprocal. One such study examined the way blacks, Puerto Ricans, and whites perceived one another in a sample of 14 high schools in eastern Pennsylvania. The study was conducted in various income-level neighborhoods in Philadelphia, in other middle-size cities, and in a semirural area. Minority/white attitudes differed significantly from white/minority perceptions.[31] This was demonstrated by minorities being more willing to participate with whites in social functions than vice versa.

Sense of Place

Humans, like other living things, possess a sense of *territoriality* that separates them from their external environment. "Territoriality, a basic concept in the study of animal behavior, is usually defined as behavior by which an organism characteristically lays claim to an area and defends it against members of its own species."[32] The human sense of territoriality is typically not as pronounced in comparison with lower

species of animal life, but it has become highly differentiated over time. Modern people "defend" territory through an intricate network of boundaries, such as fences, walls, and markers.[33]

The intense feeling generated for a particular site, whether a plot of land or an apartment in a high-rise building, is manifest in our society through a sentimental attachment we identify with a particular location. It is thought of as "my place." Concepts of territoriality can also be transferred to residents' perceptions of neighborhoods, where groups of people display authority over a larger space.

Images of neighborhoods often present a dichotomy based on both an "insider's" and an "outsider's" view. Local neighborhood residents may maintain a positive image of their surroundings, while residents from other areas perceive the location as undesirable. This positive local image can persist even when major problems surface as a result of strong attachments of citizens to their neighborhood. These strong attachments have been described in the literature as a *sense of place* (Figure 1-2). A sense of place can refer to an attachment to a particular dwelling unit, but attachment often operates in the community as a whole as well. A level of neighborliness may exist that allows individuals to develop close ties with other residents and to the activities that make the neighborhood function. This attachment is generally higher in lower-income neighborhoods in contrast to middle-class communities.

A perceptual problem often faces housing planners with regard to the sense-of-place concept. Housing standards are frequently viewed as the most critical factor in neighborhood planning in making a community stable. Planning dogma suggests that housing that includes all accepted amenities of open (or green) space, low densities, and uncrowded living areas is necessary to create a desirable living environment. These planners, holding middle-class values, often view homes without such amenities as debilitating to inhabitants. Planners appear to have little regard for maintaining a resident's sense of place. Rarely do they consider community interaction as an important source of psychological support for local residents. It is for this reason that in recent years many low-income residential

[31]Robert C. Williamson, "Social Distance and Ethnicity: Some Sub-cultural Factors among High School Students," *Urban Education*, 11 (1976), 295–312.

[32]Edward T. Hall, *The Hidden Dimension*, Anchor Books, Garden City, N.Y., 1966, p. 7.

[33]Robert Ardrey, *African Genesis*, Atheneum, New York, 1961; R. Ardrey, *The Territorial Imperative*, Dell, New York, 1966; R. Ardrey, *The Social Contract*, Dell, New York, 1970; Edward Hall, *The Silent Language*, Doubleday, Garden City, N.Y., 1959; E. Hall, *The Hidden Dimension*, op. cit.

areas have succumbed to the federal bulldozer. One example where planners misjudged the importance of neighborhood interaction was in the West End community in Boston.

West End was a predominantly low-income, ethnically mixed community located near Boston's central business district. The average Bostonian rarely entered the West End. From a distance an outsider saw

> . . . a series of narrow winding streets flanked on both sides by columns of three- and five-story apartment buildings, constructed in an era when such buildings were still called tenements. Furthermore, he saw many poorly maintained structures, some of them unoccupied or partially vacant, some facing on alleys covered with more than an average amount of garbage, many vacant stores; and enough of the kinds of people who are thought to inhabit a slum area.[34]

A physical description of West End leaves the reader with the impression that this neighborhood was indeed little more than a blighted slum. To the residents of West End it was home—a more viable place than evidenced by the eye. The people, even though living in marginal housing, identified strongly with the neighborhood. They disregarded most housing problems and viewed the total community as an extension of their living area. The level of neighborliness was very high and the majority of the people living in the area were extremely satisfied with the West End as a home.

Residents in West End maintained strong identification and feelings about their neighborhood, but the planners in Boston did not share the same view. They perceived West End to be just another slum and a likely site for urban redevelopment. In 1959, West End was demolished as part of Boston's urban renewal program. This resulted in the dislocation of 7500 persons in the area, an action that may have been unnecessary and certaintly was undesirable.

One question that has become critical over the years is how the many images of a neighborhood can be unified so that the planner and the resident can work together to solve neighborhood problems. The answer is both complex and elusive, but it will have to be found if planning at the local level is to be properly implemented.

Neighborhood Perception

Studies dealing with resident perceptions of neighborhoods have also increased. The intent of such studies varies, but much of the research has focused on one of three themes: (1) residential desirability; (2) neighborhood viability as related to the desire to move away; and (3) housing satisfaction. We will discuss the connection between neighborhood perception and intraurban movement in more detail in Chapter 14.

Residential desirability studies have proved especially useful to architects. An attempt has been made to evaluate various socioeconomic groups to determine which factors each group felt was important in maintaining satisfaction levels. "Predictors" have been described to indicate how inhabitants judge an area, based on landscaping, noise levels, and neighborliness.[35]

QUALITY OF LIFE

When speaking of people places, one is reminded of the subjective nature of interpretations of social well-being or, as the concept is more popularly known, the *quality of life* of an area.[36] While there are no universal indicators with which to measure the quality of life, nor precise definitions of the concept for that matter, a general consensus does exist as to what constitutes social well-being. David Smith indicates that

> in a well society, people will have income adequate for their basic needs of food, clothing, shelter, and a "reasonable" standard of living. In a well society, people do not live in poverty. Good quality education and health services are available to all, and their use is reflected in a high level of physical and mental health. People live in decent houses and neighborhoods, and enjoy a good quality of physical environment. They have access to recreational facilities, including culture and the arts, and adequate leisure time in which to enjoy these things. In a healthy society, a low degree of disorganization is shown with few social pathologies, little deviant behavior, low crime

[34]Herbert Gans, "The West End: An Urban Village," in Michael E. Eliot-Hurst, ed., *I Came to the City*, Houghton Mifflin, Boston, 1975, p. 151.

[35]J. B. Lansing and R. W. Marans, "Evaluation of Neighborhood Quality," *Journal of the American Institute of Planners*, 35 (1969), 195–199.

[36]Susan L. Cutter, *Rating Places: A Geographer's View on Quality of Life*, Resource Publications in Geography, Association of American Geographers, Washington, D.C., 1985.

incidence and high public order and safety. The family is a stable institution, with few broken homes.[37]

As this definition suggests, the quality of life of an area should be judged on a wide range of physical, environmental, social, economic, political, and health indicators. Cities exhibit a very high level of variation on these indicators and rarely do cities consistently rank high or low on all measures. Indeed, there is wide variation over both space and time. Recent evaluations of the 333 largest metropolitan areas in the United States by the *Places Rated Almanac* confirm this assessment, as the rankings shown in Table 10-1 indicate. In the 1980s, three different cities were cited in various years as the best places to live—Atlanta, Pittsburgh, and Seattle.[38]

The most crucial (and controversial) task in a comparative study of city living is to select the appropriate measures to assess an area and give them proper weighting. The *Places Rated Almanac*, for example, ranks cities on the basis of nine factors—climate, housing, health care, crime, transportation, education, the arts, recreation, and economics. The arbitrariness of combining variables reflecting facilities (health care, education, recreation, transportation, and the arts) with other indicators based on jobs, money, and the incidence of crime is open to question.

In the *Places Rated* evaluation, each factor counts equally. The ranking of a particular city is based on its cumulative score on all nine factors with the lowest-scoring city receiving the highest ranking. Applying appropriate weights, if any, to each of these factors presents additional problems.

Geographer Robert Pierce tried to resolve the weighting issue by questioning a large sample of New York state residents about the perceived importance of the nine factors used by Boyer and Savageau in their *Places Rated Almanac*.[39] The "bread and butter" issues of economic opportunity and housing costs were deemed most important by the sample. These were followed closely by personal safety (i.e. the crime factor) and then climate. Had the survey not been

TABLE 10-1

Top 25 Metropolitan Areas Ranked by *Places Rated Almanac*, 1989[a]

Rank	Metropolitan Area
1	Seattle
2	San Francisco
3	Pittsburgh
4	Washington, D.C.
5	San Diego
6	Boston
7	New York
8 (tie)	Anaheim-Santa Ana
8 (tie)	Louisville
10	Nassau-Suffolk
11	Atlanta
12	Cleveland
13	Philadelphia
14	Cincinnati
15	Los Angeles
16	Salt Lake City
17	Baltimore
18	Chicago
19	Oakland
20	Miami
21	Syracuse
22	Santa Barbara
23	Raleigh-Durham
24	Portland
25	San Jose

[a]Based on composite score of nine factors.

Source: Rick Boyer and David Savageau, *Places Rate Almanac: Your Guide to Finding the Best Places to Live in America*, Prentice Hall, Englewood Cliffs, N.J., 1989. Reprinted by permission of the publisher, Prentice Hall Travel, A division of Simon & Schuster, Inc. New York, N.Y.

conducted in mid-winter, climate might have been rated less important. Not surprisingly, factors relating to higher order needs such as the arts, were perceived as the least important element in the quality of urban life equation.[40]

Applying these perceived weights to the *Places Rated* data shuffled the rankings of cities such that Greensboro, North Carolina and Knoxville, Tennessee tied for first place. Pierce's findings made the front

[37]David M. Smith, *The Geography of Social Well-Being in the United States*, McGraw-Hill Problems Series in Geography, McGraw-Hill, New York, 1973, p. 69.

[38]Rick Boyer and David Savageau, *Places Rated Almanac: Your Guide to Finding the Best Places to Live in America*, Prentice Hall, Englewood Cliffs, N.J., 1989.

[39]Robert M. Pierce, "Rating America's Cities: A Perceptual Analysis of Objective Measures," paper presented at Annual Meeting, Association of American Geographers, Washington, D.C., April 1984.

[40]Abraham H. Maslow, *Motivation and Personality*, Harper & Row, New York, 1970.

page of *USA Today*, resulting in a wave of urban boosterism and temporary notoriety for Pierce. He later reworked his weighting method when the second edition of the *Places Rated Almanac* was released in 1985. Using the then-new (post-1983) census definition of metropolitan areas, the Nassau-Suffolk MSA (suburban Long Island, New York) had risen to first place.[41] A careful examination of the measurement procedures employed in the 1985 edition of the *Places Rated Almanac* showed that the Census Bureau's designation of a tripartite hierarchy of metropolitan areas (i.e. CMSA, PMSA, and MSA) had given an edge in the ratings to larger and more agglomerated metropolitan areas.[42]

Cities in the Pacific Northwest and the interior southeast generally rank the highest in these evaluations. New England cities, agricultural market centers in the Central Valley of California, and industrial cities near Chicago generally rank the lowest in these studies. Favorable (or unfavorable) press reports can be valuable or detrimental to a particular area and used to guide investment decisions. The rivalry between Pittsburgh and Atlanta following the release of the 1985 rankings led to the construction of billboards in Atlanta by Pittsburgh interests, touting Pittsburgh as the best place to live.

SUMMARY AND CONCLUSION

The image of the city is a complex phenomenon. Physical facilities, social conditions, and people themselves create an enormous range of conditions. Some areas of the city are viewed as safe and secure, while others are tagged as unsafe and undesirable. Much of this labeling is based on familiarity. Unknown and unfamiliar places are often viewed as unsafe. The urban mental map is also conditioned by social distance and emotional attachment to a place. Many planning implications are connected to these images. The creation of more people places in the city, and responsible plans that take local attitudes into account along with the "outsider's" advice, is extremely important. What peo-

ple *think* reality is may be more important than the actual situation. In a similar sense, the social and psychological variable may be just as important as the economic force in explaining urban land uses and activity patterns. In Chapter 11, we will concentrate on the more traditional economic principles and mechanisms that have been utilized to explain land uses in the city, as well as examine the structural interpretation of city space.

Suggestions for Further Reading

Andrews, Frank M., ed. *Research on the Quality of Life*, Survey Research Center, Institute for Social Research, University of Michigan, Ann Arbor, 1986.

Appleyard, Donald, Kevin Lynch, and John Meyer. *The View from the Road*, MIT Press, Cambridge, Mass., 1964.

Ben-chieh Liu, *Quality of Life Indicators in U.S. Metropolitan Areas, 1970*, U.S. Environmental Protection Agency, Washington, D.C., 1975.

Boal, F. W., and D. N. Livingstone, eds., *The Behavioral Environment: Essays in Reflection, Application and Re-Evaluation*, Routledge, New York, 1990.

Boyer, Rick, and David Savageau. *Places Rated Alamanac: Your Guide to Finding the Best Places to Live in America*, Prentice-Hall, Englewood Cliffs, N.J., 1989.

Burke, D., *et al. Behavior Environment Research Methods*, University of Wisconsin Press, Madison, 1977.

Clay, Grady. *Close-up: How to Read the American City*, Praeger, New York, 1973.

Cutter, Susan. *Rating Places: A Geographer's View on Rating Places, Resource Publications in Geography, Association of American Geographers*, Washington, D.C., 1985.

Downs, Roger, and David Stea, eds. *Image and Environment*, Aldine, Chicago, 1973.

Eliot-Hurst, Michael E., ed. *I Came to the City*, Houghton Mifflin, Boston, 1975.

Frick, Dieter, ed. *The Quality of Urban Life*, Walter de Gruyter, New York, 1986.

Garreau, Joel. *The Nine Nations of North America*, Houghton Mifflin, Boston, 1981.

Golledge, Reginald, and Gerard Rushton. *Spatial Choice and Spatial Behavior*, Ohio State University Press, Columbus, 1976.

Gould, Peter, and Rodney White. *Mental Maps*, Penguin, New York, 1974.

Hall, Edward T. *The Silent Language*, Doubleday, New York, 1959.

Hall, Edward T. *The Hidden Dimension*, Anchor Books, Garden City, N.Y., 1966.

Jackson, J. B. *Discovering the Vernacular Landscape*, Yale University Press, New Haven, 1984.

Ley, David. *A Social Geography of the City*, Harper & Row, New York, 1983.

---

[41]Robert M. Pierce, "Rating America's Metropolitan Areas," *American Demograhics* (July 1985), 20–25.

[42]Robert M. Pierce and Thomas L. Bell, "Comparing the First and Second Editions of the Places Rated Almanac," *Urban Resources*, 3 (Spring 1986), 37–42, 51; Robert M. Pierce and Thomas L. Bell, "Has Urban Livability Changed Dramatically? A Comparison of the Places Rated Almanacs," *Professional Geographer*, 39 (August 1987), 351–357.

Lynch, Kevin. *The Image of the City*, MIT Press, Cambridge, Mass., 1960.

Lynch, Kevin. *What Time Is This Place?* MIT Press, Cambridge, Mass., 1976.

Marlin, John Tepper, et al. *Book of World City Rankings*. The Free Press, New York, 1986.

Michelson, William. *Man and His Urban Environment: A Sociological Approach*, Addison–Wesley, Reading, Mass., 1970.

Moore, Gary T., and Reginald Golledge, eds. *Environmental Knowing: Theories, Research and Methods*, Dowden, Hutchinson & Ross, Stroudsburg, Pa., 1976.

Mukherjee, Rambrishna. *The Quality of Life Valuation in Social Research*, Sage, Newbury Park, Calif., 1989.

Newman, Oscar. *Defensible Space*, Macmillan, New York, 1972.

Piaget, Jean, and B. Inhelder. *The Child's Conception of Space*, Humanities Press, New York, 1956.

Pocock, Douglas, and Ray Hudson. *Images of the Environment*, Columbia University Press, New York, 1978.

Porteous, J. Douglas. *Environment and Behavior: Planning and Everyday Life*, Addison-Wesley, Reading, Mass., 1977.

Proshansky, H., *et al.*, eds. *Environmental Psychology*, 2nd ed., Holt, Rinehart & Winston, New York, 1976.

Rappaport, A. *Human Aspects of Urban Form*, Pergamon, New York, 1977.

Saarinen, Thomas G. *Environmental Planning*, Houghton Mifflin, Boston, 1976.

Smith, David M. *The Geography of Social Well Being in the United States*, McGraw-Hill, New York, 1973.

Thrift, N., *et al. Timing Space and Spacing Time*, Aldine, London, 1978.

Tuan, Yi-Fu. *Topophilia*, Prentice Hall, Englewood Cliffs, N.J., 1974.

Tuan, Yi-Fu. *Space and Place*, University of Minnesota Press, Minneapolis, 1977.

11

LAND USE DYNAMICS

Cities and metropolitan areas of all sizes provide many supportive functions for their constituents—the residents, transients, and employees that live, visit, and gain their livelihood there. In response to these roles, a complex pattern of land use has evolved. Generally, these land uses conform to a regular, predictable pattern, but strong historical-, cultural-, and technological-based traditions at work mean that cities around the world exhibit tremendous differences in form. Perhaps the biggest contrasts exist between and among cities in the developed and developing world, but significant differences also exist within each of these categories. We have previously discussed cities in the developing world in Chapter 3, and we know that their traditions contrast strongly with those in the developed world. We will examine models of third world structure later in this chapter, but the primary focus will involve structural characteristics that have developed in more advanced market economies. We will begin by examining the principles that allocate land uses in these market-based economies.

Prior to the industrial revolution, precapitalist cities were much more conservative in terms of land use variety and the spatial separation of functions than they are today. Work and residence frequently occurred on the same street, if not in the same structure, in the preindustrial era. Less mechanized forms of transportation, typically limited to walking or horse-drawn carriages, limited the range of alternatives and flexibility that we now find in choosing among sites for business/residence locations. With the innovations in transportation, as discussed in Chapter 9, the city opened up, so to speak, as it became not only larger in land area, but also more differentiated internally. With the coming of the streetcar and rail transit, work and residence became more widely separated, and more specialized administrative, commercial, and industrial zones emerged in the city. Land use allocations increasingly responded to price-bidding, with those uses most able to pay higher prices capturing more central locations, as we will discuss in following sections.

LAND VALUES AND LAND USES

Land uses in the city, in market economy nations, generally conform to a regular, predictable pattern. Most decisions to develop land for a particular use are made independently by a variety of private entrepreneurs—but within the context of the existing land use structure of the city and planning controls.

Economics and the profit motive provided the primary tool for allocating a specific use for a piece of land. The notion of the *highest and best use* came to refer to the tendency for owners to develop land to its optimal advantage (Figure 11-1). Tastes, preferences, values, and perceptions, such as those discussed in Chapter 10 also tempered land use investments. Other factors influencing uses include political variables, the

Figure 11-1. Downtown Chicago. The highest and best use of land in downtown areas invariably involves mixed-use high-rise development. This view of Chicago looking north on North Michigan Avenue along the so-called magnificent mile shows the old water tower (foreground) in the midst of a new upscale mixed-use commercial district, including Water Tower Place vertical retail mall, center right. (Ron Schramm)

physical aspect of the land, its topography, and drainage. The time frame when the investment is made, the state of transportation access, level of affluence, parcel size, ownership status, speculation, and zoning all bear on the resulting pattern.

Landowners often operate in a monopolistic framework, within which a parcel of land can be developed, and while each parcel improvement occurs in isolation, many forces tended to encourage similar, if not identical, uses for adjacent properties. The collective result creates a land mosaic that conforms to sound principles.

Land uses are rarely static. Successive uses occur over time. This dynamic aspect of land use change

presents an interesting topic for study by the urban geographer. Part of the change emanates from growth itself, which mainly affects outlying areas of the city as they are converted from rural to urban use. Just as important, and far more complex, is the rearrangement of existing uses in the city as one use succeeds another while the size and functions of the city adapt to changes in employment, accessibility, lifestyles, income, and technology (building types, layouts, etc.). A study of Toronto has shown the land use dynamics exhibit four processes of change: (1) suburbanization (growth on the periphery); (2) renewal (mainly downtown); (3) expansion of public uses and utilities (parks, expressways, telephone service, etc.); and (4) growth or decline of nucleations containing specialized functions (converting buildings to parking use, expansion of hospitals, parks, and airports).[1]

The Marxist perspective suggests that the built-in structural instability of capitalism itself accounts for much of this change as investments are withdrawn from some areas, such as the central city (Figure 11-2), and reinvested elsewhere, such as the suburbs. The very existence of capital mobility and the opportunity for alternative investment locations as transportation innovations arise, such as the automobile-based suburb in the post-World War II era, provide a good case in point. We often hear that investors seek cheaper suburban land to develop as an alternative to overpriced central city parcels in this context. This central city–suburban dynamic, in fact, has created the most profound change in the city in the last half of the twentieth century than at any time since the dawn of the Industrial Revolution itself.

As we noted in Chapter 9, we now have polycentric cities with more than one commercial center. This reality does not represent a trivial change as it casts asunder traditional models of urban land use that assumed a single-centered metropolis. Before we examine these traditional models and their more recent successors, it is important that we review land use inventory and classification techniques.

Categories of Land Uses

Classifying land use in the city is a very important first step in understanding the spatial structure of the city.

---

[1] Larry S. Bourne, "Urban Structure and Land Use Decisions," *Annals of the Association of American Geographers*, 66 (1976), 531–547.

Figure 11-2.   Slum Housing in the Central City. The withdrawal of investment in housing in the central city creates uninhabitable slums, and the housing market collapses. Shown here, row houses in northeast Washington, D.C. (Ellis Herwig/Stock, Boston)

Geographers, planners, and traffic engineers have busied themselves with such land use inventories for many decades. The most general land use inventory involves identifying the dominant economic function at a particular location. Broad categories such as commercial, industrial, or residential use appear in such inventories. Transportation planners need information on land use mixes and development intensities in order to project traffic flows, while utility companies and public-service groups need data on locations of existing facilities and growth projections to plan for future energy demand. Local housing-code enforcement agencies and tax assessors require information on building types in terms of design, square footage, or height. Information on ownership (public or private) might be needed for other types of inventories dealing with the adequacy of open-space resources. About two-thirds of all land in the city is privately held in the United States (Table 11-1). The remainder is devoted to either streets or public uses.

Residential Land

The residential function occupies the largest share of the land of the city. The exact proportion of residential uses varies, depending on whether one includes the entire land area of the city, including undeveloped vacant land as a base, or just the *built environment*.

TABLE 11-1
General Land Use Allocation in Large Cities

Type of Use	Percentage of all Land Areas[a]	
	Cities of 100,000+	Cities of 250,000+
Private	67.4	64.7
Residential	31.6	32.3
Commercial	4.1	4.4
Industrial	4.7	5.4
Railroads	1.7	2.4
Undeveloped	22.3	12.5
Streets	17.5	18.3
Public	13.7	16.2
Recreational areas	4.9	5.3
Schools and colleges	2.3	1.8
Airports	2.0	2.5
Cemeteries	1.0	1.1
Public housing	0.5	0.4
Other	3.0	5.1
Total	98.6	99.2

[a]Because of the method of derivation, subtotals do not always correspond with totals.

Source: Modified after Allen D. Manvel, "Land Use in 106 Large Cities," in *Three Land Research Studies,* Research Report No. 13, The National Commission on Urban Problems, Washington, D.C., 1968, p. 20.

TABLE 11-2
Standard Coding System for Residential Land Use

One-Digit Code	Two-Digit Code	Three-Digit Code	Four-Digit Code
1 Residential	11 Household units	110 Household units	1100 Household units
	12 Group quarters	121 Rooming and boarding houses	1210 Rooming and boarding houses
		122 Membership lodging	1221 Fraternity and sorority houses
			1229 Other membership lodgings, NEC *a*
		123 Residence halls or dormitories	1231 Nurses' homes
			1232 College dormitories
			1239 Other residence halls or dormitories, NEC
		124 Retirement homes and orphanages	1241 Retirement homes
			1242 Orphanages
		125 Religious quarters	1251 Convents
			1252 Monasteries
			1253 Rectories
			1259 Other religious quarters, NEC
		129 Other group quarters, NEC	1290 Other group quarters, NEC
	13 Residential hotels	130 Residential hotels	1300 Residential hotels
	14 Mobile-home parks or courts	140 Mobile-home parks or courts	1400 Mobile home parks or courts
	15 Transient lodgings	151 Hotels, tourist courts, and motels	1510 Hotels, tourist courts, and motels
		159 Other transient lodgings, NEC	1590 Other transient lodgings, NEC
	19 Other residential, NEC	190 Other residential, NEC	1900 Other residential, NEC

a NEC = not elsewhere classified.
Source: Modified after *Standard Land Use Coding Manual,* USGPO, Washington, D.C., 1965, p. 32.

Thirty percent of the total land area of the city is residential, and about 40 percent of the developed land. Since the residential component is the largest user of space, it will be discussed here as the first among several activities within the city (in Chapters 12–14).

Residential land use incorporates all housing activity, including individual household units (single or multiple-family), group living accommodations (dormitories, retirement homes), hotels, motels, and mobile-home parks. An example of a standardized coding system designed for a residential area survey appears in Table 11-2. Categories are broken down at the one-, two-, three-, and four-digit level.

Transportation Space

Streets, railroads, airports, and parking functions are very large land users in the city, often exceeding 20 percent of the total land area of the city. This makes transportation use the second-largest user of space. In the downtown business district, even higher portions of ground space are devoted to transportation. A study of the retail business district in East Lansing, Michigan, indicated that 65 percent of the land was devoted to the automobile. This automobile territory has been labeled *machine space.* It incorporates the area in which the automobile is given priority. This machine space includes land devoted to moving, storing, and servicing motor vehicles.[2] Aerial photographs of downtown areas readily confirm the large amount of space devoted to parking and streets. The aerial view of downtown Atlanta shown in Figure 11-3 provides an example of the extent of parking facilities (garages and ground-level lots) encircling high-rise commercial nodes.

[2]Ronald J. Horvath, "Machine Space," *The Geographical Review,* 64 (1974), 169–188.

Figure 11-3.   The Open and Intense Development of Downtown Atlanta. A large share of space in many downtown areas is devoted to the automobile. Streets, surface parking lots, and parking decks consume nearly as much space in downtown Atlanta as high-rise buildings themselves. The central business district office/hotel complex along Peachtree Street stretches across the center of the photograph with Peachtree Center complex at right center. Freeways, arterials, and over 50,000 parking spaces create islands of the several downtown development nodes. (Copyright © 1991 Dillon-Reynolds Aerial Photography, Inc.)

Commercial and Industrial Land

A big surprise to most students, as revealed in Table 11-1, relates to the small contribution that commercial and industrial land makes to the total city area. About 5 percent of the total space in the city falls in each of these groupings. Of course, the economic impact of such uses, in terms of employment and sales, far outweighs this meager space allocation. These activities involve some of the most valuable property in the city and, as we discussed in Chapter 9, they are major traffic generators and of great concern to transportation planners.

Public Land

Public uses are normally dominated by parks and golf courses, in terms of space use. Such activity is often classified as open space, even though access to it may be restricted. Floodplain areas often become parks because of their unsuitability for residential or commercial development. Schools and colleges, airports, and cemeteries are other significant public-space occupants. Their collective importance in land use planning is far more significant than many other categories of use because of permanence (especially in the case of cemeteries) or the selective nature of development that can occur in close proximity (e.g., building-height limitations near airports). Transportation planners must be very cognizant of cemetery locations when projecting future corridors, because they are prohibitively costly to move and often too sacred legally and politically to disturb.

The undeveloped portion of the city is normally held in private hands, but in some instances it may be in government ownership. The size of such property varies widely with city size, with smaller cities generally having more vacant land (see Table 11-1). Obviously, the proportion of land that is undeveloped increases with distance from downtown. Much of this land, especially in outlying areas, is typically held by large investors for speculative purposes.

Centrifugal and Centripetal Forces

A pioneer American urban geographer, C.C. Colby, made a lasting contribution to an understanding of the spatial structure of the city by showing that dynamic behavioral forces continually interact to encourage activities to concentrate and disperse at the same time. His contribution, *the centrifugal and centripetal force model*, helps explain activity concentrations in the city core and at other specialized locations, and at the same time demonstrates the continuous lure of suburbanization.[3] That model has since been applied to the processes of change that have affected all urban activities.

Many functions have responded to the centrifugal and centripetal force model by adopting suburban locations almost exclusively, while others have developed distinctive forms adaptable to both downtown and suburban situations. Selected consumer retail operations have developed outlets that can prosper downtown in one environment, and with a different emphasis also thrive in suburbia. Downtown shoe store outlets, for example, are typically intensive, space-conserving operations that depend on large volumes of pedestrian traffic. Their suburban counterparts are space-extensive, self-service operations, oriented to the automobile-based consumer. We will be continually referring to the central city/suburban trade-off in terms of commercial activity locations in later chapters.

The most dramatic testimony to the power of centrifugal/centripetal force model of urban spatial structure to date has been the emergence of the polycentric city, albeit after Colby's time. The essence of this change can be observed in Figure 11-4, which compares the relatively simple structure of the pre-World War II monocentric city with that of its polycentric counterpart that emerged after World War II, in concert with the growing influence of the automobile on urban mobility and capital investment. In this latter conceptualization, several suburban downtowns occur that emulate the business mix formerly associated only with the traditional downtown. These centers emerged for

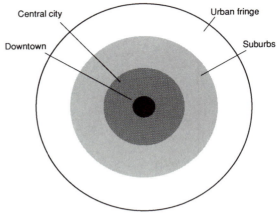

Moncentric City with Suburbs
Pre-World War II

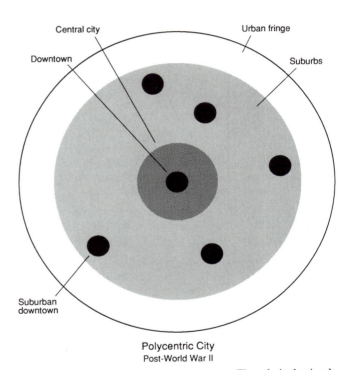

Polycentric City
Post-World War II

Figure 11-4. Changing Urban Morphology. The relatively simple structure of the pre-World War II city contrasts sharply with the post-World War II polycentric city. The automobile has created a city with several downtowns that each emulate the business mix formerly associated with the traditional downtown.

the most part at key intersections of radial highways and circumferential beltways in the suburbs. Recall the discussion of the impact of freeways on urban structure in Chapter 9. We will discuss suburban downtown developments in more detail following a closer examination of traditional land use theory.

[3]C. C. Colby, "Centrifugal and Centripetal Forces in Urban Geography," *Annals of the Association of American Geographers*, 23 (1933), 1–20.

TRADITIONAL LAND USE THEORY

The increasing complexity of urban form associated with an expansion in the number of major outlying centers raises questions about the validity of traditional land use theory. That theory, based on land uses being sorted out around a single downtown center, provided the basis for the bulk of the generalizations that have been promulgated on urban morphology. Before suggesting alternatives to this traditional theoretical framework, it will be instructive first to show its applicability to the traditional land use pattern.

Agricultural Origins of Urban Land Use Theory

As quaint as it may seem, modern urban land use theory derives from principles first expressed in terms of an agricultural land use model by J.H. von Thünen in the early 1800s.[4] On second thought, this situation should not be surprising, as the same market-based forces that shape agricultural decisions also influence urban land uses. The basic premise of the von Thünen conceptualization was that agricultural land uses conformed to general and predictable patterns around cities, which were the markets for farm goods. Those items in greatest demand, or having the highest transport costs, in the context of favorable production conditions (growing season, soil, fertility, precipitation, etc.), were grown closest to the market, and those with lesser requirements (in terms of demand, transport cost, etc.) occurred in more remote locations.

Von Thünen used the term *land rent*, which is roughly equivalent to *economic rent* in classic economics, to explain the type of agriculture that would occur at any given location.[5] It referred to the monetary return a farmer received from producing a particular commodity after all costs of production were deducted. Presumably, the farmer would specialize in producing the crop or livestock that yielded the highest land rent return at the particular location.

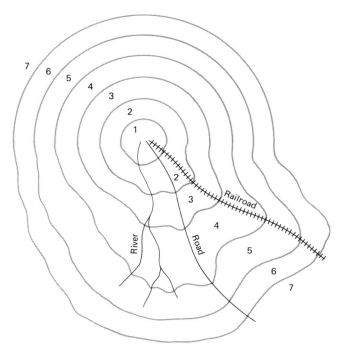

Zones of land use

1. Urban area
2. Market gardening
3. Dairying (fluid milk)
4. Dairy products (butter, cheese)
5. Grain production (wheat, corn)
6. Livestock and general farming
7. Grazing

Figure 11-5. Agricultural Land Use Model, after von Thünen. Agricultural land use rings can be constructed around the city that reflect actual production patterns. In response to market factors such as product selling prices, distance to market, and production costs, farmers produce more perishable and intensively cultivated crops closer to the market and more extensive crops/uses farther from the market.

A diagram of the agricultural land use zones around a hypothetical city appears in Figure 11-5. The crops von Thünen identified were based on the experience in Germany in the early 1800s and are not necessarily similar to those one would find today, but the principles remain the same. He said the particular type of production depended on three items: (1) distance to the market; (2) selling prices of the product at the market; (3) and land rent.[6]

Market gardening is identified with the ring immediately surrounding the city in Figure 11-5. Dairying (fluid milk production) occurs in the next closest ring to the city. Farther out, the dairy farms produce milk that is processed into manufactured items (butter, cheese, etc.). Beyond that zone are rings of crop production.

[4]J. H. von Thünen, *Der Isolierte Staat in Beziehung auf Landwirtschaft und Nationalokonomie*, 3rd ed., Berlin, 1875. Part I, which contains the original isolated-state statement, was originally published in 1826. For an English translation, see P. Hall, ed., *von Thünen's Isolated State: An English Version of "Der Isolierte Staat,"* translated by C. M. Wartenberg, Pergamon, New York, 1966.

[5]Andreas Grotewold, "von Thünen in Retrospect," *Economic Geography*, 35 (1959), 348.

[6]Hall, *von Thünen's Isolated State*, op. cit., p. 1.i.

Intensive cropping (wheat and corn) occurs in zone 5, followed by a zone of livestock and general farming farther away in zone 6. In the most distant zone 7, grazing is the major occupation.

Graphing Bid–Rent Curves

In graphic form, one can show the relationship between economic rent and distance from the market for one or several products. The so-called *bid-rent curve* slopes down to the right for each item, because with increasing distance from the market, additional transportation costs are incurred that decrease the monetary return. For example, production located at the market would incur no transportation costs. At any given distance away from the market, economic rent would decrease in direct proportion to transportation cost increases. The height of the curve at any distance can be determined by subtracting production and transportation costs from the price received for the product at the market.

Figure 11-6A shows the return from a ton of wheat at the market at $50.[7] This figure can be determined by subtracting the cost of production ($50) from the selling price at the market ($100), which leaves $50 economic rent. At any distance from the market, the rent is reduced in proportion to the level of transportation charges. Assuming transportation costs are $5 per mile, at 5 miles from the market, an additional $25 decrease in rent occurs, leaving a return of $25 (see Figure 11-6A). At 10 miles, with an added transportation charge of $25, the rent becomes zero, making it uneconomical to produce wheat at any greater distance from the market where returns would become negative. The line that connects the economic return at varying distances is the bid–rent curve. Any increase in market price would raise the curve and allow production to extend farther outward. Decreases in market prices would contract the production area. Changes in transportation charges would similarly alter production areas. As shipment costs increased, the curve would become steeper and contract the production area. Decreases in rates would flatten the curve, encouraging production at greater distances.

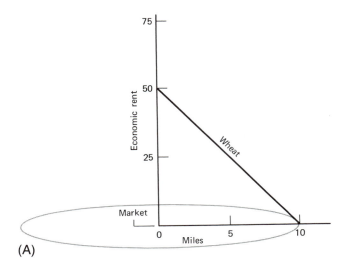

(A)

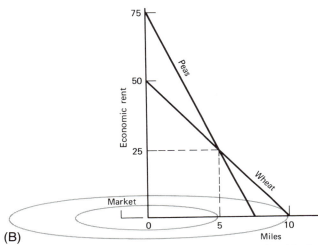

(B)

Figure 11-6. Agricultural Rent Gradients. The relationship between economic rent and distance from the market can be shown in graphic form for one (A) or several products (B). The curve in the top position at any given distance from the market gives the highest return, and that product is the preferred choice for production. *Source:* Redrawn with permission from *Papers and Proceedings*, Regional Science Association, 6, 1960, "A Theory of the Urban Land Market," William Alonso, pp. 151 and 153.

Agricultural Land Use Rings

In comparing the bid–rent curves of two products, the basis for rings of production around the market can be determined. In Figure 11-6B, a bid–rent line is shown for two products (wheat and peas). The curve for peas starts out in a higher position than that of wheat, because its market price is significantly higher than that for wheat ($150), more than offsetting the increased cost of production ($75). A return of $75 is indicated at

---

[7]This example is reported in William Alonso, "A Theory of the Urban Land Market," *Papers and Proceedings of the Regional Science Association*, 6 (1960), 149–157.

the market. Transportation charges are also higher for peas than for wheat. At 5 miles from the market, $50 of transportation charges are incurred, leaving economic rent levels at $25. Ten miles from the market, another $50 charge occurs, plunging the rent level below zero. By connecting the points with a straight line, it appears that it becomes uneconomical to produce peas beyond 5 miles from the market, because at greater distances, wheat becomes more profitable. The curve in the top position at any given distance from the market will give the highest return. In this example, peas will be produced closest to the market and wheat farther away.

Urban Land Use Zones

The allocation of urban land uses closely parallels that of rural land. Activities that need to minimize transport costs, as discussed earlier, traditionally clustered in the city center. High land prices reflected this access advantage. Commercial activities located in high-rise facilities normally bid the highest prices for such land. Specialty shops and outlets with high markups (i.e., jewelry stores) also easily adapted to expensive real estate. Other activities that might prefer downtown locations could be easily outbid. As a result, space-extensive industrial uses sought locations farther from the city center.

One observer has indicated that downtown land is occupied on the basis of its *positional advantages*.[8] Central-area sites provide *low transfer costs* owing to the high pedestrian flow rate and access that this setting provides to so many activities. The value of such sites comes from their ability to offer a convenient means for parties to interact with one another. Maximum exposure to pedestrians alone, for example, could justify paying high rents for some specialty retailers that depend on impulse buying. Locations away from high-activity nodes would be disastrous to such businesses, and they have very steep bid–rent curves. Activities with flatter curves are more flexible in their location decision and could sustain *higher transfer costs*.

A general model of urban land use along a bid–rent curve is shown in Figure 11-7. As in the agricultural case, the curves slope downward to the right, reflecting lower rents per unit of land with increasing distance. Offices, banks, hotels, and other commercial establish-

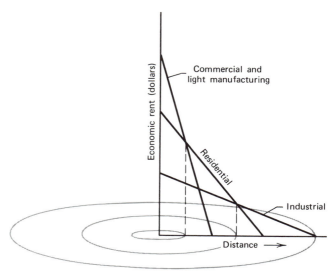

Figure 11-7. Classic Form of Urban Rent Gradients. As in the agricultural case, urban land rents decline with distance from the center of the market. Commercial uses capture close-in locations due to their ability to pay. Residential uses generally capture intermediate locations, and industrial uses occur at greater distances from the center.

ments capture close-in locations. Normally, government and public institution facilities cluster nearby. Warehousing and light manufacturing frequently identify with a *zone of transition* between commercial and residential uses.

The residential curve occupying an intermediate position in Figure 11-7 is actually a composite of several distributions. Lower-income residences, mainly apartments (sometimes public housing) or rooming houses, occur highest on the curve. The poor have traditionally lived on relatively expensive land in North American cities to save on the cost of transportation and to meet the need for close proximity to employment. They are mainly renters and live at relatively high densities.

With increasing distance from the city center, moderate-, middle-, and high-income residential areas appear in succession. Typically, the higher-income family is willing to substitute more land at a greater distance from the city center for less accessibility. Relatively large transportation expenditures to overcome this relative isolation do not represent important cost factors for the well-to-do.

Manufacturing and distribution facilities are shown as industrial uses in suburban settings on the graph, probably near radial freeways or circumferential beltways. Beyond this zone, land may be predominantly

---

[8]Edgar M. Hoover, "Land Use Competition," *The Location of Economic Activity*, McGraw-Hill, New York, 1948, pp. 90–102.

rural with some nonfarm residential activity. Rural residences and agricultural land occupy the extreme fringes of the metropolitan area, comprising the *exurban* fringe. Other land in the fringe is idle, typically held in large tracts by corporate and institutional investors for speculative purposes.

CRITICISM OF TRADITIONAL LAND USE THEORY

In addition to the criticism leveled at the traditional bid–rent model regarding the evolution of the city away from one central focus to a multinodal complex, a more fundamental philosophical problem also exists. The bid–rent model suggests that land uses are flexible and that the best combinations of uses are made. But owners of property in a free-market economy can also be regarded as having monopoly powers over the use of the land, thwarting optimal allocations. The rich are particularly well served by the land allocation process, because they get the first chance to buy property, based on their ability to pay. The poor bid last and are left with the least desirable space. This problem is particularly evident in the housing market, which will be discussed in Chapter 12.

Three types of rent have been elaborated in the literature to show imperfections in the land use allocation system:[9] (1) *monopoly rent*—given the finite quantity and locational uniqueness of a particular piece of land, the "purchaser's eagerness to buy and ability to pay"[10] can bid up the price of the land, giving a higher return to the owner than otherwise envisioned; (2) *differential rent*—returns that arise from excess profits to landowners due to an advantageous locational situation; and (3) *absolute rent*—differential returns that occur because of barriers among the allocation of land uses due to social and capital immobility, private property ownership, and distance from the market.

Critics of the urban bid–rent model have noted that monopoly rent and absolute rent have become more important; differential rent on which the bid–rent model is based is less important. Capital typically flows to areas of most profit in a free market, not the area most in need. In this context, the urban poor suffer the most, because social impacts and need are often not considered in the allocation process.

LAND VALUE SURFACE

Land values exhibit a tremendous amount of variation within the city,[11] with location and accessibility being the prime determinants. In the very heart of a large metropolitan area exceeding 1 million in population, values often exceed $1 million per acre, but only for a few blocks adjacent to the primary street intersection or along a major commercial street.[12] This central point is often labeled the *peak land value intersection* (PLVI) or 100 percent corner.

Land values drop sharply with distance from the CBD, with higher-priced pieces located adjacent to major transportation corridors. Higher values also occur at major commercial nodes. Relatively uniform but declining values per acre characterize residential areas with increasing distance from the city center. Values rise again around perimeter beltways, especially where they intersect major radial arteries, the sites preferred for suburban downtowns. Values in these areas can approach $1 million per acre or more, only to taper off abruptly toward the urban fringe.

The land value envelope of the modern American metropolitan area resembles the diagram shown in Figure 11-8, with the very high values in the CBD dropping off sharply within a relatively short distance. Local increases to the prevailing downward trend occur at outlying commercial nodes and at major freeway and arterial highway intersections, especially around circumferential beltways and suburban downtowns. One must journey many miles from large cities (100 miles or more) to find land that can be purchased nominally, given the residual effect of the urban land market. Even then, land may not be readily available if it is desirable for agricultural or recreational purposes.

Land uses respond to land values in a predictable fashion. The high price of land in downtown commercial districts restricts its use to only those functions that can pay high prices for space. The normal response in commercial areas to high-priced land is for more vertical expansion. This point will be covered in detail

[9]David Harvey, "Use Value, Exchange Value and Urban Land-Use Theory," in *Social Justice and the City*, David Harvey, ed., Johns Hopkins University Press, Baltimore, 1973, pp. 153–194.

[10]Ibid., p. 179.

[11]Duane S. Knos, *Distribution of Land Values in Topeka, Kansas*, Center for Research in Business, Lawrence, Kansas, 1962.

[12]Parcels are rarely sold by the acre downtown because they are held in relatively small lots. Usually, one observes prices quoted in terms of dollars per square foot or front-foot values, based on a standard depth.

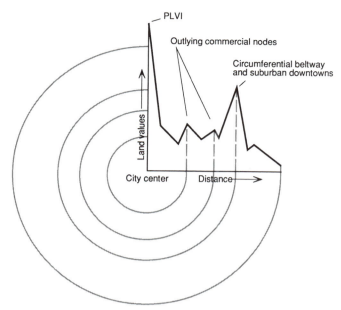

PLVI

Outlying commercial nodes

Circumferential beltway
and suburban downtowns

Land values

City center   Distance →

Figure 11-8. *Urban Land Value Surface.* High land values occur in the city center, but drop off rapidly with increasing distance. Local increases to the prevailing trend occur at outlying commercial nodes and at major freeway and arterial highway locations. Values at suburban downtown locations again reach the peaks found in the downtown areas, but drop off rapidly at short distances.

in Chapter 15, which deals with the central business district. Land assessments for taxation purposes often reflect both the value of the land itself and improvements (buildings) to it. Higher rates occur for developed rather than undeveloped land, and often higher rates are assessed against commercial rather than residential uses. This taxation arrangement causes some

problems in renewal and reduces the incentives for the redevelopment of run-down properties.

POPULATION DENSITY

The population *density–decline* profile, which shows densities falling with increasing distance from the city center, resembles the land value model quite strongly. The exact form of the classic population density–decline model has been described in many ways (Figure 11-9). Colin Clark, writing in the early 1950s, described the profile in terms of a *negative exponential* decline with increasing distance from the city center.[13] He noted that a greater rate of decline occurred nearer the center of the city, with a slowing of the drop farther outward, creating a concave form (Figure 11-9A).

Converting the density values to logarithms creates a straight-line density–decline profile, as also shown in Figure 11-9A. Subsequently, researchers have refined Clark's model to reflect real-world situations more exactly. Bruce Newling, for example, has shown that population densities in modern North American cities are not highest at the very center of the city but in a ring around the downtown core.[14] His model (Figure 11-9B) shows lower densities in the city center with increases occurring just outside the CBD; densities peak a few miles from the city center, followed by a

[13]Colin Clark, "Urban Population Densities," *Journal of the Royal Statistical Society,* A114 (1959), 490–496.

[14]Bruce Newling, "The Spatial Variation of Urban Population Densities," *Geographical Review,* 59 (1969), 242–252.

Figure 11-9. Population Density Gradients. The form of the classic population density–decline model has been described in many ways. The negative exponential form is shown in (A), while a modified negative exponential model occurs in (B). *Source:* Adapted with permission from *Journal of the Royal Statistical Society,* Series A 114 (1951), "Urban Population Densities." Colin Clark, 490–496; and the *Geographical Review,* 69 (1969), with the permission of the American Geographical Society.

negative exponential decline farther outward. The term *density rim* refers to the peak itself and the *crater effect* to the depressed level of density in the very center. Since the Newling modification of the negative exponential model involves the curve changing from a positive to a negative gradient, it is called a second-degree curve or polynomial. A logarithm transformation created the form shown in white in Figure 11-9B.

Population density profiles have changed markedly over time, just as they do in cities of varying sizes. The nineteenth-century city was more compact and the density gradient was quite steep with distance from the center (Figure 11-10A). American cities today exhibit lower central densities and correspondingly higher suburban concentrations of population, which has tended to flatten the curve over time (Figure 11-10A).

European cities offer a contrast, because their central densities tended to grow proportionally with those in outlying areas in the past, and the rate of decline with distance remained relatively constant (Figure 11-10B). Stronger planning and zoning controls, the lack of cheap developable land, and less dependence on the private automobile make European cities more compact than their American counterparts. Moreover, the lesser dependence on single-family homes in deference to mid- and high-rise housing, even at the edge of the city, reduces the potential for density declines from the city center outward. The incentive for suburbanization has not been as strong in Europe as in North America, for residential or commercial purposes, but it is a growing trend. Edges and boundaries of cities are also more clearly distinguished in Europe as a result of weaker pressures for suburban sprawl.

Smaller cities are generally more compact than larger metropolitan areas. They have steeper density–decline gradients (Figure 11-10C and 11-10D) and greater population densities at the city center because of less specialized nonresidential functions in the core area. There are frequently fewer low-density suburban units in these smaller cities. Newer cities in the United States, such as those in the South and West, also have much lower population densities than older cities in the Northeast.

Figure 11-10. Density Gradient Patterns Found in North American and European Cities. Population density profiles have changed markedly over time. Density profiles in American cities are less steep than those in European cities, and they decline less steeply with distance from the center in larger cities than in smaller ones. *Source:* Adapted from *Geographical Review*, 53 (1963), with permission of the American Geographical Society; and by permission from the *Annals of the Association of American Geographers*, 60, 1970, pp. 273–278, John S. Adams.

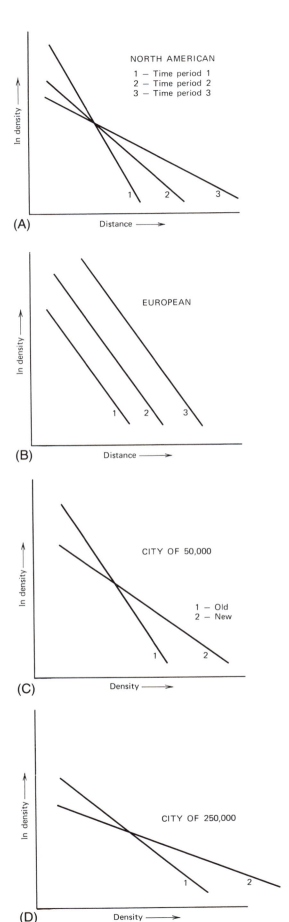

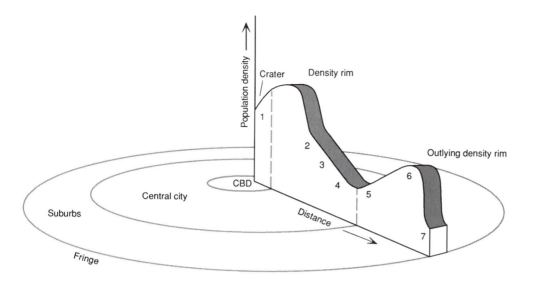

1. High-rise apartments and public housing
2. Lower-density apartments
3. Detached single-family units, duplexes, and condominiums
4. Single-family detached
5. Garden apartments, patio homes, and condominiums
6. Mid- and high-rise town-homes and condominiums
7. Single-family detached

Figure 11-11. Population Density Profile for a Metropolitan Area of 2 Million Persons. Population densities increase with distance from the city center (crater) to the density rim then decline steadily with distance up to 15 miles from the center. Density increases then resume around perimeter beltways due to a greater share of apartments and high-rise units, only to decline again as the share of single family units increases again beyond the outer density rim.

A contemporary density profile of a North American city of 2 million population appears in Figure 11-11. Note that the core density is relatively low, rising to a peak within 5 miles of the center, then dropping again, with another reverse in the trend at about 15 miles from the center. The precise distance at which these density changes occur varies among cities.

The tendency for increases around perimeter beltways in larger centers reflects the growing number and scale of garden apartment complexes, townhouses, and high-rise acommodations in an area traditionally dominated by single-family detached units. Suburban areas attracted a larger share of multifamily units in the 1980s. Densities also increased in rural fringe settings, creating a flatter density curve. The modified negative exponential decline model still fits, but the scale of the application has changed dramatically, and the curve has flattened as suburbs have become more like the central city.

DESCRIPTIVE MODELS OF URBAN STRUCTURE

Three classic spatial models of urban growth describe the land use pattern in the traditional North American city. Every student of urban studies encounters at least one or two of these conceptualizations because they are so widely accepted by all social science disciplines. Only one of the models can be credited to geographers,

the others having been developed by sociologists and economists.

Concentric Zone Model

The earliest of these models, the *concentric ring model*, emerged from a study of Chicago by sociologists at the University of Chicago in the early 1900s and is attributed to the work of E.W. Burgess.[15] That model posited a central business district at the center (zone 1) around which all other uses formed (Figure 11-12A). Surrounding the CBD, a factory, slum, and ethnic community zone existed (zone 2). This area became known as a *transition zone* or *gray zone* between the commercial core and residential communities farther out. The transition concept refers to the tendency for older residential areas to be converted to commercial uses as the business district grew. Such an area often attracted immigrants and was generally run-down and a center of crime and vice. Frequently, the land is held by speculators and the housing function is only an interim use. Zone 3 consisted of lower-income working people's homes. Other successive zones consisted of higher-income residences, with a commuter zone lying on the periphery.

[15]R. E. Park, E. W. Burgess, and R.D. McKenzie, *The City*, University of Chicago Press, Chicago, 1925, pp. 47–62.

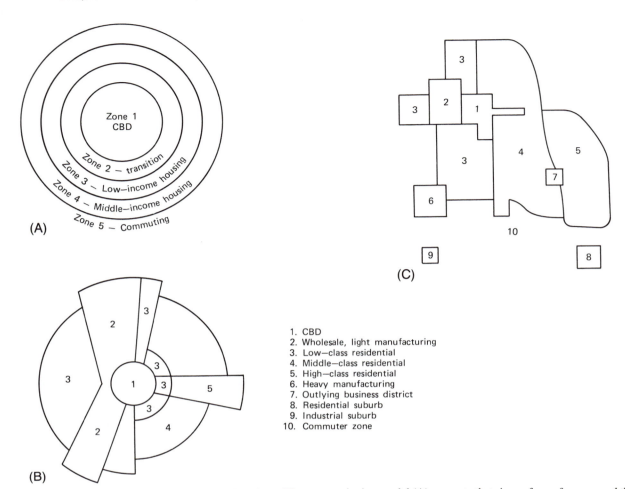

(A)

(B)

(C)

1. CBD
2. Wholesale, light manufacturing
3. Low–class residential
4. Middle–class residential
5. High–class residential
6. Heavy manufacturing
7. Outlying business district
8. Residential suburb
9. Industrial suburb
10. Commuter zone

Figure 11-12. Descriptive Models of Urban Structure. The concentric ring model (A) suggests that rings of uses form around the central business district. The sector model (B) posits that uses follow transportation corridors. The multiple nuclei model (C) recognizes that uses form around several nodes. *Source:* Redrawn with permission from Chauncy D. Harris and Edward L. Ullman, "The Nature of Cities," in Harold M. Hayer and Clyde F. Kohn (eds.), *Readings in Urban Geography*, University of Chicago Press, p. 281. Copyright © 1959 by the University of Chicago.

The ring model has several deficiencies, but its elegance and simplicity have stood the test of time. It evolved at the University of Chicago at the same time as the new field of *human ecology*, which had roots in plant ecology and social Darwinism.[16] The concepts of *dominance, specialization*, and *succession*, taken from the biological community, helped account for rings of specialized land use.

The concentric ring model inadequately accounted for the development of specialized clusters of industrial uses. It also failed to explain the impact of transportation routes on land use. Some later students of the ring

model did adjust it to meet these deficiencies by superimposing a radial highway system on it, which had the effect of stretching the rings outward where they intersected transportation corridors, creating a starlike rather than a circular urban form.

Sector Model

The land economist Homer Hoyt published a landmark article setting forth the notion of a *sector model* of urban land uses in 1939 after an exhaustive study of patterns in over 100 cities.[17] He suggested that once

---

[16]James Hughes, "Social Area Analysis," in Michael Greenberg, ed., *Urban Economics and Spatial Patterns*, Center for Unban Policy Research, Rutgers University, New Brunswick, N.J., 1974, pp.41–45.

[17]Homer Hoyt, *The Structure and Growth of Residential Neighborhoods in American Cities*, USGPO, Washington, D.C., 1939.

similar uses emerged around the CBD (at the center of the city), activities would remain in that particular area and extend over time in the same direction as the city grew (Figure 11-12B). The intuitive appeal of this argument is strong, because similar uses do, in fact, grow in specific directions, often following rail or highway arteries, high or low ground, or simply clustering on the same side of the city.

High-income residential areas are notorious for being on high, rolling, or wooded ground, and low-income areas for being in less-desirable low-lying valleys and industrial basins. Hoyt's model also easily accommodates growth, because it allows new activities to be added to the periphery, rather than requiring redevelopment of existing areas as the ring model implies. The model is also consistent with the observation that cities grow more rapidly in the direction of the high-income sector, as entrepreneurs seek business sites near the affluent market.[18]

The wedges that form the basis of the sector model have particular relevance to the residential function. The distribution of families by income in a metropolitan area is highly differentiated by neighborhood, conforming to a zonal pattern. Even with the random mobility afforded by the automobile, and the locational flexibility it promotes, land use areas have remained relatively distinctive. Particular uses continue to cluster together and grow along specific axes.

Multiple Nuclei Model

The geographers Chauncy Harris and Edward Ullman are responsible for the *multiple nuclei model*.[19] This model provides an alternative conceptualization of urban form, one based on the premise that uses do not evolve around a single core, but at several nodes or focal points (Figure 11-12C). The CBD is not necessarily at the center of the city in this situation. The model recognizes that different activities have varying accessibility requirements. For example, a commercial area could develop around a government complex, a cultural center such as a university, or a theater district, or simply at major transportation intersections. The airport could also induce commercial or industrial uses.

Each of these areas could develop its own satellite residential communities.

The multiple nuclei model acknowledges not only that specific functions have unique locational and functional needs, but also that some activities are detrimental to one another and need widely separated locations. Historical inertia that maintains relatively unique districts can also be an important factor as cities grow and envelop existing industrial and commercial nodes.[20]

Harris and Ullman philosophized that none of the three models just discussed was universally applicable and that all cities exhibited patterns identifying with aspects of one or more of the models. This observation was later picked up by social area analysts who agreed that cities tended to identify with each of the three conceptualizations, rather than one exclusively.

Urban Realms Model

On the basis of his analysis of the evolving morphology of the San Francisco Bay area, James Vance proposed the *urban realms model*.[21] Peter Muller and others later applied this scheme to the Los Angeles region and greater New York, among others.[22] The key element of the realms model (Figure 11-13) is the emergence of large self-sufficient suburban sectors each focused on a downtown independent of the traditional downtown and the central city. In the ideal form, several suburban downtowns coexist with the traditional central business district as anchors of each realm. The entire metropolitan area becomes reorganized into a set of independent urban realms according to this conceptualization. Popularly known to students as the pepperoni pizza model, this conceptualization may represent the culmination of the impact of the automobile on urban form.

The extent, character, and internal structure of each

[18]Hughes, "Social Area Analysis," op. cit., pp. 45–46.

[19]C. D. Harris and E. L. Ullman, "The Nature of Cities," *The Annals of the American Academy of Political and Social Science*, 242 (1945), 7–17.

[20]Hughes, "Social Area Analysis," op. cit., pp. 46–47.

[21]James E. Vance, Jr., *Geography and Urban Evolution in the San Francisco Bay Area*, Institute of Government Studies, University of California, Berkeley, 1964; *The Scene of Man: The Role and Structure of the City in the Geography of Western Civilization*, Harper's College Press, New York, 1977.

[22]Peter O. Muller, *Contemporary Suburban America*, Prentice Hall, Englewood Cliffs, N.J., 1981, pp. 8–11; Truman A. Hartshorn and Peter O. Muller, *Suburban Business Centers: Employment Implications*, Final Report prepared for U.S. Department of Commerce, Economic Development Administration, Project No. RED-808-G-84-5, Washington, D.C., 1986; Truman A. Hartshorn and Peter O. Muller, "Suburban Downtowns and the Transformation of Metropolitan Atlanta's Business Landscapes," *Urban Geography* 10 (1989), pp. 375–395.

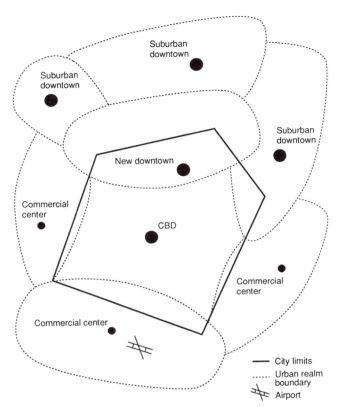

Figure 11-13. **Urban Realms Model.** The key element of the realms model is the emergence of large self-sufficient suburban sectors, each focused on a downtown independent of the traditional downtown and the central city. Popularly known to students as the pepperoni pizza model, this conceptualization may represent the culmination of the impact of the automobile on urban form.

urban realm is shaped by four criteria (Vance, 1977, pp. 411–416): (1) terrain, especially topographical and water barriers; (2) overall size of the metropolis; (3) the amount of economic activity contained within each realm; and (4) the internal accessibility of each realm vis-à-vis its dominant economic core. Interaccessibility among suburban realms is also important, particularly circumferential links and direct airport connections that no longer require them to interact with the central realm in order to reach other outlying realms and distant metropolises.

An application of this urban realms concept to the metropolitan Los Angeles region is illustrated in Figure 11-14. Each suburban realm is anchored by a major mixed-use downtown core area. In the Orange County realm (realm 5 in Figure 11-14), the Irvine area achieved preeminence over its older rivals, nearby Newport Beach, Santa Ana, and Anaheim, by the

mid-1980s. Paced by the recent expansion of the South Coast Metro downtown in neighboring Costa Mesa, this area emerged in the 1990s as the leading suburban complex in the Los Angeles region (Figure 1-7).

Social Area Analysis

Another approach to modeling the internal structure of the city, of particular relevance to the residential function, is provided by *social area analysis*.[23] Originally developed by the sociologists Eshref Shevky, Marilyn Williams, and Wendell Bell as a theory of social differentiation, social area analysis shows how family characteristics, economic status, and ethnic patterns interrelate to produce distinct spatial patterns within the city.[24] The first studies were conducted in Los Angeles and San Francisco just after World War II. Since that time, geographers and sociologists have conducted studies in many additional cities, particularly since large-scale computers became available to handle large data sets.

Social area analysis studies involve the delineation of uniform subareas in the city using three constructs: *social rank*, *urbanization*, and *segregation*. Shevky and Bell assigned census tracts to a position on a scale for each of the three indexes. For example, the *social rank* index (more recently referred to as an *economic status* indicator) consisted of an education and an occupation variable. Individual census tracts were assigned to a low, middle, or high position on a scale based on the values they showed on these two variables. Tracts were next evaluated on the basis of an *urbanization* index, sometimes referred to as a *family status* measure. Three variables—fertility, proportion of women in the labor force, and the percentage of housing in family units—defined this composite score. Tracts were again assigned as low, average, or high on these scores. Finally, a *segregation index*, often called *ethnic status*, was calculated by determining the distribution of minority persons.

[23]For a discussion of the evolution of social area analysis, see David Herbert, *Urban Geography*, Praeger, New York, 1972, pp. 139–142; Brian J. L. Berry, ed., *City Classification Handbook: Methods and Applications*, Wiley–Interscience, New York, 1972, pp. 273–278.

[24]Eshref Shevky and Marilyn Williams, *The Social Areas of Los Angeles*, The University of California Press, Berkeley/Los Angeles, 1949; Wendell Bell, "The Social Areas of the San Francisco Region," *American Sociological Review*, 18 (1953), 39–47; Eshref Shevky and Wendell Bell, *Social Area Analysis: Theory, Illustrative Application, and Computational Procedures*, Stanford University Press, Stanford, Calif., 1955.

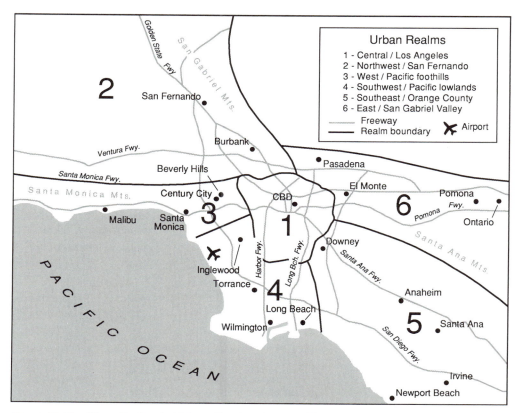

Figure 11-14. Urban Realms in Metropolitan Los Angeles. The urban realms model provides a better conceptualization of the region's complex structure than any other current approach. Each realm is anchored by a major mixed-use downtown core area. Paced by the recent expansion of the South Coast metro downtown in Costa Mesa, realm #5 has emerged as the leading suburban complex in the Los Angeles region. *Source:* Peter O. Muller, *Contemporary Suburban America*, Prentice-Hall, Englewood Cliffs, N.J., 1981, p. 10. Used by permission.

Researchers originally chose these indexes as indicative of the social space of the city because of a belief that they reflected basic societal trends—that cities were becoming more specialized and ordered on the basis of status and profession (social rank), that changes in family lifestyles were occurring (urbanization), and that ethnic groups were separate and isolated from the rest of the population (segregation). The proponents of social area analysis argued that industrialization, affluence, and gains in productivity were changing the lifestyles of urban dwellers. They felt the family was declining in importance as a nuclear unit and that more separation of home and workplace was occurring. Tracts showing high scores on the social status dimension, for example, were predominantly neighborhoods with white-collar workers, whereas blue-collar communities identified with low-scoring tracts. The early studies did not attempt to map findings, so no spatial interpretation was given.

The *urbanization index* separated subareas of the city on the basis of family composition (size, age) and type of dwelling unit (single family, multiple family). Areas with many young children and low participation rates of women in the labor force scored high on this index, whereas low-scoring tracts had more working women, more multiple-family dwelling units, and fewer children. The ethnic dimension separated out racial subcommunities, particularly black neighborhoods.

Considerable criticism of the theoretical foundation of these three factors surfaced, based mainly on the idea that they were not universal and were too narrowly conceived. But by the late 1950s, researchers had tested the model empirically, using data from a wide variety of cities. A larger number and variety of measures reflecting conditions and activity levels became common in these studies, and they generally confirmed the validity of the three dimensions.

A list of commonly used variables in a social area analysis study showing three dimensions appears in Table 11-3. As the approach to studying social areas became more broadly based in terms of the types of variables employed, the term *factorial ecology* became identified with this work.[25] This term referred to the comprehensive nature of the studies, which used up to 50 or more characteristics to develop common dimensions of variation.

Geographers began mapping the results of their factor analyses of social areas in the 1960s. They found that the three components of urban space had distinct spatial regularities that corresponded with the spatial interpretation of the ring, sector, and multiple nuclei models (Figure 11-15).[26] Each of the patterns was treated as independent of the other, and all three added together comprised a complete replication of urban structure. In this manner, the city became a "spatial sandwich" with three layers: (1) an economic status layer; (2) an urbanization component; and (3) an ethnic segregation part. The economic status layer generally exhibited sectoral characteristics, while the urbanization component produced a concentric ring pattern, and the ethnic segregation phenomenon produced a multiple nuclei arrangement.

Cross-cultural comparisons also confirmed the general validity of the rings, sectors, and nuclei in cities in various countries. The social class and family status factors were not as clear-cut in European and Asian cities as in North America, but studies in Calcutta, Cairo, and Helsinki each indicated that the social area analysis approach yielded useful generalizations.[27] Some more exhaustive factorial ecology studies have expanded the number of factors employed beyond the original three to reflect local conditions more thoroughly The social area analysis approach will be uti-

TABLE 11-3
Variables Typically Employed in Social Area Analysis Studies

Dimension	Variables
Socioeconomic status	Population indicators
	Education
	Occupation
	Income
	Housing indicators
	Quality
	Value or rent
	Household facilities and possessions
Urbanization index, family status, or life-cycle stage	Population indicators
	Age
	Family size
	Fertility
	Marital status
	Housing indicators
	Type of unit
	Age
Segregation, ethnicity, or minority group status	Racial group
	Linguistic group

Source: Adapted from Brian J. L. Berry, *City Classification Handbook, Methods, and Applications,* Wiley-Interscience, New York, 1972, p. 285.

lized in the discussion of residential communities in Chapter 12.

TOWARD A TYPOLOGY OF URBAN LAND USE

A somewhat more functional approach to explaining urban land use structure than that provided by social area analysis has been provided by Larry Bourne in a study of Tóronto.[28] Land use measures that he employed to create a composite view of the city's spatial structure included: (1) several distance and travel time indicators; (2) seven employment categories; (3) eight building stock variables; and (4) selected occupancy rate items. A total of 29 land use types were analyzed. With the aid of factor analysis, a smaller number of common dimensions of variation were revealed.

[25] Robert A. Murdie, *The Factorial Ecology of Metropolitan Toronto, 1951–1961: An Essay on the Social Geography of the City,* Research Paper No. 116, Department of Geography, Chicago, 1968; Philip H. Rees, "The Factorial Ecology of Metropolitan Chicago, 1960," in Brian J. L. Berry and Frank L. Horton, eds., *Geographic Perspectives on Urban Systems,* Prentice Hall, Englewood Cliffs, N.J., 1970.

[26] Brian J. L. Berry, "Internal Structure of the City," in Larry Bourne, ed., *Internal Structure of the City,* Oxford University Press, New York, 1971, pp. 97–103, reprinted from *Law and Contemporary Problems,* 30 (1965), 111–119.

[27] Brian J. L. Berry and Philip Rees, "Factorial Ecology of Calcutta," *American Journal of Sociology,* 74 (1969), 445–491; Janet Abu-Lughod, "Testing the Theory of Social Area Analysis: The Ecology of Cairo, Egypt," *American Sociological Review,* 34 (1969), 198–210; Frank L. Sweetser, "Factor Structure as Ecological Structure in Helsinki and Boston," *Acta Sociologica,* 8 (1965), 205–225.

[28] Larry S. Bourne, "A Descriptive Typology of Urban Land Use Structure and Change," *Land Economics,* 50 (1974), 271–280.

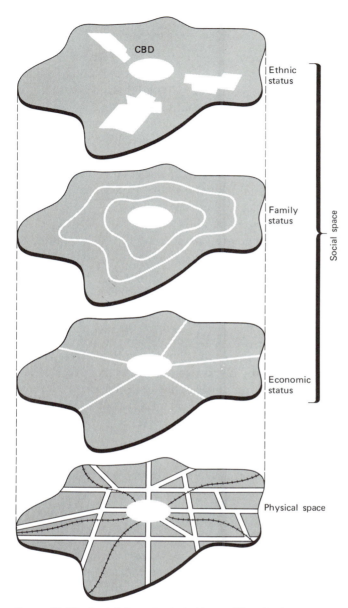

Figure 11-15. Social Area Analysis Model. The city becomes a "spatial sandwich," with the social area analysis model comprised of three layers adapted to the physical space of the city. *Source:* Redrawn with permission. From Robert A. Murdie, *Factorial Ecology of Metropolitan Toronto, 1951–1961*, Department of Geography Research Paper #16, 1969, p. 9. Copyright by the University of Chicago, Department of Geography.

The first element of the Toronto model consisted of the *high-density core area*, based on the distinctive concentration of offices, parking, and specialized service employment found there. The second factor, *distance–density contrasts*, identified accessibility differences between the city center and its hinterland. A third item distinguished *older residential areas* in the inner city. The linear pattern of *industrial and warehouse space* along rail lines provided another dimension, and the last three components singled out high-density, centrally located *luxury apartments, open space and recreational land*, and various *institutional nodes,* such as hospital and government complexes. Mixed-use suburban developments also appeared in this last grouping.

AN EXPLOITIVE MODEL OF URBAN STRUCTURE

A dynamic model of city structure—one that shows how various subareas function together—emerged from William Bunge's analysis of Detroit.[29] He discussed three interdependent units in the city: (1) the *city of death*; (2) the *city of need*; and (3) the *city of superfluity* (Figure 11-16). This model is somewhat controversial but intriguing. Poor inner-city residents comprise the city of death. They are exploited by the rest of the city because they pay a "machine tax" to others in the form of job exploitation. The owners of the machines are the wealthy entrepreneurs living in the zone of superfluity who pay them less than their worth for work. In addition, the poor also pay a "death tax," which takes the form of a surcharge for the higher prices they pay to obtain food, housing, insurance, loans, etc. A lower level of city services and cultural opportunities in their neighborhoods adds to the severity of the "death tax."

The suburban city of superfluity benefits from this exploitation. Money flows from the city of death to the city of superfluity. The city of superfluity is the home of the powerful elite class, the professionals, the business people, and the politicians. It is a small area and not overly conspicuous, but highly exploitive.

The city of need lies between the city of superfluity and the city of death. It is a buffer city that is also exploited by the city of superfluity. "Here are the white workers, the 'hard hats,' the solid union members of Middle America."[30] This city is large and relatively stable.

---

[29]William Bunge, "Detroit Humanly Viewed: The American Urban Present," in Ronald Abler *et al.,* eds., *Human Geography in a Shrinking World*, Duxbury Press, North Scituate, Mass., 1975, pp. 149–181.
[30]Ibid., p. 158.

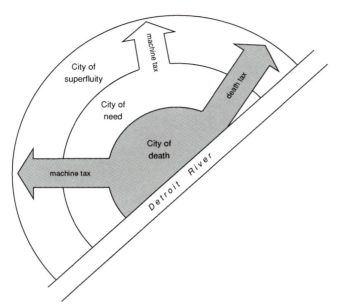

Figure 11-16. Exploitive Model of Urban Structure. Three interdependent units of the city can be found from the center outward in this model: 1) the city of Death; 2) the city of Need; and 3) the city of Superfluity. Based on the exploitation experienced by the poor and working class, this model emphasizes the control over the city exerted by the wealthy. *Source:* Redrawn with permission from William Bunge. In "Detroit Humanly Viewed," Ronald Abler et al., eds., *Human Geography in a Shrinking World*, Duxbury Press, North Scituate, Mass., p. 153.

Bunge compares the city of death to that of a foreign country. It represents another America, sharing few of the American dreams or amenities. It contains tremendous numbers of rats, which can be used as a means of defining the region (Figure 11-17). There are few doctors in the area, food is scarce, and nutritional deficiencies are common. It has a problem with filth and garbage. In short, it is a city with a miserable existence and little hope. It is a permanent and ever-declining slum according to this conceptualization.

Bunge constructed a von Thünen type of bid–rent model to show how rents determine the relative location of cities of death, need, and superfluity. He indicated that the slum dwellers living in the city centers were powerless, but that they were located "on the most convenient land, often within walking distance of downtown." The middle-class city of need is shifted outward by the presence of the city of death, and the city of superfluity occupies spacious settings farthest from the city center.

THIRD WORLD STRUCTURE[31]

Most third world cities, despite long settlement histories, remained small by contemporary standards until the post-World War II era. The largest of these cities today, however, are not those with long traditions, but settlements dating to the colonial era associated with European domination in the eighteenth and nineteenth centuries. Peculiar circumstances associated with the colonial era have also given these cities a legacy and structure quite different from the experience shared by North American and European cities.

One characteristic of these cities, a direct carryover from colonial days, is the presence of a small but powerful elite class that controls the economy and maintains strong international ties. The vast majority of the urban population remains poor and unskilled, having strong emotional and cultural ties to their recent rural past. This situation occurs in Latin America, Africa, the Middle East, and Asia.

From a spatial perspective, the third world city often takes the form of a reverse concentric ring model, owing to the presence of the elite business/administrative group in the city center adjacent to the central business district and progressively lower-income groups located farther from the city center. A large middle class, as in developed areas, is conspicuously absent. Often, substandard *squatter housing* forms the outermost ring of the city.

Model of Latin American Cities

Latin American cities differ somewhat from their counterparts in Asia and Africa. The Spanish Law of the Indies guidelines strongly influenced the form of the colonial Latin American city, as discussed in Chapter 3. Inspired by the Roman tradition of a formal grid pattern and central plaza, land uses in the European-dominated Latin American city demonstrated a strict hierarchical social order. These cities were important trade and administrative centers, an activity that occurred close to the central plaza.

As elsewhere in the third world, very little industrialization occurred in Latin American cities in the

[31]This section is adapted from Truman A. Hartshorn and John W. Alexander, *Economic Geography*, 3rd. ed., Prentice Hall, Englewood Cliffs, N.J., 1988.

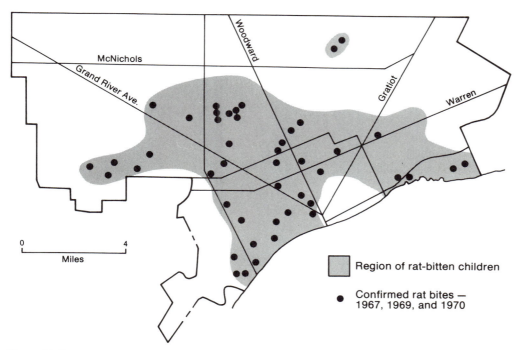

Figure 11-17. City of Death as Defined by Rat Bites in Detroit. The City of Death is an ever-declining slum, according to the exploitive model. One can use the frequency of rat bites to define the region, which provides a surrogate measure of the lower level of service and cultural opportunities available to the poor inner-city resident. *Source:* Redrawn with permission from William Bunge. In "Detroit Humanly Viewed," Ronald Abler et al., eds., *Human Geography in a Shrinking World*, Duxbury Press, North Scituate, Mass., p. 161.

colonial era, and very few opportunities existed to support the growth of a middle class. Instead, cities housed elites near the center and unskilled low-income groups elsewhere in areas notorious for their lack of public services. Typically, only the elite residential sector had access to the full range of urban services, such as paved and lighted streets, water, sewage, police and fire protection, and public parks. The central business district and industrial sector usually developed in close proximity to the elite spine (see Figure 3-6). Around these central areas one observed a series of zones of lower-quality housing.

The elite residential sector located along the spine presents a good example of the Hoyt sector model discussed earlier in the U.S. context. Typically, new growth of exclusive residences occurred toward the fringe of this area and middle-class residents moved into adjacent closer-in neighborhoods. Outward from the central spine, rings of residential areas occur, showing an inverse relationship to that demonstrated in North America. Rather than increasing in value and quality with distance from the center, housing decreased in quality. The *zone of maturity* encompasses

an area of modest houses built by residents that were upgraded over time, creating a relatively uniform residential environment. Typically, this area houses older residents, is relatively stable, and has developed a full complement of city services over time.

The *zone of in situ accretion* represents a newer residential area having a wider variety of house styles and quality levels. Typically, it is a mixed area in terms of services since streets may not all be paved and electricity not available. Some squatter shacks may be found among better-quality units. In general, the area is being upgraded, however, as more permanent housing is built and renovations occur, such as adding a second story to the house, which may have had origins as a squatter shack.

The *squatter settlement zone* typically surrounds the city (see Figures 3-1 and 3-11). Practically no city services exist in this area. Housing is built in a makeshift fashion based on the availability of materials, such as scrap galvanized metal roofing, cardboard, and discarded lumber. Rather than having an attitude of despair, however, residents in these areas often have an upbeat macho reputation in the city because they have taken the initiative to solve their housing problems and provide for themselves. The root of the problem is not that the people are lazy or shiftless, but that so many unskilled rural peasants are moving to the city so rapidly that there are neither jobs, housing opportunities, nor resources to build housing for their needs in either the public or private sector. Thus the poverty present on the fringe of the Latin American city provides a great contrast to the affluence of the North American city found in the United States and Canada.

The recent experience of Mexico City provides a graphic example of problems associated with mushrooming growth, largely in the form of squatter housing. So great has been the growth of Mexico City—a process that will probable continue—that many observers predict that it will be the world's largest city by the turn of the century, rising from a 15 million population in 1980 to 31 million. "By 1950, Mexico City was the fifteenth-largest city in the world, with a population of 3 million. Thirty years later, its population had swelled fivefold, to make it the third-largest city in the world. Within 20 years, more people will live in Mexico City than have ever lived in any city before."[32] Others have said that Mexico City is the archetype of third world urbanization problems.

The contradictions of Mexico City are legion. On Paseo de la Reforma, an eight-lane, tree-lined boulevard running 2 miles from the city core, the Zocalo, westward to Chapultepec Castle and Park, one finds fancy homes, high-class shopping opportunities, embassies, and museums, not unlike the Champs Elysées in Paris. This is the classic manifestation of the elite spine described in the preceding model (Figure 11-18). On the other hand, the city also has shantytown suburbs such as the Santa Fe squatter settlement surrounding the city dump (Figure 3-11).

SUMMARY AND CONCLUSION

The study of land uses in the city has resulted in a large theoretical body of literature dealing with both the sorting mechanisms and the behavioral changes that occur over time. To the earlier emphasis in urban geography on inventorying and mapping land uses has been added the construction of both descriptive and behavioral models of land uses, including the formulation of factorial ecologies and exploitive typologies of

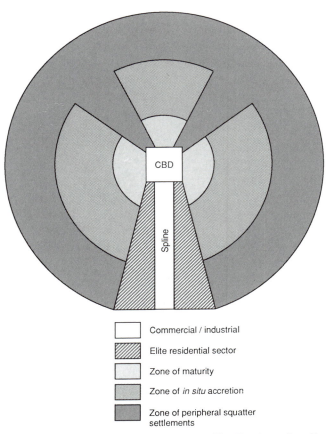

Figure 11-18. Model of Latin America City Structure. An elite residential sector typically surrounds a fashionable boulevard (spine) leading from the CBD. Rings of residential areas of successively lower quality occur at greater distance from the center. The zone of maturity includes modest homes that have been upgraded overtime. The zone of in situ accretion is a newer residential area having a wider variety of house styles and quality levels. The outer ring includes squatter settlements. *Source:* redrafted after E. Griffin and L. Ford, *Geographical Review*, 70(1980), with permission of the American Geographical Society.

the city. The study of land use changes has similarly broadened to incorporate more spatial and behavioral characteristics. The role of zoning in promoting desired land use management goals has also become a formidable force in many cities. The greater concern for minimizing and mitigating negative environmental factors has reinforced the role of planning in promoting land use compatibility. We will turn next to the first of three chapters on housing to learn how this land use affects urban form.

Suggestions for Further Reading

Alonso, William. *Location and Land Use*, Harvard University Press, Cambridge, Mass., 1964.

Bartholomew, Harland. *Land Uses in American Cities*, Harvard University Press, Cambridge, Mass., 1955.

[32]Clifford D. May, "Mexico City: Omens of Apocalypse," *Geo Magazine* (1981), p. 31.

Bourne, Larry S., ed. *Internal Structure of the City*, Oxford University Press, New York, 1971.

Firey, Walter. *Land Use in Central Boston*, Harvard University Press, Cambridge, Mass., 1947.

Gale, Stephen, and Eric Moore, eds. *The Manipulated City: Perspectives on Spatial Structure and Social Issues in America*, Maaroufa Press, Chicago, 1975.

Hartshorn, Truman A., and Peter O. Muller, Suburban Downtowns and the Transformation of Atlanta's Business Landscapes, *Urban Geography* 10 (1989), 375–395.

Hoover, Edgar, and Raymond Vernon. *Anatomy of a Metropolis*, Anchor Press, Garden City, N.Y., 1959.

Hoyt, Homer. *One Hundred Years of Land Values in Chicago*, University of Chicago Press, Chicago, 1933.

Hughes, James, ed. *Suburbanization Dynamics and the Future of the City*, Center for Urban Policy Research, Rutgers University, New Brunswick, N.J., 1974.

Johnston, R. J. *Spatial Structure*, St. Martin's Press, New York, 1973.

Kain, John, ed. *Essays on Urban Spatial Structure*, Ballinger, Cambridge, England, 1975.

Markusen, J., and D. Scheffman. *Speculation and Monopoly in Urban Development*, University of Toronto Press, Toronto, 1977.

Muller, Peter. *Contemporary Suburban America*. Prentice-Hall, Englewood Cliffs, N.J., 1981.

Murdie, Robert. *The Factorial Ecology of Metropolitan Toronto, 1951–1961: An Essay on the Social Geography of the City*, Research Paper No. 116, Department of Geography, University of Chicago, 1968.

Papageorgiou, G. J., ed. *Mathematical Land Use Theory*, Heath, Lexington, Mass., 1976.

Rushton, Gerard. *Optimal Location of Facilities*, Compress, Inc., Wentworth, N.H., 1978.

Scott, Randall, ed. *Management and Control of Growth*, The Urban Institute, Washington, D.C., 1975.

Shevky, E., and W. Bell. *Social Area Analysis: Theory, Illustrative Application and Computational Procedures*, Stanford University Press, Stanford, Calif., 1955.

12

HOUSING AND NEIGHBORHOODS

Housing constitutes the largest space user in the city and has played a large role in shaping urban regions (Figure 12-1). Residential areas were among the first land uses to decentralize and remain a prime mover in the continued expansion of suburbia. The housing supply of the city is very dynamic, due to fluctuations in additions to the stock, demolitions, and conversions. The mismatch between demand and supply for affordable housing traditionally affected the central city the most, but grew to metropolitanwide proportions in the 1980s.

The political economy of the housing market provides a useful framework to assess the performance of the housing sector. Private enterprise provided almost the entire housing supply in the United States until the 1930s. Since then, government involvement at the local and federal level has increased dramatically, especially in the provision of mortgage finance assistance for homeowners, through urban renewal programs, and in the supply of rental units for the lower- and moderate-income groups.

Home ownership rates increased dramatically as a result of liberal public and private finance programs from 1945 to 1980. Since that time, dramatic increases in housing costs and less favorable tax rates have slowed home ownership levels among young adults and low- to moderate-income families.

Geographers are concerned with the spatial and behavioral aspects of housing, the neighborhoods these units encompass, and residents themselves. Their work traditionally emphasized ownership, tenure, and density patterns, especially as they related to *housing quality* (sound or deteriorated or whatever). They have also studied various processes that affect the serviceability of neighborhoods and expansion of the supply of housing. Studies on *residential decline, gentrification, growth on the urban fringe*, and *interurban mobility* patterns of the populace are examples of this work. The following sections of this chapter deal with many of these topics. The housing stock and market will be covered first, followed by a discussion of neighborhoods and suburbanization processes. Ethnic residential space and intraurban mobility will be covered in later chapters.

POPULATION AND HOUSING DYNAMICS

At any given time, the housing stock, or supply, is a relatively static, fixed quantity. A rule of thumb of the past suggested that new building added no more than 1 percent to the inventory in any given year. At this rate, about 10 percent new housing would be created in any given decade. In general, most people live in stock built

Figure 12-1. Residential Subdivisions in the Suburbs. Housing constitutes the largest space user in the city and has played a large role in shaping urban regions. A grid arterial street network and curvilinear neighborhood street system with cul-de-sacs ties the area together. Note the haphazard pattern of development with vacant parcels interspersed with developed tracts. (Courtesy Urban Land Institute)

in previous time periods, in what can be described as *used homes* (Figure 12-2). The typical life span of any given unit is 80 years by current standards. This creates a situation requiring many adaptive responses by the inventory over time. Successive occupants, together with neighborhood changes, place housing in a very stressful environment over time, particularly in our highly mobile society.

Housing Stock Trends

Even though the housing stock is relatively stable, strong contrasts in the age and tenure status of units exist between the central city and suburbs. Lower survival rates of housing units occur in central cities because the housing stock is older and more of it is demolished for redevelopment. The central city also has more multiple-family, relatively high-density units because so much of its housing occurs in mid- and high-rise structures.

Construction rates for new housing in MSAs in the 1980s continued at record levels for much of the decade. The building of more upscale units on smaller lots characterized a major trend in single-family-unit construction in the suburbs, but nearly as many new multiple-unit structures as single-family homes also appeared in the suburbs in the 1980s. This balance in housing construction between single and multiple units suggests that more suburbs are becoming more densely inhabited and more like the central city (Figure 12-3). The result, in turn, is that ownership rates have decreased in outlying areas and the tenure status of the population became more like that of the central city.

Notwithstanding the trend toward convergence of the housing stock types, there are city/suburban contrasts in racial composition, age, stage in life cycle, income, and family status. Central cities are increasingly the home of the younger, single- or two-person household, the elderly, the poor, the homeless, the very wealthy, and minorities, whereas the suburbs are home to larger child-raising families, the middle class, the middle-aged, and the white.

Central City Housing

In the past 30 years, in only a few central cities did the population increase significantly. Beginning with the 1960s, in fact, in many central cities, especially in older, larger metropolitan areas in the North, a trend began that showed a net loss of population and housing units. In the 1970s and 1980s, the loss of central city housing inventory began to plague cities throughout the country, including several in the South and West, with the notable exception of cities with liberal annexation policies such as Phoenix.

In the 1980s, several converging trends led to a turnaround in the housing unit inventory of central cities. White flight to the suburbs slowed in many metropolitan areas and the immigration of both lesser skilled, low-income populations and affluent young professionals, often referred to as "Yuppies" (young urban professionals) or "Dinks" (dual income, no kids), kept the demand for housing units strong.

Figure 12-2.   Older Residential Neighborhood in Rochester, New York. House types show strong regional variations. These two-story homes on relatively small lots date to the trolley car era and have been maintained very well over the years. Most people live in housing built in earlier decades, as no more than 10 percent of the inventory is built in a given decade. (Courtesy of the City of Rochester)

Figure 12-3.   Higher Density Housing in the Suburbs. Nearly as many new multiple-unit structures as single family units were added to the suburban housing stock in the 1980s. Nevertheless, strong city/suburban contrasts exist in the racial composition, age, and socioeconomic status of the population. (Department of Housing and Urban Development)

The 1990 census revealed that fewer persons live in the typical household today. The traditional family unit has given way to more one- and two-person households. Higher divorce rates, the preference of singles to live alone, the attraction of childless couples to central city neighborhoods, and the aging of the population all contribute to the trend for smaller households. In midtown Manhattan, for example, half of the rental units now house only one person. And in Atlanta, the central city continued to lose population in the 1980s despite the net addition of over 10,000 housing units to the stock during the decade. These units typically housed only one or two persons—not enough to offset the loss of larger family units.

The growth in the number of new central city households reflects a changing lifestyle. This trend supports new construction, gentrification of older neighborhoods, subdividing of existing units, and loft conversions in many cities.

Nevertheless removals of lower-cost rental housing from the existing central city housing stock, due to displacement related to gentrification, continued demolitions, commercial investment, and code enforcement, created a chronic housing shortage for the urban poor in the 1980s. Gentrification typically involves the conversion of houses previously subdivided into rental units to single family use. It is not uncommon for such conversions to displace six to eight persons. This shortage came at a time when a cutback occurred in federal programs.

The responsibility for housing programs was shifted to the state and local level during the 1980s by the Reagan administration. Other state and federal policies also contributed to the problem, especially the deinstitutionalization trends in mental health treatment programs which led to a greater demand for low-cost rental units.

Homelessness

Removals from the low-income housing stock and an increase in the number of persons needing inexpensive housing led to a housing crisis in nearly all major cities in the country in recent years. Single room occupancy (SRO), hotels, missions, churches, and even the streets increasingly became the homes for a growing share of the urban poor (Figure 12-4). Homelessness, in fact, grew significantly during the 1980s.

The definition of the homeless includes those indi-

Figure 12-4. Single Room Occupancy (SRO) Housing in Los Angeles. SRO hotels provide a housing option for the homeless, but the supply of these units declined significantly in the 1980s even as demand for them increased. Many cities are now developing plans and programs to increase the supply of these units in an attempt to provide an alternative to temporary shelters. (Robert Marien/RO-MA Stock)

viduals or families without permanent shelter in which to sleep or receive mail. Traditionally, the homeless have been associated with "skid row," typically a small group of middle-aged or older men with alcohol and/or physical problems. But the new homeless include mentally ill persons (up to one-third of the total number), chronic substance abusers (another one-third), the physically handicapped, families unable to afford housing, including women and young children, as well as the traditional skid row resident.

The growing national scope of the homelessness issue led to increased federal involvement during the decade. The McKinney Act, passed in 1987, signaled the first major federal commitment to solving the problem. That act established a grant-in-aid program to assist with the development of emergency shelters, single room occupancy (SRO) units, and demonstration programs to facilitate the transition of the homeless back into the housing market. Critics have said the program neither adequately addresses "at-risk" groups nor offers a solution for the mentally ill or the substance abusers in the homeless population.

The deinstitutionalization process of mentally ill patients, which began in the late 1960s nationally, was not replaced by an adequate social services program or housing support, such as that offered by neighborhood-based halfway houses. As a result, many individuals needing assistance and counseling had to cope by themselves, and many ended up on the streets without adequate attention. Such individuals constitute the *chronic homeless*, along with substance abusers. "The group includes most of the bag ladies and the vagrants, the disoriented individuals historically described as 'street people.' "[1]

In a book-length treatise on the problem—*Landscapes of Despair*—Michael Dear and Jenifer Wolch chronicle the deinstitutionalization problem in American cities. This process created a *service-dependent ghetto* in the inner city. The experience of San Jose in receiving many former mental patients provides a vivid portrayal of the problem. The downtown traditionally housed students and low-income workers in San Jose. As the high-technology economy expanded in the region, many residents sought jobs and housing in the Silicon Valley to the north. More liberal student housing policies further weakened the market. This weakened housing market then became an attractive setting to house individuals in group care facilities. Most received public assistance, and three-quarters were mentally ill and received medication. In the early 1970s, nearly 2000 individuals lived in these community-based facilities. But soon land was rezoned and demolitions increased. Eventually, gentrification displaced many units, as did industrial rezoning.

By the end of the decade, gentrification and downtown renewal had destroyed the group care community. As a result of the statewide adoption in 1978 of Proposition 13 in California a property tax rollback, reduced local government revenues and social service programs. In the early 1980s, federal support declined as well. Nearly 400 social service department positions were eliminated in Santa Clara County in 1981–1982. Displaced clients received less counseling as a result and they dispersed. Many ended up on the street, and vagrancy and petty crime problems increased. Some individuals were reinstitutionalized in mental hospitals, while others were misassigned to jails or skilled nursing facilities and received only custodial care, not health care. Others remained homeless. Similar problems occurred elsewhere throughout the country into the 1990s.

Two other groups of homeless also exist: the *economic homeless* and the *situational homeless*. The economic homeless simply lack the financial resources to find adequate housing. Typically, this group, labeled the "new homeless," includes families with young children. Many of these economic homeless have been left behind by labor force changes. The economic restructuring of the urban economy led to a decline in the demand for low-skill labor, creating a chronic unemployment problem.

> The rise of homeless populations in cities across North America has been fueled by fundamental economic shifts and population dynamics, as well as by political priorities and development practices.[2]

Central city areas have been particularly impacted by these changes.

The situational homeless include households experiencing multiple problems such as family/child abuse, domestic violence, social disorganization, and depression. These families need intensive counseling and access to social services as well as housing.

Several issues related to the housing market and public policy have contributed to the increase in homelessness in recent years. Langley Keys indicates that four issues contribute to the problem:

1. Structural changes in local housing markets
2. The feminization of poverty
3. The failure to deal with the housing issues of deinstitutionalization
4. The fraying of the federal social safety net, particularly support for subsidized housing.[3]

The following observations further crystallize the difficulty facing low-income households today:

> Between 1975 and 1983, the number of rental households earning under $10,000 annually increased by 3 million. At the same time, the number of rental units affordable to those households declined by 2 million. Two-thirds of the 23 million low-income households currently pay excessive rents or live in physically inadequate structures.
>
> Close to 75 percent of all renter households with incomes less than $10,000 continue to live in privately

---

[1] Langley C. Keyes, *Housing and the Homeless*, MIT Housing Policy Project Report No. 15, Cambridge, Mass., 1988, p. 4.

[2] Robin Law and Jennifer Wolch, "Homelessness and Economic Restructuring," *Urban Geography* 13 (1991), pp. 105–136.

[3] Ibid., p. 7.

owned, nonsubsidized housing. Those households seek to occupy a vanishing resource. Private housing at rents these families can afford continues to be either lost to abandonment or upgraded to serve higher income households.[4]

These figures graphically suggest that an even larger "at-risk" population lies on the doorstep of homelessness. Both financial support programs and the delivery of social services need to be broadened to address this problem and prevent its further growth. Federal and state rent subsidy programs, including housing vouchers, discussed in a later section, need to be incorporated into the resolution of the problem. The provision of greater numbers of affordable housing units, and resolving the substance abuse problem that has strengthened its grip on the underclass, also needs to be part of the solution to the problem.

In short, the complexity of the homeless issue confronting the American city today requires a more comprehensive approach involving more than just improved mental health care, drug rehabilitation programs, or shelter itself. Much more attention must be given to community-based facilities that can handle a variety of programs, including day care, mental health care, job training programs, adult education, and single room occupancy (SRO) units. Counseling and placement services likewise must be expanded.

In a recent study of the homeless in Chicago, Charles Hock indicates that the loss of skid row SRO hotels that formerly provided shelter led to intensified "social dependence of the poor."[5] Those units were typically removed as a part of a program to eliminate blighted housing. This situation left the homeless even more dependent on charity from various service providers such as soup kitchens, clinics, and church shelters.

> The most deprived spend their days on the streets in neighborhoods and public spaces where their poverty, illness, and unkempt physical appearance make them a public eyesore subject to the gaze and judgment of the more prosperous bypassers. . . . The wholesale destruction of skid row SRO hotels eliminated not only affordable housing, but an urban community as well. The combination of affordable single-room hotels and diverse services on skid row balanced self-reliance and social dependence in a mixed community of the working and unemployed poor. It is precisely this sort of mix that

specialized shelter programs or targeted entitlement programs alone cannot reproduce. . . . The preservation of the remaining hotels, therefore, deserves to be a major priority not only to protect cheap rental housing, but to protect a residential way of life that contributes to, rather than detracts from, the dignity and autonomy of the urban poor.[6]

THE NEIGHBORHOOD

An urban neighborhood is a grouping of homes and their environment—political, social, economic, and physical. A neighborhood is a functional area, one with which local residents identify in terms of attitudes, lifestyles, and local institutions (churches, local social service centers, and the like). In the present context, the term *neighborhood* will be used interchangeably with *community* when specifically referring to residential areas.[7]

Several geographic models of city structure suggest the importance of the neighborhood, but at a very abstract level. The ring, sector, and multiple nuclei models, for example, identify various neighborhoods according to income and status. Social area analysis and factorial ecology studies have built on this theme by showing more precisely how residents sort themselves out in the city. But neighborhood dynamics, in terms of resilience to change and residential satisfaction, is still a little-understood topic.

An institutional shortcoming, perpetuated over the years by the *Census of Housing* and various planning and development organizations that place more emphasis on the individual units rather than their setting, also contributes to the low visibility of the neighborhood as a unit of analysis. Thinking of urban housing in terms of individual units rather than as a collective whole— the neighborhood—constitutes an American perceptual bias that contributes to uncertainty. Who defends the neighborhood? Recent concerns with neighborhood preservation, grass-roots planning efforts, and neighborhood activism have also called more appropriate attention to the neighborhood as a unit.

Good or *bad* neighborhoods are subjective labels, usually based on social and physical conditions in the

---

[4]Ibid., p. 7.

[5]Charles Hoch, "The Spatial Organization of the Urban Homeless: A Case Study of Chicago," *Urban Geography*, 12 (1991), p. 150.

[6]Ibid., pp. 151–152.

[7]In a commercial (retail) context, the term *neighborhood* is not synonymous with *community*. Each refers to a distinctive level in the retail hierarchy (see Chapter 16).

area. High socioeconomic status is not a requirement for a "good" neighborhood, but stability and cohesiveness are important. Several attributes of neighborhoods can be used as yardsticks:[8]

1. *Compatibility.* Land use consistency.

2. *Variety.* Degree of land use mixing.

3. *Integration.* Linkages between land uses.

4. *Stability.* Rate of neighborhood change (population, home ownership, and so on).

5. *Land Use Demand.* Pressure to change present rates.

6. *Relative Location.* Accessibility within and between neighborhoods.

7. *Pride.* Satisfaction—relative regard that residents have for the neighborhood.

8. *Revenue Balance.* Ratio of costs of providing services to revenue generated.

9. *Distribution of Discretion.* Relative authority of residents in shaping the destiny of a neighborhood.

Other interpretations of "good" neighborhoods include the notions of "satisfaction, comfort, and control."[9] The latter refers to a sense of authority or jurisdiction over local affairs. This situation has been likened to territorial defense wherein "residents are prepared to defend their territory . . . fight off the inroads of blight and resist encroachment."[10]

In their assessment of a "good" neighborhood, sociologists typically place more emphasis on group relationships, the distribution of power, and the role of conflict in the area. Roland Warren, for example, lists nine items for assessing the good community:[11]

1. Primary group relationships

2. Autonomy

3. Viability

4. Power distribution

5. Participation

6. Degree of commitment

7. Degree of heterogeneity

8. Extent of neighborhood control

9. Extent of conflict

Rather than considering these lists as sets of criteria for a good community, they should be thought of as reflections of conditions and choices one must think about and evaluate when making comparisons. The relative strength of these factors tells us a lot about how the area will fare in coping/resisting change and in providing long-term satisfaction for its residents. An interesting exercise might involve an assessment by the reader of neighborhoods they have lived in to gain more insight into the important characteristics contributing to their strengths and weaknesses.

Social Area Analysis

One goal of a social area analysis study is to identify a relatively uniform neighborhood unit using demographic and socioeconomic variables.[12] Such an undertaking can be justified because residents typically do sort themselves out on the basis of the *principle of exclusion.* Families decide where they want to live according to lifestyle requirements, the type of housing they need, income, and the availability of units.

Families with similar requirements and tastes make similar selections. The resulting *community space* is shown graphically in Figure 12-5. The vertical axis on both the *social space* and *housing space* diagrams refers to family socioeconomic characteristics. Occupation groups are shown in the social space diagram, with professional and managerial categories at the top and the underemployment at the bottom. Similarly, education levels, ranging from college to little schooling, are displayed in the same order, because occupational and educational levels tend to coincide. Income levels, ranging from high to low, are likewise aligned from top to bottom on the diagram. The horizontal axis

[8]Julian Wolpert et al., *Metropolitan Neighborhoods: Participation and Conflict Over Change*, Resource Paper No. 16, Association of American Geographers, Washington, D.C., 1972, pp. 9–10.

[9]James Hughes and Kenneth Bleakly, Jr., "Housing Abandonment, Neighborhood Decline, and Urban Homesteading," Chapter 2, in *Urban Homesteading*, Center for Urban Policy Research, Rutgers University, New Brunswick, N.J., 1975, p. 46.

[10]Ibid.

[11]Roland L. Warren, "The Good Community—What Would It Be?" *Journal of the Community Development Society*, 1 (Spring 1970), 14–23.

[12]Social area analysis was developed after World War II by sociologists interested in the social structure of subareas of the city. The pioneer studies were by Eshref Shevky and Marianne Williams, *The Social Areas of Los Angeles: Analysis and Typology*, University of California Press, Los Angeles, 1949; and Eshref Shevky and Wendell Bell, *Social Area Analysis: Theory, Illustrative Application and Computational Procedures*, Stanford University Press, Stanford, Calif., 1955.

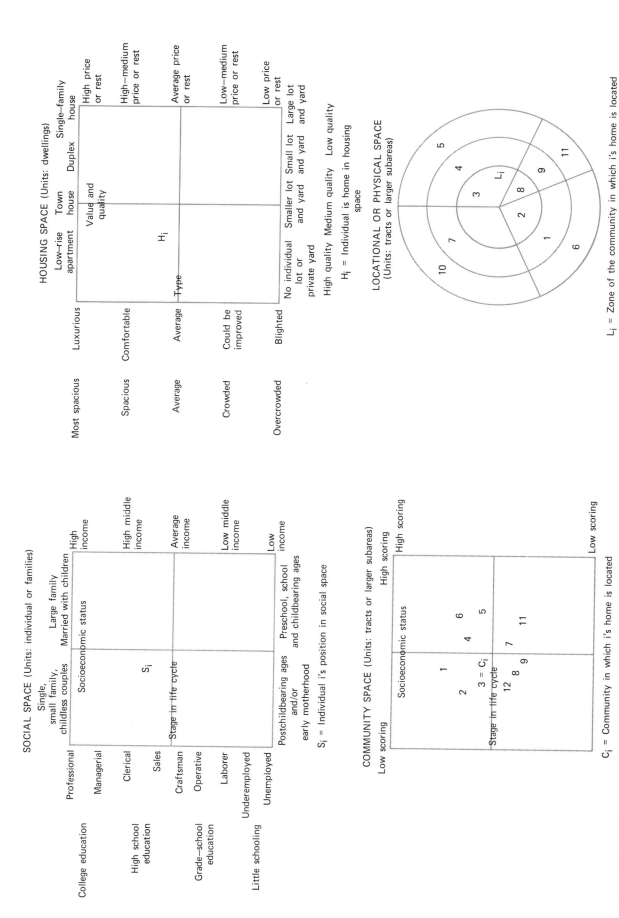

SOCIAL SPACE (Units: individual or families)

S_i = Individual i's position in social space

HOUSING SPACE (Units: dwellings)

H_i = Individual is home in housing space

LOCATIONAL OR PHYSICAL SPACE (Units: tracts or larger subareas)

L_i = Zone of the community in which i's home is located

COMMUNITY SPACE (Units: tracts or larger subareas)

C_i = Community in which i's home is located

Figure 12-5. Residential Location Decision Process. Families in the city sort themselves out on the basis of their stage in the life cycle, socioeconomic status, and house type preferences. The social space, housing space, and community space diagrams shown here can be superimposed to create the locational setting for each household according to these criteria. Relatively uniform neighborhoods are created by this process. *Source:* Redrawn with permission from Brian J. L. Berry and Frank Horton, eds., *Geographic Perspectives on Urban Systems*, Prentice Hall, Englewood Cliffs, N.J., 1970, p. 313.

249

shows a continuum of family life cycle characteristics. Small families, singles, and childless couples identify with the left side. These persons are primarily young adults, middle-age adult couples who have grown children living away from home (the so-called *empty nesters*), or the elderly. Large families, with children in the preschool or school years, fall on the far right.

Housing space shows a similar pattern to social space. The vertical axis on the housing diagram identifies various combinations of housing space (square footage), quality, and values. Large, luxurious, and prestigious accommodations (high priced) appear at the top, and crowded, blighted, low-value units are at the bottom. Dwelling unit types, densities, and lot sizes are displayed on the horizontal axis. High-density, high-rise, complete-lot-coverage complexes fall at the left extreme, and single-family, detached, low-density, large-yard homes are to the right.

An individual family can be positioned anywhere on the housing space and social space diagrams. At any given location, a household possesses a specific combination of socioeconomic characteristics and housing unit styles. For example, at location S_i on the social space diagram is a family (or household head) with an average income, sales occupation, and a high school education. The family also chooses an analogous position on the housing space diagram. In this case, the choice of housing, H_i would be a low-rise, average-rent apartment in sound condition with moderate living space.

The relative location of the Community space, C_j, for this household is shown in the Community space portion of Figure 12-6 (lower left). Note that this household (C_j) lies in the upper left sector of this diagram, reflecting its above-average socioeconomic status and relatively young life cycle stage. The zone in which this home belongs is shown in the lower right. Note that an inner ring location is preferred and that other families with similar situations (in terms of housing space and social space) locate nearby. When repeated many times over, a clustering of families with similar incomes and lifestyles unfolds. Little mixing of families of different ages, socioeconomic levels or lifestyles exists according to this thesis. Hence, the process works according to a principle of exclusion.

Uniform neighborhoods, which would result from this exclusionary process, are mapped on the schematic diagram of the Chicago metropolitan area in Figure 12-6. High-status areas with young, large families (B) occupy suburban locations, whereas high-status,

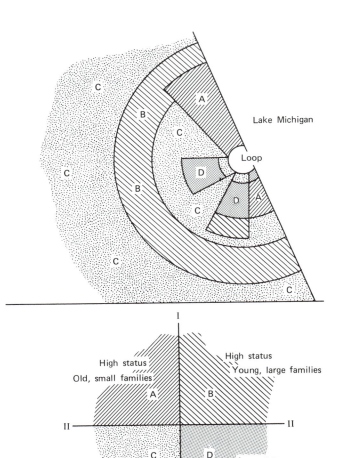

Figure 12-6. Social Areas in Chicago. The array of uniform areas created by the so-called principle of exclusion can be mapped to show high and low status areas exhibiting a wide range of family characteristics. Note high status areas along the Lake Michigan waterfront (*A*) and the ring of high status suburbs in Chicago (*B*). *Source:* Redrawn with permission from Brian J. L. Berry and Frank Horton, eds., *Geographic Perspectives on Urban Systems*, Prentice Hall, Englewood Cliffs, N.J., 1970, p. 379.

old, small families (A) are close to the city center. Similarly, low-status, old, small family areas (C) are distinct from low-status, young, large families (D). This process creates remarkably homogeneous central city neighborhoods and suburban areas, whether middle-income black communities or high-status, all-white subdivisions.

Shared Images of Housing

Public images of housing levels reinforce the concept of social area analysis. The public shares relatively consistent evaluations of neighborhoods. These evaluations, while subjective, are real. Specific addresses conjure up images of areas with a distinctive character, whether luxury residential areas, middle-class areas, or low-income sections.

A composite list of seven levels of public images of housing in Table 12-1 indicates prototypes of various categories of housing, with images ranging from *prestige* to *slum* (Figure 12-7). Two categories, *standard-comfortable* and *standard-marginal*, account for over half the housing stock in metropolitan areas. A large share of these units were built before World War II. The top-ranking prestige and bottom-ranking slum categories contain very small portions of all housing, but they are the most visible and create the strongest images because of the great contrasts in their appearance and function. The categories *very good* and *pleasantly good* contain much of the newest housing. The large *substandard* group is in poor condition. These units may have missing or faulty equipment that is not easily repaired. Such units are also a blighting influence in other housing. The social class of the occupants can be associated relatively easily with these housing groups.

The Residential Mosaic

The behavioral component of social area analysis is helpful in explaining how the sum total of many individual decisions leads to the development of uniform residential subareas in the city. It falls short of explicitly accounting for neighborhood change, but the implication is that families move as their neighbors leave or the area no longer meets family needs, in either status or style. Many residential areas, particularly central city communities, offer more heterogeneity than this scenario implies. For this reason, neighborhoods in suburban areas more likely fit this model.

Suburban Congregations

Suburban residential patterns are normally rather rigidly stratified within individual neighborhoods but heterogeneous over all. Each subdivision or residential development caters to a particular lifestyle. The distinguishing factor among neighborhoods is increasingly socially based. Comparable residential enclaves, whatever the particular lifestyle, can be found in any metropolitan area. Families who move from one city to

TABLE 12-1
Shared Images of Housing Levels

Prestige

Prototype	"Estates," mansions, fancy townhouses
Values[a]	More than $400,000
Share[b]	2 percent

Very Good

Prototype	Contemporary or older 8-room detached home or condominium; 3½–4 baths, 2- to 3-car garage
Value	$200,000 up
Share	6–8 percent

Pleasantly Good

Prototype	Seven-room post-World War II home (2 baths, 4 bedrooms or family room)
Value	$100,000
Share	15–20 percent

Standard-Comfortable

Prototype	Six-room, post-World War II tract house, prewar bungalow (3 bedrooms and 1 bath)
Value	$65,000
Share	25 percent

Standard-Marginal

Prototype	Five-room house, constructed 1920–1950 (may be in multiunit structure in East)
Value	Less than $50,000
Share	25 percent

Substandard

Prototype	Older housing with equipment and condition deficiencies
Value	Less than $25,000
Share	20 percent

Slum

Prototype	Run-down, boarded-up, but occupied structures
Value	Less than $10,000
Share	5 percent

[a]Prices vary widely by region.
[b]Proportion of total metropolitan housing, excluding public housing.

another can "plug in" to a neighborhood that is similar to the one they left with a minimum of inconvenience.

One observer has noted that the tendency of families to "withdraw into a territorially defended enclave inhabited by like-minded persons with similar attitudes

Figure 12-7. Prestige Housing in Exclusive Residential Community. Upscale housing today does not necessarily mean a mansion sited on a large acreage. These prestige houses on small lots are being used temporarily as the sales offices for the subdivision located in Aliso Viejo, California. (Courtesy Martin Public Relations/Katherine Thompson Development Co., The Seaway Collection.)

creates this *residential mosaic* of specialized social districts."[13] This situation is a little like a multilayered sandwich with several layers of filling of varying thicknesses.

At least four separate community forms occur in suburbia:[14] (1) the exclusive residential community; (2) middle-class family areas; (3) working-class/ethnic-centered settlements; and (4) cosmopolitan centers. The *exclusive upper-income* suburban area is distinguished by very large lots, appropriately screened by trees and shrubbery. It is usually located in the urban fringe or in well established inner ring suburbs. Some developments occur as minifarms with equestrian paddocks, many are built around golf courses or lakes, while most simply boast of large lots. Polo, cricket, and fox hunting, along with golf and tennis, are typical leisure-time pursuits. Social contacts are predominantly maintained by church and country club memberships, and neighboring or informal social ties with local residents are not important.

The *middle-class* area exhibits a strong family orientation and management of children is the prevailing concern. The PTA, Little League, ballet, and Scouts

symbolize this preoccupation. These families emphasize privacy and normally participate very little in city night life, preferring to stay at home. Entertainment of business associates in the home is important. Upward mobility has a high priority, and television is the prime entertainment form.

Working-class suburbs or *ethnic* areas are typically moderate-income areas. Families in such areas are typically more attached physically to their community than residents of exclusive residential and middle-class households. Neighboring is stronger, and social climbing is less important. The extended family prevails and more home entertaining of relatives than business acquaintances occurs. Participation in formal groups is less frequent and households are less conscious of material possessions. They normally live in the present instead of having high aspirations and economize on housing in order to have money for other interests. Many families in this group enjoy incomes comparable to middle-class households, especially when two or more persons work, but the unique lifestyle remains a distinguishing feature of the group.

Suburban *cosmopolitan centers* comprise the fourth archetype community. These areas cater to educated, professional families, intellectuals, and students who support cultural activities such as the theater and symphony. Often they exist as university-tied suburbs. Residents typically exhibit more varied political per-

[13]Peter O. Muller, *The Outer City: The Geographical Consequences of the Urbanization of the Suburbs*, Resource Paper No. 75-2, Association of American Geographers, Washington, D.C., 1975.
[14]Ibid.

suasions and many ethnic and religious orientations. Homes are expensive but not ostentatious.

The presence of relatively uniform residential neighborhoods in the context of an overall plethora of metropolitan lifestyles and housing forms presents an intriguing challenge for geographic analysis. The composite map of the metroplitan residential structure shown in Figure 12-8 captures much of this diversity. Note that outlying residential subareas, while areally larger, show as much variety as inner-city areas. But pockets of public housing, urban renewal, housing foreclosures, and back-to-the-city gentrification, especially in close-in areas, place much more stress on the central city market than on suburbia. This is partly due to the older age structure of the inner-city inventory.

Targeting Neighborhoods

The presence of relatively uniform residential clusters provides an opportunity for businesses to target their customers according to lifestyles and buying habits. By cross-referencing Zip Code zones (relatively homogeneous subareas of the city established by the U.S. Postal Service in the early 1960s to facilitate mail delivery) with detailed demographic and socioeco-

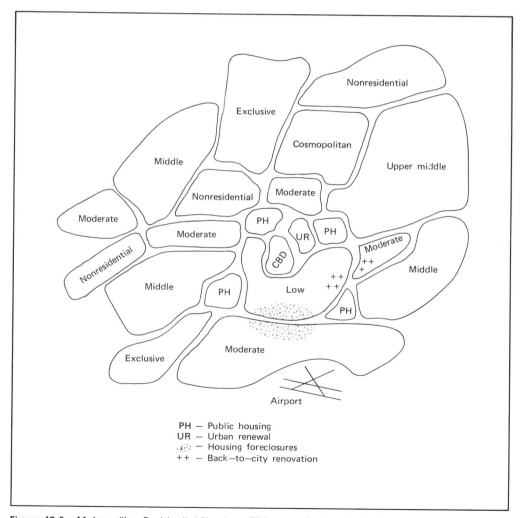

Figure 12-8. Metropolitan Residential Structure. This map of a hypothetical city shows the variety of residential communities based on various housing levels and lifestyles. Note the concentration of public housing and moderate-value homes close to the city center and the more expansive middle, and exclusive residential districts on the outskirts. *Source:* Truman Hartshorn.

nomic information from the decennial census and other sources, researchers can create in-depth profiles of households in a particular area. These neighborhood groupings provide market researchers with a wealth of information that can be used by advertisers and retailers to focus their marketing efforts. The term *direct marketing* refers to this approach of targeting customers by mail.

> During the last decade your Zip Code—actually the community it represents—has come to reveal more about you and your neighbors than any postal clerk thought possible. Those five digits can indicate the kinds of magazines you read, the meals you serve at dinner, whether you're a liberal Republican or an apathetic Democrat. Retailers use Zips to decide everything from where to locate a designer boutique to what kind of actor to use in their TV commercials—be it Mean Joe Green, Morris the Cat, or Spuds Mackenzie. College and military recruiters even rely on a city's Zip Codes to target their efforts to attract promising high school graduates. Your Zip Code is no longer just an innocuous invention for moving the mail. It's become a yardstick by which your lifestyle is measured.[15]

One target-marketing system, developed by Jonathan Robbins in the mid-1970s, grouped 36,000 Zip Codes into 40 lifestyle clusters. This system, marketed by the Claritas Corporation, goes by the name PRIZM (Potential Rating Index for Zip Markets). "Zip 85254 in northeast Phoenix, Arizona, for instance, belongs to what he called the Furs & Station Wagons cluster, where surveys indicate that residents tend to buy lots of vermouth, belong to a country club, read *Gourmet*, and vote the GOP ticket."[16] From another perspective, consider where one would find book readers.

> Last year, some 30 million Americans—17.5 percent of the population—each purchased more than six hardcover books. But book buyers are not evenly distributed across all American neighborhoods. The heaviest concentration lives in the affluent, suburban neighborhoods of college-educated, white-collar professionals—places like Highland Park in Dallas (a Money & Brains community) and Glendale, Colorado (Young Influentials). Cluster surveys show they also tend to belong to health clubs, enjoy foreign travel, attend the theater, and engage in sports like skiing, hiking, and sailing at rates well above national averages. On the other hand, they're not likely to booze

much, enjoy pro wrestling, throw Tupperware parties, buy disco records, or watch much TV. When America's book lovers aren't reading, chances are they're not turning into couch potatoes either.[17]

A complete listing of the 40 neighborhood types used in the Claritas system appears in Table 12-2.

Target marketing has become very sophisticated as retailers now use complex computer-generated profiles of their most likely customers to focus their print media advertising and direct mail promotions, using approaches like the one just described. As we will discuss in later chapters, retail operations and their markets are more segmented and competitive today, and require new approaches to maximize sales. Likewise, consumers have become more discriminating. The downside of this greater sophistication is the potential for more invasion of household privacy as the data bases that contain household information grow larger and more comprehensive.

Inadequacy of Social Area Analysis

Social area analysis provides a useful means for the outside observer to define the territorial extent of uniform subareas in the city using objective criteria. However, social area analysis does not adequately address another aspect of social space, the so-called *livability* of an area, admittedly a subjective evaluation.[18] Perceptions that local residents have of their community ties are very important, if less tangible, factors in how long a community will survive and how it will respond to outside pressure and change. This topic was partially addressed in Chapter 10 and will come up again in Chapter 14, in explaining residential change from the perspective of intraurban migration.

A second problem with social area analysis is that it is a *static approach* and does not reflect ongoing change. The stresses that residential areas face, including residential decline or gentrification, are beyond the scope of social area analysis, which reflects the community situation at a particular point in time. Residential areas occur as *patchworks* of housing and residents, with each patch referring to a local, homogeneous congregation of people.

---

[15]Michael J. Weiss, *The Clustering of America*, Harper & Row, New York, p. xi.

[16]Ibid., p. xii.

[17]Ibid., p. xiv.

[18]Anne Buttimer, "Social Space and the Planning of Residential Areas," *Environment and Behavior*, 4 (1972), 279–318.

TABLE 12-2
America's 40 Neighborhood Types (Claritas Corporation)

	Neighborhood Type	Brief Description
1	Blue Blood Estates	Wealthiest neighborhoods
2	Money & Brains	Posh urban enclaves of townhouses, condominiums, and apartments
3	Furs & Station Wagons	New money in suburbs
4	Urban Gold Coast	Upscale urban high-rise districts
5	Pools & Patios	Older upper-middle-class suburban areas
6	Two More Rungs	Comfortable multiethnic suburbs
7	Young Influentials	Yuppie condominiums and apartments
8	Young Suburbia	Outlying, childrearing suburbs
9	God's Country	Upscale frontier boomtowns
10	Blue Chip Blues	Wealthiest blue-collar suburbs
11	Bohemian Mix	Inner-city bohemian enclaves
12	Levittown, U.S.A.	Aging, post-World War II tract subdivisions
13	Gray Power	Upper-middle-class retirement communities
14	Black Enterprise	Predominantly black, middle- and upper-middle-class neighborhoods
15	New Beginnings	Suburban fringe singles complexes
16	Blue-Collar Nursery	Middle-class, childrearing towns
17	New Homesteaders	Exurban boomtowns of young midscale families
18	New Melting Pot	New immigrant neighborhoods, especially in port cities
19	Towns & Gowns	College towns
20	Rank & File	Older blue-collar industrial suburbs
21	Middle America	Midscale, midsize towns
22	Old Yankee Rows	Working-class row house districts
23	Coalburg & Corntown	Small towns based on light industry and farming
24	Shotguns & Pickups	Rural crossroads villages
25	Golden Ponds	Rustic cottage communities
26	Agribusiness	Small towns in farm regions
27	Emergent Minorities	Black, city, working-class neighborhoods
28	Single City Blues	Downscale, urban, singles district
29	Mines & Mills	Struggling steeltowns and mining villages
30	Backcountry Folks	Remote, downscale farm towns
31	Norma Rae-ville	Lower-middle-class mill towns and industrial suburbs
32	Small Town Downtown	Inner-city districts of small industrial cities
33	Grain Belt	Most sparsely populated rural communities
34	Heavy Industry	Lower working-class districts in older industrial cities
35	Share Croppers	Southern rural hamlets
36	Downtown Dixie Style	Aging, black neighborhoods in southern cities
37	Hispanic Mix	Hispanic barrios
38	Tobacco Roads	Black farm communities in the South
39	Hardscrabble	Poorest rural settlements
40	Public Assistance	Inner-city ghettos

Source: Michael S. Weiss, *The Clustering of America,* Harper & Row, New York, 1988, pp. 4–5. Copyright ©1988 by Michael Weiss. Reprinted by permission of HarperCollins Publishers.

An alternate approach to neighborhood study, a *longitudinal analysis*, incorporates change over time. Such analyses supplement the social area analysis, because the underlying assumption of uniformity in the social area analysis approach is correct. A study that portrays the interaction of a neighborhood with its environment over time provides insight that would otherwise be overlooked.

The examination of decision making from a *conflict* perspective is one type of interactional or behavioral study. Such "conflict can be between decision-making units at the same geographical scale (e.g., between households *or* between municipalities) or, it may be between decision-making units at different geographical scales (e.g., between a household and the municipality in which it is located)."[19] At the metropolitan scale, much has been written about the fragmentation of governmental organizations and the disparities this causes in terms of tax rates, educational resources, and public service delivery (see Chapter 19). This disparity is most evident between impoverished central cities and relatively affluent suburban communities. Another related problem is the decentralization of employment, which causes a housing/jobs mismatch for the lower-income central city worker in gaining access to suburban workplaces (discussed in Chapter 13).

An analysis of conflict situations like those that arise when a neighborhood faces threats by outside intrusions (a highway or public facility) or exploitation by another group suggests another level at which one could conduct a conflict study. Debates about community rezoning issues or the internal organization of inner-city ghetto areas provide another example. The fundamental difference between the approach of these conflict studies at the metropolitan or neighborhood scale and the social area perspective is that they take outside pressure, political force, threat, and other behavioral elements into consideration, whereas a patchwork study emphasizes only the uniformity of residents and their communities.

Conflict Theory

The fields of psychology and political science provide a foundation for *conflict theory* research among geographers. These geographic analyses often compare the differences between middle-class and inner-city neighborhoods in forestalling or accelerating residential change due to antagonisms and outside intrusions. An understanding of the role of the *neighborhood* in the context of a conflict requires an appreciation of the various actors and their positions and motivations, as well as the choices available to them.

One author has suggested that four categories of actions are available to a neighborhood or community for it to thrive as a unit: (1) *inducement*; (2) *maintenance*; (3) *prevention*; and (4) *elimination*. The community can invite or induce into the neighborhood people, activities, functions, and institutions that are beneficial to it. The community can promote stability (maintenance) by reducing or preventing negative effects. Finally, it can eliminate or remove unwanted facilities.[20]

The most common threat to neighborhood stability arises from land use changes that a particular property owner might want to make. These changes might involve rezoning former residential areas to more permissive uses, such as the conversion to office and institutional uses. Demolition and/or construction may be involved—or a more subtle modification of existing facilities, perhaps involving the shift of a portion of a residence to a beauty parlor, which requires a zoning change or variance. Neighbors might perceive this change as a threat to community stability because of the anticipation of increased auto traffic, parking facilities, or visual changes (signs, lighting). The homeowner who wants to make the change might just want to make the property more valuable. The zoning board or county commissioners controlling the change might in turn grant the request because it would increase the community property tax base and create more revenue to support local government needs.

There are three groups and positions involved in such rezoning cases: the property owner, neighborhood residents, and local government. Of the three, the neighborhood may be the only group opposed to any proposed action. Often it has no power to intervene because its interests may not be heard, or well articulated, until after a decision has been reached.[21]

---

[19]Kevin R. Cox, *Conflict, Power and Politics in the City: A Geographic View*, McGraw-Hill, New York, 1973, p. 15.

[20]Julian Wolpert et al., *Metropolitan Neighborhoods: Participation and Conflict Over Change*, Resource Paper No. 16, Association of American Geographers, Washington, D.C., 1972, p. 41.
[21]Ibid., pp. 13–20.

Coping with Threat: The Inner City/Suburban Contrast

Middle-class suburban areas seem to be far more effective than inner-city areas in preventing land use changes. More strategies are available to them to cope with proposed changes, and they are often more aware of the nature and long-term impact of such adjustments. Middle-class neighborhoods have access to both *formal* and *informal strategies* that help to maintain community integrity. In fact, land use change proposals occur less frequently in such areas, given the strength of such homogeneous communities. This power is derived not only from access to decision-making officials and supportive community regulations but also, more importantly, from the fact that the area is more uniform to begin with and possesses fewer zoning variances than an inner-city community.

Formal strategies available to suburban communities to prevent change mainly fall in the area of *exclusionary zoning* policies, which evolve as code or deed restrictions typically justified on the basis of "vague reasons of health, safety, public services, finance, land values, and aesthetics."[22] Examples of formal strategies include:

1. *Large-Lot Zoning.* Relatively large plots are required, effectively excluding the poor and minimizing the number of units built (which also means less need for services, including schools, and lower taxes).

2. *Exclusion of Multiple Dwellings.* Assures more uniformity of residents and less need for services.

3. *Minimum Floor Areas.* Spacious homes are mandated, excluding lower socioeconomic families.

4. *High Subdivision Requirements.* Specification of architectural style, landscape guidelines and underground utilities.

All of these rules increase the prestige, value, and exclusivity of a neighborhood and ensure continued uniformity.

Many suburban communities can be labeled *mercantilistic suburbs* because they seem to reflect a particular philosophy regarding services and governance. Such enclaves are frequently located in unincorporated areas near the central city and serve as bedroom communities for central city commuters or nearby suburban downtowns. By establishing restrictive neighborhood guidelines, they minimize the need for costly services because the poor are excluded and low densities are maintained. Fewer schools and community services are necessary, keeping taxes low. The mercantilism notion also reflects how these communities gain their support. Since residents work elsewhere, incomes are generated outside the community. Such areas can buy basic services (police, water, sewer) relatively cheaply from the outside and simply not provide other services. The incentive to maintain a relatively homogeneous-income neighborhood goes far beyond these formal means, but they are no doubt the most powerful forces.

Several *informal strategies* also reinforce the impact of written rules in maintaining community integrity. The list of informal strategies is endless, but the most obvious techniques include:

1. Public hearings, publicity
2. Pickets, demonstrations
3. Boycotts
4. Support by national citizen-advocate groups
5. Legal threats, lawsuits
6. Sit-ins
7. Election referendums
8. General influence (election of sympathetic politicians)

In middle- and upper-class neighborhoods, the value of a home appears to be more highly influenced by neighborhood amenities and attributes than a residence in inner-city areas. One pays for a *location* as well as land and improvements to it (in this case, a home) when purchasing any property, but in middle-class *uniform* areas, the neighborhood seems to be a more tangible and positive factor. The interests of the neighborhood are best served by maintaining the integrity of the *neighborhood* portion of a home's value. In inner-city areas, the value of the house is often based more on the unit itself than on its setting, lessening the need for community solidarity and uniformity.

The use of zoning regulations also reinforces the inner city–suburban contrast.

> Zoning in the suburbs is a middle-class phenomenon used to protect exclusivity, which is the backbone of homogeneity (compatibility). In low-income urban neighborhoods, homogeneity is not at such a premium, because

---

[22]Ibid., p. 34.

restrictions on land use mean restraints on possibilities for change. . . . [T]he opportunity to enhance property for monetary advantage may be more important in the low-income neighborhood than maintaining homogeneous community. . . . In the ghetto, neighborhood value is less crucial to property value, and it is possible to alter the "pure" value of a property simply by changing its use. Conversion of individual properties becomes the expression of optimal market value.[23]

Ghetto Defenses

There is also a strong central city–suburban contrast in response to threats. The grouping together of similar social groups, as in the suburbs, for example, can be interpreted as a *coping strategy*.[24] The white flight to "safe" areas is perhaps a defensive response to the threat of the expansion of black residential space. The ghetto[25] itself may be another form of this defensive protection. The ghetto provides a *cushion* against external threats and a mechanism to avoid outside pressure. The concentration of a particular group, such as the black, in ghetto areas also permits a consolidation of power and a base for action.

David Ley discusses the lower-income inner-city ghetto in this way.[26] He initially introduces the fictional ghetto community of Monroe in Philadelphia as an outpost, organized like a stockade. He describes the erroneous view of the outsider that an elaborate internal organization with a good communications network and decision-making capability to deal with community needs exists in the area. A more accurate assessment is that the ghetto is rife with internal conflict—for example, street gang activity. Stress creates *individuation* in the ghetto and residents spend an inordinate amount of energy on mere survival, and no one is trusted. Gangs patrol their own territory. More graffiti is found near the edges of the turf that a particular group controls, reflecting an increase in stress at the border.

The conclusion is that, contrary to the outsiders's view, no consensus occurs in such a community.

Residents do not have access to status and other aspects of life that provide security. Ley concluded that such areas resemble a *jungle*. Social disorder predominates and is related to stress levels. In areas with less stress, residents behave less individualistically and have broader community contact, more characteristic of the city as a whole.

A Noxious Facility in Suburbia

The case of a threat to locate a *noxious facility* in a residential community provides another illustration of conflict and community response. A *noxious facility* is normally defined as a public works project or development that is both necessary and beneficial to the community as a whole, but that produces unpleasant side effects for its neighbors. Examples would include a freeway, stadium, sewage plant, incinerator, or fire station. Frequently, cost and/or design considerations are also controversial.

Before the era of citizen participation began in the 1960s, locating a so-called noxious facility was simple and straightforward. Frequently, a politician or public works group (like the highway department or local authority) arbitrarily decided where the facility was to be built. A least-cost location was the usual choice, based strictly on the economics of buying the land and building the facility. Rarely did the public—let alone the community most directly affected—get involved or know about the impending decision in advance. This unilateral control met many challenges during the 1960s, especially as projects directly affecting middle-class neighborhoods became more common. Community action led by vocal citizens began blocking freeway construction in all major cities. Whereas little opposition surfaced when projects were initiated for lower-income areas, a very different response came when projects targeted for higher socioeconomic areas arose. The greater control that such communities exerted over their neighborhood is part of the reason, but these people were also better informed and more adept both financially and legally at challenging decisions of those in authority.

A typical series of stages of confrontation in a challenge to a proposed facility might include:[27]

1. ***Martyrdom Period.*** Bureaucrat, political, businessperson, or commission has unilateral power to make location decisions; no wide participation.

---

[23]Ibid., p. 34.

[24]F. W. Boal, "The Urban Residential Subcommunity—A Conflict Interpretation," *Area*, 4 (1972), 165.

[25]The word "ghetto" is an Italian term derived from the Hebrew word for "divorce," implying separation. First used in Venice in the early 1500s to designate an isolated section where Jews were forced to live (located near a foundry, or *getto*, in Italian), the term came to be widely used in Europe to refer to neighborhoods where Jews lived in government-imposed isolation. More recently, the term has been used to refer to separate black residential sections of the city.

[26]David Ley, *The Black Inner City as Frontier Outpost*, Association of American Geographers, Washington, D.C., 1974.

[27]Wolpert et al., *Metropolitan Neighborhoods*.

2. ***Reaction Formation.*** Citizen unrest concerning decision; people question wisdom of decision, citing negative impact.

3. ***Stalemate Stage.*** Citizen group gets injunction to delay project and hires legal assistance. Authorities consider concessions so project will not be placed in jeopardy.

4. ***Total Interdependency.*** Both sides recognize the power of the other; neither can act independently of the other. Project may be changed or citizens given other concessions.

5. ***Power Reversal.*** Citizen group gathers enough support to cancel project; accommodations usually prevent reaching this stage.

The moral of conflict theory is that neither the least-cost location for a project nor the unilateral decision of the "enlightened" power structure is always the right solution. Consideration of social costs and neighborhood opinion is important. Wider participation in the decision-making process does not ensure project success, nor is it as efficient as unilateral decision making, but it does build in safeguards for the community by minimizing adverse impacts.

Conflict Patterns in Urban Space

There are distinctive regional patterns of conflict within the city. Urban growth, both the expansion of urban services into surrounding rural areas and land use succession in built-up areas, brings considerable conflict. Aging and the changing socioeconomic character of neighborhoods produce additional problems. The different effects of these forces on various parts of the city are shown in Figure 12-9. The several areas of conflict—the core, the transition zone, established residential areas, and the periphery—generally correspond to the concentric zone model of urban structure.

At the city center, most issues revolve around rede-

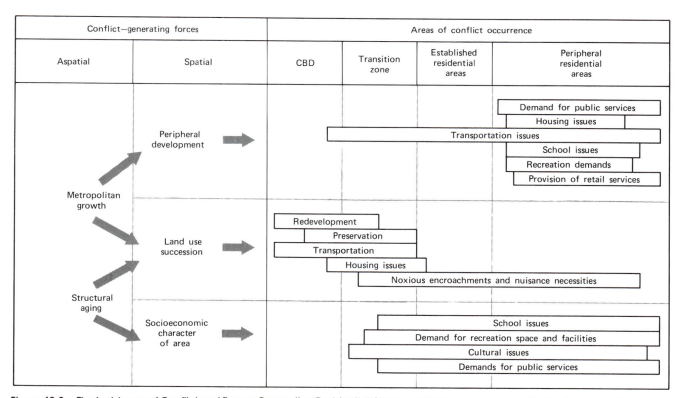

Figure 12-9.   The Incidence of Conflict and Forces Generating Residential Change in Metropolitan Areas. Distinctive regional patterns of conflict can be identified in the city. Preservation, redevelopment issues, and transportation concerns create the greatest levels of conflict in the inner city. The provision of services, school issues, and the need for adequate transportation generally lead the list of concerns in rapidly growing suburban areas. *Source:* Redrawn with permission from Donald G. Janelle and H. A. Millward, "Locational Conflict Patterns and Urban Ecological Structures," *Tijdschrift voor Econ. en Soc. Geografie,* 67, 1976, No. 2, 103, Department of Geography, University of Nijmegen.

velopment, preservation, and transportation. Outlying areas are mainly concerned with the need for additional public infrastructure services, including police protection, schools, water and sewer services, and recreational space, although transportation projects are also important.

HOUSING MARKET

The bottom line in satisfaction or dissatisfaction with a neighborhood depends on its stability in terms of both the demand for housing and their prices. The *housing market* includes the supply and demand for units, the institutions that facilitate property transactions, and the people served. Realtors, mortgage finance agencies, landlords, developers, and the government are important actors in the housing market.

A particularly visible element in the housing market system is the variety of clientele that it serves. The central city–suburban dichotomy is an example. The black housing market typically represents a totally separate market, owing to its distinctive spatial arrangement and the fact that sales are typically handled by different realtors and different marketing strategies. This separate market will be discussed in more detail in Chapter 13, which focuses on the minority residential space in the city. The shifts that occur over time in the age, sex, and income distribution patterns of residents in a particular area create stress on the housing market and will be examined in Chapter 14.

One assessment of the housing market indicated that six distinct interacting groups shape it.[28] The various actors and motivating forces that prompt the decisions of each of these groups are listed in Table 12-3. Economics (profit) motivates the behavior of most of these actors. Many of the actors are motivated by *exchange value*, while others are more concerned with the *utility*, or satisfaction, they will get from a property. *Exchange value* is the monetary worth (sales value) of a property on the market. *Use value* refers to a social evaluation of a place, such as its "niceness." Renters are almost exclusively motivated by use value, whereas owners enjoy and receive both financial incentives (exchange values) and use values from their homes.

Realtors, being motivated by economics, are not just

TABLE 12-3
Elements of Housing Market

Actor	Motivating Factor
Occupiers	Use value
Realtors	Exchange value
Landlords	Exchange value
Developers and construction industry	Exchange value
Financial institutions	Exchange value
Government	Redistributive agent

Source: David W. Harvey, *Society, the City and the Space-Economy of Urbanism,* Resource Papers for College Geography No. 18, Association of American Geographers, Washington, D.C., 1972, pp. 34–46. Reprinted by permission.

"passive coordinators" in the system, but are a very potent force, because the profit motivation encourages steady turnover of housing. Landlords and developers, who are in business to make money, are also motivated by exchange value.

The impact of financial institutions on the market is more subtle than that of other groups. Banks and savings and loan institutions not only fund housing construction and permanent financing, but also are involved in many other forms of commercial activity. Their rate of participation in housing varies, based on the attractiveness of the alternatives. Since banks have an economic motivation to maximize their return, they put their money into the most profitable and lowest-risk investments. When financial institutions invest in housing, money normally goes to new residential subdivisions, which are more profitable and more certain projects as a group than existing residential areas. This financial bias obviously discriminates against inner-city areas. In some instances, families cannot get mortgage financing at all in inner-city areas no matter how worthy their credit rating. This practice is called *redlining.* The term is derived from a policy that financial institutions are accused of following in outlining "high-risk" areas on a map in red pencil and not offering financial support to areas within that zone. This technique, is obviously illegal, but continues to discriminate against many neighborhoods.

The role of the government in the housing market ranges from providing housing units itself (usually public housing) to setting housing standards (code enforcement, zoning, and so on), guaranteeing loans, and providing financing. Some of these policies are contradictory, but they have been mainly designed to

---

[28]David Harvey, *Society, the City and the Space-Economy of Urbanism,* Commission on College Geography, Resource Paper No. 18, Association of American Geographers, Washington, D.C., 1972, pp. 34–46.

broaden access to home ownership. The impact of these programs on the spatial distribution of housing will be covered in a later section.

Housing Cycles

Expansion of the housing market rarely continues uninterrupted over a period of years. New construction more typically goes through "boom-and-bust" cycles of growth and contraction as it responds to fluctuations in the economy and the availability of mortgage money. This variability in the real estate cycle is reinforced by the existence of a *dual housing market* in most cities, one white and one black, as mentioned earlier. The demand for housing is drastically affected by metropolitan growth rates and suburbanization. These swings in the market have been described as *pulsating rhythms*.[29] Traditionally, waves of new immigrants, first from Europe, then from the South, and more recently from the Caribbean, Central America, Mexico, and Asia replenished the demand for inner-city housing as rising incomes allowed earlier groups to move out.

Filter-Down Process

The *filter-down* process represents the most typical method by which lower-income households gain access to improved housing in the city. As higher-income families move away from a neighborhood to new homes, they leave a supply of vacant structures behind. Lower-income families can then *move up* to occupy these units. At some point in the filtering process units become occupied by renters. The filtering process is frequently described as a *housing chain*, a sequence of moves that unfolds as households move from one unit to another in a deliberate sequence.

Vacancy Chains

Every move from one house to another results in a vacancy. The *chain of vacancies* that occurs as result of a move produces a ripple effect throughout the city. This sequential flow of vacancies often forms a complex spatial pattern.

The vacancy chain grows outward from the original vacancy, link by link, until the chain ends. A vacancy chain ends when a housing unit is demolished, consolidated into another unit, stands permanently vacant, or leaves the local housing market area. The length of a vacancy chain, measured in the number of links, determines the amount of local impact created by a new housing unit. If a chain has seven links, seven households were able to acquire housing more suitable to their circumstances at a given time than what they previously occupied.[30]

The length of the vacancy chain varies with location in the city and housing type. A Minneapolis study, for example, indicated that public housing vacancy chains were very short (averaging 1.6 links) and ended relatively close by, indicating that the first vacancy had only a very local impact.[31] Middle-class vacancy chains are normally longer, and the longest chains occur with the very wealthy. "As the vacancy created by an expensive house trickles down, it has much farther to go.[32] This argument is often used to justify the emphasis on construction at the top end of the market, since many people can improve their housing situation from such construction, whereas low-priced housing does not help very many other families.

RESIDENTIAL DECLINE

Among the strongest forces of change that residential areas faced in this century has been the out-migration of higher-income groups to newer peripheral housing, leaving behind a less affluent and discriminating clientele. Intrusions of unwanted uses and old and out-of-date facilities, such as the kitchen or bathroom, also contribute to a weakened demand for homes in existing residential communities. Neighborhood conditions create *negative externalities*, such as increases in crime, declining quality of schools, cutbacks in public services, nonresidential uses of neighboring properties, and lower socioeconomic status of the neighbors.

The decentralization of employment and out-migration of commercial functions (retail stores, restaurants, and personal service establishments) also weaken

---

[29]Brian J. L. Berry, "Short-Term Housing Cycles in a Dualistic Metropolis," in Gary Gappert and Harold Rose, eds., *The Social Economy of Cities, Urban Affairs Annual Reveiws*, 9 (1975), 165–182.

[30]John S. Adams and Kathleen A. Gilder, "Housing Location and Interurban Migration," in D. T. Herbert and R. J. Johnston, eds., *Spatial Processes and Form* Vol. 1, Wiley, New York, 1976, p. 187.

[31]Ibid., pp. 187–188.

[32]Ibid., p. 189.

neighborhood viability. These activities are sensitive to incomes of their clientele and follow more affluent customers as lower-income residents move into a neighborhood. The net result is an almost inevitable process of *residential decline* in an area over the years.

Residential decline develops in response to both internal and external fores. Internal forces reflect the neighborhood's "vigor and its ability to resist physical and social encroachments"[33] as structures grow older and depreciate. Combined with increasing maintenance costs resulting from the structure's age is the threat of obsolescence as newer, more fashionable residential alternatives become available. Over time, children grow up and leave home, and school enrollments drop in a neighborhood. Younger families of a lower socioeconomic level may move into the community. Frequently, the older residents who stay behind feel alienated and become less concerned about the upkeep of their houses. With physical and social maturity, the neighborhood becomes more and more susceptible to decline. In summary, obsolescence, aging, depreciation, and falling morale are all important contributors to decline.

External factors, including the encroachment of nonresidential uses such as commercial, office, or institutional and highway projects, reinforce this process. Racial succession may also be a factor. The movement of minorities into a neighborhood is often called an *invasion*, so swift is the turnover of units and rapid departure of former residents once the process starts. Racial succession does not necessarily mean neighborhood decline, as will be discussed in Chapter 13, but former residents leaving the area frequently think the area is declining because the lack of demand for housing by whites in a transition neighborhood. A large share of the former market demand often disappears with racial turnover.

The conversion of housing units to nonresidential uses is a particularly nagging problem in inner-city neighborhoods, as mentioned earlier. Increases in street traffic, the paving of lawns for parking lots, and the introduction of bright lights and signs associated with commercial uses create undesirable situations for residential sections. Many residents just decide to move and either turn the property over to commercial use or sell to a less exacting family of lower socioeconomic status in such situations. Conversions of former single-family units to multiple-family units can also have similar negative effects on traffic and the living environment.

Stages in the Decline Process

Residential changes do not occur in the same sequence or with the same speed or intensity in all areas. In fact, some communities may not be affected at all—this process is selective and gradual. Evidence gathered over the years suggests that there are distinct thresholds or stages in the process. Urban researchers have noted that it is cyclical and possibly circular.

Renewal or restoration of the most blighted areas was posited in many early models as the final stage of decline. For example, in 1959, Edgar Hoover and Raymond Vernon proposed an explicit five-stage model of neighborhood change that became a classic.[34] Analysis of changes in the New York metropolitan area suggested the stages in that study:

Stage 1 Transformation of rural land to residential use. Construction of frame dwelling units.

Stage 2 Higher-density apartment construction in inner rings (on vacant land or corner single-family sites).

Stage 3 Downgrading and conversion of a neighborhood through subdividing existing structures. Population and density increase; young families increase. Often involves influx of segregated ethnic and minority groups.

Stage 4 Thinning out as children and boarders move out; increasing vacancies.

Stage 5 Renewal of obsolete areas; frequently subsidized, moderate- or low-income multiple-family housing or luxury apartments are constructed; public sector usually involved.

This description of neighborhood change worked well in the 1950s. But by the early 1970s, several researchers began to note that a more discouraging and disturbing sequence of changes appeared to be the norm, and several alternative multistage neighborhood decline scenarios appeared. Four of these are shown in Table 12-4. A new condition appeared on the bottom of

---

[33]Hughes and Bleakley, *Urban Homesteading*, p. 48.

[34]Edgar M. Hoover and Raymond Vernon, *Anatomy of a Metropolis*, Doubleday, Garden City, N.Y., 1962, pp. 183–198.

TABLE 12-4
Housing Decline Typologies

Anthony Downs
　Racial transition from white to black
　Filtering to lower-income group
　Decline in security
　Rent default and maintenance problems
　Inability to obtain conventional mortgage assistance
　Physical deterioration
　Decline in tenant quality
　Psychological abandonment by landlord
　Final tenancy decline and departure (abandonment)
Sternlieb
　Reduction in maintenance
　Delinquent taxes
　Abandonment of reinvestment
　Cessation of services (utilities and heating)
　Landlord arranging paper sale
National Urban League
　Socioeconomic status decline
　Racial or ethnic change
　Property speculation and exploitation
　Weakened market
　Disinvestment
Linton, Mields, and Coston (vacant and derelict property)
　Vandalized
　Boarded
　Deteriorated
　Dilapidated
　Unmaintained grounds

Source: Modified after George Sternlieb and Robert Burchell, in James W. Hughes, ed., *Suburbanization Dynamics and the Future of the City,* Center for Urban Policy Research, Rutgers University, New Brunswick, N.J., 1974, p. 95.

these lists in place of renewal: *abandonment.*[35] Rather than a circular process leading to rehabilitation, as the case with the Hoover–Vernon model, they saw an open-ended and increasingly perverse situation. The problem of abandonment will be dealt with in a succeeding section, following a discussion of the reasons for failures of the renewal process.

---

[35]Housing abandonment refers to the withdrawal of a vacant housing unit from the housing market. It is frequently difficult to determine if a unit has been withdrawn. Absence of "for sale" or "for rent" signs or boarded-up windows is often an indication.

Prisoner's Dilemma

The *prisoner's dilemma* model shows very well the unfavorable environment in which property owners must operate when considering renewal and the no-win situation they face. There are a number of disincentives to renewal, and each property owner's decision and action also depend on the actions of others.

An illustration of the prisoner's dilemma scenario is shown in Figure 12-10. Alternative rates of return on property investment for two owners are shown for various options. The ideal situation would be for both parties to renew and the highest returns (7 percent) would result from this alternative. This option is, in fact, rarely chosen because there is an incentive for one owner not to renew if the other renews, and vice versa. In this example, the owner who does not renew gets a higher return (9 percent) than the owner who does renew (3 percent). The explanation for this seeming paradox is the *externality effect* that a good house has on a bad one and the costs of renewing. It seems that the individual who renews is penalized by the cost, while the holdout neighbor has no cost, and the nonrenewed home is now worth more relative to the renewed one because of the positive externality created by the renewal. A return of 3 percent goes to the owner renewing, while the neighbor received 9 percent for doing nothing. Knowing this, neither owner is willing to take the risk, recognizing that there is an incentive for the other owner not to cooperate. When both do not renew, the return is intermediate between that when both renew and when one does while the other refuses. By default, the status quo prevails, and properties are

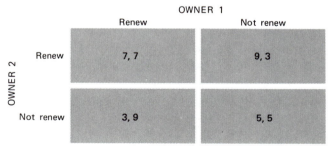

Figure 12-10. Prisoner's dilemma and urban renewal. This diagram shows the unfavorable environment in which neighboring property owners must operate when considering renewing their homes. Entry numbers refer to various rates of return (by percent) resulting from one or both owners renewing or not renewing their property. The first entry in each box refers to owner 1, and the second to owner 2.

not renewed, even though this may not be the optimal solution. The negative impact of perceptions on the process of change is also illustrated by the *arbitrage model*.

Arbitrage Model

The term *arbitrage* in financial circles refers to the simultaneous buying of securities in one market at a low price and selling them at a higher price in another market. A parallel to this situation also exists in the housing market and helps to explain rapid decline in a neighborhood.[36] As an example of how the process works, suppose that a relatively uniform housing stock is occupied by two income groups, one half low income and the other half high income. The territory that each group occupies is separate but contiguous. In the high-income area the prices of the houses are higher in the center because it is the most stable and secure part of the community. Nearer the perimeter, uncertainty increases and the house values are lower. A similar situation, in reverse, occurs in the low-income area. There, the lowest house values occur in the center and the highest on the boundary next to the high-income area.

The *arbitrage model* operates with changes in the demand for housing in the low-income area. New migrants might be moving in, causing increased pressure for additional housing, or the demand for housing might remain high while the supply dwindles as a result of demolition from code enforcement, urban renewal, or highway construction programs. This demand induces low-income residents to buy homes on the former high-income side of the boundary. High-income residents, fearing change, sell in a depressed market; the boundary shift, in turn, reduces the value of other, formerly secure housing in the interior of the high-income section.

The change can also work on the basis of expectations alone. Households on the high-income side can initiate the process by acting on their perception that house values will decline in the future because of anticipated negative developments. They rush to sell early to avoid big losses, often lower than prevailing market prices, and the low-income territory expands.

Housing Abandonment

Market failure became an increasing problem in many inner-city residential markets in the 1960s and early 1970s. Several factors contributed to wholesale housing abandonment in inner-city neighborhoods of larger, older metropolitan areas, particularly those in the northeastern quarter of the United States, including New York, Cleveland, Detroit, St. Louis, and Washington, D.C. This circumstance resulted from white flight from the city, physical deterioration of structures, the weakened demand for housing as a result of market manipulation as occurs with rent control, social disorganization, drugs, and crime in the neighborhood. Following a period of disinvestment by landowners, even utility services can be withdrawn, which signals a complete collapse of the market. Not only do owners choose to leave the area, but tenants do as well. The housing market collapses as the unit becomes a liability to the owner; it brings no income, but taxes on it still must be paid.

In such situations, the owner may arrange for a *paper sale* (by turning the title of the unit over to a wino for $1) in order to clear the record of both economic and legal liabilities. Another alternative is simply to stop paying taxes. When most people stop paying taxes, they are in essence "selling the unit to the city," as they await inevitable abandonment and pulling out themselves. In the meantime, the owner pockets the tax payment not made as a profit, eventually leaving a worthless building to the city. A *Newsweek* article by Steward Alsop in February 1972 captured the essence of the process. Alsop's essay described a tour the reader was invited to take through the South Bronx, and to 1176 Washington Avenue in particular.

> There is no mystery about what happened to 1176 Washington Avenue. The black people who lived there were terrorized by heroin addicts in need of a fix. When life became unlivable, they escaped, and there were none to replace them. The owner of the building abandoned it. The junkies moved in, stripped it clean of all nonferrous metal and everything else that could possibly be sold. Then they set the place on fire by lighting fires on the wooden floor. So 1176 is dead.[37]

In many large metropolitan areas, the federal government became a major landlord in the 1970s in areas with high abandonment rates. Federal guarantees stood

---

[36]James Little, "Neighborhood Abandonment," paper presented at the National Conference on Neighborhood Abandonment and Revitalization, Georgia State University, Atlanta, May 1978.

[37]Stewart Alsop, "The City Disease," *Newsweek*, Febuary 28, 1972, p. 96.

behind a large share of the mortgage loans in these former low- to moderate-income areas, and default meant federal takeover of the property. In 1972, Washington held title of 6000 abandoned structures in Detroit alone and was receiving more than 20 units a day.

New York City's financial crisis in the 1970s was exacerbated by huge tax arrears on abandoned property. In 1976, over $1 billion was owed; in 1978, $1.5 billion. The numbers of abandoned units are also shocking. About 95,000 units were abandoned from 1964 to 1970; 104,000 from 1970 to 1975; and 60,000 from 1975 to mid-1978, creating a total of about 260,000 units in less than 15 years.[38]

Abandonment in St. Louis

The abandonment rate in St. Louis in the early 1970s was one of the highest in the country. Overall, about 4 percent of the city's housing stock was abandoned in 1971, and up to 20 percent of the units in the worst areas (Figure 12-11). Nearly 1500 units of the 3500 units that were abandoned as of January 1971 had been given up in the previous 7 months.

The neighborhood of Montgomery, 1 mile northwest of the CBD, was particularly hard hit.[39] From 1940 to 1967, the area had remained relatively stable in terms of occupancy and number of housing units, but in the three years prior to 1970, there was an abrupt increase in the number of demolitions and abandoned units following transition of the neighborhood from white to black.

Low-quality housing had been present for decades (with half of the units being substandard since 1940), and in the late 1960s all the units were in poor condition. Nearly 80 percent of the units were rental in 1970. Vandalism was rampant. Tenants worried about losing personal property, housing fixtures, and appliances by theft, even in daytime. Market values plummeted to zero, and owners ceased making mortgage payments. Slum property dealers moved in, paying a token sum for units and then renting them very cheaply, providing little maintenance, usually not up to code levels. The high foreclosure rate eventually slowed as the low values of the property and the lack of potential resale market made the former procedure meaningless.

---

[38]Frank Kristof, "Housing Abandonment in New York City," paper presented at the National Conference on Neighborhood Abandonment and Revitalization, Georgia State University, Atlanta, May 1978.

[39]The neighborhood also bordered the infamous Pruit-Igoe housing project that itself became vacant and vandalized during the period. It has since been torn down.

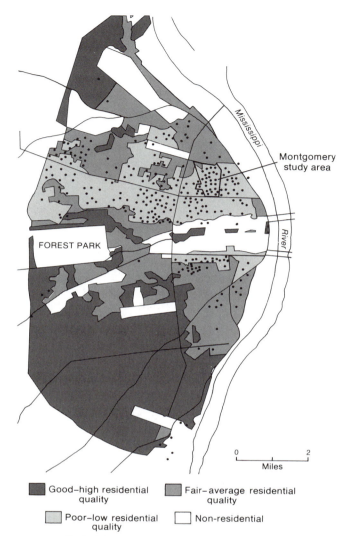

Good–high residential quality

Fair–average residential quality

Poor–low residential quality

Non-residential

• Each dot represents 5 abandoned structures

Figure 12-11.   Residential Quality and Abandoned Housing Locations in St. Louis, early 1970s. In the early 1970s, St. Louis had one of the highest housing abandonment rates in the country. In the most impacted neighborhoods, such as the Montgomery area, up to 20 percent of the units were abandoned in 1971. A domino or contagion effect served to add more and more territory to the impacted region. *Source:* U.S. Department of Housing and Urban Development, *Abandoned Housing Research: A Compendium,* USGPO, Washington, D.C., 1973, pp. 64–65.

Attempts by city and civic groups to reverse the abandonment process failed. Many units were torn down, and a mayor's task force asked for accelerated removal. Code enforcement programs became self-defeating, as they, too, encouraged abandonment. Similarly, rehabilitation was a futile exercise in the face of such severe blight. As soon as units became vacant, fixtures were stripped, frequently by the owner, leaving demolition as the only viable alternative. Fully 20 percent of Montgomery had been abandoned by 1971 and the problem was spreading. A *domino* or *contagion* effect served to add more and more territory to the blighted area.

Abandonment as a Diffusion Process

A *diffusion process* perhaps best describes the abandonment cycle. The six-stage cycle in Table 12-5 is based on a study of Philadelphia. In stage 0, preconditions develop as *neighborhood deterioration* proceeds. Initial *scattered abandonment* is followed by *contagious abandonment*. As widespread abandonment appears, some clearance and rehabilitation are normally expected, but it is usually only a holding action and not successful. In the *wholesale abandonment* phase, entire neighborhoods are junked. Pillaging and arson increase, and degenerates often move into the area. Typically venereal disease rates are high, and drug addiction and alcoholism problems abound. Ultimately many of the units are scrapped and destroyed as *clearance and renewal* are attempted. New land uses may be introduced, such as parks or parking lots, but the options are limited. The final *pathological abandonment* stage is often associated with the lack of a market for any use of the property.

A Philadelphia study recommended a "hierarchy of intervention policies" to reverse the market failure process. These included a national housing policy strategy, a public works labor force to assist rehabilitation, more public financing, and direct housing allowances to families.[40]

The widespread abandonment of housing in inner-city neighborhoods slowed dramatically by the mid-1980s. Not only had the worst housing been withdrawn from the market by that time, but also the demand for housing stabilized in the face of continued in-migration of immigrant groups to the city, particularly Hispanics and Asians. Local areas also became more sophisticated with counseling and intervention programs to avoid the encroachment of abandonment. Federal programs, including low-interest loans and rehabilitation programs, also assisted with the stabilization process. Indeed, some of the hardest-hit areas such as the South Bronx even experienced new housing investment. A

TABLE 12-5
Cyclical Process of Abandonment

Stage 0	Neighborhood deterioration	Preconditions develop
Stage 1	Scattered abandonment	Widely dispersed locations
Stage 2	Contagious abandonment	Consolidation and intensification
Stage 3	Wholesale abandonment	Units over one half abandoned
Stage 4	Clearance and renewal or rehabilitation	Widespread decay
Stage 5	Pathological abandonment	Change use

Source: John Adams, ed., *Urban Policy-making and Metropolitan Dynamics: A Comparative Geographical Analysis,* Ballinger, Cambridge, Mass., 1976. Reprinted with permission.

lesser form of abandonment, housing foreclosures, also declined somewhat, but troubled a wider array of cities and neighborhoods than did abandonment.

Housing Foreclosure

While abandonment of housing is primarily confined to run-down inner-city areas, other less impacted areas also have housing default problems. *Housing foreclosure* involves repossession by a lending agency or insurer of a property that is in arrears in loan payments. Housing foreclosures occur in neighborhoods of all classes. The circumstances of foreclosures are often quite different from those of the abandonment process. Neither the units themselves nor the neighborhoods suffer from the blighted conditions associated with abandonment, because both are typically in standard condition. Isolated units, rather than whole communities, are most frequently affected. Units are typically owner occupied, but financial overobligations and poor budgeting cause families to default on mortgage payments.

Neighborhoods are just as negatively affected by foreclosure as they are by abandonment. The visual blight associated with foreclosure (signs, boarded-up windows, unkept yards, and so on) can be devastating (Figure 12-12). A vacant house can also become a target for vandalism (Figure 12-13). The solution to the foreclosure situation lies in better counseling of prospective owners as well as more careful financial screening before the sales and possible refinancing of

---

[40]Michael J. Dear, "Abandoned Housing," in John Adams, ed., *Urban Policy-making and Metropolitan Dynamics: A Comparative Geographical Analysis*, Ballinger, Cambridge, Mass., 1976, pp. 59–99.

Figure 12-12. Housing Foreclosure and Neighborhood Image. Neighborhoods are no less negatively impacted from foreclosures than abandonment, even though individual units, not whole communities, are usually involved. This foreclosed and vacant middle-class home has been "protected" by covering picture windows with plywood. The FBI sign on the boarded window indicates that the house is now government property, probably the result of an FHA mortgage administered by HUD. (Courtesy Richard Pillsbury)

the property once problems are encountered. Lower-middle-income residents purchasing a home for the first time became a frequent victim of the process in the 1970s, following liberalization of federal lending policies related to the Great Society Programs of the 1960s. Once households found themselves several payments in arrears on their mortgage, they often reasoned that their only option was to leave. Most victims were formerly apartment renters and were not aware that they had accumulated equity in their home and might benefit from a formal sale. Realtors also contributed to

Figure 12-13. Vacant and Vandalized Foreclosed House. A vacant foreclosed unit can become the target of vandalism. Note broken windows and yard strewn with litter. Getting units back on the market and occupied as soon as possible is the best solution to the vandalism problem. (Truman Hartshorn)

the foreclosure problem because they frequently did not properly inform potential buyers of the full costs of home ownership, including maintenance and utilities. Fortunately, improved counseling programs now exist to combat this problem and the number of foreclosures appears less problematical.

GENTRIFICATION

Back-to-the-city movements and inner-city revitalization represent a countertrend to the prevailing scenario we have described (Figure 12-14). This process has stemmed decline in many communities and in some instances has resulted in a complete change in the clientele living in an area. Upper-income families frequently displace lower-income groups with this process. Attempts have also been directed to develop more sensitive programs that would minimize displacement following reinvestment, making it possible for the lower-income family to remain or return to the same unit (Figure 12-15).

Neighborhood renovation is often initiated by young, adventuresome, do-it-yourself couples who consider a run-down house to be a "challenge" to renovate. Bohemians, artists, and the gay community are also attracted to such areas. Young professionals, attorneys, brokers, and doctors sometimes follow, infusing additional capital into the community. Concerns ranging from ecology and energy conservation to nostalgia and snob appeal motivate these groups. But for most, sheer economics is also responsible. Gentrification typically occurs first in larger, older units such as close-in neighborhoods with Victorian houses. Metropolitan areas with prosperous downtown areas appear to experience inner-city renewal the most intensely and those with weaker downtowns not as much.

Rent Gap Thesis

One explanation for the growing attraction of capital to older, run-down areas such as that associated with gentrification is that it occurs when a so-called *rent-gap* becomes recognized.[41] The rent gap explanation sug-

[41] Neil Smith, "Toward a Theory of Gentrification: A Back to the Movement by Capital Not People," *Journal of the American Planning Association*, 45 (1979), 538–548; Neil Smith and P. Williams, eds., *Gentrification of the City*, Allen & Unwin, Boston, 1986.

Figure 12-14. Residential Gentrification in German Village, Columbus, Ohio. The back-to-the-city movement process has created new energy and prestige for many older run-down residential communities over the past 25 years. While a middle-class phenomenon, this rehabilitation effort is mainly associated with singles, childless couples, and retired people. Middle-class childrearing families continue to favor the suburbs. (Courtesy Larry Ford)

Figure 12-15. Revitalization Without Displacement in Savannah, Georgia. The Robbie Robinson Homes I. Project shown here involves a combination of renovation and new in-fill construction of 100 housing units in a low-income section of the Victorian neighborhood on the East Side of the city. The owner–developer, the National Corporation for Housing Partnerships (NHP), based in Washington, D.C., used a public–private financing package to underwrite the project. (Truman Hartshorn)

gests that this occurs following a period of overproduction and economic crisis. This Marxist interpretation suggests that a "capital switching" associated with gentrification occurs when investors discover that the return on investments in run-down areas exceeds that available in other areas. The gap itself refers to the difference in the "capitalized ground rent" and "potential ground rent" that a property generates. In a declining area, the price of a vacant lot often exceeds that of a run-down home and this difference is the rent gap. Once it becomes large enough, an incentive to reinvest in the area causes a turnaround or gentrification.

In a study of Adelaide, Australia, the author noted that a rent gap had existed from 1970 to 1980. "By 1970, vacant lot prices were more than double the average price of dwellings sold in the city."[42] This type of devaluation of existing properties eventually stimulated reinvestment. By 1985, house prices moved

---

[42]Blair Badcock, "An Australian View of the Rent Gap Hypothesis," *Annals of the Association of American Geographers*, 79, No. 1 (1989), 125–145.

ahead of vacant lot prices in Adelaide, neutralizing the rent gap. According to this theory, once the gap becomes large enough, capital investments are switched from other sectors of the economy, such as commercial or industrial projects, and redirected to inner-city residential areas.

Preservation

Renewal has long been practiced in the city, especially in downtown commercial areas and in slum neighborhoods. Federal funds were widely available in the 1950s and 1960s for such projects. But the majority of these campaigns resulted in very little additional housing, because the emphasis in the residential sector was on demolition. Frequently, only specially designated "historic" residential areas were restored.

The current initiative in many cities is more comprehensive. It is an indigenous grass-roots, privately financed program with a specific mission in mind—to provide central city alternatives for the middle class. The movement is financed predominantly by private sector conventional mortgages rather than by federally backed programs. Instances of whole neighborhoods being reincarnated by this *gentrification* process are becoming more common. The higher cost of housing, which places new homes out of reach of many, the increasing consciousness of emerging energy scarcity, the high cost of transportation, and a concern for growth management (less sprawl) are all good reasons to preserve inner-city housing.

> The logic of neighborhood preservation is irrefutable. Nearly half the cost of new development is infrastructure—land, roads, sewers, public utility systems. In neighborhoods, these already exist. Not only is rehabilitation cheaper, but thanks to declining standards and rising costs, a properly maintained 19th century house is probably a better investment than a brand new ticky-tacky creation.[43]

The rehabilitation effort reflects a more European attitude toward older buildings and urban form. Back-to-the-city groups generally share good feelings about the central city. Those participating in the movement cannot be described as a cross section of the middle class because the appeal remains selective. Childless couples, singles, and retired people constitute a majority. Middle-class childrearing still takes place predominantly in the suburbs.

Particularly in the industrial cities of the Northeast and North Central states, older ethnic enclaves have not deteriorated because the ethnic group has formed strong attachment and pride in the home and its neighborhood. For example, most Polish, Armenian, and German neighborhoods in Milwaukee have remained impeccably well kept. In such central city neighborhoods that have not declined, preservation is more a maintenance effort than a rebuilding problem.

One handicap that preservation efforts face in American cities, in addition to financial and institutional hurdles, is the perception people have of different architectural styles. This is called *overstructuring*, which is the association of a specific housing style with a particular income group. In North America it is frequently possible to tell the income and status of people by the style of the house in which they live. Public housing projects, for example, have a distinct institutional look (Figure 12-16). This visual overstructuring also detracts from the acceptance of attached row houses, which the middle class associates with tenement districts. In contrast, housing in European cities is not as differentiated on the exterior because high- and low-income families live in buildings of similar architectural style. In recognition of this overstructuring problem, public housing in recent years has been redesigned and densities lowered to make it appear more like middle-class units.

Neighborhood preservation is a slow process. The forces of decline are a difficult obstacle to overcome. Citizen effort must be backed up by commitments from financial institutions, governmental agencies, and neighborhood activities. Large-scale renovation programs also need the reinforcement of funding for smaller, but more flexible, homeowner maintenance projects. For example, residents who could not qualify for traditional loans for modest home improvements because of low incomes could benefit from long-term joint-venture programs set up by banks, federal agencies, and local planning departments. These programs can offer homeowners in high-risk categories small loans with very long payback periods for minor home repairs.

Urban Homesteading

One of the most innovative forms of the back-to-the-city movement is *urban homesteading*. This conjures

---

[43]Bob Kuttner, "Ethnic Renewal," *New York Times Magazine*, May 9, 1976, p. 18.

Figure 12-16. The Institutional Look of Public Housing. In the United States it is frequently possible to determine the income and status of people by observing the style of house in which they live. Public housing projects such as these units in lower Manhattan illustrate this problem of overstructuring. (Courtesy Larry Ford)

up in many minds the frontier pioneer spirit of the past.[44] Urban homesteading programs are significant because they are being applied to the residential communities that are the most difficult to recycle because of a host of community problems.

The specifics of urban homesteading are complex, but basically the process involves returning previously abandoned housing to the marketplace. Public agencies such as the Department of Housing and Urban Development (HUD) or local authorities that have repossessed units and are unable to resell them at fair market prices often offer them to an individual for a token sum (say $1) in return for the promise of rehabilitation. Section 810 of the 1974 Housing Act, administered by HUD, is one example of such a federal program that underwrites this activity.

Notable homesteading projects include those in Baltimore, New York, Boston, and Philadelphia, but dozens of cities are involved throughout the country. The greatest likelihood of success for such projects is in areas with only modest neighborhood decline. In the case of Baltimore, which had about 200 units under homesteading in the mid-1970s, some complete blocks of abandoned row houses were homesteaded in deteriorated areas (Figure 12-17).

Homesteading programs usually do not cater to the middle-class family who could finance a home in the private loan market. Neither are they attractive to the very poor, because they lack the means to underwrite expensive rehabilitation once they obtain title to such a unit. New owners must bring homes up to code requirements in a few years, and most families do the work themselves to save labor costs. *Sweat equity* refers to the use of do-it-yourself labor rather than cash to build up a property's value.

Cities frequently provide special tax concessions and other inducements so that properties are not drastically reevaluated all at once following renovation. Counseling services are frequently available to assist renovation decisions. In some instances, active community

[44]Roger M. Williams, "The New Urban Pioneers," *Saturday Review*, July 23, 1977, pp. 8–14.

Figure 12-17. Urban Homesteading in Baltimore in the 1970s. Urban homesteading programs have successfully returned many abandoned units to the housing market. Federal and local programs have recycled repossessed units by offering them to individuals for a token sum in return for the promise of rehabilitation, often with the assistance of low-interest loans and tax abatements. (Courtesy of the Department of Housing and Community Development, Baltimore)

groups carry out compliance with self-enforced codes and lobbying efforts to guarantee city service delivery. Neighborhood housing service programs exist in many communities for such purposes. Such undertakings ensure that politicians, developers, and would-be exploiters think twice before proposing the diminution of services or threats to existing conditions in areas that are undergoing revitalization.

RENT CONTROL

The recent experience with rent controls in the United States evolved from experiments with national controls imposed at the beginning of World War II. Those controls assisted the war effort by assuring that funding that could be used for the war machine not be diverted to housing. The present-day New York City experience with rent controls dates to that time. After the war, national controls were abandoned, but the shortage of housing in New York City led to the enactment of state-level controls in New York in 1950. Since that time, the city and state have shifted responsibility for the program, which since 1983 has been under the city's control.

A lesser version of rent control, *rent stabilization*, came to New York City in the 1970s. A reform package adopted in 1970 allowed for an annual increase in rents of older properties under rent controls. Many units were brought up to market rent levels in 1971 and again in 1974. Significant increases in rents could also occur when units turned over to new tenants. After a brief experience with decontrol, rent stabilization was reinstituted in 1974 after a free market rent was negotiated with the tenant.

While decontrolled units in New York rent for more than those in the stabilization program, these controls have not necessarily benefited the low- and moderate-income household, because increases in rent-stabilized unit rents have been rising faster than those in the free market as rents increase each time a unit becomes vacant. Moreover, many newer residents are less able to pay than those they replaced. An incentive therefore exists for renters to remain in place, even though the unit may be suitable for a larger family. Critics have noted that this situation has created a mismatch between household size and unit size over time as household sizes are decreasing. One-half of all renters in New York City now live alone, but as discussed earlier, lifestyle changes are largely responsible for this change, not just controls.

These changes in the past 30 years in New York have created a bewildering combination of controlled and decontrolled units, but the trend is toward decontrol. Consider the following summary of the status of controls:

All apartments built before 1947 whose tenants were in occupancy prior to 1 July 1971 continue to be subject to rent control and the MRB [maximum base rent] system. All previously controlled and stabilized apartments that saw a turnover in occupancy between 1971 and 1974 were brought up to then-market levels and entered the stabilization system. All stabilized units that have been continuously occupied prior to 1 July 1971, or that became vacant for the first time since 1 July 1974, remain under stabilization without having their rents brought up to market levels through vacancy decontrol. All apartments in buildings with less than six units that were subject to vacancy decontrol will remain permanently decontrolled and will not come under stabilization. All rent stabilized apartments, whether built before or since 1947, are therefore in buildings with six or more units. Finally, the rents in privately built structures constructed subsequent to the enactment of ETPA [Emergency Tenant Protection Act] in 1974 remain totally unregulated unless they receive some form of public subsidy, for example, real estate tax abatements or exemptions. Such buildings are subject to rent stabilization.

Under the current rent regulatory system, the size and composition of the city's inventory subject to each type of rent regulation will change each year. Because a modified form of decontrol remains in effect, the size of the controlled stock will continue to shrink as turnover in small buildings swells the permanently decontrolled stock and tenant turnover in larger buildings increases the size of the rent stabilized sector. Vacancy decontrol also means that some apartments in older buildings will be subject to stabilization while others will continue to be subject to rent control. New and rehabilitated buildings that receive a public subsidy in the form of tax benefits will add to the stabilized stock, while any new buildings built entirely without public assistance will increase the size of the never-regulated inventory.

The rent controlled sector now accounts for only about 15 percent of the city's occupied rental stock and has experienced a steady decline in recent years. The decontrolled inventory contains almost as many units as the controlled sector and has grown by 1 or 2 percent per year. With the continuation of the vacancy decontrol program for small buildings, this sector will continue to grow and will soon surpass the controlled inventory in size.[45]

Even as New York City began deregulating rents, interest in enacting rent control programs increased elsewhere. Table 12-6 summarizes rent control arguments, both pro and con. Increases in prices, inflation, and the fear of not being able to afford housing fuel arguments for rent control. Opponents argue that such

TABLE 12-6
Perceived Advantages and Disadvantages of Rent Control

Advantages

- Maintains supply of decent rental properties.
- Lowers demand for alternative housing locations.
- Keeps turnover rates down.
- Helps keep units affordable in areas with limited supply.
- Protects poor and elderly.

Disadvantages

- Keeps demand for units artificially high.
- Discourages turnover and adjustments based on family needs.
- Subsidy to middle class.
- Encourages removal of units from market and conversion to owner occupancy.
- Physical maintenance declines. May encourage racial discrimination.

Source: Modified after Paul L. Niebanck, ed., *The Rent Control Debate,* The University of North Carolina Press, Chapel Hill, 1985, pp. 107–120.

regulations discourage construction and encourage demolitions and even abandonment. Nevertheless, rent controls have gained in popularity in a growing number of communities, especially in California.[46]

In the early 1970s, Berkeley enacted such a program, which led to legislation in the state forbidding such an initiative. This was subsequently vetoed by the governor, sustaining the local program. By the late 1970s, a poll indicated that over one-half of all Californians and nearly three-quarters of all renters favored such controls. By the mid-1980s, 13 local governments had enacted rent controls in California, including the county of Los Angeles, San Francisco, Oakland, Palm Springs, San Jose, and others.

While some would say that these controls yielded no negative effects, others have argued that they weakened the housing market, especially new construction, as discussed earlier. Whatever the perspective, it has become clear in California and elsewhere that an increase in the quantity of moderately priced housing must be generated. In fact, Santa Monica, with a reputation of having the strictest rent control laws in the country, has also pioneered land use controls, along with San Francisco, that require developers involved in

[45]Michael Stedman, "The Model: Rent Control in New York City," in Paul Niebanck, ed., *The Rent Control Debate*, University of North Carolina Press, Chapel Hill, 1985, pp. 38–39.

[46]W. Dennis Keating, "Dispersion and Adaptation: The California Experience," in Paul Niebanck, ed., *The Rent Control Debate*, pp. 59–60.

major downtown commercial projects to also provide subsidized, affordable housing units in their projects.

FEDERAL INVOLVEMENT IN HOUSING

Federal involvement in housing activity has progressed through several distinct stages in the past 50 years, generally in the direction of increased involvement in actually building housing, but an abrupt reversal of this trend occurred in the 1980s. Program simplification and consolidation and less emphasis on new construction became the goals in the Reagan administration, along with shifting responsibilities to the state level. The key agency in federal housing activity, the Department of Housing and Urban Development, created in 1965, had a budget of $32 billion in 1981, declining to $9 billion in the final Reagan budget request in 1990. This downsizing of HUD became a deliberate strategy during the Reagan years to deregulate housing markets, terminate new construction programs aimed at low-income families, and introduce housing allowance programs for the poor.

HUD has primarily functioned as a financial institution over the years, making loans and grants to local housing authorities or providing guarantees for local public or private investments, but it has also sponsored research and joint projects with other agencies aimed at finding solutions to major problems.

In the 1930s, when active federal involvement in the housing industry began, public housing and home mortgage assistance received all the attention.[47] A large part of the motivation for mortgage financing at that time was to stimulate the housing industry during the depression years. After World War II, programs multiplied in many directions.

Several initiatives conflicted with overall housing goals. For example, Federal Housing Administration (FHA) loans primarily served suburban areas and promoted single-family ownership, which in turn promoted central city decline as residents moved outward in pursuit of a new home. This situation prompted urban renewal and slum-clearance programs after

World War II. These programs in turn severely hurt the poor, especially in the 1950s and 1960s as massive displacements occurred. In an attempt to improve living conditions by demolishing blighted units, urban renewal often worsened the housing situation as the poor experienced a significantly reduced market.

In the 1950–1980 period, federal programs focused on accelerated home ownership rates for families and more rental opportunities.[48] The private sector construction industry benefited considerably from these initiatives.

In the mid-1960s, a philosophy of more flexibility became the guiding principle in housing assistance. A rent supplement program began in 1965 with federal payments geared to family income rather than to project costs. Another innovation allowed public housing authorities to place low-income families in existing rental units and subsidize their rents. The Model Cities Program started to coordinate all federal programs in very impacted low-income areas in 1966, but was phased out in the early 1970s.

Section 8 of the 1974 Housing and Community Development Act created a *housing allowance* payment program permitting lower-income families to locate a unit of their choice. A family could qualify if its income was below a certain threshold based on the metropolitanwide median income. No more than 25 percent (later raised to 30 percent) of the family income went to rent, with the balance paid by the federal government. This program sought to provide more racial and income mixing as well as to permit families to leave large-scale public housing projects for more dispersed accommodations. Much of the aid went to the elderly.

Another feature of the 1974 Housing and Community Development Act involved consolidation of existing categorical grant programs, including urban renewal, open space, urban beautification, historic preservation, model cities grants, and rehabilitation loans. Title I of the act established a *block grant* approach. The goal of the program was to turn the responsibility for setting priorities and planning back to local areas and to link housing with *community development*. This program came to be known as the com-

---

[47]The Federal Housing Administration (FHA), created in 1934, is one example. Its mortgage insurance programs reduced risks taken by lenders, leading to more generous borrowing terms to the homeowner. The Federal National Mortgage Association (FNMA), called Fannie Mae and chartered in 1938, created a means for buying and selling mortgages. Over the years, it has evolved into a government-sponsored private corporation.

[48]Sections 202 and 221 FHA mortgage insurance programs in the late 1950s and 1960s liberalized loan terms for both single- and multiple-unit housing. Section 221(d)(3), established by the Housing Act of 1961, broadened opportunities for private developers to build subsidized housing. In 1968, these programs were replaced by Sections 235 and 236.

munity development block grant (CDBG) and became a mainstay of HUD activity throughout the 1980s.

A visionary and ambitious, if ill-advised, program, which was modeled after the European new town initiatives following World War II, also came into being in the early 1970s. Title VII of the 1970 Housing and Urban Development Act created a community development corporation. Through loan guarantees and grants, federal assistance became available for the development of *new towns*. Congress originally anticipated that up to 55 such communities could be developed, but by the end of 1974, only 17 had been approved for loan guarantees and thereafter support declined. In the late 1970s, the program became a fading dream and was abandoned because of excessive costs and poor management.

The concept of housing allowances, building on the Section 8 certificate program mentioned earlier, evolved into a full-blown *housing voucher* program during the Reagan years. Affordability of housing, rather than its supply, became the driving force pushing this program. Like the allowance program it supplemented, the voucher program permitted families to live in housing of their choice with the federal government providing supplementary funds to make up the difference between the market rent and the amount the household could afford. In the late 1980s, over 1 million households were enrolled in either the Housing Voucher or Section 8 certificate program.

Shifting the Responsibility

In response to the growing evidence that the supply of affordable housing available to the low- and moderate-income household had all but vanished, a report by the National Housing Task Force recommended several new initiatives in its 1988 study. In the late 1970s, over 1 million "new" federally subsidized units were added to the supply. In recent years, fewer than 25,000 units have been produced annually. And the private sector, without subsidy, cannot produce housing for low-income households.[49]

The Housing Task Force recommended that the limited federal funds available for housing be leveraged and encouraged flexible and locally developed plans to provide more housing. The group recommended tax incentives be directed to private developers to encourage their participation in low-cost housing programs.

To generate local interest in low-income housing production, the Task Force recommended the creation of a Housing Opportunity Program (HOP) to be administered by HUD. That agency would distribute federal funds to state and local governments to initiate programs. If they failed to act, private developers and nonprofit groups would be encouraged to participate in the program. The Task Force also recommended that "corporations, charitable groups, or others lend their funds at very low interest rates to help the poor" to create a "benevolent lending" program.[50] The report also called for the creation of the Housing Corporation of America (HCOA), an entrepreneurial entity designed to "stimulate benevolent lending and community development banks, to gather information about successful efforts to provide low-income housing."[51] The envisioned program also included provisions for tax credits. Housing agencies would issue tax credit certificates to projects and "conventional lenders," in turn, would receive a tax credit in exchange for charging developers a correspondingly lower interest rate.

Many state and local areas also seized the initiative in the 1980s to develop their own local programs, independent of federal oversight, to solve the growing need for more low-cost housing. One popular initiative in several states involved the creation of housing trust programs that provide matching funds to local areas seeking support for housing.

Favorable zoning support is another incentive that local areas can offer. In California, for example, developers receive a bonus of 25 percent more units per project if 20 percent of the units are built at "affordable" prices. In some instances, support goes to nonprofit developers rather than to for-profit developers. The advantage of this approach is that nonprofit organizations often enjoy an advantage in gaining neighborhood support for their programs and the permitting process is often easier for them to accomplish than for a for-profit corporation. One example of a successful nonprofit housing program is the church-based Habitat for Humanity enterprise, which has become very successful in many parts of the country in building low-cost housing (Figure 12-18). Former president Jimmy Carter has

---

[49]Diane Suchman, "Renewing the Nation's Commitment to Housing," *Urban Land* (June 1988), 2.

[50]Ibid., p. 4.
[51]Ibid., p. 4.

Figure 12-18. Habitat for Humanity Housing Program. With the assistance of tax-deductible donations and volunteer labor, local Habitat chapters build and renovate homes that are sold at no profit to partner families with no-interest mortgages. There are over 500 affiliated projects associated with Habitat in the United States, Canada, and Australia, and more than 100 sponsored projects in 28 third world countries. Headquartered in Georgia, the program's most visible volunteer and spokesperson is former President Jimmy Carter. (Courtesy Habitat for Humanity in Atlanta, Inc.)

provided high visibility for this program with his personal involvement in constructing these units.

Changing Federal Priorities over Time

Federal policies aimed at solving the housing crisis for the poor remain inadequate and it is not likely that shifting the responsibility to the state and local levels will suffice. Massive funding initiatives, as practiced in the 1960s, may not be the answer either. One analogy applied to the housing problem that reflects the complexity of the issues is that of the "square rug."[52] A different group and philosophy exist at each of the corners, "each regularly peering under the edge and probing with instruments of their own design." One corner indicates that much has been accomplished, citing the progress of recent years; another indicates there has been too much expenditure of public dollars for the undeserving. A third perspective is that government intervention is corrupt and inept. A final concern

is that the government is not doing enough and must become more involved. Given these divergent opinions, it is no wonder that no consensus exists in the area of a national housing strategy—not to mention a comprehensive growth or land use policy.

The spatial orientation of federal housing programs has vacillated widely. One reviewer suggested there have been four distinct policies, each with a different focal point: (1) emphasis on downtown; (2) emphasis on neighborhood; (3) emphasis on suburbia; and (4) emphasis on new cities.[53] It is difficult to assess where we are today in this topology in terms of public policy, in part because there is no prevailing focus for programs, other than an increasing concern for the poor.

The era of *emphasis on downtown* coincided with the period of active urban renewal in major cities during the late 1950s and early 1960s. The basis for this strategy revolved around bringing back the middle class to the city. The clearing of slums and physical redevelopment of the inner city helped change the physical environment, particularly the addition of commercial uses, but housing was not replaced in proportion to its removal. The interstate highway program aided in the removal of housing and impacted severely on inner-city neighborhoods.

A period of *emphasis on the neighborhood* followed as priorities became more people-oriented. This trend began in the early 1960s and was reinforced by the riots in major cities in conjunction with the Civil Rights Movement a few years later. The Model Cities program of 1966, part of the Johnson administration Great Society initiative, was designed to cope with neighborhood problems, including the elimination of slums, improving public health, reducing crime, enhancing cultural and recreational amenities, and improving living conditions for the poor. Neighborhood preservation forces also rediscovered the central city in the 1960s, and several activist groups began restoring declining central city housing during this period. Neighborhoods also became a cornerstone of the New Partnership Urban Policy that guided federal programs at the end of the Carter administration.

The alternative of *emphasis on suburbia* has permeated thinking throughout the post-World War II period and conflicted with other programs aimed at stabilizing the center city. Federal home mortgage and property

---

[52]John Mercer and John Hultquist, "Progress toward Environmental Goals for Metropolitan America," in John Adams, ed., *Urban Policy-making and Metropolitan Dynamics*, pp. 101–162.

[53]B. Bruce-Briggs, *The Future of Housing and Urban Development Policy*, Hudson Institute, Croton-on-Hudson, N.Y., 1972.

tax subsidies aided home ownership and suburban growth. The growing automobile-based mobility system that drove development in that era and center city decay reinforced the attractiveness of the suburbs. The *new cities* program received much attention in the 1960s as an alternative to unbridled urban sprawl and the disillusionment with central city trends. Such creations became a very popular, if too naive, solution to the urban problem, and they were short-lived.

SUMMARY AND CONCLUSION

Growing affluence and improved mobility continued to influence the American preference for low-density living in outlying locations in the late twentieth century. Housing conditions improved dramatically for most American families in the twentieth century, but the gap between housing access by the poor and middle- and upper-income groups widened during the 1980s and may continue during the 1990s. The housing problem experienced in the central city is most acute, as witnessed by the removal of many low-cost units and the paucity of new construction that is affordable to low- and moderate-income groups. The growing problem of homelessness in the city reflects this situation but is also related to weak social services programs for the mentally ill and ineffective job training programs, among others.

Geographers are also concerned with the stability of residential neighborhoods over time and the forces that perpetuate or degrade them. The formal and informal strategies available to suburban areas to maintain their neighborhoods contrast sharply with those facing central city communities. An examination of how neighborhoods respond to conflict reveals the strength and complexity of external forces that continually confront existing communities.

The housing stock at any given time is a relatively fixed commodity, but market dynamics continually add to and subtract from the stock. Traditionally, lower-income groups gained access to improved housing units through the filter-down process. The out-migration of higher-income groups and relatively constant household mobility create many stresses on the existing stock, often resulting in residential decline over time. Many institutional forces contribute to the process and housing foreclosures and abandonment have become important issues that negatively impact the housing market. Capital switching or the withdrawal of investment in a neighborhood in favor of suburban alterna-

tives is one example of a detrimental force that can impact a neighborhood.

Neighborhood reinvestment or gentrification is another countervailing force affecting older neighborhoods. A so-called rent gap partially explains the attraction of capital to older residential areas. Often, this upgrading or gentrification process is associated with displacement of lower-income families by middle- and upper-income households. Other forces that impact the residential market include rent control, the availability of financing for mortgage loans, and tax policies.

Federal government involvement in the housing market grew rapidly after World War II. Providing public housing for the poor and expanded mortgage finance funds for home ownership among the middle- and upper-income groups received the most attention. A major shift occurred in 1980 at the beginning of the Reagan administration as a rapid decrease in federal housing programs began. Responsibility for housing initiatives was shifted to state and local areas at the time and a new philosophy, that the housing market should operate more freely, gained ascendancy. Unfortunately, the private sector became less able to provide units to lower-income families in this environment, setting the stage for a new approach to providing access to housing. This emphasized housing voucher subsidies and more locally sponsored programs initiated by nonprofit developer groups and others that could qualify for tax credits in exchange for their increased involvement in providing affordable units. In Chapter 13, we will examine the structure and change of ethnic communities in the city.

Suggestions for Further Reading

Adams, John. "The Meaning of Housing in America," *Annals of the Association of American Geographers*, 74 (1984), pp. 515–26.

Adams, John. *Housing America in the 1980s*, Russell Sage Foundation, New York, 1987.

Anderson, Martin. *The Federal Bulldozer*, MIT Press, Cambridge, Mass., 1964.

Ball, Michael, et al. *Housing and Social Change in Europe and the U.S.A.*, Routledge, New York, 1990.

Birch, David L., et al. *America's Housing Needs 1970 to 1980*, Joint Center for Urban Studies, MIT and Harvard, Cambridge, Mass., 1973.

Bourne, Larry. *The Geography of Housing*, Wiley, New York, 1981.

Bratt, Rachel, et al. *Critical Perspectives on Housing*, Temple University Press, Philadelphia, 1986.

Clawson, Marion. *Suburb Land Conversion in the United States*, Johns Hopkins Press, Baltimore, 1971.

Council on Environmental Quality, *The Costs of Sprawl*, USGPO, Washington, D.C., 1974.

Cox, Kevin. *Conflict, Power, and Polities in the City: A Geographic View*, McGraw-Hill, New York, 1973.

Dahmann, Donald. "Assessments of Neighborhood Quality in Metropolitan America," *Urban Affairs Quarterly* 20 (1985), pp. 511–535.

Dear, Michael J., and Jennifer Wolch. *Landscapes of Despair: From Deinstitutionalization to Homelessness*, Policy Press/Basil Blackwell, London, 1986.

DiPasquale, Denise, and Langley Keyes. *Building Foundations: Housing and Federal Policy*, University of Pennsylvania Press, Philadelphia, 1990.

Downs, Anthony. *Residential Rent Controls: An Evaluation*, Urban Land Institute, Washington, D.C., 1988.

Evans, H., ed. *New Towns: The British Experience*, Town and Country Planning Association, London, 1972.

Frieden, Bernard J., and Arthur P. Solomon. *The Nation's Housing: 1975 to 1985*, Joint Center for Urban Studies, MIT and Harvard, Cambridge, Mass., 1977.

Grigsby, William, and Louis Rosenberg. *Urban Housing Policy*, Center for Urban Policy Research, Rutgers University, New Brunswick, N.J., 1975.

Harvey, David. *Society, the City and the Space-Economy of Urbanism*, Commission on College Geography, Association of American Geographers, Resource Paper No. 18, Washington, D.C., 1972.

Harvey, David. *Social Justice and the City*, Johns Hopkins University Press, Baltimore, 1973.

Hoch, Charles, and Robert Slayton. *New Homeless and Old: Community and the Skid Row Hotel*, Temple University Press, Philadelphia, 1989.

Hoover, Edgar, and Raymond Vernon. *Anatomy of a Metropolis*, Doubleday, Garden City, N.Y., 1962.

Howenstine, E. Jay. *Housing Vouchers: A Comparative International Analysis*, Center for Urban Policy Research, Rutgers University, New Brunswick, N.J., 1986.

Hoyt, Homer. *The Structure and Growth of Residential Neighborhoods*, Federal Housing Administration, Washington, D.C., 1939.

Hughes, James, and Kenneth Bleakly, Jr., eds. *Urban Homesteading*, Center for Urban Policy Research, Rutgers University, New Brunswick, N.J., 1975.

Hughes, James, ed. *Suburbanization Dynamics and the Future of the City*, Center for Urban Policy Research, Rutgers University, New Brunswick, N.J., 1974.

Hughes, James W. and George Sternlieb. *The Dynamics of America's Housing*, Center for Urban Policy Research, Rutgers University, New Brunswick, N.J., 1987.

Johnson, James H. *Suburban Growth: Geographical Processes at the Edge of the Western City*, Aberdeen University Press, Aberdeen, 1974.

Johnston, R.J. *Urban Residential Patterns*, Praeger, New York, 1971.

Kaplan, Samuel. *The Dream Deferred: People, Politics, and Planning in Suburbia*, Vintage, New York, 1976.

Keyes, Langley C. *Housing and the Homeless*, Housing Policy Project, Report No. 15, Massachusetts Institute of Technology, Cambridge, Mass., 1988.

Leavitt, Jacqueline, and Susan Saegert. *From Abandonment to Hope: Community-Households in Harlem*, Columbia University Press, 1990.

Ley, David. *The Inner City as Frontier Outpost*, Association of American Geographers, Monograph Series No.7, Washington, D.C., 1974.

McFarland, M. Carter. *The Federal Government and Urban Problems: HUD: Successes, Failures, and the Fate of Our Cities*, Westview, Boulder, Colo., 1978.

Muth, Richard. *Cities and Housing*, University of Chicago Press, Chicago, 1969.

National Housing Task Force. *A Decent Place to Live: The Report of the National Housing Task Force*, Washington, D.C., 1988.

Niebanck, Paul, ed. *The Rent Control Debate*, University of North Carolina Press, Chapel Hill, 1985.

Palen, J. John, and Bruce London, eds. *Gentrification, Displacement and Neighborhood Revitalization*, State University of New York Press, 1984.

Report of the National Commission on Urban Problems. *Building the American City*, USGPO, Washington, D.C., 1968.

Report of the President's Committee on Urban Housing. *A Decent Home*, USGPO, Washington, D.C., 1969.

Rosenberry, Sara, and Chester Hartman, eds. *Housing Issues of the 1990s*, Praeger, New York, 1989.

Smith, Neil, and P. Williams, eds. *Gentrification of the City*, Allen & Unwin, Boston, 1986.

Suchman, Diane. "Renewing the Nation's Commitment to Housing," *Urban Land* (June 1988), pp. 2–6.

The National Commission on Neighborhoods. *People, Building Neighborhoods*, Final Report to the President and the Congress of the United States, USGPO, Washington, D.C., 1979.

Tucker, William. *The Excluded Americans: Homelessness and Housing Policies*. Regnery Gateway, Washington, D.C., 1990.

Van Vliet, W. *Housing and Neighborhoods*, Greenwood Press, London, 1987.

Walmsley, D.J. *Urban Living: The Individual in the City*, Longman, Harlow, Essex, 1988.

Weiss, Michael J. *The Clustering of America*, Harper & Row, New York, 1988.

White, Michael. *American Neighborhoods and Residential Differentiation*, Russell Sage Foundation, New York, 1987.

Wolpert, Julian, et al. *Metropolitan Neighborhoods: Participation and Conflict over Change*, Association of American Geographers, Resource Paper No. 16, Washington, D.C., 1972.

13

ETHNICITY IN THE CITY

Even though the United States is a nation of immigrants, the diversity of the ethnic mix is nowhere more evident than in the city. In many cases, this ethnic mix can be readily observed in distinctive neighborhoods populated by specific groups. In other instances, second- and third-generation households have dispersed widely into the community. Suburbanization of these latter households often translates into assimilation into the greater community both physically and culturally. Some observers have linked this assimilation by ethnic groups into the American mainstream to an overwhelming drive to attain a middle-class lifestyle rather than maintaining a distinctive ethnic identity.

Many constraints also hamper minority advancement. An adverse economic situation often limits employment opportunities for those without work skills and fluent English language facility. Discriminatory practices affecting employment and housing opportunities also limit advancement. Often, unfavorable conditions associated with slums, poverty, crime, and drugs characterize minority communities, but this is by no means the only association.

Many middle-income, stable, ethnic communities characterize urban living today. Historically, ethnic communities evolved in inner-city areas in factory districts. As population densities increased, so did

social ills, creating negative images for such areas. But ethnic assimilation and advancement have also been a theme characterizing minority neighborhoods in a true melting pot tradition. Western Europeans (Irish, Germans), eastern Europeans (Polish, Ukranians), southern Europeans (Italians, Greeks), and others coming to America in the nineteenth and early twentieth century became assimilated in this way. Many Asian groups, especially the Chinese and Koreans, have not experienced the same level of assimilation, nor have blacks.

In this chapter, we will trace the growth and development of ethnic communities in the city, including the various migration streams from other parts of the world. Prevailing flows from Europe and Africa shifted to migrant streams from Latin America and Asia in the past century. This rich ethnic mix of migrants truly created a dynamic blend of religions, customs, dietary preferences, music and entertainment, festivals, and ceremonies in America.

Native American Indians

The original Americans, the native Indians, provide a striking example of ethnicity today, as they have maintained a unique identity despite many attempts to assimilate them into the mainstream, if not totally destroy their heritage. Confined mainly to government-administered reservations in the West for a century or more, these Native Americans have been encouraged to urbanize since the 1950s to escape the poverty and lack of opportunity on the reservation.

There are about 1.5 million American Indians in the country today. While less than 5 percent of these individuals were urbanized early in the century when their population numbered about 300,000, about one-half now live in metropolitan areas. Among the most popular cities chosen by these migrants have been Los Angeles and San Jose. Vocational and job training programs sponsored by the government have assisted these movers in attaining manufacturing jobs, especially in defense and high-technology firms. Los Angeles County, with an American Indian population of about 50,000, now has the largest concentration of these persons in the country. Other large concentrations exist in Denver, Salt Lake City, Dallas, Chicago, and Minneapolis.

IMMIGRATION WAVES

The first waves of European immigrants came to what is now the United States in the colonial period beginning in the 1600s. The English gradually established control of the East Coast and eventually pushed aside French control of the interior. But it was not until the early 1800s, following independence, that the volume of immigrants destined for cities reached massive proportions. Attracted here by employment opportunities in industry and frustrated by difficult circumstances at home due to famines and the high cost of living, these immigrants came from Ireland, Scotland, Wales, Germany, and other west European countries.

As port cities, Boston and New York became favored centers for the Irish because they lacked the money to settle in the interior, as did many other immigrant groups. These immigrants increasingly came through the Port of New York via Ellis Island (see Box), which became the gateway to a new life (Figure 13-1).

They arrived with no special farming or industrial skills, and the men soon found they were in demand primarily for manual labor. In Boston, they built the warehouses, the docks, and the freightyards, and the labor surplus in that city during the 1840s kept wages lower than in New York. This encouraged the investment that led to large scale manufacturing in Boston. In the process, that city shifted from a predominantly commercial and skilled craft center to a more mechanized, major industrial center, about the fourth largest in America in 1880. Girls and women worked as servants in the homes of proper Bostonians or

sewed garments at home. The early concentrations of the poorest immigrants in old Boston's North End and Fort Hill sections near the central business district encouraged the residential dispersal by the English-ancestry population by 1850, and the process of ethnic neighborhood differentiation and evolution that has repeatedly characterized large American cities was already evident.[1]

The Irish provided the labor for the coastal landfill work in Boston, the construction of the Erie Canal, and the building of the National Road. They also provided most of the labor for railroad building in the East.

Unlike the Irish, German immigrants settled farther inland in the nineteenth century (see Figure 13-2). Milwaukee, for example, became a favored location in the 1830s and 1840s because of its location at the western terminus of the Great Lakes navigation system. "By 1870, the other fast-growing Great Lakes cities like Buffalo, Cleveland, Detroit, and Chicago all had thriving German communities. . . . Milwaukee remained the most thoroughly German. Over one-half the population of the city registered a German heritage in 1910."[2]

By the mid-nineteenth century, waves of Scandinavians and Dutch also began arriving in the United States and settled in the upper Middle West. Rail transportation influenced the settlement patterns of these groups, as did Great Lakes water transportation. Swedes hired out as loggers or settled on farms north of Minneapolis. They also settled in the Mesabi iron ore mine area near Duluth and in Chicago. "By 1900, Chicago had more Swedes than any city in the world except Stockholm. . . . In 1920, it had twice the Swedish foreign stock population of either New York City or Minneapolis, and Swedes had probably built a third of Chicago's buildings."[3]

Prior to 1880, the dominant immigrant flow to the United States was from northwestern Europe. This "old" group (see Figure 13-2) settled in many different cities at relatively lower densities than those coming later. The majority were English speaking, such as the Irish, and cultural assimilation was relatively easy.

In the late 1800s, the flow began to be identified with a "new" immigrant group (see Figure 13-3) from southern and eastern Europe. This flow, which extended into the twentieth century, became associated

[1]James Paul Allen and Eugene James Turner, *We the People: An Atlas of America's Ethnic Diversity*, Macmillan, New York, 1988, p. 48.
[2]Ibid., p. 53.
[3]Ibid., p. 75.

Figure 13-1. Registry Room, Ellis Island. The Ellis Island immigration facility was designed to handle 5000 immigrants a day. Immigrants spent most of their time in this room. Note the huge open space with its vaulted, tiled ceiling and chandeliers. This facility has been restored, and it reopened as a museum in 1990. (AP/Wide World Photos)

with high-density residential communities located in northern manufacturing cities. Polish and Italian families constituted a large share of these migrants, and they remained impoverished over a longer period than the earlier western European migrants. Southern Europeans had more distinctive customs (language, diet) and were less easily assimilated. Tenement districts—often associated with slum living—emerged in this period (Figure 13-4). Widespread crime, high infant mortality, and social disorganization often accompanied living in these communities. A public outcry against such conditions led to the establishment of immigration quotas in the late 1920s to stem the flow into impacted areas.

Among the earliest immigrant groups from eastern Europe to the United States in the late nineteenth

century were Jews who had suffered from land ownership restrictions and persecution in their homelands. They often moved as families, not as individuals.

Czech settlers moved to farms in the Middle West, Great Plains, and Texas, as well as to cities, to take advantage of industrial jobs, especially New York, Chicago, and Cleveland. Even today, Chicago has more individuals of Czech ancestry than any other city in the country.[4]

Polish immigrants found jobs in the coal mines of Pennsylvania and slaughterhouses and steel mills in Chicago and other industrial centers.

Chicago (Cook County) came to have the largest Polish population in America. By 1890, there were already five

---

[4]Ibid., p. 87.

ELLIS ISLAND IMMIGRATION GATEWAY REBORN

About one-half of the United States' population can trace its ancestry to the immigration station on Ellis Island in the New York harbor.* That facility was officially closed in 1954, after over 50 years of use; subsequently abandoned, it was rehabilitated and reopened in 1990 as a museum, genealogy center, library, and oral history center dedicated to the 12 million persons who entered the country under the watchful eye of the immigration service.

The facility was expanded and modified, along with the island itself, over the years. Fill from New York subway construction added over 24 acres to the island. The present main building was built in 1900 (see Figure 13-1). The facility was designed to handle about 5000 immigrants a day, but in one day—April 17 1907—nearly 12,000 were processed. That year also holds the record for peak immigration to the country—nearly 12 million persons. The flow slowed during World War I, and by 1927, immigration rates were restricted by law.

Immigrants must have found the Ellis Island experience intimidating. They approached the building under a long canopy of corrugated tin, entered the central door, and found themselves in a large open space on the ground floor, the Baggage Room, where they awaited their turn to climb stairs to the vaulted Registry Room immediately above. . . .

In those days, the Registry Room was divided in half, with nearly identical facilities on each side so that two shiploads could be examined simultaneously. Channeled into railed-off lanes called "pens" (which, in 1911, were replaced with wooden benches), the immigrants were "keenly scrutinized [in] the face and body for signs of disease or deformity." . . . Doctors marked those with suspected diseases with chalk on the coat lapel. An X indicated feeblemindedness, C meant conjunctivitis, G signaled goiter, Pg branded pregnant women, etc.**

*Allen Freeman, "Ellis Island Revisited," *Historic Preservation, 42* (1990) 32.
**Ibid., pp. 32–34.

large ethnic neighborhoods, one located near the Union Stockyards and others near jobs in certain heavy industries. The Polish downtown area and the settlement near South Chicago's steel mills were intensely Polish in character, but even in the areas that were more mixed in ethnic population, the Poles tended to stay together socially. Catholicism was intimately tied to Polish ethnicity, in Chicago and elsewhere, and the establishment of parochial schools was seen as crucial.[5]

Quality farmland became less available to immigrant groups as the nineteenth century progressed. At the same time, more opportunities for industrial work opened up in northern cities. Significantly, few immigrant groups settled in the South, which remained predominantly agricultural in this period. The Ukrainians represent a late-nineteenth-century immigrant group that did not turn to farming because of the lack of opportunity in that field. Instead, they moved to coal-mining areas of Pennsylvania and to emerging industrial cities in upstate New York, such as Syracuse, Rochester, and Buffalo, as well as New York City. Many settled on the Lower East Side.

Southern Europeans also came to the United States in large numbers around the turn of the century, with the peak years occurring between 1890 and 1914. Italians and Greeks accounted for a large share of this movement. Many intended to stay only a short time and rejoin families at home once they had accumulated some wealth. Some did return, but most stayed. Italians generally settled in industrial cities, as did eastern Europeans, but usually the two groups were not concentrated in the same cities. While eastern European groups found employment in iron and steel mills and meat-packing and chemicals industries, Italians worked on the railroads (construction and operation) and in the garment industry, and generally lived in a wider array of cities than eastern Europeans. Being the predominant port of entry, many Italians settled in New York, but job availability was limited. Chicago, a major transportation hub and garment center, also

[5]Ibid., p. 99.

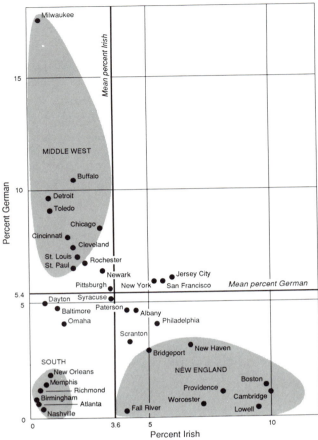

Figure 13-2. Regional Clustering of "Old" Immigrants in U.S. Cities, 1910. The Irish settled in New England (Boston, Lowell, Providence), while Germans moved farther inland. Milwaukee became a favored location, as did Buffalo, Detroit, Chicago, and Cleveland, all located in the Great Lakes area. Note that the South did not attract significant numbers of either Irish or Germans. *Source: Modified after David Ward, "Population Growth, Migration and Urbanization," in Robert D. Mitchell and Paul A. Groves, eds., North America: The Historical Geography of a Changing Continent, Rowman & Littlefield, 1987, p. 314.*

attracted large groups of Italian immigrants, as well as many eastern Europeans, an exception to the distinctive patterns just mentioned.

The association of "newer" immigrants to the United States in 1910 with the industrial cities of the northeast is shown in Figure 13-3. At the same time, central Europeans, such as the Austro-Hungarians, settled in the Middle West in cities like Chicago and Cleveland.

Greek immigrants settled in "textile- and shoe-manufacturing towns" in New England and in other industrial cities, especially New York and Chicago. Many started small retail stores and restaurants. Overall, Greek immigrants became one of the most urban-

ized of the early immigrant groups. Few worked on farms, in mines, or on the railroads. New York and Chicago had the largest number of households of Greek ancestry, a distinction they continue to hold today.

ASIAN IMMIGRATION WAVES

Immigrants from Asia mainly came to the West Coast of the United States. A wave of Chinese came to California in 1848 to participate in the so-called gold rush. Many ended up as agricultural workers, as did the Japanese and Filipinos who followed. By 1880, anti-Chinese sentiment had increased and restrictions to immigration were enacted. Nevertheless, the Chinese provided yeoman service in building railroads in the region and constructing canals and drainage systems.

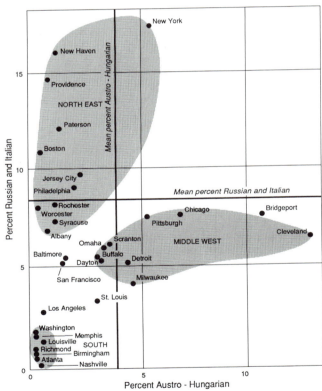

Figure 13-3. Regional Clustering of "New" Immigrants in U.S. Cities, 1910. Russian and Italian families settled in industrial cities of the Northeast such as Boston, Providence, Syracuse, and Rochester. Austro-Hungarians and other central Europeans chose to settle disproportionately in Cleveland, Chicago, Pittsburgh, and other cities of the Middle West. *Source: Modified after David Ward, "Population Growth, Migration and Urbanization," in Robert D. Mitchell and Paul A. Groves, eds., North America: The Historical Geography of a Changing Continent. Rowman & Littlefield, 1987, p. 314.*

Figure 13-4. The Turn-of-the-Century Tenement in Boston. High-density housing in northern manufacturing cities occupied by eastern and southern Europeans (Polish, Italian, Ukranian) became identified with slum living conditions. Widespread crime, high infant mortality, and social disorganization often accompanied life in these communities. (Lewis W. Hine Memorial Collection; courtesy the International Museum of Photography at George Eastman House)

San Francisco, New York, and Los Angeles eventually developed the largest concentrations of Chinese, accounting for over one-half of the total. At one time, Chinatowns in these and other cities accounted for a large share of the Chinese, but gradually Chinese residential areas suburbanized and the Chinatowns became ethnic shopping areas for the local Chinese buyers and tourists.

San Francisco's Chinatown has been the symbolic geographical center of the Chinese American experience. The area contains numerous shops, restaurants, tearooms, grocery stores, and banks, with Grant Street as the major commercial focus. But there have also been Chinese schools, temples, theaters, small factories, and residences. In the 12-block area that was the heart of Chinatown in 1980 (bounded by Kearney, Clay, and Stockton Streets and Pacific Avenue), 95 percent of the residences were Chinese. . . . In 1980, the approximately 26,000 Chinese who lived in the Chinatown area represented about a third of the Chinese in the city and county of San Francisco."[6]

However, many Chinatowns "continue to harbor the poorest, least educated, and weakest English-speaking persons. High rates of unemployment, crime, illness and drug abuse"[7] also plague these areas. The more affluent and better educated have long since left the Chinatown area for the suburbs or have never been associated with the area.

A liberalization of the immigration laws in 1965 curtailed the annual quotas that had favored European countries. Thereafter immigration from Asian countries accelerated (Figure 13-5). In the mid-1970s, over three-quarters of a million immigrants came from Indochina (Vietnam, Laos, and Cambodia) to escape the ravages of war. Many Vietnamese settled in California, especially Orange County, which has the largest concentration of Vietnamese in the country. Many live as extended families in the cities of Santa Ana, Garden Grove, and Westminster. Some have even appropriated the garage of the house to acquire needed living space (Figure 13-6).

[6]Ibid., pp. 181–182.

[7]Ibid., p. 182.

Figure 13-5. Asian Commercial Strip Development in Greater Los Angeles. Specialty retail and professional service districts have become very common in the Asian community of greater Los Angeles. Note the specialized jewelry and photography stores, as well as the specialized income tax service and dentist's office all catering to the Asian market. (Robert Marien/RO-MA Stock)

Emergence of Slum and Ghetto Neighborhoods

Most immigrants lived close to their employment in the nineteenth century, and they soon came to dominate the central residential neighborhoods in most industrial cities. Lack of housing opportunities around the time of the Civil War and before the streetcar forced other immigrants to live in "shanty towns" on the periphery.[8] As central housing densities increased, so did problems with disease and unsanitary living conditions. The term *slum* came to be synonymous with these areas. Social problems associated with alcoholism, prostitution, and crime also grew worse. The concentration of similar

ethnic and religious groups in specific areas led to the association of these areas as *ghettos*. The alleged social pathologies associated with emerging tenement districts in industrial cities were often exaggerated in the press of the day. Many problems, for example, were due to poor drainage and the proximity of slaughterhouses and other food-processing operations to residential areas rather than to the presence of immigrants in these areas. Active social reformers called for either housing reform or limitations on immigration. The terms slum and ghetto "also implied strong causal connections between poverty and social problems of the migrant poor."[9]

The indictments of the slum environment were not restricted to matters of inadequate drainage and accu-

[8]David Ward, *Cities and Immigrants: A Geography of Change in Nineteenth Century America*, Oxford University Press, New York, 1971, p. 106.

[9]Ibid., p. 2.

Figure 13-6. Vietnamese Residential Community in the Westminster District of Orange County, California. In order to provide needed housing space for the extended families living in this neighborhood, it is often necessary to convert garages to family living space. Note three cars in yard of house. (Robert Marien/RO-MA Stock)

mulations of filth, for the more immediate housing environment also attracted much critical attention. The partitioning of single-family dwellings into tenements, the infilling of their grounds with cheap new multifamily structures, and the conversion of institutional or industrial buildings into housing blocks were all viewed as a threat to light and ventilation.

The conversion of old buildings was considered a temporary adaptation to an unusually large influx of immigrants at a time when many of these neglected structures were destined to be demolished in the face of expanding business needs. In contrast, the construction of new tenement blocks covering almost an entire lot set a new and more permanent standard of housing density. "Such crowding," wrote Stephen Smith in his recollections of the early days of the housing reform movement, "amounts literally to packing." He argued for a more precise association of the environment and mortality when he concluded that "the excess of mortality is not even equally distributed over these populous poor wards, but is concentrated upon individual

tenant-houses."[10] Room overcrowding was also associated with promiscuity. Thus the connection between social environment and the urban environment became a central issue in inner-city slum areas.[11]

HISPANIC IMMIGRANTS

Several countries have contributed to the Spanish-speaking ethnic population flows to the United States. Mexico, Cuba, Puerto Rico, and several other Central and South American countries represent the most frequent origins. Not only does the United States share a common border with Mexico, but many other Hispanic areas also lie in close proximity in the Western Hemisphere. The poor economic and political conditions that residents face have encouraged outmigration.

---

[10]Ibid., pp. 29–30.

[11]David M. Ward, *Poverty, Ethnicity and the American City, 1840–1925: Changing Conceptions of the Slum and the Ghetto*, Cambridge University Press, New York, 1989, pp. 39–45.

Parts of the American southwest were populated by Spanish speaking settlers long before these territories became part of the United States. Nevertheless, the most significant immigration of Mexicans to the North occurred in the twentieth century. Agricultural workers flocked to Texas in the early twentieth century, and by the 1920s and 1930s urban growth and manufacturing growth in California began attracting larger numbers of Mexicans to that area. Depressed conditions in Mexico provided a push factor encouraging this movement, which has continued at a high rate to the present time. In 1980, California alone accounted for over 50 percent of the Mexican-born population in the United States, with about 20 percent located in Los Angeles County (Figure 13-7).

At the turn of the century, San Antonio housed the largest concentration of Mexican laborers. Later, Houston gained many immigrants who worked in construction and the petroleum industry. Chicago also attracted many Mexican immigrants in the early twentieth century to assist with railroad maintenance work.

Over 2 million persons of Puerto Rican ancestry also live in the U.S. today. In the aftermath of the Spanish-American War, Puerto Rico became a United States territory and its residents, U.S. citizens. Technically speaking, those individuals leaving Puerto Rico for the states do not enter the international migration stream. Regardless, thousands migrated to northern industrial cities in the pursuit of employment. Most moved to New York to find work in the garment industry and other low-skill fields. The flow accelerated after World War II, but most workers continued to find only unskilled low-paying employment in blue collar service trades, such as hotel attendants, porters, dishwashers, or janitors.

Puerto Ricans remain among the poorest of New York City's workers today. East Harlem, or as the area is also known, *Spanish Harlem*, attracted many of the

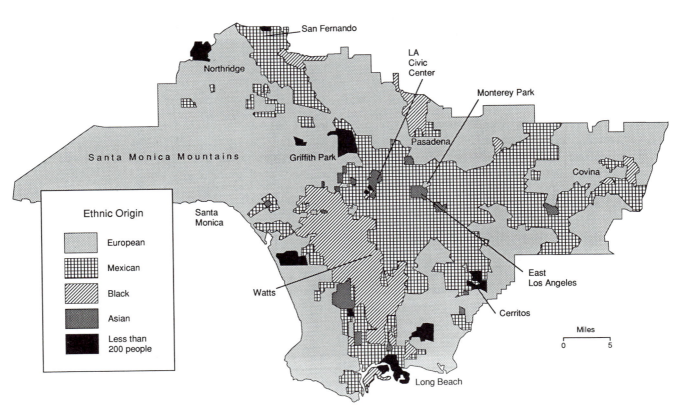

Figure 13-7. Ethnic Areas of Los Angeles. Los Angeles has been labeled a third world city by some observers, so large have the ethnic neighborhoods in the metropolitan area become. Note the distinctive Hispanic, black, and Asian communities in the region. About 40 percent of the population in the city of Los Angeles today is hispanic, primarily Mexican in origin. *Source:* Redrawn from map. *Ethnic Patterns in Los Angeles 1980.* Occasional Publications in Geography, number 5 (1989), Department of Geography, California State University, Northridge. Used by permission.

immigrants. Others live in the South Bronx, Brooklyn, and Manhattan. Most live in run-down, crowded, and poorly maintained housing typically associated with slum conditions. Housing abandonment in the South Bronx in the 1970s, as discussed in Chapter 12, particularly impacted the Puerto Rican community. Nearly 90 percent of Puerto Ricans in the United States lived in New York in 1940, and in 1980 about one-half still claimed New York as home. Several New Jersey cities, Philadelphia, and New England locations have received more Puerto Rican immigrants in recent years.

If New York is home to Puerto Ricans, Miami claims the largest concentration of Cuban-Americans. A section of Miami southwest of the downtown area, known as *Little Havana*, symbolizes the overwhelming Hispanic presence of Cuban-Americans in Miami today. Not only is this prosperous residential area predominantly Cuban, but the commercial establishments (restaurants, retailing) are also predominantly Hispanic by ownership and trade. Indeed, there are now estimated to be 25,000 Latin-owned firms operating in Miami.[12] From this core area, the Hispanic area has spread West and northwest toward the airport. Hialeah, for example, was 85 percent Hispanic in 1980.

The roots of the massive Hispanic build-up in Miami date back several decades, but gained momentum following the ascendancy of the Castro regime in the late 1950s. Well-to-do skilled immigrants were the first to migrate to Miami. Many anticipated returning home as soon as conditions improved, but instead were joined by increasingly larger numbers of fellow countrymen over time. These early migrants established a presence in the business community and a social network that provided an important role in assimilating the less advantaged who came later, stripped of all their personal possessions and wealth. Tighter emigration rules soon restricted the export of any assets from Cuba. Nevertheless, the migration flow continued unabated, creating an ever-growing Hispanic population base. By 1970, the city of Miami became 45 percent Hispanic, rising to 56 percent in 1980, and 63 percent in 1990. The Latin share in Dade County has shown parallel increases, reaching about 50 percent Hispanic in 1990.

Nicaraguans are now the second largest Hispanic group in Miami. Some estimate that up to 30 percent of the Nicaraguan professional class left their homeland in the 1980s, headed primarily for South Florida.[13] The municipality of Sweetwater has now been labeled *Little Managua* in response to its growing Nicaraguan identity.

The ethnic shift that Miami has experienced in the past 30 years is unparalleled in the annals of American history. The city of Miami also has the largest share of foreign-born population of any large American city. That number stood at 36 percent in 1980 and 40 percent in 1990. It is likely that the flow to Miami will continue in the 1990s. The weakened state of the Cuban economy and prospect of relaxed emigration restrictions should make relocation easier for dissatisfied Cubans.

BLACK URBANIZATION AND MIGRATION

In the first quarter of this century, another major migration stream emerged, again directed primarily at northern cities. The lure of manufacturing jobs encouraged this movement, along with increasingly depressed conditions in the agricultural South. This movement was distinctive because it was mainly an internal redistribution within the country and because it involved a nonwhite group—the rural southern black. Housing for this black population was initially found just beyond close-in tenement districts, in the inner suburbs being vacated by the upwardly mobile middle class. The residences were usually large single-family dwellings subdivided into rooming houses; as the migration continued to expand, densities increased along with territorial expansion.

Blacks were originally brought to the United States as slave labor to work on southern plantations, especially tobacco and cotton farms.

> After the Civil War, most blacks remained in the South, typically becoming share croppers or tenants on white-owned cotton farms, all suffering from fluctuations in production and price, and later, the ravages of the boll weevil. However, in the 1930s, tenants—both black and white—were ultimately forced out of cotton farming by federal acreage restrictions and by subsidies, which went primarily to the owners of the larger and more productive farms. By the end of the 1950s, the decreased acreage and the mechanization made possible by the subsidies had eliminated the need for most blacks on farms. The exodus of blacks from the rural South was further stimulated by growth of jobs in defense industries during World War II and the continued economic expansion of northern and western cities.[14]

---

[12]Thomas D. Boswell and James R. Curtis, "The Hispanization of Metropolitan Miami," Chapter 11 in Thomas Boswell, ed., *South Florida: The Winds of Change*, p. 151.

[13]Ibid., p. 148.

[14]Ibid., pp. 143–144.

TABLE 13-1
Black Population in Cities, 1880–1990 (000's)[a]

	1880	1900	1920	1940	1960	1970	1980	1990
New York	28	68	169	504	1088	1667	1782	2103
Chicago	6	30	109	278	813	1103	1196	1088
Philadelphia	32	63	134	251	529	654	638	632
Washington	52	87	110	187	412	538	449	400
Baltimore	54	79	108	166	326	420	431	436
St. Louis	58	78	70	166	214	254	207	188
New Orleans	58	78	101	149	234	267	309	308
Detroit	3	4	41	149	482	660	759	778
Memphis	15	50	61	121	184	243	308	335
Birmingham	—	17	70	109	135	126	158	168
Atlanta	16	36	63	105	187	255	283	264
Houston	6	5	34	86	215	317	420	458
Cleveland	2	6	35	85	251	288	251	235
Los Angeles	—	2	16	64	335	504	505	488
Jacksonville	4	16	42	62	106	118	137	164
Pittsburgh	4	20	38	62	101	105	102	N/A
Richmond	28	32	—	61	92	105	113	N/A
Cincinnati	8	15	30	56	109	125	130	N/A
Indianapolis	7	16	35	51	98	134	153	166
Dallas	2	9	24	50	129	210	266	297

[a] City ranking based on 1940 black population, in decreasing order.

Source: Richard Morrill and O. Fred Donaldson, "Geographical Perspectives on the History of Black America," *Economic Geography,* 48 (1972), 15; *Statistical Abstract,* 1990; U.S. Bureau of Census.

Urban Black Population Growth

Prior to 1910, nearly all blacks in the United States lived in the rural South, but a few cities in the South did have a significant nonwhite population. In fact, there were eight cities in the country with more than 25,000 blacks as early as 1880. All of these cities, with the exception of Charleston, are shown in Table 13-1. St. Louis and New Orleans had the largest black populations in 1880, followed by Baltimore and Washington, D.C. Philadelphia and New York were the only cities in the Northeast with large black populations at that time.

At the turn of the century, most urban blacks found employment in "fringe jobs that an industrial, commercial, society produces—janitors, servants, general laborers, strikebreakers when and where the need arises, and domestic jobs for women—the jobs that had little competition from white workers."[15] Black families serving as house help for white families frequently lived in adjacent housing, especially on side streets and alleys. Colonies of blacks living in small groups also existed in isolated districts adjacent to industrial or transportation corridors, especially along the railroad. Both of these situations produced small pockets of black residences, considerably more widely dispersed than the pattern that later evolved.

Conditions for blacks in the South had deteriorated by the turn of the present century. Strong repressive measures by the whites associated with Jim Crow laws during the Reconstruction Era, together with depressed agricultural conditions, set the stage for a tremendous out-migration to northern cities immediately before and after World War I. Improved transportation and indus-

[15]George Davis and O. Fred Donaldson, *Blacks in the United States: A Geographic Perspective*, Houghton Mifflin, Boston, 1975, p. 86.

trial expansion in the North, together with better school and health care opportunities, helped pull migrants northward.

In the 1900–1920 interval, 600,000 rural blacks left the South in pursuit of industrial jobs in northern cities. The migration streams were narrow and selective, as Figure 13-8 illustrates. Blacks from the South Atlantic states mainly headed toward Philadelphia and New York, while migrants from the South Central states moved up the Mississippi and Ohio River valleys toward Chicago and Detroit. Later, blacks from Louisiana and Texas moved westward to California.

The rapid influx of black migrants to northern cities created tremendous demand for housing. In the 1930s, for the first time, several northern cities had more urban blacks than southern cities (Table 13-1). In fact, three of the top five cities in black populations in 1940 were in the North. Black population doubled in southern cities, but increases of fourfold or more occurred in New York, Philadelphia, and Chicago during the 1880–1920 period. A tremendous regional redistribution occurred in the first half of the century, wherein a parallel decline in the black proportion of population in the South occurred simultaneously with rapid growth in the North, particularly in central city areas.

EMERGENCE OF BLACK GHETTO SPACE

Closer examination of the living space that evolved for the black indicates that spatially and behaviorally it emulated the ghetto space experience previously identified with foreign immigrant groups. A separate housing market developed to allocate this housing. Distinctive perpetuating forces, both internal and external, maintained its form and growth. Eventually, the black residential community became conceptualized as a *city within a city*.

The designation of black residential areas as ghetto space serves to explain both the context and the historical roots of the territory. Unfortunately, confusion also arises with the use of this concept. The identification of ghetto areas with poverty, slums, and blight often occurs even though much of the territory is occupied by relatively affluent families. Middle-class and wealthy blacks, living in comfortable environments, also in-

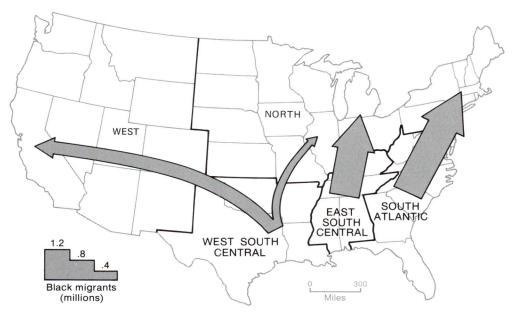

Figure 13-8. Black Migration Streams from the South, 1940–1960. Distinctive migration flows occurred from the South Atlantic to the Northeast, from the East South Central States to the Middle West, and from the West South Central to the West. By 1960, New York, Chicago, Philadelphia, Washington, Baltimore, Detroit, and Los Angeles had become the largest centers of urban black population in the country. *Source: Harold M. Rose, Social Processes in the City: Race and Urban Residential Choice* (Washington, D.C.: Association of American Geographers, Resource Papers for College Geography #6), 1969, p. 6. Redrawn by permission.

habit the ghetto subsystem. The term *ghetto* is appropriate because it demonstrates that blacks generally have not lived in random fashion throughout the city but have been confined to restricted space as a result of various social, economic, and physical pressures meted out by the community as a whole.

By using the term *ghetto centers* to apply to the black residential space in cities over 100,000 in population, with at least 25,000 black residents, one can observe the evolution of a national system of black urban nodes.[16] The original group of these cities, mainly southern, called *first-generation ghetto centers*, appeared before 1920 (Table 13-2). *Second-generation ghetto centers* emerged in the 1920–1950 period. Northern industrial cities dominated this list, particularly those in the Middle West. *Third-generation ghetto centers* joined the list after 1950. These cities were scattered throughout the country, with nearly half in the South.

The rural–urban black migration process slowed during the 1960s but not before distinctive black residential territories appeared in nearly every large American city. In fact, only six major cities with central city populations of 500,000 or more in the country did not have significant black concentrations in 1970. These cities were mainly newer regional capitals in the West (Denver, Phoenix, Seattle, Minneapolis–St. Paul, San Antonio, and San Diego).

Several southern states continued to experience absolute losses in black population in the 1960s. In Mississippi alone, 100,000 blacks moved away during the decade. A slowing of the process at the end of the decade, in comparison to the outflow in the 1940s and 1950s, lessened the importance of the rural–urban migration stream in the 1960s. In its place, intercity migration of blacks accelerated. This movement typically involved persons with greater skills, education, and income than those involved in the typical rural-to-urban movement. Contrasts from North to South in the intensity of the rural-to-urban and urban-to-rural flows also emerged. It appears that by the early 1970s, the immigration to northern cities consisted mostly of skilled migrants from other cities, whereas southern cities still received many rural poor. A counterstream of migration of skilled urban blacks moving back to the South also appeared in the 1970s in response to expanded job opportunities and the improved quality of

TABLE 13-2
Selected First-, Second-, and Third-Generation Ghetto Centers

First-Generation (prior to 1920)	Second-Generation (1920–1950)	Third-Generation (since 1950)
Atlanta	Dallas	Boston
Baltimore	Houston	Buffalo
Birmingham	Mobile	Denver
New Orleans	Boston	Milwaukee
Washington	Cleveland	Omaha
Chicago	Detroit	Phoenix
Cincinnati	Indianapolis	Rochester
New York	Kansas City	San Diego
Pittsburgh	Los Angeles	Seattle
Philadelphia	Newark	
	Oakland	
	San Francisco	

Source: From *The Black Ghetto: A Spatial Behavioral Perspective* by Harold M. Rose. Copyright © 1971 by McGraw-Hill, Inc. Used with permission of McGraw-Hill Book Company.

life in the region. This reverse flow intensified in the 1980s. Table 13-1 also indicates that the black central city population has declined in many cities according to the 1990 census.

Location of Black Residential Space

Historically, black residential space in cities exhibited one of two characteristic patterns: (1) dispersed residences located on grounds or alleys adjacent to employers; and (2) clusters of housing near rail or industrial zones or corridors. In northern cities, in-migrating blacks usually moved into housing formerly occupied by whites, as a part of the *filtering process*, similar to the pattern also followed by foreign immigrants.

In southern cities, little or no housing filtered from white to black occupancy until after World War II. Black families in the South traditionally occupied only housing built specifically for them. The dictates of segregation fostered the development of black enclaves on one side of town with totally separate supporting institutions. Such districts often grew in sectoral fashion as expansion of housing space occurred, the result of constructing new houses on the fringes of the existing space farther from the center of the city. Eventually, a sectoral pattern of black residential space also evolved in the North as additional housing space adjacent to the existing territory became available.

---

[16]This approach was introduced by Harold Rose and is discussed in Chapter 2 of *The Black Ghetto: A Spatial Behavioral Perspective*, McGraw-Hill, New York, 1971, pp. 14–25.

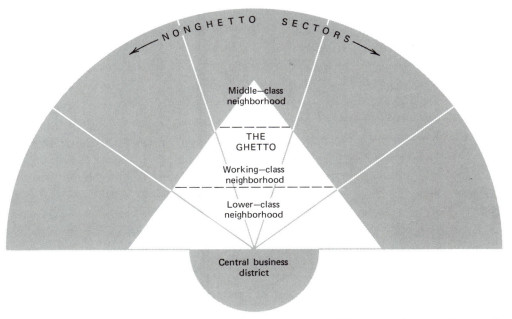

Figure 13-9. Reverse Sector Ghetto Residential Space. The base of the sector adjacent to the central business district typically houses poorer black residents in public housing or older single-family or apartment units. The moderate income working class live farther out, and the middle class in newer housing toward the apex. *Source:* From *The Black Ghetto* by Harold M. Rose, copyright © 1971 McGraw-Hill. Used with permission of McGraw-Hill Book Company.

The classic form of this segregated housing arrangement has been labeled a *reverse sector*. The ideal case, as shown in Figure 13-9, might involve the base of the sector forming near the central business district and a tapering of the space occurring farther out. The poor and moderate-income groups live in the close-in part of the space, and the middle class in newer housing toward the apex. In the context of social area analysis, this space is normally labeled as exhibiting multiple nuclei characteristics (see Chapter 11).

Comparative Residential Succession Patterns

Since blacks could not move into existing white residential areas in the South until recent decades, access to additional housing required expansion on the rural periphery outside the city limits but adjacent to the existing space. The restricted market, in the face of increasing demands for housing, also necessitated higher-density living in existing black areas as families found it necessary to double up and share space with friends and relatives.

The contrasting residential succession process in the North produced transition areas in which some blocks or tracts, even if for short periods, yielded integrated living environments. In southern areas, abrupt, permanent racial contrasts traditionally occurred at boundary points separating black and white territories (Figure 13-10). Since black housing space in the South occurred only within an existing assigned territory, frequently separated from white space with highly visible physical barriers, no transition of mixed areas existed, except in special cases. When housing succession began in the South, after World War II, neighborhood expansion in urban areas, North and South, followed the pattern of the northern case shown in Figure 13-9.

Utilizing the terminology *core, fringe,* and *transition areas* developed by Harold Rose to characterize various intensity levels of black occupancy, black housing in the South formerly fell exclusively in the *core* category.[17] *Core* areas contain more than 75 percent black population, and *fringe* areas are 50–74 percent black. The latter two categories did not become factors in the South until the 1950s.

[17]Ibid., p. 6.

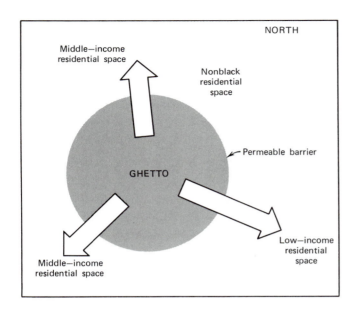

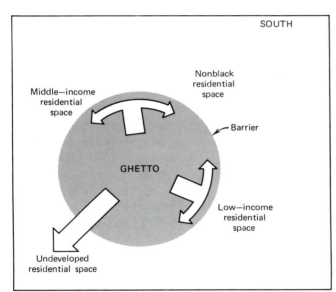

Figure 13-10. Traditional Black Residential Neighborhood Expansion Patterns: North–South Contrasts. The black residential succession process in the North allowed for movement into white neighborhoods, whereas abrupt boundaries typically separated black and white neighborhoods in the South. *Source:* From *The Black Ghetto* by Harold M. Rose, copyright © 1971 McGraw-Hill. Used with permission of McGraw-Hill Book Company.

Territorial Expansion

The prevailing pattern of black housing space expansion just discussed is a classic example of a diffusion process. Growth occurs by spreading outward from an establised node or center, not unlike the spatial adoption process of a new innovation. The node or center is

the existing black residential territory. This territorial expansion process frequently involves adding space in outlying residential areas in middle-class neighborhoods (Figure 13-10). The movement is highly directional and generally biased along the main axis of the existing territory. The growth of the black residential space in Seattle from 1940 to 1970, for example, involved adding territory along a north–south axis. Expansion was tempered on the west by the presence of apartments and on the east by a lake and more expensive homes. North–south and southwest–northeast arterial streets accommodated expansion, as did low-lying land where values were lower.

In Atlanta, a similar process of expansion occurred, beginning in the 1950s. Prior to that time, black living space was confined to the east and near-west sides of the downtown area (Figure 13-11). The 1950s expansion occurred primarily to the west and southwest, and in recent years expansion has been quite pronounced to the south and east. Northward expansion by blacks has generally not occurred in Atlanta primarily because of the blocking factor of higher-priced housing and white resistance. The channelization evident in Atlanta is partially shaped by the barrier effect of railroad corridors. As elsewhere, movement in Atlanta has been deflected away from and around areas of most resistance. Attachment by blacks to their own cultural institutions also decreased the pressure to move northward in the city. Nevertheless, nearly all census tracts on the north side contain a few black middle-class families and remnants of former rural enclaves of poor blacks still exist.

Blockbusting

Territorial accretion typically begins when one or two black families move into formerly all-white residential areas a few blocks away from the existing space. This development is often labeled *blockbusting*. It can occur when realtors or aggressive buyers pressure a white resident to sell. Panic among other white residents typically ensues, often fueled by the actions of unscrupulous realtors who warn residents of an imminent invasion of blacks, a potential lowering of house values, and the importance of leaving immediately. Such circumstances can lead to aberrations in the housing market. The demand for housing in the area among whites may drop to zero and sometimes whites sell at reduced prices, again fearing that the value of their housing has decreased as a result of the *transition*

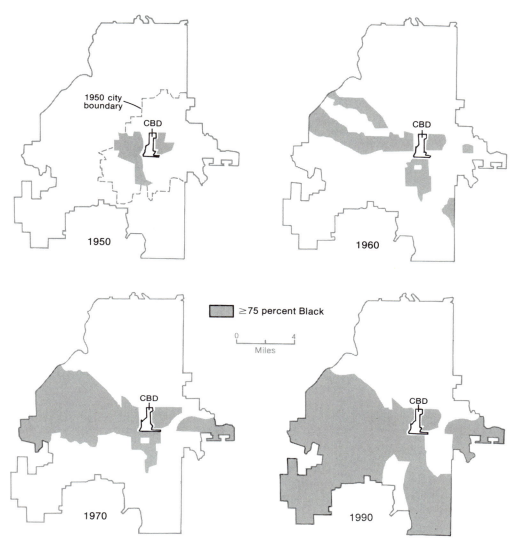

Figure 13-11.   Black Residential Expansion in the City of Atlanta, 1950–1990. Beginning in the 1950s, a black residential space began expanding to the west from its confined space to the east and near-west sides of the CBD. By 1970, that space had grown to include a large territory extending to the city limits (which were enlarged in 1952) on the west side. By 1990, this space had grown to include southwest Atlanta and the east–southeast portions of the city. Northward expansion by blacks generally has not occurred in Atlanta. *Source:* U.S. Censuses of Population, 1950–1970; Atlanta Regional Commission, *Population and Housing 1990.*

process under way. Realtors in some instances take advantage of potential sellers by advising them that values have dropped, even buying the house themselves at a reduced price and then reselling to a black family at a substantial increase.

Dozens of houses often appear on the market immediately in the days following the original sale to blacks. Sometimes whole blocks go up for sale at once. In such circumstances, temporary depressions in selling prices can occur, but studies in dozens of cities indicate that no long-term reduction in values is associated with racial turnover (see following section). In many in-

stances, the socioeconomic status of the new occupant is higher than the family moving away. Frequently the new family is younger and has more school-age children than previous residents.

Since turnover rates are so rapid, and transition so complete, little chance for long-term racial integration exists. The norm is for blocks to be all white or all black in the long run, with racial mixing occurring only temporarily during the turnover process. This is not to say that instances of integrated housing do not exist, because they do, in both the North and South. But only a small proportion of total urban housing is racially integrated. Once the wave of transition is nearly complete in one community, other adjacent communities can experience the same process, depending on the demand for housing among blacks and the strength of the white housing market.

House Values

The belief that house values fall with racial turnover remains a lively and real issue in transition areas. Many residents feel it is an inevitable by-product of the change. This observation is often reinforced by the rhetoric of anxious realtors and appraisers, who are eager for housing transactions to occur. Nearly all the evidence in housing values studies conducted in transition areas refutes the house value decline thesis. Government reports label the value decline thesis a myth.

> The fact is: there is no substance to the view that minority group residency inevitably leads to a decline in property values. The objective factors affecting property values have no relation to race at all. They depend upon the condition of the housing market and include a cluster of elements, such as the age and condition of the housing, the under-or-over supply of certain house styles, the price range of the housing, zoning changes, the under-or-over development of a neighborhood and changes in neighborhood amenities. . . .
>
> A study completed in Louisville, Kentucky in 1966 showed that of the sales of 183 houses in "changing" neighborhoods, 91 houses showed an increase in value, 73 houses showed no change in the value of the property, and 17 houses decreased in value. Another study in Plainfield, New Jersey 2 years later found that property values in a neighborhood that underwent a racial change showed the same upward trend in prices as the comparable all-white area. Other studies have drawn similar conclusions. These studies have been conducted in San Francisco, Philadelphia, Chicago, Detroit, Kansas City, Houston, and Baltimore.[18]

Tipping Point

The *tipping point* mechanism and a *self-fulfilling prophecy* partially account for the continued segregated housing market and pressure for total racial turnover once the process is initiated. The *tipping point* is that proportion of minority households that white neighborhoods will tolerate. When that critical level is reached, complete housing turnover to black occupancy is likely to occur. The precise level is debatable and highly

variable, but rarely do white households tolerate more than 10 to 15 percent minority residents. Preferences of whites to vacate areas when such levels are reached ensure that stable, racially mixed, residential neighborhoods are the exception. The *self-fulfilling prophecy* reinforces the prevailing tendency. When whites feel that their neighborhood is about to change racially from white to black, they often move. The move itself serves to facilitate the change. In other words, actual behavior patterns produce the anticipated change, once residents feel it is inevitable.

Invasion–Succession

The literature on racial change often refers to an *invasion–succession process*, based on the rapidity and completeness of turnover in a short period. Tracts, and whole neighborhoods, often change in six months or less, once the process begins. On a longer-term basis, the change also appears to be just as massive and significant. For example, in Chicago, over 1300 city blocks shifted from white to a black majority occupancy in the 1950s, and over 1000 blacks did so in the 1960s.

Ghetto Permanency

The magnitude of recent black residential expansion in central cities has created a black majority in many places. As recently as 1950, blacks comprised only a small portion of all residents. The exceptions, Washington, D.C., and Baltimore, were 35 percent and 24 percent black, respectively. Only three other cities had black populations of 15 percent or more at that time.

By 1980, the list of black centers was significantly enlarged (Table 13-3). The top 15 cities housed more than 400,000 blacks each. In Washington, D.C., 70 percent of the population was black, followed by 67 percent black in Atlanta, and 63 percent in Detroit, while Baltimore and New Orleans each had 55 percent black.

Segregated housing spaces, black and white, may have become permanent phenomena in American cities. The housing allocation system continues to operate in the context of two separate markets. Metropolitan areas are, in fact, becoming more racially polarized in a spatial context. Central cities become increasingly nonwhite, and suburbs remain predominantly white. Other minority groups, especially Hispanics and Asians, continue to expand in central cities as well, but

[18]U.S. Commission on Civil Rights, *Understanding Fair Housing*, Clearinghouse Publication 42, USGPO, Washington, D.C., 1973, p. 11.

TABLE 13-3
Highest-Ranking Cities in the United States in Absolute Black Population, 1980

Rank	City	Total Black Population in MSA (000's)	Black Percentage of Central-City Population
1	New York	3279	25
2	Chicago	1698	40
3	Los Angeles	1292	17
4	Philadelphia	1133	38
5	Washington	995	70
6	Detroit	954	63
7	Houston	689	28
8	Atlanta	653	67
9	Baltimore	607	55
10	Dallas	553	29
11	San Francisco	543	13
12	Miami	536	25
13	Cleveland	444	44
14	New Orleans	444	55
15	St. Louis	431	46

Source: Bureau of Census.

they typically do not expand into predominantly black neighborhoods.

Data from the 1980 Census confirmed that black urban population growth had slowed along with the outmigration from the South. The South, in fact, for the first time in the twentieth century experienced a net gain in black population during the 1970s, and the northeast experienced a net loss.[19] The "first and second generation ghetto centers in the northeast and north central census divisions have been the principal losers."[20] While a loss in black population has occurred in many of these metropolitan areas, a trend which continued in the 1980s, their suburban rings have gained black population. We will return to the topic of black suburbanization in a later section.

Perpetuating Forces: External Factors

The many types of *de jure* legal restrictions that formerly perpetuated racial segregation have been out-

[19]Harold M. Rose, "The Evolving Spatial Pattern of Black America: 1910–1980," Chapter 3 in Jesse O. McKee, ed., *Ethnicity in Contemporary America: A Geographical Appraisal*, Kendall/Hunt, Dubuque, Iowa, 1985, p. 67.
[20]Ibid., p. 70.

lawed. In the past, a homeowner's property deed may have specifically forbade the sale of housing or land in the white community to a black. This is an example of a *deed restriction*. Such provisions received the full support of the courts. Covenants and ordinances at the city level further solidified the practice of prohibiting racial mixing.

Restrictive Housing Policies

The private housing industry traditionally advocated residential segregation as a business necessity and moral commitment. One economic justification for this stand related to the perceived likelihood that minority resident occupancy would lower property values. The National Association of Real Estate Brokers (NAREB) code of ethics stated, as recently as 1950, that the "realtor should not be instrumental in introducing into a neighborhood . . . members of any race or nationality or any individual whose presence will clearly be detrimental to property values in the neighborhood." Federal policies also supported racial segregation. For example, FHA finance policies encouraged the status quo. One commentator described early FHA policy as "separate for whites and nothing for blacks." Less than 2 percent of FHA-insured housing built between 1945 and the late 1950s assisted blacks.

The trend of striking down restrictive housing policies began after World War II, especially at the federal level. A series of executive orders, congressional actions, and court decisions gradually required *open housing*. In the 1960s, civil rights legislation, including specific fair-housing laws, prohibited discriminatory practices by all realtors, builders, and financial institutions. For example, Title VIII of the 1968 Civil Rights Act specifically forbade any racial discrimination in housing regardless of whether federal assistance was involved or not. By the early 1970s, more than 80 percent of all housing in the country became subject to federal fair-housing law requirements. These guidelines involved more than just the sale or rental of housing; they also applied to real estate advertising and multiple-listing services.

Unwritten Discriminatory Practices

In recent years, the tools employed to foster a separate housing market were mainly unwritten real estate practices, the placement of land uses, or simply economic barriers. Even if they were more subtle than the rules they replaced, they remained just as effective. These policies will be discussed here in four groups: (1) realtor practices, (2) land use barriers and buffers, (3) community resistance, and (4) financial institution biases.

The practice of realtors not showing housing to blacks in white communities is usually camouflaged because overt refusal is illegal. The law may be circumvented by "gentlemen's agreements" whereby only white realtor agencies list homes in white communities, and blacks list only those in black areas. By simply claiming that most of their clients desire not to be shown areas either in transition or of the opposite race, this policy is rationalized. In effect, this practice results in *steering* blacks and whites in separate directions.

Potential buyers are also *screened* by the realtor, ensuring that the status quo prevails. By refusing to list homes or by not showing those in specific areas, an agent can sidestep the issue of integration and transition. By *misrepresenting homes*, such as claiming they are not for sale, indicating the unit has recently been sold, or emphasizing inadequacies of the property, a potential black buyer in a white neighborhood can be discouraged from purchasing a unit at the agent's discretion. Similar practices have been labeled *negative selling*, such as not keeping appointments to show homes, raising the price to place homes out of the buyer's range, or simply withdrawing contracts for technical reasons.

A potential black buyer can receive "cues" as to what housing is available from real estate advertisements. Phrases such as *exclusive, executive, secluded and private, country club*, and *separate school system* are often used in suburban listings to attract whites only. By handling the transaction as a private sale and not advertising or posting "for sale" signs, the seller also has greater discretion than that available to the realtor.

Land use barriers and *buffers* channel black expansion in desired directions. Classic examples of impenetrable highway and railroad corridor barriers exist in many cities. Less blatant and abrupt, but fully as effective, tools to foster racial separation are land use buffers such as the placement of cemeteries and parks, commercial and industrial corridors, and simple overzoning of vacant parcels to ensure development breaks between black and white neighborhoods. In some cases, dead-end streets and unpaved streets also serve to limit interaction and thereby promote separation. Street name changes at traditional black/white boundaries have also been used in many cities to guarantee that blacks and whites do not have the "same" address and serve as reminders of the separate living space.

Organized resistance to black occupancy in areas considered off-limits is far less vociferous and destructive now than it was 30 years ago. It is not only illegal and unethical but also bad for a city's image to practice harassment, not to mention the psychological hardship that is inflicted on families. Fraternal groups, such as the Ku Klux Klan, and in some cases the local leadership, traditionally exerted pressure to preserve the "integrity of white areas." Physical violence, financial sanctions against people and property, and intimidation by business and political leaders often created an atmosphere of fear that served to maintain the status quo, particularly in the South. The police and public transport routings and service areas also served as instruments to prevent a neighborhood transition in the past. In some areas, the increased pressure exerted by active citizen groups and homeowners associations has supplanted the more overt acts of containment, and now serves to maintain the undercurrent of separation.

Financial institution biases, such as the denial of mortgage assistance to blacks for the purchase of homes, while not as widespread as in the past, remain a problem. The rising cost of homes, growing downpayment requirements, and high income thresholds required to qualify for a loan, as well as lingering redlining practices, have also differentially affected the black family. Excessive interest rates, especially for second mortgages, and the need for some blacks to finance home mortgages through *loan shark* institutions further exacerbate the problem. Federal subsidy programs have attempted to ease the burden for blacks but have been only partially effective.

Perpetuating Forces: Internal Factors

Paralleling the impact of the external factors, several internal forces also mold the ghetto system. Preferences among blacks to live together, apart from the white community, and vice versa, also contribute to the ongoing separation. Ties to community institutions and information about housing opportunities reinforce these separate traditions. In earlier times, the ghetto provided security from outside hostilities. More recently, the black pride movement and the prospect of greater access to political institutions among black residents, paralleling the emergence of black majorities in the central city, have solidified the pride and preference for blacks to remain together as a group.

RESIDENTIAL MOBILITY AND SOCIOECONOMIC CHANGE

Housing values, incomes, and lifestyles show as much variation in the black community as in other neighborhoods. While the greater portion of black residential space has traditionally been described as lower and working class, most emerging black neighborhoods are typically of higher status than existing black areas. They are generally farther from the city center and involve the occupancy of newer housing. The movement of upwardly mobile blacks into newer, more spacious quarters also adds to the demand for higher housing consumption levels. Middle- and upper-status black residential communities, sometimes labeled *gilded ghettos*, flourish in all cities with large black populations. Sometimes these areas are located in the suburbs, but more often they are in outlying portions of the central city itself.

Older black neighborhoods decline in overall socioeconomic status as outward migration occurs. Most of this movement is explained by the same factors that entice any urban family to suburbanize. It is also fueled by a *blowout process*, which is caused by displacement of residents in older residential areas as a result of urban renewal, demolition, and code enforcement programs. This action withdraws the worst inner-city housing from the market and creates a demand for the housing being vacated by a more upwardly mobile group that is shifting to the suburbs.

Black Employment

As recently as 1930, estimates indicated that about three-quarters of black urban workers possessed no vocational skills. The high demand for unskilled labor that originally attracted blacks to the city declined by the end of the 1920s. Technological advances at that time led to a decreasing demand for manual labor. Denied access to union membership, blacks could find employment only in operative jobs (trucking, warehouse, delivery) and blue-collar service work (maintenance, janitorial, and sanitation employment). As recently as the early 1970s, the composition of the black labor force had changed only slightly in profile from that of three or four decades earlier. Blue-collar service activity characterized 70 percent of the black labor force. Unskilled manual domestic opportunities have also declined for the minority worker, such as butler, maid, yard maintenance, and chauffeur tasks.

In recent years, blacks have improved their position in the labor force, but unemployment has also increased. In older slower-growing industrial areas of the northeast, their position has slipped the most. By comparison, progress has been stronger in rapidly growing areas. Adjusting to the transition to the postindustrial information age has been particularly difficult for blacks without skills and advanced education.

POVERTY AND THE UNDERCLASS

About 20 percent of black families were at the poverty level in terms of income at the beginning of the 1970s. This poverty group occupied only a small segment of black residential space, but it was the most visible part and the one the mass media and public most often associate with black life. Nor is poverty exclusively a problem in black areas. Other inner-city minorities also share the problem (Figure 13-12).

In 1985, central city areas claimed about 43 percent of the poverty population, up from 27 percent in 1959. At the same time, the share of poor blacks in the central city rose from 38 to 61 percent.[21] From another perspective, consider that central cities in the mid-1980s housed over one-half of the nation's population trapped in poverty, up from one-third in 1972.[22] These statistics are frightening enough, but they do not, by themselves, adequately reflect the level of distress present in inner city neighborhoods. Many social and behavioral problems accompany inner city poverty, and, as a group, encompass an insidious *underclass* problem. Erol Ricketts and Isabel Sawhill

> measured the underclass as people living in neighborhoods whose residents in 1980 simultaneously exhibited disproportionately high rates of school dropout, joblessness, female-headed families, and welfare dependency. Using a composite definition where tracts must fall at least one standard deviation above the national mean on all four characteristics, they find that approximately 2.5 million people lived in such tracts and that these tracts were disproportionately located in major cities in the Northeast and Midwest. They report that in underclass tracts, on average, 63 percent of the resident adults had less than a high school education, that 60 percent of the families with

[21]John D. Kasarda, "Structural Factors Affecting the Location and Timing of Underclass Growth," *Urban Geography*, 11 (1990), p. 235.
[22]Ibid., p. 235.

Figure 13-12. Poverty and the Underclass. The inner-city poverty problem grew in magnitude over the past decade. Central cities now house over one-half of the nation's poverty population. All minority groups have been affected, but the problem is most frequently associated with inner-city blacks. This day laborer is looking for work in Austin, Texas. (Bob Daemmrich Photography)

children were headed by women, that 56 percent of the adult men were not regularly employed, and that 34 percent of the households were receiving public assistance. Their research also revealed that, although the total poverty population only grew by 8 percent between 1970 and 1980, the number of people living in the underclass areas grew by 230 percent, from 752,000 to 2,484,000.[23]

Other factors have also been associated with the underclass phenomena, including out-of-wedlock births, illicit drug and gambling activity, and the lack of role models in the most impacted areas. Mark Hughes has labeled the most isolated underclass areas as the *impacted ghetto* (Figure 13-13). These areas have continued to expand, and problems multiply in intensity despite targeted governmental assistance programs, affirmative action initiatives, and civil rights legislation.[24]

Structural changes in the economy contribute to the disenfranchisement of the less educated by making new jobs functionally inaccessible to the disadvantaged.[25] Job decentralization and white flight places central neighborhoods and black workers at a disadvantage, creating *deprivation neighborhoods*, as jobs and social institutions collapse. Black suburbanization likewise contributes to the problem by draining these areas of many cultural and social situations, clubs, churches, recreational programs, schools, and so on.[26] In short, family stability has declined, deviant behavior has increased, and the younger generation does not have access to the traditional family role model support mechanisms in these areas. To make matters worse, John Kasarda mentions four additional problems associated with these impacted neighborhoods.[27]

[23]Ibid., pp. 235–236.

[24]Mark Hughes, "Formation of the Impacted Ghetto: Evidence from Large Metropolitan Areas, 1970–1980," *Urban Geography* 11 (1990), p. 266.

[25]John Kasarda, "Structural Factors Affecting the Location and Timing of Urban Underclass Growth," *Urban Geography*, 11 (1990), p. 237.

[26]Ibid., p. 237.

[27]Ibid., p. 238.

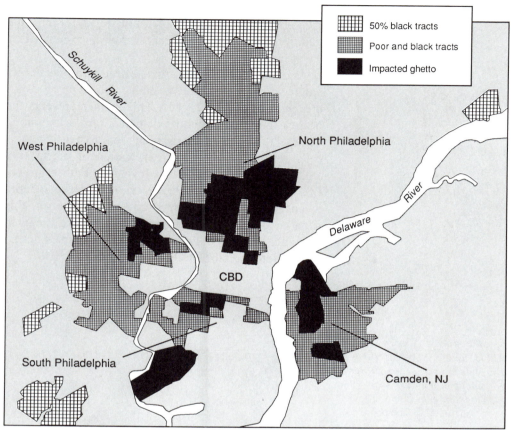

Figure 13-13.   The Impacted Ghetto of Philadelphia. Many social problems have been associated with the underclass phenomena, including out-of-wedlock births, illicit drug and gambling activity, and the lack of role models in the most impacted areas. These areas continue to expand despite intervention programs such as governmental assistance to families, affirmative action initiatives, and civil rights legislation. *Source:* Mark Hughes, "Formation of the Impacted Ghetto: Evidence from Large Metropolitan Areas, 1970–1980," *Urban Geography,* 11 (1990), p. 280. Used by permission of V. H. Winston & Son, Inc.

1. Black businesses are less prevalent in the area to provide the first work experience for the youth.

2. Protected black markets have vanished with integration, so money does not cycle into the black community, as it did in the past.

3. Affirmative action programs have not been as successful in the private sector as in the public sector.

4. Targeting aid to the most distressed areas traps recipients in the area and creates dependency.

BLACK RESIDENTIAL SUBURBANIZATION

Black suburbanization became an important phenomenon in the 1960s, but the flow was relatively modest (Figure 13-14). Suburban rings in first- and second-generation ghetto centers received the majority of the black movers. Third-generation centers participated very little in this process, but in cities in all census regions except the South, the suburban share of black population increased during the decade.

The relative proportion of blacks in surburban areas has remained relatively constant at about 5 percent. While the movement of blacks into suburbia in sheer numbers appears quite credible, the relative importance of this decentralization is far less significant, for white movement rates have been far greater. The 800,000 blacks that moved to suburbia nationwide in the 1960s accounted for only 5 percent of the population leaving the central city. The nearly 16 million whites who also shifted outward created 95 percent of the suburban

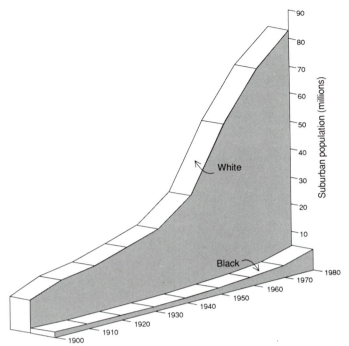

Figure 13-14.   Black-White Suburban Population Trends, 1900–1980. Black suburbanization accelerated in the 1960s and 1970s, but still remains a small share of the suburban population. Nevertheless, during the 1970s the black suburban population growth increased at three times the rate of the white population. About one-fourth of all blacks now live in the suburbs, compared to one-half of all whites. *Source:* U.S. Bureau of Census.

growth and totally overwhelmed the black migratory stream. The share of black suburban population increased by 70 percent in the 1970s and grew by 50 percent in the 1980s. In recent years three-quarters of black population growth has occurred in the suburbs. About one-half of all whites are now living in the suburbs compared to one-quarter of all blacks.

Black suburban population increases have mainly occurred in areas just outside the limits of central cities and simply represent an extension of the existing ghetto space. In Figure 13-15 this area is labeled a *spillover zone*. Other suburban increases have occurred from the growth of black residences in outlying municipalities, the centers of which have often existed for generations. Often such clusters of suburban black population occur as metropolitan growth surrounds and engulfs rural black *colonies*.

Many rural enclaves, sometimes called *shacktowns*, originally grew up along railroad lines or around factories in mill towns. Shacktowns are sometimes excluded from incorporation when suburban areas consolidate and often remain isolated from improved public service

delivery, for example, streets can remain unpaved in such areas. This circumstance illustrates not only the traditional isolation, but also the continued neglect by the greater community.

Another noncontiguous black residential phenomenon in suburban areas has been labeled *leapfrog development* (see Figure 13-15). This form represents the nearest thing to residential dispersal of blacks among whites. Rather than integration, this expansion typically represents an initial penetration of blacks into areas along a main axis of expansion. Future growth fills in the area and produces an all-black residential extension of ghetto space itself. In some cities, this situation occurs as blacks first move into apartments in all-white areas and later into owner-occupied units, proximal to the all-black territorial space.

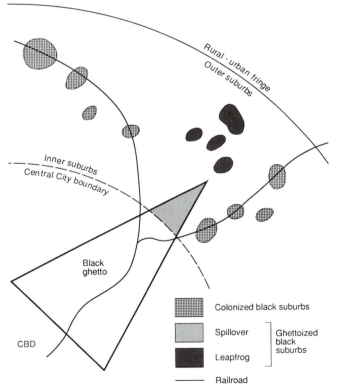

Figure 13-15.   Spatial Form of Black Urbanization. Black suburbanization began as a spillover process to areas just outside the city limits. Some leapfrog development has also occurred. Often poor black shacktowns also exist in the suburbs, frequently located along the railroad or in old milltowns. Black suburbanization today is primarily a middle-class phenomenon involving the expansion of existing black residential space. *Source:* Peter O. Muller, *The Outer City: Geographical Consequences of the Urbanization the Suburbs* (Washington, D.C.: Association of American Geographers, Resource Papers for College Geography, No. 75-2), 1976, 19. Reprinted by permission.

Filtering in the Two Housing Markets

The two urban housing markets, one white and one black, referred to as *dual market*, operate congruently in that they serve to improve housing access. Most moves by whites involve suburban shifts and the occupancy of new housing, while those of blacks are more typically central city in location and involve moves to used housing. In Chicago, for example, "two-thirds of all moves in white suburbia originate with new construction, while most of the housing available to blacks originates from turnover in the existing stock."[28]

Even within the context of a dual market, white moves appear to be the ultimate producer of added housing for blacks. These moves create a chain of additional movement by successive groups from the urban fringe inward toward the city center. This, in effect, improves the lot of all residents, but within the context of the dual market, because not all the units coming on the market are available for black occupancy.

Housing Costs and Other Deterrents to Suburbanization

At every income level, blacks typically pay more and receive less for housing for their money than whites. They occupy lower-quality housing at every rental and sales price level, and they generally live in smaller units than their white counterparts at any given income. This imbalance is often referred to as the *color tax*. Otherwise, suburban black residential areas are increasingly similar to their white counterparts in terms of density and lifestyle (Figure 13-16).

The high cost of housing and rising mortgage rates help to maintain the status quo with respect to housing patterns. Federal housing programs have had limited success in opening the suburbs to blacks.

Local environmental and ecological movements have also had negative effects on blacks. The *no-growth* movement, which is strong in many cities, has been utilized as a blocking tool, as have building permit restrictions. In the final analysis, class separation seems to remain fairly entrenched. But most disturbing is the condition that "racial rather than economic

Figure 13-16. Middle Class Black Residential Community in Atlanta. Surburban black residential areas are very similar to their white counterparts in terms of density and lifestyle. Upper-middle income residence in black community of southwest Atlanta shown here. (Courtesy Richard Pillsbury)

segregation is mainly responsible for the exclusion of nonwhites from the outer city."[29]

A much higher proportion of blacks would live in suburban settings if deterrents to outward migration did not exist. Overt discriminatory practices to thwart black suburbanization are obviously no longer legal, but underground pressures and housing codes remain as barriers to restrict minority family mobility. Several of the instruments available to white suburban areas to assist the stability and uniformity of their neighborhoods were discussed in Chapter 12. These techniques, such as minimum square-footage requirements and restrictive building codes for housing, negatively impact minority households. Superficially, they appear to prevent only the construction of low- and moderate-income housing, but they also serve to prevent minority family in-migration. "The communities argue that their opposition to low- and moderate-income housing has nothing to do with race, only with economics."[30] Nevertheless, researchers suggest that blacks continue to experience the most discrimination in the housing market, and Asians are the least segregated from whites.

SUMMARY AND CONCLUSION

While blacks represent a large share of the population in many metropolitan areas, other minority groups

[28]Brian J. L. Berry, "Short-Term Housing Cycles in a Dualistic Metropolis," in Gary Geppert and Harold Rose, eds., *The Social Economy of Cities, Vol. 9, Urban Affairs Annual Review*, Sage Publications, Beverly Hill, Calif., 1975, p. 1969.

[29]Peter Muller, *The Outer City: Geographical Consequences of the Urbanization of the Suburbs*, Resource Paper No. 75-2, Association of American Geographers, Washington, D.C., 1976, p. 27.

[30]U.S. Commission of Civil Rights, *Above Property Rights*, p. 15.

dominate the mix in other cities (Table 13-4). We have discussed the large Cuban presence in Miami and the growing Hispanic and Asian influence in the West and Southwest. But diversity is also important to recognize in the true melting pot tradition. The ethnic mix for six metropolitan areas throughout the country is shown in Figure 13-17. Distinctive regional variations in ethnic composition occur. Northeastern cities house large shares of blacks and, to a lesser extent, Puerto Ricans. Hispanics, blacks, and Asians, in more or less equal shares, coexist in several large California cities. Mexicans dominate in San Antonio, while Cubans and blacks identify with Miami (Figure 13-18). Western cities also house relatively large shares of American Indians.

The most diverse populations are generally found in larger cities. Four of the six central cities with more

TABLE 13-4

1990 Minority Population Shares in Selected Cities (percent)

	Black	Asian	Hispanic	Minority Total
New York	28	7	24	59
Chicago	39	4	20	63
Los Angeles	14	10	40	64
Detroit	76	1	3	80
San Francisco	11	29	14	54
Miami	26	1	62	89
Phoenix	5	2	20	27
San Jose	5	20	27	52
Honolulu	1	70	5	76
Houston	28	4	28	60

Source: U.S. Bureau of the Census.

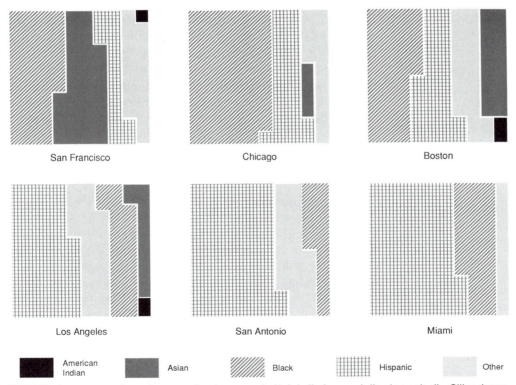

San Francisco   Chicago   Boston

Los Angeles   San Antonio   Miami

| American Indian | | Asian | | Black | | Hispanic | | Other |

NOTE: Ethnic areas are drawn in proportion to percent of total ethnic population in each city. Cities shown are not of equal size.

Figure 13-17.   **Contrasts in Ethnic Diversity in Selected U.S. Cities.** Distinctive regional variations in ethnic composition occur in U.S. cities. Northeastern and Middle Western cities (Boston, Chicago) house large shares of blacks. Hispanics (Mexicans), blacks, and Asians coexist in several large California cities (Los Angeles, San Francisco). Mexicans dominate in San Antonio, while Cubans and blacks identify with Miami. Western cities also house significant shares of American Indians. *Source:* Modified after James Paul Allen and Eugene James Turner, *We the People: An Atlas of America's Ethnic Diversity*, Macmillan, New York, 1988, p. 212.

Figure 13-18. Hispanic Architectural/cultural Influence in San Antonio. The upscale restaurants in this neighborhood near the Market, known as El Mercado, in San Antonio contribute to the Hispanic flair of the community and form a building block for the tourist industry of the city. The restaurant, La Margarita, is shown here with the Madonna statue in the background overlooking the street. (Bob Daemmrich Photography, Austin, Texas)

than 1 million population in the United States (New York, Los Angeles, Chicago, and Houston) all have a diversified ethnic mix, while Philadelphia and Detroit are the exceptions, due to the dominance of the black population in these latter two cities.[31] Smaller industrial and mining towns in the northeast and Middle West have the lowest population diversity owing to their dominance by whites.

Immigration rates to the United States increased in the 1980s, and net immigration now accounts for up to one-third of the population growth in the country. Of continuing concern is the prospect that many of these immigrants are being assimilated into the mainstream more rapidly than blacks. In a recent study, Joe Darden has noted that "color-based discrimination remains a

significant factor in American society today.... Blacks appear to have attained the lowest socioeconomic status, although they arrived in urban America much earlier than some of the other racial ethnic minorities."[32] Darden argues that "observed disparities in socioeconomic status are due primarily to color-based discrimination in housing, which, in turn, has resulted in unequal access to educational opportunities, employment, and career advancement. . . . The levels of discrimination in housing and unequal access to education and employment opportunities increase from Asian to Hispanic to Native American to black."[33]

Based on 1980 census data, researchers have found that "black–white segregation had the highest average level (69.4 percent), and the lowest average level was between Asians and whites (34.2 percent). Indeed, the level of black–white segregation was more than twice the level of Asian–white segregation. Hispanic–white segregation, at 43.4 percent, ranged between the two extremes found for Asians and blacks."[34]

In summary, "the opportunities for social, economic, and spatial mobility available to minority groups occur along a continuum. Asians experience the smallest amount of residential segregation from whites, have the highest level of suburbanization, and are provided the greatest opportunity for social, economic, and spatial mobility. Blacks, on the other hand, experience the greatest amount of residential segregation, the lowest level of suburbanization, and the least opportunity for social, economic, and spatial mobility of all racial/ethnic minority groups."[35]

Suggestions for Further Reading

Allen, James Paul, and Eugene James Turner. *We the People: An Atlas of Ethnic Diversity*, Macmillan, New York, 1988.

Bean, Frank, and W. Parker Frisbie. *Demography of Racial and Ethnic Groups*, Academic Press, New York, 1978.

Brune, Tom, and Eduardo Comacho. *Race and Poverty in Chicago*, Community Renewal Society, Chicago, 1983.

Bunge, William. *Fitzgerald: Geography of a Revolution*, Schenkman, Cambridge, Mass., 1971.

Chicago Tribune. *The American Millstone: An Examination of the Nation's Permanent Underclass*. Contemporary Books, Inc., Chicago, 1986.

Clark, Thomas A. *Blacks in Suburbs: A National Perspective,*

---

[31]James P. Allen and Eugene Turner, "The Most Ethnically Diverse Urban Places in the United States," *Urban Geography*, 10 (1989), p. 527.

[32]Joe T. Darden, "Blacks and Other Racial Minorities: The Significance of Color in Inequality," *Urban Geography*, 10 (1989), p. 563.

[33]Ibid., p. 563.

[34]Ibid., p. 565.

[35]Ibid., p. 574.

Center for Urban Policy Research, Rutgers University, New Brunswick, N.J., 1979.

Darden, Joe T. *Afro-American in Pittsburgh*, Lexington Books/Heath, Lexington, Mass., 1973.

Davis, George A., and O. Fred Donaldson. *Blacks in the United States: A Geographic Perspective*, Houghton-Mifflin, Boston, 1975.

Dewart, Janet, ed. *The State of Black America 1991*. National Urban League, Inc., New York, 1991.

Dinnerstein, Leonard, et al. *Natives and Strangers: Blacks, Indians, and Immigrants in America*, 2nd ed., Oxford University Press, New York, 1990.

Ernst, Robert, and Lawrence Huggs, eds. *Black America, Geographical Perspectives*, Anchor Books, New York, 1976.

Fuchs, Lawrence H. *The American Kaleidoscope: Race, Ethnicity, and the Civic Culture*, Wesleyan University Press, Hanover, N.H., 1990.

Gans, Herbert. *The Urban Villagers*, Free Press, New York, 1962.

Glazer, Nathan, and Daniel Moynihan. *Ethnicity: Theory and Experience*, Harvard University Press, Cambridge, Mass., 1975.

Greeley, Andrew, and William McCready. *Ethnicity in the United States: A Preliminary Reconnaissance*, Wiley, New York, 1974.

Haines, David W. *Refugees as Immigrants: Cambodians, Laotians, and Vietnamese in America*. Rowman & Littlefield, Savage, Md., 1988.

Jencks, Christopher and Paul E. Peterson. *The Urban Underclass*. The Brookings Institution, Washington, D.C., 1991.

Jones, Richard C. *Patterns of Undocumented Migration: Mexico and the United States*, Rowman & Littlefield, Savage, Md., 1984.

Kain, John F., and John Quigley. *Housing Markets and Racial Discrimination: A Microeconomic Analysis*. Columbia University Press, New York, 1975.

Lake, Robert W. *The New Suburbanites: Race and Housing in the Suburbs*, Center for Urban Policy and Research, New Brunswick, N.J., 1981.

Landry, Bart. *The New Black Middle Class*. University of California Press, Berkeley, Calif., 1987.

Lawson, Ronald, and Mark Naison. *The Tenant Movement in New York City, 1904–1984*, Rutgers University Press, New Brunswick, N.J., 1986.

Lemann, Nicholas. *Promised Land: The Great Black Migration and How it Changed America*. Alfred A. Knopf, New York, 1991.

Ley, David. *The Black Inner City as Frontier Outpost: Images and Behavior of a Philadelphia Neighborhood*, Monograph Series No. 7, Association of American Geographers, Washington, D.C., 1974.

Lieberson, Stanley, *Ethnic Patterns in American Cities*, Free Press, New York, 1963.

Lord, J. Dennis. *Spatial Perspectives on School Desegregation and Busing*, Resource Paper No. 77-3, Association of American Geographers, Washington, D.C., 1977.

Maldonado, Lionel, and Joan Moore. *Urban Ethnicity in the United States: New Immigrants and Old Minorities*, Vol. 29, *Urban Affairs Annual Reviews*, Sage Publications, Beverly Hills, Calif., 1985.

Mangiafico, Luciano. *Contemporary American Immigrants: Patterns of Filipino, Korean, and Chinese Settlement in the United States*, Praeger, New York, 1988.

McKee, Jesse O. *Ethnicity in Contemporary America: A Geographical Appraisal*, Kendall/Hunt, Dubuque, Iowa, 1985.

O'Hare, William, *et al. African Americans in the 1990s. Population Bulletin*, 16, July, 1991, 39 p.

Osofsky, Gilberg. *Harlem: The Making of a Ghetto*, Harper, New York, 1966.

Rainwater, Lee. *Behind Ghetto Walls*, Aldine, Chicago, 1970.

Rose, Harold M. *The Black Ghetto: A Spatial Behavioral Perspective*, McGraw-Hill, New York, 1971.

———. *Black Suburbanization*, Ballinger, Cambridge, Mass., 1976.

Schwartz, B., ed. *The Changing Face of the Suburbs*, University of Chicago Press, Chicago, 1976.

Simon, Julian. *The Economic Consequences of Immigration*, Basil Blackwell, Cambridge, Mass., 1989.

Spear, Allan. *Black Chicago: The Making of a Negro Ghetto*, University of Chicago Press, Chicago, 1967.

Taeuber, Karl, and Alma Taeuber. *Negroes in Cities*, Aldine, Chicago, 1965.

Tobin, Gary A. *Divided Neighborhoods: Changing Patterns of Racial Segregation*. Urban Affairs Annual Reviews, 32, Sage Publications, Beverly Hills, 1987.

U.S. Commission on Civil Rights. *Social Indicators of Equality for Minories and Women*, USGPO, Washington, D.C., 1977.

Ward, David. *Cities and Immigrants*, Oxford University Press, New York, 1971.

———. *Poverty, Ethnicity, and the American City, 1840–1925: Changing Conceptions of the Slum and the Ghetto*, Cambridge University Press, New York, 1989.

Wilson, William. *Power, Racism, and Privilege*, Macmillan, New York, 1976.

Wilson, William. *The Truly Disadvantaged: The Inner City, the Underclass, and Public Policy*, University of Chicago Press, Chicago, 1987.

14

INTRAURBAN MIGRATION AND HOUSEHOLD CHANGE

M oving is a way of life for Americans. Accelerating mobility rates accompanied growing affluence and urbanization in the past 100 years, but rates appear to be slowing today.

Moving rates for U.S. households in the 1980s averaged 2 percent lower than those in the first two decades after World War II. Urban transportation improvements and the outward movement of jobs created greater flexibility for urbanites in gaining access to work, and this situation may account for some of the decrease in movement. Higher housing prices also may have contributed to lower rates of mobility. Nevertheless, Census Bureau data indicate that 18 percent of Americans move annually and on the average make about 12 moves in a lifetime, rates considerably higher than those registered in other industrialized countries or in developing areas.

An understanding of urban mobility is critical to the study of urban growth and change, whether it be at the neighborhood level or at the metropolitan scale. Neighborhoods change, in no small part, as a result of shifting residential clientele.

Neighborhoods also change because of shifts in household composition (Figure 14-1). The study of shifts in household composition as a result of marriage,

divorce, childbearing, child-launching, job change, and/or retirement is now receiving more attention. In a recent study of Phoenix neighborhoods over a two-year period, one-third of the households experienced a change in household status, a move, or both. The authors observed that homeowners,

> especially those in older neighborhoods, are more likely to change household structure than to move, resulting in what is called *unstable staying*. The tendency for families to alter their living arrangements without moving creates the potential for enormous shifts in household characteristics without commensurate mobility in single family, owner occupied dwellings.[1]

In this chapter, we will focus on the nature and intensity of intraurban moves and the relationship between household composition and neighborhood change. The geographer's understanding of the underlying processes that explain mobility and household change has grown considerably in recent years. A large and growing literature focuses on the questions of *why* people move, *where* they move, and *who* moves.

RESIDENTIAL MOBILITY

Most individuals or households move by choice, not because of circumstances beyond their control. Forced

---

[1]Patricia Gober, Kevin McHugh, and Neil Reid, "Phoenix in Flux: Household Instability, Residential Mobility, and Neighborhood Change," *Annals of the Association of American Geographers*, 61 (1991), 86.

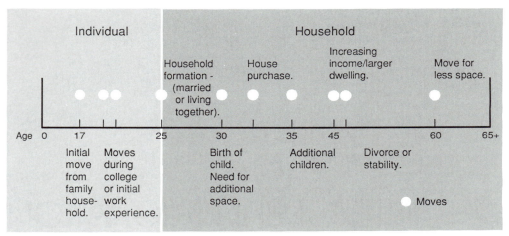

Figure 14-1. Life Cycle Perspective on Mobility. Neighborhoods change as their clientele shifts. Many moves are associated with life cycle changes. Changes in household status associated with marriage, divorce, childbearing, and others explain a large proportion of moves. *Source:* W.A.V. Clark. *Human Migration.* Scientific Geography Series, No. 7, © Sage Publications, Beverly Hills, 1987. p. 39. Reprinted by permission of Sage Publications, Inc.

moves comprise a very small share of all movement (5–10 percent). Most moves occur within the same sector of the city and do not break up established behavior patterns involving work, shopping, school, or social networks. Since moves occur in response to voluntary decisions, the movement process can be viewed as a strategy to satisfy one's preferences; hence the connection with behavioral geography. In the following sections, we will discuss movement as a process of adjustment involving the substitution of a "new" residence for another one left behind.

BEHAVIORAL PROCESSES

By its very nature, intraurban migration is a spatial process. It is also a very personal and subjective undertaking. Nevertheless, moves are predictable because regular, consistent behavior can be observed by individuals or households possessing similar needs and resources. Households of comparable socioeconomic status tend to respond in similar ways to internal and external stimuli, which, in turn, maintains the selectivity and uniformity of residential neighborhoods (recall the urban mosaic culture concept introduced in Chapter 12).

At the macro level, one can explain movement as a response to a series of *push* and *pull* factors. Changing technology standards of what constitutes a satisfactory group of appointments in the home (appliances, functional layout) provide *push factors* away from the existing inventory. The basic set of facilities found in

the home has changed dramatically since 1940 when the Census Bureau began gathering detailed household data. Modern kitchens, for example, are a far cry from the spartan appointments of their forebears. A sink, stove, and cupboards used to represent the state-of-the-art appointments. Similarly, the modern master bedroom with a tray ceiling and adjoining bath occupies a more prominent part of the home than in the past, and is often on the main floor. Support systems taken for granted in new middle-income homes today (e.g., air conditioning, a central vacuum, intercom, smoke detector, and security system) were virtually unheard of a few decades ago. In addition, leisure-oriented amenities and storage require considerably more space, such as an atrium, wet bar, deck, swimming pool, tennis court, or larger garage space. These facilities discriminate against the existing stock in favor of newer units.

An aggressive home construction industry, which produced homes at a rapid pace in desirable suburban settings in the post-World War II era, reinforced the movement trend by providing an attractive package of *pull factors*. Liberal finance terms and growing incomes encouraged families to move as household needs warranted. Improved transportation facilities in outlying areas and the association of the outer city with the good life, frequently patterned after the western suburban ethic (pool, paddock, and patio), fueled this decentralization process. Potential savings in property tax obligations (lower rates) and the prospect of better schools in suburbia reinforced the positive image that the public shared of middle-class movement to newer subdivisions away from the central city.

TABLE 14-1
Accounting for Household Relocation Behavior

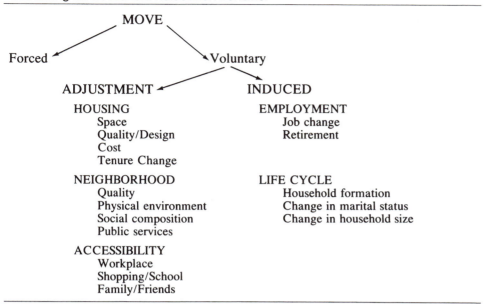

Source: W. A. V. Clark and June Onaka, "Life Cycle and Housing Adjustment as Explanations of Residential Mobility," *Urban Studies*, 20 (1983), 47–57. Reprinted by permission.

Determining the underlying behavioral processes associated with intraurban migration necessitates that researchers focus on individual decision making. Housing adjustment considerations and life cycle changes have been identified as the most crucial factors in explaining the moving behavior of Americans (Table 14-1).[2] Sociologists have cited family life cycle changes as a critical factor involved in the decision for many decades. Peter Rossi, for example, produced a classic study on the topic, *Why Families Move*, in 1955.[3] Housing adjustment factors, including characteristics of the housing unit, such as space, quality, and cost, and neighborhood characteristics have been cited more recently as even more significant factors in explaining movement than life cycle changes (Table 14-2). Rates of mobility also vary according to location and composition.

The living arrangements of certain types of households are more unstable then others, creating higher rates of residential mobility. A study of mobility in Phoenix differentiated between households with high and low rates of instability and associated mobility rates as follows:

Household Type with High Rates of Instability	Rates of Mobility, 1986–1988 (percent)
Young men (under 40 years)	91
Young childless couples (male under 40)	41
Single parents with children under 18	33
Cohabitators (opposite sex)	46
Nonfamilies (roommates of same sex)	54

Household Types with Low Rates of Instability	
Old women (over 40)	8
Old childless couples (over 40)	11
Old men (over 40)	19
Other families (three generation families, grandparents with grandchildren, and parents with adult children)	15

[2]W. A. V. Clark and J. Onaka, "Life Cycle and Housing Adjustment as Explanations of Residential Mobility," *Urban Studies*, 20 (1983), 47–57.
[3]Peter Rossi, *Why Families Move, Free Press*, New York, 1955.

Source: Patricia Gober, Kevin McHugh, and Neil Reid, "Phoenix in Flux: Household Instability, Residential Mobility, and Neighborhood Change," *Annals* of the Association of American Geographers, 61 (1991), 82.

TABLE 14-2
Reasons for Moving

Reason	Percentage
Adjustment Moves	52
Housing characteristics	41
Space	13
Quality/design	11
Cost	7
Tenure change	11
Neighborhood characteristics	7
Neighborhood quality	5
Physical environment	1
Social composition	1
Public service	1
Accessibility	4
Workplace	3
Family/friends	1
Induced Moves	30
Life-cycle change	26
Employment	4
Forced Moves	5
Other Moves	4
Total	≈100

Source: W. A. V. Clark and June Onaka, "Life Cycle and Housing Adjustment as Explanations of Residential Mobility," *Urban Studies,* 20 (1983), 47–57. Reprinted by permission.

Changes in living arrangements by these different types of households do not occur solely as a result of life cycle changes. This has led researchers to introduce the term *life course* to supplement the life cycle conceptualization. The life course stages include more broadly defined stages than life cycle groupings, such as childhood, young adulthood, middle age, later maturity, and old age (Figure 14-2). Within a particular life cycle stage, for example, household turnover rates might be high or low, depending on household composition. Households composed of young adult men, for example, have very low survival rates, but those composed of older women are much longer in duration.

Housing Adjustment Factors

By far, characteristics of the housing unit itself play the most important role in explaining movement. Typically, an individual chooses to substitute a new residence for the old one because it more closely satisfies space needs. As shown in Table 14-2, space is an important factor for 13 percent of movers, and for 11 percent of movers the quality/design of the unit is a reason cited for moving. As Americans began spending more time with family in recent years, often referred to as "cocooning," the use of home spaces changed. Demands for more informal "family room" space, larger kitchens, more bathrooms, and designs promoting better flow patterns for entertaining received greater priority. More recently, households have expressed preferences for media centers, plant rooms, and workshops in their homes. While some households "add on" a room or two to accommodate these needs, most households continue to move to provide for these needs.

Another cluster of moves can be explained by tenure changes, especially the shift from renter to owner status. While the rapid rise in the cost of housing has been cited as a factor limiting home ownership rates, with the greater variety of "starter" housing on the market today and the larger number of "two-worker" households, the demand for homes by first-time buyers remains strong. The availability of developer financing and creative loan packages assist this ownership trend.

Neighborhood characteristics, such as the quality of the community, are factors in household movement, but are not nearly as important as the characteristics of the housing unit itself (Table 14-2). Another overrated factor in explaining movement is the notion of *accessibility.* Access to the workplace is a factor for only 3–5 percent of all moves. Generally, households are willing to substitute longer work trips to gain access to houses with more amenities and less cost farther from the workplace. The distance urban residents are willing to travel to work has an upper limit, of course, and that limit generally increases with city size. Within certain travel time parameters, an *indifference zone* of travel exists for many urbanites.[4] In larger metropolitan areas, this indifference zone may peak at 30 minutes or 60 minutes travel time, whereas in a smaller community, 20 minutes may be a critical travel time. In parts of southern California commuting times are now counted in terms of hours in order to find affordable housing, but this is the exception (see Chapter 19).

Induced Moves

Moves due to life cycle changes and employment changes (retirement, job change) generally fall in the

---

[4]Clark and Onaka, "Life Cycle and Housing Adjustment," p. 48.

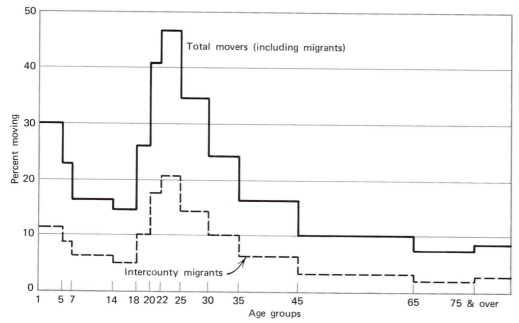

Figure 14-2. Rates of Mobility by Age. Lifecourse stages help account for varying rates of mobility. Generally, the highest rates of mobility are between ages of 18 and 35 years, and the lowest among the elderly. *Source:* Eric Moore, *Residential Mobility in the City* (Washington, D.C.: Association of American Geographers, Resource Papers for College Geography, #1), 1972, 11. Reprinted by permission.

category of induced moves (Table 14-1). A study in a small urban county in Wisconsin revealed many details of the movement process in the life cycle tradition. The study identified nine life cycle categories, each of which characterized distinct household needs and propensities to move.[5] A unique combination of marital status types and the presence or absence of dependent children distinguished each category. These stages are indicated in Table 14-3.

The first group contained young single-person households, typically apartment dwellers. The second stage identified young, childless, married couples with no dependents, sometimes referred to as being in the household-forming phase of life. The three middle categories (3, 4, and 5) involved married couples with children. Distinctions among these categories focused on the age of the children and the husband and reflect the *childbearing, child-raising,* and *child-launching* phases of family life, respectively. The preteen, teen, and young adult breaking points incorporated by these stages correspond to critical periods of household space needs.

Overall, family household needs in the Wisconsin study changed dramatically in the early movement stages, with mobility rates being highest in stages 1–3, then declining gradually through stage 5 (see Figure 14-1). Over two-thirds of the households in stage 1 had moved in the preceding year and 94 percent had moved in the past five years. The rates for renters for both the preceding one-year and five-year periods were generally higher than for owner households.

Normally, the 22 to 25-year-old category exhibits the highest rate of movement (Table 14-3). The high proportion of young adults living in rental accommodations at this age contributes to this elevated rate. A study of movers in Seattle, for example, indicated that renters had mobility rates 7–10 times as high as owners. Inner-city and nonwhite urban residents are generally associated with higher than average rates of rental occupancy and higher turnover rates. Other studies indicate that city homebuyers are more likely to move than their suburban counterparts because the former are younger and in the formative years at building a career.[6] Suburban buyers, in contrast, typically have school-age children and are "moving up" in the ownership market. Among the households less likely to move are single-parent households (because of ties to daycare), two-worker households, and working-class households.

[5]Kevin McCarthy, "The Household Life Cycle and Housing Choices," *Papers and Proceedings of the Regional Science Association*, 37 (1976), 55–80.

[6]David Varady, "The Impact of City/Suburban Location on Moving Plans: A Cincinnati Study," *Growth and Change*, 20 (1989), 35–49.

TABLE 14-3
A Life-Cycle Classification of Households[a]

Stage in Life Cycle	Definition
1. Young single head, no children	Household headed by single adult (man or woman) under 46 years old, no members under 18 years old.
2. Young couple, no children	Household headed by married couple, husband under 46 years old, no other members under 18 years old.
3. Young couple, young children	Household headed by married couple, husband under 46 years old, at least one other member under 6 years old.
4. Young couple, older children	Household headed by married couple, husband under 46 years old, at least one other member between 6 and 18 years old.
5. Older couple, older children	Household headed by married couple, husband at least 46 years old, at least one other member under 18 years old.
6. Older couple, no children	Household headed by married couple, husband at least 46 years old, no other members under 18 years old.
7. Older single head, no children	Household headed by single person (man or woman) at least 46 years old, no members under 18 years old.
8. Single head with children	Household headed by single person (man or woman) under 60 years old, at least one other member under 18 years old.
9. All other	Residual category; most are households headed by single persons over 60 years old who live with married children and grandchildren.

[a]Based on a household survey in Green Bay, Wisconsin.

Note: Household heads are designated by survey respondents. A married couple consists of a cohabiting man and woman. A single household head may have never married, or may have been married but was separated, divorced, or widowed at the time of the interview. Other household members need not be but usually are related to the household head(s); those under 18 are usually children of the head(s).

Source: Kevin McCarthy, "The Household Life Cycle and Housing Choices," *Papers and Proceedings of the Regional Science Association,* 37 (1976), 58.

Families typically reach an ebb in mobility rates at middle age. As grown children leave the household, space needs do not pose as great an issue. For example, an average of only 1 percent of the households in the Wisconsin study in stage 5 moved during the preceding year and only 15 percent during the preceding 5 years. (see Table 14-3).

Older households with no children at home exhibit slightly higher movement levels than those of the same age with children because of reduced space requirements that accompany the *empty nester* situation and the increased freedom that accompanies retirement. The upward trend of the movement rates in categories 6–8 in Table 14-3 confirms this flexibility.

Annual Rates of Movement

Over a five-year period, up to 80 percent of the population moves, creating considerable neighborhood turnover. It is also significant to note that while some families rarely move, others move continuously, keeping the average very high. About one-fifth of the households are thought to account for most of this activity.

Satisfaction and Movement

Variable movement probabilities, mainly associated with marriage and childrearing, involve a physical need for more space. Psychological factors are also involved. The desire to stay with the family's social class, other members of which are also moving, may form the basis for added pressure to move. The concept of *stress* captures the complexity of movement, incorporating both space and psychological factors. In this context, the decision process to relocate to a new residence is a very subjective undertaking involving the evaluation of many intangible factors. Often, the decision to relocate itself is more stressful than the choice or selection process in seeking a new residence.

Negative feelings about the present dwelling and positive expectations of a new residence reinforce the tendency to choose in favor of relocation. This is a classic illustration of a *push–pull factor* mentioned earlier. Frequently, not all factors indicate that a move is appropriate. Compromises often occur. Resistance to movement depends on how long the family has lived at its present address, its income, tenure status, and the strength of social ties. Once a decision to move has been made, an evaluation of the new housing unit and its neighborhood must be made.

Overcoming Inertia

The longer a family has lived in a place, the greater is the *inertial force* to remain there. Renters are more likely to move than owners because a weaker level of commitment or attachment to a place often accompanies such a lifestyle. In contrast, home ownership is typically associated with long-term responsibility. The formalities brought by mortgages and house closings tend to stabilize household movement, but increasingly flexible finance terms and comprehensive realtor services have made home ownership transfers easier and resales more routine in recent decades.

Neighborhood ties similarly serve to restrain movement but not as much as with previous generations. The poor and elderly often have stronger place ties than the middle class. Middle-class neighboring is frequently not oriented as much to the local physical community (place ties) as to dispersed locations throughout the city, which are based on work, social, and recreation networks. A distinction can thus be made between *place neighborhoods* and *social neighborhoods* for the middle class. Moves do not interrupt the latter network, removing a barrier found in lower-income neighborhoods, whose residents derive a greater share of their ties from the local community.

Negative perceptions of the neighborhood often influence the desire to move (recall discussion in Chapter 10), but dissatisfaction with the home is generally a more volatile factor than the neighborhood in inducing a move. A location near an expressway, arterial, or commercial zone where noise and light intrusions are problems illustrates the impact of environmental factors in encouraging movement.

Utility Surface

In a three-dimensional context, the movement process can be viewed as an attempt to increase one's level of satisfaction by substituting a new residence for an old one, thus permitting the family to obtain a higher position on the plane (Figure 14-3). The phrase *surface of expressed utility* can be used to describe one's position on this plane. The changing of residences essentially becomes an adjustment process in this context, involving the substitution of a new house for the old.

Middle-class families are often thought to be best able to improve their surface position because of the large number of options open to them, both locationally and economically. The poor, on the other hand, have fewer housing opportunities because of financial, locational, and informational constraints. The latter problem results from a more cramped view of the city (less familiarity and more restricted mental map), greater

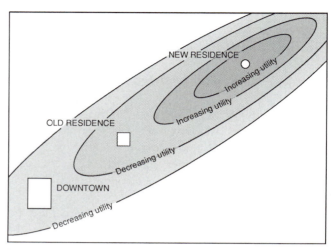

Figure 14-3. Surface of Expressed Utility. In a three-dimensional context, the movement process can be viewed as an attempt to increase one's level of satisfaction by substituting a new residence for an old one, thus permitting the family to obtain a higher position on the plane.

dependence on public transit, and greater social ties to the existing community.

The upper class often has the least flexible housing choices because of locational ties and a more limited inventory selection. The high-income group may have both social and employment ties with the downtown. Owing to its support of the arts and cultural activities, many evenings and weekends are spent downtown, in addition to daily work. Moving outward often conflicts with this attachment.

Fewer new units are being built for the high-income group, further constraining their movement options. In a Seattle study, movement rates were one-third as high for the high-income group as for the rest of the population. An inner-city high-income housing option (e.g., high-rise apartments and condominiums) is now growing in many larger cities to accommodate the affluent. Such prestige housing opportunities are expected to increase in the future, but their appeal is highly selective and involves an abrupt departure from the more general outward movement trend.

SPATIAL STRUCTURE OF MOVES

Several independent spatial dimensions create the geographic pattern of moves in the city, including distinctive distance, direction, and sectoral qualities of the process. Middle-class moves have been studied most thoroughly in this context because the flow is the largest and has made the biggest imprint on the city.

Length of Moves—Distance Bias

Most intraurban moves are *short*. Studies indicate that the vast majority of moves are less than 5 miles in length. This means that most residential shifts are within the same census tract or at most to adjacent tracts and certainly within the same socioeconomic milieu. A Seattle study indicated that the average length of a move fell under 3 miles and that fully 16 percent of the relocations involved shifts less than 0.5 mile in length. In black communities, the average distance was 1.2 miles and one-third of the activity involved moves within 0.5 mile.[7] A factor constraining the length of moves was the shortage of housing within the financial range of the family, a big problem for a large share of inner-city residents.

The area of the city with which a family is acquainted obviously tempers movement, and new homes are mainly secured in these areas. The lack of knowledge of distant neighborhoods obviously conditions the decision in favor of a nearby location, and so clustering of moves near the old residence is therefore expected. Real estate agents generally have a similar distance bias that reinforces this localization, for they typically specialize in one area and recommend houses with which they are most knowledgeable. Even real estate companies participating in comprehensive metropolitan listing services and having many branch offices show this bias. The agent, rather than the company, is usually the source of advice to the prospective buyer.

Movement is partially a decentralization process. But people do not jump from the central city to the outer suburbs in one long-distance shift; several short moves typically precede the trek to the suburban fringes. This process has appropriately been likened to a game of musical chairs. The analogy is appealing because it conjures up the local territory within which the move is exercised, its repetitive and rotational nature, as well as the fact that it is not occurring in isolation but is part of a larger chain of moves (recall the discussion of *vacancy chains* in Chapter 12).

Directional Bias

Directionally, moves are rarely random. The orientation of the move typically points outward rather than inward or laterally, considering the relationship of the new residence to the old home and the CBD. The rationale for this situation is that housing with the space and style (age, layout) frequently demanded by the growing middle-class family is most likely to be available farther from the city center. Recall that the social area analysis discussion in Chapter 12 indicated that older housing on smaller lots would be found closer in, and newer upscale housing farther out. A lateral move would not be preferred because housing similar to that being vacated by the family would be encountered. Consider this explanation:

> For a household living between the downtown and the suburbs, housing toward the downtown was older, cheaper, and cramped, but if they move outward, this would mean a newer house, bigger yard, and more room. As people moved up in the world they typically moved outward in short jumps. . . . Lateral moves are uncommon because housing in the same residential ring is similar to what is already occupied.[8]

Household Behavior Spaces

Daily movement behavior patterns also reinforce the directional bias of moves. A household operates within a so-called *activity space*, which is the territory within which daily movement takes place. The shape of the space is irregular but consistent with behavioral patterns. The extremities are normally the place of residence and the work and shopping place of the household. Within this region, most of the family's daily affairs are conducted. This area, in turn, comprises a portion of the *action space* of the family.

Action space is a concept that refers to those parts of the city about which the individual is familiar and includes a subjective evaluation of those places. In the case of a small city, one might participate in a large part of it, but as a general rule, citizens are involved regularly only with their immediate subdivision, perhaps the downtown, and one or two other major activity areas, such as the workplace, suburban downtown, or a recreation area (amusement park, stadium). In a large metropolitan area, this territory will likely be confined to one sector of the city, a so-called *urban realm*.

---

[7]Ronald R. Boyce, "Residential Mobility and Its Implications for Urban Spatial Change," *Proceedings of the Association of American Geographers*, 1 (1969), 22–26.

[8]Ronald Abler, John Adams, and Peter Gould, *Spatial Organization: The Geographer's View of the World*, Prentice-Hall, Englewood Cliffs, N.J., 1971.

Since one's action space also includes an evaluation component (level of satisfaction), it can be expressed three dimensionally. Such a surface portrays the intensity of the attachment one has to the particular area. The longer an individual lives in a city or neighborhood, the larger the action space and the greater the differentiation that an individual perceives among its various components in terms of satisfaction (Figure 14-4). New areas are assimilated as information and travel expand. The action spaces of families in a given neighborhood are often quite similar. Shared images, produced by social contact and similar lifestyles, tend to overlap among local residents. The moving process itself often may lead to an extension of the range of the family's activity space and the more extensive action space.

Measuring Directional Bias

The angle of the movement to a new location in relation to the old home can be measured to verify the direc-

tional bias tendency, as shown in Figure 14-5, based on its orientation with the CBD. Angles of less than 90 degrees indicate movement closer to the city center and those greater than 90 degrees indicate relocation farther out, assuming that the axis of movement is oriented along a line connecting the CBD with the old location. Most middle-class moves involve relatively high angles, verifying the outward tendency.

The prevailing outward movement of middle-class

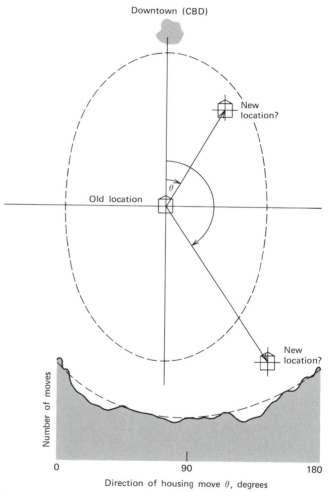

Figure 14-5. Model of Directional Bias in the Search Behavior for Urban Housing. The angle of movement to a new location in relation to the old home can be measured to verify the directional bias tendency, based on its orientation to the CBD. Angles of less than 90 degrees indicate movement closer to the city center, and those greater than 90 degrees indicate relocation farther out when the axis of movement is oriented along a line connecting the CBD with the old location. Most middle-class moves involve relatively high angles, verifying the outward tendency. *Source:* Redrawn with permission. From Ronald Abler, John S. Adams, and Peter Gould, *Spatial Organization: The Geographer's View of the World*, Prentice Hall, Englewood Cliffs, N.J., 1971, p. 501.

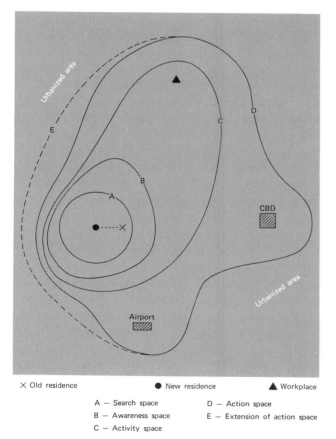

X Old residence	● New residence	▲ Workplace

A — Search space   D — Action space
B — Awareness space   E — Extension of action space
C — Activity space

Figure 14-4. Household Behavior Space for Typical Migrating Suburban Family. The search space for a new home (*A*) is typically centered on the new residence, but well within the awareness space (*B*) of the household. The larger activity space of the household also includes the workplace. Note that the household did not move closer to the workplace, but farther from it in relation to the CBD.

households, previously described in terms of a directional bias, and the general confinement of these moves to the sector location of the old residence create an *elliptical pattern* of movement. This elliptical shape results from enclosing the space composed of the CBD, the old residence, and the new residence for several households (Figure 14-6A). An understanding of social area analysis and the configuration of household behavior spaces (awareness of space, search space, etc.) help to explain this movement process.

The primary exception to the elliptical-shaped movement configuration occurs in the inner city, which has an alternative circular pattern (Figure 14-6B). Moves in that area show a more scrambled pattern because lateral moves as well as inward and outward movement occurs. This often involves cross-CBD shifts, which rarely occur elsewhere. The reasons for this complex pattern are that fewer options are typically available to households in inner-city areas in terms of unit availability and personal mobility is more restricted because of the greater reliance on public transportation.

The lower-income family, the main contributor to the inner-city flow, has fewer resources available in terms of finances, information, and transportation. The

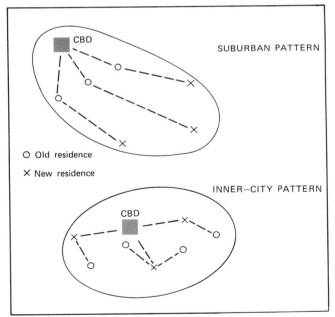

Figure 14-6. Contrasting Suburban and Inner-city Movement Patterns. The prevailing outward shift of the suburban middle-class household creates an elliptical pattern of movement. Inner-city movement patterns show a more scrambled circular pattern due to fewer options.

housing supply is also frequently much smaller than the demand (and declining) in such areas. A majority of the moves involve renters, and the preferred choice of a residence that has the desired setting and space may not be readily available, thus creating a more confused pattern.

Inner-city moves frequently involve minority households, and the restricted territorial nature of a segregated housing market (especially for blacks) must also be considered. The location and availability of public housing are factors for many movers. The prospective housing unit may also have to meet federal standards and be prequalified to be a viable alternative for families receiving housing allowances.

Forced movement rates are also higher in the inner city. When this movement is combined with voluntary shifts, excessive pressure can be placed on the housing stock, resulting in overcrowding and escalation in rental rates.

Removals from the stock are highest in the inner city. These removals result from clearance programs related to new construction, highway building, and simply physical obsolescence of structures. Enforcement of housing code guidelines designed to ensure minimum standards of health and safety or to reduce overcrowding can be counterproductive in such areas. Instead of upgrading property, such programs can result in increased demolition rates, creating more pressure on the remaining inventory. If property owners choose not to invest in housing renovation in such neighborhoods, whole blocks of housing can be condemned and removed from the inventory.

Forced movement among residents in the Atlanta model city neighborhood (Figure 14-7), resulting from urban renewal and code enforcement programs, graphically portrays this directional process. In the late 1960s, these moves occurred predominantly within a two-mile distance ring, with most involving shifts within the same census tract. Moves outside the two-mile ring were the most directionally biased, conforming to the context of the black residential space of the city (to the east, south, and west), as shown in Figure 14-9. Many moves involved shifts to public housing, further restricting the spatial choices.[9] Since those families moving in the two-mile ring remained predominantly within the low-quality housing model neighborhood area, few housing improvements accompanied

_____
[9]Mover households were usually restricted to the newer public housing developments due to a lack of vacancies in older projects.

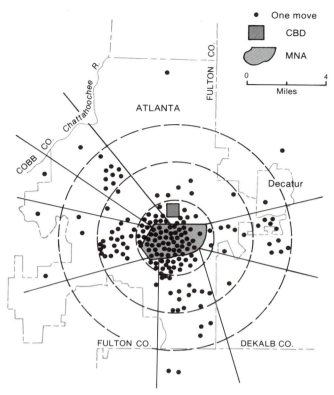

Figure 14-7. Moves by Atlanta Model Neighborhood Area (MNA) Residents. Forced moves due to urban renewal and code enforcement programs in the inner city create much pressure on other units in the vicinity. Due to transportation, economic, and informational constraints, most movers in the Atlanta MNA area remained in the low-quality housing area in a two-mile radius. *Source: Essays on the Human Geography of the Southeastern United States*, West Georgia College, *Studies in the Social Sciences*, vol. 16. Copyright © 1977, West Georgia College. Reprinted with permission.

the movement. "They were generally faced with housing conditions similar to those they had left; these conditions included very low value units, a high degree of substandardness, and overcrowding."[10]

Sectoral Bias

In addition to the distance and directional bias, a third independent *sectoral bias* also exists (Figure 14-8). The sectoral bias refers to the prevailing tendency of movers to stay in the same socioeconomic setting. Movers typically stay in the same wedge of the city when moving in relation to the CBD (recall the sector

[10]Frank V. Keller, Sanford H. Bederman, and Truman A. Hartshorn, "Migration Patterns of Atlanta's Inner City Displaced Residents," *Studies in the Social Sciences* (West Georgia College), 16 (1977), 52.

model discussed in Chapter 11), which maximizes the possibility of patronizing the same infrastructure of services (shopping centers, churches, etc.) as before. For example, residents in the southeast sector of Syracuse, New York, may be expected to stay on that side of the city when moving. Figure 14-8 indicates the context of the sectoral bias in relation to the existing housing stock of the city. The rings refer to uniform housing stock areas, the sectors to homogeneous socioeconomic zones, and the arrows to the prevailing direction of moves.

SELECTING A LOCATION

A study of how decisions are made at the individual household level reveals the location decision process that families undertake. Movers are generally described as being dissatisfied with their present situation. The most stressed households are those that think moving will be easy and are very dissatisfied with their present location. The size and facilities of the dwelling unit usually cause the most stress. Many of the initial decisions are therefore made on the basis of discussions of family needs, tastes, and preferences. These discussions mainly occur prior to physically looking at homes themselves. Residential preference discussions might incorporate thought about the house as well as its location. The proximity of schools, churches, shopping centers, and workplace receives attention, as do architecture preference, lot size, appearance, internal space configuration, square footage, conveniences offered (appliances, baths, heating), and price (see Table 14-2).

Housing Preferences

A low priority is often assigned to distance as a locational factor in selecting a residence. In terms of preferences, the size of lot and the vertical floor arrangement of the house appear to be more important than the age of the house or the neighborhood. The school system and recreational facilities also appear to be more important than other factors that are rated more indifferently, such as the friendliness of neighbors, the appearance of the neighborhood, or the availability of public services.

Space dimensions of the potential home are considered to be very important. Households typically seek

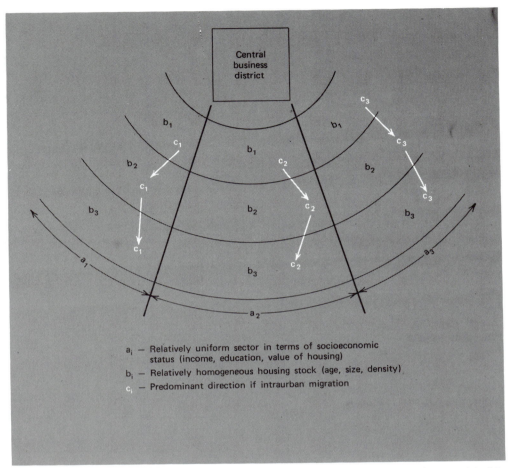

Figure 14-8. Sectoral Bias of Movers. Most movers stay within the same socioeconomic sector (*a*) of the city. They move predominantly to another ring (*b*) farther from the CBD (*c*).

more space or better quality housing (Table 14-4). These findings are consistent with the adjustment factors (space, design) and inducement factors (life cycle change) discussed earlier.

Stress–Strain Model

Several distinctive steps or stages characterize the decision to relocate. First, *household needs and expectations* must be considered, including an evaluation of the present home and environment. A choice to stay or move results from this step. The second stage (assuming the household will move) is an *active search*, which involves gathering data on alternatives and actual home inspection and selection.

Individual movement can be assessed in terms of *place utility*. This concept refers to the level of satisfaction or displeasure that a family associates with a

particular residence or location. Presumably the household moves to increase its *place utility* level, after a threshold of dissatisfaction with the present (or former) location is reached. A model of the process of location decision appears in Figure 14-9. The diagram illustrates the contribution of internal forces (household needs and expectations) and external factors (neighborhood environment, etc.) to a determination of place utility. Behavioral stress and strain factors are introduced in the model to capture evaluative procedures that families must make in regard to both advantages and disadvantages of a move. Disruption of established behavior patterns is inevitable with a move and can serve to deter or postpone such a decision.

Not all stressful circumstances result in moves because households can adjust their needs and/or modify the home environment to mitigate the problem. For example, household income may decrease when the spouse stops working in order to raise a family. Re-

TABLE 14-4
Primary Reasons for Local Moves[a]

Primary Reason for Moving	Characteristic Responses Included	Response Frequency	
		Number	Percent
Change in family circumstances	Change in marital status; change in family size; establish own household; family or health problem; new job; job search; attend school.	4285	26.8
Wanted cheaper housing	Wanted lower rent, cheaper place to live.	1033	6.5
Wanted change in tenure or structure type	Wanted to own; wanted to rent; wanted single-family house.	3114	19.5
Wanted change in space or quality	Wanted larger or smaller unit; larger rooms; specific floor plan; nicer, cleaner place; better quality.	3784	23.6
Wanted more convenient location	Wanted to be closer to work, schools, retail stores.	756	4.7
Wanted better neighborhood	Wanted quieter neighbors, friendlier neighbors, more neighboring children, nicer neighborhoods, safer area, more open space, more trees and yards.	1538	9.6
Had to leave former residence	Residence no longer available; problems with landlord.	1494	9.3

[a]Based on data gathered in Brown County, Wisconsin.
Source: Kevin McCarthy, "The Household Life Cycle and Housing Choices," *Papers and Proceedings of the Regional Science Association,* 37 (1976), 73.

duced income, together with a potential need for more living space with an expanding family, can lead to financial problems. Rather than seek a new residence, the family can decrease its consumption and spending and convert existing space to more important needs rather than seek a new residence.

Search Space

When the decision to seek a new residence is made, an active *search* begins. Normally this search takes less time than the thought process leading up to it. Most people "spend longer, on the average, in *deciding* to look for new housing than they do in actually inspecting and choosing it. The median length of thought before starting an active search in our whole sample is over two months, while the search itself is typically less than one month."[11] Research in Toronto confirmed that the length of the search period depended on the type and location of housing sought. Apartment hunters in the suburbs, for example, took less time than those house hunting, whether in the suburbs or downtown (Table 14-5). About half of the house hunters took less than a month in locating a home, while over two-thirds

of the apartment movers made the decision within a month.

Phase II of the location decision process, the *relocation decision,* shown in Figure 14-9, spells out the various stages in the relocation choice process. First, information sources must be sought and evaluated. The biggest source of information on alternative housing is the mental map one has of the existing housing stock in the neighborhood. For example, a family's *awareness space* (see Figure 14-4) indicates the spatial extent of the territory on which a family has information concerning housing opportunities. Obviously, this area is conditioned by the household's action space. The family's circle of acquaintances as well as work trip and discretionary travel patterns (social trips, shopping trips, etc.) influences the extent of this awareness area. Within the awareness space is a *search space.* Vacancies considered by a household will most likely be in the most desirable portion of this search space, usually farther from the center of the city than the existing home (see Figure 14-4). The shape of the search space is normally circular, but it is not clear whether it is typically centered on the old or new residence.

Households also obtain data from institutional sources (mass media, realtors), but their own personal experiences are the most important. Personal contact with realtors frequently produces more usable data than newspaper ads because personal discussion allows

[11]William Michelson, *Environmental Choice, Human Behavior, and Residential Satisfaction,* Oxford University Press, New York, 1977, p. 97.

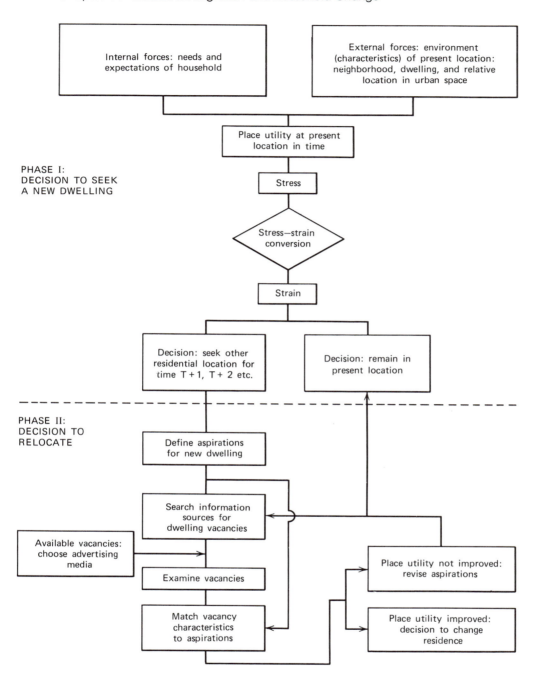

PHASE I:
DECISION TO SEEK
A NEW DWELLING

PHASE II:
DECISION TO
RELOCATE

Figure 14-9. Model of Residential Location Decision Process. Phase I of the decision process involves deciding whether or not to seek a new residence by assessing internal and external factors related to satisfaction (place utility) with the current dwelling. Phase II involves evaluation of the new residence if the decision is to relocate. *Source:* Redrawn with permission. From *Geografiska Annaler*, Series B, Vol. 52B, No. 1, 1970, "The Intra-urban Migration Process: A Perspective," Lawrence A. Brown and Eric Moore, 1–13. Swedish Society of Anthropology and Geography, Stockholm.

TABLE 14-5
Search Period, Type of Move

Destination Environment	Length of Search Period	
	One Month or Less (%)	More Than One Month (%)
House in suburbs	46	55
Apartment in suburbs	68	32
House downtown	48	52

Source: William Michelson, *Environmental Choice, Human Behavior, and Residential Satisfaction*, Oxford University Press, New York, 1977. Copyright © 1977 by Oxford University Press, Inc. Reprinted by permission.

questions to be answered and debated with instant feedback. Real estate agents are most important in situations involving moves to single-family homes (Table 14-6). Expertise concerning availability and the neighborhood is underscored by the analogy that the realtor is, in effect, a "geography teacher" for the house hunter.[12]

The biggest data source for suburban moves is simply *driving around*. Friends and relatives and a builder's reputation are clearly secondary sources of information, as shown in Table 14-6. Situations where the newspaper appears most influential involve moves to apartments and to a house downtown. But even in the case of suburban moves, nearly 60 percent of the households consulted newspapers in the Toronto study.

Most metropolitan newspapers list houses by location to assist the search process. They also provide considerable *social cue* information in individual want ads. In many instances, more social and lifestyle

information on potential houses is provided than economic or architectural data. Several phrases touting the virtues of homes in the Atlanta market taken from a single Sunday's newspaper want ad listings are shown in Table 14-7. The emphasis on nature, leisure, and amenities in marketing homes is readily apparant from the leads: "Rustic," "High on a Hilltop," "Spoil yourself," "Your ship comes in," "Sit and sip and watch the golfers."

By generalizing the search behaviors of a sample of metropolitan Toronto residents, one researcher has developed an *index of search intensity* incorporating the length of the search time and the number of houses examined.[13] The majority of house hunters looked at only a few houses. Research in Cedar Rapids, Iowa, has also indicated that few families actually look at more than one house during the search.[14] Another study found that 40 percent of intraneighborhood movers "did not look even casually at more than one unit before moving."[15] These findings suggest that families apparently exercise considerable *mental screening* of homes prior to actually looking at them, and the overall familiarity with the area assists in early stages of the process.

Most movers are satisfied with their selections, indicating that they do find what they are looking for. But city movers, as opposed to suburban ones, may not be as well satisfied. This occurs because more risk may be involved in such moves because of the potential for more environmental and other conflict problems (recall discussion in Chapter 12).

[12]Risa Palm, "The Role of Real Estate Agents as Information Mediators in Two American Cities," *Geografiska Annaler*, 58 B (1976), 34–35.

[13]Frank Barrett, "The Search Process in Residential Relocation," *Environment and Behavior*, 8 (1976), 169–198.

[14]Lawrence Brown and John Holmes, "Search Behavior in an Intra-urban Migration Context: A Spatial Perspective," *Environment and Planning*, 3 (1971), 307–326.

[15]Edgar Butler et al., *Moving Behavior and Residential Choice: A National Survey*, Report 81, Highway Research Board, Washington, D.C., 1969.

TABLE 14-6
All Sources Consulted[a] in Finding Housing (Percentage)

Type of Housing	Newspaper	Friends	Real Estate Agents	Relatives	Driving Around	Builder's Reputation
House in suburbs	58	27	62	15	77	12
Apartment in suburbs	71	23	13	10	56	1
House downtown	70	34	95	10	54	5

[a]More than one answer permitted.

Source: William Michelson, *Environmental Choice, Human Behavior, and Residential Satisfaction*, Oxford University Press, New York, 1977. Copyright © 1977 by Oxford University Press, Inc. Reprinted by permission.

TABLE 14-7
Social Cues Found in Newspaper Ads to Aid
in Home Selection[a]

Paradise in the woods	Imagine yourself
Home for pro	Love entertaining?
Rustic	Golf club
High on a hilltop	Country club gem
Rated "X" excellent	Dogs n' children
Often admired	Horse lovers
Too good to be true	Equestrian park
Cream puff	Nature whispers
Teens or tots	Soaring trees
Walk to pool	Looking for privacy
You too can live on the river	Plant your garden
Special and private	Heart of horse country
Quiet	Heated pool
Picturesque beauty	Parents happy
Consider the pool yours	Elegance in European manner
Swim-tennis buffs	Tennis and garden party
Azaleas	Vacation at home
Executive home	Terraced garden
Private fenced back yard	Secluded acre
Young executives	Club estates
Utmost in privacy	Follow the winding drive
You've just found it	Your ship comes in
Spoil yourself	Sit and sip and watch the golfers
Want life of leisure?	

[a] Phrases selected from home want ads, *Atlanta Journal Constitution,*
Sunday, May 1, 1977.

Compromise and Adjustment

While it appears that the search behavior, in terms of
actual house visits, is a shallow process, considerable
research and knowledge are accumulated prior to physically visiting houses. Apparently, searching involves
both *space covering* and *space organizing* steps.[16] The
former refers to casting a wide net concerning alternative options in the area. Much of this can be done
mentally. The second stage, space organizing, refers to
a concentrated effort in a relatively confined search
space. "When this stage occurs, the searcher alters his
behavior to a highly concentrated pattern and the
general probing patterns cease."[17]

Compromises usually occur at some stage in the
decision process, arising in response to time pressures,
diversities of opinion in a family, or failure to find
acceptable alternatives. Husband and wife preferences
and priorities, for example, differ relatively frequently.
In a Toronto study a high degree of agreement between
spouses existed on the size and layout of the proposed
home, the number of bathrooms and bedrooms, and the
exterior setting.[18] Women seemed to emphasize the
specific facilities in the home, the size of the kitchen,
and such housekeeping factors as noise and dirt. Men
emphasized fiscal matters, access to employment, and
overall floor space.

At any given time, only a limited number of residences are on the market and this may further affect
family decisions by forcing reevaluation of needs.
Decisions often must be made relatively quickly so that
a potentially satisfactory housing alternative will not be
lost to another bidder.

Structure versus Setting Trade-off

In recent years, the housing choices available to middle-class movers have broadened. More options with
respect to structural design and the interior layout of
space have appeared. Flexibility in the organization
and use of private outdoor space (patios, pools, tennis
courts) has increased, along with the selection of
community facilities (day-care centers, playgrounds,
open space). One survey indicated that

> each time the choice involved something nearer or further
> from the structural characteristics of the unit itself, the
> feature closer to the structure was chosen; more indoor
> space preferred over larger private outdoor space (the
> larger dining room was preferred in this instance, even
> though a one-story house and enclosed parking were both
> preferred over the dining room).[19]

The concern is directed predominantly toward the basic
structure itself, rather than to the outdoors or the
community. This suggests that families place greater
emphasis on the unit itself rather than its setting.

Criticism of the Perception Approach

A study of intraurban migration in Milwaukee suggested that exclusive preoccupation on perception as an

---

[16] Peter Gould, *Space Searching Procedures in Geography and the Social
Sciences*, Working Paper Series, No. 1, University of Hawaii Social Science
Research Institute, Honolulu, 1966.

[17] Frank Barrett, "The Search Process." p. 174.

[18] William Michelson, David Beluge, and John Stewart, "Intentions and
Expectations in Differential Residential Selection," *Journal of Marriage*, 35
(1973), 189–196.

[19] Patricia R. Rosenzweig, "Research and the Sensitive Housing Market,"
Urban Land, 35 (April 1976), 16.

explanatory device can be misleading.[20] The author argued that the basic determinants of housing choice were the bread-and-butter issues related to economics and the neighborhood environment. While not denying that attitudes and preferences play a role, this study indicated that knowing family income and housing cost is the most important factor in predicting migration patterns. Once these constraints are known, distance and perception factors then entered the equation to explain movement.

SUMMARY AND CONCLUSION

While household movement is a locational adjustment process, intrinsic to the individual family, distinctive patterns and processes emerge in the aggregate. The choice of new housing is very much tempered by the family's existing location and its network of information about the city. Housing changes involve considerable thought prior to the search process itself. Families are generally satisfied with their moves, but they continue shifting residences with each changing life cycle need. The predominant pattern of moves is outward, with inner-city residents not having as flexible a movement space within which to operate as the middle and upper classes.

Suggestions for Further Reading

Allen, James P. "Changes in the American Propensity to Migrate," *Annals of the Association of American Geographers*, 67 (1977), 577–587.

Apgar, William C., and Henry O. Pollakowski. *Housing Mobility and Choice*, Working Paper W86-6, Joint Center for Housing Studies of MIT and Harvard University, Cambridge, Mass., 1986.

Balan, Jorge. *Why People Move: Comparative Perspectives on the Dynamics of Internal Migration*, UNESCO, Paris, 1981.

Butler, Edgar, et al. *Moving Behavior and Residential Choice: A National Survey*, Report 81, Highway Research Board, Washington, D.C., 1969.

Cadwallader, M. T. "Neighborhood Evaluation in Residential Mobility," *Environment and Planning, A*, 11 (1979), 393–401.

Clark, Gordon, and J. Whiteman. "Why Poor People Do Not Move:

Job Search Behavior and Disequilibrium Amongst Local Markets," *Environment and Planning, A*, 15 (1983), 85–104.

Clark, W. A. V. *Modeling Housing Market Search*, St. Martin's Press, New York, 1982, pp. 209–223.

————. *Human Migration*, Scientific Geography Series, Sage Publications, Beverly Hills, Calif., 1986.

Clark, W. A. V., and June Onaka. "Life Cycle and Housing Adjustment as Explanations of Residential Mobility," *Urban Studies*, 20 (1983), 47–57.

Clark, W. A. V., and T. R. Smith. "Housing Market Search Behavior and Expected Utility Theory: 2. The Process of Search," *Environment and Planning, A*, 14 (1982), 717–737.

Clark, W. A. V., et al. "Housing Consumption and Residential Mobility," *Annals of the Association of American Geographers*, 74 (March 1984), 29–43.

Frey, William H. "Mover Destination Selectivity and the Changing Suburbanization of Metropolitan Whites and Blacks," *Demography* (1985), 223–243.

Frey, William H., and Francis E. Kobrin. "Changing Families and Changing Mobility: Their Impact on the Central City," *Demography*, 19 (1982), 261–277.

Frey, William H., and Alden Speare, Jr. *Regional and Metropolitan Growth and Decline in the United States*, Russell Sage Foundation, New York, 1988.

Gratz, Roberta Brandes. *The Living City*, Simon & Schuster, New York, 1989.

Laska, S., and D. Spain. *Back to the City: Issues in Neighborhood Renovation*, Pergamon, Elmsford, N.Y., 1980.

Long, Larry. *Migration and Residential Mobility in the United States*, Russell Sage Foundation, New York, 1988.

Michelson, William. *Environmental Choice, Human Behavior and Residential Satisfaction*, Oxford University Press, New York, 1977.

Moore, Eric. *Residential Mobility in the City*, Resource Paper No. 13, Association of American Geographers, Commission on College Geography, Washington, D.C., 1972.

Myers, Dowell. *Housing Demography: Linking Demographic Structure and Housing Markets*, University of Wisconsin Press, Madison, 1990.

Roseman, Curtis C. *Changing Migration Patterns within the United States*, Resource Paper 77-2, Association of American Geographers, Washington, D.C., 1977.

Rossi, Peter. *Why Families Move*, Free Press, New York, 1955.

Simmons, J. M. *Patterns of Residential Movement in Metropolitan Toronto*, Research Publication 13, Department of Geography, University of Toronto, Toronto, 1974.

Speare, Alden, Jr., et al. *Residential Mobility, Migration, and Metropolitan Change*, Ballinger, Cambridge, Mass., 1974.

Varaday, David. "Determinants of Residential Mobility Decisions: The Role of Government Services in Relation to Other Factors," *Journal of American Planning Association*, 49 (1983), 184–199.

---

[20]W. A. V. Clark, "Migration in Milwaukee," *Economic Geography*, 52 (1976), 48–60.

15

CENTRAL BUSINESS DISTRICT DYNAMICS

Nowhere in the city are *form* and *function* more interrelated than in the downtown central business district (CBD)—and nowhere are they more charged with meaning. This area contains prime metropolitan real estate, the high value of which necessitates very specialized uses. A large number of high-rise skyscrapers typically occupy its center. The downtown skyline, in fact, becomes the spatial fix around which many Americans base their reference framework for a particular city (see skyline ranking box). The so-called postcard identification of the downtown skyline creates strong images for the visitor, and that perspective is often shared by others familiar with the city, so strong is its mental signature (Figure 15-1). But the role of the downtown greatly transcends its physical structures. The CBD has traditionally symbolized the socioeconomic vitality and strength of the city. The intense levels of personal and professional interaction in a relatively small area create a very dynamic atmosphere. But change is also the norm for the CBD and it has had to cope with many new roles over time.

HISTORICAL EVOLUTION

The center of the city in most large metropolitan areas evolved from a retail–commercial district at the turn of

the century to an office–commercial complex at mid-century, and most recently to a convention–tourist–entertainment center. In smaller cities, the CBD remains largely a retail center, whereas the expansion of service and government employment has diversified the employment mix in larger cities. Change continues, and evidence points to future growth of the CBD in larger metropolitan areas in the area of cultural–entertainment–convention facilities and perhaps more office–commercial activity. Changing occupational structures, ever-changing lifestyle patterns, and continued activity decentralization account for these transitions.

As we mentioned in Chapter 2, the Greek market-place, the *agora*, was the precursor of the modern CBD. The Royal Exchange, established in the 1560s in London, was perhaps the nucleus of the first modern CBD.[1] It specialized in the trade of luxury goods and spices. In early American cities, the market function may have taken place around a central square or park, at the wharves, or interspersed among residences. This lack of specialization in land uses was natural in an era when personal transportation was limited. Frequently, shopkeepers lived upstairs over their businesses or behind them. Land use separations came later with

---

[1]Martin J. Bowden, "Growth of Central Districts in Large Cities," in Leo F. Schnore, ed., *The New Urban History*, Princeton University Press, Princeton, N.J., 1975, pp. 79–80.

DOWNTOWN SKYLINE RANKINGS

A dramatic downtown skyline, measured in terms of the number of tall buildings, generally corresponds to the size of the metropolitan area in which that downtown area is located. Downtown New York (Manhattan) claims the overwhelming lead in skyline ranking, with over 115 buildings exceeding 500 feet in height (over 40 stories) in 1988. Chicago and Houston ranked as second and third, with about 30 tall buildings each. Note that Los Angeles ranks sixth in tall buildings and second in population. This discrepancy can be explained by the traditional dispersed nature of employment in the region and by the fact that tall buildings were discouraged in Los Angeles because of earthquake dangers.

Today, Los Angeles is catching up with other leading cities in its share of tall buildings as building codes and building technologies now permit skyscraper construction, and the demand for high-rise space has accelerated. Houston, Pittsburgh, and Denver have high-profile skylines due to the presence of many banking and energy company headquarters. Other cities that one might expect to find with many high-rise buildings do not rank highly, as they lie in the market shadow of other major centers. Such is the case with Boston and Philadelphia, both in the shadow of New York. Nor do traditional manufacturing centers, such as Cleveland, Baltimore, and Detroit, have high skyline rankings, as their office sector is relatively weak. Tenth-ranking Washington (in terms of population size) is also missing from the list of high-profile skyline cities because of building height restrictions in deference to the national monuments that the city showcases.

Most of the high-profile buildings in cities today have downtown locations, but outlying locations have also become homes for high-rise structures as their office function has matured. Office towers in the 30- to 50-story range now populate many suburban downtowns in larger metropolitan areas (see Figures 9-14 and 17-3).

Source: Real Estate Research Corporation, *Tall Office Buildings in the United States,* The Urban Land Institute, Washington, D.C., 1985.

Skyline Rankings of U.S. Metropolitan Areas, 1988

Metropolitan Area	Number of Tall Buildings	Skyline Rank	1986 Metro Pop. Rank
New York	119	1	1
Chicago	32	2	3
Houston	27	3	8
Dallas	16	4	9
San Francisco	15	5	4
Boston	13	6 (tie)	7
Los Angeles	13	6 (tie)	2
Pittsburgh	8	8 (tie)	15
Seattle	8	8 (tie)	18
Atlanta	7	10 (tie)	13
Philadelphia	7	10 (tie)	5
Minneapolis	6	12 (tie)	16
Denver	6	12 (tie)	22

Source: The World Almanac and Book of Facts, 1988 edition, copyright Pharos Books, 1987, New York, NY 10166.

New York

Toronto

St. Louis

Figure 15-1 Postcard "Fixes" of the Downtown. The postcard identification of the downtown skyline creates a strong image for the visitor, a perspective often shared by others more familiar with the city. The intense levels of personal and professional interaction in a relatively small area create a very dynamic atmosphere in the CBD.

mechanized transportation improvements and industrialization.

In port cities, where merchants dealt with long-distance buyers as well as local customers, wholesale and retail functions became separated first. Merchants (wholesalers), trading with nonlocal customers, congregated near the docks or railroad terminals, whereas local customer-oriented retailers clustered nearer the local residential market as transportation improvements warranted. Custom houses, commodity exchanges, and brokerage activities blossomed near the docks to support the trade function, joined later by financial and legal services. In New York, for example, the original settlement occurred near the docks in lower Manhattan, and a specialized wholesale function gradually expanded in that area, even as the city grew northward. Eventually this area became identified almost exclusively with finance activity, as still reflected by the Wall Street area.

Retail activity gradually emerged along *main street* in most cities nearer residential areas or at rail transportation terminals. Streetcar lines and subways had a big impact on the emergence of these retail districts in the late 1800s, such as the expansion in midtown Manhattan near Grand Central and Penn Stations. Improved access in midtown Manhattan allowed for the development of a mass-appeal shopping district, most prominently symbolized by the department store. Specialty shops, such as apparel and jewelry stores, also congregated in the retail district, taking advantage of opportunities provided by the intense pedestrian traffic. Later, in the early twentieth century, office skyscrapers were assembled around the shopping district, also taking advantage of the accessibility due to the convergence of public transportation routes in the area (see skyscraper evolution box). Similar trends created retail districts in cities throughout the country near the intersections of the main streets.

Location and Size

The central business district is usually located in the oldest part of the city and has usually undergone several periods of redevelopment. In recent decades, demolition in many cities has far outstripped new construction, leaving considerable vacant land and generally decreasing the density of development. In many respects, a present-day cross-section of the skyline is consequently more variable in texture (height) than in earlier times when the area was more evenly and continuously built up. Building sites may not be redeveloped following demolition, and "interim" parking lots can become permanent features. Pressure for redevelopment, together with tearing down structures to save on tax assessments, threatens the oldest and most historic CBD buildings.

In the 1980s, new downtown construction outpaced that of earlier decades even in sunbelt cities that historically never had strong business cores. This activity intensified the demolition threat facing older struc-

tures. As in earlier eras, the CBD typically grew toward the higher-income side of the region and discarded space on the opposite side of the city.

The intensity of CBD uses traditionally depended on the era in which the city developed. Older, nineteenth-century cities typically displayed very high density CBD core areas, whereas those that developed after the turn of the century emerged with lower land use densities. Compare the two CBDs shown in Figure 15-2, which contrast the high-intensity land use in the Montreal CBD with the less intense San Diego downtown. Note the greater quantity of land devoted to street-level parking in the latter city. But as mentioned earlier, a convergence in CBD land use intensities may now be occurring in the late twentieth century. Downtown Los Angeles, Houston, and Dallas, among the largest sunbelt cities with traditionally weak downtowns, now boast robust CBD cores as a result of recent office and hotel construction, and San Diego has also added considerable commercial space in its core area in the past 25 years.

Centrality

The singular advantage of the CBD has been its *centrality*. The convergence of transportation lines in the area and the many activities that have evolved in response traditionally made the CBD the center of action and prestige, as exemplified in the saying "all roads lead downtown." Large numbers of working people and visitors have traditionally moved in and out of the downtown each day, and very strong relations, or linkages, developed among the multitude of activities located there. Over time, the downtown evolved into a highly refined business and service center machine with a very specialized white-collar work force supported and aided by a large unskilled or semiskilled group. It also became the government center, the tourist center, and the sports center of the metropolis. This relationship between accessibility and intensity of activity was discussed in Chapter 9 as a major determinant in urban form.

Daytime–Nighttime Contrasts

There are great contrasts between day and night in the downtown in American cities as a result of its specialized function. Most activity takes place during weekday business hours, except for the conventions, enter-

Today we take the skyscraper for granted, but it did not assume its present form without considerable experimentation and controversy over the past century. The office skyscraper is a relatively new building form. "The skyscraper is both quintessentially American and quintessentially of the twentieth century."[1] Today's skyscraper grew out of experiments in New York and Chicago, where there was money to invest in new designs and demand for more space as the white-collar revolution unfolded. Several technological revolutions in building technique also contributed to the process: the electric elevator, and the iron and steel frame.

Prior to the 1880s, buildings generally were limited to 10 stories by the available elevator technology and the massive walls required by masonry construction. Some taller structures did exist, but they were ceremonial towers or church spires. The Cologne Cathedral, for example, was the tallest structure in the world prior to the Eiffel Tower, which was built for the Paris World's Fair in 1895 and which used a bridge technology placed on end.

The experimentation in new building design that occurred in the late nineteenth century took many forms, but the greatest design impact emanated from the so-called "Chicago School" of architecture. Chicago, not New York, made the early design innovations. Chicago, which had burned in 1871, was a young city and was striving to become a great frontier city. The famous Columbian Exposition in 1873 stimulated both local and national interest in the City Beautiful movement; it not only called attention to America's international presence, but also stimulated the drive for new initiatives in urban design. The large grid street blocks in Chicago also provided good grounds for experimentation, especially when contrasted with the cramped irregular street block pattern of lower Manhattan. But the architects themselves played the most influential role.

Several distinguished names are associated with the Chicago School: Louis Sullivan, Daniel Burnham, and John Root. Their influence was felt not only in Chicago, but in New York, St. Louis, Buffalo, and other cities. The early buildings these men designed brought a new technology and exterior look to buildings rather than a new skyline, as most were scarcely taller than their predecessors. Their designs emphasized vertical lines to give the feel of a tall structure rather than ponderous masonry look. Continuous thin piers typically rose many stories above a base with expanses of slightly recessed large windows placed between the piers. Dramatic sculptured cornices usually capped the building.

Meanwhile, in New York, new structures were being financed by aggressive investors trying to build taller and taller buildings, but they did not have the same design impact as those in Chicago. New York builders continued to be influenced by classic European Renaissance and Beaux Arts Designs. Those buildings emphasized domes, mansard roofs, and/or Gothic pyramidal tops. The 600-foot Singer Building (1908) in lower Manhattan, for example, made a dramatic impact on the skyline heretofore dominated by the spire of Trinity Church (see Figure 15-5). The Singer Building had a mansard roof positioned atop a slender tower. The infamous Woolworth Building (1913) further solidified the Beaux Arts tradition with its strong Gothic flair. One observer called it "the Cathedral of Commerce—a nickname that, not surprisingly, so satisfied the Woolworth Company that in 1917 it published a brochure about the building with that as its title."[2]

New York's Flatiron Building (1903), designed by Daniel Burnham, also emphasized size by shoehorning a massive structure on a small triangular lot (Figure 10-4). Although an ornate building, in the Chicago School tradition its vertical lines—if somewhat masked by classical ornamentation—distinguished the building, as did its shape. Its location at the angular intersection of two streets also created more interest by generating a stronger image of size and mass.

The Art Deco period in the 1920s and 1930s brought both new design innovations and new standards for height. Flat terra cotta (tile) or limestone surfaces, often embellished with metal alloys, typicaliy faced these buildings which emphasized vertical lines. A sleeker, more modern curvilinear look also characterized these structures. Setbacks often occurred at upper-story levels. This "wedding cake" design (see text discussion and Figure 15-19) was promoted by the zoning guidelines that also evolved during this period, led by the New York movement. A strong negative public reaction had occurred in New York following the construction of the Equitable Building (1915) in lower Manhattan, which massed over 1 million square feet of space into 39 stories, intimidating surrounding structures.

Many public and private buildings built in the art deco style still grace the downtown areas of both large and small cities. Post offices, city halls, fire stations, and schools built during the Depression years reflect this tradition. Department stores, office towers, and hotels also adopted the art deco design.

The tallest buildings of the period, located in New York City, utilized the art deco style. The flamboyant Chrysler Building (1930) was the first structure to top 1000 feet with its 77 stories. A white brick and stainless steel facade remains an impressive sight and an important symbol on the city skyline. But the Chrysler Building was eclipsed with another art deco structure in 1931, the Empire State Building. The height and mass of the Empire State Building immediately captured international acclaim, even if its design lacked distinction.

The 1930s became a watershed era in New York, not only for the heights of new skyscrapers, but also for sowing the seeds of a new design format—the Postwar Modern slab building—and for conceiving clusters of buildings that blended together well as a group. One complex, Rockefeller Center, remains one of the most distinctive office complexes in the world today (see text description and Figure 15-15). While the Rockefeller Center slab-sided buildings anticipated the feature, they also appealed to the past with their classic details.

After World War II, some builders continued utilizing the designs of the past, but several innovative architects brought an entirely new form: the slab-sided tower. This design, also known as the "glass box," came to be called Modern or International Style. One early entry in this tradition was the 39-story Secretariat Building (1950) built for the United Nations in New York. The Lever House (1952), designed by Skidmore, Owings, and Merrill (see Figure 15-20), also boasted a glass curtain wall. This modern architectural style became the dominant form in the United States in the 1950s and 1960s.

The Seagram Building (1958) in New York, designed by Mies van der Rohe, also became a prominent contributor to this tradition. It had a deep plaza set back from the street (Park Avenue) with fountains and marble paving. The success of this design stimulated zoning changes in New York to encourage the greater use of setbacks and plazas at ground level. Later, I.M. Pei designed the striking John Hancock Tower (1975) in Boston in this tradition.

The Embarcadero Center (1971) in San Francisco

(Figure 15-14) and Peachtree Center (1967-on) in Atlanta, designed by John Portman, also follow the modern slab form, but place more emphasis on mixed uses (office, hotel, retail) in one complex. The IDS Center (1972) in Minneapolis, designed by Philip Johnson and John Burgee, also reflects the advantage of the mixed-use center. This work also anticipated the postmodern era to come, with its angular glass court lobby and its flattened octagon shape with a vertical zigzag setback at the corners creating more corner offices and visual appeal.

Postmodernism developed a more distinctive look with the Pennzoil Building in Houston (1976), also designed by Johnson and Burgee (Figure 15-22). The Transamerica Building (1976) in San Francisco also emphasizes the eccentric with its tapered spire pyramidal shape (Figure 15-13). Another unusual form was created by the 95-story tapered lines of the John Hancock Center (1969) in Chicago (see text discussion). The world's tallest structure at 110 stories, the Sears Tower (1974) also exhibits an unconventional form:

> It is in effect a set of square tubes, virtually separate 132 towers, bridled together. The tubes stop at different heights, giving the building a varied, stepped-down profile. It is a splendid allusion to the elaborate tops of old, but it emerges directly and logically out of structural expression. So at Sears, architects [Skidmore, Owings, and Merrill] found a way in which the modernist idiom could be used for the creation of a romantic and rather nonmodernist result, the ornate top.[3]

Several other postmodern structures are notable for their defiance of the traditional box form. First, the Citicorp Building (1977) in New York offered a roofline angled at a 45° angle, giving it a strong skyline statement. The AT&T building (1980) in New York caused a stir with its Chippendale Highboy opening at the top. Finally, consider the setbacks of the three towers of the Republic Bank Center in Houston, shown in Figure 15-23, or the Portlandia Public Services Building in Portland, Oregon, designed by Michael Graves. They introduce several classical nuances to the traditional square box, using color and juxtaposition to create a complex form. Indeed, the postmodern tradition continues to evolve using classical forms—pediments, arches, towers, spires—to embellish the exterior of an otherwise traditional office tower.

[1]Paul Goldberger, *The Skyscraper*, Knopf, New York, 1981, p. 3.

[2]Ibid., p. 44.

[3]Ibid., p. 132.

(A)

(B)

Figure 15-2 Contrasting CBD Development Densities in Montreal and San Diego. Older nineteenth-century cities, such as Montreal (*A*), typically have very high-density CBD core areas. Modern skyscrapers now cover most of the ground area. By way of contrast, a twentieth-century city such as San Diego (*B*) traditionally has had much lower land use densities. Intense uses increased vertical development in San Diego in the 1980s, but considerable low density uses still characterize the area. (*A*, Courtesy City of Montreal; *B*, Reed Kaestner/Zephyr Pictures)

tainment, and dining activities that primarily occur in the hotel district. In the evenings and on weekends, streets and sidewalks, along with businesses themselves, are largely empty (Figure 15-3). Middle- and upper-income citizens who come to the area by day leave for suburbia in the off-hours. The few pedestrians in the downtown at night are mostly out-of-town visitors and inner-city residents.

Street vehicular traffic is typically quite heavy both day and night. During the day, workers in private automobiles, taxis, and buses fill the streets. At night, families and teenagers cruising the main arteries, especially on weekends, create automobile traffic. Even so, traffic at night is far lighter than daytime volumes.

POPULATION AND WORK FORCE TRENDS

The modern downtown business district is primarily a work center and has relatively few permanent residents. Most of those who do live downtown are renters or transients, although there may be high-rise housing for the elderly and wealthy. Hotels house many transients and, to a lesser degree, lease space to tenants on a long-term basis. Especially in smaller cities, there may be housing space in the upper stories of commercial buildings and in older mansions converted into apartments and rooming houses. There is also a trend to include housing in new mixed-use developments for the affluent in larger cosmopolitan centers such as New York and Chicago. A back-to-the-city movement of young professionals has also benefited the housing

market on the CBD fringe. The homeless constitute yet another important and growing segment of the downtown population, as discussed in Chapter 12.

The housing inventory in and around the CBD is old and blighted in many slow-growing cities. Frequently, it is owned by absentee landlords for speculative purposes, in anticipation of future redevelopment. The area immediately adjacent to the CBD has been labeled a *zone of transition* in the concentric ring model of urban structure (see Chapter 11). The mixed land uses in this area, which lies between center-city commercial areas and lower-income residential areas farther out, make it a buffer as well as a reservoir of potentially renewable land for CBD or residential uses. In rapidly growing sunbelt cities, much of this older housing stock has been demolished for parking or in anticipation of future commercial development. Public housing facilities are also frequently located in areas close to the downtown.

The one family group most conspicuously absent from downtown housing in nearly all cities is the middle class. As a result of the residential sorting process, discussed in Chapter 12, this group has become largely suburbanized, even though some middle-class families, particularly childless professional individuals and couples, have moved to close-in neighborhoods in many cities. One common explanation for this movement is a desire among downtown workers to minimize travel costs and time.

The population levels of downtown areas are expected to remain relatively low in the future, except in cities with a strong tradition of downtown living, which

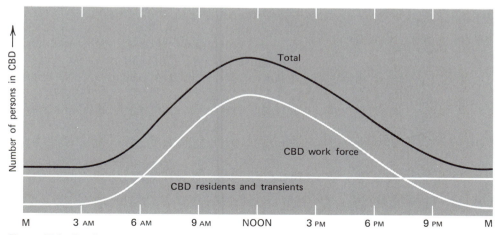

Figure 15-3 Daytime–nighttime Contrasts in Downtown Population. In the CBD of the United States city, most activity takes place during weekday business hours. In the evening and on weekends, little activity occurs as the daytime work force leaves for residential neighborhoods.

includes the cities of New York, Boston, and Chicago, among others (Figure 15-5). Expanding the inventory of the middle-class housing stock became a priority in many cities in the 1980s as a way to revitalize the area, especially to restore flagging retail sales.

The evidence most often cited to confirm the strength and dominance of the downtown area is its *employment level.* Given the traditional function of the CBD as a workplace for the city, this indicator has considerable merit. The CBD remains the largest single center of employment in nearly every large metropolitan area. Employment growth slowed in the downtown area in recent decades and many shifts occurred in its mix. Whereas the downtown formerly dominated the city both absolutely and relatively in employment, its relative strength has declined in recent decades due to the decentralization of business activity.

Breakaways

As recently as the turn of the century, the downtown in most cities had a much wider variety of employment and residential functions. Single-family and multiple-family housing was still intermingled with commercial and industrial activity, much as it still is today in smaller towns. Even in the largest and oldest metropolitan areas, physical evidence of the greater range of earlier functions still exists. Churches, cemeteries, and old mansions in the heart of the city now appear misplaced, but remain as reminders of former land use patterns (Figure 15-4).

Residential and Retail Dispersion

Residential dispersion occurred first, typically followed by the exodus of low-order population-serving commercial functions. Included in this category were neighborhood services (groceries, taverns, and the like), churches, and schools. As recently as the pre-World War II period, higher-order retail functions remained strongly entrenched downtown and were growing in importance. Retail and cultural activity dispersal came after World War II as the size and affluence of the suburban market grew. Included in this exodus were department stores and apparel shops, automobile sales and service, retail banking, restaurants, and movie theaters.

In the 1950s and 1960s, the decline in CBD retail sales acclerated as the competition from regional malls

Figure 15-4 Trinity Church and Cemetery at Wall Street and Broadway in Lower Manhattan. Churches, cemeteries, and old mansions in the heart of the city now appear misplaced, but remain as reminders of former land use patterns. The Trinity Church, built in 1846, was the tallest building in the city until 1892. (UPI/Bettmann)

intensified (Table 15-1). The more rapidly a city grew in that period, the faster the relative rate of CBD decline. Newer cities in the West and South experienced particularly rapid CBD sales drops. By the late 1980s, many downtowns had lost their last remaining department store, and CBD retail sales rarely accounted for more than 2–3 percent of metropolitan totals.

Employment Decline

Some downtown areas have maintained employment levels in the face of prevailing decentralization because of their continuing competitiveness and responsiveness to change; in some cities employment numbers are even rising. But despite an enormous investment in physical planning and construction of new facilities in their downtown areas, many cities have been unable to boost downtown employment. In some instances, renewal

TABLE 15-1
Downtown Retail Sales Decline, 1948–1963

| | Change in CBD Sales (%) | | |
SMSA Size (1960)	1948–1954[a]	1954–1958	1958–1963[b]
3 million +	−11.6	−5.0	−9.0
1–3 million	−7.8	−7.8	−12.0
500 thousand–1 million	−7.0	−8.0	−11.8
250–500 thousand	−4.3	−6.7	−11.5
100–250 thousand	−2.3	−7.1	−8.8
Average	−6.6	−7.0	−10.7

[a] 1948–1958 and 1958–1963 changes have been deflated by the Consumer Price Index (1948 = 100). All figures are for United States data.

[b] Twelve more SMSAs are included in this tabulation than in the 1948–1958 series; some CBD and SMSA definitions were changed in the 1958–1963 interval; rough comparisons can still be made.

Source: Edward Ullman et al., *Trends in CBD and SMSA Retail Sales, 1948 to 1963,* Washington Center for Metropolitan Studies, Washington, D.C., 1967.

has created net increases in floor space, but the types of activities occupying the new space are not as intensive as those that were displaced. The amount of space per employee has increased because of equipment requirements and the growth in the share of executive-level offices. As hotels replace office buildings, a net employment decline occurs. Hotels employ not only fewer persons per square foot of space, but also individuals of lesser skill. More ground-level public open space, parking space, and vacant land also usually result from redevelopment. While these investments increase the appeal of the downtown area, the addition of amenities often decreases employment.

Direct competition from the surburbs for downtown-type activities has also grown. Former disadvantages of locations away from the CBD, such as accessibility, the lack of class A office space, and weak markets, have all but disappeared, and many new, expanding, and relocating businesses now prefer the suburbs. A more detailed discussion of the downtown–suburb trade-off follows in a later section and in Chapters 16 and 17.

Comparative Job Shares

The average percentage of MSA employment located in downtown areas in a sample of 30 cities declined from 15 percent in 1963 to 7 percent in 1972 (Table 15-2). Government and institutional centers such as Washington, D.C., and Austin, Texas, register stronger as downtown work nodes than do manufacturing centers such as Akron, Dayton, and Milwaukee. Similarly, newer western and southern cities such as San

Jose, Salt Lake City, and Jacksonville exhibit relatively modest downtown employment levels in comparison to older cities in the Northeast (Trenton and Providence).

The cities showing the most robust CBD employment are those with strong office and institutional roles, including regional service center functions such as corporate headquarters. In the 1970s and 1980s, these trends continued as larger cities, especially first- and second-order cities, acquired more office space for expanding producer service and corporate activity associated with the information age.

Abstract Transactions

In addition to direct business and consumer ties, there are also many less structured but significant benefits that accrue to activities clustering in downtown areas. These factors, all associated with centrality, can be grouped into nine categories.[2] Nearly all relate to advantage offered by the CBD as a work center for the handling and disseminating of information, referred to as *abstract transactions.*

The first factor is *accessibility.* The downtown is generally the one place most easily reached by the entire city population. Partly for this reason, most government functions are housed downtown, as well as

---

[2] These factors have been extremely well documented by Jean Gottmann, "Urban Centrality and the Interweaving of Quarternary Activities," in Gwen Bell and Jacqueline Tyrwhitt, eds., *Human Identity in the Urban Environment,* Penguin, Baltimore, 1972.

TABLE 15-2
Retail Sales for Selected Cities, 1963 and 1972

SMSA	1963 SMSA Retail Sales	1963 CBD Sales as Percent of SMSA	Adjusted 1972 SMSA Sales[a]	1972 Adjusted CBD Sales as Percent of 1972 Adjusted SMSA Sales[a]	CBD Sales Change, 1963–1972[a] (percent)
Boston	$3,819,070	10.7	$5,286,804	6.3	−17.7
Washington	3,301,690	12.3	5,725,828	6.4	−10.5
Pittsburgh	2,819,984	10.6	3,696,738	7.1	−12.6
St. Louis	2,791,372	6.9	3,920,117	3.6	−26.6
Cleveland	3,671,884	11.4	3,388,957	6.3	−29.5
Baltimore	3,184,465	8.0	3,497,396	4.6	−8.1
Seattle	1,697,963	13.3	2,510,740	6.2	−30.8
Buffalo	1,646,855	9.1	2,107,611	4.6	−25.3
Milwaukee	1,651,611	9.0	2,322,273	5.4	−9.9
Atlanta	1,651,052	19.3	3,372,475	7.4	−17.8
Denver	1,485,271	11.3	2,670,290	4.4	−30.8
Indianapolis	1,345,784	17.4	1,461,820	9.2	−40.7
San Jose	1,205,795	9.4	2,110,169	3.2	−40.5
Columbus	1,118,162	20.2	1,912,464	9.3	−20.8
Rochester	1,087,066	18.8	1,653,490	9.7	−21.1
Providence	1,064,456	9.6	1,505,529	4.2	−37.4
Dayton	971,262	15.6	1,410,752	7.4	−31.3
Louisville	953,441	22.0	1,525,846	12.0	−12.9
Akron	797,088	12.3	1,120,933	4.5	−48.4
Birmingham	752,655	19.9	1,316,160	11.5	+0.5
Jacksonville	658,271	14.4	1,208,897	7.2	−7.9
Salt Lake City	653,853	15.6	1,286,267	8.7	+8.8
Richmond	652,560	19.0	1,050,335	10.6	−9.9
Grand Rapids	649,717	13.1	1,028,324	4.4	−46.9
Wilmington	623,248	12.3	950,786	5.0	−38.2
Nashville	610,842	21.0	1,308,572	8.2	−15.0
Charlotte	468,942	34.7	1,068,609	11.1	−27.2
Trenton	430,763	16.8	560,268	8.6	−33.7
El Paso	373,512	9.8	607,736	14.7	−18.7
Austin	281,837	25.3	650,364	10.0	−9.3
Mean (percent)		15.0		7.4	−22.7

[a]Figures adjusted for inflation, 1963–1972. A deflation factor of 0.7742 was used.

Source: calculated by author.

many cultural and sports centers. *Information flows* have also traditionally favored CBD locations. Face-to-face, direct, personal contact, which is very easy in the CBD, facilitates this flow, supplemented by electronic, telecommunication, and data processing networks. This factor is not as decisive as it once was for many

activities, but it may be crucial at the top management level. The downtown may still offer the best location for this interaction, but the trend for corporate headquarters to decentralize intensified in the 1980s, challenging this former locational monopoly of the downtown. The third factor, *transactional performance*, or the work environment, was also traditionally considered a benefit associated with core locations due to the proximity of many support personnel. Suburban downtowns now compete equitably in this category, further eroding the former CBD advantage.

A readily accessible *labor market* constitutes a fourth factor. While this does not apply exclusively to the downtown, a large and diverse pool of skills can be found there. Fifth, *entertainment* and *spectator sports* activity for leisure-time diversion are readily accessible in the typical downtown. The theater, opera, and symphony, as well as museums, galleries, exclusive restaurants, and sports stadiums and arenas, are usually in or near downtown and add luster to the area as a cultural center. Today, however, five-star restaurants may be more frequent in the suburbs than downtown, except in the largest cities.

A sixth factor deals with *expert consultation*. Professional expertise in many disciplines, including medical, legal, financial, governmental, and management specialists, is often most readily available in the downtown. The presence of the *money* and *credit market* itself constitutes a seventh factor that draws other firms. The eighth factor, access to *high-order-shopping* facilities, is another part of the infrastructure traditionally available to downtown workers, but now largely absent except in New York, Chicago, San Francisco, and a few other instances. Last, *educational opportunities*, including university programs and facilities, commercial trade schools, libraries, specialized bookstores, and media centers, continue to cluster close to downtown in many cities.

Operating together in a mutually reinforcing fashion, these nine interwoven factors gave the downtown its primacy as an employment center, and generally continue to serve the area well. But the tremendous decentralization of jobs and activities that has occurred in the past 25 years now provides suburban downtowns with many of these same advantages, hence the ascendancy of these centers for retail activity, office jobs, and corporate headquarters.

DELIMITING THE CBD

We all have a mental map of the location and orientation of the CBD for cities we have experienced firsthand. Tall buildings, crowds of pedestrians, and busy hotels and restaurants are cues, as are office skyscrapers and skyline vistas. Recall the postcard fixes dis-

cussed in the chapter opening.[3] Closer examination of the CBD reveals the presence of many functional areas distributed in regular fashion in a relatively small area.

Defining precise boundaries of the CBD and functional areas within it is a very difficult task. One might start by locating the *peak land value intersection* (PLVI) or 100 percent corner, which is typically located at the major intersection of the main streets. Land values and uses are often hypothesized to be the most intense for frontages at this location,[4] which can be thought of as the heart of the CBD. Its primacy is the result of its unparalleled accessibility. The classic land use models of the city, notably the *bid–rent* model discussed in Chapter 11 and the ring and sector models, posited that all land uses in the city were arranged around this point.

Comprehensive attempts at defining the boundaries of the CBD have involved the construction of indexes showing building heights, intensities of land usage, and the determination of typical CBD uses for land. The indexes are useful but entail arduous calculations that are frequently unique to the particular city. Data on street-level uses are needed for these surveys, but few published sources of such uses exist.

Raymond Murphy and James Vance Jr., are most often associated with work on CBD delimitation.[5] Their definition involves two indexes. First, a *central business height index* is calculated, block by block, based on a ratio of the total ground-floor space of a block to the floor area occupied by CBD uses. The second calculation, the *central business intensity index*, is determined by dividing the total floor area in the block devoted to CBD uses by the total block floor area. Blocks with high values on these two indexes form the CBD.

The *Census of Business*, published by the Bureau of the Census, has been the major source of comparative information on CBD retailing over the years. In 1972, for the first time, a separate *Census of Retail Trade* was published and thereafter every five years a new survey was completed. The significance of this publication to

[3]Grady Clay, *Close Up: How to Read the American City* Praeger, New York, 1973, pp. 23–32; see also Donald Appleyard, Kevin Lynch, and John R. Meyer, *The View from the Road*, Joint Center for Urban Studies, Harvard University and MIT, Cambridge, Mass., 1964.

[4]A pioneering work noting the importance of land values in accounting for downtown land uses is Richard M. Hurd, *The Principles of City Land Values*, The Record and Guide, New York, 1903.

[5]Raymond E. Murphy and James Vance, Jr., "Delimiting the CBD," *Economic Geography*, 30 (1954), 189–222; Raymond E. Murphy, "A Comparative Study of Nine Central Business Districts," *Economic Geography*, 30 (1954), 301–336.

the CBD is that it contained a definition of the CBD area using census tract boundaries for all cities, as well as providing data on the retail sales level in the area. Unfortunately, the 1987 *Census of Retail Trade* deleted that designation, a major loss to the researcher.

The CBD boundary delimitation process is arbitrary, because there are no comprehensive rules as to what constitutes such an area. The census definition became the best-known overall statement of the CBD area for comparative purposes, but the retreat of the *Census of Retail Trade* from this determination means that only locally developed delimitations will be available in the future.

A more conceptual approach at defining the CBD is provided by the *core–frame* method (Figure 15-5). The *core* of the CBD is the most intensively utilized part, while the *frame* is a surrounding support area. The core is distinctive for its high-rise structures, internal business linkages, pedestrian traffic, limited parking space, and near-complete use of sites (Table 15-3). The frame is typically composed of warehouses, parking lots, medical services, light industry, and wholesale functions (Table 15-4). Vehicular traffic predominates in the frame. Many of its functions support core activities (parking, warehousing services), and there is a high level of interaction between the two areas. The frame also services a large portion of the city. A considerable amount of land may be vacant, and older buildings may not be intensively used in this area. Public housing is frequently located on its margins, as are older industrial functions. The core is relatively small in area (a few dozen city blocks), whereas the frame is quite extensive and may take up to three-quarters of the CBD space.

Functional Areas

Several functional subareas make up the CBD. Those typical of a metropolitan area of 2 million population are shown in Figure 15-6. The intensively built-up core normally consists of a group of high-rise office buildings, a financial district, a hotel–convention district, and a retail section. Surrounding these areas are support functions, municipal and medical districts, government office facilities, a skid row, and wholesaling and warehousing areas, among others. The larger the city, the more distinctive and specialized such sections become. A notable change in land use in the frame occurred in the past 25 years when the automobile sales

and service district (the so-called automobile row) moved to the suburbs.

Continuous movement, although slow, of CBD territory over time is the norm. The CBD typically discards older, run-down sections, characterized by marginal retail businesses and skid row uses, and assimilates new territory, especially on the side toward higher-income sections of the city. These areas are known as the *zone of discard* and *zone of assimilation*, respectively. In the case of the city shown in Figure 15-6, the *zone of discard* is to the south, while the *zone of assimilation* lies to the north. Northward expandion of offices and hotels toward higher-income sections is the prevailing force of the movement for that city. Marginal retail–commercial sections and wholesaling areas to the south are abandoned as the CBD migrates northward into former auto, retail, and medical sections. Other cities would show growth and decline in different directions depending on the location of high and low income areas.

The shape of the CBD varies from city to city and normally responds to the city street plan. In some instances, the CBD is square or rectangular, consisting of several blocks surrounding the PLVI, assuming a grid street pattern and no single dominant street corridor. It can also be elongated along one or two major arteries if they are more important than cross-streets. Frequently, the CBD is cut off in one or more directions by physical features (topography, a river, expressways, and the like).

Skid Row

A *skid row* is an integral part of nearly all CBDs in large North American cities.[6] It functions as a haven for the homeless and societal "dropouts" and as an area for adult entertainment. Skid row is typically part of the zone of discard, but it may be fragmented rather than one compact area. With its own internal structure and unique land uses, including run-down loft buildings, cheap SRO hotels, a farmers market, and marginal retail uses, the skid row presents a distinct contrast to the nearby glitz of the financial district. Pawnshops, bars, low-grade cafes, cheap movie houses, repair shops, credit jewelry and gun shops, and low-quality clothing and furniture stores are common in the area.

The most characteristic group of individuals who inhabit the skid row are the homeless. They cluster here

---

[6]Richard M. Smith, "Skid Row: An Overview for Geographers," *Journal of Geography*, 78 (1970), 7–12.

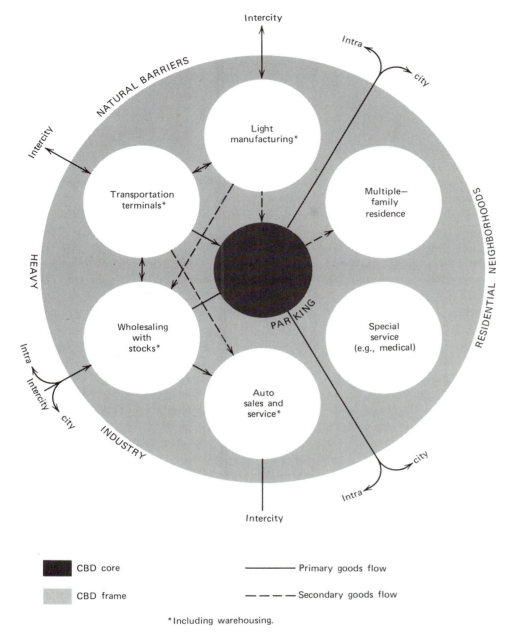

Figure 15-5   Core-frame Concept. The core of the CBD is the most intensively utilized part, with high density uses, strong internal linkages, and heavy pedestrian traffic. The frame is typically composed of warehouses, parking lots, and less intense uses loosely tied to the core. *Source:* Redrawn with permission. From Edgar Horwood and Ronald Boyce, *Studies of the Central Business District and Urban Freeway Development*, University of Washington Press, Seattle, 1959, p. 21.

to take advantage of a compatible, tolerant environment. Many permanent residents of skid row reflect an unconventional lifestyle because of their unsavory personal histories, eccentric behavior, and distinctively ruddy and coarse physical appearance. When youthful and vigorous, most residents worked regularly, but over time employment became more sporadic and alienation typically increased. Lacking skills, and often having suffered occupational injuries, many were gradually displaced from the work force. *Panhandling* (begging for money) to support drinking habits is commonplace. Selling blood and collecting bottles for

TABLE 15-3
Characteristics of the CBD Core

Factor	Characteristics
Intensive land use	Multistoried buildings; highest retail productivity per unit ground area; land use characterized by offices, retail sales, consumer services, hotels, theaters, and banks.
Extended vertical scale	Easily distinguishable by aerial observation; elevator personnel linkages; grows vertically rather than horizontally.
Limited horizontal scale	Greatest horizontal dimension rarely more than 1 mile; geared to walking scale.
Limited horizontal change	Very gradual horizontal change; zones of assimilation and discard limited to a few blocks over long periods of time.
Concentrated daytime population	Location of highest concentration of foot traffic; absence of permanent residential population.
Focus of intracity mass transit	Major mass transit interchange location for entire city.
Center of specialized functions	Extensive use of office space for executive and policy-making functions; center of specialized professional and business services.
Internally conditioned boundaries	Pedestrian and personnel linkages between establishments govern horizontal expansion; dependency on mass transit inhibits lateral expansion.

Source: Edgar M. Horwood and Ronald R. Boyce, *Studies of the Central Business District and Urban Freeway Development,* University of Washington Press, Seattle, 1959, p. 16. Reprinted by permission.

sale to recycling centers are other sources of income. Homelessness was discussed earlier in Chapter 12.

Skid row provides an *external labor* function. Local day labor agencies utilize workers on a temporary basis. In some cities, farm workers are recruited regularly from skid row areas. Handbill distributors, non-union contractors, and warehouses with fluctuating, short-term labor requirements also use skid row residents as a labor pool.

Along with the cafes and hotels that cater to the skid row inhabitant, other businesses are bars, soup kitchens, liquor stores, pawnshops, barber colleges, and missions. Many business establishments in the skid row do not depend on the internal market for their support but on their location near the CBD core. They are also attracted by relatively cheap rent and a tolerant business climate. Printers, apparel distributors, and wholesale outlets in these areas are often interspersed among the skid row functions. The overall permissive attitude within the area and neglect by the outside

TABLE 15-4
Characteristics of the CBD Frame

Factor	Characteristics
Semi-intensive land use	Building height geared to walk-up scale; site only partially built on.
Prominent functional subregions	Subfoci characterized mainly by wholesaling with stocks, warehousing, off-street parking, automobile sales and services, multifamily dwellings, intercity transportation terminals and facilities, light manufacturing, and some institutional uses.
Extended horizontal scale	Most establishments have off-street parking and docking facilities; movements between establishment are vehicular.
Unlinked functional subregions	Important establishment linkages to CBD core (e.g., intercity transportation terminals, warehousing) and to outlying urban regions (e.g., wholesale distribution to suburban shopping areas and to service industries).
Externally conditioned boundaries	Commercial uses generally limited to flat land; growth tends to extend into areas of dilapidated housing; CBD frame uses fill in interstices of central focus of highway and rail transportation routes.

Source: Edgar M. Horwood and Ronald R. Boyce, *Studies of the Central Business District and Urban Freeway Development,* University of Washington Press, Seattle, 1959, p. 20. Reprinted by permission.

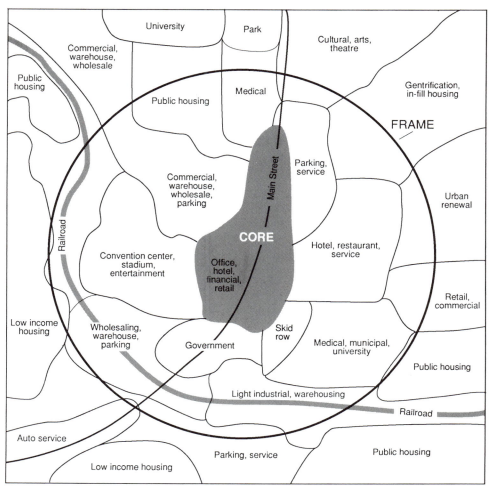

Figure 15-6 Functional Areas of a Hypothetical CBD. Several functional subareas occur in the CBD. The core encompasses the office/financial/hotel/retail core, while the frame includes parking areas, convention/entertainment district, wholesale/warehouse area, government cluster, medical area, public housing, skid row, and an urban renewal zone.

community has often led to the development of strip shows, X-rated adult entertainment, and activities catering to subculture groups.

An association of skid row functions with adult bookstores, SRO hotels, taverns, and pawnshops is shown in Figure 15-7. The name *skid row* may have originated in Seattle, referring to activities catering to loggers who frequented the area. Skid row functions evolved along Skid Road, which lumbermen used to skid logs downhill to the harbor.

Some interesting geographic studies have been conducted in an attempt to define the skid row habitat in a cross section of cities.[7] One technique has been called

the *bottle count method*, wherein counts of wine bottles are made and mapped to show blocks of high incidence; the map is then used to delimit the skid row.

The skid row presents many problems to the larger society. Planners and downtown business groups continually exert pressure for renewal of these areas. Unfortunately, this renewal is often conceived as merely a physical demolition and rebuilding process that does not address the more basic problem of human rehabilitation. In some cases, such as in Denver, physical displacement of skid row in the late 1960s resulted in creating two new enclaves in place of one former zone.[8] It also created additional problems for the skid row resident to find housing and increased food

[7]Jim Ward, "Skid Row as a Geographic Entity," *Professional Geographer*, 27 (1975), 286–296.

[8]Smith, "Skid Row," pp. 10–12.

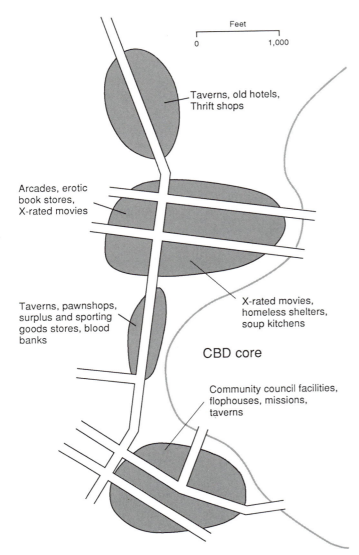

Feet

0 — 1,000

Taverns, old hotels, Thrift shops

Arcades, erotic book stores, X-rated movies

Taverns, pawnshops, surplus and sporting goods stores, blood banks

X-rated movies, homeless shelters, soup kitchens

CBD core

Community council facilities, flophouses, missions, taverns

Figure 15-7 Distribution of Skid Row Activities. An association of skid row areas with adult bookstores, SRO hotels, taverns, pawnshops, homeless shelters, blood banks, drug treatment centers, missions, and similar uses gives this district a unique function and role in the downtown area. Public policy often vacillates between containing and dispersing these activities as business groups and planners seek to revitalize and upgrade these areas.

costs, serious problems for both the elderly pensioner and the typical skid row occupant.

Many adult entertainment areas have recently decentralized outside skid row to more "respectable" areas nearer hotel and convention districts, which are the major source of patrons. Such operations lease older wholesale and commercial facilities. Nude or topless shows and tattoo and massage parlors also expand in these "honky tonk" sections. These functions are fre-

quently criticized for their base character, and city officials are not tolerant of the newer locations for fear they will tarnish the city's image. Bright lights and gaudy signs further downgrade these areas, and associated crime, drug, and prostitution activity often add to the problem. Underground organizations often own or manage these businesses and seem to be constantly engaged in legal battles with city officials over their right to remain in business.

In some cities an attempt is being made to use zoning laws and licensing restrictions to contain commercial sex establishments and other pornography institutions within prescribed districts. Such "adult business districts" are similar to the so-called Combat Zone in Boston where strip shows and adult bookstores have clustered. In some cities the approach is the opposite—the dispersal of such activities.

RETAIL CHANGE

Several trends in retailing in recent decades have dramatically changed the CBD role in this traditional downtown anchor activity. As recently as the immediate post-World War II era, downtown was synonymous with retailing, and it was essentially the only place one could find specialty shops or department stores. But changes came rapidly as the impact of activity decentralization accelerated in the 1950s. Perhaps these retail shifts can be best captured by a decriptive three-stage model: CBD dominance (1850s–1950s); CBD decline (1950s–1970s); and CBD replacement (1970s to the present).[9]

CBD Dominance (1850s–1950s)

The era of the modern CBD began in the 1850s with improvements in mechanized transportation and the invention of the large general merchandise retail unit, the department store. For the first time, it became possible for large-scale retail operations to operate in a centralized location. Other stores also clustered near the department store, including other department stores, to take advantage of heavy pedestrian traffic that facilitated comparative shopping. This attraction of

[9]This classification is adapted from J. Dennis Lord and Clifford M. Guy, "Comparative Retail Structure of British and American Cities: Cardiff (U.K.) and Charlotte (USA)," *International Review of Retail, Distribution and Consumer Research,* vol. 1, no. 4 (July 1991), 391–436.

like stores to one another is called a *competitive linkage*.[10]

The so-called GAFE index traditionally accounted for the greatest share of CBD sales.[11] Typically, the larger the city, the greater the concentration of specialized retailing that occurred in the downtown area, due to the greater drawing power of the city for customers seeking specialized goods as opposed to convenience items such as groceries, which were available in smaller towns. Department stores captured about one-half of the total sales and one-quarter of the sales occurred in apparel stores. Furniture sales and eating and drinking sales accounted for the remaining quarter of sales.

This grip on the downtown seemed invincible for over a century, but the massive suburban residential growth that accelerated after World War II soon ushered in a new era. We will discuss retail growth in the nineteenth and twentieth centuries in more detail in Chapter 16. It is sufficient to indicate here that the era of the dominance of the CBD as retailer passed in the 1950s as function after function moved away. This decentralization generally affected large cities first, and then the trend diffused throughout the urban hierarchy (Figure 15-8).

CBD Decline (1950s–1970s)

In the early 1950s, as CBD retailing dominance began eroding rapidly, about one-third of the commercial downtown floor space was devoted to retailing and up to 20 percent of the CBD labor force was employed in retailing.[12] The share of retailing occurring downtown varied considerably from city to city at that time, with a 25 percent CBD share being typical. By the early 1960s, that share dropped into the 10–20 percent range, with a 15 percent average for 30 cities.[13] An even more precipitous decline occurred between 1963 and 1972, with an average of 7 percent of sales in the CBD for the latter year. Decline continued in the 1970s and 1980s. It is now rare to find downtown areas accounting for

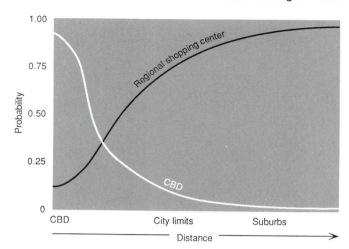

Figure 15-8 Probabilities for CBD and Suburban Mass-goods Shopping by Residential Location in Large Metropolitan Areas The downtown has become the regional shopping center for the inner-city market. For residents living away from the city center, the probability of shopping downtown falls off dramatically. Proportionately higher percentages for shopping at a regional shopping center occur with distance away from the downtown.

more than 2–3 percent of metropolitan area sales. In all fairness, it should be pointed out that individual regional malls today rarely account for more than 2 percent of total sales either, so dispersed has the retail landscape become. We will discuss this point further in Chapter 16. Even more dramatic has been the loss of downtown department stores and apparel shops. Many cities have no remaining downtown department stores today.

CBD Replacement (1970s to the present)

In response to the continued decline of retail sales, downtown leaders and government officials sought to stem the outflow with a variety of responses by the 1970s. In some cases, specialty retailers moved into arcades, galleries, and mini-malls, and developers began offering newer mixed-use centers. Examples include the Omni International in Miami, Peachtree Center in Atlanta, and Renaissance Center in Detroit. These mixed-use centers, sometimes called *megastructures*, offered the amenities and security advantages of a suburban mall.

Exceptions to the pattern of retreat of individual outlets in the CBD occur in the nonwhite ethnic shopping districts in many cities. A range of store types, from convenience establishments to junior department

[10]John Rannels, *The Core of the City*, Columbia University Press, New York, 1956, pp. 29–30.

[11]The *G* stands for general merchandise (normally department store sales), the *A* accounts for apparel and accessories (men's and women's clothing, shoes), *F* refers to furniture and appliances, and *E* to eating and drinking.

[12]Truman A. Hartshorn, *Interpreting the City: An Urban Geography*, Wiley, New York, 1980, pp. 321–322.

[13]Ibid., Table 15-2, p. 322.

stores, to apparel, dry goods, and furniture firms, as well as personal services, continue to thrive there, despite threats from renewal projects. Examples of these ethnic markets might include "Chinatowns," "Little Italy," or "Little Havana."

Fast-food chain restaurants are also growing in number in busy pedestrian districts. Such facilities often replace the traditional downtown cafeteria and sandwich shop, because they offer fast service, carry-out, and an appealing menu. Elegant restaurants in hotels and in nearby office complexes cater to growing convention and tourist business. Many cities have also added festival marketplaces such as Faneuil Hall in Boston and Harbor Place in Baltimore. These centers will be discussed in Chapter 16.

Downtown Malls

Another response to the need for a more competitive retail atmosphere downtown has been a movement toward *downtown malls*. This broad concept incorporates many types of treatments, some resembling traditional suburban shopping centers with anchor stores and smaller specialty shops, while others assume a

vertical mall format, as in the case of Water Tower Place in Chicago (see Chapter 16). Often a combination of new construction and refurbishing older structures occurs in such projects. The Gallery in downtown Philadelphia, for example, involved linking Gimbels and Strawbridge & Clothier department stores together with a 125-store enclosed mall. Horton Plaza in downtown San Diego presents an even more ambitious example of downtown retail investment. Located on 11 acres, the 1 million-square-foot center brought four new department stores to the downtown market—Mervyn's, Robinson's the Broadway, and Nordstrom—when it opened in the mid-1980s. The mall is not enclosed, but rather is an open-air emporium that plays off the traditional street with its tasteful architectural style inspired by existing theaters, fountains, and roofline embellishments. The renovated old Spanish Renaissance Revival style Balboa Theatre, dating to 1924, became an integral part of the new complex (Figure 15-9).

The largest downtown mall in the world is the Eaton Centre in Toronto, which opened in 1977. Built by the noted Canadian-based Cadillac Fairview Corporation, Ltd., the mall encloses a 15-acre area, encompassing two office towers with a Simpson's department store

Figure 15-9 Horton Plaza in San Diego. The Horton Plaza downtown mall brought new life to a declining market by adding four department stores and over 1 million square feet of retail and commercial space to the market. The mall plays off local architectural themes inspired by existing theaters, fountains, and roofline treatments. Note diagonal pedestrian spine cutting through the project anchored by Robinson's Department Store in lower right. Existing Balboa Theatre with cupola to left of Robinson's facing Fourth Avenue. Existing Golden West Hotel at lower left and Nordstrom's Department Store at top left. (Aerial Fotobank, Inc.)

anchoring one end and a new nine-story Eaton's department store the other, with each department store showcasing about 1 million square feet of retail space. It surrounds historic buildings of the Trinity Church and parallels the Yonge Street subway line. Linking the two department stores is a three-story glass-domed mall containing about ½-million square feet of retail space and over 300 stores (Figure 15-10). Enclosed parking garages are integrated into the design.

At the other end of the spectrum are street and infrastructure treatments aimed to assist existing retailers. Widening sidewalks and narrowing streets, often combined with restricting cars and giving priority to transit and emergency vehicles, represents one such approach. Banning all vehicular traffic and creating a total pedestrian zone in a section of a downtown street is yet another. The latter can include the installation of pools, fountains, playgrounds, and street furniture on

Figure 15-10 Eaton Centre in Downtown Toronto. Eaton Centre resembles a suburban mall placed in a high-density commercial area. The three-level shopping mall, anchored by Eaton's and Simpson-Sears department stores, is flanked by parking garages on either side on the upper levels. Note resemblance of vaulted glass roof to a European-style shopping arcade. (Photo by Arthur Jame, The Canadian Architect, Toronto)

the former right-of way. The mall can be temporary or permanent. It can be open or enclosed. In most cases, the concept involves the use of existing buildings rather than massive new construction, with the emphasis on the exterior environment.

The pedestrian mall approach has been very popular in small cities (50,000 to 100,000 population) in the United States. These cities have the most to lose from retail decentralization because few other functions are located in their CBDs. The core of their shopping district is relatively compact and readily adaptable to the mall concept. Consensus on a mall project can also be easier to obtain in the smaller city. Nevertheless, many pedestrian malls have failed due to a weakening market, including one of the first such facilities in Kalamazoo, Michigan, and the mall in downtown Burbank, California. Pedestrian malls also exist in larger cities, such as the Chestnut Street transitway opened in 1975 in Philadelphia and Nicollett Mall in Minneapolis, dating from 1967 (Figure 15-11).

Malls are not automatic panaceas to downtown problems, and retail sales do not always increase following their construction. Massive public–private partnerships are often required to undertake these projects. In many cases, private reinvestment increases and existing structures are spruced up because of the psychological boost such investments give to the business district. But if the overall downtown trend is for retail sales to decline in a particular city, that decline may continue even with a mall. A crucial requirement is that the mall be planned properly and be well located so that deliveries will be efficient and parking or transit access convenient.

Downtown mall failures became more frequent in the 1980s because poor designs gave them a short life expectancy. One author has suggested that four designs predominate, each of which has inherent problems:[14]

1. *Tiffany Mall*. Overdesigned with expensive materials creating an empty, cold, artificial environment.

2. *Versailles Mall*. Paintings, fountains, and shrubbery overdone, creating a jungle atmosphere that impeded interaction.

3. *Star Trek Mall*. Massive sculptures and monuments create an intimidating appearance.

4. *Walter Mitty Mall*. Superficial, noncommittal,

[14]Michael C. Cunningham, "Can Downtown Be Reinvented," *Ekistics*, 256 (March 1977), 159–164.

Figure 15-11 Nicollett Pedestrian Mall in Minneapolis. By narrowing the street and restricting its use to bus transit and emergency vehicles, the sidewalks could be widened and new street furniture and landscaping provided in this section of the downtown. Unfortunately, this program has not been as successful as planned in keeping retail activity strong along the corridor. Second-story skybridges have also moved people off the street to second-level stores. (Courtesy of the Greater Minneapolis Chamber of Commerce)

cosmetic design with no comprehensive theme or integration.

In the future, retail activities in many downtown areas will have to regroup spatially in order to remain competitive. Large-scale anchor outlets must be centrally located near major office and hotel facilities, not widely dispersed along the traditional shopping streets or at opposite ends of the CBD as is presently the case in many cities.

A comprehensive treatment of the metropolitan retail landscape is undertaken in Chapter 16. It is sufficient to note here that the downtown area is now often surrounded by a clientele of lower socioeconomic status and that its operations have been scaled back to a level reflecting the lower buying power of that market. The downtown area sells convenience and shoppers' goods to this inner-city market and to people who are

downtown for reasons of employment, business, or tourism.

OFFICE FUNCTION

For many larger metropolitan areas, the growth of the CBD office industry in the post-World War II era offset retail declines. This growth paralleled the boom in white-collar employment. During this period, offices clustered in the CBD to take advantage of the accessibility of the downtown area for large concentrations of workers. New freeways and public transportation modes provided good access to the downtown market even as residences decentralized rapidly. Powerful complementary linkages evolved among financial institutions, legal firms, insurance companies, and corporate headquarters that occupied the office buildings. The downtown setting fostered easy face-to-face contacts for professionals and a prestigious work environment.

Evolution of Control Centers

Office functions traditionally clustered in the core areas of the very largest metropolitan areas, which also claimed the largest share of corporate headquarters locations. New York and Chicago, as the largest metropolitan areas in the country, also possessed the greatest quantity of office space. More recently, office activity has decentralized down the national urban hierarchy and dispersed geographically throughout the country to all national and regional centers as defined in Chapter 5.

A descriptive four-stage process model of the spatial evolution of corporate office command and control centers, developed by R. Keith Semple and Alan Phipps, provides a framework to comprehend the vast changes that have occurred in the office industry since World War II and continue to unfold:[15]

Stage 1: **Dominant Center**—up to 1950

Stage 2: **Regional Centers**—1950s–1970s

Stage 3: **Regional Maturity**—1980s to ?

Stage 4: **National Maturity**—2010 to ?

---

[15]R. Keith Semple and Alan G. Phipps, "The Spatial Evolution of Corporate Headquarters within an Urban System," *Urban Geography*, 3 (1982), p. 259.

A diagram showing the evolution of these stages over time appears in Figure 15-12.

In Stage 1, corporate control is concentrated in a single dominant center. New York City, the traditional financial and corporate center of the United States, plays this role. The authors estimated that this control peaked around 1950. Thereafter, decentralization of office functions to regional centers began to accelerate, creating Stage 2, or Regional Centers. In two decades, many such centers evolved in older metropolitan areas in the Northeast, Middle West, and the sunbelt. At the same time, an absolute decline occurred in the number of corporate headquarters centered in New York. The discussion here will be limited to Stages 1 and 2 of the model. Stage 3, Regional Maturity, in which regional centers become robust alternatives to the national centers, began to come into focus in the 1980s, with the growth of new high-technology and service corporations in the sunbelt and the continued shifting process of corporate locations away from New York City. Headquarters functions also relocate to the suburbs in this stage. It is yet to be seen whether Semple and Phipps accurately forecast Stage 4, National Maturity, in which no regional or national center dominance exists. Recent evidence suggests that this may, in fact not be the end result. Because of the reemergence of major international centers with the globalization of world economies, the largest urban centers, such as New York, London, and Tokyo, may well play enhanced roles in the future.

In the immediate post-World War II era, elite business interests eagerly took advantage of urban renewal progams and supportive municipal zoning and permitting progams to accommodate growing office functions. Major corporations, hungry for the greater visibility and prestige associated with new headquarters buildings, willingly invested in new towers with their names emblazoned on top.

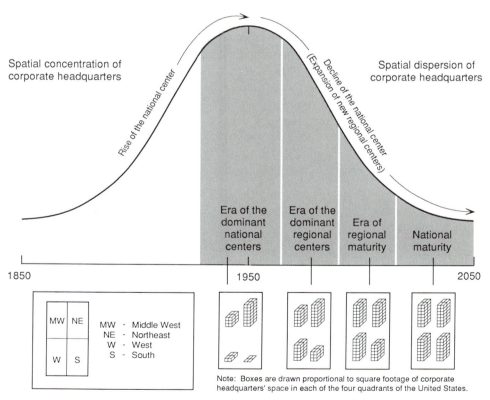

Spatial concentration of corporate headquarters

Spatial dispersion of corporate headquarters

Rise of the national center

Decline of the national center (Expansion of new regional centers)

Era of the dominant national centers

Era of the dominant regional centers

Era of regional maturity

National maturity

1850   1950   2050

MW | NE
W | S

MW - Middle West
NE - Northeast
W - West
S - South

Note: Boxes are drawn proportional to square footage of corporate headquarters' space in each of the four quadrants of the United States.

Figure 15-12 Spatial Evolution of Corporate Command and Control. This four-stage process model shows that prior to 1950 a single dominant center controlled office functions (Stage 1). Regional centers (Stage 2) emerged in the 1950s–1970s era. We are now experiencing regional maturity (Stage 3) and may enter national maturity during the next century (Stage 4). *Source:* Modified after R. Keith Semple and Alan G. Phipps, "The Spatial Evolution of Corporate Headquarters within an Urban System," *Urban Geography*, 3 (1982), 259; and R. Keith Semple, et al. "Perspectives on Corporate Headquarters Relocation in the United States," *Urban Geography*, 6 (1985), 372. Reprinted with the permission of V. H. Winston & Son, Inc.

Pittsburgh's renowned Gateway Center started with a real estate survey that identified a market for larger and more prestigious offices to be used by the city's big businesses. In the office towers that went up in the 1950s, most of the space was committed in advance to large Pittsburgh corporations. U.S. Steel, Mellon Bank, and Alcoa put up new headquarters, and with a gift from the Mellon Foundations, the city built and underground garage topped with a landscaped public plaza named Mellon Square.[16]

Other major office growth centers in the 1950s included San Francisco, Chicago, and Philadelphia.

The 1960s witnessed an office construction boom that was more than twice as large as that of the 1950s in the 30 largest metropolitan areas (132 versus 58 million square feet of space).[17] New York City alone accounted for one-half of the expansion in the 1950s and one-third of the total in the 1960s. Cities with active urban renewal programs and a strong demand for office space, due to their growing service center functions, paced this expansion, including San Francisco, Boston, Chicago, and Atlanta. "The downtown business centers of the 30 largest metropolitan areas captured some 20 percent of all office construction in the nation in the 1960s."[18]

Further insight into the emergence of strong office core areas in the 1960s and 1970s can be gained by

examining individual city trends. In addition to the strong cores that evolved in New York and Chicago, San Francisco, Pittsburgh, Houston, and Atlanta continued to build office cores in the 1960s. But the office building boom became a national phenomenon in this period, benefiting suburban as well as urban markets. The burgeoning suburban market will be discussed in more detail in Chapter 17.

San Francisco Office Core

The growth of the downtown San Francisco office sector in the post-World War II era is primarily due to the growth of the finance, insurance, and real estate industries (FIRE). The city had emerged as the financial capital of the West and the U.S. broker for Asian investments by the 1960s. In the 1970s, San Francisco headquartered 40 major firms. An office boom of unprecedented proportions engulfed the downtown area from 1960 to 1985, associated with the buildup of a massive office function (Table 15-5). Downtown office space more than doubled in this period, raising total square footage to 70 million square feet. Clerical workers occupied a large share of this space, especially in the FIRE employment group and in the government category (Table 15-6), while professional and technical workers accounted for a large share of workers in the services category.

This explosive office activity growth generated considerable controversy, as it displaced many workers whose jobs were not replaced, and it dramatically

---

[16]Bernard J. Frieden and Lynne B. Sagalyn, *Downtown, Inc.: How America Rebuilds Cities*, MIT Press, Cambridge, Mass., 1989, p. 40.

[17]Ibid., p. 57.

[18]Ibid., p. 57.

TABLE 15-5
Office Employment Growth in San Francisco CBD, 1960–1974[a]

	1960	1965	1970	1974
Office space (millions gross ft²).	27.0	33.2	42.3	50.0
Office work force	115,000	137,000	169,000	186,000
Periodic increases of office workers	—	22,000	32,000	17,000
CBD office workers as percent of total CBD employment	56	58	60	61
Total employment in CBD	204,000	235,000	283,000	305,000
CBD office workers as percent of county (city) office jobs	44	50	56	61

[a]CBD definition based on tracts 110–125, 176, and 178–80. Census CBD definition is more restricted and includes tracts 117, 121, 123–125, and 176 only. Employment in the SPUR CBD definition is about 1.36 times the census CBD in 1960 and 1.33 times the 1970 census CBD. Employment in study areas was 39 percent of employment in city in 1960 and 47 percent of county employment in 1970.

Source: SPUR, *Impact of Intensive High Rise Development in San Francisco*, Final Report, San Francisco, San Francisco Planning and Urban Renewal Association, June 1975, Table 3 modified, p. 65.

TABLE 15-6
Distribution of Office Jobs in San Francisco CBD, 1974 (%)

Industry Group	Professional, Technical	Managers, Officers, Proprietors	Clerical	Sales
Manufacturing	23.7	22.4	37.5	16.4
Transportation and other public utilities	25.5	15.2	52.5	6.8
Wholesale and retail trade	2.0	18.2	30.8	48.9
Finance, insurance, and real estate	12.4	19.7	63.8	4.0
Services	44.8	14.2	37.6	3.4
Government	22.5	14.7	62.6	0.2

Source: SPUR, *Impact of Intensive High Rise Development on San Francisco,* Final Report, San Francisco, San Francisco Planning and Urban Renewal Association, June 1975, p. 85.

changed the skyline, raising many environmental concerns. At the same time, comparable construction rates for new housing did not materialize, creating a housing supply crisis and corresponding long-distance work trip commuter problems. Moreover, controversy festered over the question of whether or not the downtown paid its fair share of taxes. These problems culminated in a clamor to restrict new high-rise downtown development, dubbed the Manhattanization of San Francisco (Figure 15-13).

A "Downtown Plan" endorsing draconian restrictions on new developments passed the Board of Supervisors in 1985. It limited new citywide development of

high-rise buildings to two or three 30- to 35-story towers a year, most of which could not be located in the downtown core. The plan also reduced the bulk of new buildings in half and required that buildings have "stepped setbacks" on upper floors and distinctive tapered rooflines to add more appeal to the skyline. The permitting process for building approvals became very cumbersome and encompassing. Not only were developers henceforth required to contribute funds for housing and transit subsidies, but also to contribute to a downtown parks fund, the development of child-care centers, and an arts fund for public spaces, among others. Needless to say, this strategy dramatically

Figure 15-13   Manhattanization of San Francisco. The explosive growth of the downtown San Francisco skyline in the 1960s and 1970s led to draconian measures in the 1980s to limit development. The change in development philosophy in the city reflected the flourishing no-growth movement in the area. Embarcadero Center is in center. Dark high-rise building in center is Bank of America (778 feet), and spire to right of center is Transamerica Pyramid (853 feet) the elevated Embarcadero freeway along the waterfront was removed in the early 1990s following the 1989 earthquake. (San Francisco Convention & Visitors' Bureau)

reduced development activity in downtown San Francisco.

The change in development philosophy in San Francisco reflected the flourishing no-growth movement in the area and the growing involvement of community-based groups in decision making, or what has been called "reactive planning." Until then, the private sector had experienced an era in which business interests controlled their own destiny. Unfortunately, the need for a more regional approach to planning in San Francisco was not addressed by the new policy, nor was a solution to the transportation or housing problems forthcoming. Increasingly, Bay Area residents sought their own solutions by moving to the suburbs in the search of a lower-cost living and working environment. The growing trend toward growth management programs to guide growth will be discussed in more detail in Chapter 19.

Manhattan: National Headquarters Function

In the 1960s, New York City (Manhattan) added tremendous capacity to its office inventory, averaging 9 million square feet of new space yearly. A study by the New York Regional Plan Association indicated that this surge in capacity represented the culmination of a third construction boom in the city beginning after World War II and ending in the early 1970s.

The initial New York City office space boom began in the 1870s and continued until after the turn of the century. The financial district of lower Manhattan (Wall Street) evolved during that period. A second cycle of growth came in the 1920s. The number of buildings greater than 20 stories tripled at that time, growing to 188 in number. Midtown Manhattan emerged as a headquarters center in that era, taking advantage of lower land costs than those farther downtown. The Depression did not stymie this growth, which continued unabated into the 1930s, and landmarks such as the Chrysler Building, the Empire State Building, and Rockefeller Center took shape at that time (Figure 15-14).

Major United States firms traditionally turned to Manhattan for their headquarters. The city serves as the financial capital of the country and this role, coupled with the entrepôt and distribution functions, helped attract and hold many other activities. But it is the national headquarters activity that makes the city unique.

> The market area of headquarters activity is often national or international in scope; the degree of complexity in this type of operation is at its greatest. . . . The need for external economies and the benefits of concentration increase so rapidly at this level that only the highest order of urban centers are capable of supporting the ancillary services, specialized labor pools, and inter-firm communication that are required by most national market functions.[19]

The continued dominance of Manhattan in headquarters activity seemed inevitable as recently as 1970. But a relative decline in its hold emerged in that decade as the local suburbs became more competitive and other cities enticed firms to move away. The high costs of space, high taxes, and expensive housing all contributed to a growing dissatisfaction with the Big Apple as a place to work and live. These trends continued in the 1980s, eventually giving the suburbs a clear majority in corporate headquarters. The downtown–suburban locational tradeoff will be disucssed in Chapter 17.

HOTEL MARKET

The hotel function became a growth industry in the downtown area in the past 25 years. In many cities, this growth helped offset employment declines in other sectors such as retailing and corporate office activity. Historically, most hotels were small independent operations and the room inventory was relatively static in most cities during the first half of the century. Moreover, the stock of rooms was relatively aged when construction activity gained momentum in the 1960s. Most of these hotels had downtown locations, often adjacent to railroad passenger terminals.

Surviving older downtown hotels are now prospering from increased convention activity in major cities. Many were demolished in the 1950s and 1960s, while others struggled to keep up with the new competition. Recent data suggest that many of the remaining older "grand" facilities can be restored more cheaply than new space can be constructed. Hotels in Chicago (Conrad Hilton), Kansas City (Muehlebach), New York (Plaza), Boston (Parker House, Copley Plaza), Salt Lake City (Hotel Utah), and Houston (Rice), among others, experienced renovations in recent years

---

[19]Ibid., p. 18.

Figure 15-14 Rockefeller Center in Midtown Manhattan. Originally, Rockefeller Center included 14 buildings built from 1931–1940, with 5 million square feet of office space on 12 acres. Over 4,000 tenants were removed and 228 buildings were demolished on the site. Today the complex includes 19 skyscrapers arrayed around the flagship 70-story 30 Rockefeller Plaza Tower, boasting a total of 15 million square feet of space. Japanese investors purchased the center from the Rockefeller interests in 1989. St. Patrick's Cathedral (spire) and Fifth Avenue to right. (Courtesy of Rockefeller Center.)

(Figure 15-15). Such older hotels, with their elegant appointments restored, have proven just as successful as new luxury hotels.

As hotel occupancy rates increased after World War II, entrepreneurs began offering new products for the business traveler, especially the downtown motor hotel and suburban facilities catering to the automobile. The interstate highway system, the expansion of motels, and the emergence of national chains in the 1950s, for example, vastly changed the city/suburban hotel mix.

Perhaps the most significant factor in the recent growth of the downtown hotel industry has been the tremendous growth in convention activity and air travel. These downtown properties are generally larger high-rise facilities than those in other locations owing to the higher cost of land in the CBD and the heavy demand placed on them by large conventions. It is not uncommon for the newer downtown hotels in the major

convention cities of New York, Chicago, Washington, D.C., and Atlanta to have 1500–2000 rooms and offer a wide array of support facilities, including ballrooms, meeting rooms, exhibit space, and a variety of food and beverage services. Suites account for up to 10 percent of the rooms in some convention hotels, with the expanded space providing opportunities for hospitality functions. Food and beverage sales, in fact, account for about one-third of the revenue in a hotel.

Often, convention hotels are built as part of a larger mixed-use facility such as the Hyatt Regency in Illinois Center in Chicago or the Westin Peachtree Plaza and Marriott Marquis in Peachtree Center in Atlanta. They also cluster near major convention halls, such as the Hyatt Regency at the Miami Convention Center or the Hyatt Regency at Reunion Square in Dallas. Convention hotels often set aside a few top floors for frequent business travelers and executives, offering them spe-

Figure 15-15   Conrad Hilton and Towers Hotel, Chicago. New life came to this old downtown property in the 1980s when it was acquired by the Hilton chain and restored to its former elegance. The number of rooms was dramatically reduced by converting former cramped single-bed units to large queen-size units with double baths. This hotel faces Lake Michigan and is the largest hotel in close proximity to the McCormick Place Convention Center. (Courtesy Chicago Hilton)

cial services such as express check-in/check-out, complementary breakfasts, honor bar service, daily papers, separate lounge/lobby space, controlled floor access, and other amenities.

Full service commercial hotels with fewer rooms and facilities than convention hotels also flourish in the downtown market. In the largest metropolitan areas, luxury hotels fill another market niche. Such facilities pamper the traveler with superior service. Typically they have 500 rooms or less and limited meeting space for small groups.

CONVENTION AND BUSINESS MARKET

The major clientele for the hotel industry is the business and commercial market (Figure 15-16), which typically accounts for 60 percent of the demand for rooms. Traveling sales and management personnel, who must constantly visit corporate offices to function effectively, provide the bulk of this business. They are out of town many days a week as a part of their job. Many of the meetings and conferences that these people attend take place in hotels.

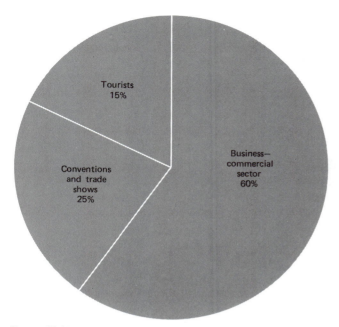

Figure 15-16 Downtown Hotel Room Markets in a Metropolitan Area. The major clientele for the hotel industry is the business and commercial market. Convention and trade show activity account for another large block of space followed by the tourist sector. *Source:* After C. Dewitt Coffman, *Marketing for a Full House*, Cornell University, School of Business Administration, Ithaca, N.Y., 1972, p. 48.

The second major component of the hotel market is the convention and trade show business (about 25 percent of the total). While the largest conventions (those with more than 15,000 delegates) are restricted to regional capitals with the best air service and specialized services, most conventions are relatively small so that even cities of 250,000 can compete effectively for this trade.

Over 20,000 conventions and trade shows are held in the United States each year, but only one-third of them are international, national, or regional in scope. Historically, trade shows have primarily required exhibit space with

> few or no meetings, food functions, or assemblies. By contrast, conventions have used meeting rooms, ballrooms, and assembly halls, and have had relatively small exhibit space needs. In recent years, however, trade shows have scheduled more meetings and food functions (to increase attendance), and conventions have discovered the financial benefits of having large trade shows in conjunction with their meetings. . . .
>
> In second and third tier cities, the convention center or civic center will function more frequently as a multipurpose or community center. The major convention users will be state-based organizations. The smaller city's

building will attract public or consumer shows, boat shows, car shows, home/garden shows, etc. The dominant category of users may be local civic and social groups or fraternal groups, which would include high school graduations, political rallies, religious crusades/revivals, local concerts, amateur athletic contests, and the like.[20]

The appeal of the convention trade to hotels is that it generates lucrative demand for many support services (banquets, luncheons, cocktail parties, exhibits, audio-visual, entertainment, catering). In addition to the full-fledged convention meetings, many other types of seminars and exhibitions are also sought by hotels.

The top convention and trade show cities in the United States are Chicago, New York, Atlanta, Washington, Dallas, and Las Vegas. Each has many large hotels and meeting room facilities to accommodate a full range of trade shows and meetings. Most major convention cities also have publicly supported convention halls that provide massive space for meetings under a single roof. The World Congress Center in Atlanta, for example, has a continuous one-floor exhibition space of 350,000 square feet and a total square footage of 650,000 square feet, providing 42 acres of floor space in one facility (Figure 15-17). A larger facility is McCormick Place in Chicago, which has 750,000 square feet of exhibit space in one building and another 350,000 in an adjacent facility. The Dallas Convention Center is also very competitive with over 600,000 square feet of space.

The third component of the hotel market is the tourist and nonbusiness visitor (15 percent of the trade). This market is not only the smallest of the three support groups but also more seasonal (see Figure 15-16). Depending on the city and its location, the demand may be mainly a summer or winter phenomenon. Resort areas and large cities stand to gain the most from this market. The Miami, Orlando, and Las Vegas markets are examples of major resorts that benefit disproportionately from this business, and New York, Washington and Chicago illustrate the draw of a major metropolitan center as a tourist mecca.

Tourists, Entertainment, and Spectator Sports

Downtown locations have also provided favored sites for sports arenas for football, baseball, basketball, and

[20]Laventhol and Horwath, *Convention Centers, Stadiums, and Arenas,* Urban Land Institute, Washington, D.C., 1989.

Figure 15-17   Sports, Convention, and Entertainment Complex in Downtown Atlanta. The support for the downtown is increasingly coming from out-of-town visitors, as these facilities demonstrate. The Georgia World Congress Center convention facility is to left center, and the Georgia Dome stadium under construction in 1991 is in foreground. The Omni Sports Arena lies at top center (pyramidal roof), flanked by the CNN Communications Center. All lie in the former railroad corridor and will showcase 1996 Summer Olympics venues. (Copyright © 1991 by Dillon-Reynolds Aerial Photography, Inc. Used by permission.)

ice hockey venues, musical entertainment pavilions, museums, and live theater facilities that serve both an out-of-town clientele and the local citizenry. These latter facilities have been called *collective ritual centers*, in recognition of the role they play in attracting a massive clientele to spectator events.

The nonlocal fan patronizing these facilities spends considerable time and money on downtown hotel accommodations and shopping as a part of the visit, providing support for many service jobs. In some cities, such as New York, Detroit, Dallas, and Kansas City, sporting facilities began to leave downtown in the 1970s, but in others the downtown arenas remained an important institution and continue to expand; witness the Superdome in New Orleans, the Metrodome in Minneapolis, and the Georgia Dome in Atlanta (see Figure 15-17).

The number of out-of-town tourists and sightseers in CBD areas has also increased dramatically in recent years. In larger cities, visits by foreigners have increased very rapidly. This phenomenon has been demonstrated most conclusively in European cities, but it is also an increasing factor in North America, especially for nationally prominent cities with superior commercial air service.

ZONING

Change and adaptation have become synonymous with the downtown, as we have discussed. The resilience and strength of the CBD in the face of these adjustments are phenomenal. Security to neighboring properties from negative land use impacts poses a complex problem for the city and the CBD in particular. Deed restrictions and protective zoning provide instruments to mitigate negative impacts. Zoning, as an instrument of the government to protect and guide development, got its start in downtown New York City early in this century.

The negative impact of the high-rise structures on neighboring properties in blocking out the daylight, in part, prompted this first legislation in New York. Concern at the time also focused on the potential threat of encroachment of the apparel industry into the department store and office market of midtown Manhattan. The zoning guidelines set standards for building designs—the so-called wedding-style office building in New York, wherein upper stories are stepped-back—and grew out of these early zoning laws (Figure 15-18). The goal of zoning was to prevent one use from creating negative impacts on another by permitting only compatible uses in close proximity. This approach helped maintain or enhance property values.

Gradually the scope of zoning was expanded beyond this approach, often labeled a *nuisance power* solution, to a more comprehensive *police power* perspective. Based on the health, safety, and welfare of the community, zoning guidelines became more prescriptive as to appropriate uses and densities for land. A 1929 court case, *Euclid v. Ambler Realty Company*, affirmed for the first time that municipalities could "regulate and restrict land use."[21]

Modern zoning guidelines are closely related to long-range planning criteria and are considerably more flexible regarding approved uses than the first regulations.[22] More categories of residential, commercial, and industrial use now appear in ordinances, and many more zoning principles or guidelines have been invoked to provide both incentives and limits to development, depending on the location, scale, and function of a particular project. For example, in New York, the zoning ordinance adopted in 1961 specified guidelines for "building height, bulk, open space, and space between buildings"[23] (Figure 15-19). Buildings that provided more open space and plazas at the street level were given a "bonus" that allowed them to build higher structures. The aim was to have more "tall slim buildings" rather than the "wedding cake" styles that formerly prevailed.[24]

The number of different zoning concepts now in use is overwhelming. A partial list of several popular tools appears in Table 15-7, along with a short description of each. Some of the approaches are meant to encourage selective redevelopment and foster preservation of historic facilities such as *transfer zoning*, while others are aimed at preserving the status quo, such as *exclusionary zoning*, or managing growth, usually labeled *impact zoning*.

One criticism of traditional zoning legislation that has gained stature in recent years is that it was too segregative and did not permit mixed uses, even when they were compatible. For example, a neighborhood grocery store could not be placed in a housing subdivision. Many cities now have enacted *planned use development* (PUD) guidelines to allow more land use mixing, especially different housing forms (single-family detached, row houses, and apartments) in a single development in response to a demand for more

Figure 15-18 Wedding Cake Office Building Style. The New York Telephone Building in midtown Manhattan exemplifies this architectural style, wherein upper stories are stepped back to minimize the negative impacts of one structure on another adjacent land use (block views, sunlight, and so on). Zoning guidelines developed in New York in the 1920s encouraged this style. (Courtesy New York Telephone)

[21]Edward Reiner, "Traditional Zoning: Precursor to Managed Growth," in Randall Scott et al., eds., *Management and Control of Growth*, Urban Land Institute, Washington, D.C., 1975, pp. 211–223.

[22]Norman Marcus and Marilyn Groves, eds., *The New Zoning: Legal, Administrative and Economic Concepts and Techniques*, Praeger, New York, 1970.

[23]John Delafons, *Land-Use Controls in the United States*, 2nd ed., MIT Press, Cambridge, Mass., 1963, p. 43.

[24]Ibid., p. 45.

Figure 15-19 Lever House, New York. Zoning changes in New York in the 1960s promoted the construction of the tall slab office tower to replace the wedding cake style. This design left more open space for plazas and fountains at ground level. Often referred to as a glass box, this style became synonymous with modern (International) architecture (see box). (Courtesy Lever House/Photo by Harry Willes.)

variety of housing options. An emphasis in the future on making subdivisions more energy effective and less automobile dependent will certainly extend this type of zoning to encourage more work, living, and shopping facilities in close juxtaposition.

Zoning has also changed away from a "rigid standards for building height and placement" to allow for more "administrative discretion, which, in full-blown form, means political deal making."[25] Instead of prescribing exact uses, broad goals and performance standards related to densities, design, and types of uses are specified in flexible zoning ordinances, leaving the exact mix to the negotiation process, which may vary over time depending on market conditions, city priorities, developer expertise, and the availability of financing.

DOWNTOWN REDEVELOPMENT

The debate as to whether a strong downtown is necessary for a healthy city is more than an academic issue. Subscribers to the strong downtown theory have not only theoretical arguments in their favor, but also practical evidence that there is a trend for renewed vitality in many cities that formerly lacked strong core areas. Los Angeles, for example, historically has not had a strong CBD, but a resurgence of construction in the last two decades dramatically changed its role in the metropolitan economy. Many new high-rise hotels and office towers emerged in downtown Los Angeles in the 1970s and 1980s. The latter were prohibited by building height regulations until 1957, but few noticed, at the time, because hardly anyone was interested in high-rise construction.

Some would say that downtown redevelopment has been a defensive tactic, an attempt to defeat the prevailing *centrifugal forces* that attract activity to the suburbs. Downtown business interests claim otherwise. Their argument is that a strong downtown core is a crucial prerequisite for a viable metropolitan area. To accomplish this rebirth, the typical strategy involves a public–private partnership. The public sector often provides access to financing and land cost write-downs for projects, thus enabling developers in the private sector to undertake projects that otherwise would not be economically feasible.

Design Innovations

Many innovations in building design have accompanied CBD renewal in the last 25 years. The *megastructure* concept, which places retail, commercial, residential, office, and entertainment facilities in a single massive building or a series of interconnected buildings, has received the most attention. This type of development emphasizes round-the-clock occupancy and attempts to design facilities with user needs and amenities in mind. The Embarcadero Center in San

[25]Douglas R. Porter, "Flexible Zoning: How It Works," *Urban Land*, (April 1988), 6–7.

TABLE 15-7
Selected Zoning Concepts

Type	Description
Density zoning	Traditional controls of height, building-to-floor ratio, lot size, lot coverage, footage, etc.
Conditional-use zoning	Specifies uses that are permitted if certain guidelines are followed.
Floating zoning	Sets strict controls on each type of development (residential, retail) but does not designate locations; useful in new subdivisions.
Impact zoning	Relates demand for land use to capacities and consequences of change; a form of land management that requires an evaluation of consequences of develoment.
Transfer zoning	Permits owner of property (historic buildings) to sell development rights to another who can build elsewhere at a higher density; promotes historic preservation.
Percentage zoning	A desired land use mix is specified in advance in terms of minimum proportions.
Contract zoning	Specific guidelines negotiated with developer.
Special-use zoning	Separate category for a particular use such as a theater district or hotel-motel area.
Agriculture and forestry zones	Designates areas for continued agricultural use, preventing speculative development.
Bonus or incentive	Permits higher densities or heights if certain design guidelines are followed (parking, open space, plazas); combines offices and theaters in one building in New York, for example.
Exclusionary zoning	Specifies performance standards; used frequently in suburban areas to maintain exclusivity and uniformity.

Source: Author.

Francisco, Renaissance Center in Detroit, John Hancock Tower in Chicago, and Trump Tower in New York are all examples of such mixed-use developments. Earlier attempts to bring people back downtown (such as Marina City in Chicago) emphasized mainly housing and parking facilities, but the recent strategy is more comprehensive. Developments are self-contained and provide for a total urban environment (work, shopping, entertainment, and often home).

The many megastructures that now line North Michigan Avenue in Chicago provide an impressive example of mixed-use facilities (Figure 11-1). The 100-story John Hancock Tower, first occupied in 1969, showcases a megastructure of nearly 3 million square feet. The innovative layout of the building includes office space on floors 13–41, retailing on levels 1–5, topped by parking on levels 6–12. Housing occupies the upper stories except for a few of the highest levels, which are devoted to commercial activity.

Other downtown innovations include underground shopping malls and passageways among buildings and transitways. Particularly elaborate developments of this type have been built in Toronto, Montreal, and Houston. In some cities, such as Des Moines, Spokane, Minneapolis, St. Paul, Cincinnati, and Charlotte, *sky bridges*—enclosed pedestrian overpasses above street level—facilitate downtown pedestrian traffic. In Minneapolis and St. Paul, for example, over 25 city blocks can be accessed in each city on grade-separated walkways at the second- or third-story level.

In effect, these corridors become climate-controlled retail corridors with no street-level entrances. Their installation often causes retail decline on the street level in response to the decline in foot traffic. In Minneapolis, for example, retail sales along Nicollett Mall have shifted from the street to second-story levels in response to the skywalk system (see Figure 15-11). Critics have also noted that the withdrawal of retailing from the street level is also discriminatory by walling off the poor and homeless from the glitz and glamor of the retail boutique. Esthetic considerations are also involved as street-level uses wither in these settings.

Sky bridges often involve awkward architectural fits between buildings and they can impair visual sight lines. Nevertheless, their use continues to expand. More coordination and planning can mitigate most problems. In their favor, enclosed sky bridges can create a retail atmosphere that is more competitive with that of the suburban mall in a climate-controlled environment. In cities with cold winters, and those with hot, humid summers, the advantage seems obvious. Navigating slushy, icy, windy streets in winter on foot, for example, can be minimized in a skywalk or underground mall environment (see Figure 19-10).

Historic Preservation

Renovating older buildings to create prestigious office and retail spaces provides another opportunity to make downtown environments more competitive. These initiatives received a boost in the 1980s in the aftermath of the passage of federal tax credit legislation as a part of the Economic Tax Recovery Act of 1981. This federal tax credit was short-lived, but the seed had been planted, and initiatives at the local and state levels continued to flourish. Historic preservation ordinances enacted in many cities encouraged the designation of historic districts, not just the preservation of individual buildings. There are now thousands of properties listed on the National Register of Historic Places.[26]

The National Trust for Historic Preservation oversees the "Main Street" program, which has been very successful in rehabilitating many downtown commercial districts across the country. Although historic district designations occur widely throughout the city and involve both city and suburban properties of all types, downtown commercial structures comprise an important and highly visible portion of these districts.

Some of the boldest and most elaborate downtown reinvestment programs have emerged in the largest and oldest American cities. CBDs of these cities have experienced the most dramatic shifts in clientele and the longest period of decentralization, but continue to exhibit an innate vitality. The massive renewal and renovation of downtown Boston around the Government Center (including a new city hall, subway station, open plaza, and the renovated Faneuil Hall and Quincy Market), the Prudential Center, and Copley Place office–retail complexes are examples. Downtown Philadelphia renovations in the Society Hall residential area and Penn Central office section are also significant. No less important is the Loring Park Development District in Minneapolis. In this nine-block area, new housing, hotel space, and a pedestrian/bicycle greenway connect Nicollett Mall and Loring Park.

The Metro Center concept in Baltimore built upon two earlier projects—Charles Center and the Inner Harbor Shoreline Development (Figure 15-20). Charles Center is an office complex with some commercial, residential, hotel, and entertainment facilities. The Inner Harbor renewal program, completed in 1977, involved low- and mid-rise developments, both residential and commercial, and parks and walkways along the waterfront.

The goal of the Metro Center program is to coordinate private and public development in the center of Baltimore in a 1000-acre section. The redevelopment is not a single technical plan, but a series of strategies by businesses and local government to improve center-city services, decrease congestion, and increase the number and variety of jobs. Joint team efforts by public and private capital have also unfolded in many other cities and offer the best prospect yet to remake the central city and keep it competitive. Federal Urban Development Action Grant (UDAG) funds were used in many cities to stimulate this reinvestment. The UDAG program, administered by HUD, used federal funds to leverage private investment in distressed areas. The program was withdrawn in the late 1980s.

Downtown building styles in the past 25 years have received their share of criticism. A trend toward homogeneous designs, creating anonymous downtown skylines with less distinctive images, is part of the critics' concern. The high-rise glass box that reappeared many times contributed to the criticism.

In some cities, such as New Orleans, critics noted that the new high-rise buildings, often more than twice as high as the surrounding structures, created an undesirable intimidating effect on older facilities. The One Shell Place office structure, built in the 1970s to a height of 51 stories in an area of 20-story buildings, was dubbed "One Square Shell" by critics. Megastructures themselves have been called a menace by some observers.

Postmodernism

Dramatic change in architecture occurred in the 1970s with the first postmodern structures. An early entry in the "new look" of buildings was the Pennzoil Place Building in Houston (Figure 15-21). The appeal of the Pennzoil Building is its unconventional geometric form; actually, it is a two-tower structure: each tower is partly square and partly a right triangle, creating a trapezoidal shape. A 10-foot space or slot separates each building, and the roofs are at a severe 45-degree angle. This design avoids the traditional rectangular box. The prestige image of the development gave it many financial advantages. Innovative designs typi-

[26]Robin Datel, "Preservation and a Sense of Orientation for American Cities," *Geographical Review*, 75 (1985), 125–141.

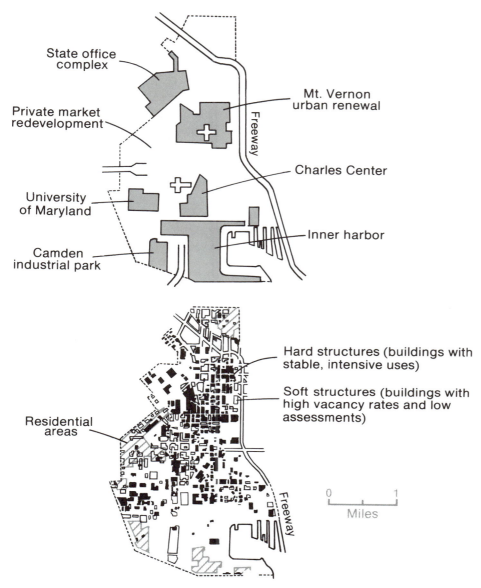

Figure 15-20   Metro Center Redevelopment in Baltimore. The metro center redevelopment effort linked the Charles Center and Inner Harbor renewal areas in the 1970s, paving the way for the "new" Baltimore CBD. The Harbor Place festival market has now replaced the old waterfront docks area, and a new hotel/convention center has revitalized its western flank. Note Mt. Vernon urban renewal area referred to in Figure 1-1. *Source:* Redrawn with permission from *Metro/Center Baltimore*, Baltimore City Department of Planning, 1975.

cally make good business sense, as they give a structure a distinctive image in the community and a marketing advantage (see box).

The Pennzoil Place Building has since been eclipsed in size and style by many other downtown Houston skyscrapers built in the early 1980s before the mid-decade recession drew new development to a halt (Figure 15-22). These buildings include the Republic Bank Center and Allied Bank Plaza, which take the postmodern design concept several steps beyond the Pennzoil Place design. Examples of striking postmodern designs emerged in other cities with active downtown markets in the 1980s as well, including Atlanta, Chicago, and New York.

Figure 15-21 Pennzoil Place, Houston. One of the first postmodern skyscrapers in the United States, this building built in the 1970s boasts an unconventional geometric form. This innovative architectural design gave the building a distinctive marketing advantage. (Courtesy Johnson Burgee Architects)

Lively Streets

Rather than creating an appealing new exterior design, many observers in recent years noted that planners and developers should pay more attention to street-level pedestrian needs when designing downtown facilities. In what William Whyte has dubbed a "brutal rejection of the street," many megastructures have drawn people inside a fortresslike facility that turns its back on the street and indeed the urban fabric of which it is a part.[27] What is needed, critics say, is a more inviting streetscape. For many years, zoning guidelines have encouraged building setbacks, plazas, and open spaces, but often cold or impersonal blank walls face the pedestrian. The traditional shopping street, with its multitude of storefront uses, gave way to impersonal office building and hotel facades with no street-level public uses, separated by greater space devoted to motor

[27]William H. Whyte. *City: Rediscovering the Center*, Doubleday, New York, 1988.

vehicle access, parking facilities, and a sharp break between megastructure buildings. Often buildings appeared to be designed for viewing and access from the freeway rather than for the pedestrian. More emphasis on visual continuity, street furniture, water features, and informal meeting places appears to be gaining popularity today as planners and developers seek to restore the street to the pedestrian. A design competition was held in Atlanta in 1991 for example to select a plan to restore a pedestrian quality to Peachtree Street, long a bastion of the automobile.

THE PROS AND CONS OF A STRONG DOWNTOWN

Eager to protect their investment, downtown business interests aggressively support the area. Some arguments advanced seem more emotional than real, while others do make good economic and ecological sense. Suggestions that the CBD is the heart of the city and that no city can prosper without a strong CBD illustrate the emotional tie. Downtown business interests in the past typically enjoyed good access to both the political and economic machinery of the city to back up their concern and have not been hesitant to use federal programs to bolster their investment as well.

The clamor for rail rapid transit systems in many cities in the 1970s to increase downtown access was typically associated with downtown business interests. Such rail systems were mainly geared to bringing more people downtown, as in the case of the systems built in Washington, DC., Atlanta, and Miami. More downtown parking space and better access for automobiles to the CBD area are other typical business concerns.

Energy consumption debates spark other arguments concerning the future of the CBD. The role of the CBD in an energy-scarce, high-cost environment is not as obvious as some would lead us to believe. Can the downtown compete more effectively than suburbia in an era of higher energy costs? Does high density save energy? What is the cost of sprawl? Definitive answers to these questions are not available, but arguments have been advanced supporting both downtown and suburb. The suburban proponent would say, for example, that living and working in suburbia saves transportation costs because of shorter work trips. Similarly, CBD proponents say public transportation is more readily available to that area, so that it can offer real cost savings on transportation despite long trip lengths.

Figure 15-22 Postmodern Houston Skyline in the 1990s. The 75-story Texas Commerce Tower frames one corner of the skyline, along with the gable-like profile of the Pennzoil building (see Figure 15-21), the multiple spires of the 56-story Republic Bank Center, and the rounded face of the 71-story Allied Bank Plaza. The Houston central business district contains nearly 40 million square feet of office space. (Courtesy Greater Houston Partnership)

Lingering Downtown Issues

Parking, crime, racial polarization, and middle-income housing are four issues that appear to be central to the debate on the future of the downtown. In each case, it is the perception that leaders and citizens have of these issues, as much as the real situation, that creates positive and negative attitudes. For example, parking may be perceived as inadequate even if there is sufficient capacity. Similarly, it is quite common to associate high crime rates with downtown areas in American cities even when the statistics show that crime is typically not a severe problem in the core commercial area. Racial polarization is another concern. Suburban white families often dislike coming downtown because the inner-city market has increasingly shifted to a black minority clientele in many metropolitan areas. Typically, only those suburbanites that either work downtown or frequent it have positive images of the area today.

Another pressing need for the downtown, in order to enhance its retail market and help it function more strongly in evening hours, involves expanding its market share of middle-income housing. Gentrification and in-fill housing have assisted in some cities, but in the majority of American cities today, the downtown remains surrounded by low-income residential neighborhoods.

A study of suburbanites in Radnor, Pennsylvania, a suburb of Philadelphia, indicated that nearly 20 percent of its citizens virtually never went downtown.[28] About half went downtown about once a month, and the rest said they went downtown only once every six months. Families with no children tended to use the downtown more, and middle-income families used the downtown less than those with higher or lower incomes. People working downtown used it more for social and recreation purposes than nondowntown workers. But the people who had lived in Radnor the longest did not use the downtown as much as newcomers. The conclusion of the study was that suburbanites have little use for the center city. This finding supports the view that a strong CBD may not be crucial to urban living.

---

[28]Joseph Zukmund II, "Do Suburbanites Use the Central City?" *Journal of the American Institute of Planners*, 37 (1971), 192–195.

Parking

The automobile provides the major mode of access to the downtown in most cities. Parking became a crucial issue as a result of increasing dependence on the automobile in the post-World War II era. The downtown has the most parking spaces in the metropolitan area, with only large airport parking facilities rivaling it in terms of capacity. Downtown businesses have led the crusade for more parking in response to worker and shopper demand. A widespread belief has evolved that "there is no parking space downtown." People in business have, in turn, traditionally felt that the provision of more parking space was a crucial factor in continued downtown viability.

Data on the actual need and trend in downtown parking are scarce. There is some evidence that there is adequate parking in many cities, but that it is not located where the customers want it—just outside the store or office they frequent. Another view is that better use of existing parking should be made by pricing it higher to allocate its use more rationally (discourage all-day parking). In other words, incentives should be given to encourage short-time parking use and disincentives to all-day users because of the high cost of land for such an idle activity. Providing cut-rate all-day parking encourages downtown commuting by car on a regular basis, causing traffic jams and pollution. A third approach is to ban cars from some streets and downtown zones and cut back on parking capacity. Catering to the pedestrian by eliminating the hazard of motor vehicles and developing secondary transport (buses, people movers) would create a more compatible environment according to this argument.

As cities grew in the post-World War II era, the demand for parking downtown grew much more rapidly than employment. The number of persons traveling per car decreased as did dependence on transit, creating a great need for off-street parking. As the number of cars increased, street parking had to be banned to add to the capacities of the streets. In large cities, the proportion of lot and garage parking increased more than enough to offset this loss (Figure 15-23).

Guidelines were developed in the 1960s that related the number of parking spaces required downtown to urbanized area populations. For example, in cities of 100,000, 16 spaces for each CBD destination by auto were suggested and 26 slots for cities of 1 million.[29] This translated into 4500 required spaces in an urbanized area of 100,000 and 18,000 spaces in cities of 1 million. Parking demand changes in relation to trip purposes and city sizes were also noted. Business and work trips created the most demand in larger areas, whereas shopping was most important in smaller cities (Figure 15-24). Downtown merchants and civic leaders called for greatly expanding parking space and inventories grew correspondingly.

In the early 1980s, environmentalists and planners began to question the wisdom of continued large-scale parking expansion in the downtown area. Not only had this approach encouraged greater dependence on the automobile, and concomitant freeway congestion, but the link with increasing air pollution had also become critical.

[29]Wilbur Smith and Associates, *Parking in the City Center*, Wilbur Smith and Associates, New Haven, Conn., 1965.

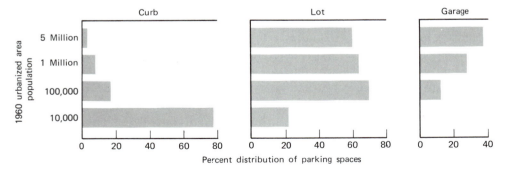

Figure 15-23 Downtown Parking by City Size and Type of Facility. The mix of curb, lot, and deck parking varies by city size. In a city of 10,000, most of the parking occurs on the street (curb), whereas cities over 100,000 primarily use parking lots; in larger cities, extensive parking hold most of the parked vehicles. *Source:* Adapted from Wilbur Smith and Associates, *Parking in the City Center*, New Haven, 1965, p. 6.

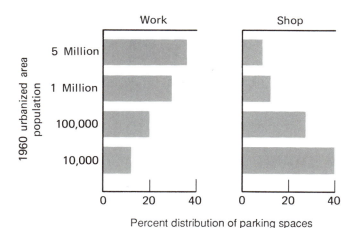

Figure 15-24 CBD Parking and Trip Purpose by City Size. Parking demand varies in relation to trip purpose, with work trips creating the highest demand in larger cities, whereas shopping creates the greatest demand in smaller centers (100,000 or less). *Source:* Adapted from Wilbur Smith and Associates, *Parking in the City Center*, New Haven, 1965, p. 6.

Today, many cities are implementing parking management strategies to offset perceived parking shortages. Preferential treatment for carpool and vanpool riders, employer-subsidized transit fares, and zoning ordinances that require fewer parking spaces with new construction near transit facilities are all options being implemented. Higher fees and increased municipal taxes on parking also serve to dampen demand. Park-and-ride lots in outlying areas and shuttle services provide other alternatives to CBD parking.

SUMMARY AND CONCLUSION

Despite decades of decentralization and years of intense use, the downtown area still plays a strong economic, social, and psychological role in the city. It has adapted to change very well in the past. But immense problems remain and will continue to require the attention of skillful planners and the infusion of large amounts of capital to ensure future competitiveness. Even though the distant view of the skyline suggests a young and vibrant city, most downtown areas remain burdened with a declining local resource base. The employment level has typically declined, and many local residents view the downtown as irrelevant to their daily lives. Increasingly, the new economic support for the downtown is coming from out-of-town business people, conventioneers, and tourists who pa-

tronize the hotels, convention facilities, and entertainment and cultural centers. Those working downtown do support local retail outlets, but increasingly the focus of their lives, like those who work in the suburbs, lies elsewhere.

Suggestions for Further Reading

Berk, Emanuel. *Downtown Improvement Manual*, American Society of Planning Officials, Chicago, 1976.

Corgel, John B., and Truman A. Hartshorn. "Measuring the Impact of the Inner City Markets on CBD Retail Sales," *Urban Geography*, 1 (1980), pp. 130–139.

Datel, Robin, and Dennis Dingemans. "Why Places Are Preserved: Historic Districts in American and European Cities," *Urban Geography*, 9 (1988), pp. 19–36.

Firey, Walter. *Land Use in Central Boston*. Harvard University Press, Cambridge, Mass., 1947.

Frieden, Bernard J., and Lynne B. Sagalyn. *Downtown, Inc.: How America Rebuilds Cities*, Massachusetts Institute of Technology, Cambridge, Mass., 1989.

Friedman, J. J. "Central Business Districts: What Saves Sales," *Social Science Quarterly*, 69 (1988), pp. 325–340.

Halpern, Kenneth. *Downtown USA: Urban Design in Nine American Cities*, Whitney Library of Design, New York, 1978.

Horwood, Edgar, and Ronald Boyce. *Studies of the Central Business District and Urban Freeway Development*, University of Washington Press, Seattle, 1959.

Hurd, Richard M. *The Principles of City Land Values*, The Record and Guide, New York, 1903.

Huxtable, Ada Louise. *Have You Kicked a Building Lately?* Quadrangle Books, New York, 1976.

International Downtown Executives Association and Real Estate Research Corporation. *Analysis of Major Commercial Districts*, Department of Housing and Urban Development, Washington, D.C., 1978.

Morrill, R. "The Structure of Shopping in a Metropolis," *Urban Geography*, 8 (1987), pp. 97–128.

Moudon, A. V. *Public Streets for Public Use*, Van Nostrand Reinhold Company, New York, 1987.

Murphy, Raymond. *The Central Business District*, Aldine-Atherton, Chicago, 1972.

Parking Consultant Council, National Parking Association. *The Dimensions of Parking*, Urban Land Institute and National Parking Association, Washington, D.C., 1979.

Paumier, C. B., et al. *Designing the Successful Downtown*, ULI—The Urban Land Institute, Washington, D.C., 1988.

Rannels, John. *The Core of the City*, Columbia University Press, New York, 1956.

Redstone, Louis. *The New Downtowns: Rebuilding Business Districts*, McGraw-Hill, New York, 1976.

Robertson, K. A. "Pedestrian Skywalk Systems: Downtown's

Great Hope or Pathways to Ruin?" *Transportation Quarterly*, 42 (1988), 3, pp. 457–483.

Smedcof, Harold R. *Cultural Facilities in Mixed-Use Development*. Urban Land Institute, Washington, D.C., 1985.

Ullman, Edward, et al. *Trends in CBD and SMSA Sales, 1948–1963*, Center for Metropolitan Studies, Washington, D.C., 1967.

Urban Land Institute. *Adaptive Use: Development Economics, Process and Profiles*, Washington, D.C., 1978.

Whyte, William H. *City: Rediscovering the Center*, Doubleday, New York, 1988.

Wilbur Smith and Associates. *Parking in the City Center*, Wilbur Smith and Associates, New Haven, Conn., 1965.

16

METROPOLITAN RETAIL STRUCTURE*

The distribution of goods and services between merchants and consumers is among the chief economic activities of urban areas. One of the most notable events in any city is the movement of people to shop or the movement of vehicles to deliver articles to customers. In the United States as a whole, and in all metropolitan areas, approximately 20 percent of all employed workers are engaged in retail and wholesale pursuits. Retailing accounts for over $1.5 trillion in sales annually in over 1.5 million establishments. It is not surprising, therefore, that the retail function in cities has received a good deal of attention by geographers.

Because urban geographers are interested in process and pattern, this chapter will focus on the spatial arrangement of retail activities in metropolitan areas. The retail landscapes evident today in the North American city have emerged slowly and are the result of numerous marketing and technological achievements. Retail units have become more specialized over time and the niche they serve in the marketplace more segmented and clearly defined. We witness today fewer entrepreneurs and a larger share of retail business controlled by huge multinational firms.

The spatial patterns that have emerged in the retail landscape are entirely logical, if constantly changing. We can discover the underlying order by an examination of the historical trends that have led to present spatial arrangements. Why are certain functions where they are? Why do some retail functions cluster? These and other questions will be answered in this chapter. Concepts introduced in Chapter 8 in dealing with central place theory will be heavily utilized.

The primary unit in the urban retail landscape is the individual store. Most of these units congregated in downtown areas at the beginning of this century, but have since dispersed throughout the metropolitan region. Today we find major concentrations of stores in suburban locations in addition to those in the central city. The growth of the population, its greater mobility, increases in personal income, and changes in transportation technologies have all led to the *centrifugal drift* of retail units outward to peripheral areas. This suburbanization of retailing has dramatically affected metropolitan sales patterns. In Chicago, for example, $12 billion in retail sales occurred in the central city out of a total of $50 billion in the metropolitan area in 1987, creating a 76 percent suburban share.[1] In Atlanta, 85 percent of retail sales occurred in the suburbs in 1987.

---

*Chapter in First Edition authored by Borden D. Dent, Georgia State University; revised in this edition by author.

[1]Bureau of the Census, *1987 Census of Retail Trade, Geographic Area Series, United States*, RC 87-A-52, U. S. Government Printing Office, Washington, D.C., 1989.

HISTORICAL ROOTS

Retail stores as we know them today—providers of specialized shoppers' goods—are a product of the mid-nineteenth century, but the retail market concept itself dates back to antiquity, as we discussed in Chapter 2 and Chapter 15. For example, recall the discussion about the agora being the predecessor of the modern-day central business district.

In the colonial period, so-called *frontier stores*, named for their location on the leading edge of settlements, provided many items for sale, but they were primarily taverns and blacksmith operations rather than retail outlets (Table 16-1). Indeed, *peddlers* provided the first true retail function in America, but they were itinerant travelers, not in-store retailers as we know the concept today. Peddlers were very important institutions in rural and small-town America as recently as the early twentieth century. The *general store* gradually replaced the peddler in the latter part of the nineteenth century and still provides a role in rural America today (Figure 16-1). The general store was the first organized in-store retailer selling a wide range of goods from food to household supplies to livestock and farm provisions.

As cities grew in the mid-1850s, new forms of retailing emerged to serve the growing demand for goods. Clusters of these stores emerged in downtown areas, including "the butcher, the baker, and the candle stick maker" store, as the rhyme goes. These and other units as a group created the first *specialty retail* centers in American cities.

The *department store*, a large unit offering a collection of clothing, household goods, furniture, bedding, and other supplies, in several sections, also emerged at the same time. This store type drew customers from throughout the city, offering quality merchandise, credit, and personal customer service. Many of the big name retailers that we still associate with department stores—Marshall Field (1867), R. H. Macy (1858), William Filene (1851), and others–date to this time (Table 16-2). By the turn of the century, the department store experienced growing competition from a new mass seller form—the variety store.

The *variety store* represented the first of several innovations in the mass merchandising of goods, a trend that continues to generate new forms today. Often referred to as the "five and dime," the variety store offered a small selection of a wide range of clothing and household supply items. Many of these stores grew into national chains with their appeal focusing on low prices, self-service, and minimal sales assistance. S. S. Kresge (the predecessor of K-Mart), F. W. Woolworth, and W. T. Grant, among others, became mainstays in downtown retailing in all cities in the immedi-

TABLE 16-1
Selected Merchandise at McCorkle's Store in 1774[a]

Apparel	Household Items	Medicines	Miscellaneous Items
Raccoon hats	Pewter tableware	Spirits of turpentine	Pig iron
Gloves	Toddy ladles	Brimstone	Locks
Shoes	Toddy spoons	Alum	Grindstones
Coat strops	Skillets	Turlington's drops	Claw hammers
Razors	Brass kettles	Turlington's balsam	Putty
Looking glasses	Frying pans	Stoughton's bitters	Hand saws
Watch chains	Butcher knives	Bateman's drops	Files
Stockings	Rugs	Anderson's pills	Rope
Garters	Trunks	Glauber salts	Cat gut
Fans	Candle molds		Soap
Bonnets	Candle snuffers		Bags
Handkerchiefs			Chisels
Breeches			Scales
Gowns			Quills

[a]Adapted from Conway Howard Smith, *The Land that is Pulaski Country,* ©1981 by Conway Howard Smith for Pulaski County Library Board.

Figure 16-1. The General Store. The general store, which still can be found in rural America today, was the first organized in-store retailer selling a wide range of goods, from food items to household supplies to livestock and farm provisions. Coffey's General Store in Edgemont, North Carolina, has been in the same family for over 50 years. (Bruce Roberts/Rapho/Photo Researchers.)

TABLE 16-2
Department Store Pioneers

Name	Place	Year
William Filene	Boston	1851
Arthur Letts ("The Broadway")	Los Angeles	1896
Adam Gimbel	New York	1910
J. L. Hudson	Detroit	1886
R. H. Macy	New York	1858
Marshall Field	Chicago	1867
Morris Rich	Atlanta	1867
John Wanamaker	Philadelphia	1861
Richard Sears ("Sears & Roebuck")	Minneapolis	1886

Source: P. J. Reilly, *Old Masters of Retailing,* Fairchild Books, New York, 1966.

ate pre- and post-world war II era. But hard times emerged by the 1960s for the traditional variety store as suburbanization of retailing accelerated and more discriminating shoppers turned to name brand merchandise and more expensive fashion-oriented merchandise. Today it is rare to find a variety store in the city, but some do exist.

A new wave of mass merchandisers rapidly captured the growing demand for more upscale name brand merchandise at discount prices in the 1960s. Led by the success of K-Mart created by the Kresge Company, many established chain stores created discount divisions. Woolworth spawned Woolco, and Dayton Hudson launched the Target store, and new retailers also entered the scene, such as Zayre and Wal-Mart. We will discuss other contemporary types of mass merchandising concepts in later sections, following a discussion of retail decentralization and the hierarchy of retail centers in the metropolitan area that have evolved in the past 50 years.

METROPOLITAN RETAIL LANDSCAPE

Before post-World War II suburbanization, the retail sales network was organized around a downtown that contained the only mass selling units (department stores) in the city (Figure 16-2). Convenience selling units, primarily food stores, were located throughout the urban area. After major suburbanization in the post-World War II era, mass selling units vastly multiplied in number, decreasing the centrality of the CBD for such sales. The number of convenience selling units also grew substantially. These changes actually involved three specific tendencies in the suburbs: (1) filling-in of retail units in newer residential areas; (2) expansion of retailing along arterial streets; and (3) opening of department stores in larger shopping centers.

The outward shift of major department stores actually began in the 1920s. By following a series of *interceptor rings*, it is possible to trace this process (Figure 16-3). Interceptor rings are best described using a map where a line or ring joins together department stores at similar distances from downtown areas at various points in time. Department stores that moved out initially were usually located at relatively close-in intersections of major arterial routes leading to and from city centers. They became interceptors in that they offered competition for the older downtown units. In the case of Detroit, the first ring (now an inner ring) was structured around several Sears & Roebucks (a pioneer developer of outlying stores) and Federal department stores (Figure 16-3). By 1958, two additional rings had formed connecting several more Federal and Wards (Montgomery Ward) stores. The interceptor ring concept has been used more recently to conceptualize the location of large department stores in many other cities.[2]

---

[2]See Joseph D. Enedy, "The Department Store in Metropolitan Baltimore, 1945–Present: A Geographical Analysis," unpublished Ph.D. dissertation, Department of Geography, Kent State University, 1973, pp. 92–94; Borden D. Dent, "The Challenge to Downtown Shopping," *Atlanta Economic Review*, 28 (January 1978), 29–33.

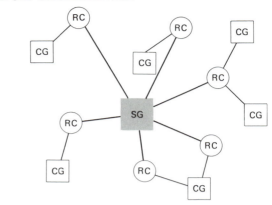

BEFORE SUBURBANIZATION

AFTER SUBURBANIZATION

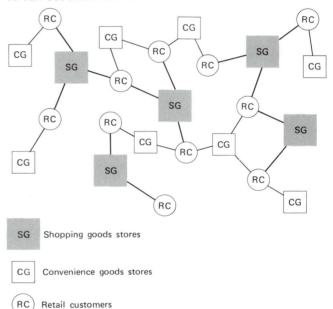

SG   Shopping goods stores

CG   Convenience goods stores

RC   Retail customers

Figure 16-2. Changing Metropolitan Retail Patterns Before and After Urbanization. Before post-World War II suburbanization, the retail sales network was organized around a downtown that contained the only mass selling units (department stores) in the city. Convenience selling units, primarily food stores, were located throughout the urban area.

A wide variety of other retail units also found advantages in locating along major traffic arterials adjacent to shopping centers, and indeed along entire suburban strips, as automobiles became more widely used for commuting. These retail districts provided services for the automobile as well as for the expanding needs of the increasingly leisure-oriented and do-it-yourself suburban family. We will examine arterial retail activity in a later section.

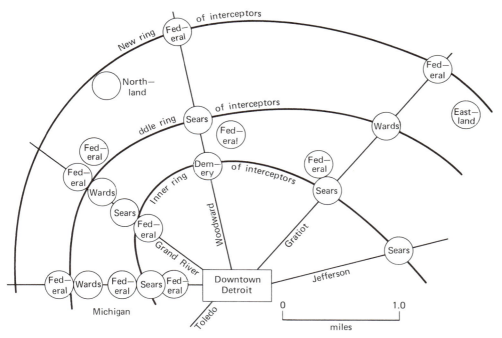

Figure 16-3. Interceptor Rings of Department Store Locations in Detroit. The outward shift of department store locations can be traced by mapping sites at similar distances from the downtown at various points in time. *Source:* Redrawn from *The Selection of Retail Locations*, by Richard L. Nelson. Copyright © 1958, F.W. Dodge Corporation. Used with permission of McGraw-Hill Book Company.

A Classification of Urban Commercial Structures

A casual glance at a current urban land use map may not reveal to the novice much spatial order regarding commercial patterns. Upon closer inspection and study, it becomes apparent that certain land use organizations do exist. Examination of these patterns led Brian Berry and fellow workers to group similar business areas in Chicago in the early 1960s.[3] The classification that emerged is reminiscent of earlier work by Malcolm Proudfoot for Philadelphia in the latter 1930s.[4] Proudfoot's classification included five types of retail structures: (1) CBD, (2) outlying business center, (3) principal business thoroughfare, (4) neighborhood business street, and (5) isolated store cluster.

Three major classes comprised Berry's classification: (1) *centers,* (2) *ribbons,* and (3) *specialized areas*

(Figure 16-4). Urban business *centers* demonstrated a hierarchical arrangement beginning first with the low-order isolated convenience store (grocery-drugstore), then a neighborhood business center containing small supermarkets, drugstores, dry cleaners, and the like. Next in the hierarchy was the community shopping center comprising not only those functions of the neighborhood center, but also stores offering higher-order goods (variety and clothing stores, bakeries, jewelry stores, florists, and perhaps a post office). At the regional level were the most specialized stores, including large department stores, apparel stores, shoe shops, music and record stores, hobby shops, and other specialized functions. The apex of the pyramidal hierarchy was identified with the CBD, which offered the most specialized retail functions.

Ribbon developments refer to the collections of unplanned retail units that evolve along highway corridors due to the good automobile access they offer. These units include gasoline stations, fast-food restaurants, automobile dealers, tire dealers, and the like. They also encompass space extensive functions such as furniture stores, mobile home sales, and home supply stores (see later section).

[3]Brian J. L. Berry, *Commercial Structure and Commercial Blight: Retail Patterns and Processes in the City of Chicago,* Research Paper No. 85, Department of Geography, University of Chicago, Chicago, 1963, p. 19.

[4]Malcolm Proudfoot, "City Retail Structure," *Economic Geography,* 13 (1937), 425–428.

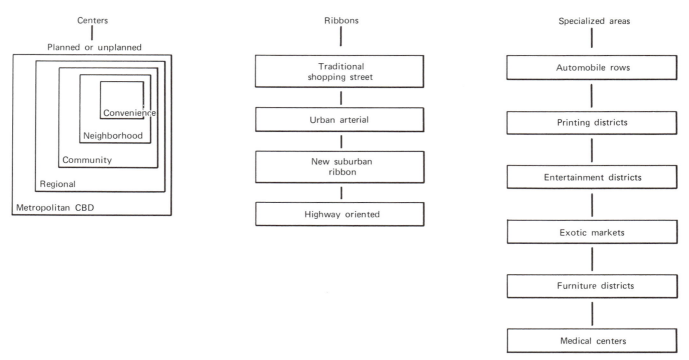

Figure 16-4. Metropolitan Retail Structure, after Berry. Three major classes of retail forms exist in this classification: 1) centers; 2) ribbons; and 3) specialized-function areas. This conceptualization is especially appropriate in accounting for the hierarchy of shopping centers and the role of the retail strip corridor. *Source:* Redrawn with permission. From Brian J. L. Berry, *Commercial Structure and Commercial Blight*, University of Chicago, Department of Geography, Research Paper 85, 1963, 20. Copyright by the University of Chicago, Department of Geography.

Large metropolitan areas also contain *specialized-function* areas. These are characterized by automobile rows, professional office clusters (doctors, dentists, paramedical colleges, and clinics), furniture districts, antique districts, and others. Many of these areas were unplanned originally, the clustering being the result of mutual attractiveness (economies in advertising, referrals, and the like). Today we find that more formalized planning is integral in their development, especially with regard to medical centers. The architectural requirements of these latter complexes (plumbing, electrical, air handling) often necessitate a more unified approach. Specialized-function areas require good accessibility because they draw customers from throughout the metropolitan area.

It is important to point out that many retail functions will be represented in several locational environments, and that the classes in the Berry classification are not mutually exclusive. For example, we may find dry cleaners as a ribbon-oriented function or in a neighborhood shopping center. It is important to remember, too, that Berry's classification is *spatial* in that it is an attempt to organize the commercial pattern conceptu-

ally on the land use map. This classification remains the most suitable today to describe the retail landscape and is especially appropriate to explain the hierarchy of shopping centers.

A dominant role in the explanation of the various functional centers in retail space is the concept of *hierarchy*. The various levels of shopping centers within metropolitan areas correspond with the central place hierarchy of service centers discussed in Chapter 8 (Figure 16-5). Several behavioral traits and economic characteristics that explain the intraurban commercial hierarchy are:[5]

1. Different functions have *thresholds* and minimum *trade areas* of varying sizes (i.e., they require differing minimal numbers of customers for their support).

2. Customers demand various goods at different frequencies. Low-threshold, high frequency-of-

---

[5]Brian J. L. Berry and Frank E. Horton, *Geographical Perspectives on Urban Systems*, Prentice Hall, Englewood Cliffs, N.J., 1970, p. 456.

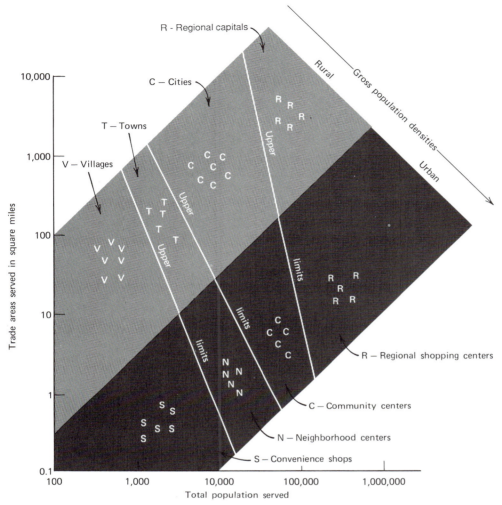

Figure 16-5. Hierarchies in Urban and Rural Settings. The central place hierarchy of settlements, discussed in Chapter 8, has an urban counterpart in the shopping center hierarchy. Note that the trade area served (square miles) is much higher in rural areas due to lower population densities, but the total population served at any level is much higher in an urban setting. *Source:* Brian J. L. Berry/John B. Parr, *Market Centers and Retail Location: Theory and Applications,* ©1988, p. 30. Adapted by permission of Prentice Hall, Englewood Cliffs, New Jersey.

purchase items are found at lower-level nucleations having small trade areas. High-threshold, low frequency-of-purchase items occur in higher-level nucleations having larger trade areas.

An actual count of functions indicates more lower-order outlets (e.g., supermarkets) dotting the land use map and fewer high-order functions (large furniture or appliance stores). The urban consumer travels only short distances to obtain groceries because these purchases are made frequently. To obtain major home appliances, a purchase that is practiced infrequently, consumers will make a longer trip. The key to under-

standing the commercial pattern in cities lies in these behavioral characteristics of consumers.

The same type of *nesting* of trade areas that occurs at the regional scale also occurs inside metropolitan areas of various sizes. Figure 16-6 portrays a hypothetical spatial arrangement of these patterns, indicating the traditional role of the CBD at the top of the hierarchy in providing goods and services to the entire metropolitan area. It is quite apparent from this figure that trade areas of lower-order goods offered at the neighborhood- and community-level centers are quite small when compared to those of the regional shopping centers that offer higher-order goods and services.

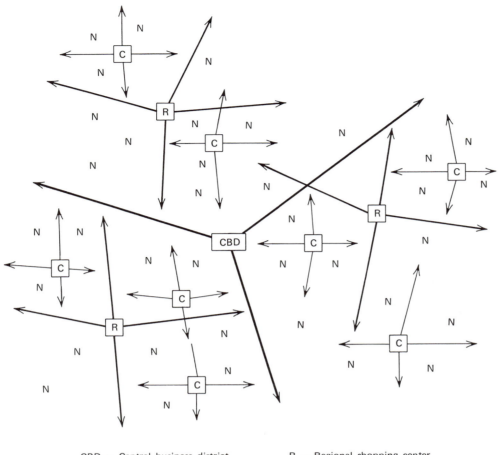

CBD — Central business district   R — Regional shopping center
C — Community shopping center   N — Neighborhood shopping center

Figure 16-6. Spatial Expression of the Retail Center Hierarchy, after Berry. This traditional model of the structure of retailing in metropolitan areas indicates that the CBD falls at the top of the hierarchy in providing goods and services to the entire metropolitan area. The reach of regional centers, community centers, and neighborhood centers is also shown. The length of the arrows indicates the composite ranges of goods and services at each level.

Dynamic Aspects of Urban Commercial Patterns

Further insight into the dynamic aspects of shopping behavior was provided by James Vance in the early 1960s.[6] Research in the San Francisco–Oakland SMSA area led him to identify three chief periods in the development of city retail patterns. Initially, retailing occurred in *downtown central locations*. The second phase began in the late 1800s, coinciding with the rise of public mass transportation. Commercial activity began to spread out along the *transport lines* at that time, clustering at main intersections bisecting these routes. Vance identified a third phase, which began in the 1930s, with the rise of private automobile ownership and the beginning of new *mass-appeal* merchandising techniques (high-volume, brand name identification approaches).

Vance highlighted the following dynamic factors influencing the overall commercial pattern of cities:[7]

1. The automobile, giving the consumer more mobility and freedom of choice.

[6]James E. Vance, Jr., "Emerging Patterns of Commercial Structure in American Cities," in K. Norborg, ed., *Proceedings of the IGU Symposium in Urban Geogrpahy, Lund 1960*, Gleerup, Lund, Sweden, pp. 485–518.

[7]Ibid.

2. Changing purchasing power and tastes, causing greater sales volumes and the demand for more retail space.

3. New housing patterns, especially the centrifugal drift of population outside older downtown locations.

4. Changes in land use zoning policies, leading especially to large land parcels for planned centers.

5. Changes in merchandising (commodity combining), leading to larger stores and thus causing frequent building design changes and alterations.

In addition to the identification of these historical trends and dynamic factors, Vance also made several predictive overtures. First, recall that the CBD traditionally functioned to supply the metropolitan region with all forms of goods and services. Vance argued that this pattern would tend to break down in large metropolitan regions. In effect, he suggested that the CBD would become several downtowns—one, the office district for the region; another, the specialty goods seller to the urbanized area; and a third, the mass-appeal goods seller to inner-city residents. Outlying regional shopping centers would provide mass-appeal goods for the suburban market. Vance argued convincingly that throughout history the seller always attempted to locate as close to the consumer as possible. Over time, this decreased the size (area) of trade areas.

More recently, further changes in retail structures have occurred, again altering the role of the CBD, as discussed in Chapter 15. The CBD is now one of several regional shopping centers and no longer at the top of the retail hierarchy (Figure 16-7). Often both outlying *regional* and *superregional* centers have more extensive trade areas than the downtown and equivalent or greater retail space square footage. Malls in suburban downtowns now generate sales levels above those of the CBD. In many cases, the CBD today ranks fifth or lower in sales volume among all centers in a particular metropolitan area.

SHOPPING CENTER EVOLUTION

Modern zoning practices favor the planned, nucleated shopping center, and thus it is natural to find that store cluster arrangement to be the most dominant retail form in outlying portions of urban areas. But this is a relatively new arrangement. Older streetfront shopping

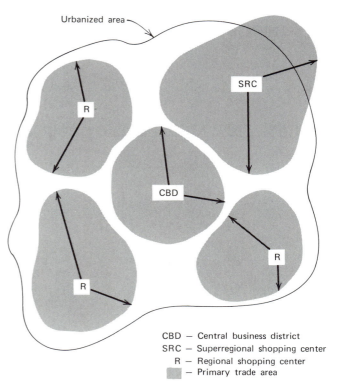

CBD — Central business district
SRC — Superregional shopping center
R — Regional shopping center
░ — Primary trade area

Figure 16-7. Contemporary Retail Trade Area Structure for Large Metropolitan Area. The CBD now functions as one of several regional shopping centers and no longer lies at the top of the retail hierarchy. Often both outlying regional and superregional centers have more extensive trade areas than the downtown.

districts were located at major arterial intersections and not planned as a group. Remnants of these older centers still exist in older central city residential neighborhoods, dating back to the streetcar era. With greater dependence on the automobile for access, shopping districts needed to provide more parking, which led to considerable experimentation in shopping center design, beginning in the 1920s and culminating with the emergence of the regional mall in the 1950s.

Shopping Center Prototypes (1900–1930)

Several design innovations shaped the development of the modern shopping center, and these advances occurred in stages following years of experimentation (Figure 16-8). One such advance first appeared in Baltimore with the construction of the Roland Park shopping center in 1907 (Figure 16-9). Built in a fashionable residential suburb, this retail center contained several neighborhood stores in a unified building structure with a liberal setback from the street, permitting off-street parking in front of the businesses.

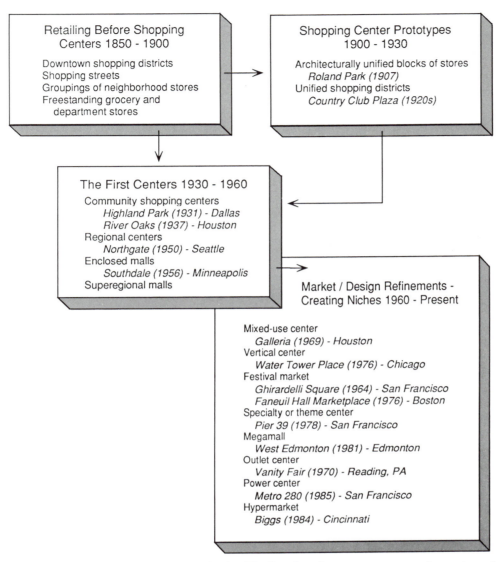

Figure 16-8. Evolution of the Shopping Center. The first shopping centers grew out of groupings of stores dating to the mid-nineteenth century; not until the twentieth century, however, did unified shopping districts emerge. Several innovations, or "firsts," occurred after World War II, including the first department store in a regional shopping center, and the first enclosed regional mall. Since 1960, many refinements have occurred with shopping center design, including the development of specialized formats for particular market niches. *Source:* Modified after A. Alexander Bül and Nicholas Ordway, "Shopping Center Innovations: The Past 50 Years," Urban Land (June 1987), 24.

Country Club Plaza in Kansas City, developed in the 1920s, took the emerging concept of a shopping center prototype one step further with the creation of a unified shopping district (Figure 16-10). Again, the suburban site catered to the automobile with the liberal provision of parking spaces around several buildings planned as a unit in the context of a traditional street pattern. This was not a true shopping center as we know it today, isolated from through street traffic and surrounded by massive parking lots. Although located in the suburbs, the center reflected a more traditional downtown design.

The First Centers (1930–1960)

By 1931, another forward leap in design came with the Highland Park Center in Dallas. Many consider this center to be the first planned center in the United

Figure 16-9. Roland Park Shopping Center, Baltimore. Built in 1907, this retail center was a "first" in that it contained several stores in a unified building structure with a liberal setback from the street, permitting off-street parking in front of the businesses as automobiles came into wider use. The tudor architectural style of the center blended in well with fashionable suburban residences built in the community at the same time. Note horse and carriage making delivery. (Courtesy Peale Museum, Baltimore City Life Museums.)

Figure 16-10. Country Club Plaza, Kansas City. Developed in the 1920s, this shopping center pioneered the concept of a planned suburban shopping district by incorporating several buildings in one setting clustered together around a traditional street network, with liberal provisions for automobile parking. Developer J. C. Nichols built the center in conjunction with a residential subdivision. This center still flourishes today with minor modifications (see Figure 9-8). (Courtesy Plaza Association.)

States.[8] The site was not bisected by public streets and the plan provided for the development of stores and parking under a unified management umbrella. We would call this a strip shopping center today. Remarkably, it still remains very competitive in the Dallas market.

Shopping center management concepts came of age with the development of the River Oaks Center in Houston in 1937. It pioneered innovations such as the percentage lease as a means to determine rent based on sales performance and a merchants association. These techniques and others have become hallmarks of the shopping center industry whereby centers carefully orchestrate the tenant mix, advertising and promotion activities, common area maintenance, security, and the overall image of the center in order to maintain a competitive edge.

While early shopping centers included specialty stores, none contained a major department store anchor along with other specialty stores, until the Northgate Center in Seattle pioneered the concept in 1950. To be sure, outlying department stores existed before this time, but they were free-standing stores on major arterial streets. While Northgate became the first regional shopping mall in the country, another design innovation yet to come meant that it would have to share the limelight with another center, Southdale Shopping Center in Minneapolis, as a regional mall innovator.

Southdale, developed in 1956, enjoys the distinction of being the first enclosed regional center in the country (Figure 16-11). This design innovation truly turned the mall inward away from the street, creating a totally controlled shopping environment that revolutionized the retail shopping experience. Gradually centers emerged with two or more department store anchors, and the number of these center mushroomed nationwide, along with sales levels. Nationally, shopping center sales remained under $100 million annually in 1967, but leaped to over $100 billion by 1977.

Creating Niches (1960 to the Present)

Further refinements to the shopping center concept have occurred in the past 30 years, but they represent fine-tuning of a proven concept rather than the revolutionary change that occurred in the 1930–1960 era. The

mixed-use center, for example, which combines retail, office, and hotel functions in one integrated complex, came of age in 1969 with the introduction of the Galleria in suburban Houston (Figure 16-12). That complex became the nucleus of the City Post Oak suburban downtown, which evolved to national prominence in the 1970s (see box). Taking the mall concept back downtown in the form of a *vertical mall* made headlines in 1976 with the opening of Water Tower Place on North Michigan Avenue in Chicago (Figure 16-13). Water Tower's seven levels of retailing include department stores and specialty shops linked by escalators and glass-enclosed elevators in an open central atrium providing views of all levels. Unlike traditional shopping centers, sales volumes are highest on the top levels of this complex, reflecting its superior design. Water Tower Place is part of a mixed-use complex that also includes housing, office, and hotel space.

The *megamall* concept, pioneered by the West Edmonton Center in 1981, wraps an extraordinarily large retail mall having 3.8 million square feet of space including eight department stores and literally dozens of specialty stores around an enclosed amusement entertainment complex. The recreation facilities include four operational submarines in a lake, an ice skating rink, a 400,000 square foot amusement park, a scale model of the Pebble Beach golf course, a water park with wave machine, and a replica of Columbus' Santa Maria, among other activities. This center draws its clientele from western Canada and the northwestern United States, completely overpowering traditional thinking on shopping center trade areas. The potential for a large number of megamalls appears limited because of the sheer scope and scale of these complexes and the difficulties in securing permitting in the face of potential environmental and infrastructure support problems.

Festival markets and specialty or *theme centers* also entered the retail scene in the 1970s. This concept was pioneered by Ghiradelli Square with the renovation of abandoned brick factory buildings near the San Francisco waterfront in 1964 (Figure 16-14). The complex houses about 70 specialty retail shops and a dozen restaurants on about 8 levels in 10 buildings on a sloping hillside. It catered to a tourist/convention clientele and became an often-copied specialty center in the 1970s.

Another pioneering example of a festival market, developed by regional mall builder James Rouse, is the Faneuil Hall marketplace opened in Boston in 1976

---

[8]A. Alexander Bül and Nicholas Ordway, "Shopping Center Innovations: The Past 50 Years," *Urban Land* (June 1987), 22.

Figure 16-11. Southdale Regional Shopping Center, Minneapolis. This contemporary photograph shows the first enclosed regional shopping center in the United States, built in 1956. It revolutionized suburban retailing by creating a totally inward-facing, climate-controlled environment in the midst of a huge parking lot. (Courtesy Southdale Shopping Center.)

Figure 16-12.   The Galleria at City Post Oak, Houston. The Galleria regional shopping center, first developed in 1969, became a prototype for a mixed-use center which combines retail, office, and hotel space into one integrated complex. The Galleria is nearly lost in this photograph showing the large number of high rise facilities that now blanket the area. It is located to the right foreground of the tall dark building (Transco Tower) at top left of photograph, anchored by two high-rise structures. (Urban Land Institute.)

Figure 16-13. Water Tower Place, Chicago. This pace-setting vertical mall located on fashionable North Michigan Avenue opened in 1976. Unlike traditional shopping centers, sales volumes are the highest on the top levels of this complex, reflecting its superior design. A high-rise hotel tower rises above the retail block with a lobby on the 13th floor. Exterior view of complex shown in Figure 11-1. Several other vertical malls now complement Water Tower Place on North Michigan Avenue. Water Tower's seven levels of retailing include department stores and specialty shops linked by escalators and glass-enclosed elevators in an open central atrium, affording the shopper a vista of all floor levels. (Courtesy JMB Properties Urban Company.)

(Figure 16-15). As with Ghiradelli Square and other festival markets, this center offers specialty shop/restaurant/entertainment functions in an anchorless setting. The anchor in a sense is the setting—a historic district, the waterfront, or Main Street. Early festival markets like Faneuil Hall were located in run-down downtown neighborhoods having historical architectural significance to the community. Other examples of festival markets include Harbor Place in Baltimore,

South Street Seaport in New York, the Underground in Atlanta, and Riverwalk in New Orleans.

Two successful innovations of the 1980s in shopping center retailing include the emergence of the *factory outlet center* and the so-called *power center*. Both represent a blurring of traditional lines of retailing and demonstrate how competition and price squeezing can lead to new trends in the industry. The factory outlet center provided an opportunity for manufacturers to enter the retail field directly. Most of the stores in these centers are factory owned. Few are located in the midst of metropolitan area markets because manufacturers traditionally marketed their name brand goods exclusively through department stores. Locating close to department store competitors would only serve to erode traditional sales opportunities and anger department store retailers.

Department stores typically sell goods at a markup to cover their higher overhead costs. Outlet centers, on the other hand, offer discounted prices. To avoid retaliation, most outlet centers typically locate 20–30 miles away from their department store competition, along major highways leading to and from metropolitan areas or in resort/recreation settings where national retailers are typically underrepresented. Tourist areas also offer an opportunity to capture a larger, more affluent market predisposed to shop as a part of the holiday experience. Indeed, some of the earliest and most successful outlet centers can be found in vacation/resort markets such as North Conway, New Hampshire (gateway to the White Mountains); Myrtle Beach, South Carolina; Orlando, Florida; and Niagara Falls, New York.

Outlet centers also located in derelict factories as an outgrowth of initiatives taken by a particular firm (e.g., Boaz, Alabama, got started as an outlet for Blue Bell jeans as did the first such center in Reading, Pennsylvania), opened by Vanity Fair in a closed factory building in 1970. The firm manufactured hosiery, sleepwear, and lingerie, giving it access to several products for outlet center distribution. Vanity Fair also leased space to other businesses. By 1983, there were 183 of these stores in the country, employing 2000 persons and generating over $250 million in sales. Other companies sought out existing but weak community shopping center locations, and yet another group began from scratch, building new centers, some with a village theme and others as an indoor mall.

A list of major manufacturers and their products frequently occurring in outlet centers appears in Table

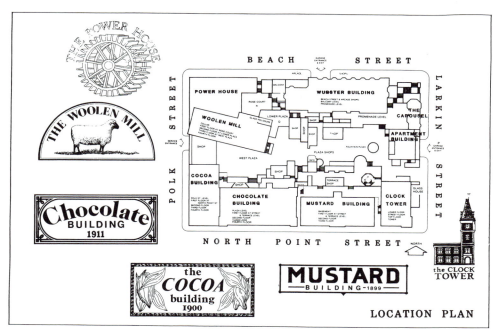

Figure 16-14. Ghirardelli Square, San Francisco. This festival market became a prototype following the renovation of abandoned factory space for an integrated specialty shopping complex in 1964. Located near the waterfront in a tourist district, the complex houses about 70 specialty shops and a dozen restaurants on about 8 levels in 10 buildings on the sloping hillside. The complex was renovated and redesigned in the mid-1980s, preserving its historic character. Signs now call out the names of the old factory buildings (Woolen Mill, Cocoa Building, Mustard Building, and others). (Courtesy Benjamin Thompson & Associates)

16-3. By the early 1990s, over 200 outlet centers posting total annual sales of more than $5 billion flourished in the United States, all of which had opened in the past 10 years.

We will postpone the full discussion of the *power center* until after the presentation of the traditional shopping center hierarchy. The power center represents a modification of that hierarchy. Suffice it to say here that the mix of retailers in a power center differs from that of a more conventional center in that several large off-price anchor stores, rather than many smaller specialty stores, account for the majority of the space. With such added complexity to the types of shopping centers available today, competition between and among types has increased dramatically. Traditional uniform market areas for these centers have given way to more overlapping and uncertainty in the business. To increase our understanding of the retail landscape, it will be useful to examine traditional marketing and consumer behavior characteristics.

SHOPPING CENTER HIERARCHIES

Shopping center clusters today may contain as few as 6 units or as many as 200 or more outlets. Megamalls and superregional centers, at the top end of the hierarchy, locate in cities of a million or more in population. One of the largest superregional malls in the world, and the largest on the West Coast, is South Coast Plaza and Town Center, which boasts 2.8 million square feet of retail space and generates over 1.5 billion dollars of sales annually (Figure 16-16). This retail center forms the nucleus of the South Coast Metro suburban downtown in Orange County. The sales acumen of this center occurs in an environment with keen competition as well. There are over 75 million square feet of retail space in Los Angeles County, for example, and no fewer than 45 regional malls.

Regional malls occur in cities as small as 25,000–50,000 in population, depending on the location of the city and competing markets. Each of the different size

Figure 16-15. Faneuil Hall Festival Marketplace, Boston. This festival marketplace developed by James Rouse in 1976 became a much-copied model for festival markets involving the adaptive reuse of run-down buildings. Faneuil Hall and the Quincy Market buildings date to the 1700s and had been slated for demolition. This project pioneered the concept of the food court. There are now 22 restaurants, 40 food stalls, and 125 specialty shops in the complex. (Peter Southwick/Stock Boston.)

TABLE 16-3
Leading Firms with Outlet Stores

West Point Pepperell—fabrics, linens, domestics

Van Heusen Co.—shirts, sweaters

Calvin Klein—men's sportswear

American Tourister—luggage

London Fog—rainwear

Burlington Coat Factory—outerwear

Dexter Shoes—shoes

Corning—housewares

Pfaltzgraf—stoneware, china

Champion—knitwear

Carolina Pottery—pottery, household goods

Leather Loft—handbags, luggage, leather goods

The Paper Factory—paper goods, gifts

Source: Author.

nucleations has its own distinctive combinations of retail types and mix of sales, depending on its level in the hierarchy. As each type displays its own retail character, its size and composite trade area will also be distinctive. The urban geographer is interested in the role of each of these different forms in the commercial structure of the city.

Studies to determine the minimum threshold size for market entry of several different kinds of establishments found in these centers have produced interesting results. Table 16-4 lists those functions commonly found in city retail nucleations at several shopping center levels and presents the findings of two major research efforts. Individual threshold populations vary depending on population density, but the threshold sizes are nevertheless revealing in a relative sense. Those thresholds reported by Brian Berry and W. L.

Figure 16-16. South Coast Plaza and Town Center, Orange County. This superregional mall with four department stores and nearly 3 million square feet of retail space forms the nucleus of the South Coast Metro suburban downtown. Note the integration of cultural/entertainment facilities into the mall complex, including the South Coast Repertory Theatre and the Orange County Performing Arts Center. (Courtesy South Coast Plaza.)

TABLE 16-4

Minimum Threshold Populations for Retail Units in Four Different Shopping Center Sizes

	Threshold Sizes	
Establishments and Services by Shopping Center Levels	*Berry and Garrison (1958)*	*Noble et al. (1976)*
Neighborhood shopping center		
Beauty shop	480	423
Supermarket	254	437
Physicians	380	488
Barbershop	386	648
Dentist	426	827
Drugstore	458	840
Cleaners and dryers	754	1234
Community shopping center		
Restaurant	—	372
Insurance agency	409	460
Women's clothing	—	748
Apparel store	590	758
Variety store	549	1352
Hardware store	431	1267
Regional shopping center		
Bank	610	1216
Men's clothing	—	1362
Department store	1083	1388
Jewelry	827	1882
Movie theater	—	2234
Superregional shopping center		
Florist	729	2276
Sporting goods	928	22,740
Optometrist	1140	6078
Photo	—	8785
Stationery	—	12,298

Source: Michael S. Noble et al. in Edwin W. Rams, ed. *Analysis and Evaluation of Retail Locations,* Reston Publishing, Reston, Va., 1976. Reprinted with permission of Reston Publishing Company, Inc., a Prentice-Hall Company, 11480 Sunset Hills Road, Reston, Virginia; and Brian J. L. Berry and W. L. Garrison, "Functional Bases of the Central Place Hierarchy," *Economic Geography,* 34 (1958), 145–154, with permission.

Garrison were obtained in Snohomish County, Washington, and those by Michael Noble et al. from places in Arizona, Nevada, New Mexico, and Utah having more than 20,000 population.

There are differences in the order of entry for a given level of retail operation because of regional and time variations, but the overall trend is consistent. It is readily apparent that as the shopping center class level increases, the unit unique to each class requires a greater threshold population for support. These threshold size changes are most obvious between the community and regional center classes.

A most helpful and relatively current source of data on retail operations for the geographer is *Dollars and Cents of Shopping Centers: 1990,* published by the Urban Land Institute.[9] That organization identifies four major shopping nucleations: *neighborhood, community, regional,* and *superregional* centers. For each, facts are reported on operating expenditures, leasable floor space, and tenant characteristics.

Other inventories of shopping center trade include the census conducted by *Shopping Center World.*[10] This publication reports, for example, that in 1988 there were about 33,000 centers of all sizes operating in

[9]Urban Land Institute, *Dollars and Cents of Shopping Centers: 1990,* Urban Land Institute, Washington, D.C., 1990.

[10]*Shopping Center World,* February issues. Published by Communication Channels, Inc., Atlanta.

the United States, accounting for over 600 billion dollars of sales. In 1964, by contrast, there were only 7600 centers, with sales of 78 billion dollars.

Convenience Store

At the lowest end of the shopping center hierarchy lies the *convenience store*. An isolated grocery or drugstore or tavern typifies this class. The "mom-and-pop" grocery store, often found at a streetcorner in an older residential subdivision, best fits this description. The store provides convenience goods for the immediate neighbors, who normally walk to it for purchases. The convenience store is largely disappearing today, typically being replaced by a small chain-operated market that is open for extended hours (e.g., 7-Eleven, Stop-n-Shop, Circle K) and offering a limited line of the most frequently demanded food items and gasoline. It has also been supplanted to some extent by the neighborhood shopping center, which serves a larger trade area and offers large store sizes which are preferred by consumers who can reach them just as easily by car as an earlier generation could get to the convenience store on foot. Moreover, Americans do not shop as frequently for convenience items as they did in the past before the advent of the refrigerator, fast food, and greater participation rates of women in the labor force. This being the case, a preference for a large store to find goods has grown.

Neighborhood Center

The functions found in the *neighborhood centers* are dominated by low-order goods and services. These centers typically serve a market area with a population of 7000 to 15,000 persons. These neighborhood centers average just under 70,000 square feet in size. They provide for the daily needs of their customers, principally the provision of convenience goods such as food, drugs, liquor, and/or hardware, and personal services such as beauty shop, dry cleaners, or video rental store.

Because neighborhood centers offer goods demanded frequently, they are the most common type of center. The neighborhood center class accounts for over one-half of all shopping centers in the United States.

A superstore or supermarket occupies the most floor area in these centers and it is the major anchor (Table 16-5). The concept of the superstore, an innovation of the 1980s, refers to "a supermarket with more than 30,000 square feet of sales area, an annual sales volume of at least \$5 million, and 20 to 25 percent of sales in nonfood items."[11] A superstore typically offers many of the following in addition to food items: drugs, cosmetics, a bakery, a delicatessen, film processing, cards and gifts, books, pharmacy, wine, automotive supplies, fast food, florist, small appliances, video film rentals, and a branch bank. Therefore, this store typically absorbs some functions formerly found in other competing stores in the neighborhood center. In short, the superstore consolidates in one operation several low-order functions and seems to compete better in the marketplace than the traditional supermarket.

Drugstores, video tape rentals, and legal offices make up the next largest share of activity. Beauty shops, restaurants, and fast food occur most frequently in neighborhood centers. Duplication of functions exists but is not the common experience. As the figures in Table 16-5 indicate, the average number of stores in each group is not high (averaging less than 1 in each category). The functions that occur most frequently represent the kinds of goods and services that have low thresholds for market entry.

The neighborhood shopping center can be either planned or unplanned, but most occur as planned centers on major arterial highways. These centers exist in communities of all sizes and might be the only shopping center level present in small villages. Although the superstore or supermarket is the anchor and most prominent business, it occurs less frequently than a fast-food unit or dry cleaners. Considerable shifting of the tenant mix has occurred in neighborhood centers in the past 15 years. Medical and dental offices, real estate offices, and hardware stores are not found as often today. In their place one now finds fast-food outlets, video tape rentals, and florists, among others, which did not occur as frequently in the past. Overall, the median size of these centers increased by one-third from 1975 to 1990, paced by the growth in size of the superstore and by the greater number of eating establishments.

---

[11] Urban Land Institute, *Dollars and Cents of Superstore Centers: A Special Report*, Urban Land Institute, Washington, D.C., 1988.

TABLE 16-5
Characteristics and Tenants Most Frequently Found in Neighborhood Centers

Characteristics	
Median gross floor area	68,000 square feet
Anchors	Supermarket: 22,413 GLA[a] or Superstore: 36,953 GLA

Tenant	Frequency of Occurrence,[b] Rank	Average Number of Stores[c]	Median GLA
Beauty shop	1	.6	1200
Restaurant (with liquor)	2	.5	3200
Dry cleaner	3	.5	1475
Fast food	4	.5	1434
Restaurant (without liquor)	5	.4	2200
Drugstore	6	.3	7060
Video tape rental	7	.3	1538
Legal office	8	.3	1347
Women's specialty	9	.3	1590
Supermarket	10	.3	22,413
Florist	11	.3	1320
Cards and gifts	12	.3	2050
Superstore	13	.2	36,953
Women's ready-to-wear	14	.2	2100
Barbershop	15	.2	898
Bank	16	.2	2835
Jewelry	17	.2	1000
Liquor/wine	18	.2	2400
Radio, video, stereo	19	.2	2228
Family shoes	20	.2	3000

[a]GLA refers to gross leasable floor area in square feet.

[b]Frequency of occurrence refers to the number of times a function is found among centers of this class. A rank of 1 means that this function was found most frequently; 2, less frequently; and so on.

[c]This number reflects the relative frequency of a store of this type in the center. Typically, six or fewer stores occur in a neighborhood center, so this list of 20 types includes many entries less than 1 (e.g., .6, .3, etc.).

Source: Urban Land Institute, *Dollars and Cents of Shopping Centers: 1990* (published triennially), 625 Indiana Ave., N.W., Washington, D.C. Reprinted with permission.

Community Center

A comparison between Tables 16-5 and 16-6 demonstrates the functional difference between the neighborhood and the *community shopping center*. As the next higher level in the functional hierarchy, the community center offers, in addition to those functions at the neighborhood level, more specialized shoppers' goods stores, such as women's apparel, a bank, or bookstore.

Approximately 30 percent of all shopping centers fall into this class, and each center is designed to serve about 30,000 to 50,000 people.

Included at the community shopping level are junior department stores, discount stores, supermarkets, or superstores as anchors. While junior department stores (Woolworth, Walgreens, etc.) still predominate, it is more typical to find a discount store as the primary anchor today (e.g., K-Mart, Wal-Mart, or Target). The

TABLE 16-6
Characteristics and Tenants Most Frequently Found in Community Shopping Centers

Characteristics	
Median gross floor area	161,000 square feet
Anchors	Discount department store: 60,000 GLA[a]
	Superstore: 37,000 GLA
	Junior department store: 35,000 GLA

Tenant	Frequency of Occurrence,[b] Rank	Average Number of Stores[c]	Median GLA
Women's ready-to-wear	1	1.2	3000
Restaurant (with liquor)	2	.8	3537
Fast food	3	.7	1500
Beauty shop	4	.6	1300
Family shoe	5	.6	
Jewelry	6	.6	1260
Cards and gifts	7	.6	2600
Restaurant (without liquor)	8	.6	2807
Women's specialty	9	.5	1600
Bank	10	.5	2955
Cleaners and dryers	11	.4	1600
Junior department store	12	.4	35,390
Superstore	13	.4	37,430
Radio, video, stereo	14	.4	2000
Discount department store	15	.4	59,537
Video tape rental	16	.3	2000
Books	17	.3	2400
Unisex hair	18	.3	1217
Superdrug	19	.3	14,600
Drugstore	20	.3	7532

[a] GLA refers to gross leasable area in square feet.

[b] Frequency of occurrence refers to the number of times a function is found among centers of this class. A rank of 1 means that this function was found most frequently; 2, less frequently; and so on.

[c] This number reflects the relative frequency of a store of this type in the center.

Source: Urban Land Institute, *Dollars and Cents of Shopping Centers: 1990* (published triennially), 625 Indiana Ave., N.W., Washington, D.C. Reprinted with permission.

junior department store form differs from a major department store in that the quality and price of goods are generally lower, item selection is more limited, fewer departments are present (i.e., no furniture or appliance sales), and its physical size is smaller. In the past, more than one supermarket often appeared in these centers, but the superstore usually does not locate in centers with another food store.

The more specialized goods found in the community center require a higher threshold of entry than activities in neighborhood centers and as such normally have larger trade areas. The stores in a planned community center typically occur in rowlike fashion, hence the label strip center is used for these complexes. The anchors in the community center typically exist at the ends or well spaced between the smaller stores. The total length of the center is critical because shoppers do not like to walk long distances from one end to the other. It is not uncommon to find covered walkways linking the stores, but complete climate control along passageways is usually lacking. Sites are selected to guarantee easy accessibility to major thoroughfares and a plentiful supply of offstreet parking is provided.

In the 1980s, many changes occurred in the frequency of functions offered in community shopping centers. Prominent new additions to the list of top 20 functions included fast food (ranking third), the superstore, video tape rental, books, unisex hair salons, and the superdrugstore. Dropouts from the list included the traditional supermarket, medical and dental offices, men's wear, the barbershop, yard goods, and insurance offices. These changes reflect adjustments in marketing strategies, especially the tendency to develop larger stores offering a broader range of goods, as in the case of the discount department store, the superstore, and the superdrugstore. These changes came at the expense of losing the traditional supermarket and variety store from the list of most frequently occurring store types.

Lifestyle changes are also reflected in the business mix in community centers, including the growing tendency to eat more frequently away from home. The strong presence of fast-food outlets and the high ranking of restaurants serving liquor reflect this trend. The emergence of the video tape rental store at both the neighborhood and community center levels also testifies to the trend for more time spent at home for entertainment. The highest sales volumes in community centers occur in superstores, which registered about $350 per square foot in 1990. These units perform better than their supermarket predecessors as a result of the greater emphasis on nonfood items with higher markups, such as flowers, pharmacy, and household items. The lowest sales volumes in community centers came from cinemas and laundry units, which typically register volumes under $50 per square foot.

Regional Center

The *regional shopping center*, as we discussed earlier, is distinguished by the inclusion of at least one major department store. These centers became the dominant outlying retail form in terms of sales in the latter 1950s and 1960s. They contained on average 500,000 square feet of floor space, and a wide variety of shoppers' goods and services were provided, typically as much as available in the CBD. As many as 50,000–200,000 people formed the principal trade area. Today these centers account for about 4 percent of all shopping

nucleations, but they are very visible on the landscape because of their large size.

The kinds of goods and services found in regional centers are listed in Table 16-7. The most frequently occurring functions are women's and men's clothing and shoe stores, along with jewelry, gift, and book stores. Note that, on average, a regional center provides 11 apparel stores, 5 shoe stores, and 3 jewelry stores, according to information in Table 16-7. As in the case of neighborhood and community centers, fast-food stores also occur frequently, typically clustered in food courts. Food courts offer a dozen or more fast-food alternatives with a central seating area serving all outlets. The range of food typically includes ethnic offerings, hot dogs, seafood, and dessert items (Table 16-8).

The *duplication* of functions is very evident at the regional mall level. Many stores offer similar goods. Most of the functions are of higher order than those found at the community or neighborhood level, thus requiring larger population thresholds to compete in the market. The range of goods has now widened, so that composite trade areas of the regional shopping center are quite large. Shoppers normally patronize the nearest regional shopping center exclusively; they rarely split purchases among two or more centers. In turn, the shopping opportunities available at that center reflect the buying power of its trade area and its patron's retail goods preferences.

Regional shopping center design has changed remarkably over the past two decades. At first, regional centers were usually laid out with a department store at each end of a large open or enclosed mall connecting the two. Small shops adjoined this center mall. Most such centers were predominantly single story, but the department store usually contained more than one level. As these centers evolved and grew in size, there was a tendency to reduce the linear dimension. It is quite common today to find multitiered architectural designs and most are totally enclosed, making them completely environmentally controlled. Many older complexes are now being refurbished to make them more competitive, often adding new wings of stores, as well as additional anchors. The highest sales volumes in the regional center occur with camera and jewelry stores and kiosks, which have become very popular on mall concourses. Sales levels in these operations often reach $500 per square foot. Low sales volumes on a per-square-foot basis occur in arts and crafts stores and shoe repair shops, which may not exceed $300.

TABLE 16-7
Characteristics and Tenants Most Frequently Found in Regional Shopping Centers

Characteristics			
Median gross floor area	469,520 square feet		
Anchors	One or two major department stores		

Tenant	Frequency of Occurrence,[a] Rank	Average Number of Stores[b]	Median GLA[c]
Women's ready-to-wear	1	7.1	3510
Jewelry	2	3.1	1241
Fast food/carry out	3	2.7	860
Family shoe	4	2.4	3129
Women's specialty	5	2.2	2413
Women's shoe	6	2.0	1467
Men's wear	7	2.0	3038
Cards and gifts	8	1.9	2699
Books	9	1.1	2991
Unisex/jean shop	10	1.1	3077
Toys	11	1.1	3426
Eyeglasses—optical	12	1.0	1250
Records and tapes	13	1.0	2594
Athletic footwear	14	1.0	2594
Special apparel—unisex	15	1.0	1290
Radio, video, stereo	16	.9	2539
Restaurant (with liquor)	17	.8	3842
Department store	18	.8	110,184
Costume jewelry	19	.8	712
Candy and Nuts	20	.8	604

[a] Frequency of occurrence refers to the number of times a function is found among centers of this class. A rank of 1 means that this function was found most frequently; 2, less frequently; and so on.

[b] This number reflects the relative frequency of a store of this type in the center.

[c] GLA refers to gross leasable area in square feet.

Source: Urban Land Institute, *Dollars and Cents of Shopping Centers: 1990* (published triennially), 625 Indiana Ave., N.W., Washington, D.C. Reprinted with permission.

Superregional Centers

Superregional centers also provide a wide variety of shopping goods and extend the shopping center concept beyond that of a typical regional mall. General merchandise, apparel, furniture and furnishings, services, and recreational opportunities are all features of the superregional center. These nucleations usually have over 1 million square feet of space in enclosed environments, and frequently house up to 150 individual selling units (Table 16-9).

Many showcase examples of these centers now abound in addition to the South Coast Plaza mentioned earlier. Columbia Mall (Maryland) expanded in the late 1970s to nearly 2 million square feet of space. The three-level Woodfield Mall at Schaumburg, Illinois, in suburban Chicago near O'Hare Airport, is now one of the largest suburban centers in the United States, with 2 million square feet of retail space.

These centers will be dwarfed in the early 1990s with the opening of the Mall of America in Bloomington, Minnesota, in suburban Minneapolis. It will offer 800

TABLE 16-8
Most Frequent Food Lines in Food Courts
in Regional Malls

1. Hot dogs/corn dogs	9. Greek
2. Pizza	10. Pastries/croissants
3. Oriental/Chinese	11. Ice cream
4. Sandwich/subs	12. Drinks/juice
5. Hamburgers	13. Cookies
6. Mexican	14. French fries
7. Yogurt	15. Seafood/fish/chips
8. Chicken	16. Potatoes

Source: Urban Land Institute, *Dollars and Cents of Shopping Centers: 1990* (published triennially), 625 Indiana Ave., N.W., Washington, D.C., p. 306. Reprinted with permission.

stores, 18 theatres, and 100 restaurants— a true mega-mall. In addition, there will be an amusement park in the mall. Planners speculate that it will draw customers from up to 400–500 miles to shop, clearly setting it apart from the more traditional superregional center. Trade areas for superregional centers are very large, often serving as many as 250,000 people, drawing not only from the surrounding areas, but also from all parts of the city and adjacent rural hinterlands.

At least three major department stores, each having 100,000 square feet of floor space (each larger than most neighborhood centers), generate the drawing power for superregional centers. Apparel, shoe, fast-food, and jewelry stores are the most prevalent units, along with other specialty stores, such as decorative accessories and eyeglasses/opticians. The main difference between the superregional and regional centers is not in the mix of goods but in the number of units offering them. Not only are there more department stores in the superregional centers, but also more specialty stores of a given type. The average number of women's ready-wear stores in superregional centers, for example, is 14, while the average is 7 in the regional center.

The superregional shopping center provides for many family activities other than just retailing. Several functions are recreational in nature (restaurants, theaters), and the center provides a *social nexus* for its clientele. It becomes a meeting place for the young, and retailers take advantage of this affinity by providing record and video stores, unisex jeans stores, athletic footwear for the yuppie market, along with video arcades and fast-food outlets. In many ways, the shopping center has become a replacement for the "corner drugstore" as a meeting place for youth in an earlier generation. It also provides restful places for the elderly (e.g., bench clusters).

Many large regional shopping centers provide settings for cultural exhibits, fairs, craft shows, art exhibits, community workshops, day care and other programs of local interest. Local governments often use the centers as public meeting places and dissemination points for public service programs.

SUBURBAN TOWN CENTER

The regional or superregional shopping center has essentially become the *town center* for suburbia. Americans now spend more time at shopping malls than anywhere else outside their homes and jobs. "You can buy anything from diamonds to yogurt in them, go to church or college, register to vote, give blood, bet, score, jog and meditate in them, and in some you can get a motel room, apartment, or condominium—and live there."[12] Teenagers spend their evenings there, as do families and the elderly. The suburban shopping center has evolved into a total environment of entertainment and culture.

Some have called the mall a fantasy land in the tradition of Disneyland with its fountains, trees, ice-skating rinks, and amusement arcades (pinball, pong). It is also

[A] timeless space. Removed from everything else and existing in a world of its own, a mall is also placeless space and the beauty of the form is that this space can be filled with all kinds of fine-tuned fantasies. Malls can host the ideal image of the small-town street or embody nostalgic themes—an anesthetized version of early America is particularly popular in the Northeast. Or they can create new hybrids with elements otherwise found in amusement parks, public markets, sports arenas and symphony halls—encased in structures that partake of the opulence of grand hotels, European city plazas and the great American railroad stations. (Not surprisingly, malls on the West Coast are the most ebulliently rococo, while the Midwest leans towards a kind of mall classicism and the Sunbelt goes for glassy elegance.)[13]

---

[12]William Kowinski, "The Malling of America," *New Times*, 10 (May 1, 1978), 33; see also William Kowinski, *The Malling of America*, William Morrow, New York, 1985.
[13]Ibid.

TABLE 16-9
Characteristics and Tenants Most Frequently Found in Superregional
Shopping Centers

Characteristics			
Median gross floor area	985,153 square feet		
Anchors	At least three department stores		
Tenant	Frequency of Occurrence,[a] Rank	Average Number of Stores[b]	Median GLA[c]
Women's ready-to-wear	1	13.6	3410
Jewelry	2	6.9	2200
Fast food	3	5.1	812
Men's wear	4	5.0	2709
Women's shoe	5	4.6	1500
Women's specialty	6	4.4	1732
Family shoe	7	3.8	3014
Cards and gifts	8	3.4	2521
Department store	9	2.5	156,000
Unisex apparel	10	2.5	1900
Men's and boy's shoe	11	2.2	1206
Decorative accessories	12	2.1	1295
Books	13	2.1	3301
Athletic footwear	14	2.0	2063
Restaurant (with liquor)	15	2.0	4734
Unisex/jean shop	16	1.9	3511
Candy, nuts	17	1.8	710
Eyeglasses—optician	18	1.8	1303
Toys	19	1.7	3367
Records and tapes	20	1.7	2508

[a] Frequency of occurrence refers to the number of times a function is found among centers of this class. A rank of 1 means that this function was found most frequently; 2, less frequently; and so on.

[b] This number reflects the relative frequency of a store of this type in the center.

[c] GLA refers to gross leasable area in square feet.

Source: Urban Land Institute, *Dollars and Cents of Shopping Centers: 1990* (published triennially), 625 Indiana Ave., N.W., Washington, D.C. Reprinted with permission.

With more emphasis on cultural and civic functions, the mall complex as the hub of the suburban downtown has become a true town center. The South Coast Metro, for example, includes the Orange County Performing Arts Center, the summer home of the Los Angeles Symphony, the South Coast Repertory Theater, and a sculpture garden. The art galleries, museums, day care, and exclusive membership club functions now found in malls offer additional evidence of their growing town center role.

Assigning Centers a Niche

Now that the classic hierarchy of centers is understood, it is appropriate to return to the task of assigning recently developed shopping center formats to their appropriate place in that hierarchy. The difficulty of this assignment becomes obvious when one observes that the traditional assignment criteria—square footage, tenant mix, number of anchors, types of stores, trade area size, and sales volume—are all blurred or redefined by many of the newer center formats. As shown in Figure 16-17, most of the new types of centers sit on the fence, so to speak, as they bridge the distinctions of traditional centers. In the long run, this may lead to the redesignation of the hierarchy and the elimination of one or more levels. It is clear, for example, that the trend is for larger centers, and most lie on the community center/regional center boundary line. The roles of two types of centers shown in Figure 16-17, the power center and the hypermarket, have not yet received appropriate coverage and their role in redefining the center formats deserves discussion.

Hypermarket

The *hypermarket*, a concept borrowed from Europe, combines food, apparel, and general merchandising functions together in one very large operation—about 200,000 square feet. A lack of competition from other forms of retailing, unlike the situation in the United States, largely explains the success of hypermarkets in Europe. Neither supermarkets nor discount stores existed in Europe before the hypermarket. But in the United States, market saturation by both superstores and discount stores preceded the hypermarket, making the process of carving out a niche more difficult. Hypermarkets, for example, must draw from a larger trade area than their predecessors. To do this, they emphasize their size and vast array of products, often touting themselves as malls without walls. They boast competitive pricing due to rapid turnover of stock and bulk merchandising displays reminiscent of a ware-

house, and they typically emphasize only fast-selling items in a particular category, rather than offering many choices.

Considerable experimentation is still occuring with hypermarkets in the United States, and the number of these centers is still limited. Names in this category include Sam's Wholesale Club and Hypermarket USA, divisions of Wal-Mart; American Fare, operated by K-Mart and Brunos Foods; Price Club, based in San Diego; and Carrefour, a French transplant. To keep sales volumes high and to generate high traffic flows, hypermarkets must seek locations in relatively high density urban areas and in areas with affordable land prices. For these reasons, many observers feel that land prices are too high in the Northeast and Far West to make these outlets appealing and that population densities are too low in the South to make them attractive. According to this reasoning, the Middle West may be the most appealing future locations for hypermarkets in the United States.

Power Center

The *power center* also bridges the community/regional shopping categories, but for different reasons than the hypermarket. Sometimes labeled a super-community center, the power center emphasizes a large number of anchor discount stores at the expense of smaller specialty stores. A typical community center, for example, has a 60/40 space assignment in terms of the anchor/

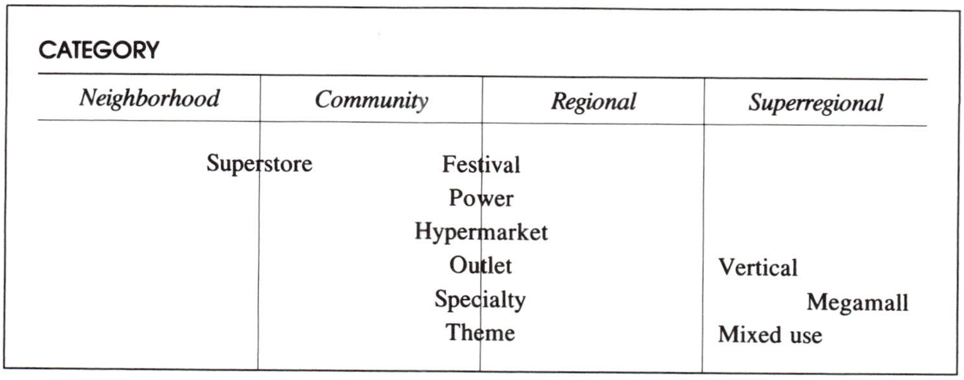

CATEGORY			
Neighborhood	*Community*	*Regional*	*Superregional*
Superstore	Festival		
	Power		
	Hypermarket		
	Outlet		
	Specialty	Vertical	
	Theme		Megamall
		Mixed use	

Figure 16-17. Newer Shopping Center Forms in Relation to the Traditional Hierarchy Classification. Many of the newer shopping center formats do not fit the traditional classification as they bridge established distinctions. This may lead to the redesignation of the hierarchy and the elimination of one or more levels in the future.

small store mix, while the power center provides an 80/20 split. The term "power" refers to the "power retailers" that occupy the anchor stores (Figure 16-18). Beginning in the mid-1980s, so-called "category killer" stores began dominating their merchandising group. Toys 'R' Us began dominating toys, for example, as Marshall's, T.J. Maxx, and Upton's began dominating apparel, and Circuit City became prominent in electronics. A list of these "power retailers" appears in Table 16-10. The range of store types having entries in the power retailer listing is growing rapidly. In addition to apparel and electronics, it includes home

TABLE 16-10
Fast-Growing Power Center Stores

Toys	Furniture
Toys 'R' Us	Levitz
Family Clothing and	Drugs
Accessories	Phar Mor
T.J. Maxx	Drug Emporium
Uptons	F & M Distributors
Marshalls	Children's Store
Mervyn's	Children's Palace
Dress Barn	Kiddie City
Electronics/Appliance	Kids 'R' Us
Circuit City	Arts and Crafts
Lechmere	Michaels
Silo	Cineplex
Highland Appliance	AMC
Home Centers	General Cinema
Home Club	Cinemark
Home Depot	Food
Builders Square	Cub Foods
Hechingers	Sporting Goods
Office Supplies	Herman's World of
Office Depot	Sporting Goods
Office Max	
Catalog Showroom	
Service Merchandise	

centers, sporting goods, drugs, catalog showrooms, movie theaters, arts and crafts, and others.

Many early entrants in the power center shopping center industry chose locations adjacent to regional malls to take advantage of their drawing power; indeed, some regional mall developers built competing power centers themselves on property adjacent to the regional mall. Like the regional center, the power center needs a large middle-class market base to thrive. But unlike the situation in a traditional mall, analysts have noted that there is little *cross-shopping* in the power center. That is, few customers patronize several stores on a single trip. The design of the centers contributes to a hostile environment for "casual shoppers" because the large number of anchors takes up a lot of space, creating long walking distances. Most of these centers are not enclosed, creating an environment more tied to "easy in, easy out" by automobile rather than cross-shopping. Pedestrian passageways between stores rarely exist. In summary, the power center is a collection of destination stores sharing a common site.

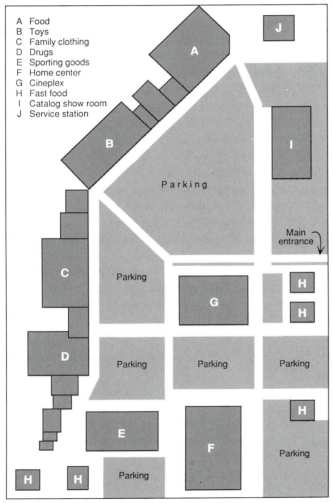

A Food
B Toys
C Family clothing
D Drugs
E Sporting goods
F Home center
G Cineplex
H Fast food
I Catalog show room
J Service station

Figure 16-18. Space Allocation in the Power Center. Sometimes labeled a super-community center, the power center mix places more emphasis on anchor discount stores at the expense of smaller specialty stores. A typical community center has a 60/40 space assignment in terms of the anchor/small store mix, while the power center provides an 80/20 split.

Costs of operation are lower in power centers, offering another competitive advantage over the regional mall. Common area maintenance is lower, as are heating, ventilation, and air conditioning (HVAC), electricity, and security charges for common areas. Overall, rents in power centers are typically about one-half those at nearby regional malls.

Some power centers include traditional discount retailers such as Target or K-Mart stores, while others may have a department store in their midst. A grouping trend toward including more national chain restaurants (Olive Garden, Red Lobster, Chilli's) in outlets at these centers also appears to offer considerable future growth potential.

Power centers may replace the regional mall altogether in medium-sized cities as well as curtail community center growth in larger markets. Others speculate that we are now in the midst of a phase change and that the regional center will cease to exist in the future, shifting either to a superregional center or to a power center. With the greater buying power that family households now enjoy as more women have joined the workplace, and the less time now available for shopping by the busy family, the power center seems to be providing an appealing alternative. By offering value-oriented goods and prices in a setting requiring less time to shop and easy access, the power center appears to represent a format with much growth potential. The key to their success appears to be the anchor selection. Most observers suggest that each anchor retailer should be the dominant seller in its category. In this way, the trade area will remain strong, as it is typically defined by the draw of the strongest stores in the center. We will now turn to a more in-depth examination of how trade areas are derived.

The recent changes to the retail hierarchy may have even more far-reaching implications for the future of the department store itself as a retail institution than for the regional mall. The new power stores, for example, essentially replace specialized departments in the traditional department store. Consumers today are willing to forego the intensive customer service that is the department store standard to gain price advantages, rapid service, and easy access. Some department stores have responded by eliminating many departments altogether and by streamlining operations. One national retailer, Sears & Roebuck, has instituted everyday low prices in its stores and is also taking a leadership role in developing power centers through its real estate subsidiary Homart.

TRADE AREA ANALYSIS

The study of metropolitan retail patterns is often encompassed in a much broader study identified as *marketing geography*. Marketing geography can occur at two scales: global (such as international trade, e.g., the European Common Market) or the local and regional levels that deal with individual business centers and their trade areas.[14] Marketing geography is a good example of applied geography. The determination and feasibility of retail store locations, evaluating markets, delimiting trade areas, and identifying consumer behavior all are major contributions made by this discipline. On the basis of theoretical concepts developed by central place theorists, the retailing geographer has been able to explain the patterns on metropolitan retailing land use maps.

The quality of the *form* and *function* of urban retail patterns is a central theme of the geography of retailing. Study of form as explained by function allows us to understand spatial retail preferences.[15] Form refers to the arrangement of retail shopping districts and the common features that they share. Function includes, among others, the analysis of kind and frequency-of-use of goods and shopping area organization. In our discussion thus far in this chapter, we have dealt with both aspects by examining the predominant forms that have resulted from the spatial organization of the functional hierarchy. Applied geographers have also contributed to our understanding of the retail system by looking at the intraurban shopping behavior of consumers. It is in the area of delineating trade or market areas that geographers have contributed most.

Kinds of Trade Areas Defined

Market or trade areas are defined as those areas around a single retail establishment or group of establishments (shopping center) from which the unit draws its customers (recall discussion in Chapter 8). There are three kinds of retail trade areas: general, composite, and proportional (Figure 16-19).

[14]Ross L. Davies, *Marketing Geography with Special Reference to Retailing*, Retailing and Planning Associates, Cambridge, England, 1976, pp. 1–2.

[15]Saul B. Cohen and George K. Lewis, "Form and Function in the Geography of Retailing," *Economic Geography*, 45 (1967), 4.

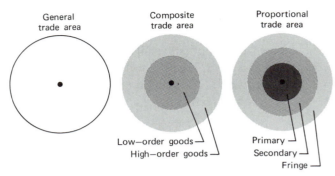

Figure 16-19. Three Main Types of Retail Trade Areas. The general trade area typically encompasses a region enclosing all customers, while the composite trade area defines a territory for several different goods or services based on a customer survey. The proportional trade area indicates various levels of customer attraction to a particular retail area. *Source:* Redrawn with permission from Ross L. Davies, *Marketing Geography with Special Reference to Retailing,* Retailing and Planning Associates, Cambridge, 1976, and Methuen, London, 1977, 201.

General Trade Area

The *general trade area* is the simplest kind, represented on maps by a single bounding line. That area may represent a region that encloses all customers (really defining an outer range) or it can encompass an area within which a certain percentage of the customers come. These trade areas are usually delineated by obtaining address information of store customers through sample surveys.

Composite Trade Areas

A *composite trade area* defines a territory incorporating trade zones for several different goods or services. Such designations are used for shopping center analyses where information is ordinarily obtained by customer surveys.

Proportional Trade Area

Recognizing the variable nature of trade area boundaries, *proportional trade area* diagrams indicate various levels of customer attraction to a particular retail area. The bounding lines enclose areas depicting proportions of customers coming to a center according to distance and/or travel time to that center. This form of trade area delimitation can be developed by shopping surveys or by employing one of several mathematical models. This type of trade area designation is more realistic than the others. Since urban residents are provided with so many alternative choices for shop-

ping, they rarely fit uniquely into a single shopping trade area. A customer may be in one trade area for grocery shopping and in another for clothing.

Proportional trade zones can be subdivided into primary, secondary, and tertiary areas. The primary trade area (or core) surrounds the retail unit(s) and usually contains 60–70 percent of its customers. The secondary area, surrounding the core, contributes an additional 15–25 percent of the customers. The remainder of the customers travel from the tertiary or fringe of the total trade area.

Shape and Size of Trade Areas

There are no definite rules governing the size and shape of retail trade areas. In general, size and shape will be determined by location, population density, accessibility, geographic features (especially barriers), competition, and store image.[16] Contrary to the generalized shapes represented in Figure 16-21, most trade areas are not completely circular. Convoluted, irregular shapes are the norm, especially because of competing center locations and the influence of the road network leading to the store or center. Geographic barriers such as major toll bridges, hilly topography, or traffic congestion tend to distort (constrict) market areas. Trade area sizes are also affected to a large degree by travel time and the size of store or center (recall Figure 1-7). The level of the good or service in question primarily affects the trade area size. Recent research has shown that distance expressed in time rather than miles is an important limiting factor on trade area size (to be discussed more fully below). But in our age of dwindling gasoline resources, the distance in miles could become a more compelling reason to shop at a closer center in the future.

Drawing power is a term frequently used in trade area analysis. It is calculated by determining the proportion of customers attracted to a center at a specific distance (time or miles). In comparing two stores (or centers), the one with the most drawing power attracts a larger percentage of its customers from a greater distance. Department stores ordinarily have more drawing power, for example, than supermarkets. Drawing

---

[16]William Applebaum and Saul B. Cohen, "Guideposts for Store Locations Strategy," in *Guide to Store Location Research,* William Applebaum, et al., Addison-Wesley, Reading, 1968, p. 33.

power is really another way of expressing the range of a good in the central place theory context.

Delineating Trade Areas

Store location research and trade area analysis is a relatively young field, only dating back to the early part of the century.[17] Previous attempts at such demarcation were based on intuition. Some recent contributions have been made using more "formalized" (i.e., mathematical) approaches. In practice, most analyses remain an empirical activity.

Empirical Methods

There are two chief aims of store location analysis: to define the characteristics of the probable customer and to delineate the trade area. Population characteristics such as age, structure, income, education, and occupation are gathered to develop customer "profiles." Demographic attributes of the area, such as number and density, are also part of the fact-finding. This information is customarily obtained from the Bureau of the Census.

Trade area delineation is accomplished through customer surveys, conducted at the place of business by asking a sample of customers their residential street address (or closest intersection), how often they shop at the store or center, and what goods or services they buy when shopping. Information from these surveys enables developers and center managers to direct future planning for the center. They are also used in the preparation of advertising campaigns and for guiding future store location decisions.

Address information taken from these surveys is used to place approximate trade area limits around stores or shopping centers, such as determining primary trade areas. With this information, the researcher then collects census data (e.g., income, education, and number of families) from those census tracts lying within the primary trade area. Generalized customer profiles can then be assembled.

Mathematical Methods

Early attempts at defining trade areas with more mathematical rigor included the use of Reilly's law of retail gravitation, explained in Chapter 5. Reilly's gravity formulation proved moderately successful in defining trade areas around cities (by using the breaking point), but it has been shown to be too deterministic and coarse for intracity applications. There are so many closely spaced intervening opportunities within urban areas that this rigid model is inadequate. When used, it works best for stores having the very lowest level of goods and services. Whenever large regional or superregional center trade areas are being plotted, alternative behavioral methods must be employed.

One such alternative method was developed by David Huff.[18] That model incorporates the conceptual framework of Reilly and other gravity models, but is focused on the spatial behavior of consumers. Huff identified two useful trade area components when measuring the *utility* of a shopping center to a customer: shopping center offerings and travel time.

Shopping center offerings are an expression of the center's mass (its attractive force). The fundamental argument is that the larger the number of items carried by the shopping center, the greater will be the consumer's expectation of a successful shopping trip and willingness to travel to that center. Travel time is inversely related to a shopping center's utility. The farther the customer lives from the center, the less likely a trip will be made to the center.

The unique feature of the Huff model is the generation of a *probability surface* associated with trading at a specified shopping center (Figure 16-20). A consumer living farther from a center is less likely to shop at that center. Eventually, this probability tapers off to a very small level and the customer chooses to shop at an alternative center. In practice, Huff's probability surface can be used to delineate trade areas by determining specific equal probability contours to two or more centers that form the trade area boundary, usually the 50 percent probability line. Here again, the analyst can obtain census information for those tracts lying within the specified boundary to learn more about shopper income and age characteristics.

By way of summary, it should be pointed out that the Huff model is realistic in that it implicitly states that customer behavior in urban areas is flexible and complex, not rigid, and that shopping behavior is governed by choice. While a shopper may trade at a given center

---

[17]William Applebaum, "Can Store Location Research Be a Science?" *Economic Geography*, 41 (1965), 234–237.

[18]David L. Huff, "A Probabilistic Analysis of Shopping Center Trade Areas," *Land Economics*, 39 (1963), 81–90.

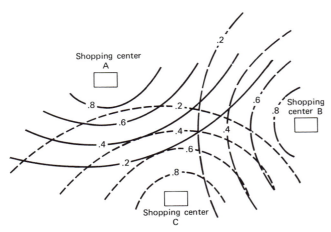

Figure 16-20. Probabilities of Shopping at Competing Centers. This model, developed by Huff, focuses on the spatial behavior of consumers by incorporating both travel time and the attractiveness of a center to a shopper based on size. Using these factors, the probabilities of shopping at a particular center can be determined.

Figure 16-21. Retail Strip Corridor. A significant share of retail activity occurs along arterial highway corridors. Attracted to such areas are many highway-oriented activities such as automobile sales and service, fast food, and gasoline sales, as well as space extensive functions such as furniture sales and home improvement stores. (Courtesy Richard Pillsbury.)

most of the time, the shopper may occasionally frequent another center for goods and services not offered at a center nearer home. For these reasons, the Huff interpretation is referred to as a *behavioral model*.

Retail Corridors

As mentioned in an earlier section, a significant share of retail activity, one-third or more in most cities, occurs on arterial strips of highway corridors totally separate from the activity occurring in the hierarchy of retail centers (Figure 16-21). Many of these retail corridors extend from the city center outward for miles, extending into the rural fringe. In recent years, this activity has intensified and attracted larger and larger retail outlets.

Numerous geographic studies have attempted to define exactly what constitutes the functional linkages within ribbons, but there has been no definite consensus. Regional and intraurban variation abound, making analysis and classification difficult. What is apparent is that the arterial site is a desirable location for a number of different kinds of establishments, particularly functions that benefit from easy highway access, especially the many businesses tied directly to the automobile. These include auto sales and service, auto repair, gasoline sales, and auto accessories, as well as space-intensive functions requiring good auto-based accessibility such as furniture, home improvement stores,

garden nurseries, and lumberyards. Recreation vehicle and boat sales, contractors (swimming pools, home repair, landscaping, irrigation/sprinkler), and various vendors (coffee, soft drink, candy, beer/wine/liquor) also find corridor locations attractive for the same reasons. Still other functions such as fast food, restaurants, banking facilities, copy centers, and others take advantage of the traffic flows and visibility offered by the highway setting.

CHANGING CONSUMER DEMAND AND SPATIAL PREFERENCES

Several factors have been shown to affect consumer spatial behavior. Chief among these are location, attractiveness, and time.[19] All else being equal among all shopping destination choices, travel time is the most important variable. All else not being equal, the center's location, attractiveness, and image will play a major role in determining consumer choices. Location involves the center's position relative to competing centers, and also the occurrence of natural or artificial barriers. Attractiveness includes several factors, notably total center floor space, anchor store space, supermarket space, parking space, and whether or not the

---

[19]Ken Jones and James Simmons, *Location, Location, Location*, Methuen, New York, 1987.

center has an enclosed, environmentally controlled mall. Images and subjectively held mores of shoppers also affect a center's drawing power. For example, customers are willing to travel farther to centers thought to have "good" images.

As a controlling factor in consumer choice, travel time rather than travel distance has been shown to be very important, as mentioned earlier. In one study of Toledo, the most significant time dimension for trade area analysis was the 15-minute travel time distance, as that time frame enclosed nearly 74 percent of the customers among each of the surveyed centers.[20] In a study using several shopping centers in Atlanta, similar results were achieved.[21] There 75 percent of potential volume of sales was found within 15 minutes of each center. Other research by geographers has substantiated this general trend.[22]

Time spent traveling to a shopping center will also be affected by its size. Frequency of visiting a center is inversely proportional to the size of the development. Consumers tend to make more stops per week at the neighborhood or community level than at the regional center level. This simply reflects the kinds of goods and services offered at the lower-order centers (i.e., convenience goods). There is also a relationship between a center's store *variety* and consumer travel. At close distances, variety will have a greater impact on spatial choice, but as distances increase, the variety of the retail mix had less impact.[23] Eventually, at some outward distance, greater variety will not attract those customers living farther away.

There are also indications that patterns of consumption are favoring higher-order goods in response to rising income levels.[24] This results in longer, but less frequent, trips. As a result, there are fewer convenience goods stores, and a greater number of specialized centers serving wider trade areas. Frequently specialized function centers concentrate to create nucleations such as fashion centers, "boutique" clusters, furniture

fashion centers, and others. These may locate in satellite malls that are separate, smaller, add-on units adjacent to larger regional centers and that share common management, parking areas, and promotion.

As pressures have mounted to create maximum accessibility and parking space, it has become less likely that unplanned centers will continue to prosper. Many are now located in older, lower-income neighborhoods. The demand for higher-order goods typically increases in newer outlying areas closer to higher-income residents. In pursuit of the growing urban market, retailers tend to leave lower-order nucleations and locate in higher-order centers as conditions permit. There has been a trend involving the gradual disappearance of small, isolated retail stores, with larger units strung together along arterial ribbons often taking their place.

Retail Succession and Blight

The typical city's commercial landscape is always changing. These changes result from alterations in either demand (the market) or supply (the commercial system). The fundamental components of any demand change in metropolitan retail systems are the result of changes in its population and income. Supply changes result chiefly from technological advances in delivery systems, plant structures, or transportation. Any of these factors may cause a disequilibrium in the overall organization.

The changing character of the retail picture yields continuous patterns of retail *succession*, and often *retail blight*. Most studies of retail succession and blight refer to those situations where neighborhoods change from higher to lower income levels. But retailing patterns also change as the result of increasing incomes (leading usually to more specialty stores and higher-quality goods).

Retail Blight Defined

Several kinds of commercial blight can be defined: (1) economic, (2) physical, (3) functional, and (4) frictional.[25] *Economic blight* results from losses in market demand. This may occur because of lowered population numbers, changes in socioeconomic levels, or increased competition. Casual inspection of commer-

[20]James A Brunner and John L. Manson, "The Influence of Driving Time upon Shopping Center Preference," *Journal of Marketing*, 32 (1969), 50.

[21]Borden D. Dent, "Mapping Regional Shopping Center Trade Volumes in Atlanta, Georgia," *Southeastern Geographer*, 12 (1972), 69–77.

[22]William J. Young, "Distance Decay Values and Shopping Center Size," *Professional Geographer*, 27 (1975), 309.

[23]Bert Rosenbloom, "The Trade Area Mix and Retailing Mix: A Retail Strategy Matrix," *Journal of Marketing*, 40 (1976), 61.

[24]James W. Simmons, *The Changing Pattern of Retail Location*, Research Paper No. 92, Department of Geography, University of Chicago, Chicago, 1964.

[25]Berry, *Commercial Structure and Commercial Blight*, pp. 179–185.

cial areas suffering from this kind of blight will reveal store vacancies, fewer specialty shops, or a lower quality of goods carried by the remaining stores (Figure 16-22). These changes can be noticed in shopping centers as well as along ribbons or in unplanned nucleations exhibited in many older city neighborhoods.

Blight that occurs through the deterioration of buildings is *physical blight*. Usually this type of decline is simply the result of structural aging of the building. Such dilapidation may be accelerated by a lack of maintenance by entrepreneurs in areas suffering from other forms of blight, notably economic. In anticipation of falling revenues, the owner is less likely to invest in upgrading older structures.

Figure 16-22. **Declining Market Demand and Retail Blight.** Casual inspection of commercial areas suffering from vacancies, a lower quality of goods in surviving stores, and fewer specialty retailers, suggests that the buying power of residents in the trade area has declined or that customers have been lured away by competing retail opportunities. (Teri Leigh.)

Functional blight results from changing technology. As retailing has grown in North America, so has the method of retailing. Many units have increased in size to operate more efficiently. As older and smaller buildings become obsolete, they become less attractive to consumers. It is often difficult for older downtown department stores to compete with even their own newer suburban branches, which are more spacious and better planned. Greater use of the automobile and the wider choices it provides also frequently lead to functional blight. For example, retail outlets built during the streetcar era often have difficulty providing convenient offstreet parking for automobiles.

Whenever a commercial area generates environmental problems, such as traffic congestion, the need for increased fire or police protection, or the like, it is said to be experiencing *frictional blight*. Frictional blight may also be the result of the intrusion of other land uses close to the commercial district, making it less desirable as a retail site. Commercial areas may show evidence of all or some of these forms at a given time.

Retail Succession

As neighborhood composition changes, so does its retail character. Retailing is seen as a social process and the retail firm as a social institution.[26] As such, then, retailing is a kind of surrogate for the population it serves. Furthermore, retailing mirrors the changing attributes of an entire urban population, or of a neighborhood, its use of leisure time, its expectations, and even its goals.

Identifying commercial blight can lead to an understanding of neighborhood transition, because the two are closely related. Berry has identified three stages in retail succession or change:[27]

1. **Anticipation of Neighborhood Transition.** In this stage, vacancies rise as normal replacement lapses. Also, stores are not maintained as well as before because of a lack of economic confidence in the area. Beginning deterioration is the result.

2. **Population Turnover.** This state is characterized by a real loss in demand, and specialty shops drop out of the system. Large department stores

[26]Edwin M. Rams, ed., *Analysis and Valuation of Retail Locations*, Reston Publishing, Reston, Va., 1976, p. 14.

[27]Brian J. L. Berry, *Geography of Market Centers and Retail Distribution*, Prentice–Hall, Englewood Cliffs, N.J., 1967, p. 123.

may change product lines, switching to lower quality goods.

3. **Stabilization.** The retailing activities in this phase have responded to the neighborhood change. Buildings continue to suffer from a lack of maintenance and rents drop. Vacancies are at a high level, and deterioration is most noticeable.

One result of the process of succession is that lower-income areas are usually left with two levels in the intraurban functional hierarchy rather than four. As demand decreases with the lowering of incomes, higher-order goods offerings in more specialized centers cannot be sustained and they withdraw from the market.

The general results of commercial blight—deterioration, vacancy, low maintenance and rents—are indeed very depressing. These changes produce tangible, observable landscape features that can lead to the development of negative images of the city. Retail units are also social institutions, so the responses and solutions to the problem of blight must be directed to a much larger and more significant problem than the outlets themselves.

SUMMARY AND CONCLUSION

This chapter dealt with the retail structure of the American city. The retail land use map is dynamic. It exhibits constant disequilibrium as the forces governing supply and demand of retail goods and services change. As urban populations grow and redistribute, as incomes rise or fall, and as retail marketing strategies change, the effects are manifested in retail patterns. The structure evident 25 years ago is different from today's, and today's structure will be different from tomorrow's.

The prevailing retail pattern in the United States is a dispersed one, with a variety of shopping levels accounting for the bulk of sales. These nucleations or centers exhibit a nested, functional hierarchy, akin to a central place system. As the spatial organization of the retail pattern developed, a sorting of the functions occurred.

The CBD will likely continue to develop as a regional center supplying mass-appeal foods to inner-city residents and those working downtown. Outlying regional and specialty centers will primarily supply these goods for regional markets in their areas, while some centers will draw more widely, especially those positioned in niches with little competition.

The future of the traditional hierarchy of centers is uncertain. Regional centers no longer function as they once did— at the top of the retail hierarchy. Many are being expanded into superregional centers while others undergo restructuring as power centers having a greater concentration of anchors in relation to the number of smaller specialty centers. Outlet centers are also creating increased competition for the traditional regional center.

Higher-order retail centers of all types are offering more nonretail functions within, as they become more integrated with their communities, both architecturally and functionally. Nonretail commercial facilities, including office and hotel space, as well as more entertainment and recreation activity, continue to expand adjacent to shopping centers, as in the case of growing suburban downtowns. Retail corridors are also very dynamic retail markets accounting for a greater share of urban retail sales. In the past, retailers and cities have gone hand in hand; the future will bring new technologies and dimensions to this old but continuing symbiosis.

Suggestions for Further Reading

Applebaum, William, et al. *Guide to Store Location Research*, Addison-Wesley. Reading, Mass., 1968.

Bacon, Robert W. *Consumer Spatial Behavior: A Model of Purchasing Decisions over Space and Time*, Oxford University Press, London, 1984.

Berry, Brian J. L. *Geography of the Market Centers and Retail Distribution*, Prentice-Hall, Englewood Cliffs, N.J., 1967.

Berry, Brian J. L. et al. *Commercial Structure and Commercial Blight*, Research Paper No. 85, Department of Geography, University of Chicago, Chicago, 1963.

Cohen, Yehoshua S. "The Diffusion of Planned Regional Shopping Centers in the United States," Chapter 3 in *Diffusion of an Innovation in an Urban System*, Research Paper No. 140, Department of Geography, University of Chicago, Chicago, 1972, pp. 25–42.

Davies, Ross L. *Marketing Geography with Special References to Retailing*, Retailing and Planning Associations, Cambridge, England, 1976.

Davies, R.L. and D.S. Rogers. *Store Location and Store Assessment Research*. Wiley, New York, 1984.

Dawson, John A., ed. *Retail Geography*, Croom Helm, London, 1980.

Dawson, John A. and J. Dennis Lord, eds. *Shopping Centre Development: Policies and Prospects*, Croom Helm, London, 1985.

Downtown Research and Development Center. *Downtown Malls: Feasibility and Development*, New York, 1974.

Duncan, Delbert J., and Stanley C. Hollander. *Modern Retailing Management: Basic Concepts and Practices*, 9th ed., Richard D. Irwin, Homewood, Ill., 1977.

Fitch, Rodney and Lance Knobel. *Retail Design*. Whitney Library of Design, New York, 1990.

Garner, Barry J. *The Internal Structure of Retail Nucleations*, Studies in Geography, No. 12, Department of Geography, Northwesten University, Evanston, Ill., 1966.

Goldstucker, Jac, et al., eds. *Retail Trading Area Analysis and Site Selection*, Reserach Monograph 78, Georgia State University, College of Business Administration, Publishing Services Division, Atlanta, 1978.

Hines, M.A. *Shopping Center Development and Investment*. John Wiley and Sons, New York, 1988.

Horwitz, Richard. *The Strip: An American Place*, University of Nebraska Press, Lincoln, 1985.

Jones, Ken, and Jim Simmons. *Location, Location, Location*. Methuen, Toronto, 1987.

Jones, Ken, and Jim Simmons. *The Retail Environment*, Routledge, New York, 1990.

Kowinski, William. *The Malling of America*, William Morrow, New York, 1985.

Lion, E. *Shopping Centers: Planning, Development and Administration*, Wiley–Interscience, New York, 1976.

McKeever, J. R., et al. *Shopping Center Development Handbook*, Urban Land Institute, Washington, D.C., 1977.

Nelson, R. L., *The Selection of Retail Locations*, F. W. Dodge Corporation, Chicago, 1958.

Pillsbury, Richard. *From Boarding House to Bistro: The American Restaurant Then and Now*. Unwin Hyman, Boston, 1990.

Potter, Robert B. *The Urban Retailing System: Location, Cognition and Behavior*, Gower Publishing, Aldershot, Hants, England: Gower, 1982.

Rams, Edwin M., ed. *Analysis and Valuation of Retail Locations*, Reston Publishing, Reston, Va., 1976.

Redstone, L. G. *New Dimensions in Shopping Centers and Stores*, McGraw-Hill, New York, 1973.

Simmons, James W. *The Changing Pattern of Retail Location*, Research Paper No. 92, Department of Geography, University of Chicago, Chicago, 1964.

Urban Land Institute. *Dollars and Cents of Shopping Centers: 1990*, Urban Land Institute, Washington, D.C., 1990.

Vance, James E., Jr. *The Merchant's World: The Geography of Wholesaling*, Prentice Hall, Englewood Cliffs, N.J., 1970.

Worley, William S. *J.C. Nichols and the Shaping of Kansas City Innovation in Planned Residential Communities*. University of Missouri Press, Columbia, 1990.

17

THE OFFICE FUNCTION

The commercial function of the city was discussed in Chapters 15 and 16 in terms of the changing dynamics of retail, office, and hotel activity. The focus on downtown commercial activity in Chapter 15 was followed by a metropolitan perspective of retailing in Chapter 16. We will continue the metropolitan perspective in this chapter, which emphasizes the role of office activity in the modern postindustrial service economy. In the suburbs, retailing traditionally captured most of the commercial space, whereas more balance existed downtown. Now, retailing has declined downtown and a diversified economy has emerged in the suburbs. In this chapter, we will examine the growth of the office function in the city, placing an emphasis on suburban growth. The expansion of corporate headquarters activity and producer services will be highlighted (Figure 17-1).

CHANGING LOCATION POLICY

The explosive growth of service occupations and the boom in office building construction in the past 25 years totally revamped the economic base of many cities, fostering the emergence of new work settings for a large segment of the urban work force. Unlike the situation with retail decentralization, the market for office space often triggered an interventionist public policy aiming to steer investment decisions. Economic factors such as rental rates and the availability of a skilled labor pool also play an important role in choosing office locations. In addition, amenity-based factors, management preferences, and residential locations of decision makers enter the decision process.

Public policy toward new office development vacillated dramatically in the 1960s and 1970s as cities began coping with the growing demand for office space and pressures for decentralization intensified. In several large metropolitan areas, such as Toronto, Paris, and London, a *containment* response emerged.[1] Restrictive planning, financing, and taxation policies shaped this framework as fear grew of an impending decimation of the downtown work center.

In the immediate post-World War II era, it was assumed that the downtown area would continue to serve as the single office space nexus for the urban region. Face-to-face contact among decision makers could be maximized in that setting. Moreover, this was the only area of the city where office towers existed. The initial public sector response to the prospect of office space decentralization was that it would be detrimental to the future of downtown, especially in the face of the exodus of retailing activity at the same time. But alas, another perspective soon emerged that encouraged selective office decentralization. London, in

---

[1]Peter Hall et al., *The Containment of Urban England*, 2 vols., Allen & Unwin, London, 1973.

Figure 17-1. Pepsico World Headquarters, Purchase, N.Y. Opened in suburban New York in 1970, this building consisting of seven square blocks linked at the corners frames three courtyard gardens around a central fountain. The lavishly landscaped grounds include 42 pieces of sculpture set in 112 acres of specialty gardens, and ponds ranging from formal manicured hedges and shrubs to perennial and wildflower gardens. Pepsico is now the 23rd largest corporation in the U.S., with operations in 150 countries. Subsidiaries of the firm include Frito-Lay, Kentucky Fried Chicken, Pizza Hut, and Taco Bell. (Courtesy Pepsico, Inc.)

fact, pioneered a policy encouraging office decentralization.

A ban on office development in London and the West Midlands first became public policy in 1964 to thwart increasing centralization and congestion.[2] Development moved to the southwest thereafter, but in 1966, the no-build region was expanded to include the southeast, East Anglia, and the East Midlands. This policy was designed to direct growth to the southwest (Bristol area) in the early 1970s, but the machinery marshaled to thwart growth was only partially successful. Financial inducements for building in outlying areas had little effect because they mainly took the form of issuing selective building permits to developers for new facilities. Since office firms were mainly renters, not developers themselves, they were scarcely affected. The net result of the limited central growth policy and ineffective suburban incentive policy resulted in a pent-up demand for core office space and pushed up rental rates because new supplies of space were not built.

In 1963, a Location of Offices Bureau (LOB) was created in London to assist the dispersal of offices away from central London. Between 1963 and 1977, it assisted in the relocation of firms accounting for 150,000 jobs. During this period, pressure on the inner-city area decreased, but the trend was not recognized until the mid-1970s. Commuter traffic decreased and there was a 10 percent decline in employment in the core area. When this situation became known, an abrupt policy role reversal for the LOB was enacted. Beginning in 1977, that group began encouraging office activities to locate in the central area. It was feared that if the decentralization trend continued, the heart of London would experience a serious decline in employment.

Control of office development in central Toronto provides another example of public policy involvement. That control gradually stiffened as a result of tougher zoning regulations.[3] A density-control provision first appeared in 1959, which regulated the "bulk"

[2]Material in this section is synthesized from J. Goddard, *Office Locations in Urban and Regional Development*, Oxford University Press, London, 1975, pp. 36–43.

[3]David Newland, "Land Policy in the Central City: A Toronto Perspective," paper prepared for the Management of Land for Urban Development Conference, Canadian Council on Urban and Regional Research, April 1974.

of buildings by specifying a relationship between their height and the portion of lot areas covered. The taller the building, the smaller the percentage of the lot that could be occupied. The maximum ratios varied for different uses, but an overall ceiling of 12 times the lot area became the rule. This guide turned out to be very permissive, as building activity in the downtown financial district continued at a fever pitch during the 1960s and early 1970s. A city council elected in 1973 began a crusade to limit development in the core city. A holding bylaw was enacted that called for a height limit of 45 feet and 40,000 square feet maximum floor area for all new downtown buildings.

In Janary 1976, an amended bylaw took effect that would deflect commercial development from the downtown and at the same time encourage residential growth. In essence, this plan represented a form of downzoning. Instead of 12 times coverage, only 8 times coverage of commercial space was permitted.

But with the addition of residential uses to the building, development intensity to 20 times lot coverage could be restored. The intent of this guideline was to encourage more mixed uses downtown, primarily to stimulate family-type apartments in the core city and fewer work complexes.

The so-called Central District (CD) of Toronto contained virtually all the office space in the region through the 1950s and over 90 percent of the space as recently as the early 1960s (Figure 17-2).[4] Today, that share remains more than half, but the largest quantity of growth now occurs in the suburbs. Outlying office development accelerated in the 1970s with the adoption of a downzoning policy for the CD area and the implementation of a policy favoring the development of suburban centers located at sites with rail service.

---

[4]Gunter Gad, "Office Location Dynamics in Toronto: Suburbanization and Central District Specialization," *Urban Geography*, 6 (1985), 333–334.

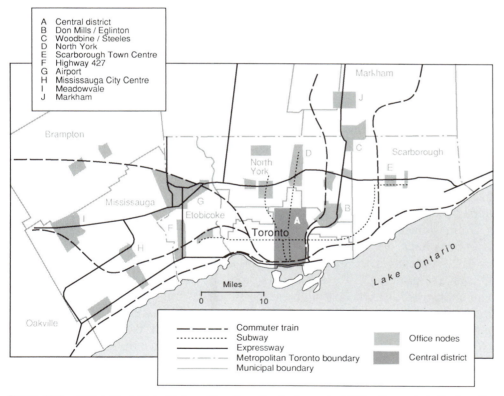

Figure 17-2. Office Markets in Metropolitan Toronto. In the early 1960s, the central district of Toronto (A) contained over 90 percent of the office space in the city. That market now contains just over one-half of the metropolitan office inventory. Several outlying districts now claim large office shares, including North York (D), Mississauga (H), Scarborough (E), and Markham (J). Note the light and heavy rail transit connections to these centers and the freeway network. *Source:* Gunter Gad, (*Inner City and Suburban Office Nodes*), Field Trip Guide book, Association of American Geographers Annual Meeting, Toronto, 1990. p. 9. Used by permission.

Major banks and investment functions connected to the stock exchange continue to occupy sites in the CD, which remains the financial control center for the country. "Overall, the CD is becoming more and more exclusively a high order decision-making center, gradually shedding much of its traditional components, be they characterized in terms of low order service functions, branches of various rank and size, or clerical labor."[5]

Even though local government policy began promoting the growth and development of suburban office centers in Toronto 25 years ago, these centers remain modest in employment levels in comparison to the market-directed centers that have emerged in the United States in the past two decades. Scarborougth City Centre, for example, employs only 16,000, wheras a comparable suburban downtown in the United States may employ 75,000 or more (Figure 17-3). The Canadian centers enjoy better public transportation access than their U.S. counterparts, but weaker highway access. Poor limited-access highway capacity, rather than government policy or the lack of developer interest, appears to limit the office development potential in these areas.

The core of the Scarborough town center is dominated by a classic suburban shopping center, and other commercial uses are strung out around it in a highly regulated fashion. Much open space and carefully planned pedestrian paths and zones have also been incorporated into the plan. Residential population densities in and around suburban centers in Canada are also much higher than in their U.S. counterparts. The Scarborough municipal population approached 500,000 in the late 1980s, and it contained 50,000 apartment units. While high-rise housing is envisioned for the core of Scarborough, it has not yet been built. Nevertheless, nearby apartment towers of 20 stories or more contribute to the urban flavor of the area (Figure 17-3). Arterial roads, vacant land, and industrial districts fragment the area and prevent it from functioning as a cohesive unit. One observer notes that "its greatest deficiency is [that] the area is so thoroughly planned and neat that it lacks the spontaneity and vitality that is associated with real downtowns."[6]

One of Toronto's newest suburban centers, and most free-wheeling in the sense of being more market driven

than the rest, is the Markham Town Center. Formerly horse farm country, Markham got its start because it was located just outside the more restrictive North York community in the northern suburbs. This area hosts firms with high concentrations of back-office or clerical-intensive activity, and many of Toronto's high-technology businesses, giving it a "silicon valley" flair. Major banks have concentrated their processing offices here, as have book publishers, insurance companies, and major corporations such as Hyundai. This area received its first big corporate commitment in 1981, when American Express chose the area for a major office, followed by other high-profile corporations such as IBM and A.C. Nielson. Among the major high-technology corporations present are Apple Computers, Hewlitt-Packard, and Samsung.

The North York suburban center, located in an older section of the city than Scarborough, along Yonge Street, benefits from main line transit service, whereas a light rail system serves Scarborough. Fully 40 percent of the work trips to the North York downtown depend on rail service. It became an important goverment work center and a media center in the 1980s. Civic and cultural centers play a large role in Canadian suburban centers than in their counterparts in the United States, and North York fills this role best. In fact, it is Toronto's most mature suburban downtown.

> When seen from Highway 401 just east of Yonge, it presents a view of a substantial wall of skyscrapers. This view is deceptive in that North York has an awkward linear form, like the modern metropolitan equivalent of a *strassendorf*. It has developed between two subway stations on the Yonge line, with an extension south to the interchange of Yonge Street and Highway 401.[7]

The area is now developing into both a downtown and uptown subcenter and together they are projected to employ 65,000 and house about 23,000. But the area also has its problems due to its linear layout along a major arterial street. Its imposing high-density structure negatively impacts an adjacent single-family residential community, and a lack of parking and associated vehicular congestion detract from its attractiveness as a work center.

In the 1980's, prevailing market conditions, more than overt government-induced steering, guided office activity growth in Toronto and London as in U.S. cities. Some would argue, however, that the invisible hand of the government still influenced the process as

[5]Ibid., pp. 346–347.

[6]Edward Relph, "The Toronto Guide: The City, Metro, The Region," Field Guide, Association of American Geographers Annual Meeting, Toronto, April 1990, p. 67.

[7]Ibid.

(A)

(B)

Figure 17-3. Suburban Downtowns: Scarborough City Centre (Toronto) and Perimeter Center (Atlanta). Suburban office centers in Toronto remain modest in employment levels in comparison with more intensively developed centers in the United States. Scarborough City Centre (*A*) employs fewer than 20,000 persons, whereas a comparable suburban downtown in the United States such as Perimeter Center (*B*) may employ 75,000 or more. Canadian suburban centers enjoy better public transportation access than their U.S. counterparts, but weaker highway access. (*A*) Courtesy Trilea Centers, Inc., (*B*) Courtesy Dillon-Reynolds)

an overbuilding binge overtook the market, as we will discuss in a later section. The choices for office locations also expanded greatly in the 1980s for high-order headquarters functions, professional and administrative offices, and back-office operations.

Back offices refer to clerical-intensive, routine processing functions often associated with the record-keeping operations characteristic of the insurance and finance industry. Back-office operations emphasize internal transactions to the firm that require minimal external face-to-face contact with persons from other firms or government agencies. An insurance firm's operations, for example, include two major tasks: underwriting new policies and (2) record keeping services for existing policies. The former function involves processing new insurance applications, including acceptance or rejection. These operations are conducted by phone or mail and do not depend on any particular location. Record-keeping functions involve routine computer-assisted operations. All associated financial tasks involving life expectancy forecasts and policy yields are similarly routinized. Neither outside personal contact nor proximity to other firms is required to perform these tasks. One study of an insurance company has shown that clerical workers (typists, computer terminal operators, and clerks) account for 67 percent of the labor force in that industry.[8]

METROPOLITAN OFFICE GROWTH

The growth of suburban downtowns, as presented in Chapter 9, represents the most important structural change in the metropolitan area of the late twentieth century. Unlike the situation with retailing, which remains widely dispersed in hundreds of centers and corridors in a typical metropolitan area, the proclivity of office activity is to cluster in 4–6 centers in a region of 1–3 million population (such as Atlanta and Toronto), and no more than 10–12 centers in regions of 8–10 million population (such as Chicago). To be sure, retailing often provides the hub location around which office centers evolve both downtown and in the suburbs, but the share of metropolitan retailing in any given location rarely exceeds 1–2 percent, whereas 15–20 percent of the metropolitan office market may be associated with a particular cluster (Figure 17-4).

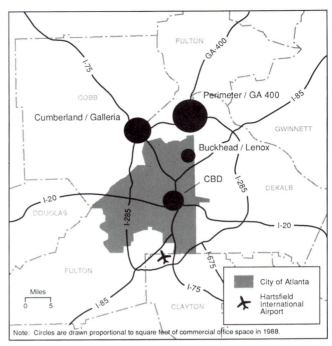

Figure 17-4. Atlanta's Downtowns. Four major downtown markets exist in Atlanta based on the presence of large concentrations of office space. Note that the CBD ranks third in size and that the three suburban centers are all located on the affluent north side of the region. Predecessor office parks were also disproportionately concentrated on the north side (see Figure 17-7).

The quantity of office facilities in a city does not depend on that city's population size as much as it does on its function. Financial centers, regional service centers, government, and major headquarter cities all have large office empolyment concentrations, and in nearly all cases, the locational needs of these activities are similar. Nearly all first-, second-, and third-order centers discussed in Chapter 4 fit in this category. The exceptions include industrial centers, resort cities, and cities in the shadow of larger metropolitan areas. An example of a city in the shadow of a larger center that demonstrates a weak office function would be Philadelphia, situated as it is so close to New York.

Whereas suburban office growth in the 1950s and 1960s typically occurred in campuslike settings provided by office parks, that which occurred in the 1980s primarily gravitated to massive high-rise towers associated with suburban downtowns (Figure 17-4). This most recent period of office growth occurred during the Reagan-era economic expansion. Increases in office space resulted from favorable financing and taxation policies, as well as growing demand for space. Savings

---

[8]Jack M. Nilles, et al., *The Telecommunications–Transportation Trade-off, Options for Tomorrow*, Wiley, New York, 1976, p. 20.

and loan institution deregulation, real estate syndication, and the massive infusion of funds into the construction industry by pension funds and foreign investors, especially by the Japanese, also drove this expansion (Figure 17-5).

In the past two decades, the postindustrial service economy came of age, making it more obvious that the office buildings served as the factories of the information age, as mentioned in Chapter 1. The growth of the service economy, paced by the corporate activity of the *Fortune 500* service firms, complemented the traditional presence of the *Fortune 500* industrial firms' headquarters in downtown and suburban markets.

Not only did an absolute increase in the number of major corporate headquarters office space users appear in this period, but also a specialized office services group came of age, exemplified by the emergence of the *producer services* industry. We will consider this aspect of the service economy before returning to a discussion of the headquarters office function.

GROWTH OF THE SERVICE SECTOR

The growing share of service sector jobs in the national economy provided a major part of the expanding employment base in large cities in the 1970s and 1980s. The service sector, in fact, increased from 64 to 72 percent of total U.S. employment from 1969 to 1985. At the same time, the manufacturing function declined from 25 to 19 percent.[9]

The growth of the service sector can be attributed to the expansion of several work categories, including retail, wholesale, government, nonprofit, and transportation functions, but none grew as fast in the past 15 years as producer services (Table 17-1). Producer services grew by over 60 percent from 1977 to 1986, whereas the total economy grew by only 29 percent.

---

[9]Edwin Mills and John McDonald, eds., *Sources of Metropolitan Growth.* New Brunswick, NJ: Rutgers University center for Urban Policy Research 1992.

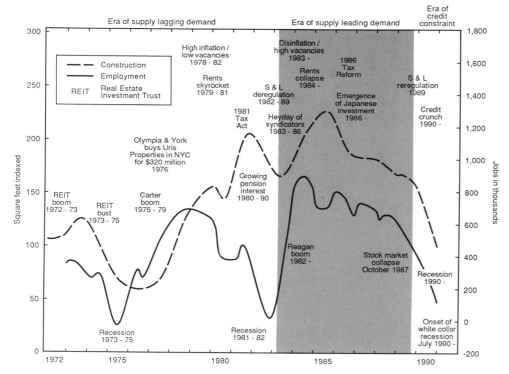

Figure 17-5.   Office Construction and Office Employment Trends in the United States, 1972–1990. Economic cycles and the availability of financing have dramatically affected the construction of office space. The supply of space lagged demand for the first 10 years of this period, but after 1983—following the S&L deregulation and tax reform—supply led demand. Note the impact of the 1973–1975 and 1981–1982 recessions on employment, a pattern that reemerged in 1990–1991. *Source:* Salomon Brothers. Used by permission.

TABLE 17-1
U.S. Producer Service Job Growth, 1977–1986 (millions)

Sector	Total Change	Percent Change
Finance, Insurance, Real estate	1.8	32
Business services	2.5	44
Legal services	0.3	05
Membership organizations	0.04	01
Miscellaneous professional services	0.3	05
Social services	0.7	12
Total	5.7	61

Source: William Beyers, "Producer Services and Metropolitan Growth and Development," Chapter 6 in Edwin Mills and John F. McDonald, eds., *Sources of Metropolitan Growth.* New Brunswick, NJ: Rutgers University, Center for Urban Policy Research, 1992, p. 128.

TABLE 17-2
Leading Producer Service Sectors, by Employment, 1986

	000s of Jobs
Finance, Insurance, Real Estate (FIRE)	6.3
Business Services	4.7
Legal Services	0.7
Membership Organizations	.6
Misc. Professional Services	1.3
Social Services	1.4

Source: William Beyers, "Producer Services and Metropolitan Growth and Development," Chapter 6 in Edwin Mills and John F. McDonald, eds., *Sources of Metropolitan Growth.* New Brunswick, NJ: Rutgers University, Center for Urban Policy Research, 1992, p. 128.

Over 1.8 million jobs were created in the Finance, Insurance, and Real Estate (FIRE) industry in that period, 2.5 million in business services, and 5.7 million in producer services overall (Table 17-1). Producer services, defined as operations that provide business and professional services to other professional or business activities, cluster in areas with a strong corporate or government office presence, as those functions represent the primary clients for these services. Producer services typically include "intermediate" services used in the provision of other services or in the processing of extractive (mining) or manufacturing activities. Those activities most frequently associated with the producer services group are finance, insurance, and real estate employment, business services, legal and accounting services, management, public relations, and social services. Distributive functions, such as transportation, communication, utilities (TCU), and wholesale and retail activity, are not included in the grouping, nor are nonprofit functions (health, education) or consumer service (hotel, personal services, repair services, motion pictures, and amusement) functions.

The significance of the producer services category to the metropolitan economy is that it represents a rapidly growing, specialized, white-collar, office-based function (Table 17-2). All types of businesses use producer services and they have become more capital-intensive as telecommunications needs, information processing, and office networking have grown in importance. Their growth is directly related to the tendency for more division of labor due to technological changes that continually reshape business practices. Producer services occupy the largest share of Class A office space[10] and pay the highest salaries to their employees, as these positions require specialized professional and managerial skills.

Many firms externalize (i.e., farm out) more operations as they grow, through the use of consultants and/or outside firms that can provide specialized services more efficiently (e.g., legal work, investment services) than in-house offices of the firm. This process, also known as a *decoupling of functions*, intensified in the 1980s as competitive pressures increased and will likely continue to reshape business practices in the future. Innovations in business practices related to computer applications and other technology advances create new market niches for specialized producer service functions and will generate new work opportunities in the future.

The concentration of these producer services in larger metropolitan areas is an example of an *agglomeration economy*, or clustering of services available to businesses. The producer service function also provides a good example of the city's role in fostering the exchange of ambiguous information. *Ambiguous information*, as referenced earlier in Chapter 1, refers to the sharing of specialized information during meetings and negotiation sessions. These discussions typically include "an interactive and convergent set of exchanges before the final exchange can be consum-

---

[10]Office markets in the city can be segmented into Class A and Class B space based on the quality of the space and public amenities of the building. (See footnote 18.)

mated."[11] The "information exchanged between a corporation's research and prodution activities" provides a good example of ambiguous information sharing.

> If a research team comes up with a bright new product idea, elaborate and sequential discussions may be required between research, production, product design, marketing, accounting, and legal specialists. Furthermore, continuing discussions may be advantageous as the research and development (R&D) activity proceeds. It is easy to believe that face-to-face communication may be advantageous in such circumstances.[12]

Not only do the agglomeration economies that cities provide assist such exchange, but *localization economies* (the availability of many services and support functions at a location) reinforce the advantage of office-based functions congregating in larger cities. No less then 90 percent of producer services jobs are located in metropolitan areas, and that share will likely continue to grow in the future.[13]

---

[11]Edwin Mills, "Sectoral Clustering and Metropolitan Development," Chapter 1 in Edwin Mills and John McDonald, eds., *Sources of Metropolitan Growth.* New Brunswick, NJ: Rutgers University, Center for Urban Policy Research, 1992, pp. 3–18.

[12]Ibid.

[13]William Beyers, "Producer Services and Metropolitan Growth and Development," Chapter 6 in Edwin Mills and John McDonald, eds., *Sources of Metropolitan Growth.* New Brunswick, NJ: Rutgers University, Center for Urban Policy Research, 1992, pp. 125–146.

A detailed breakdown of the fastest-growing producer service activities in the United States from 1974 to 1985 appears in Table 17-3. Computer and data-processing functions grew a phenomenal 247 percent in this period. Membership organizations and personnel supply firms (temporary labor) grew by over 500,000 jobs, and banking by nearly 400,000 jobs. Other important producer services grew by over 300,000 jobs, including architecture and engineering, legal services, management and public relations, and credit agencies (other than banking). In addition, several other groups with lower absolute total numbers, but nevertheless exhibiting a high percentage growth (more than 100 percent), included accounting and auditing, research and development labs, and mail and reproduction services. Many of these job categories did not exist as recently as 25 years ago, so profound has been the impact of technology and change on this segment of the labor market.

CORPORATE DECENTRALIZATION

The growing importance and complexity of the command and control function of the corporate headquarters office led to a more concentrated pattern of corporate power in one or more major metropolitan areas of

TABLE 17-3
Fastest-Growing Producer Services, 1974–1985[a]

Service	Employment Change, 1974–1985	Percent Growth
Membership organizations	550,194	55
Computing and data processing	365,275	247
Architecture and engineering	329,834	96
Banking	391,216	33
Real estate agents	299,822	36
Legal services	366,052	115
Personnel supply	507,411	143
Management and public relations	333,874	189
Credit agencies (other than banking)	300,018	68
Retail administration and auxiliary offices	263,818	52
Insurance agents	208,082	60
Building services	226,837	60
Accounting/auditing	213,415	112

[a]More than 200,000 growt' in employment, 1974–1985, in each category.

Source: William Beyers, "Producer Services and Metropolitan Growth and Development," Chapter 6 in Edwin Mills and John F. McDonald, eds., *Sources of Metropolitan Growth.* New Brunswick, NJ: Rutgers University, Center for Urban Policy Research, 1992, pp. 132–133.

developed countries in the early to mid-twentieth century. Tokyo provided this function in Japan, London in England, and New York for the United States. The need for close and frequent interactions with specialists in finance, the stock market, management, and legal affairs, including other chief executive officers (CEOs), attracted the headquarters office to the downtown areas of these cities. One author labeled this trend as the era of *dominant national centers*, representing the first of four stages of a descriptive model of office location patterns.[14] (recall Figure 15-12).

After World War II, regional centers developed more specialized and national ties, and this growth led to a decentralization of headquarters offices to these centers. That trend intensified in the 1960s and 1970s, creating an era of the *dominant regional center* by the 1980s. Headquarters offices also migrated to the suburbs of both the emerging centers and the traditional corporate centers in this period. The model also suggests that a third stage of the process, the era of *regional maturity*, will unfold early in the twenty-first century, leading into an era of *national maturity* by 2050. In this last stage, no dominant national center exists.

The evidence available to date suggests that we may be in the midst of an era of dominant regional centers, given the rapid decentralization of corporate office activity in the past 25 years to the cities and suburbs of sunbelt metropolitan areas and to the suburbs of the traditional corporate leaders, namely, New York and Chicago. Corporate merger and acquisition activity intensified this process, as has the structural shift of the national economy to services and away from manufacturing. The decline of older manufacturing firms located in traditional centers, compared to the more rapid growth of new sunbelt-based service firms, further accentuates this contrast.[15]

Despite years of decentralization to older cities, New York and Chicago continue to claim the largest share of corporate headquarters in the United States. Both the traditional downtown and the suburbs share these activities today. The skyline rankings for metropolitan areas in 1988 show the dominance of New York; Chicago and Houston rank number 2 and 3, respectively (see box in Chapter 15).

As recently as 1970, Manhattan claimed 117 corporate headquarters of the *Fortune 500* industrial firms, and its suburbs claimed another 34 firms (Table 17-4). Manhattan lost 39 of those corporate headquarters in the 1970s, while the suburbs gained 30 headquarters offices (Figure 17-6). In the 1980s, Manhattan lost another 28 firms and the New York suburbs lost 4 companies. Chicago also lost firms in this period, declining from 39 in 1970, to 24 in 1979, to 21 in 1988. During this same period, Chicago suburbs increased from 15 to 21 firms from 1970 to 1979, then falling back to 20 in 1988. The near equal share of headquarters in Chicago (21) and the suburbs (20) in 1988 shows that the suburbs have now reached parity, as they have in Los Angeles. Far fewer *Fortune 500 Service* firms (Table 17-5) have located in New York (see Table 17-4). The Manhattan share of these firms increased from 56 to 66 in 1988, while the suburban share declined from 23 to 17. The experience in Chicago was similar. Los Angeles, on the other hand, has more service firm headquarters in the suburbs than in the city.

Evidence in support of the regional decentralization of offices is also provided by Table 17-4, which indicates that, as a group, Dallas, Atlanta, Minneapolis–St. Paul, and Washington, D.C., gained 5 *Fortune 500* industrial firms from 1970 to 1979 and 23 from 1979 to 1988. Their share of *Service 500* firms increased by 9 from 1983 to 1988. The decentralization of *Service 500*[16] firms is more pronounced as one-half of the total is now accounted for by nine areas outside the traditional headquarters group. These areas include San Francisco, Houston, Dallas, Atlanta, Boston, and Minneapolis–St. Paul. These metropolitan areas captured just under one-half of all the *Service 500* firms in 1989 (218 of 500), with many of these sites occurring in the suburbs.

The situation for manufacturing firms shows a more conservative location pattern, with a greater concentration of headquarters in the Northeast in the old manufacturing belt. The one major exception to this tendency is the more decentralized pattern of newer high-technology firms that have clustered disproportionately in the Silicon Valley to the south of San Francisco in the shadow of San Jose.

Not all corporate growth of manufacturing firms has occurred in the sunbelt, however. A recent article on

[14]R. Keith Semple and Alan G. Phipps, "The Spatial Evolution of Corporate Headquarters within an Urban System," *Urban Geography*, 3 (1982), 258.

[15]R. Keith Semple et al., "Perspective on Corporate Headquarters Relocation in the United States," *Urban Geography*, 6 (1985), 370–391; and John D. Stephens and Brian P. Holly, "City System Behaviour and Corporate Influence: The Headquarter Location of U.S. Industrial Firms," *Urban Studies*, 18 (1981), 285–300.

[16]The *Fortune 500* industrial firms and *Fortune 500* service firms are sometimes referred to as the *Fortune 1000* firms.

TABLE 17-4
Location Changes of *Fortune 500* Industrial and *Fortune 500* Service Firm Headquarters, 1970–1988

	Fortune 500 Industrial			*Fortune 500* Service	
	1970	*1979*	*1988*	*1983*	*1988*
New York (Manhattan)	117	78	50	56	66
City of Chicago	39	24	21	18	20
City of Los Angeles	13	12	10	19	18
City of Philadelphia	10	7	6	9	9
	179	122	87	102	113
Change		−57	−35		+11
New York suburbs	34	54	50	23	17
Chicago suburbs	15	21	20	12	11
Los Angeles suburbs	10	12	8	26	21
Philadelphia suburbs	4	5	3	3	5
	63	92	81	64	54
Change		+29	−11		−10
Dallas	7	8	16	19	20
Atlanta	3	4	10	7	10
Minneapolis-St. Paul	11	11	16	11	14
Washington, D.C.	0	3	7	7	9
	21	26	49	44	53
Change		+5	+23		+9

Source: Thomas Stanback, Jr., *The New Suburbanization: Challenge to the Central City,* Westview Press, Boulder, Colo., 1991, p. 79.

corporate headquarters changes from 1980 to 1987 suggests that Charlotte and Atlanta benefited among the sunbelt cities, but so did Boston and Philadelphia.[17] The emergence of the service and high-technology economy in Boston and the growth of pharmaceuticals and service activity in Philadelphia explain this latter realignment.

MARKET SEGMENTATION

The downtown office market offers an *information-rich* environment for face-to-face contact and ready access to other support functions. Opportunities to interact with government bureaucrats and politicians,

corporate executives, high-profile cultural leaders, and entertainment personalities can be maximized in the downtown. The infamous businessman's lunch at a membership club epitomizes the opportunity for information sharing in the downtown area. The exchange of *uncodified knowledge* is maximized in such a setting.

Specialized financial institutions, such as a federal reserve bank, stock exchange, holding company, or brokerage house, benefit from locational centrality. Many contacts occur by telecommunications transmissions, but regular personal contact at the local level is also important. These functions also maintain strong ties with legal and business advisors and outside consultants with central locations.

Government offices—city, county, metropolitan, state, and federal—also remain centrally located in most cities. The CBD traditionally offered the best accessibility for the largest number of people to these

[17]Steven R. Holloway and James O. Wheeler, "Corporate Headquarters Relocation and Changes in Metropolitan Corporate Dominance, 1980–1987," *Economic Geography* (1991), pp. 54–74.

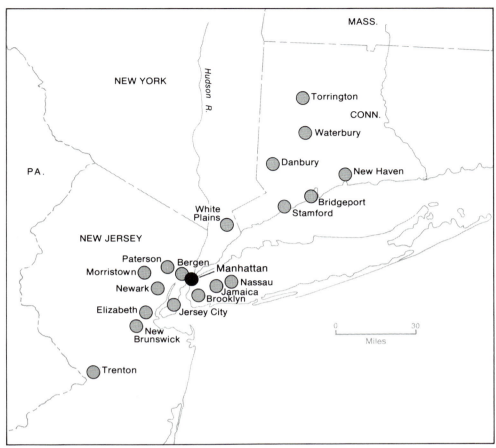

Figure 17-6. Suburban Office Headquarters in Greater New York. Four regions share the suburban corporate headquarters market: 1) Long Island; 2) New Jersey; 3) Westchester County, N.Y.; and 3) Connecticut. These suburban centers claimed 67 corporate headquarters in 1988 (see Table 17-4).

public service functions. Interagency contact also benefits from such centrality. Nevertheless, many governmental operations are routine paper-processing tasks that could be accomplished in decentralized settings, but official policy often dictates that offices remain concentrated.

Corporate headquarters functions that need information-rich office settings now find that suburban downtowns offer competitive alternatives to the traditional downtown. In the 1980s, suburban downtown markets became just as competitive as the downtown for Class A office space.[18] Corporate headquarters activities

responded by moving to suburban sites to take advantage of the amenities they offered and the high-profile opportunities associated with new signature office towers. Proximity to prime residential communities influenced many corporate leaders to select the suburban

TABLE 17-5
The *Fortune Service 500:* The Corporate Mix

100 largest diversified service companies
100 largest commercial banking companies
50 largest diversified financial companies
50 largest savings institutions
50 largest life insurance companies
50 largest retailing companies
50 largest transportation companies
50 largest utilities

Source: Fortune, June 4, 1990.

---

[18]Class A office space occurs in mid- or high-rise office buildings and commands premium rental rates, reflecting its quality. Professional offices and headquarters functions typically occupy this space. Class B space may be in older structures or may not offer as many amenities (lobby space, high-speed elevators, etc.). It is typically occupied by nonprofit businesses, government offices, or clerical-intensive operations.

alternative. Access to airports and a skilled labor market for professional staff positions is also maximized in suburban settings today.

SUBURBAN OFFICE SHARES

There is little doubt that in terms of favorable public relations, the suburb is often ranked higher than the city by both professionals and the citizenry. Those who do move to the suburbs invariably praise the decision and willingly recite problems of former locations. A study of office decentralization in Cincinnati, for example, reported that 92 percent of the respondents indicated there would be no advantage in being downtown.

In the early 1970s, it appeared that the decision to move was sequential, with small consumer-oriented firms relocating first and large national corporate headquarters last:

> Office suburbanization in the larger SMSAs has been pioneered by the sales offices of manufacturing industry. These have generally been followed by the more routine clerical activities of the insurance companies. Various

computer and research services have tended to follow, pursued by some lawyers, accountants, and real estate concerns. The regional offices of national organizations have then moved out of the central city. Somewhat later in the sequence the corporate headquarters of the larger national enterprises have also left the CBD.[19]

By the late 1970s, it became apparent that an entirely new situation existed. First, the emerging generation of executives had become accustomed to the suburban workplace and eagerly promoted it for all office endeavors. Second, expansion of suburban office space began to come more from the growth of firms already in suburbia than from decentralization. Finally, it became obvious that suburban interstate beltway freeways had opened up many new locations for potential development around all metropolitan areas.

The phenomenal suburban office expansion in major metropolitan areas continued in the 1980s, creating a suburban employment mix very similar to that in the city (Table 17-6). The suburban manufacturing share

[19]Gerald Manners, "The Office in Metropolis: An Opportunity for Shaping Metropolitan America," *Economic Geography*, 50 (1974), 101.

TABLE 17-6

Employment Profile comparisons (percent share) Selected Cities and Suburban Counties, 1987

	Manufacturing	*Retail*	*FIRE*	*Other Services*	*Government*
New York					
City	10	11	15	36	14
Westchester County	13	15	8	33	11
Chicago					
City	17	13	12	29	12
DuPage County	13	18	8	32	8
Philadelphia					
City	11	14	10	34	19
Montgomery County	19	16	10	31	7
Atlanta					
City	9	14	10	30	14
DeKalb County	10	18	10	28	12
Detroit					
City	23	16	7	27	13
Oakland County	18	22	9	36	8
Washington, D.C.					
City	2	8	6	37	39
Fairfax County	4	17	10	34	17

Source: Thomas Stanback, Jr., *The New Suburbanization: Challenge to the Central City*, Westview Press, Boulder, Colo., 1991, p. 70.

generally exceeded that of the city by that time except for strong manufacturing centers such as Detroit and Chicago. Suburban retailing, of course, exceeded that in the downtown. The suburban FIRE employment share also matched that in the city for the first time in the 1980s, except for New York and Chicago, which retained a slim central city lead. The "other services" share was comparable in both subareas at that time as well. Only in government office employment did the central city consistently outpace the suburbs, but the suburban share was surprisingly strong.

The higher concentration of skilled executive and professional employment in the suburbs in the 1990s further validates the emerging image of the suburbs as the preferred workplace for the information age professional. The figures for the three largest metropolitan areas in the country (Table 17-7) consistently demonstrate the larger share of employment in the suburbs among three prominent office groupings: executive/managerial, professional, and sales.

Suburbanization of Headquarters

Leading the move to the suburbs in the late 1970s were headquarters operations of major firms. The top management of 135 of the top *Fortune 500* industrial firms and 178 of the second 500 had their headquarters in the suburbs in 1975.[20] In 1965, only 47 of the top 500 had outlying locations.

> Boston lost 75 large companies to its suburbs in 1970–1971, and St. Louis 43 in 1970 alone; Los Angeles saw several major banks desert its CBD; and in Detroit, which recently lost S.S. Kresge, Bendix, Budd, and both its daily newspaper offices to the suburbs, things are so depressing that fomer Mayor Cavanaugh refers to "Detroit's sister cities—Nagasaki and Pompeii. . . ."[21]

Suburban New York captured the majority of office firms vacating Manhattan. "From 1960 to 1974, suburban New York registered a spectacular rise in *Fortune's* annual directory of the nation's 500 largest industrial firms, at the same time, New York City's share of these home offices dwindled from 140 in the mid-1960s to just over 90 in 1976."[22] This decentralization is shared among three areas: southwestern Connecticut; West-

TABLE 17-7
Occupational Mix of City and Suburban Resident Workers (percent) in Selected Metropolitan Areas, 1986

	New York City	New York Suburbs
Executive/manager	13	17
Professional	16	19
Sales	10	13

	Los Angeles City	Anaheim
Executive/manager	13	15
Professional	13	11
Sales	11	15

	Chicago City	Chicago Suburbs
Executive/manager	10	15
Professional	14	14
Sales	10	19

Source: Thomas M. Stanback, *The New Suburbanization: Challenge to the Central City,* Westview Press, Boulder, Colo., 1991, p. 52.

chester County, New York; and northern New Jersey (see Figure 17-9). Connecticut's Fairfield County is

> expected to surpass Chicago as the nation's second largest concentration of headquarters after New York City; with 75 major former Manhattan firms having arrived since the mid-'60s, and at least another 50 now on the way, Fairfield might well someday find itself the number one head office complex if the current popularity of that suburban New York sector persists.[23]

OFFICE PARKS

In the early post-World War II days of office suburbanization, a few firms selected smartly landscaped sites for new facilities on major arterial highways. This trend was gradually built upon to produce full-fledged office parks by the late 1950s. Many of the latter accommodated several smaller firms that shared space in single-story or mid-rise buildings. Eventually, these were joined by an elaborate mix of small and large firms and associated business services. Back offices, sales offices/warehouse functions, and showrooms also gravitated to these areas (Table 17-8). By the 1960s, the greatest share of suburban office space in medium to large cities had gravitated to controlled office park environments, with single-story and mid-rise buildings

---

[20]Peter Muller, *The Outer City: Geographical Consequences of the Urbanization of the Suburbs,* Resource Paper No. 75-2, Association of American Geographers, Washington, D.C., 1976, p. 37.

[21]Ibid

[22]Ibid.

[23]Peter O. Muller, "The Suburbanization of Corporate Headquarters: What Are the Trends and Consequences?", *Vital Issues,* 27 (April 1978).

TABLE 17-8
Office Functions Associated with Suburban Office Facilities

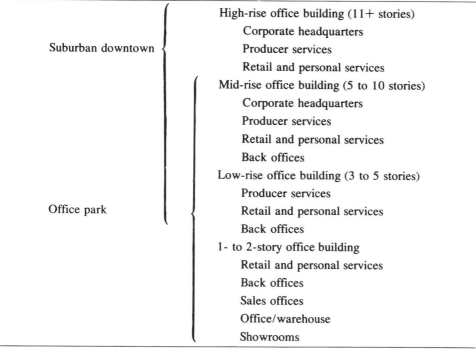

Suburban downtown
- High-rise office building (11+ stories)
  - Corporate headquarters
  - Producer services
  - Retail and personal services

Office park
- Mid-rise office building (5 to 10 stories)
  - Corporate headquarters
  - Producer services
  - Retail and personal services
  - Back offices
- Low-rise office building (3 to 5 stories)
  - Producer services
  - Retail and personal services
  - Back offices
- 1- to 2-story office building
  - Retail and personal services
  - Back offices
  - Sales offices
  - Office/warehouse
  - Showrooms

Source: author.

in one environment adding considerable geographical prestige to the area (Figure 17-7). This situation fits the second stage, Independence, of the Hartshorn–Muller model of suburban development discussed in Chapter 9. Recall that retail, office, and industrial activity growth in the suburbs makes these areas independent from the central city as an employment center in this stage.

Accessibility and Amenities

Outlying office park alternatives grew as a result of the aggressive leadership of their developers, but not until the accessibility of outlying areas became competitive with downtown. The lure of site amenities, particularly campuslike settings near fashionable residential areas, differentially benefited the office park concept. The advantages of suburban office parks are summarized in Table 17-9. Although many of these points have already been covered, a brief recounting of the suburban advantage is useful because the office park nurtured

and shaped most of the advantages now taken for granted.

The attractiveness of suburban sites for *work environments*, for example, has been cited as a factor in reducing psychological stress and as a source of employee satisfaction, which reduces worker turnover. Second, suburban locations often provide shorter journey-to-work trips for both clerical and executive workers. Some firms have even noted that executive work weeks have increased 10–20 percent as a result of the proximity to home and short work trip commute.[24] These locations also opened up a new employment market for the firm—the college-educated homemaker. This group, often hesitant to work downtown, eagerly engages in workplaces near home.

Few, if any, sacrifices had to be made by the employee who chose to work in office parks rather than downtown. The first parks often lacked the proximity to shopping that the downtown offered, and employees lamented not having the opportunity to shop during

---

[24]"Executives Can Work Longer in Suburbia," *Office*, 79 (1974), pp. 24ff.

Figure 17-7. The Office Park Alternative. Suburban office park facilities initially catered to the small sales office market and the back offices of firms emphasizing intensive clerical operations, followed by regional sales offices seeking the advantages of expressway accessibility. (Ted Schmoll/Photo Network)

TABLE 17-9
Advantages of Office Park Locations

1. Good access to high-capacity transportation, especially freeways and airports; good internal circulation, offstreet parking, and freedom from vehicular congestion.

2. Location close to high-income residential areas; proximity to executive residential areas and to suburban working homemaker market.

3. Near other national and regional headquarter firms and supporting service companies; good offpeak hour access to downtown.

4. Prestige site location; quality campuslike suburban atmosphere; low development intensity; landscaping with lawns and/or wooded setting.

5. Strict building/land ratios; proper setbacks and color coordination; underground utilities; screening of service areas; controlled signs; comprehensive architectural control.

6. Access to suburban shopping centers; on-site personal and professional services (banking, postal, dining, beauty parlor, health, and recreational facilities).

7. Comprehensive protective planning and zoning; protective covenants; continuous management and coordination with park occupants; round-the-clock security; immediate occupancy.

8. Taxation advantages; lower insurance rates, easier financing and resale; more investment protection; flexible leasing and/or building options; ease of expansion.

Source: Truman A. Hartshorn, "Industrial/Office Parks: A New Look for the City," *Journal of Geography,* 72 (1973), 36. Reprinted by permission.

lunch hours. Later, the simultaneous development of office and shopping center complexes in one setting neutralized this disadvantage.

Traffic congestion and restricted downtown parking opportunities also encouraged office park expansion. Instead of expensive downtown parking rates, suburban office parks frequently offered plenty of free or low-cost parking. Usually five or six spaces per 1000 square feet of office space were provided. But suburban congestion increased as activities expanded, and public transportation was limited.

Together, office parks and suburban shopping centers led the movement of commercial activity toward high-income areas. The primary location of office parks on the affluent north side of Atlanta in the early 1970s provides a classic illustration of this affinity. Office parks in Atlanta evolved along the interstate radials and the perimeter highway (Figure 17-8). Office parks also reached a high level of sophistication at the time in New York, Chicago, Toronto, and in California cities.

Virtually all metropolitan areas of 50,000 or more now have office parks. The parks often have incubator space for new firms and a wide variety of lease/purchase options. Some have been developed in close proximity to general aviation fields to take advantage of

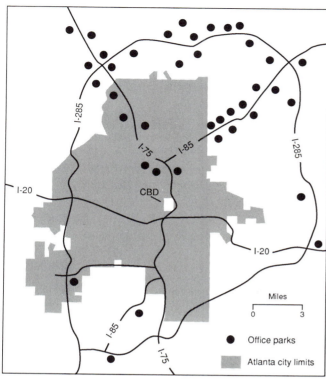

Figure 17-8. Office Park Locations in Atlanta, 1970. The affinity of Atlanta's office parks to the northside radial and circumferential freeway network dramatically increased white-collar employment in the area. The regional service function of the Atlanta economy attracted branches of many Fortune 1000 firms in this period. *Source:* Truman A. Hartshorn, "Industrial/Office Parts: A New Look for the City," *Journal of Geography,* 72 (1973). Reprinted by permission.

air accessibility, and convenient sites for operations bases for corporate aircraft. This approach, know in the trade as the *fly-in* concept, can also be especially useful to smaller cities with no scheduled commercial air carrier service. Other specialized office parks have used research and development as a theme. Such parks cater to manufacturing firms, governmental agencies, nonprofit corporations, and think-tank operations. They will be discussed more fully in Chapter 18 as a specialized example of an industrial park.

Another adaptation of the office park is the *business park,* which combines office, hotel, restaurant, showroom, and warehouse/distribution functions in one setting. These projects became very popular in the 1980s. We will discuss business parks in more detail in Chapter 18 in conjunction with the industrial/distribution function of the city.

In the 1970s, the office park and regional shopping center played a catalytic role in generating more intensive commercial centers in the suburbs, by attracting

more specialized producer service functions and other retail and service activity, including hotels and restaurants. Stage 3 of the Hartshorn/Muller suburban development model, *catalytic growth,* describes this growth process:

> By 1973, the suburbs had pulled ahead of the central cities in total employment, and that gap has widened steadily ever since—signaling that a critical mass of urban economic activity has irreversibly suburbanized. The parallel expansion of high-income housing communities, and the growing tendency for ever more specialized office functions to migrate to emerging suburban business centers with expressway exposure [characterized this process]."[25]

URBAN CORES

The stage was now set for the emergence of true downtown centers in the suburbs in the 1980s. Christopher Leinberger has described six types of *urban cores* (Table 17-10) that emerged. Some of these centers blossomed around regional malls, some involved revitalization of *old town centers,* and yet others were planned from the ground up for locations at strategic transportation sites (Figure 17-9).

While observers still thought in terms of office parks to describe suburban office centers in the early 1970s, it was the high-rise office building late arriving in the suburbs in the late 1970s that revolutionized its market role. The Leinberger model classifies centers as either class A, class B, or class C urban cores (Table 17-11) based on the role of office, retail, and business park/industrial park uses, and their intensity. Class A centers have strong office/hotel functions along with a major retail presence. Class B centers lack important high-rise office activity as measured by the presence of producer services and corporate headquarters. Many cater to back-office functions in mid-rise offices or lack an office function entirely. Class C centers place more emphasis on business park/industrial park uses and generally have a weak retail presence. Some centers have evolved from Class C to Class B to Class A status overtime such as King of Prussia in suburban Philadelphia in Montgomery County (Table 17-11). In other cases the upgrading or intensification of uses has been

[25]Truman A. Hartshorn and Peter O. Muller, "Suburban Downtowns and the Transformation of Metropolitan Atlanta's Business Landscape," *Urban Geography,* 10, No. 4 (1989), 381.

TABLE 17-10
Six Types of Urban Cores, after Leinberger

Type	Name	Description
1. Class A	Central Business District	Class A downtown core; many new offices and hotels as well as renovations of older buildings; shrinking role as office center for region.
2. Class B	Revitalized Suburban Town Center	Class B old town centers that have declined; may be government center in role as county seat; former retail space may be largely vacant and/or demolished; new high-rise construction transforms area into office center; examples include Towson, Md., and Pasadena, Calif.
3. Class A	Revitalized Suburban Town Center	More upscale version of type 2; more emphasis on corporate headquarters; may be evolving from Class B to Class A center; examples include Bethesda, Md.; Fort Lauderdale, Fla.; and Clayton, Mo. (suburban St. Louis).
4. New Class C	Suburban Core	Origin as industrial or business park, now acquiring more office and high technology businesses; examples include Peachtree Corners in suburban Atlanta (Gwinnett County) and South Orlando, Fla.
5. New Class B	Suburban Core	New core areas evolving around shopping centers in metropolitan peripheries with starter housing and middle-income residential communities; examples include San Bernardino and Riverside, Calif. (in greater Los Angeles); Gwinnett Place (suburban Atlanta); and Great Northern in Cleveland.
6. New Class A	Suburban Cores	High-rise office development around upscale regional mall (Heathrow, Orlando; Owings Mills, Baltimore; or as mixed-use centers (Las Colinas, Dallas); others began as Class B centers, evolving into Class A over time, such as Perimeter Center (Atlanta), Tyson's Corner (Washington, D.C.), or Bellevue (suburban Seattle); yet others originally began as Class C centers, such as King of Prussia (Philadelphia) or Hunt Valley (Baltimore), which began as industrial and distribution centers.

Source: modified after Christopher B. Leinberger, "The Six Types of Urban Village Cores," *Urban Land* (May 1988), 24–27.

partial, as in the case of the shift in Ontario, California from Class C to Class B status. Some centers simply remain Class B or C Centers and have not taken on new roles. Type 6 in the Leinberger model, the New Class A Suburban Core, is generally recognized as having the most significance in defining the new suburban downtown form. It generated the most dramatic skylines and rapidly transformed a suburban landscape into an urban setting. Among the most impressive of these centers today are Tyson's Corners in Fairfax County in suburban Washington, D.C., the Buckhead/Lenox area (Figure 9-13) and Perimeter Center in suburban Atlanta (Figure 17-3); The City Post Oak in suburban Houston may be a pioneer in this regard (Figures 9-14 and 16-12). Built as The Galleria regional mall by developer Gerald Hines in 1971, this center now has the distinction of housing the tallest office building in suburban America, the 65-story Transco Tower.

As with the emergence of any new form, achieving consensus on a definition of the suburban downtown has been difficult (see box). As these downtowns matured, other high-order functions gravitated to them, including upscale restaurants, more specialty retailing, full-service hotels, suite hotels, luxury hotels, convention/conference facilities. They also attracted more high-rise housing, hospitals, and branch campuses of universities, among other functions. With greater commercial densities came increased pressure to add more parking facilities. Former surface parking sites were replaced with multilevel parking decks, which released "found" space for further commercial development.

It is now common to encounter master-planned mixed-use downtowns type 6 cores in the Leinberger model, designed from the beginning as class A centers, now that we know the mix of functions that such centers will support. The Galleria in suburban Dallas and Las Colinas, also in suburban Dallas, provide examples. The Galleria boasts three levels of shopping surrounding an ice rink, a luxury hotel, several restaurants and

SUBURBAN DOWNTOWNS

The high-order, multifunctional activity centers that have so swiftly emerged in the outer suburban city go by many different names in the literature, among them "nucleation," "minicity," "activity center," "urban subcenter," "suburban business district," and even "urban village." Although no consensus yet exists as to how to define these complexes precisely, it is becoming clearer what they are and what they are not. For definitional purposes, the largest of these centers best characterizes the genre because they are the most clearly demarcated on the landscape, the most diversified in function, and have the heaviest impact on metropolitan economic-spatial structure. They possess increasingly well-defined labor markets, trade areas, and identities as social centers for their surrounding populations. They are clearly more than urban villages; they are also more than suburban-activity centers, a term that has been used to denote a broader category encompassing all suburban commercial areas. In our view, these burgeoning complexes have reached a scale of development warranting their designation as *suburban downtowns*. To set them off from second-order and smaller suburban-activity concentrations, these first-order centers should contain (1) at least one regional shopping center of more than one million square feet of selling space; (2) three or more high-rise office buildings housing at least one *Fortune 1000* firm headquarters; (3) an office complex of at least 5 million square feet; (4) at least two major hotels of more than 400 rooms each; and (5) an employment level of 50,000 persons.

A case can readily be made for considering these centers to be full-fledged "downtowns" in the classic sense, because they have become the crossroads of their portion of the outer suburban city with superior freeway/highway access and have attracted a diversified mix of commercial activity. To be sure, they look different from the traditional central-city CBD. Suburban downtowns are more loosely knit together, so to speak, with islands of nearby development often scattered across a sea of parking lots and/or decks. And, of course, they are far more auto-oriented than pedestrian-oriented, but they still function along the lines of the CBD-type downtown. Office rents for Class A space match or exceed those downtown. Typically, these centers serve as corporate headquarters locations as well as the nexus for high-order support services, including legal, accounting, and finance functions. The one activity conspicuously absent is the government function.[26]

In a recent book Joel Garreau calls this phenomena an *edge city*.[27] He says we have taken the function of the city (the machine), and transported it to the edge of urbanity (the frontier), and tried to merge the two creating an unsettled environment punctuated by office buildings. Garreau identifies 17 edge cities in greater New York and 16 each in the Washington, D.C., and Los Angeles areas. There are now about 200 such edge cities compared with 35 large CBD's in the country. Garreau says that "By moving the world of work and commerce out near the homes of the middle and upper middle class, it [the Edge City], has knocked the pins out from suburbia as a place apart. It has started the reintegration of all our functions. . . ."[28]

[26]Ibid., p. 376.

[27]Joel Garreau, *Edge City: Life on the New Frontier*, Doubleday, New York, 1991.

[28]Ibid., p. 399.

theaters, structured parking, and two major office towers with about 1 million square feet of space in one high-density setting.

Las Colinas now serves as the world headquarters of Exxon, having moved from New York in 1991. GTE Corporation has also recently relocated to Las Colinas in consolidating its headquarters from Connecticut and other locations. This mixed-use complex includes housing, a people mover system connecting commercial centers, and a series of lakes and canals offering water-based ferry service.

For the future, it appears that a fifth stage in the evolution of suburban downtowns is unfolding, that of the *mature town center*.

Whereas the economic function of this future center will not change significantly from its role today, it will be much different politically and socially. Nor will it differ significantly physically. True, interior design problems

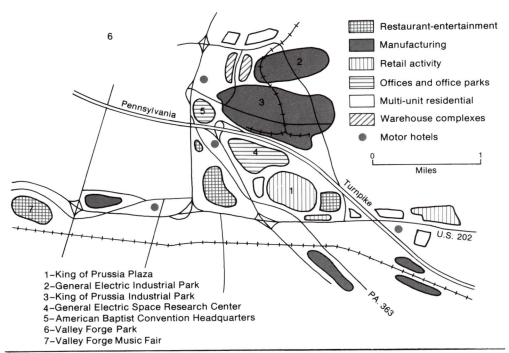

1–King of Prussia Plaza
2–General Electric Industrial Park
3–King of Prussia Industrial Park
4–General Electric Space Research Center
5–American Baptist Convention Headquarters
6–Valley Forge Park
7–Valley Forge Music Fair

Figure 17-9. King of Prussia Suburban Downtown, Philadelphia. The name of this complex derives from an historic tavern of that name in the area. This area became a favored site for development due to its location at an intersection of the Pennsylvania Turnpike (completed in the area in 1954), and the then-new Schuylkill Expressway. One of the first developments in the area was the General Electric aerospace production facility. By 1965, the regional shopping center established a new identity for the area. Later, office and hotel activities and a greatly expanded mall created a more diversified character for the area (see Tables 17-10 and 17-11). *Source:* Peter O. Muller, *The Outer City: Geographical Consequences of the Urbanization of the Suburbs* (Washington, D.C., Association of American Geographers, Resource Papers for College Geography, 75-2), 1976, 41. Redrawn by permission.

will be worked out and considerable infilling will occur, and secondary transportation systems—automated light-rail systems and the like—will develop to assist access. But the most significant changes will come in the cultural opportunities associated with these centers and in their governance. These areas will become centers for the arts, boast important entertainment and sporting facilities, and become true town centers.

These downtowns are in a political never-never land at present, often positioned astride multiple political jurisdictional boundaries and lacking "official"designation or status such as that conferred by a postal address or incorporation. Nevertheless, local governance will come of age, probably evolving out of the private associations and special districts that are now appearing to address the issue of financing transportation solutions and infrastructure improvements. . . .

Over time some of the organizations have expanded their involvement to include the management of day-care facilities, security, and other services.[29]

Other problems also plague these centers, but their overall vitality is a testament to the confidence the public places in them. One issue that begs solution is the critical jobs/housing balance found in these centers. While satisfaction exists among the higher skilled employee in terms of housing access, many lesser skilled clerical and blue-collar service workers cannot afford to live near these centers and long-distance commuting poses critical problems. We will discuss this issue in detail in Chapter 19.

THEORETICAL CONSIDERATIONS

No single body of theory explains the location of office facilities. While costs and accessibility considerations are important, so are the agglomeration economies associated with clustering. In this case, the sharing of information is very important. Management and operational considerations also become important in this context, placing emphasis on face-to-face contact con-

---

[29]Ibid., Hartshorn and Muller, "Suburban Downtowns . . ." pp. 391, 393.

TABLE 17-11
Types of Regional Urban Village Cores

Historical Background		Physical Characteristics		
		Class A Space	*Class B Space*	*Class C Space*
New Suburban Cores		Heathrow (Orlando) Owings Mill (Baltimore) Las Colinas (Dallas)	Gwinnett (Atlanta) San Bernardino/Riverside (Los Angeles) Whitemarsh (Baltimore) Great Northern (Cleveland) Burlington County, N.J. (Philadelphia) Ontario (Los Angeles) ◄─────── X	Peachtree Corners (Atlanta) City of Industry (Los Angeles) City of Commerce (Los Angeles) South Orlando (Orlando) X
		Hunt Valley (Baltimore) ◄─────── X ◄───────		X
		King of Prussia (Philadelphia) ◄─────── X ◄───────		X
		Tysons Corner (Washington, D.C.) ◄─────── X		
		Newport Beach/Irvine/Costa Mesa (Los Angeles) ◄─────── X		
		Perimeter Center (Atlanta) ◄─────── X		
		Princeton (New York) ◄─────── X		
Revitalized Suburban Towns		Beverly Hills (Los Angeles) Stamford (New York) White Plains (New York) Bethesda (Washington, D.C.) ◄─────── X Clayton (St. Louis) ◄─────── X Fort-Lauderdale (Miami) ◄─────── X	Pasadena (Los Angeles) Long Beach (Los Angeles)	
Downtowns		Nearly all CBDs		

Source: Christopher B. Leinberger, "The Six Types of Urban Village Cores," *Urban Land* (May 1988), 24–27.

siderations, telecommunications behavior, and the nature of work performed in the particular office. We have already discussed the role of information, but the role of the organizational behavior of the firm deserves more attention.

Orientation Network

The management philosophy of a firm and its organizational structure create a very complex *orientation network* specific to that firm. This philosophy and the nature of the functions performed greatly affect the potential for the whole firm or specific operations to decentralize. Several types of office organizations and associated communication and *contact patterns* are

shown in Table 17-12. The two activities that require personal contact are the advertising agency and the executive group. Interaction in a relatively controlled environment is essential for these functions. Routine operations, such as those represented by general accounting and design work, are more internalized and outside contact is minimal. The operational space needs of the latter group are very flexible and sites with many amenities are typically preferred.

Office operations flexibility is typically greater for specific functions than for firms as a whole. Several stages in the evolution of location patterns for a business are shown in Figure 17-10. *Centralization* characterizes Stage 1 when all operations are clustered in one setting. In Stage 2, *fragmentation* occurs as specific units break away to take advantage of particular envi-

TABLE 17-12
Types of Office Organizations and Contact Patterns

Type	Communications	Technology	Contact with Outside World
Personal contact required			
Advertising agency	Responsive to outside demands	Coordination internally and externally; creative	Visitors must be impressed, backroom people keep out of sight
Executive group	Controlled and relatively infrequent	Meetings; telephones; fax; slide/graphics presentations; talking	Controlled access to visitors; desire to impress
Routine operations			
General accounting	Follow predetermined paths	Use of computers quick data retrieval	Cut off
Design office	Continual discussion of work in progress	Long-term projects; drawings; computer graphics; special problems of information retrieval	Unimportant except at a day-to-day working level

Source: Modified after F. Duffy, "Office Design and Organizations: 1. Theoretical Basis," *Environment and Planning, B,* (1974), 113.

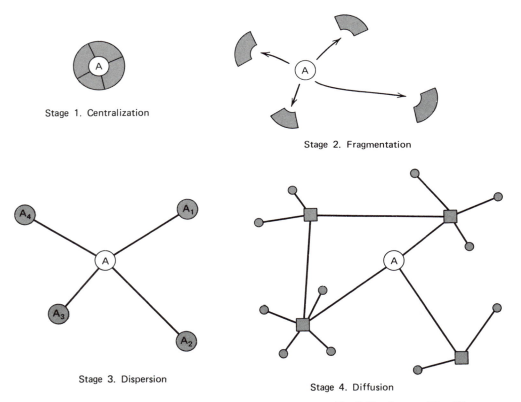

Stage 1. Centralization

Stage 2. Fragmentation

Stage 3. Dispersion

Stage 4. Diffusion

Figure 17-10. Spatial Evolution of Corporate Facility Locations. Flexibility for specific office operations is typically greater than for firms as a whole. Centralization (Stage 1) is typically followed by the
splitting up of operations (Stage 2), followed by dispersion (Stage 3), and a hierarchial arrangement at a
later time (Stage 4). *Source:* Redrawn with permission. From Jack M. Nilles, et al., *The Telecommunications—
Transportation Trade-off, Options for Tomorrow,* Wiley, New York, 1976, p. 12.

ronments for their specific operation. Stage 3 shows a *dispersion* of offices that occurs when all functions of a firm move to satellite centers, not just specific operations. In Stage 4, a *diffusuion* of functions occurs away from the outlying centers and a hierarchy of linkages emerges. Small core staffs in each of these remote locations depend on telecommunication service for work coordination. The networks of ties that these decentralized offices maintain are called *occupancy chains* reflecting informational interdependencies that remain strong, even with the physical separation.

The larger the firm and the more specialized its work, the greater the incentive to disperse operations within a metropolitan context. An illustration of the various functions of single firms, each with unique needs, is revealed by considering three broad levels of business administration (Table 17-13). *Top management* sets long-term goals and strategies for the company. It depends on contact from many outside sources, including financial institutions, researchers, government, and other business organizations. This function must be conducted in large cities to maximize contact. Traditionally, most top firms maintained corporate financial offices in New York City for this level of decision making, but this activity is increasingly becoming more dispersed. Such activity can be conducted at outlying centers as well as downtown because meetings are prearranged and lengthy. Often, it may occur at remote "retreats" where personnel can devote their full attention to the appointed agenda. The recent moves of Union Pacific from Manhattan to Allentown, Pennsylvania, and J.C. Penney from Manhattan to Plano, Texas (in suburban Dallas), illustrates these decentral-

ization tendencies, as does the move of Sears from its namesake tower in Chicago's downtown loop to suburban Hoffman Estates.

The second level of organizational structure refers to *middle management*. Decision making among this group involves implementing company goals. Planning, research and development, and supervisory applications work are involved. Small teams of workers familiar with specific tasks translate the goals into action. Since the work is largely internalized, there is considerable flexibility in location. Regional offices dispersed among many second- and third-order centers, characterized by both downtown and suburban locations, claim many middle management operations.

Contact Patterns

Office work does not involve a product per se but rather a service. One definition of office work indicates that it is basically "communications control."[30] Much of the activity is encompassed by the term *abstract transactions*, discussed in Chapter 15, and involves a wide range of business contacts, both within an organization and with outside clients. Knowledge and information are the raw material.[31] Face-to-face contact may be useful but hardly necessary or most efficient for the conduct of much office business. Routine exchanges, such as placing orders or asking for advice, can best be handled by telephone. Among individuals who are familiar with one another, remote telephone contacts suffice for the conduct of most business, lessening the need for physical proximity.

The Impact of the Telephone

The versatility of the telephone conversation in handling both routine daily business and the resolution of problems via an unlimited network of contacts has perhaps had the most profound effect of any development on the deconcentration of office activity. The telephone, in its advanced digital format, can be used for voice mail, paging, and faxing documents, in addition to its more traditional role of providing instantaneous audio contact. Telephones can be easily con-

TABLE 17-13
Levels of Business Administration

Level	Function and Location
Top management	Long-term goals; strategies; orientation relations; central location; large prearranged meetings; input from outside
Middle management	Planning and application; research and development; small groups of familiar individuals work with specific objectives
Day-to-day management	Routine operations coordination; internal discussion; can be done by phone

Source: John Goddard, *Office Location in Urban and Regional Development,* Oxford University Press, London, 1975. Used with permission.

---

[30]F. Duffy, "Office Design and Organizations: I. Theoretical Basis," *Environment and Planning, B,* 12 (1971), 111.

[31]Michael Bannon, "The Office Industry: A Facet of the White-Collar Revolution," *Geographical Review,* 65 (1975), 404.

nected with word processors to generate documents or linked to computer systems to conduct a variety of tasks.

The phone is a great tool for personal communication. A study of office behavior in London, for example, found that 20 pecent of all office contacts could be handled via telephone.[32]

High-level decision making or negotiations involving hard bargaining on sensitive issues, by contrast, require more participant interaction. The necessity for feedback in such sessions often requires face-to-face meetings in order to assess positions and to work out compromises. These sessions often occur regularly (e.g., daily) among executives. They usually involve only two persons and are short.

Mixing Business and Pleasure

Luncheon meetings in one of the principal's offices or in a neutral setting at a restaurant or private club are important activities for decision makers. "Nothing quite replaces the business conference lunch. The complex relationship between people and offices, between offices and governmental functions, between sales and management, financing, trading, and other business activities are traditionally linked—downtown."[33] But the growing suburban hotel room inventory in and around office parks and the growing array of restaurants in adjacent commercial districts that cater to the noontime business conference have also broken the former CBD monopoly in this area. In addition, the suburban setting offers another specialized but growing form of business contact substitute—the tennis, golf, or fitness club. The home-based party has also grown in popularity. This phenomenon, usually organized around cocktail parties, buffets, or barbecues, has grown rapidly.

Downtown versus Suburban Meetings

Scheduled face-to-face business meetings themselves are not necessarily well served by downtown settings. Long business sessions and conferences involving many persons are held infrequently and organized well in advance. Often, some participants come from out of town and, quite likely, many work in offices in suburban centers. Given these circumstances, locations for meetings are very flexible.

Meetings involving new contacts normally entail several persons engaging in general discussion, and again are planned so that participants can assemble at any mutually convenient location. Follow-up sessions can be handled as routine business, often by telephone. Few persons are usually involved at such times and personal on-site involvement is rarely required. For these reasons, phone conversations suffice for contact once participants know one another.

The phone can be used as a substitute for 20–60 percent of local business transactions according to one estimate.[34] However, there is no substitute for participants knowing each other, which is a must for successful use of the phone for sensitive negotiations.

The use of the videophone to enhance communication decision making is more limited than envisioned a decade ago. There is no advantage to this type of conversation for many tasks and it has several disadvantages. Essentially, the videophone makes interaction too formal because participants are not relaxed and comfortable. By comparison, simple audio teleconferencing involves minimal intrusion, unlimited contacts, and low cost.

Contact by telephone is generally impromptu and advance arrangements are not usually necessary. Several comparisons are made between telephone and face-to-face meetings in Table 17-14. The data suggest that telephone conversations are rarely longer than 10 minutes, whereas face-to-face meetings are much more time-consuming, typically 30 minutes or more in length. The frequency of contact via telephone is significantly higher than that for face-to-face meetings and usually the discussions are more specific and cover fewer topics.

Research conducted in London found that 80 percent of all personal and routine business contacts among downtown offices could be accomplished just as regularly as in outlying places. The remaining 20 percent of office contacts that were more dependent on downtown sites presumably involved highly sensitive negotiations undertaken by finance executives (stockbrokers, bank officers, and bond dealers), corporate attorneys, commercial realtors, and commodity traders. The strong

---

[32]J B Goddard, *Office Linkages and Location, Progress in Planning*, Vol. 1, Part 2, Pergamon, New York, 1973.

[33]J. Ross McKeever, *Business Parks: Office Parks, Plazas and Centers: A Study of Development Practices and Procedures*, Technical Bulletin, 65, the Urban Institute, Washington, D.C., 1970, pp. 2.

[34]Nilles, *The Telecommunications–Transportation Trade-off*, p. 132.

TABLE 17-14
Characteristics of Telephone and
Face-to-Face Meetings

	Telephone (percent)	Face-to-Face (percent)
Length of contact		
2–10 minutes	87	19
10–30 minutes	12	29
More than 30 minutes	1	52
Arrangement of contact		
Not arranged	83	17
Same day	9	13
1–7 days before	6	43
More than 1 week	2	27
Frequency of contact		
Daily	18	14
Once a week	23	10
Once a month	14	13
Occasional	34	38
First contact	11	25
Range of subject matter		
One specific subject	84	57
Several specific subjects	15	35
Wide range of subjects	1	8

Source: J. B. Goddard, *Office Linkages and Location, Progress in Planning,*
Vol. 1, Part 2, Pergamon, Oxford, England, 1973.

center-city ties of these activities would make them
unlikely candidates for dispersal.

An office operations study in London also revealed
that firms rejecting movement to the suburbs depended
more on face-to-face meetings, and those that did move
used the telephone more intensively. The firms that
moved had 58 percent fewer outside calls and 55
percent fewer external meetings than firms that did not
move. This finding supports the generalization that
office movement can be highly selective based on the
functions performed.

Parity in Rental Costs

When comparing the total package of costs (land, rent,
tax, mortgage, and utility payments) for downtown and
suburban locations, one finds virtual parity in physical
space costs. This means that rental costs do not become
obvious locational determinants, because significant
savings in rent do not occur in the suburbs. One major
exception to the parity thesis of downtown/suburban
office space costs occurs in New York City, where land
and taxes are higher in Manhattan than in outlying
locations.

By considering the long-term productivity of employees and their accessibility outlays, cost advantages
can easily tilt toward outlying places for many types of
firms. Lower employee turnover, less travel time, and
more amenities all contribute to higher job satisfaction.
Greater potential for future expansion of space also
usually exists in the suburb. In all instances, these items
can be translated into indirect long-term cost savings,
even though they are not reflected in direct rental rates.

Labor Costs and Other Considerations

Labor costs dominate the operating expense ledger for
the office firm, for this industry is very labor intensive.
Labor typically accounts for half to three-quarters of
operations costs, whereas space costs themselves constitute only 10 to 15 percent of the total. A survey in
London indicated that these estimates are on the conservative side.[35] In the British case, labor costs totaled
73 percent of operating costs, whereas rent accounted
for 18 percent and communication costs (telephone,
postage, etc.) were 8 percent.

Locations that promote payroll savings cannot be
ignored. For many clerical positions, it is possible to
pay lower wages and yet obtain a higher level of skilled
workers in the suburb than downtown. This obviously
reinforces the attraction of the suburban job market.

The suburb offers other conveniences that may not
translate into direct cost savings. Such offices are
frequently closer to the airport; crime rates are typically
lower; the schools are better; and living costs may be
lower. The savings in corporate and personal income
taxes, as well as sales tax advantages experienced by
moving to the suburbs, have been cited as a major
factor by firms leaving Manhattan for outlying communities. Typically, this involves extra tax savings by
shifting to other states in the New York case (i.e.,
moves to Connecticut or New Jersey), a factor with
which few cities have to contend.

---

[35]Goddard, *Office Linkages and Location*, p. 40.

SUMMARY AND CONCLUSION

The office function came of age in the twentieth century with the white collar occupational revolution, but the growth of this activity over the past 30 years has had an even greater impact on the city. During the first half of this century, office activities were restricted to downtown locations and mainly concentrated in the largest metropolitan areas, such as New York, London, Paris, Tokyo, Toronto, and Montreal. Corporate headquarters and government operations claimed the majority of the space. But in the post-World War II era, office functions decentralized, shifting from dominant centers like New York to regional centers throughout the country, and they broke away from downtown locations to include suburban settings. These activities also mushroomed in scope and intensity.

Public policy intervention schemes have attempted to influence the office location pattern, but market conditions have generally shaped the growth. Younger *Service* 500 firms' corporate headquarters now exhibit a decentralized pattern throughout the country, especially visible in the sunbelt. Older *Industrial* 500 firms' corporate headquarters remain more clustered in the Northeast, even if they have been suburbanized.

Suburban office growth began in the 1960s as office parks chose sites offering freeway accessibility. Sales offices, back offices, and regional headquarters activities filled these facilities. As the suburban commercial market matured, it attracted more specialized office functions, including corporate headquarters and a wide array of producer services. Today, suburban office functions are concentrated in downtown cores that rival or exceed the size of the central business district. Unlike retailing, however, suburban office space is much more clustered.

Innovations in the telecommunications industry and the growing complexity and specialization of functions in the service economy, including the expansion of computer operations, legal and accounting services, personnel agencies, and others, collectively known as producer services, are creating the bulk of the demand for office space today. As firms grow in size and complexity, they increasingly "farm out" specialized office operations. Labeled a decoupling of functions, this process has disproportionately benefited the suburbs of larger metropolitan areas.

Suggestions for Further Reading

Alexander, Ian C. *Office Location and Public Policy*, Longman, London, 1978.

Armstrong, Regina. *The Office Industry: Patterns of Growth and Location*, Report of the Regional Plan Association, MIT Press, Cambridge, Mass., 1972.

Barratt, Robert N. *Exodus from New York City*, Louis Schlesinger Co., Clifton, N.J., 1977.

Conway, Donald J., ed. *Human Response to Tall Buildings*, Dowden Hutchinson, and Ross, Stroudsburg, Penn., 1977.

Cowan, P., et al. *The Office: A Facet of Urban Growth*, Heinemann, London, 1969.

Daniels, P. W. *Office Location: An Urban and Regional Study*, G. Bell and Sons, London, 1975.

————. *Service Industries: A Geographical Appraisal*, Methuen, London, 1986.

Garreau, Joel. *Edge City: Life on the New Frontier*, Doubleday, New York, 1991.

Goddard, J. *Office Location in Urban and Regional Development*, Pergamon, Oxford, England, 1975.

Hall, Peter, et al. *The Containment of Urban England*, 2 vols., Allen & Unwin, London, 1973.

Hartshorn, Truman, and Peter O. Muller. *Suburban Business Centers: Employment Implications*, Final Report, U.S. Department of Commerce, EDA, Project No. RED-808-6-84-5, Washington, D.C., 1986.

————. "Suburban Downtowns and the Transformation of Metropolitan Atlanta's Business Landscape," *Urban Geography*, 10, No. 4. (1989), pp. 375–395.

Holloway, Steven R., and James O. Wheeler, "Corporate Headquarters Relocation and Changes in Metropolitan Corporate Dominance, 1980–87," *Economic Geogrpahy* (1991), pp.

Holly, Brian. "Regulation, Competition, and Technology: The Restructuring of the U.S. Commercial Banking System," *Environment and Planning A*, 19 (1987), 633–652.

Huxtable, Ada Louise. *Have You Kicked a Building Lately?* Quadrangle Books, New York, 1976.

Johnston, J. E., ed. *Suburban Growth*, Wiley, London, 1974.

Marshall, J. N. "Services in a Postindustrial Economy," *Environment and Planning A*, 17 (1985), 1155–1167.

McKeever, J. Ross. *Business Parks: Office Parks, Plazas and Centers: A Study of Development Practices and Procedures*, Technical Bulletin 65, The Urban Institute, Washington, D.C., 1970.

Nilles, Jack M., et al. *The Telecommunications–Transportation Trade-off, Options for Tomorrow*, Wiley, New York, 1976.

Noyelle, T., and Thomas Stanback. *The Economic Transformation of American Cities*, Allenheld and Roman, Totowa, N.J., 1983.

Noyelle, Thierry J. *Beyond Industrial Dualism: Market and Job*

Segmentation in the New Economy, Westview Press, Boulder, Colo., 1986.

Quante, Wolfgang. *The Exodus of Corporate Headquarters from New York City*, Praeger, New York, 1976.

Semple, R. Keith. "Toward a Quarternary Place Theory," *Urban Geography*, 6 (1985), 285–296.

Semple, R. Keith, and Alan G. Phipps. "The Spatial Evolution of Corporate Headquarters within an Urban System" *Urban Geography*, 3 (1982), 258–279.

Stanback, Thomas M., Jr., *The New Suburbanization: Challenge to the Central City*, Westview Press, Boulder, Colo., 1991.

Stanback, Thomas M., Jr., et al. *Services: The New Economy*, Allenheld, Osmun and Co., Totowa, N.J., 1981.

Wheeler, James O. "The Corporate Role of Large Metropolitan Corporate Hierarchy in the U.S. South," *Economic Geography*, 61 (1985), 66–78.

Wheeler, James O., and Ronald L. Mitchelson. "Information Flows among Major Metropolitan Areas in the United States, "*Annals of the Association of American Geographers*, 79 (1989), 523–543.

18

INTRAMETROPOLITAN INDUSTRIAL AND WHOLESALE SPACE

Manufacturing activities within the city are more *footloose* than they have been in the past. The term "footloose" refers to the locational flexibility available to the firm to choose among several production sites. Access to water, rail, freeway, pipeline, and/or air service tempers locations for many industrial firms, but a larger share of firms today are assembly and fabricating industries that require fewer bulky raw materials in the manufacturing process and a greater share of their output is high-value-added products. These types of operations can choose among diverse locations with a skilled labor pool and favorable costs, good educational facilities and many amenities. Suburban areas have become more competitive in this regard, as have smaller towns. The preferred locational choices for new automobile assembly plants by Japanese manufacturers in Kentucky and Tennessee illustrate this point. Expansion of high-technology facilities on the urban fringe also occurs for the same reason.

As corporations have grown in complexity, more separation by function also occurs, splitting up the administrative/control function from production opera-

tions. The use of branch plants and automation has also increased to contain costs and keep the firm competitive. More businesses are also vertically integrated today as a firm may control all phases of the manufacturing process from raw materials to intermediate products and fabricated goods for the consumer. This helps them control costs and internalize more of the production process.

Clustering of industrial activity still occurs, largely in *industrial park* settings. Such an environment provides needed services for the firm, a prestigious location, and room for expansion. High-technology activity and the warehouse/distribution function provide a large market for industrial park operations.

LOCATIONAL SIFTING

No urban activity, except the residential function, has had a longer history of decentralization from the city center than manufacturing. Industrial jobs have been moving outward continuously since mechanized transportation first made it possible in the mid-1800s. Many of the outward shifts have been indirect locational adjustments. As the demand for products shifts with various stages of the *product cycle*, some businesses fail as others gain market share. The product cycle refers to the process of birth, growth, maturation, and decline of a product or firm. Plants may close or shift their output to other products as demand for output changes. The net result is that over the years, older central city firms close, while newer expanding plants appear in the suburbs. We also know that manufacturing now supports a smaller share of the labor force as the service economy has grown. But, as we noted in Chapters 7 and 17, the restructuring that occurred with industry in the 1980s has made this sector more competitive as productivity levels advanced during the decade.

As the mix of manufacturing activity became more technologically sophisticated following World War II, plant obsolescence increased. Scale economies and production process changes encouraged more activities to be housed in larger single-story complexes, located farther from the city core. Two- and three-story factories in the central city were abandoned in greater numbers. This decentralization explained much of the locational adjustment affecting industry at that time.

Most of the locational changes in a given city today come from firms in a particular area that are expanding their operations. Up to 85 percent of new manufacturing jobs in an urban area are created in this way, rather than from firms new to the area.

HISTORICAL EVOLUTION OF INDUSTRIAL PATTERNS

At the turn of the century, population and manufacturing were distributed at relatively similar density levels (Figure 18-1 and Table 18-1). Accelerated dispersal developed thereafter, but residential areas spread outward more rapidly than manufacturing in the period through World War II, because site requirements for new houses were far more flexible and responsive to the automobile during that time. Goods movement has traditionally been more expensive than people movement and generally favored closer-in locations for manufacturers. Historically, land has been cheaper on

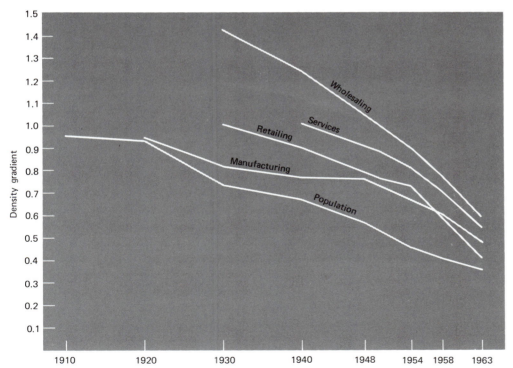

Figure 18-1. Historical Evolution of Urban Activity Density Levels, 1910–1963. At the turn of the century, population and manufacturing activities occurred at relatively similar density levels. A sharp drop in the density gradient for manufacturing occurred after World War II with the expansion of light manufacturing facilities in industrial parks served by the motor truck and freeway system. *Source:* After E.S. Mills, "Urban Density Functions," *Urban Studies,* 7, 1970, 14.

TABLE 18-1
Characteristics of Industrial Plants That Either Abandon or Cling to Central Sites

Abandon	Cling
1. Comparatively large size	1. No specialized buildings required
2. Time or service factor unimportant	2. Time or service factor an important element
3. Large ground area per person required	3. Specialized, unstandardized, highly skilled work
4. Nuisance features (odors, noise, high fire hazard, etc.)	4. Low ground area per worker required
5. Specialized buildings required	5. Comparatively small scale
6. Serious problem of waste disposal	6. Obsolete buildings suitable
7. Large quantities of fuel and/or water required	7. Close contact with market required
	8. Highly seasonal, fluctuating labor force
	9. Style factor important

Source: Robert M. Haig, *Major Economic Factors in Metropolitan Growth and Arrangement*, Regional Survey, reprinted by Arno Press Inc., New York, 1974, pp. 104–105 (reprint of original 1927 work).

the periphery, but physical proximity to the downtown was also important to industry for transportation and communication purposes.

The Depression of the 1930s affected decentralization by almost completely halting industrial relocations. After World War II, changes in manufacturing activity patterns again accelerated. The sharp drop of the manufacturing density gradient line in Figure 18-2 shows that manufacturing decentralization gradually closed the density gradient gap between it and other activities in the 1950s and 1960s with the coming of the freeway era.

Craft Shop Roots

In the late 1700s, manufacturing activity resembled present-day craft shop operations with emphasis on producing consumer household items in small-scale operations. Such endeavors could easily be accommodated in downtown areas, interspersed among other shops and services. Much production actually occurred in the home in early New York and Boston, as elsewhere. One can still observe such craft production in an authentic setting in colonial Williamsburg in the jewelry, silversmith, brass, and pewter shops. Specialized industries such as shipbuilding usually required special locations near the waterfront.

Migration to Water Power Sites

With the advent of the Industrial Revolution when durable goods production came of age, machines began

replacing hand-labor operations, and the locational needs of all manufacturers gradually became more exacting. Access to water power and the need for more specialized buildings created factory alignments along the waterfront in manufacturing cities.

Lowell, Massachusetts, located at Pawtucket Falls on the Merrimac River, typifies the internal morphology of the early industrial city in North America. Textile factories in Lowell expanded in linear fashion along the river and canals that supplied the power. The city housed over 30 such facilities by the mid-1840s. Lowell became the second largest city in Massachusetts and the largest textile center in the country by 1850.[1] Other distinctive features of the mill town included rows of boarding houses (Figure 18-2) built by companies to house factory workers, primarily single women.

Transition to Steam Power

Urban transformation occurred on an even larger scale during the age of the steam engine. This transition was initially felt in Middle Atlantic states such as Pennsylvania, rather than in New England. These states offered closer access to the fuel source—coal. Philadelphia, for example, adapted its industry to steam in the first half of the 1800s. Other cities located on rail lines also benefited tremendously from the conversion to steam

---

[1]In the 1970s, a plan to preserve this manufacturing complex unfolded, becoming a reality in the 1980s. Many historic structures remained even though the textile function itself had failed in the 1920s. See Lowell Historic Canal District Commission, *Report of the Lowell Historic Canal District Commission*, USGPO, Washington, D.C., 1977.

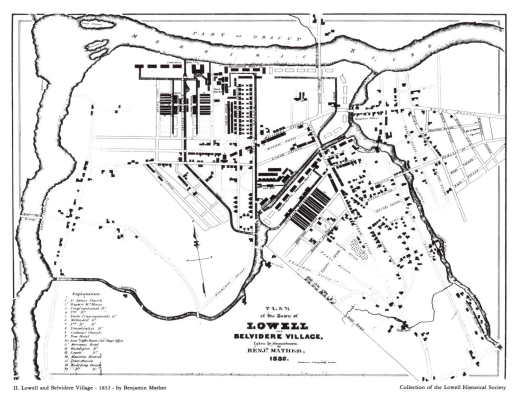

II. Lowell and Belvidere Village - 1832 - by Benjamin Mather   Collection of the Lowell Historical Society

Figure 18-2.   Textile Mills and Water Power Sites in Lowell, Massachusetts. Access to water power and the need for more specialized buildings created factory alignments along the waterfronts of manufacturing cities in the early 1800s. Located at Pawtucket Falls on the Merrimac River, Lowell typifies the internal morphology of the early industrial city in North America. Water often was diverted into artificial canals above the falls location to provide additional water power sites, as was the case in Lowell. (Courtesy of the Lowell Historical Society)

power because quantities of coal could be delivered to them relatively inexpensively by train.

Rail Transportation

Downtown sites served by rail became magnets for durable goods industry sites in the late 1800s. Rail corridors leading in and out of the CBD became very important heavy industrial sites. The need for handling large quantities of raw materials, not to mention the warehousing and distribution of final products destined for national and regional markets, created a linear manufacturing pattern along the railroad. Liberal extensions of rail spur lines that formed beltways around inner-city locations also assisted in the development of industrial districts with good transportation access.

The Motor Truck

Before the use of the motor truck in intraurban goods movement in the first part of the twentieth century, the horse and wagon provided the most flexible form of transport. The limited application of wagon movement, because of time and load restrictions, reinforced the status quo regarding industrial location patterns. Movement costs were also very high. A 1918 survey, for example, indicated that horse and wagon transport cost $0.33/ton-mile, while trucks could do the job at the much lower rate of $0.15/ton-mile.[2]

The drastically lower shipment rates offered by

---

[2]Leon Moses and H. Williamson, "The Location of Economic Activities in Cities," *Papers and Proceedings of the American Economic Association*, 62 (May 1, 1967), 211–227.

trucks opened many more parts of the city for industrial sites. The introduction of the truck also came at a time when technological changes affected industrial processes. The trend toward single-floor assembly-line operations adversely affected older multistory close-in sites where expansion space was limited. Aggressive marketing of suburban sites by railroads and local government authorities also produced greater industrial location flexibility.

AGING INDUSTRIAL CORE

As recently as World War II, much industry remained localized in the pre-1900 sites. Industrial locations in Boston, for example, illustrated the continuing attachment to the downtown area. About one-half of Boston's industries clustered in a band around the CBD *zone of transition* in 1940 (Figure 18-3). The remaining activities in Boston had either migrated outward along railway lines, primarily to the north and west, or remained at waterfront sites.

As early as the 1920s, professional observers foresaw the coming of a manufacturing exodus from the central city. One study of New York catalogued several important factors that either attracted or repelled industry, based on plant size, nuisance, and market factors (Table 18-2). After World War II, the decentralization impetus gathered momentum. Transportation modes changes (trucks substituted for horses and trains), new

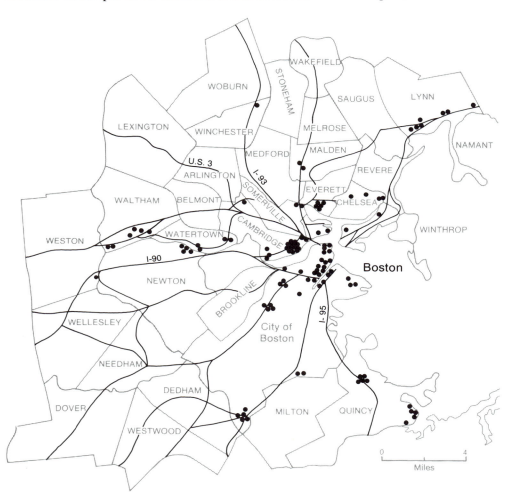

Figure 18-3. Industry Clusters in Boston, 1940. As recently as World War II, much industry remained located in pre-1900 sites. A clustering of about one-half of Boston's industry at the time occurred in a band around the CBD in the zone of transition. The remaining activity had gravitated to railway lines to the west and north or remained at sites near the waterfront. *Source:* Redrawn with permission. From Walter Firey, *Land Use in Central Boston.* Harvard University Press, Cambridge, Mass., 1947, p. 84. Copyright © Harvard University.

TABLE 18-2
Manufacturing Employment Shares in Selected Metropolitan Areas, 1958–1987
(000's of Jobs)

City	1958	1967	1977	1987
Atlanta				
City	49.6 (59)[a]	54.0 (46)[a]	39.9 (31)[a]	40.3 (20)[a]
MSA	83.5	117.2	128.7	200.4
Baltimore				
City	113.4 (56)	106.7 (51)	79.9 (48)	50 (35)
MSA	201.0	209.7	165.9	145.2
Boston				
City	90.2 (30.0)	79.6 (25)	50.9 (19)	42.5 (16)
MSA	301.0	316.2	267.7	272.4
Charlotte				
City	21.2 (76.5)	25.6 (65.1)	27.8 (32)	44.0 (28)
MSA	27.7	39.3	87.1	155.4
Houston				
City	68.8 (65.8)	97.9 (70.9)	147.4 (70)	112.8 (70)
MSA	104.5	138.1	210.1	160.2
Milwaukee				
City	126.6 (64.9)	118.6 (54.8)	91.4 (45)	63.9 (37)
MSA	195.1	216.5	204.1	172.5
Minneapolis–St. Paul				
City of Minneapolis	58.5 (43)	69.2 (34)	52.0 (24)	44.3 (18)
City of St. Paul	41.8 (31)	54.4 (27)	36.9 (17)	34.6 (14)
MSA	146.0	203.7	216.9	250.9

[a]( ) percent.

Source: U.S. Bureau of the Census, *Census of Manufactures,* various years.

technological standards evolved (single-story buildings substituted for multistory factories), and the locational requirements for a greater share of businesses became more flexible within the metropolitan labor market.

Post-World War II Decentralization

During the 1950s, central cities experienced an average decline in manufacturing activity of 1 percent per year, while suburbs grew an average of 5 percent annually. The city/suburbs disparity in employment change narrowed slightly in the 1960s and 1970s, but the same overall trends continued (Table 18-2). In 1958, for example, it was rare to find a city, such as Boston, that registered less than a 50 percent central city manufacturing share. A sample of seven cities (Table 18-2) averaged 60 percent central city manufacturing employment in 1958. This share dropped to 52 percent in 1967, to 41 percent in 1977, and to 33 percent in 1987.

Historically, industries requiring rail access were often assigned to the least desirable urban land. Such prohibitive zoning often yielded sites at "the wrong end of town." In addition, "this prejudiced planning rarely located industry on main streets with 'front sites,' and thereby forced industrial traffic to penetrate residential neighborhoods."[3]

It became clear after World War II that old industrial areas needed upgrading or faced the prospect of accelerated decline. Old red-brick, multistory factories had deteriorated and their neighborhoods experienced a similar fate (Figure 18-4); vandalism, crime, and pollution grew in such areas. Employee satisfaction, and even company survival, often dictated abandonment of such locations. Incompatible land uses had sapped the vitality of such areas. Tenement housing, narrow potholed and dead-end streets, blighted commercial enterprises (bars, outlet stores, and skid row functions), and undesirable vagrants often detracted from the working environment.

[3]Truman A. Hartshorn, "Industrial/Office Parks: A New Look for the City," *The Journal of Geography,* 72 (March 1973), 38.

Figure 18-4. Stetson Factory, Philadelphia, 1943. It became clear after World War II that older industrial areas needed upgrading or faced the prospect of accelerated decline. Employee satisfaction, access to parking, the need for truck loading docks and turning aprons, and a better image for the firm often dictated the abandonment of existing sites. (The Historical Society of Pennsylvania)

Firms wanted not only more spacious sites to accommodate newer production and distribution techniques, but also areas with more amenities and a better image. The *pull* of plentiful expansion space, improved transportation accessibility, and amenities in the suburbs was coupled with *push* factors associated with negative conditions in the central city.

By the late 1960s, entire metropolitan areas began reporting losses in manufacturing employment in their central cities. Cities most dependent on manufacturing experienced the most change. Four cities (Milwaukee, Boston, San Francisco, and Baltimore) with heavy manufacturing concentrations lost more than 20,000 manufacturing jobs each in the 1958–1972 period. This bleak scenario of conditions in the central city was also observed in 1972:

> Executives complain about the abominable phone service in many cities, horrendous commuting conditions, rapidly rising crime. . . . Then there are problems with the work force. Many young women seem to be avoiding the big cities, while young execs no longer consider a move to the New York office a promotion; indeed, they demand differential pay to cover the increased cost of living. There is also the desire to get away from it all, which was

one of the big reasons why Xerox moved its top men from Rochester to pastoral Connecticut: the company president felt that they would get a better perspective of the whole company from the new, more isolated locale. . . . But the biggest appeal of the suburbs, of course, is that much of the population, housing, and development is there, or headed there.[4]

The Truck–Auto–Freeway Trilogy

The so-called *truck–auto–freeway trilogy* that emerged in the 1960s contributed mightily to suburban expansion (Figure 18-5). The interstate highway system, for example, opened suburban areas for efficient motor freight movement for the first time. It also enhanced employee access. Circumferential bypass roads around cities, as well as radial downtown-oriented corridors, promoted outlying industrial growth by providing highly visible and imageable settings for firms striving

---

[4] R. Cassidy, "Moving to the Suburbs," *The New Republic*, 166 (January 22, 1972), 20–23.

Figure 18-5. Truck Freight Terminals and Freeway Sites. The truck–auto–freeway trilogy contributed significantly to the decentralization of manufacturing. Truck freight terminals are strongly attracted to arterials and freeways large acreages are required for storage and maintenance facilities, necessitating locations on the urban fringe, as is the case with this west coast facility. (Courtesy of the American Trucking Association)

to enhance public awareness of their plants. Immaculately landscaped and appointed industrial parks overlooking freeways are an important manifestation of the increasing emphasis that businesses have placed on their corporate image.

In Situ Suburban Expansion

Suburban industrial growth by the late 1970s was no longer primarily fueled by the decentralization process so important in earlier decades. Rather, simple growth of stationary firms explained the bulk of such expansion. Decentralization was still occurring, but the majority of potentially mobile firms in the central city had already exercised this option. The less competitive central city firms increasingly went out of business rather than choose to relocate when faced with such an adjustment. Firms that remained most competitive in central city locations often served special markets or had unique site requirements.

INDUSTRIAL PARK ALTERNATIVES

The majority of post-World War II industrial growth has occurred in industrial parks. A widely accepted definition of an industrial park states:

> An Industrial Park is a planned or organized district with a comprehensive plan which is designed to insure compat-

ibility between the industrial operation therein and the existing activities and character of the community in which the park is located. The plan must provide for streets designed to facilitate truck or other traffic, proper setbacks, lot size minimums, land/use ratio minimums, architectural provisions, landscaping requirements, all for the purpose of promoting the degree of openness and parklike character which are appropriate to harmonious integration into the neighborhood.

The Industrial Park must be of sufficient size and must be suitably zoned to protect the area surrounding it from being devoted to lower uses. The management is charged with the continuing responsibility of preserving compatibility between the park and the community as well as protecting the investments of the developers and tenants.[5]

The forces that have contributed to the accelerated development of industrial parks were summarized by a recent United Nations report.[6]

1. The expansion and dispersion of light assembly and distribution of facilities.
2. Lack of suitable industrially zoned land in older central cities.
3. Blight, traffic congestion, and cramped conditions of older industrial areas.
4. Change in plant design from multistory mill-type buildings to single-story plants permitting horizontal-line production methods and demanding larger sites.
5. More dependence on the automobile for commuting.
6. Increased truck transport of industrial products, requiring more unloading space.
7. Preference by institutional investors for financing construction in planned districts where investment security is more certain.
8. Convenience and economy of details being taken care of by a development and management organization.

Distribution of Industrial Parks

Planned industrial parks, sometimes referred to by the more inclusive term *districts*, are not a new develop-

[5]William Lee Baldwin, *A Report on the Dartmouth College Conference on Industrial Parks*, Arthur D. Little and the State of New Hamsphire, Hanover, June 1958, p. 27.
[6]United Nations, Department of Economic and Social Affairs, *Industrial Estates: Policies, Plans and Progress*, New York, 1966.

ment, for many such parks in the United States date back to the turn of the century. In Europe, South America, Asia, and Africa, industrial parks are also widespread and are referred to as *industrial estates*.

In the United States, the earliest industrial parks were founded in Chicago (the Clearing Industrial District, 1899, and Central Manufacturing District, 1905), Kansas City (Fairfax, North Kansas City Industrial District), and New York. The Central Manufacturing District in Chicago was first organized in 1890 as a joint venture between the Chicago Junction Railways and the Union Stock Yards as an industrial complex, while the Clearing Industrial District was orginally envisioned as a freight car interchange when it was consolidated by the president of the Chicago and Great Western Railway. By 1917, the Central Manufacturing District housed 200 establishments. Both of these developments have been enlarged over the years and now comprise several physically separate tracts.

The growth of industrial parks nationally was a slow and dispersed process until after World War II. In 1940, there were fewer than 35 parks. Over 200 parks were developed in the 1950s, but the proliferation of parks in the 1960s was unprecedented. The majority of the 2500 parks in the United States by the 1970s had been developed in the previous decade.[7] As one might suspect, the growth pattern was uneven.

California claims the greatest concentration of industrial parks. Other leading states (Texas, Florida, Georgia, Minnesota, Wisconsin, and Missouri) are for the most part located outside the traditional northeastern manufacturing belt. The recent growth of light-industry and high-technology activity in these states partially explains the industrial park boom.

In 1965, there were 23 planned industrial districts in the city of Chicago, opccupying over 2500 acres of land, and another 149 districts outside the city. In the 1970s, the number of parks in the metropolitan area approached 300. Plant locations and relocations in Chicago from 1966 to 1970 are shown in Figure 18-6. Note the large number of installations on the western periphery of the city limits just inside I-94 near O'Hare airport. Many of these parks house plants that moved from the city of Chicago.

In recent decades, railroads declined in importance as a locational factor in siting industrial parks in the Chicago region, as elsewhere. The demise of the stockyards and meat-packing activity paralleled this withdrawal of emphasis on rail lines as a park locator. The freeway has now taken over as a major locational determinant. In the 1980s, in fact, many developers removed their rail spur line network, for they had become a detriment to leasing space to image-conscious firms seeking high-amenity, landscaped locations. Some parks with rail access acquired the pejorative label "iron park," reflecting their outmoded image. Truck-high loading docks have now replaced the rail as an important locational consideration. Landscaping, building setbacks, signage, and architectural control have become big selling points for newer industrial parks, as has good freeway access.

Industrial parks have assumed three different forms, each with a unique function and role as well as a specific locational affinity: (1) fabrication, distribution, and warehouse parks; (2) technology parks; (3) business parks.

Fabrication, Distribution, and Warehouse Facilities

Most industrial parks provide space for light manufacturing, distribution, or warehousing functions. These sectors of the economy have expanded greatly and have become increasingly market-oriented in recent years. Increased product differentiation and the functional complexity of their component parts require more suppliers and a highly sophisticated and decentralized procurement and distribution network. Additional stages in the manufacturing process have accompanied these developments. This elaborate product mix requires more plants to assemble and distribute goods. The growth of industry (and industrial parks) in California and the South is in no small part explained by plant expansions to serve rapidly expanding sunbelt markets.

As mentioned earlier, railroad interests were early promoters of the industrial park concept. But public agencies such as county commissions, industrial development authorities, and private developers have also been active. Railroads still account for about 25 percent of industrial park management.

An excellent example of the industrial park phenomenon is provided by the Great Southwest Industrial Park in suburban Dallas–Fort Worth. It incorporates one of the largest planned industrial/office complexes in the

---

[7]Linda Liston, "Proliferating Industrial Parks Spark Plant Location Revolution," *Industrial Development*, 139 (March/April 1970), 7–11.

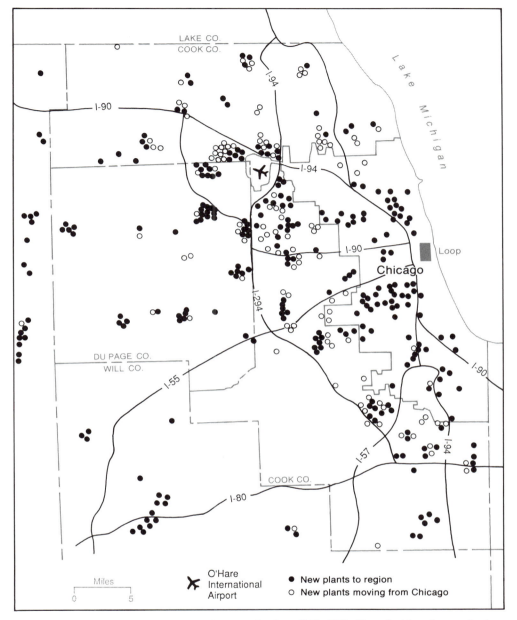

Figure 18-6.   Industrial Changes in the Chicago Region, 1966–1970. New plant locations and relocations to the Chicago area in this period chose locations near the western city limits along I-94, especially
in the area of O'Hare International Airport. *Source:* Redrawn with permission from *Chicago: Transformations
of an Urban System*, copyright © 1976, Ballinger Publishing Company, p. 39.

Western Hemisphere (Figure 18-7). The Great Southwest Industrial Corporation, a subsidiary of the Penn
Central Railroad, began developing the park as a goods
distribution and warehouse center as well as a commercial recreation complex in 1956. More than 600
companies are located on 7000 acres of prime commer-
cial-industrial property, including shopping centers,

retailers, hotels, offices, and industrial firms. The
property lies astride one of the biggest growth corridors
in the United States, midway between Dallas and Fort
Worth and immediately south of the Dallas–Fort Worth
Metroplex Airport. The Six Flags Over Dallas amusement theme park occupies a perimeter of the industrial
zone. Other notable features of the area include the Six

Figure 18-7. Great Southwest Industrial Park, Dallas–Fort Worth. In recent decades, the railroad declined in importance as a locational factor in siting industrial parks, and the freeway became the major locational determinant. This complex in suburban Arlington, Texas, is one of the most distinctive industrial park complexes in the world. (Courtesy of Vantage Companies, Dallas)

Flags and Forum 303 shopping centers, the Texas Stadium in Arlington, several hotels, and a complement of service industries. Downtown Dallas and Fort Worth lie only 12 minutes away to the east and west, respectively, via the Dallas–Fort Worth Turnpike, which bisects the park.

Most of the firms located in the Great Southwest Park are small (Table 18-3), and over 80 percent have fewer than 50 employees and nearly one-half have fewer than 10. These firms locate either in their own separate buildings or in multitenant single-story facilities. A full range of functions are present, but the distribution and warehousing function prevails in terms

TABLE 18-3
Size of Firms in Great Southwest Industrial District, Dallas

Size Category	Number of Firms	Percent of Total Firms
Fewer than 10 employees	256	47
11–49 employees	187	35
50–99 employees	47	9
100–299 employees	44	8
More than 300 employees	8	2
Total	542	101

Source: Great Southwest Industrial Park Directory, 1976–77, Spartan Printing, Arlington, Texas, June 1976.

of the number of firms. Among the largest facilities (with greater than 300 employees) are food processing, apparel manufacture, machinery and machine parts fabrication (Bell Helicopter), electronics (Voight Corporation), and plastics (Textan).

Technology Parks

Technology parks represent a specialized adaptation of the industrial park designed for the needs of research and development companies. The most famous are the Stanford Industrial Park (Palo Alto, California), with 17,000 employees in the Silicon Valley south of San Francisco, and the Research Triangle Park (North Carolina), having 12,000 employees.

The Research Triangle Park is named for its location in the center of a triangle formed by three university cities—Duke University at Durham, the University of North Carolina at Chapel Hill, and North Carolina State University in Raleigh (Figure 18-8). Among the research facilities nestled in the 5500-acre tract are the Triangle Universities Computation Center, which is linked with the three universities, the North Carolina Science and Technology Research Center, and the nonprofit Research Triangle Institute, which performs contract research. Several federal government agencies maintain research facilities at the park, including the National Institute of Environmental Health Sciences, the Environmental Protection Agency, the National Center for Health Statistics Laboratory, and the Forest Sciences Laboratory. These activities impart a heavy emphasis in the park on environmental and life science research.

The majority of the park's occupants are research and development subsidiaries of private corporations, including IBM (computers). Burroughs-Wellcome (pharmaceuticals), and several textile and fiber enterprises. A few nonprofit corporations also conduct research at the center, including the National Laboratory for Higher Education and the National Driving Center Foundation. A comprehensive service plaza with hotel and conference facilities is also a part of the development. The area now boasts that it has the highest per capita concentration of Ph.D.'s in science and engineering in the world.

Electronics, electrical apparatus, and aerospace firms are typical tenants in technology parks. Most are located in major metropolitan areas, frequently within easy access of major universities. Proximity to campus

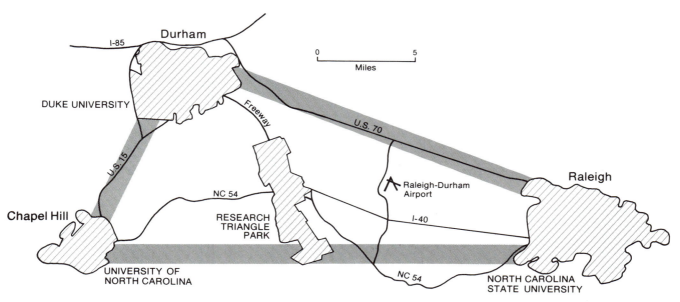

Figure 18-8. Research Triangle Park, North Carolina. This technology park caters to the needs of research and development operations of public and private firms. This 5500-acre park is named for its location in the center of a triangle formed by three university cities—Duke University at Durham, the University of North Carolina at Chapel Hill, and North Carolina State University in Raleigh.

activities, including library and computer facilities and associated educational programs (symposia, short courses, etc.), creates an attractive package to the firm and employee alike. Among the facilities frequently available at technology parks are incubator buildings that serve as nurseries for newly formed high-technology companies.

A classic example of a high-technology complex is the "Technology Region" corridor (Route 128) in suburban Boston. Route 128 is a circumferential highway that served as a beltway around Boston (about 10 miles from the CBD) when completed in the early 1950s (Figure 18-9). There were 396 firms on the route in 1962 and 729 firms in 1967.[8] Employment in the same period rose from 40,000 to 66,000. Twenty industrial parks lined Route 128 in the late 1960s. Along the southern half of the arc, goods distribution centers predominated, whereas firms to the north were mainly scientific and technological in character. Many firms in these centers regard highly their proximity to MIT. Harvard, and other educational institutions in the area.

Subsequently, Boston has acquired another beltway (I-495) (see Figure 18-11) that has also attracted high-technology firms, particularly electronics companies.

This area is now called the "Platinum Perimeter." The top 20 establishments along I-495 in 1973 are shown in Table 18-4.

The world's largest high-technology complex occurs in the Silicon Valley, stretching from Palo Alto southward to San Jose in the Santa Clara Valley. Hewlitt-Packard, Lockheed, and Apple Computers all have major production and research facilities in the area. Recall the discussion in Chapter 5. That area is blanketed with one- to two-story-high technology facilities. The relatively high standards used in the fit and finish (exterior materials, plentiful windows, signing, and landscaping) give high technology facilities a "top-of-the-line" image in the industrial park group. Often they combine sales offices, administrative functions, production, and warehousing in one facility.

Business Parks

A hybrid industrial park form, the *business park*, represents the most popular version of the form today because of the flexibility it offers. Business parks combine the office and industrial park function with business and commercial services, including showrooms, eating establishments, and hotels (Table 18-5). Such a diversity of land uses, catering to several markets, creates a functional complex especially ap-

[8]Carl O. Ojala and Paul F. Rizza, "Route 128: A Study of Industry Location Factors," *Atlanta Economic Review*, 20, No. 10 (1970), 37.

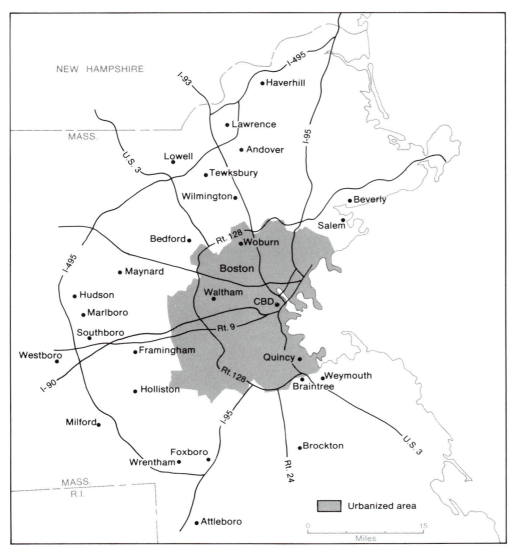

Figure 18-9. Boston's Technology Regions. Boston's Routes 128 and I-495 encompass locations for a large share of the electronics, computer, instruments, defense, and pharmaceutical high-technology firms for which the metropolitan area is so famous. Many firms in these fields regard highly their proximity to centers of higher education in the region including the Massachusetts Institute of Technology (MIT) and Harvard University.

propriate to the needs of many metropolitan submarkets, as well as smaller urban areas. These business parks vary widely in size, from small single-story strip centers to dozens of multistory buildings. They can range from 3 to 5 acres to 1000 acres or more. The largest and most specialized of these parks resemble mixed-use centers previously found only in downtown markets.

An example of a multiuse business park having space devoted to commercial (office, hotel, retail), service (personal and professional), and industrial

functions is Gateway Plaza in Kansas City, adjacent to the International Airport terminal (Figure 18-10). It is one of more than a dozen industrial parks in the airport vicinity but is distinctive because of the integration of several different activities in one controlled environment.

Business parks have a particular appeal to prospective leasers because of the complement of services they offer. It is possible to locate both office and distribution facilities in one setting in these parks even though the buildings might be physically separated. Developers

TABLE 18-4
The 20 Largest Establishments on I-495 in Boston

City	Firm	Product
Andover	Standard International Corp.	Electronic, medical, and surgical apparatus
Tewksbury	Wang Laboratories	Computers
Wilmington	Compugraphic Corp.	Computer graphics
	Dynamic Research	Electronic research and development
North Bedford	Aerovox Corp.	Electronic components
Maynard	Digital Equipment Corp.	Electronic equipment
Westboro	Parke Davis	Pharmaceutical products
Hudson	Arrow Automotives	Automotive alternators
	Cutwisle	Construction machinery
	Byrd and Zayre	Electronic equipment
Marlboro	RCA Corp.	Components
	Philipps Screw	Electronic equipment
Holliston	Clark Equipment	Electric equipment
Shewsbury	Simplex Industries	Laboratory equipment
Milford	S.O.S. Consolidated	Control Instruments
Wrentham	American Science and Engineering	Scientific research
	Electronics Corp. of America	Electronic controls
Foxboro	Foxboro Company	Control instruments
Attleboro	Augat	Medical instruments
Southboro	Data General	Minicomputers

Source: Reprinted with permission, © Jacques Soppelsa, *Annales de Geographie, 85,* No. 471 (Sept.–Oct. 1978), A. Colin, Paris.

TABLE 18-5
Functions Associated with Business Park Facilities

Mid-rise office building (6–10 stories)
Low-rise office building (3–5 stories)
One- to two-story office building
Office-warehouse
Incubator office
High-technology (office/assembly/distribution)
Research and development
Showroom/wholesale
Retail service
Business service
Personal service
Hotel/conference center
Restaurant
Distribution/warehouse
Miniwarehouse
Light industrial

and bankers also benefit from this concept because it provides a diversified investment. A faster sellout rate is another feature due to the simultaneous appeal to several markets. The business park is also competitive on higher-priced land such as that ajdacent to airports, theme parks, or regional malls. The Inverness Industrial Park in Denver, for example, offers a wide variety of office, recreational, commercial, and industrial space uses. Erin Mills in Toronto and the Irvine Industrial Complex in Irvine, California, have mixed residential and industrial uses coexisting quite successfully. Montebello, in Denver, and Elk Grove Village, in Chicago, also have integrated industrial and residential functions.

Adjustments to the business park concept continue. Not only is the mix of activities in the center constantly under review, but so are marketing strategies and infrastructure improvements. At the Hacienda Business Park, the largest such development in northern

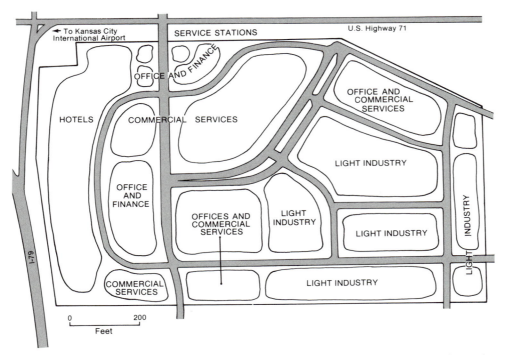

Figure 18-10. Gateway Plaza Business Park, Kansas City. The business park is the most popular version of the industrial park today. It combines the office and industrial park function with business and commercial services, including restaurants, showrooms, and hotels. Such a diversity of uses creates a functional complex especially appropriate to the needs of many metropolitan submarkets as well as those in smaller urban areas. *Source:* After Airport Entrance Development Co., Kansas City.

California, located in Pleasanton in the East Bay Area only 40 minutes from downtown San Francisco, the developer has attracted major corporations to a self-contained business community (Figure 18-11). Primarily an office center, the complex offers two hotels, a retail center, restaurants, a child development center, and recreation facilities and will eventually house 1000 units for on-site residents. The park's success is enhanced by the presence of a large bedroom community of highly skilled workers that formerly commuted to downtown San Francisco. A free bus shuttle system ferries employees between the park and the nearest BART station. A computerized ride-sharing system is offered, with carpoolers receiving preferential parking, and a heliport, bicycle lanes, and parking decks round out the transportation system. Underground utilities, a 24-hour security system, public fountains, and lush landscaping are other advantages of this complex.

The nearby Bishop Ranch Business Park in San Ramon, California, is another "master planned, fully integrated business community." It houses many *Fortune 1000* firms, including Chevron, USA, and Pacific Bell. Its award-winning internal transportation system includes computerized matching for car and van pools and a shuttle bus system.

LOCATION TRENDS

In the post-World War II era, the transport surface of the city became increasingly uniform with respect to movement costs, as discussed earlier. Firms increasingly made locational decisions on other factors such as amenities. A major factor in the industrial park selection process, as with office locations, was the desire among chief executives to locate facilities close to home and thus to minimize commuting distances. This factor has carried over into the location pattern of industrial parks, which have increasingly sought out the higher-income side of the city and the rapidly growing side of town, a process similar to that experienced by office parks, as discussed in Chapter 17. The growth of the East Bay area of San Francisco discussed above provides a classic example of this process.

Figure 18-11. Hacienda Business Park, Pleasanton, California. This 876-acre complex, the largest in northern California, is located in suburban San Francisco in the East Bay area, 40 minutes from downtown San Francisco. Primarily an office center, the complex offers two hotels, a retail center, restaurants, a child development center, and recreation facilities. On-site housing for 1000 residents is also planned. (Courtesy Hacienda Business Park)

Airport Corridors

A location factor that is of growing importance is the proximity to metropolitan airports. Recent expansion around Chicago's O'Hare International Airport, or Dulles Airport in suburban Washington, D.C., reflects a national trend. The rapid air freight deliveries that such locations offer allow firms to forego elaborate parts warehousing depots of their own and to rely instead on computerized overnight deliveries of needed items.

Intercity postal distribution services are also being increasingly housed near airports. The U.S. Postal Service began locating its Area Mail Processing Centers in the 1970s near airports to speed the processing of all letters and parcels that moved between cities by air. Firms interested in speedy intercity mail service will no doubt increasingly locate closer to such facilities in the future.

The concept of an *industrial airport* took on new meaning with the opening of the Alliance Airport in Fort Worth in 1990. The 800-acre airport, owned by the city of Fort Worth, lies in the center of a 3000-acre business/industrial park developed by private interests (the Perot Group). American Airlines is building an aircraft maintenance hub at the complex and several other corporations have announced plans to locate in the area, including IBM, Tandy, Santa Fe Railway-owned Honda automobile distribution center, Texas Instruments, and others. It is being touted as the first industrial airport in the country designed and built to serve business tenants. Some observers speculate that the growing demand for greater air cargo capacity will lead to the development of several other specialized air freight airports around the country in the future.

Just 15 miles from the Dallas–Fort Worth airport, the Alliance airfield boasts top-of-the-line facilities and a 10,000-foot runway capable of handling the largest jets. It "will allow aircraft to carry raw materials directly to manufacturing facilities around the airport."[9] The potential exists for an extensive foreign trade zone in the area, and it is expected to be a development hub for the northwest sector of the Dallas–Fort Worth Metroplex.

---

[9]*Jet Cargo News*, 22, No. 9 (January 1990).

Figure 18-12. Apparel Fabricator in the Inner City of Los Angeles. Many single-story windowless apparel fabricator plants using unskilled immigrant labor have found inner-city locations desirable for their operations. Rows and rows of these facilities operate near downtown Los Angeles, giving the area a "third world" atmosphere. (Robert Marien/RO-MA Stock)

Central City Opportunities

Urban development planners and business interests have increasingly promoted the reindustrialization of central city land parcels in recent years (see box). They sought to provide jobs for central city residents and to stabilize a declining tax base. Among the advantages of such locations are access to transport facilities (rail and freeway), a plentiful blue-collar labor supply, adequate utility services, and, sometimes, favorable tax rates. Use of such land for warehousing often has more potential than its use for manufacturing, especially because older buildings can be converted for storage purposes. Businesses serving a local or regional market, particularly the downtown, could benefit the most from such initiatives. Among the industries that have considerable promise for central city expansion are apparel fabricators, paper products, food purveyors, interior design and decorators' showrooms, and recycling centers (Figure 18-12).

A study of the reuse of industrial buildings in the black community of Chicago in the 1970s indicated that nearly 60 percent were reclaimed for nonindustrial uses related to community needs (churches, eating and drinking establishments, furniture and upholstery shops, recreation buildings, and funeral parlors).[10] The remaining 40 percent that reconverted to industrial functions were used for fabricated metals manufacture, construction depots, and printing and publishing functions.

Defunct military bases similarly offer considerable potential for development because of their large size and accessibility to utility and transportation services. The redevelopment of the Brooklyn Navy Yard in New York and the Raritan Center Industrial Park created on the site of the former Raritan Arsenal in New Jersey illustrates this type of land use succession. Many such installations have airfields already in place.

Waterfront sites also have potential for development. Many industrial planners foresee increased pref-

---

[10]Charles Christian and Sari F. Bennett, "The Reclamation of Industrial Building Vacancies: Chicago's Black Community," *Urban Affairs Quarterly*, 13 (1977), 109–116.

ENTERPRISE ZONES (EZs)

In conjunction with two cornerstones of federal economic development initiatives in the 1980s, privatization and public/private partnerships, several new programs were proposed. Urban enterprise zones, for example, were seen as one such vehicle to energize impacted central city economies. The goal of the enterprise zone was to encourage investment in designated areas with high levels of economic distress by providing a package of public sector incentives to encourage the private sector to invest in them. These incentives might include several of the following: property tax relief, corporate tax credits or deferments, low-interest loans, job training assistance, technical and management assistance, sales tax exemptions for building materials, machinery and equipment, and others.

The history of the enterprise zone concept is interesting because a British geographer, Peter Hall, is generally credited with selling the idea to the Thatcher government in Great Britain in the late 1970s, based on the dynamism that capitalism demonstrated in Hong Kong. The Reagan administration then became a proponent of the program in the United States.

Proposals to initiate federal enterprise zone programs in the United States were consistently defeated by Congress for most of the 1980s, despite strong Presidential lobbying efforts. In 1987 Congress finally passed Federal legislation authorizing the Secretary of the Department of Housing and Urban Development to designate 100 such zones, but the program was eventually suspended because Congress did not authorize any federal tax incentives to support them. Nevertheless, many states initiated their own programs with an urban emphasis. By the end of the decade, 36 states and the District of Columbia had such programs.

Despite the attractiveness of the enterprise zone concept to policy makers, academic observers often have been critical of the program. They argue that it is an example of a "worst first" economic policy. Rather than focus on such impacted areas, the argument goes that a more efficient policy would focus on areas with more potential. Observers contend that such programs do not create "net new jobs," but simply transfer investment from more productive areas and reduce tax revenues. Moreover, these programs might prolong the life of inefficient firms and encourage investment in outmoded technologies. Critics also mention that inner-city sites may not be the best locations for the firms due to noise, traffic, and logistical considerations and their impact on struggling residential communities.

"A majority of academics believe that tax credits and incentives, particularly those aimed at reducing capital costs, fail to significantly influence business decisions."[1] In other words, the firms that one might want to build up an economy are not looking for a subsidy and are not interested in locating in an enterprise zone. Still another argument against these firms is that they would pay low wages and that it would be more appropriate to invest the service economy in these areas, not manufacturing.

An assessment of state level programs conducted in the late 1980s indicates that enterprise zones have indeed created a favorable environment for economic development when coupled with commitments from the business community and governmental agencies.[2] The number and type of jobs created has been favorable, silencing some critics. Many local residents from impoverished areas have received jobs in these zones. But the study concluded that the successful enterprise zone program must be part of a more comprehensive economic development initiative utilizing the resources of several agencies and programs.

---

[1]Rodney A. Erickson, "Enterprise Zones: Lessons from the State Government Experience," in Edwin Mills and John McDonald, eds., Chapter 8, *Sources of Metropolitan Growth.* New Brunswick, N.J.: Rutgers University, 1992, pp. 161–182.

[2]Ibid.

erences among industries for locations with three or four types of transportation available so as to maximize "through" transport.[11] Such sites would offer cheaper movement of containerized goods. The port of Stockton, California, for example, has a water channel connection with San Francisco and is serviced by several rail and truck lines and an airport. This quadra-modal (four modes) access has created prime industrial land. Similar advantages exist at Port Newark–Port Elizabeth on the New Jersey waterfront in the New York area and at many other declining port areas in coastal and river cities.

Truck Terminals

Truck terminals are strongly attracted to arterials and freeways, particularly those near perimeter highway beltways or city bypasses referred to as truck routes. Often truck terminals cluster together on land bypassed for more intense development on the lower-income side of town. Frequently, this land is not suitable for other development because of drainage characteristics or other undesirable physical constraints, such as a lack of utilities. Because relatively large acreages are required for storage and maintenance facilities, some of the newer truck terminal sites are largely confined to rural fringes of the urban area. Such sites offer savings on taxes, avoidance of neighborhoods with expensive city services, and stricter zoning regulations.

Truck terminals may also used abandoned warehouses and manufacturing sites in the central city, especially if they offer easy freeway access. Such locations provide good work access for employees, cheap facilities for storage of vehicles and goods, and enclosed space for repair and maintenance of vehicles. In some instances, truck terminals prefer locations near rail spur lines or classification yards where freight interchanges between truck and rail can be easily accomplished.

WHOLESALING AND WAREHOUSING OPERATIONS

Wholesaling and warehousing functions involve specialized distribution services rather than a product in

the traditional sense. In part, such an activity represents a transportation service involving a hierarchical flow of goods from factory to depot (storage), and then movement of products on to the retailer or consumer. Students of the activity process have identified two stages in this movement: *trunking* and *delivery*.[12] The trunking stage refers to the movement of large lots or bulk shipping to warehouses for storage and classification. The delivery stage refers to small-quantity shipments to a wholesaler, retail outlet, or individual consumer.

Each industry has its own distribution characteristics depending on the product and transportation costs. Many warehouses are owned by an individual firm and stock solely proprietary items, while others are independently operated and function as brokerage houses serving many firms and products. Wholesaling also frequently involves breaking bulk and redistributing goods in smaller lots, extending credit, and promotion through advertising and demonstration.

Changing Regional Patterns

Even before wholesaling became a sedentary occupation of urban entrepreneurs in the mid-nineteenth century in the United States, traveling merchants, manufacturers' agents, brokers, and factors traveled extensively to peddle wares and establish distribution channels. Gradually, wholesaling became identified in the late nineteenth century with larger cities near settlement frontiers in the West. Collections of manufactured goods accumulated at these centers for distribution of rural consumer markets. Railway hubs and *break-of-bulk* transfer points gained prominence in wholesaling activity at that time. Such centers have been described as *unraveling points*.[13]

In the South, wholesaling centers were traditionally either coastal ports, from which railroads fanned into the interior (Charleston, Savannah, and Mobile), or outright rail junction cities (Atlanta, Roanoke, and Charlotte). In the interior Middle West and Great Plains, wholesaling expanded in river cities, especially along the Mississippi and Missouri river system and in

[11]"Opportunities in Intermodal Transportation," *Industrial Development* (March/April 1976), 2–6.

[12]H. D. Watts, "The Market Area of a Firm," in Lyndhurst Collins and David F. Walker, eds., *Locational Dynamics of Manufacturing Activity*, Wiley, New York, 1975, pp. 364–366.

[13]James E. Vance, Jr., *The Merchant's World: A Geography of Wholesaling*, Prentice Hall, Englewood Cliffs, N.J., 1970.

Figure 18-13.   The St. Louis Gateway Arch as Symbol of the City. Wholesaling activity traditionally flourished in river and port cities like St. Louis. The arch rising on the banks of the Mississippi River frames the downtown skyline symbolizing the role of St. Louis as a gateway city to the west, a role that propelled its early growth. (Courtesy St. Louis Convention and Visitor Bureau)

cities in its vicinity—Minneapolis–St. Paul, Sioux Falls, Sioux City, Omaha, St. Joseph, Kansas City, and Dallas–Fort Worth.[14] These latter cities exemplify the role of the *gateway city* as a wholesale area. The Gateway Arch on the river in St. Louis symbolizes that role for the city in opening up the West (Figure 18-13).

Large cities also prospered as major wholesalers. New York, Chicago, Los Angeles, San Francisco, Denver, and Cincinnati have all assumed important roles in this regard, as have smaller subregional centers. These cities all demonstrate the importance of central place theory in explaining the location of wholesale centers at the top of the urban hierarchy.

In the early part of the twentieth century, unraveling points shifted from the Great Plains to the Mountain West (Salt Lake City and Denver) as the settlement frontier moved westward. As a group, cities with strong wholesale functions today include large regional centers in agricultural areas, particularly in the South (Charlotte, Raleigh, Jacksonville, Shreveport, Lubbock, and Amarillo). But all cities serve as wholesalers, even if only for the local market.

New York remains the prime distributor because of its financial and headquarters role. It has been described as a "*summit of convergence*, an *arbiter market*," that establishes taste, in recognition of its function as the cultural capital of the country.[15]

Patterns within the City

The spatial break between retailing and wholesaling that occurred in the 1800s was covered in Chapter 16. In the 1800s, wholesaling clung to rail sites, while retailing moved nearer the consumer to main street. The wholesale district remained concentrated in a central rail-oriented setting well into the twentieth century. But by the 1920s, outward movement began, due to the increased flexibility created by the motor truck. The expansion of chain general merchandise stores at that time also struck a hard blow to the merchant wholesaler. On the other hand, the growth of catalog retail sales and the introduction of Rural Free Delivery of postal mail items in the 1930s buoyed up

---

[14]Ibid., p. 42.

[15]Ibid., p. 118.

the industry at the same time as it encouraged decentralization. Distributors no longer needed to congregate near railway express shipment offices, because parcels could be delivered by mail through the post office to remotely located customers. Mail-order houses such as Montgomery Ward and Sears, Roebuck greatly benefited from this development.

Location Affinities of Specific Functions

Wholesaling today involves a much greater variety of marketing systems than ever before. A few very large and specialized wholesaling operations are located in downtown areas to provide access to *professional buyers*, such as at *merchandise marts* (Figure 18-14). These facilities often specialize in displays of particular products. Some exhibits are usually permanent, such as home furnishing displays, carpets, furniture, apparel, and others. Other exhibits are seasonal, such as gifts, technology, sports/recreation, and food. Facilities for these shows are often adjacent to the hotel district,

catering as they do to out-of-town buyers representing the regional or national market. Good access to banks and other financial institutions for credit is also maximized at these locations.

Other types of wholesale outlets serve local markets, providing for the needs of city residents, including antique/flea markets and *farmers' markets* or *produce markets* (fish, fruit, vegetable distributors). These operations were traditionally located near the city center or at waterfront sites, but many are now located in suburban environments. Outdoor settings, partially enclosed booths, or indoor facilities house these functions. Commercial accounts, including grocers, restaurants, and institutions (schools, hospitals), as well as individual consumers, patronize these operations.

Arterial streets frequently cater to other locally based wholesale operations. Most visible in this group are automotive parts distributors, building trades suppliers (plumbers, roofers, sheet-metal fabricators, contractors), salvage and scrap materials handlers, and recycling centers. These corridors have been called *customer-access* wholesaling districts in recognition of their function as primarily suppliers to independent custom-

Figure 18-14. Chicago Merchandise Mart. This facility was the biggest building in the world when built in the 1930s by retailer Marshall Field. Located on the bank of the Chicago River, the building remains a major employer in downtown Chicago. (Courtesy Merchandise Mart Properties)

ers (contractor, automobile service stations, or the individual homeowner).[16]

The *stockroom supplier* represents yet another type of wholesaler. Such firms cater to small businesses by replenishing needed stock (parts, tools, and perishable merchandise).[17] Companies often specialize in particular fields, such as vending operations (cigarettes, candy, sandwiches, coffee, soft drinks), art supplies, cameras, flowers, or amusements (billiards, video game machines). They often choose suburban locations where economical space for parking fleets of delivery vans, storage, and employee parking is readily available.

Most mass goods retailers maintain their wholesaling and warehouse operations in outlying areas, including grocery store distributors, commercial bakeries, department store warehouses, and restaurant supply houses. The need for larger single-story warehouses, truck access, and lower taxes (frequently items in inventory are taxed more heavily in the central city) has encouraged more dispersed sites. Often it is also easier and quicker to move products from the edge of the city inward than it is to accomplish the reverse, especially in off-peak hours.

As business products have grown more complex and marketing more competitive, a need for specialists that demonstrate and sell products has also increased. *Sales agency* arms of electronics and computer firms, for example, have expanded in recent years because showroom demonstrations are required to project the potential impact of a particular piece of equipment.[18]

Salespeople are also important in other areas where product applications are very specialized and intricate or customized in design (hospital equipment, medical billing/invoicing systems, etc.), or where fashions or seasonal markets are involved (apparel, gifts). Company representatives in any of these areas often operate out of their homes and cars and do not require a centralized office or work center. Those requiring offices frequently locate in suburban office parks.

In some instances, sales personnel operate exclusively from their office, serving only as brokers who coordinate the transfer of titles to goods that are shipped directly from plant to consumer. Much of this contact is handled by telephone, fax, or mail service. Other types

of sales work require ongoing personal contact between retailer and producer because of style changes (shoes, clothing, novelties, and gifts). In either case, locations near the wholesaler's residence are preferred working locations.

SUMMARY AND CONCLUSION

Manufacturing was the mainstay of city employment for over 100 years, beginning in the early 1800s. Even now it remains a significant force in those areas first identified with textile factories or iron and steel mills. The facilities that house manufacturers, and locations within the city, have changed markedly over time. So has the mix of industry as high-techology activities have become more visible.

Technology and accessibility advancements have produced accelerated activity decentralization in all cities. The linear pattern of industry, once concomitant with rail spur lines, has given way to clusters of factories and warehouses around interstate beltways, airports, and in more remote rural locations, frequently in industrial park settings. The motor freight industry is the prime mover of industrial goods within and between cities today, except for very long transcontinental trips or for bulky low-value goods. Warehouses and truck terminals have also become major tenants of industrial parks.

Even in the face of the dominant outward flow, the suburbanization process has been selective. Some manufacturing activities still cling to central city locations. Those functions serving local markets and relying on a central city labor supply find close-in locations competitive. Other activities continue to exhibit strong ties to waterfront sites, either downtown or in fringe areas. Business parks now exist in a wide variety of urban locations. Wholesaling activity has also become more specialized spatially. Downtown sites remain competitive for functions requiring professional buyers, arterials cater to locally based distributors, and suburban sites predominate for mass goods storage and distribution.

As the competitiveness of suburban locations has increased, central city planners have attempted to make abandoned industrial sites marketable for reuse. Newly recruited activity to such sites is predominantly oriented to the surrounding community itself and frequently involves a nonindustrial service or recreation function rather than a manufacturing activity.

---

[16]James E. Vance, Jr., *This Scene of Man*, Harper's College Press, New York, 1977, p. 384.

[17]Ibid.

[18]Ibid., p. 385.

Suggestions for Further Reading

Bredo, William. *Industrial Estates: Tool for Industrialization*, Free Press, Chicago, 1960.

Collins, Lyndhurst, and David Walker, eds. *Locational Dynamics of Manufacturing Activity*, Wiley, New York, 1975.

Groves, Paul A. *Towards a typology of Intermetropolitan Manufacturing Locations*, University of Hull, Hull, England, 1971.

Hamilton, F. E. Ian, and G. J. R. Linge, eds. *Spatial Analysis, Industry and the Industrial Environment*, Vol. 1, *Progress in Research and Applications*, Wiley, New York, 1979

Kitawaga, E. M., and D. J. Bogue. *Suburbanization of Manufacturing Activity within Standard Metropolitan Statistical Areas*, Scripps Foundation, Oxford, Ohio, 1955.

Proctor, Mary, and Bill Matuszeski. *Gritty Cities*, Temple University Press, Philadelphia, 1978.

Struyck, James, and Franklin James. *Intrametropolitan Industrial Location*, Lexington Books, Lexington, Mass., 1975.

Urban Land Institute. *Industrial Development Handbook*, Urban Land Institute, Washington, D.C., 1975.

Vance, James E., Jr. *The Merchant's World: A Geography of Wholesaling*, Prentice Hall, Englewood Cliffs, N.J., 1970.

———. *This Scene of Man*, Harper's College Press, New York, 1977.

19

PLANNING, REGULATION, AND THE FUTURE*

The cities as we will know them in the early twenty-first century already exist. No significant regional or internal land use reallocations are anticipated in the 1990s in cities in developed countries. The polycentric form produced during the 1960–1990 growth boom that created a much larger and more decentralized city is largely in place. In many cities, the 1990s are expected to be primarily a time for catch-up, involving the absorption of vacant commercial space built in the boom years, and a time to develop new growth management techniques to mitigate chronic housing and transportation problems. Other social problems, including poverty, crime, and drug abuse, must also be addressed.

Third world urbanization will continue at a rapid rate, creating more and larger cities. Those cities will generally remain impoverished and continue to offer limited opportunities for socioeconomic advancement.

These situations suggest that planning, education, and economic development initiatives for cities should be actively pursued. There are many socioeconomic and environmental ills that must be addressed in both the developed and developing world. In the former, more balance must emerge in the transit/motor vehicle work trip mix, more balance must unfold in the jobs/housing mix in various parts of the city, and more balance must come to the inner-city/suburban income mix. The private sector will increasingly be called upon to provide leadership with these issues and will be influenced in the process by stronger public sector planning and growth management programs. Higher residential densities can be expected to be part of the solution to provide affordable housing for a larger spectrum of the population.

URBAN PLANNING

The systematic planning of cities began long ago, and urban planning as we know it today has become a sophisticated, comprehensive process directed at assisting an urban region in achieving its socioeconomic goals. This process went through a metamorphosis with the advent of the first zoning laws and over the decades has evolved from an administrative function to a broad-based interdisciplinary process that addresses and solves a broad range of urban problems. Several movements in recent decades have heightened public awareness of the need for more effective urban problem-solving approaches. The environmental movement, for example, led to more concern for energy conservation, recycling, and alternatives to the automobile for commuting. Energy price fluctuations associated with the Arab oil embargo in 1973–1974 and continued unset-

*Chapter authored by Frederick P. Stutz, San Diego State University.

445

tled conditions in the Persian Gulf called attention to the sensitive nature of United States' dependence on imported petroleum.

Escalating housing prices, rising crime rates, a plunging national economy, and the financial crisis faced by several of the nation's larger cities caused America to realize in the early 1980s and again in the early 1990s that a sense of vulnerability gripped nearly every central city in the country. As attention began to focus on critical problems, it was now time to meet the challenge.

This chapter will focus on the strategies followed in urban planning to meet and address these challenges. This complex process can be divided into four broad categories: (1) planning for physical development; (2) planning for economic development; (3) planning for capital improvements and public facilities; and (4) long-range planning for social well-being.

Challenges in Planning

Providing opportunities for the physical growth and development of a city is central to the idea of urban planning. The physical layout of a city has a great deal to do with determining the quality of life of its residents. It is a contributing factor in how far one lives from work or school or friends, it places limitations on opportunities for recreation and shopping, and it affects neighborhood aesthetics.

Contemporary land use planning must also take into account the dynamic nature of the city. While some city features, such as climate, topography, and cultural history, remain relatively constant, features such as population, economic activities, and physical upkeep can experience rapid change. Urban planning must deal with the constant change in these economic, social, and environmental processes and conform to broad regional and national goals.

Yet another challenge to urban planning involves public participation and community identity. Successful urban planning relies not only on the quality of the planning staff and leadership, but also on the active support of the community. Planning programs with active community involvement generate a much higher success rate, a fact that has been recognized by the federal government. Many federal, state, and local guidelines now called for participation by the citizens of the community in establishing development priorities (Figure 19-1).

Service Provision

The provision of adequate public services represents a primary goal of the urban planning process. These functions include health services, recreation, utilities, social welfare programming, and environmental and hazard protection. Although it is not a responsibility of urban planning to provide services per se, say health services, the delivery of community health services is a primary consideration in the urban planning decision-making process. Providing an adequate number of hospital beds and health delivery personnel, for example, falls under this planning rubric. The placement and provision of recreational and open spaces represent another major area of concern to urban planners.

It is now a common practice for the developers of residential subdivisions to set aside land for, or actually construct, neighborhood parks or open spaces within the subdivision. The award of density bonuses, whereby builders can build more dwellings per acre than zoning guidelines permit, provides an incentive for developers to allocate large tracts of open space within their subdivision (Figure 19-2). The placement of and provision for libraries, once considered part of the educational process, now fall under the recreational agenda in many areas, as more citizens seek better access to this amenity. It has also become common practice for cities to provide centers for the performing and fine arts, often housed in a community civic center.

As urban regions continue to grow outward, planning for the future provision of sewage treatment, water, trash collection, and street lighting requires constant attention. Not only must urban planners project future needs and plan the layout of such facilities, they must also propose methods by which these facilities will be financed.

While utilities such as telephone, cable TV, and street lighting are often paid for by developers or residents, facilities for sewage treatment, the water supply, and trash collection/disposal present major communitywide challenges. As areas continue to grow, sewage treatment facilities and sanitary landfills for trash disposal must keep pace with demand. Urban planners are therefore called upon to find either additional space for these facilities or new methods for dealing with the problem. However, no one wants a sewage treatment plant or a sanitary landfill in their neighborhood, which is called the NIMBY (not in my backyard) or LULU (locally undesirable land use) syndrome (Figure 19-3). Residents also balk when

Figure 19-1. **Community Involvement in the Planning Process.** Planning initiatives that incorporate active community involvement generate a higher success rate for projects. Citizen groups can also be helpful in establishing development priorities within the community. (Bohdan Hrynewych/Stock, Boston)

asked to pay higher fees for the transport and processing of wastes to satisfy more stringent environmental standards for landfill operations. When planners turn to new solutions, such as trash-to-energy plants that burn trash, they often face other problems, such as atmospheric pollution, exorbitant costs, and unproven technologies.

Housing

The will of the people is often the deciding factor in determining how much and what type of housing is adequate for an area. While developers may desire to build as much housing as market conditions may warrant, pressures may also exist to slow the process by placing limits on the amount of new housing that is built. In some instances, residents want developers to

provide adequate monies to fund the new levels of service needed by the growing populace—an idea that many planners find not only acceptable, but necessary—while in other areas, residents simply do not want any projects, conditions or not. In an era of planning that demands careful monitoring of the public's desires, constant education of the public regarding the needs of the city and the development of alternative strategies to accomplish these ends must be ongoing programs. The needs of the community and those of the private sector development community must be reconciled.

The issue of housing cost is dealt with by ensuring a mix of housing types and values and appropriate densities. Unfortunately, federal- and state-level subsidies for low-income housing do not begin to keep pace with the current need, and the problem is likely to worsen in the future. Builders and planners alike have attempted

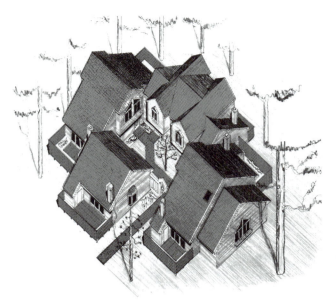

Figure 19-2. Higher-Density Housing and Open Space Amenities. Whitman Pond Village in Weymouth, Massachusetts, includes a townhouse community of 11 7-unit clusters on 6 acres. The design consists of a courtyard layout that minimizes road and utility infrastructure costs, allows most units to have outside exposures on more than two sides, and preserves open space. This design also promotes socialization. (Courtesy Urban Land Institute)

to address the problem by promoting the use of smaller homes on smaller lots, including zero lot line units. This is only a partial solution, however, and often disproportionately benefits middle-income, first-time buyers (Figure 19-4). A recent book, *Density by Design*, discusses several ways that densities can be increased without sacrificing quality of life.[1]

Transportation

Planning for transportation systems is among the most crucial elements of modern urban planning, because freeway traffic is increasing and average trip distances are lengthening (Figure 19-5). Planning in this area involves both short-term and long-term projects at several different geographic levels. *Regional planning* concerns the overall transportation system for an entire urban area and deals with both the building and maintenance of the transportation network and the develop-

---

[1] Lloyd Bookout and James W. Wenting, *Density by Design*, ULI—The Urban Land Institute, Washington, D.C., 1988.

Figure 19-3. Citizen Opposition to Toxic Dump Site. When New York State authorities identified a Cortland County site as a possible location for a toxic dump, citizen opposition intensified. This NIMBY response has complicated the siting process for many noxious facilities. In this winter scene, citizens have signed their names in protest on this wall on the grounds of the county courthouse. (Kirk Condyles/Impact Visuals)

Figure 19-4. Density by Design. Using innovative designs to increase housing densities lowers the cost of housing, allowing a wider range of socioeconomic groups to live in an area. Increasing densities also shortens work trip lengths and uses land more efficiently. (Courtesy Urban Land Institute)

ment of different modes of transportation. *Subregional planning* usually deals with specific areas within an urban area, such as the CBD or individual communities. *Corridor planning* involves linear projects such as freeways and railway lines, either subway, heavy, or light rail. *Spot improvement* planning is aimed at specific projects—bridges, freeway interchanges, short segments of road, or intersections (see Chapter 9).

URBAN DESIGN

Urban design is a difficult term to define. One might say that the physical form of an urbanized area represents its urban design. Therefore, it is correct to say that urban design involves both planned and unplanned efforts. The term urban design as used today, however, usually refers to a planned effort at producing results that are aesthetically pleasing, as well as socially redeeming. Since it involves an overlap between planning, architecture, and landscape architecture, urban design should be thought of as a multidiscipline effort. As such, development of large projects, such as residential communities or regional shopping centers, in-

volves a team effort by specialists from a variety of fields.

The ideology of urban design usually involves one of three philosophies. One ideology is concerned with creating an ideal social environment. Many such proposals follow utopian concepts and may not be practical. One such concept that worked successfully in England during the first half of this century was proposed by Ebenezer Howard.[2] His *garden city* proposal sought to provide a low-density living environment where social life could be promoted on a human scale by limiting the population to 30,000 persons. Several of these landscaped small cities could then be clustered around a central city whose growth, in turn, would be limited by the presence of garden cities.

A second ideology is that of creating a city based on aesthetic principles. There are many examples of this philosophy. The *English Renaissance* style found in colonial Charleston, Williamsburg, and our nation's capital are classic examples of this type, as discussed in Chapter 2.

[2]Ebenezer Howard, *Garden Cities of Tomorrow*, 1902; reissued by MIT Press, Cambridge, Mass., 1970.

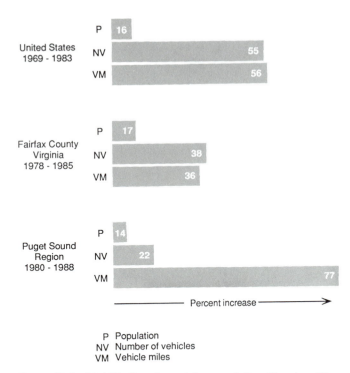

P Population
NV Number of vehicles
VM Vehicle miles

Figure 19-5. Mobility Trends and Transportation Planning. The number of licensed drivers and motor vehicles on the streets has risen far more rapidly than the population. When coupled with the dramatic increase in vehicle miles traveled, the implications for transportation planning become obvious. To resolve the problem, short- and long-term solutions will require additional highway capacity, as well as management solutions. *Source:* adapted from Urban Land Institute, "Myths and Facts about Transportation and Urban Growth," Urban Land Institute, Washington, D.C., 1989.

Another ideology combines social and physical ideals. Le Corbusier and Frank Lloyd Wright developed proposals for cities of this nature. Le Corbusier proposed a city with high-rise development situated in an extensively landscaped common public space in a parklike setting. Wright's proposal suggested an environment that would maximize individual freedom. In his Broad Acre City, each lot occupied one acre. C.A. Doxiadis proposed yet another style, called *ecumenopolis*, based on a human scale.

Ecumenopolis

Ecumenopolis grew out of Doxiadis' work on *ekistics*, the scientific study of human settlement.[3] It refers to a

[3]C. A. Doxiadis, *Ecumenopolis: The Settlement of the Future*, Doxiadis Associates, R-ERES-18 Athens Center of Ekistics, Athens, Greece, 1961. See also C. A. Doxiadis and J. G. Papaioannou, *Ecumenopolis: The Inevitable City of the Future*, Norton, New York, 1974; and C. A. Doxiadis, *Ekistics, An Introduction to the Science of Human Settlements*, Oxford University Press, New York, 1968.

continuous form of settlement consisting of cities and their surrounding agricultural support areas that Doxiadis envisioned evolving across the earth. He conceived of humans as creating, in 150 years, a hierarchical urban organization that would contain a balance between developed and open space. The end product of this urbanization was an ecumenopolis.

The key element to the ecumenopolis form is its focus on proportions that are suitable for humans. A city in this system would be limited to dimensions that are humanly manageable, such as walking distances of a maximum comfortable range of about 10 minutes. To maintain this viability, the paths of humans and vehicles do not cross. Connections with other modes of transportation are quick and easy.

A population of about 50,000 is seen as the maximum community size for physical, mental, and social well-being. An area of 7000 square feet would contain a single city cell. Several cells would be linked into an integrated whole by communication and transportation systems. The self-contained mixed-use developments unfolding today in the CBD and suburban downtowns and the renewed emphasis on minimizing the length of the journey to work appear to fit perfectly with the ecumenopolis approach.

The Arcology Alternative

Not all urban designers agree that cities must be built on a modest scale to incorporate the human dimension. Paolo Soleri, for example, believes that his high-density, three-dimensional cities are also designed to accommodate the human scale. The concept of *arcology*, based on a blending of architecture and ecology, infuses Soleri's city. Each city fuses with nature because of placement to take advantage of natural heating and ventilation processes, to conserve land, and to minimize energy consumption. His cities can be up to several hundred stories in height, housing a half-million people or more. They incorporate all functions (industry, commerce, housing, shopping, agriculture, and transportation) under a single roof.

Soleri's cities are expansive, vertical megastructures quite unlike the sprawling two-dimensional cities we have today. He feels that the present city style alienates people because of the separation of activities and their irrational placement. He views streets and highways as barriers and dead spaces that waste land, segregate land uses, and mutilate the city. He refers to this as savagery. Families are separated because of the distances between home and workplaces, and the young and elderly are unnecessarily isolated from their families. According to Soleri, the low-density flat city, in short, debilitates and suppresses the individual.

The arcologies that Soleri proposes could be built anywhere, on dams of lakes, on cliffs of a mountain face, or afloat at sea. He argues that they would crowd human beings together—something they need inasmuch as people are cultural beings—and that the compactness would create a wholeness and fullness missing in today's city. The living and working spaces would be "turned on complexity, the vectoriality of life."[4]

Since the Soleri arcologies are in effect pedestrian villages, there is little need for the private automobile, except to travel between cities or for treks in the countryside. Some of the cities have aircraft runways on their roofs to facilitate air travel. Internal movement within the complex is handled by various modes—escalators, elevators, moving and stationary sidewalks, and stairways.

> Imagine a ride on a curving, 30-story escalator suspended or cantilevered into the center of an arcology: rising in minutes through a commercial center, then a terraced layer of playing fields, theaters, and auditoriums, now a zoo, above it the city senate—all of them festooned with footbridges and elevators and hung in great shafts of light. For the more fantastic cities, the setting would determine the spirit of the place: The arcology called Stonebrow is intended to span a canyon, where the successive geological, fossil and floral layers would "remind man of the miracle of life emerging and perpetuating itself in endless ways." Soleri's Arcoindian cities would be cut into great gashes in cliff faces; life would take place in a vast amphitheater facing the desert or the sea under a broad semidome of sky. Novanoah I is intended to float free on the seas, harvesting them in pursuit of "an all-new and fantastic culture, adding new folds to the human condition."[5]

An architectural rendering of one Soleri city, Babel IIC, appears in Figure 19-6.

Critics of this type of urban design abound. Many observers have likened this approach to a "rat colony," pointing out that when overcrowded rat behavior degenerates. But Soleri argues that rats, while being social animals, do not have culture, and the comparison cannot be made. He suggests that crowding among people is natural, and that life is diminished without it. Sociologists also point out that density and crowding are not synonymous. High-density living environments do not necessarily require crowding.

Critics of the Soleri philosophy also point out that rather than bringing nature back into the city, arcology is the antithesis of pastoral living. Soleri purports that his approach creates minimal environmental disruption and energy exploitation, whereas traditional cities gobble up excessive quantities of land and green space in search of the good life.

One prototype city, Arcosanti, is currently being built in a rural environment north of Phoenix by Soleri and his students. It has been under construction for nearly two decades and appears to have lost momentum (Figure 19-7). To date, it houses only a small dedicated staff that gives daily tours and sells wind chimes and other mementos, but it was originally envisioned to house about 5000 persons. It is a low-budget operation, but an enthusiastic and dedicated group of followers has taken up the cause. As with all of Soleri's designs, Arcosanti incorporates many arches, apses, and domes and is designed to take advantage of the natural landscape.

While it is unlikely that cities using the arcology concept will become commonplace, high-density centers with some of its attributes may evolve around Tokyo or New York, where the public could be expected to be most receptive to the approach and where a need exists for high-density housing space. Indeed, in denser downtown environments, in both cities and suburbs, we are already witnessing mixed-use redevelopment, as discussed in Chapters 15 and 17. Perhaps, too, settlements in outer space or on the moon may someday adopt the arcology approach to counteract a hostile environment.

Physical Environment Perspectives

The idea that the physical environment affects the social environment has long enjoyed support among professionals. The urban environment is made up of a number of elements, and the process of manipulating these elements is a major part of the designer's concern. The urban designer must give the space around a building a positive relationship both to adjacent buildings and to the urban pattern as a whole. All space,

---

[4]Paolo Soleri, *Arcology, The City in the Image of Man*, MIT Press, Cambridge, Mass., 1969, p. 13.
[5]David Butler, "In the Image of Man," *Playboy* (June 1972), 210.

Figure 19-6. Arcology and the Three-dimensional City. Paolo Soleri envisions an ideal urban environment in which residential, cultural, and work spaces cluster together in one setting in conjunction with public and commercial uses. The design for Babel II C, built on a mountainside, is shown here. (See Figure 19-7.) (Reprinted from *Arcology, the City in the Image of Man*, by Paolo Soleri. By permission of the MIT Press, Cambridge, Massachusetts. Copyright © 1969 by the Massachusetts Institute of Technology.)

interior and exterior, filled and unfilled, must be tied together to create an environment that fulfills the needs of the society it serves (Figure 19-8).

All too often, when seeking to fulfill aesthetic demands, modern urban design follows current fashion, making it difficult to define principles that may be applied over time to a variety of cultures. Gordon Cullen, in his work called *Townscape*, enumerated three factors in aesthetics that he regards as constant: perception, anthropometrics, and stimuli.[6]

---

[6]Gordon Cullen, *Townscape, Architectural* Press, London, 1961.

Perception is a visual function. While that which the eye sees is translated by a brain that is influenced by culture, the mechanics of what is visualized is much the same for everyone. Blue is the same shade regardless of who is viewing it, just as are texture, hue, and physical dimensions. The way the color is accepted, however, is influenced by perceptions that are influenced by cultural factors. For example, the color red is a dominant color in some Oriental cultures, and used widely in design, while it is considered hedonistic in some Southwest Asian cultures and therefore would not be acceptable.

Anthropometrics, the relationship of body measure-

Figure 19-7. Arcosanti, a Prototype Three-dimensional City. Paolo Soleri is currently building this community in a rural environment north of Phoenix. It has been under construction for two decades and appears to have lost momentum, but originally was designed to house 5000 persons. (Courtesy of Cosanti Foundation, Scottsdale, Arizona; used by permission)

Figure 19-8. The Edinborough Mixed-use Center in Edina, Minnesota. This innovative 26-acre complex in suburban Minneapolis includes affordable condominium housing for first-time buyers, high-rise housing for the elderly, an indoor public park, an office building with ground-floor retailing, and structured parking, in a unified setting. The design goal for the project was to create a pedestrian environment and a unified aesthetic appearance, yet maintain a separate identity for each unit. "These objectives were achieved through the use of color, building materials, and the repetition of design elements such as archways that identify major entrances. The tall buildings were placed at the south end of the site to achieve visual access from the freeway, to provide shade for the park. . ., and to buffer the low-rise residential buildings from the freeway." (Source: "Edinborough, Minneapolis, Minnesota," Project Reference File, No. 17, vol. 17 (October–December 1987), Urban Land Institute, Washington, D.C. Used by permission.

ments to that which is encountered, can also be seen as being fairly constant between cultures and over time. The height and size of stairs, walls, fences, and furniture affect our relationship to our environment and elicit a response from the user. This factor has led to the development of child-size furniture and public telephones, water fountains, and elevator controls for the physically impaired.

Sensory perception creates *stimuli* to the environment. Thus, desired human responses can be evoked by the use of materials and forms that tend to produce them. Sound levels can be decreased by the use of sound absorbing materials, temperature can be influenced by the type of building materials chosen, and foot traffic can be directed toward chosen paths by the choice of ground coverings. Similarly, open prows have been used on the corners of skyscrapers to mitigate wind problems at ground level.

The physical form of a city is usually classified as either orthogonal or organic. Orthogonal refers to that which is right-angled, as in a grid system, and by its very nature infers conscious planning. Organic refers to everything else, and while it may be consciously planned, it is usually thought of as unplanned. An example of planned organic form is the geometric or axial order of St. Peter's Square in Rome (Figure 19-9). The geometric layout produces a symmetrical pattern with a clearly defined axis. Buildings may also be kinetically or sequentially ordered. Using the elements of change and modulation, the environment is divided into a series of zones, which creates a progression of visual experiences.

Another important factor that influences the physical form is the transportation network. It divides public and private areas and channels the flow of traffic, both foot and vehicular. Transportation networks are geometric and can usually be classified as either net or tree type. The grid pattern is an example of the net form. The tree

Figure 19-9. Geometric Order of St. Peter's Square, Vatican City, Rome. A symmetrical pattern with a clearly defined axis creates order and a ceremonial setting for the approach to St. Peter's Cathedral. At one time, Vatican City was a separate community divided from Rome by the River Tiber, but the city of Rome now surrounds this small city-state. (AP/Wide World)

form has a main trunk with branches off that trunk, and a cul-de-sac is the smallest branch of the tree. This type of form is quite useful in creating a sense of community in a residential area, but when applied to a system as a whole, it limits growth and development and is not a desirable form if the goal is to provide easy public transportation access. The traditional grid form, in fact, offers an ideal form for bus transit access.

While many factors help shape the urban form, transportation is among the most important. Most major cities have been located where the transportation advantages provided easy access. The economic well-being of a city today is still influenced by the transportation advantage it enjoys. The widespread use of automobiles in this country has had a major impact on the physical form of our cities. The compact city of the last century was a result of the need for workers to live close to their work. The development of streetcar and subway mass transit first allowed workers to move farther from their jobs, and reliance on the automobile has contributed to this pattern. Suburban downtowns, for example, are a definite by-product of the modern transportation network.

The provision of open space within the urban form has become a major concern of many urban design critics. While parks are the most evident result of this concern, they are not the only type of open space that satisfies the need. Public space that is a daily part of city life is, perhaps, the most successful use of such space, but it has not played the major role in the United States that it has in European cities. An important element in the design of any open or public space is uniqueness of character, and thus such space cannot be copied and duplicated within every urban design.

The incorporation of amenities into urban design is important and is unique to both the culture and the setting of the city. Each culture has amenities that it considers vital, such as climate, location, and the predominant recreational activities. The presence of an enclosed shopping mall might be considered a major amenity to an urban dweller in a hot climate, while those in a mild year-round setting, such as in southern California, might consider it extravagant. Along downtown waterfronts, an urban design that limits the height and bulk of buildings and calls for gradually increased heights as you move away from it provides an amenity for a large area by simply preserving the view. Similarly, an urban design encouraging large buildings that can provide shelter from wind or sun in climates with extreme temperature variations is also creating an amenity. An example is the downtown underground mall concept developed in several Canadian cities to ameliorate the impact of harsh winters on pedestrian shopping (Figure 19-10).

Figure 19-10. Underground Retail Mall in Winnipeg, Manitoba. This regional mall is located in an underground setting in downtown Winnipeg. This design draws the people inside, creating a problem at street level, but it offers an innovative solution to the difficulties of coping with a harsh winter. (Courtesy Trizec Properties)

THE ROLE OF GOVERNMENT

Almost every level of government is involved in urban planning, from the city, county, and regional levels to state and national levels. However, the basic form of urban planning takes place at the local level. Municipal governments almost always have a comprehensive or "master" plan that prescribes how long-term physical development of the community should proceed. Within a city, planning also involves subareas or sections of a city, such as the central business district, specific residential neighborhoods, educational centers, and industrial or business parks.

Except for those counties that comprise only one city, such as Denver or San Francisco, planning at the county level usually involves a number of incorporated places (cities), as well as unincorporated territory within the county. Although the county government may not have jurisdiction over planning decisions made by the incorporated cities within the county, decisions made by county planning staff can have definite impacts on the member cities. A housing tract that is built in unincorporated territory just outside the boundary of an incorporated city will fall within that city's sphere of influence, and its residents will impact the transportation, educational, recreational, and medical facilities of the city. On the other hand, such tracts will also contribute to the economic well-being of the city by providing additional consumers for businesses. While the territories of the different levels is usually quite distinct, there is usually a sense of cooperation between the planning agencies.

Regional planning, like county planning, influences the quality of life for residents in a number of cities. The regional agency may have authority over one element of service or may be responsible for planning in a number of different areas. The Bay Area Rapid Transit District (BART) controls rail mass transit in part of San Francisco Bay area. While the provision of rapid transit and the placement of lines and stations can have a definite economic impact on cities within the district, economic planning is not one of BART's responsibilities. On a broader scope, the San Diego Association of Governments (SANDAG) is the regional planning agency for San Diego County and as such includes economic development, air and water quality, and transportation among its concerns. Regional planning agencies have been established in almost every major area of the country in response to a requirement set forth by the federal government; these regions can then receive federal funding provided by several different congressional acts.

State government is involved in planning in a number of different ways. Every state has a department that is responsible for the planning, development, and maintenance of its highway system. Although primary and secondary education comes under control of locally elected school boards, basic standards are set by the state and the distribution of educational funds is handled at the state level. The public university system in most states is guided by a state agency. State government can also have agencies that are involved in any number of planning issues, such as community development or park and recreational planning. The right to form cities and establish political boundaries is granted through state statutes and legislation.

Unlike many European countries, the United States has no national planning agency, and in fact the Federal government has no right to regulate land use planning. The few national programs that are centrally regulated, such as Social Security and Internal Revenue, are self-administering. The federal government, however, affects issues like transportation and housing through its fiscal policies, which offer aid to state and local governments for construction and development in these areas. President Carter issued a statement in March 1978 that called for a "new partnership" between federal, state, and local governments, as well as neighborhood groups, voluntary associations, and the private sector. This was the first comprehensive urban policy statement issued by a president of the United States. The Reagan administration did not continue this program, believing instead that this issue was better left for the states to handle. While the Departments of Transportation (DOT) and Housing and Urban Development (HUD) have not been abolished, the funding they offer states has been cut back considerably since 1980. However, the new transportation initiative announced by President Bush in 1991 did call for a return of more flexibility and funding to the states for transportation programs.

Cooperation between Levels

Effective urban planning requires a good deal of cooperation between all levels of government, particularly city, county, and regional. Unfortunately, this does not always occur. Goals for one agency may not be compatible with those of another, and the process requires give and take. At the regional level, problems are sometimes encountered if one city is considerably larger than other member cities and uses its voting power, usually apportioned according to population, to control the issues without regard to the needs of the smaller members.

Legislation

Legislation involved in urban planning includes zoning and subdivision ordinances, building codes, and requirements set forth by the state. We discussed zoning activities in Chapter 15.

Subdivision ordinances, typically to control growth, establish minimum requirements with which developers and builders must comply. They are useful for preventing the improper layout of lots and poor street arrangement, and for ensuring that development conforms to the general good of the community. Frequently, subdivision ordinances require the developer to provide land for parks, schools, and streets, and to pay a good portion of the cost of developing these facilities.

Building codes set minimum requirements for things such as the types of materials that may be used in construction, the amount of support to be used for roofs, the thickness of foundations and sizes and numbers of windows, and the design and capacity of electrical systems. Permits are issued only for those plans that meet the minimum requirements, and inspections are made to ensure that the plan is being followed. As technology progresses, codes are updated to reflect changes. A recent example of this is the requirement by many cities that smoke alarms be installed in residential structures and that overhead water sprinklers for fire protection be included in many new commercial and business structures.

Zoning, subdivision ordinances, and building codes are shaped by a city's comprehensive master plan. This plan, called the General Plan in California, is a formal document that has been adopted by the city council and attempts to describe and direct future development. The General Plan is required by the State Planning and Zoning Law in California and is defined, in part, as "a comprehensive, long-term . . . plan for the physical development of the . . . city." It contains a statement of policies and goals and must be updated every 10 years. Once adopted, a city must make sure that development does not violate the plan. The law requires the inclusion

of the following 10 areas, known as elements: (1) land use; (2) housing; (3) circulation; (4) conservation; (5) open space; (6) noise; (7) seismic safety; (8) scenic highway; (9) safety; and (10) air quality. Additional elements can be addressed and usually are in larger cities.

POLITICAL FRAGMENTATION

One analogy of the city likens it to a computer system, suggesting that while its *hardware* components work well, failure occurs in the *software* arena. Housing, health, and transportation programs that work relatively efficiently as separate units (the hardware system) generally do not have access to effective management and administrative systems (the software) to make them run smoothly. The major hardware components of the city can be described in a systems context, using the human body as a model:

1. Metabolic System. Air, water, food, fuel, and waste distribution and management.
2. Cardiovascular System. Transportation network, vertical and horizontal (streets, airports, elevators, etc.).
3. Nervous System. Information and communication network (telephone, mail service, radio, television).
4. Enclosure System. Private and public buildings (residential, commercial, industrial, churches, arenas, stadiums).[7]

Coordinating and managing the operations of these components is a complex process. The difficulty posed by political fragmentation at the local government level adds to the problem. Local governments often compete with one another for revenues or the right to deliver services. Rarely have city governments been innovative in terms of new administrative programs or solutions to problems, because they are managed by political forces more interested in garnering votes to win elections than in effective program development. Even when local governments have been more professional, they are typically tied to traditional management styles fraught with the limitations imposed by political patronage and civil service bureaucracies. Other institu-

[7]John P. Eberhard, "Technology for the City," *International Science and Technology*, 57 (1966), 18–29.

tional barriers that thwart solutions to problems include the presence of autonomous bureaus and authorities and simply a lack of funds.

Even though cities function as a single interactive metropolitan entity socially and economically, they are highly fractured politically. This political fragmentation is reinforced by a perceptual split as well. Often, the suburbanite identifies with central city issues and reads the major city paper, even though living in a totally separate, autonomous, political enclave. When out of town, the resident also identifies with the central city, but the nearer the person gets to home, the greater the differentiation that occurs. At that scale the person typically declares loyalty to the subdivision, shunning identification with the central city.

The suburbanization process dates to the beginnings of urban growth. But after World War II, suburban areas in the United States became more independent from the central city. The corporate city ceased to expand areally even as urban growth accelerated. In the 1950s annexation of outlying areas stopped, except in the South and West, and suburban areas developed their own municipal service and utility systems. In the aggregate, this addition of new political entities completely encircled a given central city with many competing governments.

The reasons for the weakening of central city territorial growth are complex, but include transportation improvements, growing affluence, the rapid rate of urban growth, and growing dissatisfaction with the city itself. The automobile, coupled with a rapid road-building process, opened up a very large and formerly rural area adjacent to the city for urbanization after World War II. The housing boom of the late 1940s, in response to a pent-up demand for units following the war and liberal governmental incentives (e.g., FHA loans), reinforced the decentralization process. Prospective homeowners felt they could get along without costly city services in their new suburban homes. The prospect of lower tax rates in the urban fringe also encouraged outward movement, as did the possibility for whites to escape from an increasingly minority-dominated central city.

As people, industry, and commercial activity congregated in outlying areas, expanded governmental services were also required, but citizens usually looked to local authorities for these services rather than the more remote central city. Initially, many areas contracted with the city for delivery of these services as an alternative to developing their own delivery capability.

Eventually, most were forced to develop their own infrastructure because of heavy demands and a reluctance of cities to contract with them.

Simultaneously with the emergence of politically independent suburbs, central cities fell on hard times. Population growth generally ceased and the size of the tax base shrank following the out-migration of the middle class. The central city government became increasingly hard-pressed to provide costly services to its growing share of needy persons. Central cities faced added burdens from the cost of services provided for those working or recreating in the city but not living there and paying for them. Recall the problems associated with the mercantilistic suburb discussed in Chapter 12.

The number of local governments in metropolitan areas proliferated to staggering proportions by the 1960s. Over 20,000 such entities existed in metropolitan areas and over two-thirds of them administered to fewer than 5000 persons each.[8] In 1967, the average number of governments in each of the 233 SMSAs was nearly 100. Fragmentation had clearly become a major problem facing metropolitan areas because areawide problems were not being solved comprehensively but on a piecemeal basis. For example, the many sewer districts that evolved in metropolitan areas frequently led to enormous pollution problems. Within a particular city, some of the districts treated sewage effectively, others merely dumped it untreated into streams, and many had no municipal sewer programs at all, relying instead on septic systems. The point is that utilities, including sewers, are vital urban services that should be available throughout the metropolitan area on an equitable basis in the form of an integrated system. "With political power chopped up into little pieces and parcelled out among a large number of municipalities, no one local government can do very much about traffic, zoning, pollution, and other problems that go beyond the existing municipal boundaries."[9]

Financially, fragmentation also creates problems. *Effective tax rates* among metropolitan municipalities vary widely. The effective rate is a ratio between the taxes levied and the total assessed valuation of the community. Central city effective rates are invariably high, whereas the effective rate in an outlying area

---

[8]David B. Walker, "Regionalism: Defining the Terms," *Public Management* (1970), 4–7.

[9]Harold Kaplan, *The Regional City,* Canadian Broadcasting Corporation, Toronto, 1965, p. 44.

may be low. The problem of inequitable tax rates is illustrated in Figure 19-11, which shows the relationship between tax rates and areal sizes of municipalities. On the left side of the diagram, which describes many small political units, tax rates can vary widely. As the number of governments decreases, tax rate variations decrease, approaching a midrange value.

Many overtures have been made in recent years to consolidate or integrate city and suburban governments. Each new solution is typically met with cries from vested interests of discrimination and disenfranchisement. In reality, the city and suburbs do have much in common, but neither wants to yield any power to another jurisdiction or suffer any financial penalty. Central cities have treated the suburbs as stepchildren in the past, and the suburbs in turn feel that central cities are too decrepit and exploitive and therefore inferior.

Among the metropolitan solutions that have been

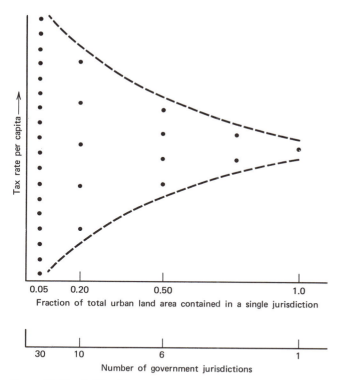

Figure 19-11. Political Fragmentation and Fiscal Capacity. Effective tax rates among metropolitan counties and municipalities vary widely. In areas with small political units (left side of diagram), tax rates can vary much more widely than in communities where fewer governmental jurisdictions (right side) levy taxes. In the latter instance, tax rates approach a midrange value. *Source:* Redrawn with permission from Wilbur R. Thompson, *A Preface to Urban Economics*, The Johns Hopkins University Press, Baltimore, 1965, p. 271. Copyright © 1965 by The Johns Hopkins University Press, Baltimore, Maryland 21218.

proposed in the past to solve this dilemma, in addition to annexation, are: (1) federation; (2) city–county consolidation; (3) county–city consolidation; (4) special districts; (5) council of governments; and (6) tax-base sharing.

Federation

The *federation* concept involves creating a new level of government, a superagency, to coordinate areawide problems, while existing governments remain active at the local and community levels. Very little success has occurred in the United States with this type of reform, but since 1954, the approach has been successfully used to govern the Toronto metropolitan region. In addition to representatives from the city of Toronto, that metropolitan government originally had delegates from 12 suburban areas. These outlying areas were themselves consolidated into five municipal governments in 1967 (Etobicoke, North York, Scarborough, East York, and York) as seen in Figure 17-2.

The scope of activities handled by the Toronto metropolitan government is very broad.

> In the areas of education, water supply, and sewage disposal, many of the earlier problems have been arrested if not eradicated; a metropolitan park district of many thousand acres has been established; an extensive expressway system has been launched; an attempt has been made to control air pollution; a system of unified law enforcement has been implemented; and public transportation has been consolidated and improved.[10]

Many problems remain unsolved in Toronto in spite of these accomplishments, particularly in the area of housing. Critics have also noted that the trend for broader metropolitan solutions has been at the expense of local neighborhood input, thus creating a possibly tyrannical situation.

Consolidation

City–county or county–city *consolidation* has successfully reduced the number of governmental agencies in many urban areas. When the county unit encompasses the entire urban area, such consolidations become, in

---

[10]Maurice Yeates and Barry Garner, *The North American City,* 2nd ed., Harper & Row, New York, 1976, p. 441.

effect, metropolitan governments. Where urbanization is much more broadly based, only partial metropolitan governance is involved. In Miami, following the 1957 consolidation of the city government into an urban county form, most areawide functions were handled exclusively by Dade County. Municipalities retained the right to perform some functions if they so chose. Even with a metropolitan police system, for example, the city of Miami maintained its own police force. The biggest problem with this "Metro" government, as it is now called, is that south Florida has grown rapidly in recent years and urbanization in the Miami area has spilled far beyond Dade County boundaries.

For a variety of reasons, the urban county form of governance has not been very popular nationally. Among the problems are state laws prohibiting such an action, including frequent limitations on the authority of counties to levy taxes, and the reluctance of cities to give up existing authority. In larger metropolitan areas such consolidation is only a partial solution because MSAs typically extend into several counties.

Another more popular form of consolidation, the city–county merger, has been widely utilized in United States metropolitan areas. Jacksonville–Duval County, Florida; Nashville–Davidson County, Tennessee; and Indianapolis–Marion County, Indiana, are among the many areas that have permitted the city to govern on a countywide basis.

Special Districts

Special districts refer to the wide variety of commissions and authorities created in metropolitan areas to take the lead role in solving one or more areawide problems. The advantage of the special district is that it is very effective when dealing with a particular problem and does not interfere with existing governmental arrangements. It can often levy taxes, but in many cases it acts as more of a coordinator than a provider of services.

When special districts are used to oversee the work of existing agencies, problems can occur in setting criteria for allocating resources among the agencies, and setting priorities can be problematical. Once established, unfortunately, authorities often take on an identity of their own and become unresponsive to the needs of those they serve. One example of how large and controversial a special district can become is illustrated by the case of the Port Authority of Greater

New York, which deals with public transportation matters in the tristate area. It is responsible for the operations of the harbors, bridges, and airports in the region. But it also has become a major realtor and developer, having built the World Trade Center twin office towers and many other facilities peripheral to its original mission. Special districts have received wide attention in recent years in the area of mass transit. Such agencies were created in San Francisco and Atlanta, for example, to develop the rail rapid transit systems, which are separate from existing departments of transportation as noted earlier in the chapter.

Council of Government

Some attempts at regional governance have simply involved elected officials setting up intergovernmental discussion groups. One example is the *council of government* approach. Some of these agencies are merely forums for debate, others have taxing and development authority, while still others function as clearinghouses and coordinators in terms of planning for consistent regional development programs. The latter format has been promoted by the A-95 review process, which requires that all projects with federal funding be commented upon and reviewed by a single regional planning agency in each metropolitan area. Such agency reviewers do not normally have veto authority over projects, but they make recommendations and suggest alternatives that would make projects more compatible when necessary. In some cities this local review agency is the metropolitan government (e.g., Metropolitan Dade County in Miami); in others, it is an umbrella multicounty planning agency (e.g., the Atlanta Regional Commission in Atlanta, the North Central Texas Council of Governments in Dallas–Fort Worth, and the East–West Gateway Coordinating Council in St. Louis). Most of these areawide review agencies have jurisdictions over only a few counties (5 or less), while a few have jurisdiction over a vast area (10 or more).

Tax-Base Sharing

Fiscal disparities in the form of great variations in revenue-producing ability cause many hardships in metropolitan areas. Municipalities that are primarily low-income residential typically have a low revenue-producing ability, while younger affluent suburban areas have a much greater ability to raise tax dollars. Commercial and industrial areas similarly have more lucrative tax bases than residential communities. An areawide government would be one possibility to remove the inequitable burden of providing needed supporting services, shifting the responsibility for taxation and services to a broader geographic jurisdiction. *Revenue sharing* and *tax-base sharing* are other possible remedies to such fiscal problems. The former involves a higher-level government agency (i.e., state) returning to the local government a share of its tax revenues, usually in proportion to the number of people in the area. The latter approach usually returns money to local jurisdictions on the basis of need rather than population.

A good illustration of the tax-base sharing concept is provided by the metropolitan government in the Minneapolis–St. Paul region. Begun in 1971, the fiscal disparities program diverted 40 percent of the increase in the nonresidential tax-base revenues each year to local areas based on a formula calculated according to the population and property tax base in the particular area. That pool of money, generated from expansion in commercial and industrial property assessments, went disproportionately to areas with a high demand for services and lower tax bases, which lowered inequities between poor and affluent areas.

Each local area continued to levy taxes and determine its own millage rate under the program, so minimal disruption of the traditional taxation system occurred. Only the increase in the value of the tax digest in the area was subject to sharing.

The effect of tax-base sharing in Minneapolis was to relieve local residential property tax burdens, minimize competition for new commercial/industrial projects among local areas, and promote tax equity in the area by providing a means to "share the wealth."[11] This program loosened the dependence of the local community for service delivery from the relative wealth of that community, while at the same time helping to preserve local autonomy. Many other metropolitan areas are now contemplating similar municipal funding arrangements.

Fiscal Problems

Over the last two decades, urban areas have been faced with growing financial problems, to the extent that several have approached bankruptcy. While the debt problems faced by cities such as New York and Cleveland have been among the worst, almost every city has faced cutbacks in services and, frequently, a delay in implementing a variety of plans. The fiscal problems have been a result of a combination of factors. The recent economic recessions came at a time when an increasing population in the urban areas created higher demand for the provision of public goods and services that could not keep pace with the supply. Urban residents in the twentieth century have come to expect a dramatic expansion of government services over time, while the conservative movement that has gained increasing support since the 1970s has demanded lower taxes, as the case with California's Proposition 13. While such tax-cutting measures have given needed relief to the middle class, they have seriously reduced funding for public services. In other areas of the country, fees collected from developers have increased dramatically, but they rarely generate sufficient revenues to offset the additional service costs that these developments require over time.

THE PLANNING PROCESS

Brian Berry (1973) has suggested a model of urban policy and he has put forth four different planning frameworks (Figure 19-12). Planning policies and programs are first established (Box 4) as inputs for the urban system. Additionally, external forces beyond the control of the planning department are also at work (Box 3), such as prevailing regional economic conditions. Box 1 in the center incorporates the long- and short-term activities and operations of the city system. Two sets of outputs occur. Goals and objectives (Box 2) are targeted developments that have been strategized and planned. However, undesirable results can and do occur (Box 3), whose causes are beyond the abilities or role of the urban planner or policy maker.

Four Approaches

As an expansion of this simple urban policy model, Berry proposed four types or approaches to planning:

[11]David L. Sjoquist, "Sharing the Property Tax Base: An Alternative to Metropolitan Government," *Atlanta Economic Review*, 28 (1978), pp. 56–62.

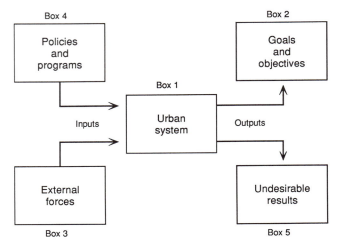

Figure 19-12. Urban Policy Planning Framework, after Berry. Local policies and programs established by the community, (Box 4) and external forces (Box 3) such as economic conditions, influence the operations of the city system (Box 1) and converge to help focus goals and objectives for future development in the community (Box 2). Notwithstanding the best efforts of the planning process, undesirable results beyond the control of the planner (Box 5) may often occur. *Source:* Reprinted from *The Human Consequences of Urbanization: Divergent Paths in the Urban Experience of the Twentieth Century* by B.J.L. Berry, Fig. 17, p. 173. Copyright © 1973 by St. Martin's Press, Inc. Reprinted by permission of the publisher.

(1) exploitive opportunity-seeking; (2) ameliorative problem solving; (3) allocative trend-modifying; and (4) normative goal-oriented.

The first, *exploitive opportunity-seeking,* is the approach used by small cities attempting to quickly develop an economic base. Both policy makers and leaders of private industry seek ways to develop and maximize profits without great regard for the consequences of growth or future problems that may be created by it.

The second type of planning is *ameliorative problem solving,* wherein nothing is done until the urban problems become unmanageable. This is a short-term reactive planning style in which the planning staff goes about "putting out fires" or taking care of emergencies on a day-to-day basis, with no time or inclination to develop long-term plans. This type of planning usually is the result of a greatly understaffed or underfunded planning department, or an urban system where there is a rapid turnover of elected officials producing a lack of continuity. Neither of these first two styles of planning is adequate for large urban areas in North America today.

The third approach is the *allocative trend-modifying*

form of planning, which is typical of large North American cities in the 1990s. With this strategy, considerable effort and cost are expended to measure the past trends in population, land use, housing, and transportation, and these are then projected into the future. By predicting the future of such urban conditions, urban policy makers may then allocate resources in the best possible fashion before the changes have taken place so as to avoid major conflicts or undesirable results. This allows cities to modify existing trends to gain the desired results through regulatory processes, for example, zoning processes. A more elaborate description of the allocative trend-modifying form of planning follows in the next section.

The fourth and last form of planning is the *normative goal-oriented* form. Normative means developing the best possible outcome and adjusting the urban system to meet this outcome in the future. This is a long-term planning process in which firm goals and objectives are established and regulatory mechanisms are adjusted in accordance with them to develop the ideal urban system. While this style of planning is more typical of socialist and communist forms of government, which possess stronger control of various regulatory mechanisms, most major cities in North America today have a branch of the planning department, usually called the "long-term planning division," whose major focus is normative goal-oriented planning.

While the first three approaches are typical of planning in United States and Canadian cities, and the last form more typical of European and centrally planned economies, it is not uncommon for all four types of planning to be represented by different groups or jurisdictions within the same North American urban regions. Within large urban regions, literally scores of metropolitan service districts may exist, each with its own planning staff. It is not uncommon for a large MSA to have hundreds of planners and policy makers, many with different goals, objectives, and interests.

Steps in Planning Process

Over the past three decades, there has evolved a process of planning that has been called the *system planning* or *system design process* (Figure 19-13). The basic steps include problem definition, requirements for solution, generation of alternatives, evaluation of alternatives, selection of alternatives, and implementation.

Once the decision to plan has been established,

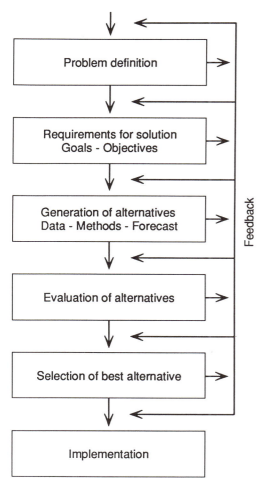

Figure 19-13. The System Design Planning Process. The basic steps in this comprehensive process, as shown here, include problem definition, developing goals and objectives, gathering information and establishing alternatives, evaluating and selecting alternatives, and implementing the desired solution. *Source:* Adapted from San Diego Association of Governments.

which usually means a conscious effort to allow government intervention into the laissez-faire forces that have operated in the city, a detailed *problem definition* must be made of the current state of the urban system. This step is most important because it says that users are dissatisfied with the present operation of the urban system (or expect to be dissatisfied if the process continues as observed) and want to see a better management of the functioning of the urban system in the future. This step really determines, to a large extent, the nature of the activities to follow in each of the following steps.

The next broad step is the *requirements for solution* to the urban problems observed or expected in step one.

This is a broad step because it encompasses several important stages. The first stage of this step requires the planner to understand, as fully as possible, the present urban system as it currently exists. This task is ongoing and it is never fully completed. College courses such as this one, as well as public administration and urban economics courses, are frequently aimed at understanding the present urban system. A part of this process is to formulate *goals and objectives* for the urban system. Goals are broad in scope while objectives are more specific. A goal may be to improve access and reduce congestion, while an objective might be to provide express bus lanes and service in major travel corridors. John Levy has identified five sets of goals: (1) political goals; (2) economic goals; (3) social goals; (4) environmental goals; and (5) redistributive goals.[12]

The next step is the *generation of alternatives,* which usually involves gathering data and employing computerized statistical methods to generate forecasts. A set of alternative plans offering various courses of action should strongly reflect the goals and objectives from the previous step. In principle, many designs or possibilities should be explored before the best design is chosen. But planners are faced with practical limitations: finite time periods for projects and limited funds to spend. Thus, typically, they must frequently rely on their own personal judgments, on only approximate analytical treatments, and presumably on a very structured process to help them in selecting the best set of alternatives. Once a set of alternatives has been narrowed down, each one must be detailed in relation to (1) the overall direct and indirect costs in light of the available funds, (2) the time span over which the project could reasonably be implemented compared to the available time span of when it is needed, and (3) the positive and negative social and economic impacts of the alternative, for both the short run and the long run.

These three steps, when estimated for each alternative, help in the next stage of the planning process, which is the *evaluation of alternatives* stage. In this stage, an attempt is made to ascertain what would happen if an alternative were implemented. Sometimes, this is done by observing what has happened in another city where such an alternative has already been tried out. For many large-scale urban systems, frequently there is no effective analogy, either because

[12]John Levy, *Contemporary Urban Planning,* 2nd ed., Prentice Hall, Englewood Cliffs, 1991, p. 97.

conditions of the area under consideration are unique or because the kind of alternative envisioned has not been tried out in the same form before. However, much of what is frequently termed *professional judgment* is no doubt developed through analogy with other areas.

Another means of transferring knowledge gained in one city to a situation in another city is by using a model. Mathematical models consist of relationships between certain numerical characteristics of the actual urban system. Mathematical relationships are developed that will help explain the use of various parts of the urban system. Such modeling has been found to be the only effective approach in large urban systems to predict the results of possible alternative plans, and hence it is the most widely used approach.

The next stage is the actual *selection of the best alternative*. The most widely used method involves a *benefit–cost analysis* whereby expected benefits in monetary terms are compared to expected costs. Usually, the alternative with the highest ratio of benefits to

costs is selected. However, at least two obvious problems result from this analysis. First, some social and environmental impacts are impossible to monetize, such as the negative value of displacement of persons or the destruction of a bird's nest or wildlife habitat. Second, plans typically have very different impacts on different groups, leading to a net gain for some groups and a net loss for other groups. Other less objective approaches for the evaluation of alternative plans (which suffer from the same problems as the benefit–cost analysis) are the *planning balance sheet* and the *goal attainment matrix* (Figure 19-14).

Once the best alternative is selected, it, as well as the other alternatives, must be presented to urban governments for approval. Only after such plans have been given the green light will they be moved to the *implementation* stage. Randall Scott (1975) has identified three major ways in which urban governments can facilitate the adopted plans: through (1) fiscal policies, (2) land regulation policies, and (3) development poli-

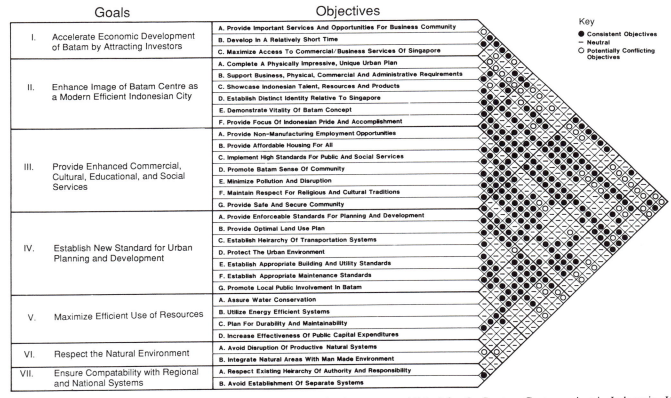

Figure 19-14. Goal Attainment Matrix. This set of goals and objectives was established for the Bantam Centre project in Indonesia. It identifies consistencies and conflicts between and among objectives, as well as suggesting instances where no positive or negative impacts exist (labeled as neutral situations). Objective A, for example, seeks to provide services for the business community, which is noted as consistent with 11 objectives and conflicting with 4 others (short time development, distinct identity from Singapore, respecting existing hierarchy of authority, and avoidance of establishing separate systems). *Source:* Courtesy P & D Technologies (formerly PRC Engineering, Inc.)

cies. An example of the first is the property tax or a state sales tax rebate to the local area for the construction of a major project, for example, the Bay Area Rapid Transit in San Francisco. Other fiscal policies besides direct taxation include rent controls, issuance of permits, and subsidies or grants for everything from low-income housing to parks, to industrial location incentives (see Chapter 7).

Land regulation policies over the years have centered on the zoning ordinance, which we discussed in Chapter 15. Other techniques include construction codes, setback requirements, height limitations, density requirements, and sewer hook-up restrictions. Finally, development policies include areas of the city targeted for redevelopment, direct new housing development, or the creation of industrial parks.

Naturally, all of these planning stages assume that the planner can operate in a detached, objective manner and not be swayed by his or her own bias or those of lobbying groups. Additionally, it is assumed that the planner can predict all the effects of each alternative plan. These assumptions have been strongly criticized by Marxist theorists, including David Harvey who has suggested that planning is really a technique of redistribution of public goods, and therefore must be separated from the normal political-economic establishment in order to be fairly allocated.[13] Some evidence suggests that location biases of public goods have favored low-income as well as high-income groups.

LAND USE REGULATION

Urban land use regulations evolved from straightforward zoning controls and master plans into full-blown experiments with growth restrictions, fair share housing guidelines, and other techniques to guide and manage growth in the 1960s and 1970s. These initiatives altered the traditional roles of the public and private sectors in development and generated considerable litigation in the courts. Some guidelines have evolved into linkage laws out of more traditional bonus zoning guidelines, while other initiatives evolved from greater concerns with equity, environmental, and/or transportation issues. In many cases, the availability or affordability of housing has motivated such initiatives.

San Francisco, for example, exacts fees on downtown office buildings over 25,000 square feet and in turn offers payments to housing providers averaging about $15,000 per unit. This policy resulted in the construction or renovation of several thousands of housing units. In Boston, the program encompasses office, retail, and institutional buildings over 100,000 square feet throughout the city. From 1983 to 1985, this program generated commitments of $45 million for housing programs. Such programs have expanded throughout California and have also been widely adopted in New Jersey. Both states require that local governments enact programs to promote affordable housing. A jobs/housing balance issue also became an important public policy issue in the 1980s, along with a broader growth management concern.[14] Both of these topics will be addressed in succeeding sections.

Jobs/Housing Balance

A relatively new solution to the problem of increased suburban traffic congestion caused by explosive employment growth gained credibility in the late 1980s in many areas of the United States. This problem resulted from the increased commuting times to these work centers from low-density residential subdivisions that shifted farther into the suburban fringe. Some observers have noted that if "nearby affordable housing development [had] accompanied job center growth, perhaps less auto traffic would have resulted."[15] This led to a ground swell of support for the concept of a *jobs/housing balance*. Local and regional planners increasingly support the notion of expanding the supply of housing in "job-rich" areas and the quantity of jobs in "housing-rich" areas. Ideally, a ratio of one job for every dwelling unit (a ratio of 1:1) would represent a balance. But in many households, more than one person is employed, so that more jobs than housing units would be a better balance.

The Southern California Association of Governments (SCAGS) has studied this issue for nearly 20 years and projected in the mid-1980s that a growth of nearly 6 million persons would occur in the region

[13]David Harvey, *Social Justice and the City*, Edward Arnold, London, 1973.

[14]Douglas R. Porter, "The Office/Housing Linkage Issue," *Urban Land*, (September, 1985), 16–21; Douglas R. Porter and Terry Jill Lassar, "The Latest on Linkage," *Urban Land* (December 1988), 7–11.

[15]Lloyd W. Bookout, "Jobs and Housing: The Search for Balance," *Urban Land* (October 1990), 5.

between 1984 and 2010, along with the addition of 3 million jobs.[16] Moreover, the projections indicated that most of this job growth would occur in Los Angeles and Orange County, while housing growth would occur in the fringe counties of San Bernardino, Riverside, and Ventura. The projections indicated that this imbalanced growth would further overload freeways and average speeds on them would drop 50 percent to an average of 19 m.p.h. The SCAGS growth management plan adopted in February 1989 recommended a jobs/housing ratio of 1.22:1 within each subregion of the area. This ratio represents the projected regionwide balance between jobs and housing in 2010. Now the question

becomes how can one achieve such a balance? What is the appropriate geographic area in which to achieve balance? What price ranges should be encouraged? As answers to these and other questions are worked out in California and elsewhere in the coming years, evidence mounts that the crisis is worsening (see box).

Affordable housing for most workers is not being provided in adequate quantities near growing suburban employment centers, commuting trips are becoming longer, and pollution levels from automobile emissions continue to increase. The problem is graphically portrayed by the experience of commuters from Moreno Valley, located in Riverside, the fastest-growing county in California according to the 1990 census (Figure 19-15). A decade ago, only 28,309 people lived there, and now the population is 116,427. The

[16]Ibid., p. 8.

Figure 19-15. Residential Boom in Moreno Valley, Riverside County, California. Labeled the boomdocks, this rapidly growing bedroom community 70 miles east of Los Angeles offers affordable housing in an idyllic setting. This artist's conceptualization of the Moreno Valley Ranch shows a master-planned community, designed for 12,000 families on 4000 acres, that boasts a myriad of recreational and entertainment features. (Courtesy The Warmington Company).

METROPOLITAN FUTURE VISIONS

The current vision of a desirable metropolitan area, according to Anthony Downs, Senior Fellow at the Brookings Institution, is based on four pillars:

1. Ownership of single-family homes on spacious lots.

2. Ownership and use of a personal, private motor vehicle.

3. Low-density suburban office or industrial workplaces and shopping centers.

4. Living in small communities with self-governance.

These four visions of metropolitan living create four corresponding flaws based on inconsistencies among the key elements of these visions:

1. Low-density residential and work patterns generate tremendous vehicular travel and traffic congestion.

2. There is no provision for housing for low- and moderate-income families.

3. There is no consensus regarding how to finance the required infrastructure.

4. There is no mechanism to resolve conflicts arising from facility locations (due to NIMBY and LULU syndrome).

A new vision for suburban America can be crafted from key elements of existing visions, according to Downs, if residents begin to think and behave more in terms of community and the "collective impacts of individual decisions" rather than the way they currently think and behave. Key elements of the new vision are as follows:

1. Sizable areas must be set aside for moderately high-density residential and workplace uses.

2. Residents must live closer to work.

3. The governance structure must include provisions for local authority administered in the context of area-wide needs.

4. Incentive arrangements are required to encourage individuals and households to take into account more realistically the collective costs of their decisions. (Examples include peak hour pricing on highways and linkage zoning requiring the simultaneous development of housing and workplaces.)

5. Equitable strategies to finance infrastructure must be developed.

Source: This box is based on Anthony Downs, "The Need for a New Vision for the Development of Large U.S. Metropolitan Areas," Salomon Brothers, *Bond Market Research, Real Estate,* August 1989.

nearest major employment centers are in Orange County, 45 miles to the west, or Los Angeles, 70 miles to the northwest. "The drive to L.A. takes two hours on a good day, three when an accident ties up traffic on the Pomona Freeway."[17] The article discussing this and similar communities in southern California is entitled "The Boomdocks" Distant Communities Promise Good Homes But Produce Malaise; Census Shows People Moving So Far from Jobs They Lack Time to Enjoy Life."

The authors call rapidly growing communities like these the *boomdocks,* because they lack urban amenities and are located in remote areas for one reason—access to affordable housing. The article discusses the stress of the long commute and the strain it places on family relations. This problem has now spread to most large metropolitan areas of the country, including New York, Chicago, and San Francisco, and to many areas in Florida. Long work commutes have fueled the clamor for growth management in which the jobs/housing balance issue and traffic congestion play an important role.

[17]Rodney Ferguson and Eugene Carlson, "The Boomdocks: Distant Communities Promise Good Homes But Produce Malaise; Census Shows People Moving So Far from Jobs They Lack Time to Enjoy Life," *Wall Street Journal,* October 25, 1990, pp. A1, A6.

GROWTH MANAGEMENT

While there is no simple definition of *growth management* as practiced in many urban areas of the United States in the early 1990s, the emphasis on most programs occurs in one or more of three areas: (1) orderly infrastructure provision; (2) environmental preservation; and (3) quality of life and design considerations.[18] Most initiatives have occurred in response to rapid growth, especially in California, which has experienced several taxpayer-induced initiatives on the ballot to roll back taxes and/or restrict growth. Programs have also been proposed in Oregon, Florida, and Georgia, among other areas.

The orderly infrastructure provision guidelines typically provide mechanisms to support the programming of utilities and services that keep abreast of development. The use of *impact fees* exacted on developers of new projects has proven increasingly popular as a means to pay for facilities and avoid capacity shortages. On the transportation side, these initiatives often involve the creation of transportation management associations (TMAs), which attempt to reduce traffic congestion. In some instances, *urban service boundaries* are prescribed that designate areas that can and cannot be developed.

In San Diego, for instance, the city enacted restrictions on development in fringe areas, called an *urban reserve* in 1979, and sought to redirect development to existing neighborhoods.[19] The program called for four tiers of management in the city: (1) urbanized; (2) planned urbanizing; (3) future urbanizing; and (4) parks and open space. The city invested its resources to provide capital improvements in the urbanized area, while developers funded improvements in planned urbanizing areas. The future urbanizing areas could not be developed for 20 years. That program worked well in terms of directing growth, but an active citizenry initiated even stricter controls in 1985 that limited the number of building permits issued annually. Pressures for growth continued nonetheless, leading to a leapfrogging of development outside the city to other municipalities. Restrictions also bid up house prices

and the cost of developing projects in the city. The regional effect of these restrictions has been counterproductive in terms of commuting and dependence on the automobile. Longer work trip lengths have resulted, creating more imbalance in the jobs/housing mix.

Environmental preservation/protection initiatives related to growth management gained prominence in the United States in the 1980s, especially in sensitive areas such as wetlands, coastal areas, and mountain environments. National, state, and local development guidelines became more specific and restrictive in these areas. The preceding San Diego guidelines, for example, included specific requirements for the protection of hillsides, canyons, floodplains, and wetlands. These areas are an important part of the city's commitment to preserve open space.

The third focus of growth management involves quality of life issues and design guidelines for development, such as architectural control, setbacks, and land use mixing, that are akin to the more traditional police power of zoning. The activist planning approach followed in Bellevue, Washington, a suburban downtown in greater Seattle, provides an example of such initiatives (Figure 19-16).

Located on the eastern side of Lake Washington in suburban Seattle, between two arteries feeding the downtown area, Bellevue began evolving as a bedroom community in the 1950s. Later, a regional mall became the focal point for the commercial development of the area. However, the market continued to evolve along the lines of the Hartshorn–Muller 5-stage process model of suburban development discussed in Chapters 9 and 17.

Using an urban design team and a public–private planning process, the city developed a strong set of policies and procedures, primarily with zoning regulations in the 1980s to shape growth. The goal of the process was to ensure that a pedestrian corridor would provide the backbone of this new downtown. Named the Major Pedestrian Corridor, this promenade was planned as a main street.

> More than 2000 feet long, with three major public open spaces situated on its alignment, this east/west link will connect the retail hub and regional shopping center with high-rise office and mixed-use development to the east. The corridor is a required element of the city's 1981 incentive zoning code, which intensified building densities within the downtown and called for a variety of uses. The corridor will be built in increments by private developers whose projects abut it. In exchange, developers

---

[18]Based on remarks by Douglas Porter, Urban Land Institute, at the Annual Meeting of the National Council for Urban Economic Development, Washington, D.C., April 1989.

[19]Regional Growth and Planning Review Task Force, *Growth Management in the San Diego Region*, Final Report, San Diego Association of Governments, November 1988.

Figure 19-16. Pedestrian Corridor in Bellvue, Washington. Compared with the wide swaths of many pedestrian malls, Bellvue's corridor is compact. Pedestrian movement takes place along corridor edges, where sidewalk cafes, shopping, and other uses are concentrated. Passive recreation and special activities occur in the middle of the corridor, which is reserved for plantings, seating, kiosks, and other furniture. Note the apple motif on the lamppost, which hearkens back to an earlier time when apple farming prevailed in the area. (Courtesy Mark Hinshaw)

may exceed the maximum height limit and earn density bonuses. The bonuses may be banked for use in a later development phase or sold to another project within the core. . . .

Compared with the wide swaths made by many pedestrian malls, Bellvue's corridor will be compact; it may be no less than 45 feet and no more than 60 feet wide. The city intends that pedestrian movement take place along the corridor edges, where sidewalk cafes, shopping, and other active pedestrian uses will be concentrated (Table 19-1). Passive recreation and special activities will occur in the middle of the corridor, which will be reserved for plantings, seating, kiosks, and other furniture. (Figure 19-16) Between these two sectors, two pedestrian pathways will run. Secondary pedestrian-movement paths with commercial frontages will cut through development superblocks and feed into the Major Pedestrian Corridor.

TABLE 19-1

Selected Design Guidelines for Bellvue Pedestrian Corridor, from City Code

Topic—Pedestrian Amenities

Purpose—Ensure that corridor emphasizes pedestrian use

Accomplished by—

- providing generous amounts of seating in a variety of forms.
- providing appropriate lighting.
- providing drinking fountains, litter receptacles, and restrooms.
- providing directories and maps.
- establishing a graphic system using a logo and international symbols.
- encouraging artwork and decorative fountains.
- providing handicap access.
- vegetation to complement pedestrian use (e.g., shade, wind protection, seasonal flowers, etc.).
- considering safety, security, and fire protection.

Source: modified after Terry Jill Lassar. *Carrots & Sticks: New Zoning Downtown.* Urban Land Institute, Washington, D.C., 1989, p. 149.

These secondary paths may lead to enclosed atriums and landscaped spaces.

The corridor design guidelines also contain massing provisions addressing sun-access and street-wall enclosure concerns [Table 19-2].[20]

The first major high-rise building along the corridor, the 1.5 million-square-foot Koll Center, opened in 1987. This 27-story office–retail mixed-use center qualified for corridor density points, as it provided pedestrian amenities along the corridor. A civic center and more high-rise mixed-use facilities are planned for the corridor in the 1990s.

SUMMARY AND CONCLUSION

The role of urban planning has evolved from an administrative function to a broad-based interdisciplinary process focused on a broad range of urban problems. The environmental movement, the need for improved transportation access, the growing housing mismatch between the "haves" and "have-nots," and growing social problems afflicting the central city all call for more effective planning. Such a process must include a

[20]Terry Jill Lassar, *Carrots and Sticks: New Zoning Downtown*, Urban Land Institute, Washington, D.C., 1989, pp. 148–149.

TABLE 19-2
Guidelines to Insure Appropriate Scale of Facilities on
Bellvue Pedestrian Corridor, from City Code

Topic—Massing of Abutting Structures

Purpose—Create an intense urban place, giving consideration
to open spaces and public areas, and giving special
consideration to sun, shade, and air.

Accomplished by—

- Ensuring that the form and placement of buildings
consider year-round conditions of sun and shade within
the corridor.

- Encouraging lower portions of buildings to be built to
the corridor edge, but not necessarily in the same
manner. Variations in use, design, and configuration
should be encouraged.

Source: modified after Terry Jill Lassar. *Carrots & Sticks: New Zoning
Downtown.* Urban Land Institute, Washington, D.C., 1989, pp. 149–150.

significant public participation component and programs with strong community support. More cost
sharing with the private sector will also be necessary to
fund improvements due to public sector budget cutbacks in recent years.

Idealists have proposed alternative urban designs to
better meet the needs of urban residents over the years.
Most such plans have not moved far beyond the
drawing-board stage, but higher residential densities
and more mixed-use developments appear to be gaining
favor to meet the need for more affordable housing and
less dependence on long-distance automobile-based
commuting. More emphasis on open space and amenities in urban developments, long a concern of urban
design professionals, also appears to be yielding more
exciting and attractive residential subdivisions and
commercial development designs.

The fragmentation of government service delivery in
urban areas, especially pronounced in the areas of
water supply, wastewater treatment, police and fire
protection, solid-waste management, public transportation service delivery, and regional planning has
scarcely been resolved, despite years of study and a
myriad of proposed solutions. Financial exigencies
faced by urban areas have multiplied as their tax bases
have eroded, voter-supported tax rollbacks have been
implemented, and demands for urban services have
accelerated.

Growth management initiatives mushroomed in several parts of the country in the early 1990s, as urban
areas faced increased pressure by their constituencies to
address infrastructure inadequacies, environmental

concerns, and quality of life issues. While such concerns are understandable and the goals of these programs were generally laudable, implementing financial
solutions to these problems lagged. As a result, the cost
of housing and the cost of doing business in these areas
increased, and solutions remained elusive. Developers
were increasingly called upon to finance these infrastructure improvements, and local governments were
encouraged to develop master plans for their communities to make growth more orderly in the future. A
growing trend to link the approval for the construction
of new commercial and industrial buildings to the
provision of additional housing also gained momentum. Finding a satisfactory solution to this jobs/housing
balance dilemma will remain a central political issue
facing a growing number of urban regions in the future.

Suggestions for Further Reading

Ausubel, Jesse H. and Robert Herman, eds. *Cities and their Vital Systems: Infrastructure Past, Present, and Future*, National Academy Press, Washington, D.C., 1988.

Appleyard, Donald, *Livable Streets*, University of California Press, Berkeley, 1981.

Baldwin, John H. *Environmental Planning and Management*, Westview Press, Boulder, Color., 1985.

Barnet, Jonathan. *An Introduction to Urban Design,* Harper and Row, New York, 1982.

Banerjee, Tridib and Michael Southworth. *City Sense and City Design: Writings and Projects of Kevin Lynch.* The M.I.T. Press, Cambridge, Mass., 1990.

Berry, Brian J.L. *Patterns of Urbanization and Counter-Urbanization*, Sage Publications, Los Angeles, 1976.

———. *Human Consequences of Urbanization.* St. Martin's Press, New York, 1973.

Brotchie, John, et al, eds., *The Future of Urban Form*, Croom Helm, New York, 1985.

Brower, David J., David Godschalk, and Douglas Porter, *Understanding Growth Management*, Urban Land Institute, Washington, D.C., 1989.

Buck, Peter L., ed., *Modern Land Use Control*, The Practicing Law Institute, New York, 1978.

Catanese, Anthony J., *The Politics of Planning and Development*, Sage Publications, Beverly Hills, Calif., 1984.

Clark, Gordon L. *Judges and the Cites. Interpreting Local Autonomy.* The University of Chicago Press, Chicago, 1985.

Clavel, Pierre, *The Progressive City: Planning and Participation, 1969–1984*, Rutgers University Press, New Brunswick, N.J., 1987.

Cullen, Gordon, *Townscape*, Architectural Press, London, 1961.

De Chiara, Joseph, *Urban Planning Design Criteria*, 3rd ed., Van Nostrand Reinhold, New York, 1982.

Doxiadis, C.A., and J.G. Papaioannou, *Ecumenopolis: The Inevitable City of the Future,* Norton, New York, 1974.

Fleming, Ronald L. and Renata von Tscharner. *Place Makers,* Harcourt Brace Jovanovich Publishers, New York, 1987.

Gallion, Arthur B., and Simon Eisner, *The Urban Pattern: City Planning and Design*, Van Nostrand Reinhold Co., New York, 1986.

Gratz, Roberta, *The Living City,* Simon & Schuster, 1989.

Harrigan, John J., *Political Change and the Metropolis*, Little, Brown, Boston, 1985.

Hart, John Fraser, ed. *Our Changing Cities,* Johns Hopkins University Press, Baltimore, 1991.

Harvey, David, *Social Justice and the City*, Edward Arnold, London, 1973.

Howard, Ebenezer, *Garden Cities of Tomorrow*, 1902; reissued by M.I.T. Press, Cambridge, Mass., 1970.

Lake, Robert ed. *Resolving Locational Conflict.* Center for Urban Policy Research, Rutgers University, New Brunswick, N.J., 1987.

Lassar, Terry Jill, *Carrots and Sticks: New Zoning Downtown,* Urban Land Institute, Washington, D.C., 1989.

LeCorbusier. *The City of Tomorrow and its Planning.* Translated from 8th French edition of *Urbanisme,* Paris, 1924, by Frederick Etchells and Published by John Rodker in 1929; 3rd Reprint ed., published by MIT Press, Cambridge, Mass., 1971.

Levy, John M., *Contemporary Urban Planning*, 2nd ed., Prentice Hall, Englewood Cliffs, 1991.

Levy, John M., *Economic Development Programs for Cities, Counties & Towns*, 2nd ed., Praeger, New York, 1990.

Marcus, Clare Cooper and Carolyn Francis. *People Places: Design Guidelines for Urban Open Space.* Van Nostrand Reinhold, New York, 1990.

McHarg, Ian, *Design with Nature*, Natural History Press, Doubleday & Co., Inc., New York, 1969.

Miles, Mike, et al., *Real Estate Development: Principles and Process*, Urban Land Institute, Washington, D.C., 1991.

Mills, Edwin and John McDonald, eds. *Sources of Metropolitan Growth* Center for Urban Policy Research, Rutgers University, New Brunswick, N.J., 1991

Moudon, Anne Vernez, ed. *Public Streets for Public Use,* Columbia University Press, 1991.

Schofield, J.A., *Cost Benefit Analysis in Urban and Regional Planning*, Allen & Unwin, Boston, 1987.

Scott, Randall, *Management and Control of Growth*, Urban Land Institute, Washington, D.C., 1975.

So, Frank S., and Judith Getzels, *The Practice of Local Government Planning*, International City Management Association, Washington, D.C., 1988.

So, Frank S., Irving Hand, and Bruce W. McDowell, *The Practice of State and Regional Planning*, The American Planning Association, Chicago, 1986.

Soleri, Paolo, *Arcology, The City in the Image of Man*, M.I.T. Press, Cambridge, Mass., 1969.

Trancik, Roger, *Finding Lost Space: Theories of Urban Design*, Van Nostrand Reinhold, New York, 1986.

Wenting, James W., and Lloyd Bookout, *Density By Design*, Urban Land Institute, Washington, D.C., 1988.

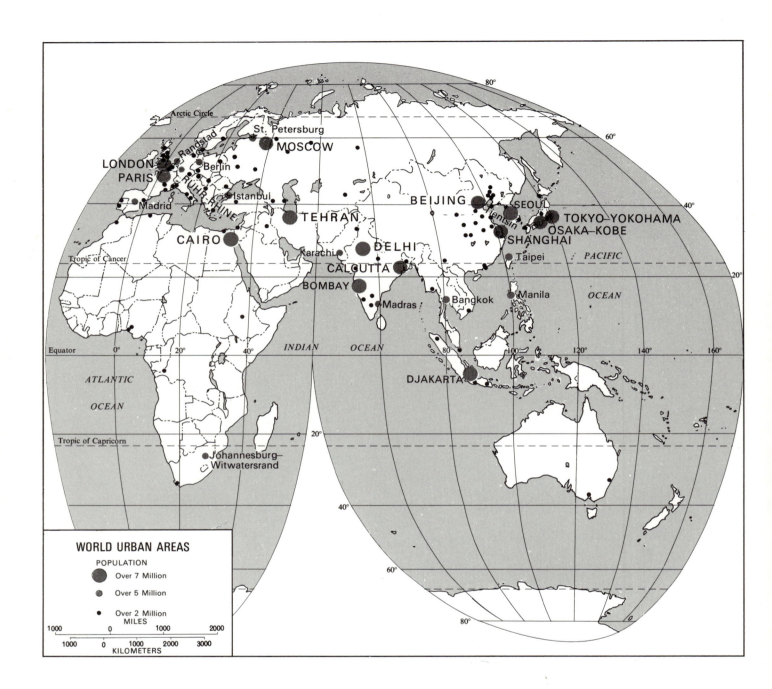

WORLD URBAN AREAS

POPULATION

● Over 7 Million

● Over 5 Million

• Over 2 Million

MILES

1000   0   1000   2000

KILOMETERS

1000   0   1000   2000   3000

LONDON
PARIS
Madrid
RUHR-RHINE
Berlin
Randstad
St. Petersburg
MOSCOW
Istanbul
TEHRAN
CAIRO
Tropic of Cancer
Karachi
DELHI
CALCUTTA
BOMBAY
Madras
BEIJING
Tientsin
SEOUL
TOKYO-YOKOHAMA
OSAKA-KOBE
SHANGHAI
Taipei
PACIFIC
OCEAN
Bangkok
Manila
INDIAN   OCEAN
DJAKARTA
Equator
ATLANTIC
OCEAN
Tropic of Capricorn
Johannesburg-
Witwatersrand
Arctic Circle

80°
60°
40°
20°
0°
20°
40°
60°
80°

0°   20°   40°   80°   100°   120°   140°   160°